Biological Perspectives on Motivated Activities

edited by
RODERICK WONG
University of British Columbia

 boilerplate Ablex Publishing Corporation, Norwood, New Jersey

Library of Congress Cataloging-in-Publication Data

Biological perspectives on motivated activities / edited by Roderick
  Wong.
    p.   cm.
  Includes bibliographical references and indexes.
  ISBN 0-89391-889-X
  1. Motivation in animals. 2. Motivation (Psychology)   I. Wong,
R. (Roderick), 1944-
QL781.3.B56 1994
591.51—dc20   94-31177
                                               CIP

Ablex Publishing Corporation
355 Chestnut Street
Norwood, New Jersey 07648

To Bernice and Kristi

CONTENTS

PART II
Early Experience and Motivation

PART III
Motivation of Ingestive Behavior

PREFACE

This book consists of a collection of essays, reviews, and experimental reports on selected topics in motivation. Rather than surveying the general field, this volume restricts its coverage to biological perspectives on selected aspects of this topic. This perspective is concerned with the function as well as the mechanisms of behavior. From this orientation, behavior analysis involves identification of ultimate causes responsible for the shaping of proximate mechanisms that enable an organism to respond adaptively to environmental conditions. These proximate mechanisms involve anatomical, physiological, psychological, or behavioral traits. An analysis of ultimate causes focuses on two questions: (a) the function of a trait, and (b) its evolution (i.e., the preadaptations and genetic mechanisms that, in conjunction with ecological pressure, shaped the proximate mechanisms). Although most physiological and behavioral researchers in psychology study proximate mechanisms in depth, functional considerations are less likely to dominate their thinking. In this book most of the chapters give consideration to both levels of analysis.

Although human behavior is discussed and analyzed in some chapters, the emphasis in this book is on animal motivation. The chapters are grouped into the following units: (a) evolution and proximate mechanisms, (b) early experience and motivation, (c) motivation of ingestive behavior, (d) aversive motivation, and (e) sensory pleasure and motivation. The contributors to this volume were chosen because of their biological orientation to the myriad topics they chose to study. In a variety of ways, the authors consider the interplay of functional factors and proximate mechanisms in their analysis of motivated behavior. When this approach was not explicitly taken, I have raised such possibilities in the commentary and synopsis section that precedes each chapter. The unifying theme that provides cohesion to the range of topics covered in the chapters is that of adaptive function and its mechanisms.

The lead chapter in this book, by Cosmides and Tooby, provides the framework for the perspective taken in most of the succeeding chapters. You will encounter references to various aspects of their chapter in the Introduction as well as in the commentaries on the individual chapters. The last chapter, by Cabanac, is an attempt to show the relationship between the affective aspects of sensory stimuli and motivated behavior. Cabanac's discussion offers suggestions, often provocative, for the conceptual integration of many of the issues discussed in the chapters sandwiched between it and the lead chapter. Although production of this volume was delayed for three years from the completion of the chapters, the substance within them remains substantial and undated.

I wish to thank all of my contributors for taking time from their busy research schedules to write their thoughtful chapters, as well as for their supportive cooperation. I am also very thankful for the support and guidance from Barbara Bernstein of Ablex Publishing Corporation. Working with her was a pleasure. Thanks also to Linda B. Pawelchak, who was contracted by Ablex to complete the production process of this volume during the final stage. I also received help from Georg Schulze and Neil V. Watson in their comments and corrections on some chapters, especially mine. Bernice Wong has been a wonderful source of encouragement and inspiration by her example and emotional support. This project would not have been completed without her.

Introduction

RODERICK WONG
University of British Columbia

For more than a decade, research on cognitive processes among human and non-human species has been the focus of the majority of volumes in experimental psychology. Such a focus reflects the centrality of cognition in contemporary psychology. The other major influence on psychology during the same period, ethology, has been represented in numerous volumes focusing on behavioral ecology/animal cognition as well as on mating systems/reproductive behavior. There have been interesting developments and advances in research dealing with the interaction of biology and behavior on issues *other than* animal cognition/behavioral ecology and mating behavior, and we offer a sampling of some of these developments. The chapters in this volume deal with selected topics on biological aspects of human and animal behavior, with emphasis on animal motivation.

Behavior can be explained in terms of two levels. One level concerns the way in which proximate causal mechanisms combine to control the behavior of individuals, and the other focuses on how natural selection has, in the past, acted as a designing agent in shaping the proximate physiological and psychological control mechanisms responsible for the behavior. The latter explanation is called a "functional" explanation and is predicated on the assumption that natural selection tends to maximize fitness. Fitness depends upon the design criteria or the features of the system upon which selection acts.

An evolutionary perspective provides us with a comprehensive explanation of many characteristics of both human and nonhuman behavior. The seminal work in this field, E. O. Wilson's (1975) *Sociobiology*, provided subsequent scholars with an overall comprehensive framework from which to develop specific theories and models. Although the field of animal behavior had been considerably advanced as a result of this monumental work, the social sciences have not been revolutionized by it as promised by its author. This volume begins with a revised, expanded, and updated version of an important paper by Cosmides and Tooby (1987) that should have as great an impact on animal behavior scholars as it has had on

1

those in human evolutionary psychology (e.g., Buss, 1990). In this chapter, they discuss some of the reasons why traditional sociobiological analysis has not been incorporated into mainstream social science. The primary reason is that "classical" sociobiological analysis applied evolutionary theory directly to the level of manifest behavior, rather than using it as a heuristic guide for the discovery of psychological mechanisms. Cosmides and Tooby argue that natural selection cannot select for behavior per se but can select only for mechanisms that produce behavior. The latter is elicited by information arising from the organism's external environment and its internal states. This message is as relevant for the analysis of animal behavior as it is for the application of evolutionary theory to the understanding of human behavior, and this theme will be documented in many of the chapters that follow.

The psychology of an organism consists of the total set of proximate mechanisms that cause behavior. Natural selection shapes these mechanisms so that the behavior of the organism enhances its fitness. Organisms process information from their environment in ways that lead to fit behaviors while excluding unfit behaviors. Cosmides and Tooby argue that evolutionary oriented students of human behavior have neglected the most important level of proximate causation: the cognitive level. They assume that cognitive programs are species-typical traits, but that the parameters that feed into them differ with individual circumstance. Thus variations in these parameters will produce variation in manifest behaviors among animals of motivated activities such as feeding/hoarding, drinking, mating, maternal care, stimulus seeking, and other goal-directed behaviors. This theme recurs in the subsequent chapters.

In their chapter, Cosmides and Tooby propose an evolutionary approach to understanding the cognitive level of proximal causation. This approach is concerned with the kind of programming necessary for the organism to be able to extract and process information in a way that will lead to adaptive behavior. They discuss material demonstrating a number of cognitive "adaptive specializations" that have evolved among human and nonhuman animals for dealing with different, evolutionarily important domains. These include sexual behavior, mate choice, parenting, kinship, resource accrual and distribution, predator avoidance, and disease avoidance, among other motivated activities. In many respects there is continuity between the material treated in Cosmides and Tooby's chapter and those covered in traditional cognitive psychology. However, their perspective is novel relative to the latter and has much in common with that taken by the other contributors in this volume, especially those writing on animal motivation.

Parent–offspring interactions are complex processes, and it is likely that a kind of "Darwinian algorithm" of the sort postulated by Cosmides and Tooby (1987), as well as other proximate mechanisms such as genotypic and environmental variables, guide the manifestation of maternal behavior. The next chapter, by Richard Porter and Frédéric Lévy, focuses on the role of olfactory learning in early social interactions and maternal behavior in rodents and sheep/lambs. In doing so they point out similarities and differences among rodents and ungulates in their analysis. Although olfactory cues play an important role in mediating maternal behavior in several species of rodents as well as in ewes, they appear to have less influence on lambs. In their section on rodent behavior, Porter and Lévy discuss the role of olfactory cues in the development of typical rodent behavior. These include pup responsiveness to maternal chemical signals, the role of odors in social discrimination, and the development of specific food preferences via transmission of chemical information from mother to young. In their section on ungulates, Porter and Lévy deal with maternal acceptance and selectivity, and the importance of olfactory regulation for these phenomena. Variables such as sensitive periods and the timing of acquisition and retention are considered. These authors provide a coherent analysis of parent–offspring interactions from a biological perspective that includes evolutionary, hormonal, sensory, dietary, and experiential factors. In doing so, they provide us with a model analysis incorporating proximate and ultimate causation.

Early experiences also receive prominent attention in the chapter by Mary-Lou Cheal. In it she discusses her ideas on how environmental factors interact with ontogenetic development to allow the expression of species-typical behaviors. These ideas are illustrated by data from some of her various research projects in seemingly very diverse areas. These include courtship behavior of tropical fish, developmental changes over the lifespan of the Mongolian gerbil, as well as attentional processes in humans and gerbils. The unifying concept of her research is that each topic is related to determinants of motivated behavior with likely adaptive consequences. In her early work, Cheal demonstrated that environmental factors in adulthood interact with species-typical behavior of a particular species of fish to determine motivation for courtship behavior. In more recent work, Cheal and her colleagues have shown that the rearing environment can influence a wide range of reactions such as ventral gland growth and marking behavior, response latencies in finding food in a novel apparatus, and the ontogeny of bone growth in developing gerbils. It appears that a diverse environment facilitates many processes, although one should be cautious about inferring possible adaptive advantage arising from such a manipulation. In general, Cheal's results and discussion on the lifetime continuity of behavior indicate the interaction of multiple factors that motivate behavior and influence the direction of behavior development.

The chapter on feeding behavior in rodents, by Lyn Raible, provides us with a very useful service, the integration of an almost overwhelming mass of data on this topic. In contrast to most review papers on feeding, which seem to regard the behavior as an endpoint for the evaluation of the effectiveness of various physiological manipulations, Raible's review presents a synthesis of information on physiological, psychological, as well as ecological aspects of the feeding system. This system is viewed from a larger perspective in its incorporation of foraging and hoarding activities. The discussion of the interplay between energy depletion/repletion cycles and environmental/psychological factors in the regulation of feeding is particularly valuable and original.

The outcome of Raible's review of physiological factors influencing feeding was a proposal on the integrative function of neural regions such as the paraventricular nucleus, ventromedial hypothalamus, and lateral hypothalamus. She hypothesizes that every neurotransmitter, sex steroid, and peptide that has been found to influence food intake appears to do so by its effects on some aspect of this system. The implications of this suggestion are developed in the chapter.

In dealing with aspects of feeding other than consumption, Raible shifts her analysis from physiological factors to the role of learning mechanisms, mainly of the associative sort. These aspects include diet selection as well as foraging and hoarding behaviors. However, ecological variables such as response cost are also salient in influencing these behaviors. As the cost of a specific macronutrient increases, animals become more selective. The composition of their diet is adjusted if the preferred item is too "expensive." Similarly, increases in procurement cost lead to decreases in foraging frequency and increases in meal size. Although learning and memory may be the primary forces guiding foraging behavior, mechanisms dealing with energy regulation also are involved.

The example of a prodigious hoarder, the Syrian golden hamster, also illustrates the effects of response cost and learning mechanisms on their food procuring behavior. Although these animals normally do not manifest postfast compensatory behavior and deal with deprivation by hoarding, they consume more of their hoard and decrease the amount they add to it as the cost of procurement is increased. Raible suggests that these animals act proactively to prevent the occurrence of food shortage and thus reduce the amount of time and energy required to forage when food is scarce. In contrast to the hamsters' strategy, rats are more reactive and alter meal size and frequency when food is scarce. Mongolian gerbils show a mixed strategy, which seems to be intermediate to that of hamsters and rats. These species-specific strategies may be regarded as examples of the adaptive specializations discussed in Cosmides and Tooby's chapter in this volume.

Possible adaptive specializations of Mongolian gerbils and Syrian golden hamsters that result in unique reactions are also discussed in R. Wong's chapter on flavor neophobia. Although wariness of novel-tasting foods, particularly those adulterated with bitter-tasting quinine, is a universal reaction in almost all animals, this is not the case with the aforementioned rodents. These animals show strong neophobia to sweet and salty tasting nuts and substantial wariness to sour-tasting nuts. However, neither quinine nor another bitter-tasting substance, sucrose octa acetate, elicits hesitation when the animals are exposed to nuts flavored with them. There is substantial evidence indicating that the processes involved in neophobia and conditioned taste aversions are not necessarily dependent. Such findings challenge the common assumption that neophobic reactions have been selected for as a primary defense against the ingestion of toxic substances. Instead, learned aversion mechanisms may be the most effective vehicle to ensure this defensive function.

Because taste aversions are acquired easily and quickly, unconditioned aversions to novel substances may not be critical and would be redundant. Although many plants contain chemicals that are toxic and frequently taste bitter, a priori rejection of bitter substances may limit the quantity of food available to some herbivores, which may have evolved some tolerance for the alkaloids in the plants of their native habitat (Jacobs, 1978). Thus, a mechanism enabling the animals to learn flavor–consequence relationships rapidly may be the optimal device for avoiding potentially toxic substances. Consequently, acquired flavor aversions ensure adaptive food selection in a potentially changing habitat where earlier labeled "safe" foods may be scarce. These processes are examples of adaptive specializations or behavioral phenotypes that have specifically evolved in response to environmental pressures. The demands of the natural situation provide a framework for the types of domain specific psychological mechanisms described in the Cosmides and Tooby chapter.

Motivational analysis requires consideration of proximate mechanism(s) required for the manifestation of goal-achieving behavior. In his chapter, Georg Schulze proposes that homeostasis provides the mechanism for motivated activities that maximize the organism's fitness. In contrast to Cosmides and Tooby, who emphasize cognitive programs in proximate causation, Schulze argues that the innate psychological mechanisms that process information leading to adaptive behavior are regulated by homeostatic mechanisms. These mechanisms are essential for motivation because they regulate the consequences of behavior. The effects of environmental stimuli that affect the integrity of the organism are counteracted by homeostatic mechanisms. Schulze utilized control theory to explain how environmental stimuli and internal state articulate. This analysis involves comparisons between signals indicating the current state of the system with some input reference signal (called *set point*). Control theory and references to the set point notion are indicated in discussions in the chapters by Raible on feeding and by Cabanac on affective aspects of sensation and motivated behavior. However, many critics of this approach have drawn attention to its shortcomings, and Schulze addresses some of these issues in his chapter.

Schulze defines *hedonic state* in terms of the effect of a stimulus on the current position of a regulated variable relative to some hypothetical set point for that variable. A pleasant hedonic state is attained when the stimulus moves the regulated variable in the direction of the set point; and when it is moved away from the set point, an aversive hedonic state is experienced. Animals react to stimuli according to the hedonic state produced by the stimuli, which, in turn, are influenced by their internal state. This issue receives further elaboration in Cabanac's chapter. Adaptive behavior arises from the hedonic state resulting from the response to the stimuli. Following Cosmides and Tooby's proposition that evolution selects for mechanisms that represent the manifestation of adaptive design at the psychological level, Schulze views homeostatic mechanisms and their associated hedonic states as other products of such selection.

Although most models of drinking and thirst-motivated behavior have employed the concept of homeostasis to account for the outcomes of laboratory manipulations that reliably initiate, modulate, or terminate drinking behavior or thirst-motivated behavior, there has been a persistent suggestion in the literature that "normal" drinking, rather than being triggered by deficits in the intra- or extracellular space, is a purposive act that anticipates a future water deficit, using information acquired as a consequence of individual experience. In his chapter, Fred Valle reviews evidence for this hypothesis in painstaking detail and finds it wanting. Instead, as a result of his own experiments that were designed to substantiate the "anticipation" hypothesis, Valle concludes that "normal," feeding-related drinking in rats is controlled by other factors. Drinking behavior, per se, seems to depend much more strictly on (a) local, contemporary events in the internal environment (homeostatic mechanisms); and (b) the amount of water that is required to masticate and swallow a particular type of food in comfort, although ecological variables such as the procurement cost of water can substantially modulate the effects of the first two classes of variables. Of particular interest is the suggestion that meal-related drinking is primarily a hedonically driven option for the rat. The greater the difficulty in processing the food (due to protein content), the greater is the positive hedonic value of the accompanying drink. The theoretical basis of this is discussed in Cabanac's chapter.

Although the evidence for an anticipatory mechanism mediating "normal" drinking may be subject to question, there is no question about its role in instrumental activities. When goal-achieving activities are not consummated (i.e., there are obstructions to an anticipated goal), predictable behavioral consequences ensue. These changes in behavior are assumed to arise from a hypothetical internal activating state resulting from the organism's reactions to the absence of the anticipated outcome. This state has been referred to as *frustration* and is omnipresent in the animal world. Dwindling resources, changing circumstances, competition, and a host of other constraints conspire to block the attainment of goals. For the past two decades, Paul Wong has studied frustration effects in animals and humans in a variety of situations. He has developed an approach called the *behavioral field* in which the observation and recording of collateral behaviors is emphasized. In his chapter, P. Wong presents a stage model on how organisms adapt or cope with frustrative stress. He also presents empirical evidence from both the human and animal research that demonstrates the usefulness of his model. This model postulates that the adaptation process involves four orderly stages, and each stage is characterized by certain dominant behavioral strategies and cognitions.

P. Wong's stage model provides a frustration interpretation of phenomenon as diverse as depression, obesity, addiction, and obsessive love. The model is also used to explain the development of creativity and resourcefulness. Wong suggests that frustration can induce either adaptive or nonadaptive behavior. The outcome is dependent upon whether a particular coping strategy has been repeatedly reinforced or not. P. Wong conceptualizes the coping mechanisms in each stage as preprogrammed adaptive reactions that are elicited in frustrating situations. In that respect, they may be regarded as adaptive reactions exhibited by individuals in a species. These mechanisms enable the animal to survive in an environment where dwindling resources and intraspecific competition thwart its ability to attain its relevant goals.

Competition for territory and resources is analyzed in Lincoln Chew's chapter on the elements of agonistic behavior in fish. Following an initial general treatment of the diversity of behaviors exhibited by an equally wide spectrum of piscine species, Chew proceeds with a deeper consideration of conflict behavior, drawing upon his research with two fish groups, the salmonids and the cichlids. In doing so, he describes the role that aggressive behavior plays in the establishment and maintenance of conspecific relationships. From analyses of his data, Chew presents the possibilities of two models. The first one, which accounts for salmonid behavior, is called the *classical* or *linear model of aggression*. Among these fish, as relationships are established and territories claimed and defended, the level of conflict declines. In contrast, cichlids, such as the White-Cloud minnow, show unorthodox patterns of interaction in that their agonistic behavior soars dramatically and irregularly from time to time. A nonlinear model was developed to account for the data on this minnow. In this chapter, Chew presents a resolution of two seemingly mutually incompatible views of aggression, following considerations of population composition. It is possible to view the different social structures and attendant behavior of these two fish groups as further examples of adaptive specializations.

In the final chapter, Michel Cabanac presents material that, at first sight, may appear to be misplaced in this collection. However, I believe that Cabanac's novel conceptual analysis of the question "What is sensation?" has implications for motivational aspects of behavior. Although Cabanac is an eminent physiologist who has advanced research on thermoregulation and feeding–hoarding interactions, he is also known for his influential theoretical analysis of hedonic processes in human behavior. In this chapter Cabanac reminds the reader of the multidimensional characteristics of sensation. It has qualitative, quantitative, intensity, and affective components. Our understanding of sensations stems mainly from Aristotle's classification of the senses, and from this system has evolved the notion of exteroceptive, proprioceptive, and interoceptive sensations. In contrast to this view, Cabanac regards any afferent neural pathway as a potential sensation generator. Although there may be many sensations, there is only one class of sensations. What brings the focus of attention on a given input and to consciousness is simply the density of action potentials carried by this pathway. The affective processes and their role in guiding behavior toward useful stimuli and away from noxious stimuli are important elements of sensation that have heretofore been overlooked. Such processes are also involved in guiding motivated behavior, and this theme is reflected in many of the other chapters.

Each organism is a prisoner of its own sensorium. Because attainment of the state of positive affect or pleasure is necessarily transduced through the sense organs, a clearer understanding of the structure of sensation is critical. Any consideration of the ecological factors influencing motivated behavior must include assumptions about the information content of the organism's environment. The sense filters this input, however, once by its chemicophysical window, and also by the biological and cultural format of its brain. Consequently, information processing of cognitive adaptations of the sort envisioned by Cosmides and Tooby should be concerned with the "filtered" environmental variables. The weighting given to these variables via the attainment of pleasure may constitute the proximate basis of motivated behavior. These weighting mechanisms are likely to be domain specific devices subject to selection pressures themselves.

The common element of the chapters in this volume is the theme of adaptation. Both humans and nonhumans have evolved mechanisms that allow them to be able to extract and process information leading to adaptive reactions. The cognitive programs that are responsible for people's ability to deal with aggressive threats, form pair bonds, and reason are species-typical traits that have been selected for just as are patterns of mating, parent–offspring interactions or neophobic reactions, or mechanisms of feeding and drinking. In these chapters, consideration is given to the role of both distal and proximal variables in the explanation of behavior. As a result of the material presented here, we trust that the reader will be influenced by a perspective that has more prominence in ethology than it has in psychology.

REFERENCES

Buss, D. M. (Ed.). (1990). Biological foundations of personality: Evolution, behavioral genetics, and psychophysiology. *Journal of Personality, 58,* Special Issue.

Cosmides, L., & Tooby, J. (1987). From evolution to behavior: Evolutionary psychology as the missing link. In J. Dupré (Ed.), *The latest on the best: Essays on evolution and optimality.* Cambridge, MA: MIT Press.

Jacobs, W. W. (1978). Taste responses in wild and domestic guinea pigs. *Physiology and Behavior, 20,* 579–588.

Wilson, E. O. (1975). *Sociobiology: The new synthesis.* Cambridge, MA: Belknap Press of Harvard University.

Part I

EVOLUTION AND PROXIMATE MECHANISMS

From Evolution to Adaptations to Behavior
Toward an integrated evolutionary psychology

LEDA COSMIDES
JOHN TOOBY
*University of California
at Santa Barbara*

COMMENTS
Roderick Wong

The lead article in this book is an extensive revision of a chapter originally published in John Dupré's (1987) edited volume on evolution and optimality theory, a collection that dealt mainly with theoretical issues relevant to human evolution. Although the skeleton of this article is drawn from the 1987 paper, most of the material has been revised to fit in with the theme of

The authors of this chapter would like to warmly thank David Buss, George Cosmides, Martin Daly, Roger Shepard, Don Symons, and Margo Wilson for their very helpful comments on earlier versions of this work. Our heartfelt thanks also go to Lorraine Daston and Steve Pinker, whose excellent judgment and generous help at a crucial moment brought this chapter to fruition. Needless to say, any remaining (and newly introduced) errors remain uniquely our own. The new writing and reworking of this chapter were completed while we were Fellows at the Zentrum fur interdisziplinaire Forschung (ZiF) of the University of Bielefeld, and we would like to thank Dr. Peter Weingart and the ZiF for their support, assistance, and many kindnesses. The preparation of this chapter was also supported by NSF Grant BNS9157-449 to John Tooby.

This chapter is based on several recent articles of ours, especially Cosmides and Tooby (1987) and Tooby and Cosmides (1990a, 1990b). As Don Symons is fond of saying, it is difficult to understand this book. There are new sections on motivation, emotions as they relate to motivations, and why adaptations turn out to be species typical. Material and the ideas in this work provide a framework upon which the subsequent chapters are anchored. Although most of the authors did not specifically develop their chapters to fit in with the lead article, the substance of their works dovetails with the theme of that chapter. In the synopsis and comments that precede each chapter, I attempt to indicate the connections between ideas in the Cosmides and Tooby article and the chapter under discussion.

Although the main thrust of the Cosmides and Tooby chapter is on the value of evolutionary psychology for the understanding of human behavior, their arguments and proposals are equally cogent for the analysis of animal behavior. They regard a crucial link in the causal chain from evolution to behavior to be one involving innate psychological mechanisms. They focus on information-processing systems as prime examples of such mechanisms, and although the possibility was not explicit in that chapter, motivational mechanisms may also be involved in this link. Although information may be the key to the adaptive regulation of behavior, motivational factors are required for the expression of such regulation.

When applied to behavior, natural selection theory is regarded by the authors as more closely allied with the cognitive level of explanation than with any other level of proximate causation. This is because the cognitive level seeks to specify a psychological mechanism's function. Alternatively, one could argue that a motivational level of explanation also involves a specification of the mechanism's function. From a cognitive framework, Cosmides and Tooby propose that for important domains, animals should have evolved specialized learning mechanisms, called *Darwinian algorithms*, that organize experience into adaptively meaningful schemas or frames. When activated by appropriate environmental or proprioceptive information, these innately specified frame builders should focus attention and organize knowledge that will lead to domain-specific inferences, judgments, and choices. One may question what it is that activates this information; this is where motivational factors may enter into the picture.

The goal of evolutionary theory is to define the adaptive problems that or-

---

what someone is saying until you know who they are arguing with. These papers were addressed to several distinct research communities: (a) those interested in taking an evolutionary approach to human behavior, but who are unfamiliar with cognitive science; (b) those skeptical of the value or possibility of taking an evolutionary approach to human behavior; and (c) cognitive psychologists, many of whom are unfamiliar with modern evolutionary functionalism. These papers were *not* addressed to behavioral scientists working on animal behavior, and this new chapter, built out of these earlier building blocks, unfortunately preserves the prior orientation. If we had had the time to address this new chapter to animal researchers, many things about it would be different, not least the presumptuous and hectoring tone. Animal researchers are in many respects far in advance of other communities in their focus on adaptive function, proximate mechanisms, and careful experimentation, and we suspect we are running the risk of telling animal researchers a great many things they already know. If so, we offer our apologies in advance. Another obvious flaw is that we did not have the time to bring the literature discussed fully up to date, and so have had to rely on the references that came to hand.

ganisms must be able to solve, while the goal of cognitive psychology is to discover the information-processing mechanisms that have evolved to solve them. It is reasonable to assume that both goals must be considered in the analysis of behavior. However, a more comprehensive analysis could also include motivational processes, unless one argues that an analysis incorporating evolutionary and cognitive mechanisms makes such an enterprise redundant.

The type of evolutionary psychology advocated by Cosmides and Tooby uses the methods of evolutionary biology as well as experimental psychology, particularly cognitive psychology, to study the naturally selected design of psychological mechanisms. Although the Darwinian algorithms are instantiated in neural hardware, Cosmides and Tooby argue that it is not necessary to understand the details of this hardware in order to analyze evolutionary adaptations. Hence the naturally selected design of the "mind" could be studied at the information-processing level. However, Crawford (1993) suggests that these mechanisms "come along with the computer": They are hard wired. If these algorithms were shaped by natural selection, then they can be changed only by natural selection, and then only through changes in DNA, which codes for enzymes that direct the construction of proteins. Such an inference implies that adaptive mechanisms may be analyzed at the biochemical or neural level. This type of analysis is presented in many of the subsequent chapters in this volume. However, Cosmides and Tooby assume that natural selection has fixed the alleles at loci mediating the development of Darwinian algorithms; thus, these adaptations can be studied without reference to DNA, biochemistry, or neuroanatomy. In addition to physiological analysis, then, most of the chapters in this book analyze motivational phenomena in terms of psychological mechanisms of the sort proposed by Cosmides and Tooby.

References

Crawford, C. B. (1993). The future of sociobiology: Counting babies or studying proximate mechanisms? *Trends in Ecology and Evolution, 8,* 183–186.
Dupre, J. (1987). *The latest on the best: Essays on evolution and optimality.* Cambridge, MA: MIT Press.

INTRODUCTION

Popular wisdom has it that arguments against new ideas in science typically pass through three characteristic stages, from

1. "It's not true," to
2. "Well, it may be true, but it's not important," to
3. "It's true and it's important, but it's not new—we knew it all along."

If the current state of the behavioral sciences is any indication, then the application of evolutionary biology to the understanding of human behavior has entered the "it's true but not important" stage.

Yet evolutionary biology is important for understanding human behavior, and not everyone knows it—in fact, those most involved in the scientific investigation of "human nature" are generally the most unaware of its implications. We shall argue that the reluctance of many behavioral scientists to appreciate or take advantage of the richness of the evolutionary approach is a direct consequence of a widespread tendency to overlook a crucial link in the causal chain from evolution to behavior: the level of evolved psychological mechanisms, functionally analyzed as adaptations, and described as information-processing systems. This level is pivotal, because it describes the mechanisms that actually link the evolutionary process to manifest behavior. It is these mechanisms that evolve over generations; within any single generation it is these mechanisms that, in interaction with environmental input, generate manifest behavior. The causal link between evolution and behavior is made through the psychological mechanism.

Efforts that skip this step in the evolutionary analysis of behavior, as valuable as they may be in other ways, have contributed to an erroneous caricature of the evolutionary approach to behavior as offering nothing more than post hoc compilations of correspondences between behavior and loosely reinterpreted evolutionary theory. But a rejection of the evolutionary approach based on such an incomplete and misleading characterization of its nature and valid possibilities is mistaken: As we shall discuss, the search for order in human behavior requires the application of the emerging principles of evolutionary psychology. We shall argue that an approach drawn from evolutionary psychology, consistently applied, can repair many of the deficiencies that have hampered progress in the social and behavioral sciences.

EVOLUTIONARY THEORY DOES NOT PREDICT INVARIANCE OR OPTIMALITY IN THE MANIFEST BEHAVIOR OF DIFFERENT INDIVIDUALS

Sciences prosper when researchers discover the level of analysis appropriate for describing and investigating their particular subject: when researchers discover the level where invariance emerges, the level of underlying order. What is confusion, noise, or random variation at one level resolves itself into systematic patterns upon the discovery of the level of analysis suited to the phenomena under study. The lack of success the behavioral sciences have had since their founding has been explained either by the claim that no such science is possible (e.g., human complexity intrinsically transcends any attempt to discover fundamental patterns) or by the view we share, that progress has been slow because scientific efforts have not yet, for the most part, been framed using concepts and organizing principles suitable to the phenomena under study. Can such an appropriate level of inquiry be found for a science of human behavior? Because humans are the product of the evolutionary process, the explanation for their characteristics must be sought in the evolutionary process: For a science of human behavior, the level of underlying order is to be sought in an evolutionary approach.

Using evolution as an informing concept is not enough, however. During the formative period of modern behavioral ecology in the 1970s, many researchers thought that evolutionary biology would revolutionize research in human behavior; this conviction spread after the publication of E. O. Wilson's *Sociobiology* drew widespread attention to the dramatic advances that were taking place in the application of evolution to behavior. Many thought that evolutionary theory would reveal the level of underlying order, that the apparent variation in human behavior would resolve itself into systematic patterns, that invariant relationships would be identified, and that a true social science would emerge. After more than a decade, however, this is a revolution still waiting to happen.

We suggest that the reason progress has been slow is that in the rush to apply evolutionary insights to a science of human behavior, many researchers have made a conceptual "wrong turn," leaving a gap in the evolutionary approach that has limited its effectiveness. This wrong turn has consisted of attempting to apply evolutionary theory directly to the level of manifest behavior, rather than using it as a heuristic guide for the discovery of evolved psychological mechanisms, that is, psychological adaptations.

The attempt to discover evolutionary structure directly in the behavioral level has created a series of difficulties, of which two should serve to illustrate: (a) the use of behaviorally uniform categories or behavioral universality as the signature of evolution, encouraging (among other things) forced typological approaches, and (b) using the "optimality" of manifest behavior (or the lack of it) as the measure of the success (or failure) of the evolutionary paradigm. The belief that evolutionarily structured behavior must be invariant across individuals, or inflexible in expression, has invited a brute force, typological approach to variation in, for example, cross-cultural studies and primate behavior (e.g., humans are monogamous, Hanuman langurs live in one-male groups, etc.). All too often, the researcher would take the observed variation, average it, and typify the species or group by that average (see Tooby & DeVore, 1987, for a more extensive discussion of this problem). The variation itself is considered noise, or an embarrassment to be explained away. Those social scientists skeptical that biology had anything to offer to an understanding of human behavior would dwell on the extraordinary complexity of human behavior, and its enormous and engaging variety, and counterpose this richness to the clear explanatory inadequacy of what they considered to be naive and reductive typological characterizations. Second, it is easy to catalog behaviors that appear absurdly nonoptimal, if the standard is fitness-maximization under modern conditions. Many have dismissed evolutionary approaches as weak or inapplicable to humans on the basis of this rich behavioral variation and the prevalence of obviously maladaptive behavior. Fitness-maximization does not seem to be the underlying logic that governs much of modern human behavior.

If these are the grounds for dismissing evolutionary approaches, however, they are poor ones. The theory of natural selection itself predicts that the manifest behavior of different individuals will vary enormously under many conditions according to principles hard to describe using behaviorally defined categories. Furthermore, it deductively implies that an individual's behavior will often appear far from "optimal," as, for example, when optimality is defined without respect to the individual's social environment, or without respect to the statistical distribution of situations to which a species has been exposed over its evolutionary history. In fact, difficulties emerge generally whenever optimality as a standard is applied to expressed behavior and not to the quality of the design of the mechanisms that generate it. A few of the reasons why looking for invariants or optimality at the behavioral level leads to difficulties are summarized by Tooby and DeVore (1987), in their discussion of hominid behavioral evolution. They include the following:

1. The fitness interests[1] of different individuals are often in conflict; in fact, much of modern evolutionary theory analyzes the conflicting fitness interests of different categories of individuals (e.g., self vs. kin [Hamilton, 1964], parent vs. offspring [Trivers, 1974], male vs. female [Trivers, 1972]) or even of different subsets of the genome within a single individual (Cosmides & Tooby, 1981). An interaction between individuals (or different traits within an individual) whose fitness interests conflict cannot, in principle, produce an outcome that is optimal for both individuals. The outcome will either be optimal for one party but not the other, or, very commonly, the conflict will result in an outcome that is nonoptimal for both.

2. Therefore, larger patterns of social behavior are not necessarily—or even usually—optimal for any individual or group of individuals. Instead, they will be the emergent result of the operation of evolved mechanisms situated in these interacting individuals—mechanisms selected to act in ways that reflect these con-

---

[1]The term *interests*, or *fitness interests* is a useful, but often misleading one, because it links a formal evolutionary concept to an implicit folk psychological concept, *self-interest*, without sufficiently flagging the profound differences between the two. Self-interest tends to be used to refer to conditions an individual desires to bring about because they reflect what he or she values, for whatever reason. On the other hand, the concept of *fitness interest* defines the set of potential outcomes for a specified set of genes in a specific organism that would maximally promote the replication of those genes. Because different subsets of genes in an individual are maximally replicated under different conditions, an individual cannot have a single unified fitness "interest" (see Cosmides & Tooby, 1981). Instead, only traits as defined by their genetic basis can. More significantly, selection acts on the basis of the statistical frequency of conditions, so fitness "interests" on any one occasion are important only to the extent that they reflect a large recurring class of situations that will correspondingly select for adaptations to address them. An even more serious pitfall involved in using the term *fitness interests* is that it invites teleological reasoning. Instead of viewing organisms as collections of mechanisms whose design features were selected for because under ancestral conditions they imposed behavioral outcomes that tended to correspond to fitness promotion, organisms are viewed as agents pursuing fitness as a goal. Organisms are adaptation executors, and not fitness pursuers. For many purposes, this distinction may not seem major, but in considering certain problems, it assumes major importance (see Tooby & Cosmides, 1990b, for discussion).

flicting fitness interests. Frequently, therefore, the behavior of an individual cannot be understood in isolation; its behavior will be the mutual result of adaptations selected to promote its own interests and the counterstrategies produced by the adaptations of others.

3. Organisms are selected to have adaptations that respond to features of their individual situation and social circumstances, and not simply to their local habitat ("the environment"). For example, an individual's best behavioral strategy may depend on its size, its health, its aggressive formidability, its facility at accruing resources, or the number of sibs it can rely on for support. This means that organisms will be selected to be facultative strategists (where appropriate) rather than inflexibly committed to the same behavior or morphology. Consequently, individuals equipped with the same species-typical set of evolved psychological adaptations will often manifest different behaviors in response to the different information they derive from assessing their own abilities, resources, and circumstances. Individual differences, behavioral variation, or "personality differences" that arise from exposing the same species-typical architecture and developmental programs to environmental differences relate individual differences to evolved functional design in a straightforward way. For this reason, much of the study of behavioral variation can be recast as the study of the underlying (and usually) universal psychological adaptations that generate variation in response to circumstantial input (see Tooby & Cosmides, 1990a).[2]

4. For certain social and reproductive behaviors, the favored strategy will depend on the distribution of other behaviors in the population, leading to complexly interactive dynamics. The prevailing analytic tool for dealing with this is game theory and evolutionarily stable strategies (Axelrod & Hamilton, 1981; Maynard Smith, 1982; Maynard Smith & Price, 1973). In such situations, selection can produce psychological mechanisms that are sensitive to information indicating the distribution of relevant behaviors in the local population and then respond accordingly. For example, under stable frequency-dependent conditions, behavioral strategies may be enduringly variable from individual to individual.

5. To be selected for, a trait need not be advantageous under every conceivable potential circumstance. It need only be of benefit *on balance*, against the

[2] Those researchers who are interested in applying an evolutionary perspective to individual differences can investigate the adaptive design of evolved species-typical mechanisms by seeing whether different manifest outputs are adaptively tuned to their corresponding environmental input: Does the algorithm that relates input to output show evidence of complex adaptive design? On the other hand, individual differences caused by genetic differences between individuals have to be analyzed differently and will generally be noise from a functional standpoint (Tooby & Cosmides, 1990a). Methodologically, the criterion of complex, functional design tends to segregate the two components: Complex adaptations will tend to be species-typical, or nearly so in species with a relatively open breeding structure, and so genetic differences will usually tend to be nonfunctional perturbations in species-typical (or at least population-typical) functional design.

statistical distribution of conditions encountered during its evolutionary history. This means that the frequency with which it was advantageous, scaled by the magnitude of the advantage, outweighed the frequency of disadvantage scaled by the cost. Thus, selection for a trait or mechanism has always occurred against a background statistical distribution of ancestral environmental conditions and cannot be understood when abstracted from this background. Nothing in the logic of selection precludes the emergence of designs that generate maladaptive choices under a subset of conditions, and even the most perfected, "optimal" strategy may involve producing many maladaptive acts as a by-product of producing advantageous behavior.

6. Therefore, natural selection cannot be expected to produce behavioral responses that maximize fitness under every imaginable circumstance. The situational specificity of an adaptation depends on the selective history of encountering similar situations (for discussion see Tooby & Cosmides, 1990b). The degree of situational adaptation manifested by individuals will be a matter of (a) how frequent in the species' evolutionary history that situation has been, (b) how long (in phylogenetic terms) it has been recurring, and (c) how large its fitness consequences are. Organisms will be well adapted to common, important situations, reasonably adapted to common less important situations and less common highly important situations, but not adapted to uncommon, unimportant situations.

7. The recognition that adaptive specializations have been shaped by the statistical features of ancestral environments is especially important in the study of human behavior. Our species spent over 99% of its evolutionary history as huntergatherers in Pleistocene environments. Human psychological mechanisms should be adapted to those environments, and not necessarily to the twentieth-century industrialized world. The rapid technological and cultural changes of the last several thousand years have created many situations, both important and unimportant, that would have been uncommon (or nonexistent) in Pleistocene conditions. Evolutionary researchers ought not to be surprised when evolutionarily unprecedented environmental inputs yield maladaptive behavior. Our ability to walk fails us hopelessly when we are chased off a cliff.

For these and other reasons, the search for scientifically analyzable order on the level of manifest behavior will meet with very limited success. Certain ingredients in behaviorism were, of course, a healthy and much needed antidote to attempts early in this century to base psychology on introspection and experientially derived descriptions and phenomena. Even cognitive psychologists would have to admit that in an important sense, we're all behaviorists now. But using behavioral data to test theories is not the same thing as restricting oneself to behavioral descriptive categories, and the marked emphasis by evolutionarily oriented researchers on behavior and behavioral categories has handicapped the integration of evolutionary biology with modern postbehaviorist psychology. Many (though not all) psychologists have attempted to move ahead to describe the mechanisms responsible for behavior, whereas many (though not all) of the evolutionary community have remained focused on behavior. Trying to locate optimality in behavior (a weakness too often indulged by the evolutionarily oriented), or trying to use behavioral uniformity or inflexibility as particularly diagnostic of the "biological" (a weakness often characteristic of those hostile to evolutionary approaches) are both symptoms of a misdirected focus on behavior. These symptomatic problems are alleviated when attention turns from behavior to the mechanisms that generate behavior. Viewed from such a perspective, neither behavioral variation nor frequent departures from behavioral "optimality" are an embarrassment to an evolutionary perspective, but they are instead predictions of evolutionary theory, as applied to psychological mechanisms, viewed as adaptations.

When the appropriate level of analysis is found, variation becomes fuel in the search for order: Instead of averaging out variation, one looks for systematic relations among the different varying elements. What is variable at one level manifests order—that is, invariance—at another. Instead of lamenting the complex variations in human behavior, researchers can use patterns in behavioral variation positively, as clues to the nature of the psychological mechanisms that produce behavior. We think that the appropriate level is the analysis of psychological mechanisms, described in information-processing terms. Before turning to this, however, we need to address the controversy concerning whether evolution optimally designs organisms (Gould & Lewontin, 1979; Lewontin, 1978). After all, if natural selection is only a weak force, and organisms are random agglomerations of properties, why try to gain insights through attempting to analyze their functional designs?

NOT OPTIMALITY BUT WELL-ORGANIZED DESIGN

The entire tortured debate on evolution and optimality founders on a central indeterminacy in its formulation that renders the controversy more of a distraction than an addition to our understanding of the utility of evolutionary approaches (see the papers in Dupré, 1987; Lewontin, 1978; Maynard Smith, 1978). The problem is that *optimality* is an undefined term unless all of the constraints on the problem to be solved are defined in advance. Is a given wing the best possible design for the new McDonnell–Douglas commuter jet, representing an optimal trade-off of all of the design requirements? That depends on what one considers to be possible, and what the design requirements are: How much money can be spent on the manufacturing phase? What materials are available to be used? Can the rest of the fuselage be modified as well, or are only the wings allowed to vary? What is the maximum load the plane has to carry, and the average load? How turbulent are the weather conditions it should be designed to withstand? What are the temperature conditions? Is passenger comfort a factor? And so on. Biological problems are almost always far too complex for every constraint on the possible to be identified and for every design requirement to be determined, which prevents *optimality* from having any determinable meaning. To pick only one issue, no biologist ever has a complete historical record of the statistical properties of the range of environments a species evolved in: How then could one tell if the resulting design was optimally engineered for that range of environments?

Instead, of course, most evolutionary biologists tend to use the term *optimality* for far more modest purposes. Biologists have understood for the better part of a century that the evolutionary process includes random or function-blind elements such as mutation, drift, environmental change, developmental constraints, linkage, and so on, that act to reduce the match between evolved design and adaptive requirements. Despite these processes, organisms nevertheless display a high degree of complex functional organization, and biologists need a way to describe and investigate it. The sole known scientific explanation for this complex organic functionality is, of course, natural selection, which is the only component of the evolutionary process that is not blind to function. Selection constructs adaptations through a relentless hill-climbing process driven by the positive feedback of better replicating design features (Dawkins, 1986; see also Pinker & Bloom, 1990, for an excellent discussion of these issues; and Tooby & Cosmides, 1990b).

If one is to understand the functional dimension of organisms, one needs a way of referring to the solution of adaptive problems, however well or poorly grasped they may be by biologists in any specific case. Where adaptive problems can be modeled to some reasonable approximation and some of the most significant constraints identified, *optimality* is simply the name used to refer to the privileged part of the state space where one would expect the hill-climbing process to end up given static conditions and enough time. It allows the researcher to interpret organic structure in the light of functional analysis. Given that researchers have defined a specific problem, and identified a specific set of constraints as the only ones that will be considered in the analysis, then they can report how near or far the design of the organism happens to be from what their model identifies as optimal. The hotly contested question, How close to or far from optimality are organisms in general? is not only unknowable in practice, but in fact meaningless, because there is no privileged class of defined constraints and factors that could be applied to such an analysis.

Thus, one cannot meaningfully ask how close or far from perfection an organism's design is because there is no unique and logically coherent standard of perfection. But the question can be rephrased so that one asks, instead, How improbably functional is an adaptation in solving an adaptive problem? This question is answerable because although there is no unique and privileged standard of perfection, there are identifiable and usable standards for the other end of the scale, lack of perfection, or lack of functionality. Chance conditions unshaped by functionally organizing forces can be used as the entropic floor, so to speak, and this benchmark allows the biologist to recognize adaptations by virtue of how far biological organization departs from chance in the direction of incorporating features that contribute to the solution of known adaptive problems. Given a definition of an adaptive problem (e.g., vision, resistance to infection, providing nourishment to offspring, predator evasion), functionality can be gauged by how improbably far from chance or some known prior condition an organ, mechanism, or adaptation goes toward manifesting functional properties (e.g., how much better is the eye for vision than is undifferentiated fetal tissue). By these criteria, many biological structures appear to be extremely well designed: The vertebrate eye or immune system may not be perfect (whatever that could mean), but they each involve sets of intricately coordinated elements that bring about otherwise improbable functionally exacting outcomes. Because this correspondence between evolved structures and functional requirements is astronomically unlikely to have come about by chance, we can confidently conclude that these functional systems were constructed by selection, the only evolutionary force not blind to function. Complex adaptations can be identified by the improbable degree of functional organization they show for solving an adaptive problem (Dawkins, 1986; Thornhill, 1991; Tooby & Cosmides, 1990b; Williams, 1966, 1985; see also Pinker & Bloom, 1990).

By using improbability of functional design as a standard rather than optimality, one can assess how widespread functional design is. For example, if designs are no better than chance, then chance rearrangements of their components will be as good as their present arrangements. Even on a simple biochemical level, of course, this is absurd. If one runs through the long list of complex organic molecules used in mammalian physiology, such as myoglobin, hemoglobin, ATP, RNA, DNA, serotonin, cysteine, and so on, and did the experiment of transmuting any one of these chemicals throughout the body into water, a nontoxic substance, the result would be devastating, and in most cases the organism would die. A number of other tests against random reorganization of components (in the brain, in physiology, in metabolic pathways, and so on) can be considered, all showing a marked interdependence of elements, combining to produce improbably good solutions to adaptive problems. The philosophically minded may wish to debate whether such a state of affairs represents perfection, or whether steel tubing might not be better than capillaries, but mammalian physiology and biochemistry inarguably reflect a well-coordinated functional design, whose parts fit together in an exceedingly intricate and exceedingly improbable mesh to bring about functional outcomes. To ignore the functional organization in organic structures is to miss the most important thing about them, and the primary thing that makes them intelligible.

So, instead of looking at the behavioral level, and trying to analyze whether it is optimal (fitness-maximizing, rational, or whatever), we suggest that researchers might more productively attempt to discover and map the structure of the psychological mechanisms that generate behavior. Where functional analysis is relevant and helpful in this enterprise (and we think it is often indispensable), the standard that should be used is the standard of improbably good design (based on the consequences of a mechanism's design features in conditions that resemble the species' environment of evolutionary adaptedness), rather than on the vague or indeterminate standard of optimality or perfection. Of course, assessing good design depends on carefully defining adaptive problems, an issue we will deal with later in the chapter, after discussing the relationship between behavior, mechanisms, and evolution.

FROM EVOLUTION TO PSYCHOLOGICAL DESIGN TO BEHAVIOR

To speak of natural selection as selecting for "behaviors" is a convenient short-hand, but it is misleading usage (for discussion, see Symons, 1989, 1992). The error is worth belaboring, because the failure to appreciate it has delayed the fruit-ful application of evolutionary theory to human behavior by years. When used too casually, this shorthand misleads because it obscures the most important level of proximate causation: the psychological mechanism.

Natural selection cannot select for behavior per se; it can only select for genes that guide developmental programs to construct mechanisms that produce behavior. There is nothing special about behavior in this regard; the same can be said, for example, of digestion. Natural selection can only spread rearrangements of patterns in molecules of DNA; these rearrangements have effects, and it is be-cause they have these effects that they are selected for or not. Through this chain, natural selection gives us teeth, salivary amylase, a peristaltic esophagus, an acid-filled stomach, an absorptive colon: mechanisms that produce digestion. The op-eration of these mechanisms causes certain molecules to be extracted from plant and animal tissues and incorporated into our own tissues: an effect that we call di-gestion. Natural selection gives us food-processing machinery, and the operation of this machinery results in digestion, which is an effect of the functioning of mechanisms.

Behavior, like digestion, is an effect of the functioning of mechanisms. Nat-ural selection can give you a reflex arc, and the functioning of this arc causes an effect: Your leg swings when your knee is tapped. But this effect cannot occur in the absence of a mechanism for producing it. Behavior cannot occur sui generis; behavior is an effect produced by a causal system: proximately, by psychological mechanisms. Although researchers would acknowledge these points as patently ob-vious, in practice, many simply methodologically leapfrog this level, with many unfortunate consequences.

One of the resulting confusions has to do with the nature of selection and its relationship to behavior in a given situation. Selection cannot directly "see" an in-dividual organism in a specific situation and cause behavior to be adaptively tai-lored to the functional requirements imposed by the situation. Selection is a sta-tistical process acting across generations, which "evaluates" the aggregate performance of alternative designs over the long run. This performance evaluation not only sums up design performance over the thousands of particular situations encountered by an individual over an individual lifetime, but indeed the trillions of situations encountered by millions of individuals over many generations. Be-cause single events cannot cause designs to spread throughout the species, and because selection cannot anticipate unique events that an organism will encounter in the future, there are no adaptations specialized for single instances. Consequently, there is no way for behavior to be made specifically fitness-maximizing for each individual situation the organism encounters. More generally, design properties that are too particular in the conditions they address, and hence improve performance only in very rarely encountered situations, will be selected for only weakly—or not at all, if the frequency of their benefit does not offset their metabolic cost. Equally, the more common a particular type of situation, the more such situations will select for adaptations specialized to address them. Thus, the accumulating design of organisms over evolutionary time encounters individual events as instances of large recurrent classes: Individual events are in effect lumped into classes large enough to make it "worthwhile" to build situationally specific adaptations to deal with them. Because natural selection shapes mechanisms, and mechanisms in turn generate behavior, individual situations are treated by mechanisms only as instances of evolutionarily recurrent classes.

Thus, an adaptation is more than a mere collection of phenotypic properties, which, in a particular individual on a particular occasion, happen to have the effect of enhancing reproduction—winning the lottery, wearing parkas in Alaska, and irrigating fields are not adaptations. An adaptation must be a recurrent design that reappears across generations and across individuals (caused by the developmental interaction between stable features of the world and the relevant set of genes). For selection (as opposed to chance) to have manufactured a structure, the evolved design must have had repeated encounters with recurrent properties of the world. Those encounters constitute the history of selection for that design. If characteristics emerge uniquely every generation, or haphazardly from individual to individual, then selection cannot organize them.

This means that the phenotype of an individual organism must be carefully distinguished from the design of the phenotype. Natural selection manufactures design, defined as those properties that are stable across all individuals of the same genotype. As Williams says, "the central biological problem is not survival as such, but design for survival" (Williams, 1966, p. 159). The individual phenotype manifests innumerable transient properties, which disappear with the death of the phenotype or change idiosyncratically over the life span. Although some of these transient properties may promote reproduction, they are chance-produced beneficial effects, not adaptations (Williams, 1966). An important confusion (common in the evolutionary community) is the failure to distinguish between transient properties, which cannot be adaptations, and design properties, which can (Symons, 1989, 1992; Tooby & Cosmides, 1990b).

Thus, to understand the role of selection in behavior, one needs a description of the cross-generationally stable design of the phenotype: It is this that (potentially) has a functional explanation; it is this set of adaptations or mechanisms that brings about a correspondence between the adaptive demands of a situation and the functional patterns in behavior. The task of describing phenotypic design involves the process of redescribing the phenotypically variable and the transitory in terms of the recurrent and the stable. This process of description is key: By choosing the wrong categories, everything about the organism can seem variable and transitory, to the extent that *plasticity* or *behavioral variability* can be seen as the single dominant property of an organism. By choosing the right categories— adaptationist categories—an immensely intricate species-typical architecture appears, with some limited additional layers of frequency-dependent or population-specific design as well. Discovering the underlying recurrent characteristics that generate the surface phenotypic variability is essential to the discovery of adaptations. To recover adaptive design out of behavioral or morphological observations, one needs to determine what is variable and what is invariant across individuals: Only the recurrent is a candidate adaptation. Adaptations may be variable in expression but must be uniform in design (Tooby & Cosmides, 1990a, 1990b). Because (holding genotype constant) behavior and physiology often do vary, underlying design will often have to be described in terms of conditional rules such as developmental programs or decision-making mechanisms. We have argued elsewhere for the importance of distinguishing adaptive design from its phenotypic expression (Tooby & Cosmides, 1990b). This is simply the equivalent in biological terms of distinguishing the mechanisms regulating behavior from behavior itself (Cosmides & Tooby, 1987; Tooby & Cosmides, 1989a).

By bypassing the level of mechanisms and focusing on behavior, one can easily lose sight of the distinction between the transient or variable and the recurring and stable. This has led to a research tradition of attempting to explain behavior in individual situations as tailored fitness-maximizing responses to the unique nature of each situation (e.g., How is Susan increasing her fitness by salting her eggs? Rather than: What is the nature of human salt preference mechanisms and how did they mesh with the physiological requirements for salt and the opportunities to procure salt in the Pleistocene?). Ironically, by focusing on behavior and not sifting for the stable features of the phenotype, many evolutionarily oriented researchers have thrown away one of the tools necessary to recognizing adaptations (Symons, 1989, 1992; Tooby & Cosmides, 1990b).

The motivation to finesse the level of mechanisms and move directly from evolution to behavior has two sources. The first is the rapid growth, over the last several decades, in the sophistication and power of modern evolutionary theory, especially in implications for behavior (Dawkins, 1976, 1982; Hamilton, 1964; Krebs & Davies, 1984; Maynard Smith, 1982; Trivers, 1972; Williams, 1966; Wilson, 1975). For many in the evolutionary community, the advances in evolutionary theory were so intoxicating and looked so powerful that it seemed as if the study of proximate mechanisms was unnecessary to build a science of behavior, and that their study could be postponed to some future date, as a kind of dotting of i's and crossing of t's.

Second, the widespread desire to avoid being entangled in the proximate level stems, in many cases, from the belief that the exploration of mechanisms means the exploration of the neurophysiological bases of behavior, a task that is genuinely thorny and arduous. Also, to be fair, at the present state of knowledge, neuroscience seems limited to exploring only relatively simple kinds of behaviors, offering no purchase on many issues of interest, such as—to take a thoroughly random sample of topics interesting to behavioral ecologists—mate choice, reciprocation, assistance toward relatives, communication, inbreeding avoidance, small-group dynamics, habitat selection, foraging, and so on. Both of these reasons are misguided, however; evolutionary theory cannot be turned into a theory of psychology without building models of the adaptations (i.e., the proximate mechanisms) involved, and building models of proximate mechanisms need not always involve neurophysiological descriptions. There exists an alternative approach to the study of psychological mechanisms that can be pursued without waiting decades for the requisite advances in neuroscience. This is the cognitive analysis of psychological mechanisms, and it serves, among other things, to bridge the gap between neuroscience and evolutionary biology.

LEVELS OF EXPLANATION: EVOLUTIONARY, COGNITIVE, AND NEUROPHYSIOLOGICAL

Evolutionary psychology relates evolutionary explanations in terms of adaptive function to psychological explanations in terms of proximate mechanisms (see, e.g., Buss, 1987, 1989; Cosmides, 1989; Cosmides & Tooby, 1987, 1989; Crawford, Smith, & Krebs, 1987; Daly & Wilson, 1981, 1988; Erickson & Zenone, 1976; Galef, 1990; Gallistel, 1990; Rozin & Schull, 1988; Shepard, 1984, 1987; Sherry & Schacter, 1987; Staddon, 1988; Symons, 1979, 1987, 1992; Tooby, 1985; Tooby & Cosmides, 1989a, 1990a, 1990b; and many others). The correct characterization of adaptive strategies gives precise meaning to the concept of function for proximate mechanisms. Reciprocally, a detailed analysis of the proximate mechanisms of a species gives rich insight into the past selective pressures that have acted to create and organize them. Psychological mechanisms constitute the missing causal link between evolutionary theory and behavior. Evolutionary theory frequently appears to lack predictive and explanatory value because many researchers skip this crucial predictive and explanatory level. Yet it is the proximate mechanisms that cause behavior that promise to reveal the level of underlying order for a science of behavior.

The psychology of an organism consists of the total set of proximate mechanisms that cause behavior. Natural selection, acting over evolutionary time, shapes these mechanisms so that the behavior of the organism correlates to some degree with its fitness. In the lifetime of any particular animal, however, it is the proximate mechanisms that actually cause behavior—not natural selection. If these proximate mechanisms can be understood, behavior can be predicted more exactly; understanding the fitness-promoting strategies studied by evolutionary theorists allows only approximate prediction. Behavior correlates exactly with proximate mechanisms, but only approximately with the fitness-promoting strategies that shaped those mechanisms. But in what descriptive language should proximate mechanisms be described? Although the description of behavior in terms of adaptive strategies plays an important role in evolutionary theory and modeling (see, e.g., Maynard Smith, 1982), it cannot be used for describing proximate mechanisms: Other than a few impoverished terms such as *facultative* and *obligate*, it lacks a vocabulary and method for linking the results of evolutionary modeling to proximate mechanisms.

Psychological mechanisms, themselves, can be studied on different descriptive and explanatory levels. Most evolutionarily informed studies of proximate mechanisms have described psychological mechanisms in terms of their physiological or neurophysiological underpinnings, finding, for example, that birth spacing is mediated by lactation, which generates prolactin that suppresses ovulation; that testosterone levels change with shifts in dominance, thereby affecting agonistic behavior; or that vision is subserved by an array of retinotopic maps. Neurophysiological descriptions are certainly a valid and important descriptive level, and no account of proximate mechanisms can be considered complete until the neurophysiological dimension has been worked out.

But adaptationist approaches, so far, have made only limited contributions to the investigation of neurophysiology (Tooby & Cosmides, 1989b), and vice versa. This is because, in many cases, the descriptive languages that are convenient for describing evolutionary processes and their consequences and the descriptive languages that are convenient for neuroscientists are too far apart to be intelligibly related. More important, unless you know that a particular information-processing system exists and what its function is, it is very difficult to discover its physiological underpinnings. Likewise, it is difficult to discover a mechanism simply by trying to piece together the welter of neuroscientific results. Who would look for the neurophysiological mechanisms responsible for vision unless they first knew that the eyes existed and that their function is to gather information from light striking the retina? Until researchers have an inventory of the functions of the human mind—that is, the collection of information-processing tasks the brain evolved to solve—neuroscientific approaches will be limited to an unguided empiricism that gropes its way among a forest of incredibly complex phenomena, without any way of knowing how to group results so that larger scale functional systems can be recognized.

Although presently very valuable (and ultimately indispensable), neurophysiological studies by themselves do not usually address a crucial *functional* level of explanation, a level that describes what a mechanism does, rather than how it does it. As a result, both neuroscientists and evolutionarily oriented researchers into human behavior can profit by addressing the central level of proximate causation, needed to tie the other levels together: the cognitive level, analyzed in adaptationist terms. The investigation of adaptations, described as information-processing systems, will prove illuminating to both evolutionary biology and neuroscience. Moreover, both groups seem to be converging from different directions on this level—witness, for example, the growth of cognitive neuroscience as well as of mechanism-oriented behavioral ecology and evolutionary psychology. We will argue that the cognitive level provides the previously missing common ground and conceptual tools necessary to forge richly informative relations between evolutionary biology and psychology, and then between an evolutionarily informed psychology and neuroscience.

The cognitive level is, of course, the characterization of psychological mechanisms in terms of their information-processing structure. This approach dovetails smoothly with evolution, because in the adaptive regulation of behavior, information is key. Behavior is not randomly emitted; it is elicited by information, which is gleaned from the organism's external environment, and, proprioceptively, from its internal states. Natural selection provided animals with information-processing machinery to produce behavior, just as it gave them food-processing machinery to produce digestion. This machinery selects—and frequently seeks—particular information from the environment; it manipulates such information according to structured procedures, extracts inferences from it, and stores some of it in memory in altered form; the machinery's output is used to make mental models, to inform other parts of the system, and to instruct the motor neurons responsible for behavior. Thus, behavior is one output of our information-processing machinery. Empirically, information-processing mechanisms can be explored because behavioral output differs with informational input; the information-processing machinery that maps informational input onto behavioral output is a psychological mechanism. In cognitive psychology, the term *mind* refers to an information-processing description of the operation of the brain—a description that, among other things, maps informational input onto behavioral output (Block, 1980; Fodor, 1981).

For these reasons, we suggest that the central organizing fact for psychology is that *the evolutionary function of the brain is to process information in ways that lead to adaptive behavior.* All adaptive behavior is predicated on adaptive thought: An animal must process information from its environment in ways that lead to fit behaviors while excluding unfit behaviors. Accordingly, characterizing proximate mechanisms in terms of their information-processing structure is not an arbitrary choice, but rather the most natural and appropriate course for psychologists to take. An information-processing framework provides a descriptive language excellently suited to capture the evolved design of proximate mechanisms. The cognitive level of explanation describes psychological mechanisms in functional terms, as programs that process information.

Traditionally, ethologists have—in effect—studied very simple cognitive programs: A newborn herring gull has a cognitive program that defines a red dot on the end of a beak as salient information from the environment, and that causes the newborn to peck at the red dot upon perceiving it. Its mother has a cognitive program that defines pecking at her red dot as salient information from her environment, and that causes her to regurgitate food into the newborn's mouth when she perceives its pecks.

Note that the descriptions of these simple programs are entirely in terms of the functional relationships among different pieces of information; they describe two simple information-processing systems. Naturally, these programs are instantiated in neurological machinery, and it will be informative to work out eventually what the neural substrate is. But knowledge of how such programs are implemented physically is separate from an understanding of these programs as information-processing systems. Each is a separate kind of knowledge describing different features of the situation (see, for example, Block, 1980 or Fodor, 1981, for more discussion of the nature of cognitive explanations). Presumably, one could build a silicon-based robot that would produce the same behavioral output in response to the same informational input as the herring gull's do. The robot's cognitive programs would maintain the same functional relationships among pieces of information and therefore be identical (on an information-processing level) to the cognitive programs of the herring gull. The robot's "neural" hardware, however, would be totally different. The specification of a cognitive program constitutes a complete description of an important level of proximate causation, independent of any knowledge of the physiological mechanisms by which the program is instantiated. Through information-processing descriptions of the structure of mechanisms one can develop an understanding of the workings of the mind on a functional level; in subsequent research, this can be tied to a complementary description of how such mechanisms are neurobiologically implemented (see Pylyshyn, 1984, and Marr, 1982, for a discussion of functional versus neurobiological levels of description; see also Cosmides, Tooby, & Barkow, 1992, for their relationship to other kinds of description).

When applied to behavior, the theory of natural selection is more closely allied with the cognitive level of explanation than with any other level of proximate causation. This is because the cognitive level seeks to specify a psychological mechanism's function, and the theory of natural selection is a theory about function. The theory of natural selection specifies how an organism should respond to different kinds of information from its environment. It defines adaptive information-processing problems that the organism must have some means of solving. Cognitive programs are solutions to information-processing problems.

An evolutionary explanation for behavior or structure explains why a behavior pattern or structure was selected for (that is, why it was functional) or, in the absence of a selectionist explanation, how it otherwise evolved. An evolutionary approach to understanding the cognitive level of proximate causation asks, What kind of programming must an organism have if it is to extract and process information about its environment in a way that will lead to adaptive behavior? How does the organism use information from its environment to compute what constitutes the "right" behavior at the right place and the right time (Staddon, 1987)? A cognitive explanation provides an information-processing description of how the proximate mechanisms involved operate. And a neurophysiological explanation provides a description of how the cognitive mechanism or computational design is physically implemented in the organism. Each level illuminates different issues, offers and requires distinct arrays of tools for research, and has its unique set of relationships and links to the other levels. We think each level is indispensable and emphasize the cognitive level and its links to the evolutionary level primarily because these relationships are, for too many research communities, a missing link on the path from evolution to behavior. Disregarding this level has proved crippling to many research efforts.

To understand these arguments it is important to keep clearly in mind what we mean by the cognitive or information processing level. Like all words, *cognitive* is used to mean many different things. For example, many psychologists use it in a narrow sense, to distinguish it as a kind of mental process distinct from others such as *emotion* or *motivation*—that is, as something that corresponds more or less to the folk concept of *thinking* while in a calm frame of mind. Many also associate it with so-called "higher" tasks, such as chess playing, mathematics, puzzle solving, and so on (of course, these were absent from our evolutionary history, and hence our ability to do them is an accidental by-product of evolved capacities). This characterization also builds on stereotypes; many cognitive psychologists study just these things: difficult, artificial tasks requiring deliberation and the application of culturally elaborated skills.

We are using the word *cognitive* in a completely unrelated sense, not as referring to any specific type of mental process, but rather as referring to a level of analysis and a descriptive language that can be applied to every psychological or indeed developmental process. Thus, one can have cognitive models of every aspect of an emotion (including associated physiological changes), of the regulation of breathing, or even of the development of calluses on hands (e.g., information derived from processes in the epidermal layer is procedurally evaluated to regulate whether growth rates should be increased and stabilized at a new thickness). Thus, *cognitive* in this usage is not a description of a type of process, but a method by which any regulatory process may be described—that is, in terms of functional relationships among units of information or contingent events. (One could even phrase it more abstractly: It is an explicit model of how a complexly contingent causal system interacts with a complexly contingent environment to produce predictable outcomes where both system and environment can temporally change.) Just as mathematics is an indispensable language for describing certain scientific models, procedural languages (of, for example, the kind used in computer programming) are precise descriptive languages for capturing how complex systems functionally interact with complex environments. Moreover, for reasons we will discuss, not only is this level of description methodologically convenient, but it allows the researcher to express in what is arguably the most appropriate and accurate terms the relationship between natural selection and the design of psychological mechanisms.

EVOLUTION, FUNCTION, AND THE COGNITIVE LEVEL

It is nearly impossible to discover how a psychological mechanism processes information unless one knows what its function is, what it was "designed" or selected to do. Trying to map out a cognitive program without knowing its function is like attempting to understand a computer program by examining it in machine language, without knowing whether it is for editing text, reconstructing three-dimensional images of the body from magnetic resonance data, or launching a space shuttle. It is perhaps conceivable that an inspired programmer may finally figure it out, but not probable, given that the programmer would not know what parts of the world its elements corresponded to, what was being regulated, what constituted successful or failing outcomes, and so on. If, on the other hand, the programmer knows that the program she is trying to map out is a text editor, she can begin by looking for a way of loading text, or for a command that will delete a word, or for a procedure that will move a whole paragraph. It is far easier to open up a black box and understand its architecture if one knows what it was designed to do.

Recognizing this, a number of cognitive scientists, such as Chomsky, Shepard, Fodor, and Marr, have argued that the best way to understand any mechanism, either mental or physical, is to first ask what its purpose is, what problem it was designed to solve (e.g., Chomsky, 1975; Fodor, 1983; Marr & Nishihara, 1978; Shepard, 1981).

This is exactly the question that evolutionary theory allows one to address. It allows one to pinpoint the kinds of problems the human mind was "designed" (that is, selected) to solve and consequently should be very good at solving. And although it cannot tell one the exact structure of the cognitive programs that solve these problems, it can suggest what design features they are likely to have. It allows one to develop a *computational theory* for that problem domain: a theory specifying the problem and therefore what functional characteristics a mechanism capable of solving that problem must have (Marr, 1982; Marr & Nishihara, 1978).

Many cognitive psychologists assume that the human mind is a general-purpose computer with domain-general, content-independent processes (Cosmides, 1989). From an evolutionary point of view, this is a highly implausible and unparsimonious assumption, and, in fact, one logically impossible to sustain. For virtually any vertebrate species (at least), there are domains of activity for which the evolutionarily appropriate information-processing strategy is complex, and deviations from this strategy result in large fitness costs. An organism that relied on the vagaries of, for example, trial-and-error learning for such domains would be at a severe selective disadvantage (see also Shepard, 1981). The more general and content-independent the process, the more alternatives there are to compute, and combinatorial explosion fatally cripples such systems (Cosmides, 1989; Cosmides & Tooby, 1987; Tooby & Cosmides, 1989a, 1990b).

Instead, for such domains, animal species should have evolved *Darwinian algorithms*—specialized mechanisms that organize experience into adaptively meaningful schemas or frames (Cosmides, 1985, 1989; Cosmides & Tooby, 1987). When activated by appropriate environmental or proprioceptive information, these innately specified "frame-builders" should focus attention, organize perception and memory, and call up specialized procedural knowledge that will lead to domain-appropriate inferences, judgments, and choices. Like Chomsky's language acquisition device, these inference procedures allow the organism to "go beyond the information given" in experience—to behave adaptively even in the face of incomplete or degraded information (Bruner, 1973). Such mechanisms constitute phylogenetically supplied structure designed to supply what is absent from the information available through experience, so that the two in concert can accomplish what either alone could not: the adaptive regulation of behavior.

What we call *Darwinian algorithms* have been called (sometimes with related but somewhat distinct meanings) *adaptive specializations* by Rozin (1976), *modules* by Fodor (1983), *cognitive competences* or *mental organs* by Chomsky (1975), or, more generally, psychological or cognitive adaptations. In our view, such evolved mechanisms have two defining characteristics: (1) They are (usually) most usefully described on the cognitive level of proximate causation, and (2) they are evolved adaptations. We have used the term *Darwinian algorithm* when addressing certain research communities because it emphasizes both characteristics.

There are many domains of human and nonhuman activity that should have Darwinian algorithms associated with them. Aggressive threat, mate choice, sexual behavior, parenting, parent–offspring conflict, friendship, kinship, resource accrual, resource distribution, disease avoidance, predator avoidance, and social exchange are but a few. The dynamics of natural selection shape the patterns of behavior that can evolve in such domains and therefore provide insights into the structure of the cognitive programs that produce these patterns.

COMPLEX ADAPTIVE PROBLEMS SHOULD BE DEFINED IN COMPUTATIONAL THEORIES

The signal lesson lurking beneath the surface of modern evolutionary biology is that adaptive behavior requires the solution of many information-processing problems that are highly complex—far more complex than is commonly supposed. The cognitive programs that allow the newborn herring gull to gain sustenance from its mother are relatively simple: They directly connect the perception of an environmental cue with an adaptively appropriate behavioral response. But not all adaptive problems are so easily solved, and many complex adaptive problems can be solved only by complex cognitive programs.

Discovering the structure of complex cognitive programs requires a great deal of theoretical guidance. A series of hunt-and-peck experiments may uncover a few simple cognitive programs, but it is unlikely that a research program that is blind to function will ever uncover the structure of a complex information-processing system, such as the human mind—or even an insect mind. Simple combinatorial explosion assures this result. If you analogize the structure of a psychological mechanism to a computer program, or try to write a computer program that duplicates what a psychological mechanism does, one will rapidly discover that it takes a large number of programming instructions to accomplish what even a simple psychological mechanism does. Complex psychological mechanisms might be likened to computer programs with thousands or even hundreds of thousands of lines of code. If the researcher has nothing to assist her aside from a pure faith in empiricism, the sheer number of alternative possibilities will almost always defeat the discovery of the architecture of the more complex psychological mechanisms. Without some valid expectations about what is to be found guiding the design of experiments and the strategy of investigation, psychological research will fail to capture or even to detect the complex psychological mechanisms responsible for regulating many rich domains of behavior. Thus, it has been no accident that the more theory-agnostic empirical research programs have tended to defend the position that all psychological phenomena can be explained by invoking a few, simple, general principles. Because of their research strategy, they could not have discovered more.

So, if theoretical guidance is necessary for a successful research program, what form should it take? In his pioneering studies of visual perception, David Marr argued that *computational theories* of each information-processing problem must be developed before progress can be made in experimentally investigating the cognitive programs that solve them (e.g., Marr, 1982; Marr & Nishihara, 1978). A computational theory is a task analysis; it specifies the nature of an information-processing problem. It does this by incorporating "constraints on the way the world is structured—constraints that provide sufficient information to allow the processing to succeed" (Marr & Nishihara, 1978, p. 41). A computational theory is an answer to the question, What must happen if a particular function is to be accomplished?

For example, the information-processing problem that Marr wanted to understand was how an organism reconstructs three-dimensional objects in the world from a two-dimensional retinal display. As you walk around a table with a square top, for example, light reflected from the tabletop hits your retina, projecting upon it a two-dimensional trapezoid of changing dimensions. Yet you do not perceive an ever-deforming, two-dimensional trapezoid. Instead, your cognitive programs use these data to construct a "percept" of a stable, three-dimensional, square tabletop.

To understand how we compute solid objects from data like these, Marr and his colleagues first examined relevant constraints and relationships that exist in the world, like the reflectant properties of surfaces. They considered the discovery of such constraints the "critical act" in formulating a theory of this computation, because these constraints must somehow be used by and embodied in any cognitive mechanism capable of solving this problem (Marr, 1982; Marr & Nishihara, 1978). Marr called the specification of such constraints, together with their deductive implications, a computational theory of an information-processing problem.

Natural selection, in a particular ecological situation, defines and constitutes "valid constraints on the way the world is structured," and therefore can be used to create computational theories of adaptive information-processing problems. Such constraints can be drawn from the structure of selection pressures, from the statistical structure of ancestral environments, or from their combination. For example, cognitive programs that are designed to regulate the disposition of benefits on kin will be selected to conform to the [cost to self in terms of forgone reproduction < (benefit to kin member in terms of enhanced reproduction) weighted by (the probability of sharing a gene at a random locus identical by descent with the kin member)] constraint of kin selection theory (Hamilton, 1964). The more a cognitive program violates this constraint, the more it is selected against. Equally, the more closely a cognitive program instantiates this constraint, the more strongly it will be selected for. This constraint is inherent in the dynamics of natural selection, and thus should apply to any species from any habitat at any time during evolutionary history. For various reasons, members of a species may be precluded from conferring benefits on their relatives, but if they regularly do, then understanding this constraint will help to discover the structure of the cognitive programs responsible.

The production of behavior that respects constraints imposed by the evolutionary process is a cognitive program's *adaptive function*—that is, it was the reason it was selected for. In other words, the production of behavior that more closely conforms to favored adaptive strategies is the criterion by which alternative designs for cognitive programs are filtered, so that the program (out of the alternatives that appear) that most closely implements these design requirements is the one that most often spreads through the population to become a species-typical trait.

The specification of constraints imposed by the evolutionary process—the specification of an adaptive function—does not, in itself, constitute a complete computational theory. These constraints merely define what counts as adaptive behavior. Cognitive programs are the means by which behavior—adaptive or otherwise—is produced. The important question for a computational theory to address is: What kind of cognitive programs must an organism have if it is to produce behavior that meets these adaptive criteria?

Natural selection theorists do not usually think of their theories as defining information-processing problems, yet this is precisely what they do. For example, kin selection theory raises and answers questions such as, How would a well-designed psychological architecture treat the information that individual X is its brother, and how should it regulate decisions about helping him? How should its assessment of the cost to it of helping its brother, versus the benefit to the brother of receiving help, affect the decision? Should the information that Y is a cousin alter the decision on the allocation of assistance between its newborn and its brother? In general, how should a good design treat information about relatedness and the costs and benefits of actions on individuals in order to improve its decision making?

As these questions show, an organism's behavior cannot fall within the bounds of the constraints imposed by the evolutionary process unless it is guided by cognitive programs that can solve certain information-processing problems that are very specific. To confer benefits on kin in accordance with the constraints of kin selection theory, the organism must have cognitive programs that allow it to extract certain specific information from its environment: Who are its relatives? Which kin are close and which distant? What are the costs and benefits of an action to itself and to its kin? The organism's behavior will be random with respect to the constraints of kin selection theory unless (a) it has some means of extracting information relevant to these questions from its environment, and (b) it has well-defined decision rules that use this information in ways that instantiate the theory's constraints. A cognitive system can generate adaptive behavior only if it can perform specific information-processing tasks such as these.

The fact that any organism capable of conferring benefits on its kin must have cognitive programs capable of solving these information-processing problems does not imply that different species will solve each problem via the same cognitive program. There are many reasons why such programs may differ. For example, different environmental cues may have different reliabilities and accessibilities for different species. Moreover, each species occupies a different ecological niche, and hence the value of particular actions will differ across species: The cognitive programs of a baboon will assign a different value to social grooming than will the cognitive programs of a whale. But cognitive programs that perform the same function in different species may differ in more profound ways. For example, the cognitive programs for recognizing kin might operate through phenotype matching in one species, but through early imprinting in another species (Holmes, 1983). Both programs will accomplish the same important adaptive function. Yet they will embody radically different information-processing procedures, and they will process different information from the environment. For this and other reasons, in constructing a computational theory or task analysis, it is usually not enough simply to know the relevant evolutionary theory.

COMPUTATIONAL THEORIES SHOULD CONTAIN AN ANALYSIS OF THE STRUCTURE OF THE ENVIRONMENT

Usually, in building a task analysis, understanding the relevant evolutionary theory is a necessary starting point. This may involve both a basic familiarity with models of the evolutionary process (including such things as definitions of fitness, selection, adaptation, genes, the role of stochastic factors) and the available models of the selection pressures relevant to the problem under study (such as descriptions of the selectional principles governing such domains as kin-directed altruism, reciprocation, sexual recombination, and sexual selection). But such models will rarely be sufficient, in themselves, to build a model of the task facing the organism. Almost always, it will be necessary to analyze how these principles were manifested as a species-specific array of selection pressures, refracted through the specific ecological, social, genetic, phylogenetic, and informational circumstances experienced along a given species' evolutionary history (Tooby & Cosmides, 1990b; Tooby & DeVore, 1987). This is the characterization of ancestral conditions, sometimes referred to as the *environment of evolutionary adaptedness* or EEA.

Selection acts so that the properties of evolved psychological and developmental mechanisms tend to mesh together with the recurrent structure of the world so that their interaction produces functional outcomes. Theories of selection pressures provide definitions of what counts as a functional outcome. And because of this mesh between environment and mechanism, an analysis of the recurrent structure of the world—or that portion of it relevant to the problem or problem-solving mechanism—is a rich source of information about the mechanism. For this reason, the analysis of the structure of the ancestral world is a critical part of the construction of a computational theory.

Often, of course, because most of the properties of the world stay the same, the modern world provides a satisfactory laboratory for the analysis of the structure of many ancestral environments and conditions. For example, in understanding how color vision works, or in studying the ontogeny and regulation of bipedal locomotion, the relevant parts of the modern world provide an adequate model. For many animal species studied in the field, modern conditions are doubtless as representative of these species' EEA as anything additional inference could contrive. For humans, however, many aspects of the world have changed dramatically, and so the reconstruction of hominid ancestral conditions is more necessary. The structure of cues and events in modern suburban environments, for example, is not a good model for how predators impinged on our hominid ancestors, and in such cases models of ancestral conditions must be reconstructed from the array of available sources (see Tooby & Cosmides, 1990b; Tooby & DeVore, 1987, for discussion). And as informative as evolutionary theory is, it cannot substitute for a model of ancestral conditions. Evolutionary theory cannot tell you such things as how often individual variance in foraging success was substantially greater than band-wide variance, important in understanding the psychology of hominid reciprocation (Cosmides & Tooby, 1992); nor can it tell you the mean ecological frequency of hominid-menacing predators, how far off they can be spotted in various landscapes, or what types of naturally occurring refuges were typically available (see Orians & Heerwagen, 1992, for a discussion of human habitat selection).

In developing such descriptions, it is important to remember that the environment of evolutionary adaptedness (EEA) is not a place or a habitat, or even a time period. Rather, it is a statistical composite of the adaptation-relevant properties of the ancestral environments encountered by members of ancestral populations, weighted by their frequency and fitness-consequences. For example, how often was the cue of a snake-shape linked to a venomous bite? The properties used to build the composite are selected out of all possible environmental properties as those that actually interacted with the existing design of the organism during the period of evolution. Whether or not these things are observable by the organism, they can be "known" (that is, reflected) in the structure of the mechanisms because natural selection will select those mutant designs whose structure conforms to these otherwise unobservable features of the world. Thus, organisms can act far more appropriately than can be explained by "experience," through the action of specialized mechanisms that reflect the structure of evolutionarily recurrent situations. Domain-general mechanisms, which must reflect equally the structure of every possible situation, can thus supply no specialized guidance in the solution of particular families of problems.

Thus, statistical and structural regularities define the EEA. The conditions that characterize the EEA are usefully decomposed into a constellation of specific environmental regularities that had impact on fitness and that endured long enough to work evolutionary change on the design of an adaptation. For convenience, we have called these statistical regularities *invariances*. Invariances need not be conditions that were absolutely unwavering, although many, such as the properties of light or chemical reactions, were. Rather, an invariance is a single descriptive construct, calculated from the point of view of a selected adaptation or design of a given genotype at a given point of time. No matter how variable conditions were, they left a systematically structured average impact on the design, and that systematic impact needs to be coherently characterized in terms of the statistical and structural regularities that constituted the selection pressure responsible. These invariances can be described as sets of conditionals of any degree of complexity, from the very simple (e.g., the temperature was always greater than freezing) to a two-valued statistical construct (e.g., the temperature had a mean of 31.2C and standard deviation of 8.1), to any degree of conditional and structural complexity that is reflected in the adaptation (e.g., predation on kangaroo rats by shrikes is 17.6% more likely during a cloudless full moon than during a new moon during the first 60 days after the winter solstice if one exhibits adult male ranging patterns). Thus, as a composite, it is necessarily "uniform" in the abstract sense, although that uniform description may involve the detailed characterization of any degree of environmental variability—which may, in fact, have selected for mechanisms that can track such variability and respond accordingly.

Of course, from the point of view of an adaptation or mechanism, important parts of the structure of the world include not just the external physical, biological, and social environment, but also the regularities presented by the other mechanisms in the brain and body, as well as in others' minds and bodies. The lungs are part of the EEA to the heart, and cross-cultural regularities in emotional expression or grammatical structure are part of the EEA to face interpretation mechanisms and the language acquisition device, respectively.

Thus, a computational theory of an adaptive problem is defined by the recurrent structure of the world, the structure of selection pressures, and how these combine to create demands for certain kinds of information processing. These must be directly reflected in the design of any mechanism that solves the adaptive problem, when it is expressed in information-processing terms. As we shall discuss, such computational theories are invaluable as heuristic guides for psychological research. This is true even though there may be many possible information-processing structures that could potentially solve the adaptive problem. (Moreover, one of course needs evidence that the organism actually does regularly solve the adaptive problem under EEA-like conditions more often than would be expected by chance.) In the likely event that there is more than one possible mechanism design that could solve the adaptive problem, then experimentation is needed to discover which design the organism actually has.

THE IMPORTANCE OF COMPUTATIONAL THEORIES

A computational theory is a description of the specific information-processing problems and subtasks regularly encountered by a species during its evolutionary history, including the ecological, informational, social, and physiological conditions in which the problems were regularly embedded. These problems should be catalogued and made explicit, for they are the building blocks of psychological theories. There are two reasons why this is so.

The first is obvious. These computational theories supply a great deal of the theoretical guidance necessary to construct experiments and studies, saving the researcher from groping along on blind empiricism alone. They provide suggestions about the kinds of mechanisms an organism is likely to have, about the kinds of information from the environment a mechanism subserving a given function will be monitoring, about what the goals of the mechanism are (that is, what functional outcomes it is designed to produce), and so on. Knowing, for example, that an organism—because of its ancestral social environment and inclusive fitness theory—must have some means of distinguishing kin from nonkin may not uniquely determine the structure of a cognitive program, but it does help narrow hypotheses. The cognitive program responsible must be sensitive to environmental cues that correlate with kin but do not correlate with nonkin. In most cases, very few cues from the species' environment of evolutionary adaptedness will be sufficiently reliable or accessible, and the researcher can in due course discover which are used by the organism's cognitive programs. Discovering which cues are used will illuminate other of the program's information-processing procedures: Early exposure suggests an imprinting process, whereas facial similarity suggests phenotype matching procedures. Step by step, deduction by deduction, experiment by experiment, the cognitive programs responsible for kin recognition can be mapped. In the meantime, the researcher who is blind to function will not even be looking for a program that guides kin recognition, let alone figure out which environmental stimuli it monitors, what representations are constructed from these cues, and what procedures act on these representations to regulate behavior.

The second reason why a fully elaborated computational theory is useful is less obvious, but perhaps equally important. The computational theory allows a test of adequacy that any proposed psychological theory must be able to pass. The test is this: *Is the hypothesized system of cognitive programs powerful enough to realize the computational theory? That is, is the proposed mechanism capable of solving the adaptive problem?* This allows one to rule out certain theoretical approaches without having to test each one of an infinitely expandable list of hypotheses. Many can be eliminated simply by seriously inquiring what computational architecture is being assumed by the hypothesis and analyzing its performance capabilities.

Any proposed cognitive system must be powerful enough to produce adaptive behaviors while *not* simultaneously producing too burdensome a set of maladaptive behaviors. (One can equally well use this test with a less controversial standard: Any hypothesized mechanism advanced as being responsible for certain behavioral phenomena must be powerful enough to produce the observed behavior while *not* simultaneously producing too large a set of behaviors that are not observed.) Not just any cognitive program will do: Our cognitive programs must be constructed in such a way that they somehow lead to the adaptive results specified by evolutionary theory on the basis of the information available. This test of computational sufficiency (see Pinker, 1979, 1984, 1989) or solvability (see Tooby & Cosmides, 1992) often allows researchers to eliminate whole categories of hypotheses. In particular, current research in cognitive psychology and artificial intelligence suggests that many of the general-purpose learning theories that are widely accepted by social and behavioral scientists are not powerful enough to solve even artificially simplified computational problems, let alone the complex information-processing problems regularly imposed by selective forces operating over evolutionary time. Because of the survival of extant species into the present, we know for a fact that they can successfully solve an entire suite of problems necessary to reproduction, and we need to develop theories of the architecture of the information-processing mechanisms—the cognitive adaptations—that allow them to do it.

Researchers involved in empirical debates are all to conscious of the fact that there are an inexhaustible set of alternative hypotheses that can be invented by the ingenious to avoid having to dispose of cherished intellectual positions. Therefore, the empirical testing of each hypothesis in turn from this potentially inexhaustible set cannot by itself be a practical research strategy. One must be able to integrate these empirical findings with other sources of valid inference to be able to draw larger and more interesting conclusions. For psychologists, the analysis of computational performance is one approach to doing this.

THE ANALYSIS OF COMPUTATIONAL PERFORMANCE

Thirty years ago, Noam Chomsky inaugurated a new era in cognitive psychology when he explored psychological questions by analyzing the capacities of well-specified computational systems (Chomsky, 1957, 1959). He was attempting to evaluate the adequacy of behaviorist accounts of language, such as Skinner's *Ver-*

bal Behavior (1957). To perform such an analysis, Chomsky needed models or descriptions of two components of the question. The first model essentially corresponded to what Marr subsequently called a computational theory—a task analysis defining the problem to be solved, which specifies things such as what counts as success, what are the conditions under which the candidate mechanisms must perform, what information is available to the mechanism, and so on. Language was an excellent choice for such a test of behaviorist accounts of psychological phenomena, because language—particularly syntax—involved complex but clearly specifiable patterns of behavior. Within this domain, one could define without ambiguity and with great exactitude criteria for recognizing what behavioral patterns humans could and did routinely produce and, therefore, what any mechanism hypothesized to account for this behavior had to produce as well. (In these early analyses, Chomsky focused not on the issue of whether conditioning processes could account for the initial learning of language, but on the far more restricted question of whether behaviorist mechanisms, having complete access to grammatical rules in whatever fashion they could be represented within the system, could be made to produce as output a defined subset of grammatical English sentences.)

The second description or model Chomsky needed was a formalization, in computational or information-processing terms, of the hypothesis being tested—in this case, stimulus-response (S-R) learning theory. This marked an important departure from the then widespread practice, still endemic in psychology, of failing to specify the computational architecture of the mechanism being proposed, and instead simply positing a black box described solely in terms of its assumed ability to produce certain consequences. To actually see whether a mechanism is capable of solving a problem, one needs a well-specified description of the information-processing structure of the mechanism being hypothesized. Whenever a hypothesis about a psychological mechanism is being advanced, one needs to carefully investigate what computational architecture for the mechanism is being assumed or is entailed. In this case, Chomsky (following others) settled on finite state devices as natural implementations of Hullian learners, along with some other background assumptions necessary for the analysis to proceed.

The third step in such an analysis is to apply the model of the mechanism to the model of the task and thereby explore how the proposed computational system performs, given the conditions and the goals as defined in the computational theory. What parts, if any, of the problem can the hypothesized mechanism solve? What are the strengths and weaknesses of the mechanism's performance? What information or environmental conditions does the mechanism need to be present in order to succeed? Does it require infinite memory, or immensely long periods of computation, or certain specific cues? Of course, the most basic question is, Is the design of the candidate mechanism computationally sufficient to solve the problem (Pinker, 1979, 1984, 1989)? That is, can the computational system solve the problem? If not, of course, the hypothesis can be ruled out.

In this case, for Chomsky's general analysis, the computational theory was the grammar of the English language as it is known by ordinary speakers: all the grammatical sentences of English, such as "the child seems asleep," but not the indefinitely larger set of ungrammatical sentences, such as "the child seems to sleeping." The information-processing problem to be solved was the production or recognition of sentences that conformed to this set. The question Chomsky addressed was: Can these sentences be produced by a finite state device similar to the mechanisms proposed by the behaviorists of the time? By using this approach, and related, more informal arguments, Chomsky was able to persuade many psychologists and linguists that finite state devices (and their incarnation in psychology, behaviorist theories of conditioning) were not tenable explanations for human language competence because they were incapable of solving many language-related tasks in any plausible fashion. Given realistic assumptions about memory, the total number of states allowable to the system, and similar considerations, the general-purpose, S-R learning mechanisms proposed by the behaviorists were not powerful enough to generate the set of sentences that conformed to English grammar—that is, they were not powerful enough to produce many grammatical sentences while simultaneously precluding the production of large classes of ungrammatical sentences. As one part of this analysis, Chomsky formally demonstrated that finite state grammars were completely incapable of generating a well-defined subset of grammatical English sentences. Perhaps more significant for subsequent research, Chomsky sketched other difficulties this family of mechanisms had in dealing with issues of acquisition, generalization, phonology, semantics, and so on. By performing this kind of analysis, Chomsky showed that S-R learning mechanisms could not plausibly account for the fact that people speak English. Given, of course, that some people do speak English, his computational analysis allowed Chomsky to eliminate a whole class of hypotheses for language competence: those invoking mechanisms that embody finite state grammars (Chomsky, 1957, 1959). Moreover, if there was at least one class of behaviors that could not be accounted for by standard conditioning theory, then S-R mechanisms could not therefore be a complete account of the mind. This pointed to the possibility that there might be a large array of mental mechanisms that did not operate according to S-R principles.

Chomsky's pioneering analysis, despite some controversy about the generality of its conclusions, initiated a vigorous research program into the cognitive mechanisms underlying the human language faculty. Subsequently, many researchers have worked on constructing nonbehaviorist psychological theories of language that include more powerful and more specialized computational machinery (for a review, see Wanner & Gleitman, 1982). Of more lasting significance, however, is the general strategy that continues to guide some of this work: Many psycholinguists and linguists have tended to pursue their research through (a) the empirical investigation of natural language production, acquisition, perception, and comprehension, including the structure it displays and the computational problems it poses, and (b) the use of this knowledge to construct increasingly sophisticated models of various components of the human language faculty, often through exploring and evaluating the performance of the various candidate computational mechanisms hypothesized to manage these tasks. By approaching the psychology of language in this way, psycholinguists have been able to make substantial progress in exploring one of the most complex phenomena facing psychologists.

We suggest that there are a series of lessons to be drawn from these developments in psycholinguistics that might be productively applied elsewhere in psychology. The first lesson is to focus on the mechanisms responsible for generating behavioral phenomena, and not just on the behavioral phenomena themselves. The second is to insist that these hypotheses about mechanisms be made computationally explicit, that is, that a cognitive or information-processing model of the mechanism be supplied. This element, though sometimes laborious, has become far easier given the widespread accessibility of computers and easy programming languages, as well as the broad array of other tools for formal analysis. The third lesson is the value of constructing careful computational theories or task analyses of the problem being addressed by the mechanism. And, finally, the last lesson is the value of combining these elements in order to evaluate the performance of alternative candidate mechanisms in solving the tasks or generating the observed patterns of behavior. In short, it is very productive for behavioral scientists to analyze phenomena from a cognitive, information-processing, or computational perspective. We should move beyond the hand-waving stage of theorizing, in which black boxes are endowed with miraculous abilities through the bestowal of labels. Instead, we should investigate explicitly described computational architectures and the performance they can be expected to generate. In so doing, the field of psychology has everything to gain and nothing to lose.

LEARNABILITY AND DOMAIN-SPECIFICITY

The emergence of this form of analysis in psycholinguistics serves to illustrate the value of the analysis of computational performance, and we suggest that this tool can provide an equally effective tool for psychologists in other areas, assisting in the investigation of the mechanisms responsible for generating the behavioral phenomena they study. The investigation of "learnability" in the study of language acquisition may prove particularly instructive for psychologists, because its analysis mixes two issues of widespread applicability throughout psychology. Many tasks successfully faced by organisms are complex and also involve "learning," that is, the modification of a specific competency using information derived from encounters with the world. In fact, for many social and behavioral scientists, "learning" is treated as a key explanation for many phenomena. What lessons are there in the study of language acquisition about the issue of learning?

The purpose of a learnability analysis is to evaluate whether a proposed information-processing mechanism is capable of learning to solve the problem that its advocates claim it can solve, given the information that is available to it in the environment (Pinker, 1979, 1984, 1989). In short, it is the question of computational sufficiency applied to models of learning mechanisms (Pinker, 1984). For example, to learn to solve a given problem, different information-processing mechanisms require different kinds of environmental information. If the information necessary for a given mechanism to work does not exist in the environment, yet the organism being studied solves the problem, then one knows that the mechanism under consideration is not the one that is responsible for the organism's performance. Instead, an alternative design is required, which, for example, may supply the missing information that is necessary for the learning process to succeed through the evolved structure of its procedures.

Learnability analyses have been most fully developed in psycholinguistics, where they have been used to evaluate, reject, or suggest modifications in hypotheses about how a child acquires the grammar of the language spoken by its adult community (Pinker, 1979, 1982, 1984, 1989; Pinker & Prince, 1988; see also Grimshaw, 1981; Wexler & Culicover, 1980). For example, some hypotheses about the information-processing mechanisms responsible for grammar acquisition require that adults provide reliable feedback when the child makes a grammatical error. Yet lengthy transcripts of parent–child interactions have been collected and analyzed, and these show that adults rarely correct children's grammatical errors (Pinker, 1989). In fact, children acquire grammar normally even in cultures in which adults do not regularly converse with very young children, where overheard streams of adult–adult speech constitute the only informational input available to the child's learning mechanisms (Heath, 1983; Pinker, 1991). Consequently, one can reject any hypothesis that posits the existence of a learning mechanism that will work only if the child reliably gets negative feedback when he or she makes a grammatical error.

The rise of Chomskyan psycholinguistics (especially learnability analysis) constituted an important turning point in the development of modern psychology. Up until that point, psychology had been overwhelmingly dominated by general-purpose learning and cognitive theories. These theories were *domain-general*: The same process was supposed to account for learning in all domains of human activity, from suckling at the breast to the most esoteric feat of modern technology. General-purpose mechanisms are still the favored kind of hypothesis throughout the social and behavioral sciences (Tooby & Cosmides, 1992). Yet by specifying what actually needs to be accomplished in order to acquire grammar, psycholinguists have shown that a task routinely mastered by four-year-old children was too complexly structured to be accounted for by, for example, S-R learning theory.

Of course, modern incarnations of domain-general explanations of language acquisition have fared no better against the battery of specialized computational problems posed by language than did their behaviorist predecessors. When each new computational technology appears in psychology (from telephone switching systems to holograms to computers to new programming languages), in the heady excitement of exploring the potentialities of the new technology the crippling weaknesses of associationism are forgotten. This pattern was most recently reenacted with the advent of connectionism, which was initially taken by many to be a computational model of a domain-general associationism that could work. Yet, in the careful application of this family of models to actual adaptive problems real organisms solve, all of the same difficulties reappear. For example, through careful learnability and computational performance analyses, Pinker and Prince (1988; Pinker, 1991) were able to show that the existing domain-general connectionist model for the acquisition of the past tense in English was computationally insufficient to solve the problem and can (at most) reflect only part of the relevant mechanisms. Many of the reasons the model failed were not specific to the particular connectionist model proposed, but instead were general to domain-general connectionist models (Fodor & Pylyshyn, 1988). Of course, connectionist designs—like every other possible architecture—run into such logically inescapable problems as combinatorial explosion and the need for "innately supplied" specialized structure, meaning that functional connectionist architectures that solve real adaptive problems will also turn out to require domain-specific designs (see, e.g., Jacobs, Jordan, & Barto, 1990; Miller & Todd, 1990; Todd & Miller, 1991a, 1991b). Thus, while connectionist models provide an interesting and important addition to the range of computational systems available for modeling psychological processes, they do not provide any escape from domain-specificity.

Work on language learnability has convinced many psychologists that no general-purpose learning mechanism would be powerful enough to permit the acquisition of the grammar of a natural language under natural conditions. But what kind of learning mechanism would have the requisite power? The conclusion has been that the acquisition of a natural language grammar requires cognitive programming that is not only complex, but specialized. Chomsky argued that just as the body has many different organs, each of which is specialized for performing a different function—a heart for pumping blood, a liver for detoxifying poisons—the mind can be expected to include many different "mental organs" (Chomsky, 1980). A mental organ is an information-processing system that is specialized for performing a specific cognitive function. A mental organ instantiates learning theories that are *domain-specific*: Its procedures are specialized for quick and efficient learning about an evolutionarily important domain of activity. Chomsky argued that the acquisition of a grammar could be accomplished only through a highly structured and complex *language acquisition device* (LAD): a functionally distinct mental organ that is specialized for learning a language.

The problem posed by the child's acquisition of the local grammar is that there are an indefinitely large set of grammars that can, in principle, generate whatever subset of adult language the child hears. Only one of them is correct, and the child picks the correct one, even though an infinity are logically possible. Despite the fact that the data available to the child are insufficient by themselves, the child must induce which of these grammars in fact generated that sample. This cannot be done unless the design features of the evolved mechanisms that allow the child to learn language place constraints on the child's hypothesis space that reflect actual adult grammar. If the mechanisms were content-independent and domain-general, they would have no information about the nature of adult grammar that could allow the mechanisms in the child to decide among alternatives. Only mechanisms that came specifically equipped with this "knowledge" could determine which adult grammar is actually being spoken. Where does this "knowledge"—perhaps in the form of procedures or other structural features in the mechanisms—come from? The Chomskian argument is inherently adaptationist: Nothing, apart from selection, can endow the LAD with just those adaptive specializations necessary to supply the information regularly missing from adult speech samples, coordinating the two so that the local adult grammar can be uniquely determined (Pinker & Bloom, 1990; see also Tooby & Cosmides, 1990c). The evolved procedures of a child's language acquisition device depend for their success upon stable and enduring species-typical regularities of the grammar-producing mechanisms of adults.

In this history, there are several increasingly familiar lessons. The first is that it pays to develop explicit models of the mechanisms proposed. The second is that adaptive problems, when dissected, usually turn out to be far more complex than is commonly appreciated. The third is that this complexity tends to require corresponding specialization in the psychological machinery in order to address the unique features of the specific problem type—that is, mechanisms capable of solving adaptive problems will frequently be domain-specific. Fourth, the structure of the world needs to be studied (or at least that part of it relevant to the problem to be solved), because the mechanism evolved to mesh with this structure to produce the functional consequence. And finally, the fact that a psychological phenomenon falls under the heading of "learning" makes no difference—one still needs a model of the environment, the mechanism, and their interaction.

Learnability analyses can, and should, be applied to all adaptive problems involving "learning," that is, that involve the modification of competences based on encounters with the world. Of course, no hypothesis about an information-processing device can be evaluated unless it has been made sufficiently explicit. Black boxes labeled "capacity to learn what foods have the highest number of calories per unit of toxin," "ability to learn how to be a good parent," "capacity for culture," "capacity to learn to maximize inclusive fitness," and so on do not qualify: A label is not a substitute for a hypothesis. A computational system (such as we are) cannot be given abilities through magical fiat, and to understand such a system one needs to go through the explicit enumeration of all the causal steps necessary to produce behavior. Of course, it is a laborious task to detail actual procedures for even relatively simple tasks. But it is a standard that exposes hand-waving, as well as hypotheses that depend on the operation of previously unrecognized miracles. There is a traditional lament among junior military officers who have just been given orders: Nothing is impossible for the person who doesn't have to do it. In the social and behavioral sciences, no model of a species' psychological architecture seems impossible when its proponents do not have to specify by what methods it generates the necessary behavior. In particular, domain-general, content-independent "learning" and cognitive processes have gotten a free ride by having been left unspecified as to computational architecture. They seem attractive hypotheses because being unspecified, nothing can be impossible to them.

Many psychologists think of the dispute over Chomsky's language acquisition device as a controversy about innateness, but, as we shall see later, it was not. "Innate" is not the "opposite" of "learned." Every coherent learning theory—even Hume's associationism or Skinner's brand of behaviorism—assumes the existence of innate cognitive mechanisms that structure experience. A "blank slate" will stay forever blank: Without innate cognitive mechanisms, learning is impossible (e.g., Hume, 1977/1748; Kant, 1966/1781; Quine, 1969; Popper, 1972). As Herrnstein (1977) points out, Skinnerian learning theorists were able to avoid discussion of the innate cognitive mechanisms governing generalization and discrimination only by ignoring the problem of which dimensions, out of uncountable possibilities, are used by the organism. Instead, the controversy in psycholinguistics was important because it highlighted the weakness in the most central explanatory concept in the history of psychology: learning.

"LEARNING" IS NOT AN "ALTERNATIVE HYPOTHESIS"

Many common concepts in the behavioral and social sciences are used as if they were hypotheses and explanations, when in fact they are not. "Learning" stands out as one of these: It is a concept that many people believe is heavily freighted with explanatory power. Analytically, however, the only meaning operationally coupled to the word "learned" is "environmentally influenced." As a hypothesis to account specifically and causally for mental or behavioral phenomena, it is nearly devoid of meaning.

Processes categorized as "learning" are accomplished through information-processing mechanisms, of course, and what matters is the discovery of the specific structures of these mechanisms. Their architectures may be (and arguably are) completely different from each other, and the application of the same label—learning—to describe all of them conceals this fact. Thus, such mechanisms may be simple or complex, domain-general or domain-specific, present from birth or late developing, and so on. An organism may be endowed with many different learning mechanisms, or just a few. The ubiquitous belief that the human mind, for example, contains only one domain-general cognitive process that results in "learning"—whether "induction" or "hypothesis testing" or "conditioning" or "imitation" or "rationality"—is nothing but conjecture conventionally accepted in many research communities as a fact (see Tooby & Cosmides, 1992). It has no empirical basis at all and in cognitive psychology appears to be a metatheoretical holdover from the heyday of behaviorism.

In reality, the controversy in psycholinguistics was over whether the evolved learning mechanisms that allow humans to acquire a grammar are simple and domain-general or complex and domain-specific (e.g., Atherton & Schwartz, 1974; Chomsky, 1975; Katz, 1975; Marshall, 1981; Pinker, 1979; Putnam, 1967). The behaviorists thought that the simple, domain-general processes of classical and operant conditioning were plausible accounts for language; Chomsky and his successors showed that they were not and proposed the existence of learning mechanisms that were complex and domain-specific. Both camps agreed that language is "learned" (i.e., requires exposure to language environments); they disagreed about *how* it is learned (i.e., about what the nature of the evolved mechanisms is).

The failure to grasp this point leads to enormous conceptual confusion in the behavioral sciences. The common belief that "learning" is an alternative hypothesis to an evolutionary theory of adaptive function is a category error. Learning is a label for a family of cognitive processes (defined solely by the fact that they modify some aspect of the behavioral control system in interaction with the world). An adaptive function is not a cognitive process; it is a problem that is solved by a cognitive process. Learning is accomplished through psychological mechanisms (whose nature is most often not understood), and these were created through the evolutionary process, which includes natural selection. Consequently, the issue can never sensibly be whether a particular behavior is the result of natural selection "or" learning. The issue is: What is the evolved information-processing structure of the learning mechanisms involved in producing a particular behavior? More generally, one might ask: What kinds of learning mechanisms does natural selection tend to produce?

As Symons has cogently argued, this has been the substance of the nature–nurture controversy—which could not have genuinely been about innateness at all, since all (coherent) participants must acknowledge the reliable development of some evolved structure in the psychological architecture (Symons, 1987). Instead the debate is really about whether the innate mechanisms are few and domain-general, or many and functionally specialized. Thus, when behavioral scientists are arguing about whether aggression is "innate," the substance of the debate (however they may put it to themselves) is whether there are any features of the psychological architecture that evolved specifically to regulate aggression, or whether aggression is purely a result of the same few domain-general learning mechanisms that are putatively responsible for nonsense syllable memorization or domino matching. So, one question to ask is: Are the mechanisms that constitute the human psychological architecture few and general, or do they include many specialized mechanisms for food choice, foraging decisions, mate choice, incest avoidance, aggression regulation, social exchange regulation, sexual jealousy, parental care, and so on?

As discussed, when models of cognitive programs become sufficiently well specified to actually account for empirical results, they almost always turn out to be complex and domain-specific. When researchers present such well-specified models together with the empirical results that support them, they are often met with the counterclaim that "people might just learn to think that way." Yet, the invocation of an unspecified learning process does not constitute a valid alternative hypothesis. Suggesting that "learning" is an alternative hypothesis is comparable to claiming that an alternative hypothesis to a well-specified theory of vision, such as Marr's (1982), is "light hits the retina and this causes the organism to see three-dimensional objects." This is not an explanation; it is a description of the phenomenon to be explained. All the intervening steps are missing: It does not count as an "alternative hypothesis" because no one has bothered to specify the nature of the cognitive programs that cause it to happen.

"Learning" designates the phenomenon to be explained. A complex, domain-specific cognitive program *is* a learning mechanism; how, then, can "learning" be construed as an "alternative hypothesis"?

The claim that a behavior is the product of "culture" is not an "alternative hypothesis" either. It entails nothing more than the claim that surrounding or preceding individuals are an environmental factor that has influenced the behavior under discussion in some way. It leaves the learning mechanisms that allow humans to acquire and generate culture completely unspecified (Tooby & Cosmides, 1989a, 1992).

Interestingly, evolutionary researchers are often subject to a reciprocal species of error (see discussion in Tooby & Cosmides, 1990b). Many seem to operate from the implicit premise that an organism can "decide" which course of action, however complex, will promote its inclusive fitness simply by inspecting the environment. These researchers interpret the fact that humans were produced by the evolutionary process to mean that humans must be maximizing their inclusive fitness in all situations, or at least attempting to do so, even in evolutionarily unprecedented modern environments. This view makes sense only if one believes that the organism has a cognitive program that says "do that which maximizes your inclusive fitness." Yet this is merely a veiled way of claiming that the organism "learns" what to do to maximize its fitness. It is not a hypothesis. It leaves "learning" a mysterious, omniscient, and utterly unspecified process.

It is improper to invoke an undefined process as an explanation. "Learning" should not be invoked to explain other phenomena at this point in the development of psychology, because it is itself a phenomenon that requires explanation. The nature of the cognitive processes that allow learning to occur are far from understood.

The tendency to assume that learning is accomplished only through a few simple domain-general mechanisms lingers in many branches of psychology, including cognitive psychology. We believe this metatheoretical stance is seriously flawed, and persists only because psychologists and evolutionary biologists have not joined forces to create computational theories that catalog the specific and detailed information-processing problems entailed by the need to track fitness under Pleistocene or ancestral conditions. Later, we join Daly and Wilson (1988), Gallistel (1990), Pinker and Bloom (1990; see also Pinker, 1991), Rozin (1976), Shepard (1981), Symons (1987), and many others in arguing that a consideration of such problems suggests that natural selection has produced a great many cognitive programs that are complex and highly domain-specific.

INNATENESS, SPECIES-TYPICAL DESIGN, AND INDIVIDUAL DIFFERENCES

Before discussing why evolutionary considerations suggest that most psychological adaptations will be domain-specific, that is, functionally specialized, we should briefly discuss the use of the word *innate* and several related issues. In this chapter, we are using this frequently misunderstood word as cognitive psychologists often use it: to describe reliably developing species-typical properties of the organism. We are not using it to refer to expressed phenotypic properties that are present from birth; human teeth provide an example of something that develops reliably, according to a species-typical design, that is absent at birth. "Innate" features of the human species-typical architecture could appear through maturation at any time throughout the life-cycle. We often use another phrase, *evolved*—as in evolved structure—in certain contexts as a synonym. That is, for a complex functional structure to have evolved, it needed to have appeared often enough in phenotypes to have been the target of selection.

More significantly, we do not mean to imply by using the word *innate* that something is immutable or impervious to modification or elimination by sufficiently ingenious ontogenetic intervention. Every feature of every phenotype is fully codetermined by the interaction of the organism's genes, its initial package of zygotic cellular machinery, and its "environment"—meaning everything else that impinges on it. But simply pointing to the interaction between the two misses something important: that natural selection acts on the species' set of genes so that the result of the usual interaction between the genes and the environment is to produce a stabilized, improbably functional design. Thus, developmental mechanisms are themselves adaptations, shaped to buffer environmental perturbation by ignoring dimensions of the world that were variable during the EEA and shaped to employ in their processes of organismic construction the stably recurring structure in the world. The usual result is a successfully produced complex architecture, most aspects of which are species-typical, although (depending on the breeding structure of the species), some may be population-typical or frequency-dependent.

Consequently, every individual really has two inheritances: its genes, which may be perturbed by mutations, and the environmental invariances or regularities that its developmental processes depend on. Selection acts on genes that regulate developmental programs to suppress perturbation from genetic and environmental sources. Thus, gene–environment interactionism is quite compatible with stably recurrent evolved design (Crawford & Anderson, 1989). It is this recurring structure that we are referring to when we use terms such as *innate* or *evolved* or *reliably developing* or *design*. Obviously, developing organisms are vulnerable and complex dynamic systems, and environmental intervention can change almost everything about them, so these terms entail assumptions about spontaneous development in normal or EEA-like environments. When the organism develops in environments that deviate from that to which the genotype is adapted, its phenotype may also deviate from those aspects of its design that were targets of selection. This divergence of past and present environments sometimes introduces complications for the researcher, particularly those who study humans.

WHY SHOULD DARWINIAN ALGORITHMS BE SPECIALIZED AND DOMAIN-SPECIFIC?

> Nature has kept us at a great distance from all her secrets, and has afforded us only the knowledge of a few superficial qualities of objects; while she conceals from us those powers and principles, on which the influence of these objects entirely depends. Our senses inform us of the colour, weight, and consistence of bread; but neither sense nor reason can ever inform us of those qualities, which fit it for the nourishment and support of a human body.
>
> —David Hume, 1977/1748, p. 21

Genes coding for psychological mechanisms that promote the inclusive fitness of their bearers will outcompete those that do not and tend to become fixed in the population. The promotion of inclusive fitness is an evolutionary "end"; a psychological mechanism is a means by which that end is achieved. Can the human mind be comprised primarily of domain-general and content-independent psychological mechanisms and yet realize this evolutionary end? We argue that natural selection could not have produced such a psychological architecture, nor could such a hypothetical design successfully promote fitness (i.e., regulate behavior adaptively).

Consider how Jesus explains the derivation of the Mosaic code to his disciples:

> Jesus said unto him, "Thou shalt love the Lord, thy God, with all thy heart, and with all thy soul, and with all thy mind. This is the first and great commandment. And the second is like it, Thou shalt love thy neighbor as thyself. *On these two commandments hang all the law and the prophets.*"
>
> —Matthew 22:37–40 (emphasis added)

Jesus has given his disciples a domain-general, content-independent decision rule to be used in guiding their behavior. But what does it mean in practice? Real life consists of concrete, specific situations requiring specific decisions out of an infinite set of alternatives. How, from this rule, do I infer what counts as "loving my neighbor as myself" when, to pick a standard Biblical example, my neighbor's ox falls into my pit? Should I recompense him, or him me? By how much? How should I behave when I find my neighbor sleeping with my spouse? Should I fast on holy days? Should I work on the Sabbath? What counts as fulfilling these commandments? How do I know when I have fulfilled them?

In what sense does all the law "hang" from these two commandments?

These derivations are not obvious or straightforward. That is why the Talmud was written. The Talmud is a "domain-specific" document: an interpretation of the "law" that tells you what actions fulfill the injunctions to "love God" and "love your neighbor" in the concrete, specific situations you are likely to encounter in real life. The Talmud solves the *frame problem* (e.g., Boden, 1977; Fodor, 1983) posed by a domain-general rule like Jesus'.

A domain-general decision rule such as "Do that which promotes your inclusive fitness" cannot guide behavior in ways that actually do promote fitness, because what counts as fit behavior differs from domain to domain. Therefore, like the Talmud, psychological mechanisms governing evolutionarily important domains of human activity must be domain-specific.

The easiest way to see that Darwinian algorithms must be domain-specific is to ask whether the opposite is possible: In theory, could one construct a domain-general, content-independent decision rule, that, for any two courses of action, would evaluate which better serves the end of promoting inclusive fitness? (For additional discussion on why the answer is no, see Tooby & Cosmides, 1990b.)

First, such a rule must include a criterion for assessing inclusive fitness: There must be some observable environmental variable against which courses of action from any domain of human activity can be measured. As the promotion of inclusive fitness means differential representation of genes in subsequent generations, the time at which the consequence of an action can be assessed is remote from the time at which the action is taken. For simplicity's sake, let us drop collateral fitness components and assume that number of grandoffspring produced by the end of one's life is an adequate assessment of fitness. Using this criterion, the decision rule can be rephrased more precisely as, "Choose the course of action that will result in more grandoffspring produced by the end of one's life."

But how could one possibly evaluate alternative actions using this criterion? Consider a simple, but graphic example: Should one eat feces or fruit? Will trial and error (or operant conditioning, induction, hypothesis testing, imitation, etc.— the argument is general to any system that lacks specialized procedures to deal with the stable structure of the world) work? Clearly, no individual has two parallel lives to lead for purposes of comparison, identical except that he or she eats feces in one life and fruit in the other. Each life is a single, uncontrolled experiment. The individual who eats feces is far more likely to contract parasites or infectious diseases, thereby incurring a large fitness cost. And if this individual instead eats fruit and leaves a certain number of grandoffspring, he or she still does not know whether eating feces would have been better: For all that individual knows, feces could be a rich food source (as they are for some species) that would increase fecundity.

Does learning from others constitute a solution to the problem? Imitation is useless unless those imitated have themselves solved the problem of the adaptive regulation of behavior. If the blind leadeth the blind (to retain our Biblical orientation), they shall both fall into the ditch. Imitation, as a strategy, can only supplement systems that have already solved the primary problem of the adaptive regulation of behavior.

If, however, others are monitored not as role models for imitation but instead as natural experiments, this does allow the comparison of alternative courses of action, in a limited fashion. The number of hypotheses that can be tested is a function of the number of individuals under observation and the comprehensiveness of the observation. Nevertheless, each individual life is subject to innumerable uncontrolled and random influences that rapidly outstrip the population size and that any observer would have to keep track of to make valid inferences. If the observer watches some people eat fruit and others eat feces and waits to see which will have a larger number of grandoffspring, how would the observer know whether these individuals' differential fitness was caused by their diet or by one of the millions of other things they experienced in the course of their lives? Of course, the most major problem is that of time delay between action and the cue used to evaluate the action: grandoffspring produced. It is fundamentally impractical to have to wait two generations (or even any substantial fraction of one) to determine the value of choices that must be made today—learning latencies tend to be very short because of this problem of combinatorial explosion. Moreover, where would the population of individuals living by trial and error, which supports the observer's adaptive regulation system, come from? Obviously, although social observation can and does supplement other psychological processes (e.g., Galef, 1990), potential role models would have to have solved the problem of the adaptive regulation of behavior by some other method if observing them is to provide any benefit.

Can the use of perceptual cues solve the problem? The individual could decide to eat what smells good and avoid what smells bad. This method works, of course, because such criteria are design features of evolved, domain-specific mechanisms. Nothing smells intrinsically bad or good; the smell of feces is attractive to dung flies. Admitting smell or taste preferences is admitting domain-specific knowledge or procedures. Admitting the inference that foul-smelling or foul-tasting entities should not be ingested is admitting a domain-specific innate inference.

Even if it were somehow possible to learn the fruit-eating preference using domain-general mechanisms, an individual equipped with appropriate domain-specific mechanisms would enjoy a selective advantage over one who relied on "trial and possibly fatal error" (Shepard, 1987). The tendency to rely on trial and error in this domain would be selected out; domain-specific Darwinian algorithms governing food choice would be selected for and become a species-typical trait.

There is also the problem of deciding which courses of action to evaluate, an instance of the widespread information-processing problem of combinatorial explosion. The possibilities for action are infinite, and the more truly domain-general a mechanism is, the more it would be restricted to generating random possibilities to be run through the inclusive fitness decision rule. When a tiger charges, what should your response be? Should you smile winningly? Do a cartwheel? Sing a song? One has the intuition that running randomly generated response possibilities through the decision rule would not be favored by selection. And again, on what basis and by what procedures would psychological mechanisms compute which possibility would result in more grandchildren? An alternative design that includes Darwinian algorithms specialized for predator avoidance seems reasonable, with design features such as a tendency to trade an increase in false positives in predator detection in for an increase in hits, and procedures that, upon detecting a potential predator, restrict response alternatives to flight, fight, or concealment, and orchestrate among them.

The domain-general "grandchildren produced" criterion fails even in these simple situations. How, then, could it work in more complicated learning situations—for example, when an action that increases fitness in one domain decreases it in another? Suppose the hypothetical domain-general learning mechanism somehow reached the inference that sexual intercourse is a necessary condition for producing offspring. Should the individual, then, have sex at every opportunity?

An evolutionarily well-designed organism would not, of course. There are, for example, large fitness costs associated with incest (e.g., Shepher, 1983). Given a potential partner with cues (evaluated by domain-specific mechanisms: see Buss, 1987, 1989, 1991a, 1992, 1994; Symons, 1979) that would normally elicit sexual desire, EEA-reliable cues indicating that the potential partner is a family member should inhibit sexual impulses.

How could a regulatory system like this be induced by a general purpose system? If a female engages in incest, then loses her baby after a few months, how could a domain-general mechanism identify what caused the miscarriage? Each life is a series of many events (perhaps including sex near the time of conception with nonkin as well as kin), any one of which is a potential cause. Why conclude that sex with one individual, who physically and psychologically resembles other members of his sex in many respects, caused the loss of the baby? Why not reject everyone of the same eye color, or stop having sex at a particular time of day, or start eating within six hours of having sex, and so on, ad infinitum? Even assuming that a domain-general system did settle on the "kin versus nonkin" dimension, a design that had to learn this evolutionarily stable contingency between mating with family members and fitness reduction would be rapidly replaced by a design that came equipped with specialized mechanisms that solved the problem.

Indeed, where could the correct dimensions of discrimination and generalization come from (Herrnstein, 1977)? There are an infinite number of dimensions that could be used to carve the environment into categories; there is no assurance that a general-purpose information-processing system would ever isolate those useful for creating the kin/nonkin categorization scheme, and the "grandchildren produced" criterion cannot guide such a system toward the appropriate dimensions. (In contrast, domain-specific kin recognition mechanisms can exploit evolutionarily recurring statistical regularities that link cues with kinship, such as being raised by the same caretaker.)

A general purpose system would have to solve the infinite dimensions problem not only if it is to categorize events, but also if it is to apply the knowledge acquired to new situations. Suppose the architecture had somehow correctly inferred that avoiding sex with kin had positive fitness consequences. How should one generalize this knowledge about the kin/nonkin categorization scheme to other domains of human activity? Should one, for example, avoid any interaction with kin? This would be a mistake; selectively avoiding sex with kin has positive fitness consequences, but selectively avoiding helping kin has negative fitness consequences (given a certain envelope of circumstances; Hamilton, 1964).

Thus, not only must the acquisition of the kin/nonkin categorization scheme be guided by domain-specific Darwinian algorithms, but its adaptive use for guiding behavior is also domain-specific. In the sexual domain, kin must be avoided; in the helping domain, they must be helped; when one needs help, kin are a likely source from whom to solicit it (Hamilton, 1964); when one is contagiously ill, one should avoid infecting kin to the extent this is consistent with the solicitation of help. Domain-general learning is inadequate not only because it is costly, slow, and unreliable in practice, but because in principle there is no domain-independent variable for discriminating success from error. In the sexual domain, error = sex with kin. In the helping domain, error = not helping kin given the appropriate envelop of conditions. In the disease domain, error = infecting kin. What is the common criterion of success in mate selection, predator avoidance, and foraging? One cannot escape the conclusion that motivational systems—if nothing else—driven by the evaluation of consequences must contain domain-specific features. The only general criterion of success is fitness itself, which is inherently unobservable at the time decisions must be made.

In short,

1. There is no domain-general definition of what counts as success and failure that correlates with fitness.
2. Adaptive courses of action can be neither deduced nor learned by general criteria because they depend on statistical relationships between features of the environment, behavior and fitness that emerge over many generations, and are therefore not observable during a single lifetime.
3. Combinatorial explosion cripples any insufficiently content-structured mechanism, as there are an infinite number of potential category dimensions, an infinite number of possible relations, an infinite number of potential hypotheses, and an infinite number of potential behaviors.

For these reasons, exclusively domain-general architectures are computationally insufficient to solve many adaptive problems. And even where they might be sufficient, they cannot solve them as efficiently as architectures equipped with functionally specialized mechanisms, because sets of procedures designed to take advantage of the recurrent features of defined adaptive problems will, by their nature, be more efficient than any alternative design lacking this information.

Given the complexity of the world, and the complexity of the total array of adaptive tasks faced by living organisms, the psychological architecture of any real species must be permeated with domain-specific structure. The psychological architecture appears to be more complexly specialized than anyone ever suspected.

DARWINIAN ALGORITHMS SOLVE
THE "FRAME PROBLEM"

Researchers in artificial intelligence have found that trial and error is a good procedure for learning only when a system already has a well-specified model of what is likely to be true of a domain, a model that includes a definition of what counts as error. More generally, they have found that whenever they try to build a system that can tackle a real problem, they have to build in large amounts of "domain-specific" programming structure about the problem-space. Artificial intelligence researchers call this the *frame problem* (e.g., Boden, 1977; Fodor, 1983), and it arises because general-purpose computational systems have the problems discussed earlier. To move an object, make the simplest induction, or solve a straightforward problem, the computer must already have a sophisticated model of the domain in question: what counts as an object or stimulus, what counts as a cause, how classes of entities and properties are related, how various actions change the situation, what goal is to be achieved. Unless the learning or problem domain is severely circumscribed and the procedures highly specialized and content-dependent—unless the programmer has given the computer what corresponds to vast quantities of "innate knowledge"—the computer can move nothing, learn nothing, solve nothing. The frame problem is a concrete, empirical demonstration of the philosophical objection to the *tabula rasa*. It is also a cautionary tale for advocates of domain-general, content-independent learning mechanisms.

Unfortunately, the lessons from AI have been lost on many. Although most cognitive psychologists realize that their theories must posit some innate cognitive architecture, a quick perusal of textbooks in the field will show that these still tend to be restricted to content-independent operating system characteristics: short-term stores, domain-general retrieval and storage processes, imagery buffers. Researchers who do insist on the necessity of positing content-dependent schemas or frames (e.g., Minsky, 1977; Schank & Abelson, 1977) seldom ask how these frames are built. Their approach implicitly presumes that frames are the product of experience structured only by domain-general learning mechanisms. For example, Cheng and Holyoak (1985) cite "induction" as the process that builds their content-dependent "pragmatic reasoning schemas." Yet the building of frames must also be subject to the frame problem: Where do the situation-specialized procedures or information come from that "know" how to build appropriate as opposed to the infinite set of inappropriate frames?

The chain has to begin somewhere and, as we have seen, domain-general processes alone cannot accomplish the task. What can? The conclusion seems inescapable: For the organism's cognitive architecture to solve adaptive problems, or to "learn" adaptively, it must have domain-specific procedures, that is, content-specialized Darwinian algorithms. These Darwinian algorithms can be seen as schema or frame *builders*: as cognitive mechanisms that structure experience along adaptive dimensions in a given domain and define useful problem spaces and, in general, supply the other necessary specificity to structure the developing psychological architecture so that it is equipped to frame problems adaptively. Phylogenetically supplied Darwinian algorithms solve the frame problem for the organism, just as the programmer solves it for the artificially intelligent system.

THE FRAME PROBLEM AND SO-CALLED "CONSTRAINTS" ON LEARNING

Biologists and psychologists have an unfortunate tendency to refer to the properties of domain-specific (but not domain-general) mechanisms as "constraints." For example, the one-trial learning mechanism, discovered by Garcia and Koelling (1966), that permits a rat to associate a food taste with nausea several hours later is frequently referred to as a "biological constraint on learning." Reviews or treatments of domain-specific elements in psychological systems frequently have titles such as *Biological Boundaries of Learning* (Seligman & Hager, 1972), *Constraints on Learning* (Shettleworth, 1972), or even *The Tangled Wing: Biological Constraints on the Human Spirit* (Konner, 1982). This terminology is seriously misleading, because it incorrectly implies that "unconstrained" learning mechanisms are a theoretical possibility; it implicitly denies the existence of the frame problem.

All constraints are properties, but not all properties are constraints. Calling a property a "constraint" implies that the organism would have a wider range of abilities if the constraint were to be removed. Are a bird's wings a "constraint on locomotion"? Obviously, such usage would be absurd: Wings expand the bird's capacity to locomote. On the other hand, a thick rubber band placed in such a way that it pins a bird's wings to its body is a constraint on the bird's ability to locomote, constraining the bird to walking. If anything, wings should be called "enablers," because they enable an additional form of locomotion.

Equally, there is no evidence that the domain-specific mechanisms that permit one-trial learning of an association between taste and nausea are "constraints on learning." Removing the specific properties that allow the efficient learning of this particular association would not expand the rat's capacity to learn; it would reduce it. Not only would the rat be unable to associate a food taste with an electric shock; it would also be unable to associate a food taste with nausea.

The tendency to refer to such evolved structures as "constraints on learning" shows the durability of the mistaken notion that a tabula rasa is possible and, more specifically, that learning is possible in the absence of a great deal of domain-specific structure. If the "constraint" language were accurate in its implications, then a property that "prepares" an organism to associate a taste with nausea might preclude it from associating a taste with an electric shock. However, if an organism with this prepared association also had a domain-general associative mechanism, there is no a priori reason why that mechanism should not work to pair taste with electric shocks. In order to call the prepared association a "constraint" on the learning caused by the general-purpose mechanism, one would have to demonstrate empirically that the activation of the prepared association by the presence of food somehow causes the general-purpose mechanism to shut down. Rozin and Schull (1988) have pointed out another way in which the terminology of constraints is misleading: It implies that the human mind was "built down" from a more general-purpose cognitive system present in our ancestors. Yet such a phylogenetic history seems far from likely: It presumes that our primate ancestors had a capacity to learn that was broader and more powerful than our own.

The rich, functionally specialized information-processing structures present in the psychologies of organisms should be affirmatively characterized as adaptations, rather than as constraints. They should not be characterized, implicitly or explicitly, by how far they deviate from the ideal of a nonexistent—and indeed, impossible and incoherent—general-purpose architecture. It is true that psychologies differ in the breadth of situations to which they can respond appropriately. The fact that humans can improvise an amazing and elaborate range of behaviors, from composing symphonies to piloting aircraft to writing *The Idiot* indicates a generality of achieved problem solving that is truly breathtaking. But we know from the reality of combinatorial explosion and its progeny in various fields that this cannot be the result of mechanisms that are solely domain-general, content-independent, and free of procedures poised to exploit the structure of the world. Most of all, "generality" is a description of what an architecture lacks: It means that it lacks anything particular (such as information or procedures) that suits it for some situations over others. For this reason, generality of accomplishment is not achieved, and could not be achieved, by generality of design. General designs are inherently weak designs, while specialized designs are inherently more powerful, though at the price of addressing a narrower range of problems. The solution, for an architecture that must be both powerful, yet somewhat general, is the bundling of specialized mechanisms together, so that in aggregate, they address a large range of problems and do so powerfully. Moreover, mechanisms that are "general purpose" to some degree can be embedded in this guiding matrix of functional specialization to supplement them and broaden the range of solvable problems still further. Thus, in the human case (for example), one has mechanisms incorporating (highly structured) social observation, imitation, operant conditioning, and so on that (conjointly with an expanded array of specialized mechanisms) increase the range of situations that can be responded to appropriately. It is time for behavioral scientists to turn from a nearly exclusive focus on these more general-purpose mechanisms to the crucial, and largely neglected, encompassing superstructure of evolved domain-specific functional specializations.

FUNCTIONAL SPECIFICITY IN MOTIVATION

Within this tradition of emphasizing general-purpose architectures, the field of motivation has played a subversive role (Tooby & Cosmides, 1992). As was clear from the previous analysis, motivation is the most obviously difficult thing to make general, because what counts as adaptively successful behavior for the organism differs completely from domain to domain. There is simply no uniform element in sex, eating, drinking, staying warm (but not overheating), and so on, that could be used to build a general architecture that could learn to accomplish these behaviors. Any architecture that can do these tasks requires something functionally specialized to address them. What many psychologists did was to make motivation the repository of the inescapable minimum of functionally specialized regulatory structure, while making the rest of their hypothesized architectures as general as possible. Despite the admission of functional specialization into psychological processes, the tendency has been to keep these elements restricted to as small a class as possible and to view them as external to the "important" central learning or cognitive processes. They are incorporated as, for example, reinforcers operating by drive reduction.

Modern mainstream cognitive psychologists have continued in this tradition, for the most part, and have labored to keep any such content-influenced elements extrinsic to the primary cognitive machinery. Indeed, they have usually avoided addressing how functional action—such as mate choice, food choice, or effort calculation—takes places at all. The principles of concept formation, of reasoning, of remembering, and so forth have traditionally been viewed as uninfected prior to experience with any content, their procedures lacking features designed for dealing with particular types of content. (The recent emergence of modular or domain-specific cognitive psychologists constitutes a dissenting subcommunity.)

Given this division of labor (i.e., with motivation the keeper of the functionally specific, and learning theory the keeper of the general laws of mind), much of great value was learned. However, because of the powerful prejudice against content-sensitivity or functional specialization harbored by many learning theorists, a great deal more could have been learned, even within this Procrustean framework. An attempt could have been made to comprehensively survey the list of primary reinforcers, and the conditions and contexts within which they were reinforcing. Unfortunately, the pretheoretical preference was to keep this list as short as could be accepted as credible (with credibility depending on what kinds of animal behavior one knew about). To keep this short list credible, one had to keep research organisms outside ecologically valid circumstances, away from biologically significant stimuli and, indeed, in highly stimulus-impoverished circumstances (Beach, 1955; Breland & Breland, 1961; Lockard, 1971).

Ethology (or sociobiology or behavioral ecology or animal behavior—the names have been changed to protect the innocent) has played an important corrective role in this regard (Daly & Wilson, 1984; Krebs & Davies, 1984; Lorenz, 1965; Tinbergen, 1951; Wilson, 1975). These fields have provided carefully documented, functionally interpretable behaviors that lie far outside anything that drive reduction theory and a short list of motivations could explain. Thus, one has the effort male ring doves will go to monitor the sexual behavior of their mates (Erickson & Zenone, 1976). One has reports from an entire range of species—from langurs to lions to rodents—of newly resident males killing the infants of their predecessors and thereby accelerating ovulation (Hrdy, 1977; for reviews see Hausfater & Hrdy, 1984). The now well-known selection pressure of kin selection has led to the search for and documentation of an enormous array of kin-directed altruistic acts—behaviors completely undreamt of in drive theory's philosophy (Hamilton, 1964; Williams & Williams, 1957; for review see Krebs & Davies, 1984). Similarly, the complex conditions under which reciprocation is and is not engaged in are hard to account for using traditional notions of what reinforcers are and what, exactly, it is that they reinforce (e.g., Wilkinson, 1988, 1990).

Evolutionary studies of humans similarly bristle with documented phenomena that cannot be accounted for with general architectures and a short list of drives, rewards, or reinforcers (see Tooby & Cosmides, 1992, for discussion, and the papers in Barkow, Cosmides, & Tooby, 1992, for examples). Buss's and Symons's important work in the area of human mate choice and sexuality shows that the "sex drive" is a construct completely inadequate to cope with the structural richness of the factors involved in the differentiated sexual psychologies of males and females (Buss, 1987, 1989, 1991a, 1992, 1994; Symons, 1979). Some of our own work has focused on the complex evolved structure of the inference mechanisms and associated motivations linked to human reciprocation (Cosmides, 1989; Cosmides & Tooby, 1989, 1992). Finally, Daly and Wilson have explicitly been exploring the issue of the complexity and functional subtlety of the human motivational system and how it conforms to expectations drawn from a broad array of selectionist theories (Daly & Wilson, 1981, 1982, 1984, 1987a, 1987b, 1988; Daly, Wilson, & Weghorst, 1982; Wilson & Daly, 1985, 1987, 1992). They have explored the motivational structure recoverable from such phenomena as risk taking, violence, sexual jealousy and proprietariness, parental care (and its lack), spousal abuse, and their regulation by such factors as gender, age, kinship, reproductive value, and various situational factors. Work such as Buss's, Symons's, and Daly and Wilson's leads to the conclusion that the human mind contains evolved motivational mechanisms that are specifically targeted to address adaptive problems involved in mate selection, aggression, mate guarding, discriminative child care, and so on, and that these psychological mechanisms recalibrate themselves depending on the age, sex, number of children, and so on, of the individual they are in. That is, humans have motivations specifically "about" the sexual behavior of their spouses, "about" those identified by cues as genetic kin, "about" how much to care for a sick child, and so on that are not derived from a shorter list or culturally variable socially learned "values."

Information-processing descriptions of motivational questions provide a rich language for characterizing this expanding range of behavioral phenomena. For example, the cognitive architecture of bumblebees appears to contain psychological specializations for foraging (Real, 1991). These mental organs embody rules of relevance, drawing the animal toward some aspects of its environment and not others. These rules cause the animal to search for certain kinds of environmental patterns—such as flower-shaped objects—and, upon finding these patterns, to engage in adaptively appropriate activities—such as sampling the nectar from the flower.

Its rules cause the animal to compute certain functions—such as nectar reward per unit time per flower—and use the computed value to decide which color flowers to forage on (Real, 1991). The animal might continue to forage until some consummatory function—perhaps a calculation of total nectar consumed—deactivates the mental organ and thereby causes the foraging behavior to cease. Mental organs may be arranged in hierarchical fashion, in such a way that a bee might forage as long as the predation risk is sufficiently low, but when environmental cues indicate the presence of a predator, the foraging mechanisms are deactivated and the predator avoidance programs activated.

Once one has a map of the information-processing programs that govern behavior, motivational questions can be discussed with great precision. For example, bumblebees are risk-averse foragers; given two different flower patches that have the same expected nectar payoff but different variances, they concentrate their foraging on the low variance patch (Real, 1991). Describing the bumblebee's behavior as the expression of cognitive rules encourages one to ask very specific questions about those rules, such as: Do these rules cause the bee to prefer the more variable patch if its average reward is higher? How much higher does the average reward have to be? Do the bee's decision rules compute reward as a function of time for one flower at a time, or are these values averaged over two or more flowers? Does the bee's past history with a flower of a specific color affect its foraging decisions? and so on (Real, 1991). Once one has specified all the cognitive rules that govern the bumblebee's foraging—what kinds of information these rules take as input, what transformations they perform on that information, and what behaviors they generate as output—one has a very complete and specific description of the bumblebee's motivational programs in the domain of foraging.

Theories of adaptive function, in their ranking of outcomes in terms of fitness promotion, inherently help in analyzing the design of motivational mechanisms. Moreover, computational theories that include models of ancestral conditions as well as selection pressures will provide clues as to what cues and outcomes should be rewarding, how to define goal states, and how to model an equivalence and relative value in a mental or information-processing currency of cued consequences (so-called *fitness tokens*; Daly & Wilson, 1988). Of course, the most important implication is that it will often be more productive to consider motivational mechanisms as subcomponents in separate domain-specific mechanisms, rather than as a single unitary system crosscutting through every domain. That is, one should consider a pluralism of motivational mechanisms, without expecting that the motivational dimension should operate according to the same rules from problem-solving system to problem-solving system. In such models, motivation may show up, for example, as a series of differentiated regulatory variables embedded in separate problem-solving mechanisms whose magnitudes play roles in decisions and procedure activation. Of course, given that every organism needs to arbitrate between activities, there will need to be an encompassing integrative and arbitrative motivational system that addresses the issue of task switching. This raises the issue of the organization of the entire psychological architecture, and with it, emotion.

EMOTIONS AS ADAPTATIONS
TO PHYLOGENETICALLY RECURRING SITUATIONS

All adaptations evolved in response to the repeating elements of past environments, and their structure reflects in detail the recurrent structure of ancestral environments. This ability to "know about" and exploit the complex structure of the world, based on cues that identify recurring situations, is one of the things that give domain-specific mechanisms such an edge in producing adaptive behavior. Given that animal minds consist of collections of evolved mechanisms in a world in which situations reappear from generation to generation, a functional description of emotion naturally emerges (Tooby, 1985, Tooby & Cosmides, 1990b). One simply needs to shift the focus from considering how an individual mechanism matches the environmental structure of its particular problem type to addressing how sets of mechanisms might advantageously be coordinated when dealing with evolutionarily reappearing situations.

Of course, each psychological mechanism can operate in a number of alternative ways, each of which will be more or less useful in dealing with a given situation. Taken together in their interaction with the other mechanisms in the architecture, some configurations will deal better than others with specific situations. For this reason, selection can have been expected to have shaped the system architecture to structure interactions among the different mechanisms so that they function particularly harmoniously when confronting commonly recurring (across generations) adaptive situations. Fighting, engaging in sex, needing nourishment, falling in love, escaping predators, confronting sexual infidelity, and so on, have each recurred innumerable times in evolutionary history, and each requires that a certain subset of the psychological architecture's behavior-regulating algorithms function together in a particular way to guide behavior adaptively through that type of situation. This structured functioning together of mechanisms is a mode of operation for the mind and can be meaningfully interpreted as an emotional state. Each emotion state—fear of predators, guilt, sexual jealousy, rage, grief, and so on—corresponds to an integrated mode of operation that functions as a solution designed to take advantage of the particular structure of the recurrent situation these emotions correspond to. The characteristic feeling that accompanies each such mode is the signal that activates the specific constellation of mechanisms appropriate to solving that type of adaptive problem.

To make this concrete, let us briefly describe in these terms what might happen to a hypothetical human hunter-gatherer when a distant lion becomes visible. The recognition of this predator triggers the internal "broadcast" that we call the feeling of fear; this broadcast acts as a signal to all of the diverse mechanisms in the psychological architecture. Upon detecting this signal, they each switch into the "fear mode of operation"—that is, the mode of operation most appropriate to dealing with the danger presented by a predator. The mechanism maintaining the hunger motivation switches off and cognitive activity involved in reasoning about the discovery of food is stopped, neither being appropriate. A different set of motivational priorities is created. Mechanisms regulating physiological processes issue new "instructions" making the person physiologically ready for the new sorts of behaviors that are now more adaptive: fighting or, more likely, flight. Inferential activity switches to representations of the local terrain, estimates of probable actions by the lion, sources of help and protection from the lion, and so on. The primary motivation becomes the pursuit of safety—a concept specially defined by this emotion state. The modes of operation of the perceptual mechanisms alter radically: Hearing becomes far more acute; danger-relevant stimuli become boosted, while danger-irrelevant stimuli are suppressed. The inferential networks underlying the perceptual system interpret ambiguous stimuli (i.e., shadows, masking noise) in a threatening way, creating a higher proportion of true predator detections at the cost of a higher rate of false alarms. Attention-directing mechanisms become fixed on the danger and potential retreats. Similarly, discovering one's mate in a sexual liaison signals a situation that threatens future reproduction and present investment allocation; this cue should therefore activate sexual jealousy (Daly, Wilson, & Weghorst, 1982; Daly & Wilson, 1988; Buss, 1992). The emotion of sexual jealousy constitutes an organized mode of operation specifically designed to deploy the programs governing each psychological mechanism so that each is poised to deal with the exposed infidelity: Physiological processes are prepared for violence; the goal of deterring, injuring, or murdering the rival emerges; the goal of punishing or deserting the mate appears; the desire to make oneself more competitively attractive emerges; memory is activated to reanalyze the past; and so on.

In this view, emotion and "thinking" (i.e., consciously accessible inference) are not parallel processes; rather, emotional states are specific modes of operation of the entire psychological architecture (and, indeed physiological architecture), including whatever inferential processes may be going on. Each emotional state manifests regulatory features "designed" to solve particular families of adaptive problems, whereby the psychological mechanisms assume a unique configuration. Using this approach, each emotional state can be mapped in terms of its characteristic configuration and the particular mode each identifiable mechanism adopts (motivational priorities, inferential algorithms, perceptual mechanisms, physiological mechanisms, attentional direction, emotion signal and intensity, prompted cognitive contents, etc.).

Of course, ever since Darwin (1871, 1872), emotions have been seen as the product of the evolutionary process, and usually, although not always, as functional adaptations (Arnold, 1960, 1968; Chance, 1980; Daly et al., 1982; Darwin, 1872; Eibl-Ebesfeldt, 1975; Ekman, 1982; Frijda, 1986; Hamburg, 1968; Izard, 1977; Otte, 1974; Plutchik, 1980; Tomkins, 1962, 1963; and many others). In fact, much of the best work in evolutionary psychology to date stems from an evolutionary–functional approach to emotions (e.g., Bowlby, 1969; Daly et al., 1982; Ekman, 1982). The particular interpretive framework advanced here (Tooby, 1985; Tooby & Cosmides, 1990b; see also 1990a) is consistent with much of the vast literature on emotion. It is simply an attempt to integrate into a modern adaptationist framework: (a) the idea that the mind consists primarily of a collection of evolved function-specific information-processing mechanisms with such views as that (b) emotions are coordinated systems (Arnold, 1960, 1968; Frijda, 1986; Izard, 1977; Lazarus, Kanner, & Folkman, 1980; Plutchik, 1980), that (c) organize action (Frijda, 1986; Lazarus, 1966) appropriate to situations (Arnold, 1960; Frijda, 1986; Lazarus et al., 1980; Tolman, 1932; see especially Nesse's, 1990, excellent discussion).

To characterize an emotion as an adaptation in information-processing terms, one must identify the following properties of environments and of mechanisms:

1. *A situation*—a recurrent structure of environmental and organismic properties, characterized as a complex statistical composite of how such properties covaried in the environment of evolutionary adaptedness. Examples of situations are being in a depleted nutritional state, competing for maternal attention, being chased by a predator, being about to ambush an enemy, having few friends.

2. *The adaptive problem*—the identification of which organismic states and behavioral sequences will lead to the best average functional outcome, given the situation. For example, what to do given you are being chased by a predator; what to do given you are in a depleted nutritional state.

3. *Cues that signal the presence of the situation*—for example, low blood sugar signals a depleted nutritional state; the looming approach of a large fanged animal signals the presence of a predator; seeing your mate having sex with another signals sexual infidelity; finding yourself consistently alone or avoided by others signals that you have few friends.

4. *Algorithms that monitor for situation-defining cues*—including perceptual mechanisms, proprioceptive mechanisms, and situation-modeling memory.

5. *Algorithms that detect situations*—these mechanisms take the output of the monitoring algorithms in (4) as input, and through integration, probabilistic weighting, and other decision criteria identify situations as either present or absent (or present with some probability).

6. *Algorithms that assign priorities*—a given world-state may correspond to more than one situation at a time, for example, you may be nutritionally depleted *and* in the presence of a predator. The prioritizing algorithms define which emotion modes are compatible (e.g., hunger and boredom), which are mutually exclusive (e.g., feeding and predator escape). Depending on the relative importance of the situations and the reliability of the cues, the prioritizing algorithms decide which emotion modes to activate and deactivate, and to what degree.

7. *An internal communication system*—given that a situation has been detected, the internal communication system sends a situation-specific signal to all relevant mechanisms; the signal switches them into the appropriate adaptive emotion mode.

8. *A set of algorithms specific to each mechanism that regulates how it responds to each specialized emotion state*—these algorithms determine whether the mechanism should switch on or switch off, and if on, what emotion-specialized performance they will implement.

Any controllable biological process that, by shifting its performance in a specifiable way, would lead to enhanced average fitness outcomes should come to be partially governed by emotional state (see [8] above). Such processes include:

Goals. The cognitive mechanisms that define goal-states and choose among goals in a planning process should be influenced by emotions. For example, vindictiveness—a specialized subcategory of anger—may define "injuring the offending party" as a goal state to be achieved. (Although the functional logic of this process is deterrence, this function need not be represented, either consciously or unconsciously, by the mechanisms that generate the vindictive behavior.)

Motivational priorities. Mechanisms involved in hierarchically ranking goals, or for nonplanning systems, other kinds of motivational and reward systems, should be emotion-dependent. What may be extremely unpleasant in one state, such as harming another, may seem satisfying in another state (e.g., aggressive competition may facilitate counterempathy).

Information-gathering motivations. Because establishing which situation you are in has enormous consequences for the appropriateness of behavior, the process of detection should in fact involve specialized inference procedures and specialized motivations to discover whether certain suspected facts are true or false. What one is curious about, what one finds interesting, what one is obsessed with discovering should all be emotion-specific.

Imposed conceptual frameworks. Emotions should prompt construals of the world in terms of concepts that are appropriate to the decisions that must be made. If in an angry mood, domain-specific concepts such as social agency, fault, responsibility, and punishment will be assigned to elements in the situation. If hungry, the food–nonfood distinction will seem salient. If endangered, safety-categorization frames will appear. The world will be carved up into categories based partly on what emotional state an individual is in.

Perceptual mechanisms. Perceptual systems may enter emotion-specific modes of operation. When fearful, acuity of hearing may increase. Specialized perceptual inference systems may be mobilized as well: If you've heard rustling in the bushes at night, human and predator figure-detection may be particularly boosted, and not simply visual acuity in general. In fact, nonthreat interpretations may be depressed, and the same set of shadows will "look threatening"—that is, given a specific threatening interpretation such as "a man with a knife"—or not, depending on emotion-state.

Memory. The ability to call up particularly appropriate kinds of information out of long-term memory will be influenced. A woman who has just found strong evidence that her husband has been unfaithful may find a torrent of memories about small details that seemed meaningless at the time but that now fit into an interpretation of covert activity. We also expect that what is stored about present experience will also be differentially regulated, with important or shocking events, for example, stored in great detail.

Attention. The entire structure of attention, from perceptual systems to the contents of high-level reasoning processes, should be regulated by emotional state. If you are worried that your spouse is late and might have been injured, it is hard to concentrate on other ongoing tasks.

Physiology. Each organ system, tissue, or process is a potential candidate for emotion specific regulation, and "arousal" is doubtless insufficiently specific to capture the detailed coordination involved. Changes in circulatory, respiratory, and gastrointestinal functioning are well-known and documented, as are changes in levels of circulating sex hormones. We expect thresholds regulating the contraction of various muscle groups to change with certain emotional states, reflecting the probability that they will need to be employed. Similarly, immune allocation and targeting may vary with disgust, with the potential for injury, or with the demands of extreme physical exertion.

Communication processes. What individuals communicate, whether "voluntarily" or "involuntarily," will be influenced by emotion state. The role of emotional expression as a form of functional communication of situation (including intentions) goes back to Darwin and is widely appreciated (Darwin, 1872; Ekman, 1982).

Behavior. All psychological mechanisms are involved in the generation and regulation of behavior, so obviously behavior will be regulated by emotion state. More specifically, however, mechanisms proximately involved in the generation of actions (as opposed to processes like face recognition that are only distally regulatory) should be very sensitive to emotion state. Not only may highly stereotyped behaviors of certain kinds be released (as during sexual arousal or rage, or as with species-typical facial expressions and body language), but more complex action-generation mechanisms should be regulated as well. Specific acts and courses of action will be more available as responses in some states than in others, and more likely to be implemented. Emotion mode should govern the construction of organized behavioral sequences that solve adaptive problems.

Specialized inference. Emotion mode should be one factor that governs the activation of specialized inferential systems, such as cheater detection (Cosmides, 1985; Cosmides, 1989; Cosmides & Tooby, 1989), bluff detection, and so on.

Reflexes. Muscular coordination, tendency to blink, threshold for vomiting, shaking, and many other reflexes should be regulated by emotion mode.

Learning. Emotion mode will also regulate learning mechanisms. What someone learns from stimuli will be greatly altered by emotion mode, because of attentional allocation, motivation, situation-specific inferential algorithms, and a host of other factors. Emotion mode will cause the present context to be divided up into situation-specific functionally appropriate categories so that the same stimuli and the same environment may be interpreted in radically different ways, depending on emotional state. For example, which stimuli are considered similar should be different in different emotional states, distorting the shape of the individual's psychological "similarity space" (Shepard, 1987).

Hedonic evaluation of acts, events, and stimuli. A behavioral sequence is composed of many acts. Each of these acts can be thought of as an intermediate "factor" in the production of a behavioral sequence. Determining which courses of action are worthwhile and which are not is a major informational problem. The payoff of each "factor of production"—of each act in the sequence—must be computed before one can determine whether the whole sequence is worthwhile. Every time there is a change in the world that affects the probable payoff of an act or new information that allows a better evaluation of payoffs, this value needs to recomputed. Evaluating entire chains as units is not sufficient, because each item in a chain (staying behind from the hunt, making a tool, borrowing materials from a friend, etc.) may be used in another unique sequence at a later time. Therefore, effort, fitness token-payoffs (rewards), risks, and many other components of evaluation need to be assigned continually to classes of acts. For this reason, there should be mechanisms that assign hedonic values to acts, tallied as intermediate weights in decision processes. Our stream of actions and daily experiences will be affectively "colored" by the assignment of these hedonic values. If our psychological mechanisms were not using present outcomes to assign hedonic weights to classes of acts, there would be no function to suffering, joy, and so on. Emotion mode obviously impacts the assignment of hedonic values to acts.

Energy level and effort allocation. Overall metabolic budget will of course be regulated by emotion, as will specific allocations to various processes and facilitation or inhibition of specific activities. The effort that it takes to perform given tasks will shift accordingly, with things being easier or more effortful depending on how appropriate they are to the situation reflected by the emotion. Thus, fear will make it more difficult to attack an antagonist, while anger will make it easier. The confidence with which a situation has been identified should itself regulate the effortfulness of situation-appropriate activities. Confusion should inhibit the expenditure of energy on costly behavioral responses and should motivate more information gathering and information analysis.

For a more extended discussion of emotions as architecture-organizing psychological adaptations, and how to relate them to the cue structure of ancestral environments, see Tooby and Cosmides (1990b).

INDIVIDUAL DIFFERENCES

Of course, mapping a universal evolved psychology would be an empty project if every member of a species had a fundamentally different one. But complex adaptations, including complex psychological adaptations, should tend to be nearly species-typical for humans or any species with an open-breeding system, and at least population-endemic for species with more closed population structures (Tooby & Cosmides, 1990a). Evolutionary constraints on how adaptations must be implemented, as well as recent developments in the theory of the evolution of sexual reproduction and genetic systems can help here: They show how genetic differences can exist within the shared superstructure of universal, complex, adaptively organized psychological mechanisms.

The argument is straightforward (see Tooby & Cosmides, 1990a; see also, Tooby, 1982): (a) A species is a group of organisms defined by their ability to interbreed and form offspring that can equally well reproduce. (b) To survive and reproduce in a complex world, the organism needs complex mechanisms (complex adaptations). (c) Complex adaptations require complex blueprints at the genetic level. This means that they require coordinated gene expression, involving hundreds or thousands of genes to regulate their development. (d) If the genes involved in complex adaptations differed in ways that significantly impacted the design of the component parts, from individual to individual, then, (e) every sexual generation (which breaks apart old combinations and randomly generates new ones) would lead to the break down of complex adaptations. (f) Sexual recombination makes it improbable that all of the necessary genes for a complex adaptation would be together in the same individual if the genes coding for components of complex adaptations varied substantially between individuals. Therefore, (g) humans, and other complex organisms, cannot vary significantly in those genes that underlie their complex adaptations. This applies with equal force to psychological adaptations: Even relatively simple cognitive programs or "mental organs" must contain a large number of interdependent processing steps, limiting the nature of the variation that can exist without violating the functional integrity of psychological adaptations.

These conclusions are well supported by observations on human and nonhuman physiology. One can flip open *Gray's Anatomy* to any page and discover it describes down to fine detail the architecture of any normal human from anywhere on the planet. The "architecture" or physiological and neurobiological design of humans is both distinctively species-specific and species-typical. When one examines the organs, with their complex design and interlocking architecture, one finds (within an age and sex, and to a large extent between sexes) monomorphism of design: Everyone has two lungs, one neck, blood, homoglobin, insulin, and so on. And, although there is a great deal of superficial variation—no two hands are exactly the same size—each organ system has the same basic design: The locations and connections between organs are topologically the same, and the internal tissue structures and physiological processes have a uniformity of structure and functional regulation. One has to descend to specific enzymatic pathways before design differences—as opposed to quantitative variation—start showing up: Individual proteins may indeed differ due to genetic differences between individuals, but genetically specified, coordinated functional variation in biochemical pathways between individuals of the same sex and age is very rare.[3]

In short, although there is a large amount of variation among humans concerning single or quantitative characteristics of specific organ systems, there is almost *no variation* among humans in what organs exist, or the basic design of each organ system. Everyone has a heart, and a liver, and so on, and everyone's heart and liver function in much the same way. We expect that this pattern holds for "mental organs" as well. Such variation, whether it is of "physical" or "mental" organ systems, can modify the functioning of these systems between individuals— sometimes drastically. Phenylketonuria is the result of a single gene modification. Nevertheless, such variation must be recognized as modifications of a design whose integrity is largely intact and is not likely to consist of a wholly different design, differing "from the ground up." We find implausible, on the basis of population genetics considerations, the notion that different humans have fundamentally different and competing cognitive programs, resting on wholly different genetic bases. For this reason, individuals should be slightly noisy versions of species-typical designs, perturbed in many minor fashions by genetic noise in superficial properties. Consequently, heritable psychological differences are not themselves likely to be complex psychological adaptations. Thus, we believe that behavioral scientists can most effectively devote most of their early research effort to elucidating the most commonly shared and basic design features of a species' cognitive programs. (For further development of this argument, and its application to the study of both species-typical design and individual differences, see Tooby & Cosmides, 1990a.)

In this view, individual differences are primarily explained by different environmental factors being fed into the same species-typical design: a standard psychological view. This is why regularities must be found at the level of mechanisms, and not behavior itself. For example, individual differences may be caused when wholly different cognitive programs become activated in different individuals, although they exist latently in all individuals, based on a species-typical genetic basis. Such facultative programs can be differentially activated early in the life cycle (setting individuals along different developmental tracks), by short-term situational elicitation, or even as the result of superficial (in the sense discussed earlier) genetic differences in other parts of the genome (e.g., constitutional differences or gender).

---

[3]Nonetheless, it is well established that there is a remarkable amount of genetic diversity in humans, and other similar species. What is it doing there? There seems to be good reason to believe that it is there in order to create variation that is superficial from the point of view of functional architecture but that enhances defenses against infectious disease (see, e.g., Hamilton & Zuk, 1982; Tooby, 1982). That is, it seems likely to be the result of parasite-driven frequency-dependent selection for biochemical individuality, supplemented by other by-products of the evolutionary process, such as as mutations and selectively neutral variants drifting through the population.

CONCLUSIONS

Many evolutionary biologists seem to think that once they have identified an adaptive function, their job is done: Specifying how the organism accomplishes the function is a trivial matter. This is comparable to thinking that once Einstein had derived the equation $E = mc^2$, designing a nuclear power plant was a trivial matter. Understanding what properties a cognitive program must have if it is to accomplish an adaptive function is far from trivial—it is one of the most challenging problems facing modern researchers. But it is an illuminating enterprise.

There is emerging a new approach, usually called evolutionary psychology, which is made possible by the simultaneous maturation of behavioral ecology, evolutionary biology, paleobiology, cognitive psychology, and neuroscience. Together, these disciplines allow the discovery and principled investigation of the set of evolved information-processing adaptations that constitute one important description of human and nonhuman psychological architecture. We propose that they be combined according to the following guidelines:

1. Use the principles of natural selection as a starting point to develop models of the adaptive problems that the species of interest had to solve.
2. Attempt to determine how these adaptive problems would have manifested themselves in the species' environment of evolutionary adaptedness, insofar as this is possible. Recurrent environmental features relevant to the adaptive problem, including constraints and relationships that existed in the social, ecological, genetic, and physical situation of the species should be specified; these constitute the conditions in which the adaptive problem arose and further define the nature of the adaptive problem. Such features and relationships constitute the only environmental information available to whatever cognitive program evolved to solve the adaptive problem. The structure of the cognitive program must be such that it can guide behavior along adaptive paths given only the information available to it in these conditions.
3. Integrate the model of the selection pressures with available knowledge of the relevant ancestral conditions, drawing whatever valid and useful implications can be derived from this set of constraints. Catalog the specific information-processing problems that must be solved if the adaptive function is to be accomplished. This constitutes a computational theory of the adaptive information-processing problem. The computational theory is then used as a heuristic for generating testable hypotheses about the structure of the cognitive programs that solve the adaptive problem in question.
4. Use the computational theory to (a) determine whether there are design features that *any* cognitive program capable of solving the adaptive problem must have, and (b) develop candidate models of the structure of the cognitive programs that the species in question might have evolved to solve the adaptive problem. Be sure the model proposed is, in principle, powerful enough to solve the problem defined in the computational theory.
5. Eliminate alternative candidate models with experiments and field observation. Cognitive psychologists have already developed an impressive array of concepts and experimental methods for tracking complex information-processing systems—these should be used to full advantage. The end result is a validated model of the cogni-

tive programs in question, together with a model of what environmental information, and other factors, these programs take as input.

6. Finally, compare the model against the patterns of manifest behavior that are produced by modern conditions. Informational inputs from modern environments should produce the patterns of manifest behavior predicted by the model of the cognitive programs already developed.

As previously discussed, some who adopt the evolutionary perspective attempt to leap directly from Step 1 to Step 6, neglecting the intermediate steps, searching only for correspondences between evolutionary theory and modern manifest behavior. However, because they leave the causal chain by which evolution influences behavior vague and unspecified, such attempts have sown the widespread confusion that (in the human case) hypotheses about economics, culture, consciousness, learning, rationality, social forces, and so on, constitute distinct alternative hypotheses to evolutionary or "biological" explanations. Instead, such hypotheses are more properly viewed as proposals about the structure of evolved cognitive programs and the kinds of information they take as input. They contain implicit theories about how these evolved cognitive programs interact with information derived from modern environments.

Cognitive psychology and evolutionary biology are sister disciplines. The goal of evolutionary theory is to define the adaptive problems that organisms must be able to solve. The goal of cognitive psychology is to discover the information-processing mechanisms that have evolved to solve them. Alone, each is incomplete for the understanding of behavior. Together, applied as a unified research program, they offer the promise that the level of analysis appropriate for describing and investigating behavior has, at last, been found.

REFERENCES

Arnold, M. B. (1960). *Emotion and personality.* New York: Columbia University Press.
Arnold, M. B. (1968). *The nature of emotion.* London: Penguin Books.
Atherton, M., & Schwartz, R. (1974). Linguistic innateness and its evidence. *The Journal of Philosophy, 71,* 6.
Axelrod, R., & Hamilton, W. D. (1981). The evolution of cooperation. *Science, 211,* 1390–1396.
Barkow, J. H., Cosmides, L., & Tooby, J. (Eds.). (1992). *The adapted mind: Evolutionary psychology and the generation of culture.* New York: Oxford University Press.
Beach, F. A. (1955). The snark is a boojum. *American Psychologist, 5,* 115–124.
Block, N. (1980). What is functionalism? In N. Block (Ed.), *Readings in philosophy of psychology.* Cambridge, MA: Harvard University Press.
Boden, M. (1977). *Artificial intelligence and natural man.* New York: Basic Books.
Bowlby, J. (1969). *Attachment and Loss, Volume 1.* New York: Basic Books.
Breland, K., & Breland, M. (1961). The misbehavior of organisms. *American Psychologist, 16,* 681–684.
Bruner, J. S. (1973). *Beyond the information given.* (J. M. Anglin, Ed.). New York: Norton.
Buss, D. M. (1987). Sex differences in human mate selection criteria: An evolutionary perspective. In C. B. Crawford, M. F. Smith, & D. L. Krebs (Eds.), *Sociobiology and psychology.* Hillsdale, NJ: Erlbaum.

Buss, D. M. (1989). Sex differences in human mate preferences: Evolutionary hypotheses tested in 37 cultures. *Behavioral and Brain Sciences, 12*, 1–49.

Buss, D. M. (1991). Evolutionary personality psychology. *Annual Review of Psychology, 42*, 459–491.

Buss, D. M. (1992). Mate preference mechanisms: Consequences for partner choice and intrasexual competition. In J. Barkow, L. Cosmides, & J. Tooby (Eds.), *The adapted mind: Evolutionary psychology and the generation of culture.* New York: Oxford University Press.

Buss, D. M. (1994). The evolution of desire. New York: Basic Books.

Cheng, P. W., & Holyoak, K. J. (1985). Pragmatic reasoning schemas. *Cognitive Psychology 17*, 391–416.

Chance, M. R. A. (1980). An ethological assessment of emotion. In R. Plutchik & H. Kellerman (Eds.), *Emotion: Theory, research, and experience* (pp. 81–111). New York: Academic Press.

Chomsky, N. (1957). *Syntactic structures.* The Hague: Mouton & Co.

Chomsky, N. (1959). Review of Skinner's "Verbal Behavior." *Language, 35*, 26–58.

Chomsky, N. (1975). *Reflections on language.* New York: Random House.

Chomsky, N. (1980). *Rules and representations.* New York: Columbia University Press.

Cosmides, L. (1985). Deduction or Darwinian algorithms?: An explanation of the "elusive" content effect on the Wason selection task. Doctoral dissertation. Department of Psychology and Social Relations, Harvard University, Cambridge, MA.

Cosmides, L. (1989). The logic of social exchange: Has natural selection shaped how humans reason? Studies with the Wason selection task. *Cognition, 31*, 187–276.

Cosmides, L., & Tooby J. (1981). Cytoplasmic inheritance and intragenomic conflict. *Journal of Theoretical Biology 89*, 83–129.

Cosmides, L., & Tooby, J. (1987). From evolution to behavior: Evolutionary psychology as the missing link. In J. Dupre (Ed.), *The latest on the best: Essays on evolution and optimality.* Cambridge, MA: MIT Press.

Cosmides, L., & Tooby, J. (1989). Evolutionary psychology and the generation of culture, Part II. Case study: A computational theory of social exchange. *Ethology & Sociobiology, 10*, 51–97.

Cosmides, L., & Tooby, J. (1992). Cognitive adaptations for social exchange. In J. Barkow, L. Cosmides, & J. Tooby (Eds.), *The adapted mind: Evolutionary psychology and the generation of culture.* New York: Oxford University Press.

Cosmides, L., Tooby, J., & Barkow, J. (1992). Evolutionary psychology and conceptual integration. In J. Barkow, L. Cosmides, & J. Tooby (Eds.), *The adapted mind: Evolutionary psychology and the generation of culture.* New York: Oxford University Press.

Crawford, C. B., Smith, M. F., & Krebs, D. L. (Eds.). (1987). *Sociobiology and psychology.* Hillsdale, NJ: Erlbaum.

Crawford, C. B., & Anderson, J. L. (1989). Sociobiology: An environmentalist discipline? *American Psychologist, 44*(12), 1449–1459.

Daly, M., & Wilson, M. (1981). Abuse and neglect of children in evolutionary perspective. In R. D. Alexander & D. W. Tinkle (Eds.), *Natural selection and social behavior.* New York: Chiron.

Daly, M., & Wilson, M. (1982). Homicide and kinship. *American Anthropologist, 84*, 372–378.

Daly, M., & Wilson, M. (1984). A sociobiological analysis of human infanticide. In G. Hausfater & S. Hrdy (Eds.), *Infanticide: Comparative and evolutionary perspectives* (pp. 487–502). New York: Aldine de Gruyter.

Daly, M., & Wilson, M. (1987a). Evolutionary psychology and family violence. In C. B. Crawford, M. F. Smith, & D. L. Krebs (Eds.), *Sociobiology and psychology.* Hillsdale, NJ: Erlbaum.

Daly, M., & Wilson, M. (1987b). The Darwinian psychology of discriminative parental solicitude. *Nebraska Symposium on Motivation, 35*, 91–144.

Daly, M., & Wilson, M. (1988). *Homicide.* New York: Aldine.

Daly, M., Wilson, M., & Weghorst, S. J. (1982). Male sexual jealousy. *Ethology and Sociobiology, 3*, 11–27.

Darwin, C. (1871). *The descent of man and selection in relation to sex.* London: Murray.

Darwin, C. (1872). *The expression of emotion in man and animals.* London: Murray.

Dawkins, R. (1976). *The selfish gene.* New York: Oxford University Press.

Dawkins, R. (1982). *The extended phenotype.* San Francisco: W. H. Freeman.

Dawkins, R. (1986). *The blind watchmaker.* New York: Norton.

Dupre, J. (Ed.). (1987). *The latest on the best: Essays on evolution and optimality.* Cambridge, MA: MIT Press.

Eibl-Eiblsfeldt, I. (1975). *Ethology: The biology of behavior* (2nd ed.). New York: Holt, Rinehart and Winston.

Ekman, P. (Ed.). (1982). *Emotion in the human face* (2nd ed.). Cambridge, UK: Cambridge University Press.

Erickson, C. J., & Zenone, P. G. (1976). Courtship differences in male ring doves: Avoidance of cuckoldry? *Science, 192,* 1353–1354.

Fodor, J. A. (1981). The mind–body problem. *Scientific American, 244*(1), 124–133.

Fodor, J. A. (1983). *The modularity of mind.* Cambridge, MA: MIT Press.

Fodor, J. A., & Pylyshyn, Z. (1988). Connectionism and cognitive architecture: A critical analysis. *Cognition, 28,* 3–71.

Frijda, N. H. (1986). *The emotions.* London: Cambridge University Press.

Galef, B. G. (1990). An adaptationist perspective on social learning, social feeding, and social foraging in Norway rats. In D. Dewsbury (Ed.), *Contemporary issues in comparative psychology.* Sunderland, MA: Sinauer.

Gallistel, C. R. (1990). *The organization of learning.* Cambridge, MA: MIT Press.

Garcia, J., & Koelling, R. A. (1966). Relations of cue to consequence in avoidance learning. *Psychonomic Science, 4,* 123–124.

Gould, S. J., & Lewontin, R. C. (1979). The spandrels of San Marco and the Panglossian program: A critique of the adaptationist programme. *Proceedings of the Royal Society of London, 205,* 281–288.

Grimshaw, J. (1981). Form, function, and the language acquisition device. In C. L. Baker & J. J. McCarthy (Eds.), *The logical problem of language acquisition.* Cambridge, MA: MIT Press.

Hamburg, D. A. (1968). Emotions in the perspective of human evolution. In S. L. Washburn & P. C. Jay (Eds.), *Perspectives on human evolution* (pp. 246–257). New York: Holt.

Hamilton, W. D. (1964). The genetical evolution of social behavior. *Journal of Theoretical Biology 7,* 1–52.

Hamilton, W. D., & Zuk, M. (1982). Heritable true fitness and bright birds: A role for parasites? *Science, 218,* 382–387.

Hausfater, G., & Hrdy, S. (Eds.). (1984). *Infanticide: Comparative and evolutionary perspectives.* New York: Aldine de Gruyter.

Heath, S. B. (1983). *Ways with words: Language, life, and work in communities and classrooms.* New York: Cambridge University Press.

Herrnstein, R. J. (1977). The evolution of behaviorism. *American Psychologist, 32,* 593–603.

Holmes, W. G. (1983). Kin recognition in animals. *American Scientist, 71,* 46–55.

Hrdy, S. B. (1977). *The langurs of Abu.* Cambridge, MA: Harvard University Press.

Hume, D. (1977). *An enquiry concerning human understanding* (E. Steinberg, Ed.) Indianapolis: Hackett. (Original work published 1748)

Izard, C. E. (1977). *Human emotions.* New York: Plenum.

Jacobs, R. A., Jordan, M. I., & Barto, A. G. (1990). *Task decomposition through competition in a modular connectionist architecture: The what and where vision tasks* (COINS Technical Report 90-27). Dept. of Computer & Information Science, University of Massachusetts, Amherst, MA 01003.

Kant, I. (1966). *Critique of pure reason* New York: Anchor Books. (Original work published 1781)

Katz, J. J. (1975). Innate ideas. In S. P. Stich (Ed.), *Innate ideas.* Berkeley: University of California Press.

Konner, M. (1982). *The tangled wing: Biological constraints on the human spirit.* New York: Holt, Rinehart and Winston.

Krebs J., & Davis, N. (1984). *Behavioural ecology: An evolutionary approach* (2nd ed.). Oxford: Blackwell Scientific Publications.

Lazarus, R. (1966). *Psychological stress and the coping process.* New York: McGraw-Hill.

Lazarus, R., Kanner, A., & Folkman, S. (1980). Emotions: A cognitive–phenomenological analysis. In R. Plutchik & H. Kellerman (Eds.), *Emotion: Theory, research and experience: Vol 1. Theories of emotion* (pp. 189–217). New York: Academic Press.

Lewontin, R. (1978). Adaptation. *Scientific American, 239,* 157–169.

Lockard, R. (1971). Reflections on the fall of comparative psychology: Is there a message for us all? *American Psychologist, 26,* 22–32.

Lorenz, K. (1965). *Evolution and the modification of behavior.* Chicago: University of Chicago Press.

Marr, D. (1982). *Vision: A computational investigation into the human representation and processing of visual information.* San Francisco: W. H. Freeman.

Marr, D., & Nishihara, H. K. (1978, October). Visual information processing: Artificial intelligence and the sensorium of sight. *Technology Review,* pp. 28–49.

Marshall, J. C. (1981). Cognition at the crossroads. *Nature, 289,* 613–614.

Maynard Smith, J. (1978). Optimization theory in evolution. *Annual Review of Ecology and Systematics, 9,* 31–56.

Maynard Smith, J. (1982). *Evolution and the theory of games.* Cambridge, UK: Cambridge University Press.

Maynard Smith, J., & Price, G. A. (1973). The logic of animal conflict. *Nature* (London), *246,* 15–18.

Miller, G. F., & Todd, P. M. (1990). Exploring adaptive agency: I. Theory and methods for simulating the evolution of learning. In D. S. Touretskz, J. L. Elman, T. J. Sejnowski, & G. E. Hinton (Eds.), *Proceedings of the 1990 Connectionist Models Summer School* (pp. 65–80). San Mateo, CA: Morgan Kauffman.

Minsky, M. (1977). Frame-system theory. In P. N. Johnson-Laird & P. C. Wason (Eds.), *Thinking: Readings in cognitive science.* Cambridge, UK: Cambridge University Press.

Nesse, R. M. (1990). Evolutionary explanations of emotions. *Human Nature, 1,* 261–289.

Orians, G., & Heerwagen, J. (1992). Evolved responses to landscapes. In J. Barkow, L. Cosmides, & J. Tooby (Eds.), *The adapted mind: Evolutionary psychology and the generation of culture* (pp. 555–579). New York: Oxford University Press.

Otte, D. (1974). Effects and functions in the evolution of signaling systems. *Annual Review of Ecology and Systematics, 5,* 385–417.

Pinker, S. (1979). Formal models of language learning. *Cognition, 7,* 217–283.

Pinker, S. (1982). A theory of the acquisition of lexical interpretive grammars. In J. Bresnan (Ed.), *The mental representation of grammatical relations.* Cambridge, MA: MIT Press.

Pinker, S. (1984). *Language learnability and language development.* Cambridge, MA: Harvard University Press.

Pinker, S. (1989). *Learnability and cognition: The acquisition of argument structure.* Cambridge, MA: MIT Press.

Pinker, S. (1991). Rules of language. *Science, 253,* 530–535.

Pinker, S., & P. Bloom (1990). Natural language and natural selection. *Behavioral and Brain Sciences, 13*(4), 707–784. (Reprinted in J. Barkow, L. Cosmides, & J. Tooby [Eds.], *The adapted mind: Evolutionary psychology and the generation of culture.* New York: Oxford University Press.)

Pinker, S., & Prince, A. (1988). On language and connectionism: Analysis of a parallel distributed processing model of language acquisition. *Cognition, 28,* 73–193.

Plutchik, R. (1980). *Emotion: A psychoevolutionary synthesis.* New York: Harper & Row.

Popper, K. R. (1972). *Objective knowledge: An evolutionary approach.* London: Oxford University Press.

Putnam, H. (1967). The "innateness hypothesis" and explanatory models in linguistics. *Synthese, 17,* 12–22.

Pylyshyn, Z. W. (1984). *Computation and cognition: Toward a foundation for cognitive science.* Cambridge, MA: MIT Press.

Quine, W. V. O. (1969). *Ontological relativity and other essays.* New York: Columbia University Press.

Real, L. A. (1991). Animal choice behavior and the evolution of cognitive architecture. *Science, 253,* 980–986.

Rozin, P. (1976). The evolution of intelligence and access to the cognitive unconscious. In J. M. Sprague & A. N. Epstein (Eds.), *Progress in psychobiology and physiological psychology.* New York: Academic Press.

Rozin, P., & Schull, J. (1988). The adaptive-evolutionary point of view in experimental psychology. In R. C. Atkinson, R. J. Herrnstein, G. Lindsey, & R. D. Luce (Eds.), *Stevens's handbook of experimental psychology.* New York: Wiley.

Schank, R., & Abelson, R. P. (1977). *Scripts, plans, goals, and understanding.* Hillsdale, NJ: Erlbaum.

Seligman, M. E. P., & Hager, J. L. (1972). *Biological boundaries of learning.* New York: Meredith.

Shepard, R. N. (1981). Psychophysical complementarity. In M. Kubovy & J. R. Pomerantz (Eds.), *Perceptual organization.* Hillsdale, NJ: Erlbaum.

Shepard, R. N. (1984). Ecological constraints on internal representation: Resonant kinematics of perceiving, imagining, thinking, and dreaming. *Psychological Review, 91,* 417–447.

Shepard, R. N. (1987). Evolution of a mesh between principles of the mind and regularities of the world. In J. Dupre (Ed.), *Evolution and information*. Cambridge, MA: MIT Press.

Shepher, J. (1983). *Incest: A biosocial view*. New York: Academic Press.

Sherry, D. F., & Schacter, D. L. (1987). The evolution of multiple memory systems. *Psychological Review, 94*, 439–454.

Shettleworth, S. J. (1972). Constraints on learning. In D. S. Lehrman, R. A. Hinde, & E. Shaw, (Eds.)., *Advances in the study of behavior* (vol. 4). New York: Academic Press.

Skinner, B. F. (1957). *Verbal behavior*. New York: Appleton.

Staddon, J. E. R. (1987). Optimality theory and behavior. In J. Dupre (Ed.), *Evolution and information*. Cambridge, MA: MIT Press.

Staddon, J. E. R. (1988). Learning as inference. In R. C. Bolles & M. D. Beecher (Eds.), *Evolution and learning*. Hillsdale, NJ: Erlbaum.

Symons, D. (1979). *The evolution of human sexuality*. New York: Oxford University Press.

Symons, D. (1987). If we're all Darwinians, what's the fuss about? In C. B. Crawford, M. F. Smith, & D. L. Krebs (Eds.), *Sociobiology and psychology* (pp. 121–146). Hillsdale, NJ: Erlbaum.

Symons, D. (1989). A critique of Darwinian anthropology. *Ethology and Sociobiology, 10*, 131–144.

Symons, D. (1992). On the use and misuse of Darwinism in the study of human behavior. In J. Barkow, L. Cosmides, & J. Tooby (Eds.), *The adapted mind: Evolutionary psychology and the generation of culture* (pp. 137–159). New York: Oxford University Press.

Thornhill, R. (1991). The study of adaptation. In M. Bekoff & D. Jamieson (Eds.), *Interpretation and explanation in the study of behavior*. Boulder, CO: Westview Press.

Tinbergen, N. (1951). *The study of instinct*. New York: Oxford University Press.

Todd, P. M., & Miller, G. F. (1991a). Exploring adaptive agency: II. Simulating the evolution of associative learning. In J. A. Meyer & S. W. Wilson (Eds.), *From animals to animats: Proceedings of the First International Conference of Simulation of Adaptive Behavior* (pp. 306–315). Cambridge, MA: MIT Press.

Todd, P. M., & Miller, G. F. (1991b). Exploring adaptive agency: III. Simulating the evolution of habituation and sensitization. In H. P. Schwefel & R. Manner (Eds.), *Parallel problem solving from nature* (pp. 307–313). Berlin: Springer-Verlag.

Tolman, E. C. (1932). *Purposive behavior in animals and men*. New York: Appleton-Century-Crofts.

Tooby, J. (1982). Pathogens, polymorphism, and the evolution of sex. *Journal of Theoretical Biology, 97*, 557–576.

Tooby, J. (1985). The emergence of evolutionary psychology. In D. Pines (Ed.), *Emerging syntheses in science*. Proceedings of the Founding Workshops of the Santa Fe Institute. Santa Fe, NM: The Santa Fe Institute.

Tooby, J., & Cosmides, L. (1989a). Evolutionary psychology and the generation of culture: Part I. Theoretical considerations. *Ethology & Sociobiology, 10*, 29–49.

Tooby, J., & Cosmides, L. (1989b). Adaptation versus phylogeny: The role of animal psychology in the study of human behavior. *International Journal of Comparative Psychology, 2*(3), 105–118.

Tooby, J., & Cosmides, L. (1990a). On the universality of human nature and the uniqueness of the individual: The role of genetics and adaptation. *Journal of Personality, 58*, 17–67.

Tooby, J., & Cosmides, L. (1990b). The past explains the present: Emotional adaptations and the structure of ancestral environments. *Ethology and Sociobiology, 11*, 375–424.

Tooby, J., & Cosmides, L. (1990c). Toward an adaptationist psycholinguistics. *Behavioral and Brain Sciences, 13*(4), 760–762.

Tooby, J., & Cosmides, L. (1992). Psychological foundations of culture. In J. Barkow, L. Cosmides, & J. Tooby (Eds.), *The adapted mind: Evolutionary psychology and the generation of culture* (pp. 19–136). New York: Oxford University Press.

Tooby, J., & DeVore, I. (1987). The reconstruction of hominid behavioral evolution through strategic modeling. In W. Kinzey (Ed.), *Primate models of hominid behavior* (pp. 183–237). Albany, New York: SUNY Press.

Tomkins, S. S. (1962). *Affect, imagery, consciousness* (Vol. I). New York: Springer.

Tomkins, S. S. (1963). *Affect, imagery, consciousness* (Vol. II). New York: Springer.

Trivers, R. L. (1972). Parental investment and sexual selection. In B. Campbell (Ed.), *Sexual selection and the descent of man 1871–1971*. Chicago: Aldine.

Trivers, R. L. (1974). Parent–offspring conflict. *American Zoologist, 14*, 249–264.

Wanner, E., & Gleitman, L. R. (1982). *Language acquisition: The state of the art.* Cambridge, UK: Cambridge University Press.

Wexler, K., & Culicover, P. (1980). *Formal principles of language acquisition.* Cambridge, MA: MIT Press.

Wilkinson, G. S. (1988). Reciprocal altruism in bats and other mammals. *Ethology and Sociobiology, 9,* 85–100.

Wilkinson, G. S. (1990, February). Food sharing in vampire bats. *Scientific American,* pp. 76–82.

Wilson, E. O. (1975). *Sociobiology: The new synthesis.* Cambridge, MA: Harvard University Press.

Wilson, M., & Daly, M. (1985). Competitiveness, risk taking, and violence: The young male syndrome. *Ethology and Sociobiology, 6,* 59–73.

Wilson, M., & Daly, M. (1987). Risk of maltreatment of children living with step-parents. In R. Gelles & J. Lancaster (Eds.), *Child abuse and neglect: Biosocial dimensions* (pp. 215–232). New York: Aldine de Gruyter.

Wilson, M., & Daly, M. (1992). The man who mistook his wife for a chattel. In J. Barkow, L. Cosmides, & J. Tooby (Eds.), *The adapted mind: Evolutionary psychology and the generation of culture* (pp. 289–322). New York: Oxford University Press.

Williams, G. C. (1966). *Adaptation and natural selection: A critique of some current evolutionary thought.* Princeton, NJ: Princeton University Press.

Williams, G. C. (1985). A defense of reductionism in evolutionary biology. *Oxford Surveys in Evolutionary Biology, 2,* 1–27.

Williams, G. C., & Williams, D. C. (1957). Natural selection of individually harmful social adaptations among sibs with special reference to social insects. *Evolution, 17,* 249–253.

Part II

EARLY EXPERIENCE AND MOTIVATION

_____ chapter 2 _____

Olfactory Mediation
of Mother–Infant
Interactions in Selected
Mammalian Species

RICHARD H. PORTER
FRÉDÉRIC LÉVY
Laboratoire de Comportement Animal
URA INRA-CNRS 1291
France

SYNOPSIS AND COMMENTS
Roderick Wong

Parental care ensures the survival of offspring and thereby enhances the parents' reproductive success. In that respect, there are proximate and ultimate factors that motivate the various activities that comprise this class of adaptive behavior. In mammals, parental care usually takes the form of behavioral interactions between parent (usually the mother) and offspring. One form of these interactions involves attachment of the parent and infant to each other. The ultimate function of parental and filial attachment is that of the reproductive success conferred on the parent and offspring, and it is manifested in the immediate survival of the young. The chapter by Porter and Lévy provides a beautiful example of proximate and ultimate analyses of the role of olfactory mediation in parent–offspring attachment among selected species of rodents, lagomorphs, and ungulates. In their analysis the authors integrate the influence of evolutionary, hormonal, neurobiological, dietary, sensory, and experiential factors that affect these interactions. In their description and discussion of research on two species of rodents from the family Muridae, the authors indicate how and why the Norway rat and the Egyptian spiny mouse evolved distinctively different reproductive strategies. Rats are altricial and are unable to make excursions out of the nest until they are 2 weeks old. These pups show selective responding to olfactory cues emanating from lactating females, and there is a close synchrony between the time course of production of maternal pheromone and the age range over which pups are attracted to such cues. Mothers cease to emit the maternal pheromone at about 27 days postpartum when their young are no longer responsive to such olfactory cues and when weaning is complete.

In contrast to rats, spiny mice are precocial and newborn pups are capable of independent locomotion. The pups begin to approach home-cage bedding material when only 1 day old and can eat solid food at age 4 days. They prefer chemical cues from lactating conspecific females that had been maintained on the familiar diet compared to those fed an unfamiliar diet. In that respect, the experiments on spiny mice and rats indicate that the salient characteristics of maternal pheromone involve the mother's diet. In nature, diets of omnivorous rodents are likely to vary between family groups and could provide the basis for distinctive maternal odors.

Because maternal resources are limited, natural selection processes favor the discriminative allocation of parental investment such that there is preferential treatment of the mother's biological offspring. This is made possible by the parent's ability to discriminate between its own and alien offspring. On this basis, Porter and Lévy predicted that mechanisms for accurate recognition of offspring would most likely evolve in contexts in which mothers' own and alien young intermingle in the same area prior to weaning. This is common among ungulates. Exceptions would occur among animals, such as rodents, that engage in reciprocal communal nursing. Acceptance of foster young among rats is due to the likelihood that wild-living rats will keep their newborn litters in individual nests isolated from other conspecifics. The authors suggest that in this context, caring for any young in the nest is a viable maternal strategy because those young would likely be the mother's own offspring. However, they also concede that the ready acceptance of foster young is an artifact of domestication or laboratory rearing conditions.

Certainly, the role of maternal diet is a factor that is very important. Among spiny mice, when two females and their newborn litters are housed together in a large enclosure, the mothers nurse and retrieve the alien young as frequently as their own. By the eighth day after the birth of the pups, mothers interact preferentially with their own offspring, even though they will still accept and nurse newborn alien pups. The preceding results were obtained when the mothers were maintained on the same diet. When their diets were systematically varied, lactating females preferentially retrieved alien 1-day-old pups whose mothers were fed the same diet but not those whose mothers were fed a different one from the subject females. Again, these results indicate that the olfactory phenotype of stimulus pups reflected the diet fed to their mothers.

In discussing the role of olfactory stimuli in mother–infant interactions among the European rabbit, Porter and Lévy indicated some unique characteristics of their behavior. The altricial pups are confined to the nest until 13–18 days old and receive intermittent and brief maternal care. The mothers leave the nest and return for a single nursing period each day in which they do not assist the pups in locating the nipples. This behavior, which reduces the risk of attracting animals that prey upon rabbits in secluded nests, is believed to be an adaptation to heavy predation pressure. The pups are dependent upon olfactory cues for localization of the nipple. Emission of a rabbit "nipple-search pheromone" may be under the influence of reproductive hormones. Unlike the case with rats and spiny mice, rabbits show rapid initial nipple attachment and require little postnatal learning of the odors that direct such behavior. The mothers rely on odor cues for offspring recognition and show discriminative affiliation between their own and alien pups.

Specificity of maternal responsiveness is most evident among ungulates. Being grazers, sheep live in free-ranging conditions in which females and juveniles share the use of a common area. Newborn lambs are highly precocial and often wander away when their mother leaves them to graze. Also many ewes give birth around the same time. Maternal responsiveness is maximal at parturition, and, within an initial "sensitive period," any alien newborn exchanged for the mother's neonate will elicit maternal behavior. If mother–young contact is maintained for at least 2 hours, a selective bond is formed between the ewe and the lamb. The mother will then suckle only her own lamb and reject any alien young approaching the udder. This lasts throughout the lactation period.

Olfaction is the major sensory channel involved in the regulation of maternal behavior. More specifically, the amniotic fluid (AF) on the newborn's coat is responsible for the heightened attractiveness of lambs immediately after birth. The duration of AF attractiveness is a function of the mother's motivational state but also varies with the type of behavioral test used.

There are some interesting and significant differences between the effects of AF from different sources on maternal acceptance among two species of ungulates, sheep and goats. Sheep will respond positively to lambs rubbed with AF from either the tested ewe or an alien one. In contrast, goats are attracted only to the olfactory label associated with their own. The does will accept an alien kid that had been fed an artificial milk substitute (thus unlabeled) rather than alien kids that had been licked or fed by an alien doe. However, research on sheep indicates that these effects were not observed.

Unlike the case with rats and rabbits, there seems to be little evidence that lambs depend upon olfaction in their interactions with the ewe, even though the ewes respond to the AF emanating from the lambs.

In their discussion, Porter and Lévy indicate how the functions and patterning of olfactory signals exchanged between mothers and infants are reflections of complex interactions with the environment throughout the species' evolutionary history. Comparisons between the four species that they chose provide insights into the correlation between ecological/life history variables and particular parameters of mother–infant communication. For example, enhanced individual discrimination would be expected as the opportunity for erroneous maternal investment increases. Because sheep congregate in large flocks, early offspring recognition enhances the ewe's fitness by allowing her to invest her limited resources in her own lamb rather than wasting it on aliens. In addition, lambs who indiscriminately approach alien ewes could put themselves in jeopardy by physical attacks. Among newborn rabbits, discriminative responsiveness to their own mother versus alien females would be of little adaptive value because the pups are unable to leave the nest chamber. The functionally blind pups must locate a nipple and begin sucking via stereotyped, rapid, inborn responses to odors emanating from the mother's nipple. However, mother rabbits reject conspecific pups carrying foreign labels. This is an adaptive strategy given that those carrying the odor of alien mothers would normally not be the female's offspring.

In general, the material in this chapter provides the reader with a model analysis of the mechanisms and function of maternal behavior. This material substantiates Wilson's (1975) assertion that "the pattern of parental care is a biological trait like any other; it is genetically programmed and varies from one species to the next. Whether any care is given in the first place and what kind and for how long are details that can distinguish species as surely as diagnostic anatomical traits used by taxonomist." Porter and Lévy's description and discussion about the characteristics and the circumstances of maternal behavior among these selected rodent and ungulate species indicate the intricate interaction of early experience, olfactory factors, and learning (except in rabbits) as proximate variables that shape the pattern of maternal behavior of members in each species. This analysis documents the manifestation of the complex domain-specific programs (Cosmides & Tooby, this volume) with motivational components.

Reference

Wilson, E. O. (1975). *Sociobiology: The new synthesis*. Cambridge, MA: Belknap Press of Harvard University.

INTRODUCTION

Olfaction appears to be a sensory modality of singular importance for the mediation of early mother–infant interactions among terrestrial mammals, including humans (e.g., Leon, 1983; Porter, 1991; Rosenblatt, 1983; Schaal, 1988a). In many species, one or both members of the mother–infant dyad have been found to emit olfactory signals to which their partner is discriminatively responsive, and which ultimately contribute to the optimal growth and development of the neonate. Despite such general cross-taxa similarities in the reliance on odor signals during the early postpartum period, the details of this chemosensory communication system and its functional involvement in particular aspects of behavioral and physiological development vary considerably with the life histories and ecology of the species. To illustrate this point, we will summarize and compare briefly the relevant data from three taxonomically diverse groups of mammals that have been the subjects of intensive studies of mother–infant olfactory communication—rabbits, sheep, and various species of rodents.

RODENTS

The large number of currently existing rodent species range over most of the earth's surface and display "a bewildering variety of adaptations" (Eisenberg, 1981). Although rodents are commonly used in research on mother–infant chemical communication, only a small proportion of the species comprising this order has been systematically studied. Our discussion of rodents will focus upon two members of the family Muridae, the Norway rat (*Rattus norvegicus*) and the Egyptian spiny mouse (*Acomys cahirinus*), that have evolved distinctly different reproductive strategies.

Throughout much of the world, Norway rats live commensally with humans (Eisenberg, 1981). With few exceptions (e.g., Barnett, 1958; Calhoun, 1962), however, accounts of rat social behavior have been restricted to laboratory strains. The production of large litters containing 14 or more pups is not uncommon for domestic rats. Young are born after a 21–22-day gestation period in a nest constructed by their mother and usually isolated from other conspecifics (e.g., Gubernick, 1981). In some instances, however, two (or even more) females with suckling pups have been observed sharing the same burrow (Calhoun, 1962; Lee & Moltz, 1985; Leslie, Venables, & Venables, 1952). During the first 2 weeks postpartum, the mother intermittently visits the nest where she serves as a source of food and warmth for her offspring (e.g., Jans & Leon, 1983). Altricial rat pups are functionally blind and deaf at birth, with poorly developed motor capabilities. Based on his thorough review of the literature, Gottlieb (1971) concluded that the first overt responses to auditory and visual stimuli occur on days 5 and 8, respectively. As they become increasingly mobile around 2 weeks of age, pups begin to make their initial excursions out of the nest (Leon & Moltz, 1971; Weisner & Sheard, 1933), and weaning is completed approximately 2 weeks later.

Spiny mice (*A. cahirinus*) are widely distributed in the eastern Mediterranean region (including the islands of Crete and Cyprus), northeast Africa, and southwest Asia (Haim & Tchernov, 1974; Tchernov, 1975). Members of this species typically inhabit rocky outcroppings in arid deserts, where they shelter in naturally occurring cracks and crevices (Brunjes, 1990; Dieterlen, 1962; Tchernov, 1975); but they are also found in villages and towns as a commensal of humans (Haim & Tchernov, 1974).

In marked contrast with rats (and other murid rodents), spiny mice give birth to offspring whose sensory and motor systems are well developed. At birth (or shortly thereafter), the eyes and ears are open, and the precocial pups are capable of independent locomotion (Brunjes, 1990; Ruch, 1967). Unlike most small rodents, *A. cahirinus* mothers do not construct a nest in which their pups are confined during the early postpartum period. Concomitant with the relatively large size of the neonates, and the lengthy gestation period of 38–39 days, litters tend to be small in comparison with those of altricial rodents (i.e., ranging from one to six pups, with a mean of approximately two to three; see also Dewsbury & Hodges, 1987). Pups have been observed to eat solid food as early as the 4th day after birth (Porter, Cavallaro, & Moore, 1980) and can be "weaned" successfully in the laboratory at the end of the first week (Dieterlen, 1962). Nonetheless, when pups are left with their mother, suckling shows a gradual linear decline and may not cease entirely until the 4th week (Porter, Tepper, Baumeister, Cernoch, & Matochik, 1982).

Responses of Young to Maternal Odors

General Activity and Locomotor Orientation. Nest odors, particularly those emanating from the mother, exert a marked effect on the spontaneous behavior of rat pups. Thus, isolated pups display reduced locomotor activity when tested on soiled bedding from their home cage as compared to clean bedding material (Campbell & Raskin, 1978), or when exposed to air blown over their anesthetized mother (Schapiro & Salas, 1970). Moreover, in tests conducted on their own home-cage bedding, pups that suffered experimentally induced olfactory deficits (i.e., nasal perfusion with zinc sulfate solution) evinced locomotor hyperactivity relative to saline-treated controls (Hofer, 1976). Similarly heightened ambulation on home-cage bedding has been observed among olfactory bulbectomized pups (Raskin, 1982). The rate of ultrasonic "distress" calls by rat pups also varies with their olfactory environment. Pups isolated on clean bedding emitted more ultrasonic vocalization than did those on soiled home-cage bedding (Oswalt & Meier, 1975).

One of the presumed functions of enhanced locomotor activity and rate of ultrasonic calls in the absence of nest odors is to increase the likelihood that the "isolated" neonates will regain contact with their mother or nest (Porter, 1983).

But the role of maternal odors in keeping young in the vicinity of the nest area is perhaps more evident in the directional orientation of pups toward such chemical cues. Accordingly, in two-choice preference tests, rat pups as young as 3–4 days pivot their bodies so that the head is oriented toward bedding taken from their home cage, when paired with clean bedding material (Cornwell-Jones & Sobrian, 1977; Sczerzenie & Hsiao, 1977). By day 9, pups tested in intact litters began to move toward home-cage rather than clean bedding, and at day 13 they began to respond preferentially to bedding from their home cage over that from a nonpregnant female (Gregory & Pfaff, 1971).

Selective responding by rat pups (Wistar strain) to olfactory attractants emanating from lactating females was delineated in an early report by Leon and Moltz (1971). Pups moved toward the odor of their own mother, or of a strange lactating female, simultaneously presented with either an empty goal box or the odor of a nulliparous female. Results of additional experiments by these same authors point out the close synchrony between the time course of production/emission of "maternal pheromone" and the age range over which pups are attracted to such cues (Leon & Moltz, 1972; see also Clegg & Williams, 1983, for a further discussion of the use of the term *pheromone* in this context). At 14 days postpartum, the odor of lactating females first becomes attractive to standard (16-day-old) test pups (cf. Holinka & Carlson, 1976). This coincides with the age at which pups begin reliably to approach the odor of stimulus-lactating females and is also about the time when they normally initiate excursions from the natal nest (see also Gregory & Pfaff, 1971). Mothers cease to emit maternal pheromone at about 27 days postpartum, when their young are no longer responsive to such olfactory cues and weaning is usually completed (Leon & Moltz, 1972). Thus, the temporal parameters of the production of maternal pheromone and pups' attraction to that same stimulus coincides with the developmental period when pups are fully mobile yet still dependent on their mother for the provision of basic resources.

Spiny mouse pups, like young rats, are attracted to odors from their home cage (Janus, 1988; Porter & Ruttle, 1975) and also repond positively to bedding soiled by a pair of unfamiliar parents and their litter (Birke & Sadler, 1987). In contrast with rats, however, the precocial spiny mouse pups begin to approach home-cage bedding material when only 1 day old. At this same age, *A. cahirinus* neonates prefer (i.e., selectively move toward) odors from lactating females over odors produced by other classes of conspecifics (Porter & Doane, 1976; Porter, Doane, & Cavallaro, 1978). Such positive responsiveness to maternal pheromone is still shown by 20-day-old pups but is no longer evident on day 25 (Janus, 1988; Porter et al., 1978). Thus, similar to rat pups as discussed earlier, spiny mouse young begin to move toward sources of maternal pheromone when they become capable of independent locomotion and are at risk of wandering away from the mother or home area, and they continue to do so until weaning.

There are differences between spiny mice and rats in the postpartum period during which females emit maternal pheromone. Whereas rat mothers cease producing maternal pheromone at approximately the same time that their offspring are weaned, 2-day-old *Acomys* neonates are attracted to the odor of 35–38-day post-partum mothers that had been housed with their own weanlings prior to testing (Porter et al., 1978). Although the functional significance (if any) of this prolonged emission of maternal pheromone in *A. cahirinus* cannot be explained at present, it could be an adaptation associated with communal nursing of young. Based upon his observations of captive groups of spiny mice, Dieterlen (1962) has suggested that females may provide reciprocal care of young born to members of their own social group. Unfortunately, there have been no relevant field studies of this species that might corroborate this hypothesis.

For species in which several mothers with their suckling offspring co-occur in the same area, and females reject or react agonistically to alien young, indiscriminate attraction of pups to odors from conspecific females could be very costly. In this context, one would expect the young to respond selectively to the odor of their own mother only. On the other hand, if suckling young are unlikely to encounter lactating females other than their own mother, or in a communal nursing situation wherein females reciprocally care for one another's pups, there will be less need for neonates to recognize their own mother's individual scent (i.e., distinguish between that odor and the olfactory signature of other mothers).

The manner in which wild-living Norway rat mothers treat alien young is not known, but they have been reported to attack strange pups in laboratory tests (King, 1939, cited by Leon, 1983). Lactating females of laboratory strains, however, generally tend to accept young that are not their own—even though they may respond somewhat differently to own versus alien pups (see later discussion of this issue). Investigations of whether laboratory rat pups recognize (i.e., respond discriminatively to) the odor of their own dam have yielded inconsistent results, possibly due to strain differences or artifacts of laboratory housing conditions. Long-Evans hooded rats tested at 18–20 days of age moved preferentially in the direction of their own mother's anal excreta (the route through which maternal pheromone is released) rather than to similar stimuli from a strange dam (Brown & Elrick, 1983; cf. Galef & Muskus, 1979). In comparable experiments with Wistar rats, 16–18-day-old pups approached the odor of an alien lactating female as frequently as the odor emitted by their own mother (Leon & Moltz, 1971). Leon (1975) subsequently determined that salient characteristics of maternal pheromone may be altered by the mother's diet. That is, Wistar rat pups were attracted to odors produced by lactating females fed the same diet as the mother of those test pups, but not by odors from females maintained on a distinctly different diet.

The latter pattern of results for young Wistar rats was mirrored closely in a related series of experiments with neonatal spiny mice. At both 1 and 2 days of age, *A. cahirinus* pups preferred chemical cues from lactating conspecific females that had been maintained on the familiar maternal diet, as compared to such odors from females fed an unfamiliar diet (Doane & Porter, 1978; Porter & Doane, 1977). Further experiments have elucidated the interaction between dietary variables and genetically mediated species-typical factors in determining the characteristics of maternal odors that are attractive to spiny mouse pups. Two-day-old pups that had been raised by either their own mother or a foster female of their own species preferred bedding soiled by a conspecific lactating female over bedding from a laboratory mouse (*Mus musculus*) when all the animals had been fed the same diet (Porter, Deni, & Doane, 1977). If *Acomys* pups had been raised by a *Mus* foster female, however, they developed a preference for *Mus* maternal pheromone over that from conspecific females. Furthermore, odors emanating from a *Mus* female fed the familiar maternal diet elicited more choice responses by spiny mouse young than did odors from conspecific females that had eaten an unfamiliar diet (Porter & Doane, 1977).

It appears, therefore, that the mother's diet may be more salient than genetically mediated differences between spiny mice and house mice in determining the properties of maternal chemical cues to which *A. cahirinus* pups respond (see also Clegg & Williams, 1983). In nature, diets of omnivorous rodents are likely to vary (qualitatively as well as quantitatively) between individuals or family groups and could thereby provide the basis for distinctive maternal odors. It is also evident from the previously mentioned studies of cross-species fostering and dietary manipulations that the specific characteristics of the attractive odors produced by mother rats and spiny mice are individually learned by their pups (Leon, 1975; Porter & Doane, 1977). Such an early learning process would allow more flexibility than would a genetically determined pheromone-recognition system and would also be a more parsimonious means for pups to develop the ability to discriminate their own mother.

Nipple Localization and Attachment.   The reliance of rat pups on maternal chemical signals for effective nipple attachment and suckling is evident from a number of experiments involving systematic impairment of chemosensory capabilities. Olfactory bulbectomy or peripheral destruction of the olfactory epithelium is followed by reduced weight gain and heightened mortality among preweaning rat pups, with the severity of the deficits varying to some extent according to the age at which the treatment is administered (Hill & Almli, 1981; Rouger, Tobach, & Schneirla, 1967; Singh & Tobach, 1975; Singh, Tucker, & Hofer, 1976). These developmental anomalies appear to be a direct function of disrupted nipple localization or attachment. Thus, 2-day-old bulbectomized pups fail to locate nipples from a distance but will attach and suck if held in contact with one (Teicher, Flaum, Williams, Eckhert, & Lumia, 1978). Following complete olfactory bulbectomy when 7 days old, however, pups would not even attach to a nipple held against their snout (Risser & Slotnick, 1987).

An alternative technique for assessing the mediating role of maternal olfactory cues for neonatal suckling is to directly manipulate the source of those chemical stimuli. Thorough washing or chemical lavage of the nipple region of anesthetized lactating female rats results in reduced suckling by intact pups (Hofer, Shair, & Singh, 1976; Teicher & Blass, 1976). In related studies in which thermal, tactile, and olfactory properties of the mother's nipple region were systematically altered, only the latter manipulation was found to interfere with nipple attachment

(Blass, Teicher, Cramer, Bruno, & Hall, 1977; Bruno, Teicher, & Blass, 1980). Based upon their detailed series of experiments in which they continued to use anesthetized mothers as test stimuli, Blass and Teicher (1980; Teicher & Blass, 1977) concluded that pups' initial nipple attachment is elicited by the odor of their mother's saliva or amniotic fluid, which she deposits on her ventrum while grooming herself during parturition. After this first suckling bout, further nipple attachment is under the control of saliva that the pups themselves deposited on their mother while feeding.

At present, there is only limited evidence to suggest that spiny mouse pups may likewise rely on maternal odors for effective nipple localization. Pups whose nasal passages were irrigated with zinc sulfate solution ($ZnSO_4$) on day 2 postpartum (to impair their olfactory capabilities) displayed growth retardation and behavioral deficits relative to their saline-treated and untreated control littermates (Porter, Sentell, & Makin, 1987). Anomalous physical development was more pronounced when all the pups in a litter had been treated with $ZnSO_4$, than for pups that received this same treatment but were afterwards housed with intact littermates. The most plausible interpretation of these data is that suckling by $ZnSO_4$-treated pups was disrupted because they had trouble finding and grasping the nipple. When intact littermates were present, their appropriate feeding behavior could have facilitated nipple orientation and suckling by the olfactory-impaired pups by providing visual and tactile guides to the mother's ventrum.

Development of Dietary Preferences.   Animals with omnivorous feeding habits are able to adapt more readily to unpredictable environmental fluctuations and to exploit a wider variety of habitats than are specialists who are dependent upon a very limited range of food items (e.g., Rozin, 1976). For the latter category of animals, genetically mediated dietary preferences would be an effective solution to the problem of food choice. As pointed out by Rozin (1976, p. 27), this same dietary-selection mechanism would not be suitable for species such as rats that may respond to "anything of potential nutritional value as a possible food." Spiny mice likewise vary their feeding habits according to food availability, with primary dietary constituents in their desert habitat including a variety of insects, plants, seeds, and snails (Degen, Kam, Hazan & Nagy, 1986; Harriman, 1980). Those that live commensally with humans have been reported to eat "nearly everything they can find" (Walker, 1975, cited by Harriman, 1980, p. 1076).

The problem of dietary selection by omnivorous mammals takes on special significance at the approach of weaning. At this time, the young animal may be confronted with a vast array of potentially consumable items, ranging from those that are both palatable and nutritious to others that are of little nutritional value or even poisonous. Of the various methods by which appropriate food selection might be accomplished in this context, several involve the transfer of chemical information (specific olfactory or taste cues) from mothers, or other adult conspecifics, to young.

First, as adults eat, they routinely leave residual chemical traces of their presence at the feeding site. Weanlings, in turn, may be attracted to such odorous cues and feed selectively at sites marked in this manner. For example, rat pups that are given the choice of a clean feeding site, versus one soiled with anal excreta from either a lactating or nulliparous female, consume more food at the latter location (e.g., Galef, 1981). Pups are similarly responsive to residual olfactory cues that are produced by adult females but not contained in their anal excreta (Galef & Heiber, 1976). Because the chemical cues that affect weanlings' choice of feeding sites are produced by both lactating and nulliparous females, and are also attractive to young (65-day-old) adults, they thereby differ from maternal pheromone (discussed earlier).

Aside from marking feeding sites with residual olfactory cues, mothers may deposit chemical labels directly onto the food items on which they feed. These labels may then be used by weanlings to select safe, palatable food. Accordingly, weanling spiny mice consumed more of a novel food item that had been partially eaten (and thus, presumably labeled) by their mother than a clean sample of the same food (Porter, McFadyen-Ketchum, & King, 1990). Consumption of similar food items was not affected, however, by the presence of labels deposited by the subject weanlings' father or by an alien mother. Salient maternal labels that direct early dietary choices therefore appear to be individually distinctive, enabling spiny mouse pups to recognize those produced by their own mother.

The flavor or odor of mother's milk may reflect her recent feeding habits and in this way provide an additional influence on the development of specific food preferences by her offspring (e.g., Galef & Clark, 1972; LeMagnen & Tallon, 1968; Mainardi, Poli, & Valsecchi, 1989). Galef and Henderson (1972) found that weanling rats will consume more of a normally nonpreferred diet if their mother had been maintained on that same diet during the nursing period. Further experiments by these same authors ruled out any effects due to ingestion of maternal feces or exposure to food particles clinging to the mother's body. Additional support for the hypothesis that mother's milk may serve as a vehicle for transmitting dietary information to suckling pups is provided by the behavior of weanlings who had received supplemental feeding of milk manually expressed from a lactating female eating a diet different from their own mother's (Galef & Sherry, 1973). Even though these pups ingested only 1.5 cc of milk from the unfamiliar-diet female, they nonetheless displayed slightly elevated consumption of that diet at weaning.

Direct transmission of dietary cues from one individual to another can also occur during social interactions other than suckling. Galef and his colleagues have conducted a detailed investigation of the processes by which rats acquire specific dietary information via olfactory signals emanating from conspecifics that have recently fed (summarized in Galef, 1986; Galef & Stein, 1985). Although these experiments have typically focused on interactions between adult rats, the mechanisms that have been implicated in the development of specific dietary preferences should similarly enable offspring to acquire the same type of information from their mother.

The basic observation is that rats that have the opportunity to interact with a *demonstrator* that has recently eaten (at a different location) will then show a preference for feeding on the same diet as the latter animal. In this way, individuals could provide members of their colony with information regarding food resources located nearby. Such acquired food preferences are still evident if the interacting *demonstrator* and *observer* had been separated by a mesh screen, but not if they were on opposite sides of a solid Plexiglas partition. As further evidence of the importance of olfactory cues in this social learning process, feeding preferences of anosmic animals are not influenced by exposure to a recently fed demonstrator.

Through additional experiments, it has been ascertained that salient dietary cues are effective in influencing rat feeding preferences only if they occur in the presence of another conspecific (Galef, 1986). Whereas simple exposure to a diet had no effect on feeding behavior, observers' dietary selection was influenced by olfactory cues from the digestive tract of a demonstrator that had been fed by intragastric intubation, or particles adhering to the fur at the anterior end of a conspecific (e.g., Galef & Stein, 1985). It has been shown recently that carbon disulfide in rat's breath is an important contextual cue for the development of enhanced diet preferences (Galef, Mason, Preti, & Bean, 1988). Because dead animals do not emit carbon disulfide, they are ineffective as demonstrators even when powdered with food. On the other hand, animals that were exposed to a novel diet moistened with carbon disulfide exhibited a subsequent preference for that diet. Comparable feeding preferences were not seen among control animals that experienced the same novel diet without concomitant carbon disulfide exposure.

In laboratory colonies, spiny mouse pups have been observed to lick the mouth region of their parents, especially that of the mother (Porter et al., 1980). During such interactions, the parent remains stationary with the mouth slightly open, enabling the pup to lick around the partially exposed teeth and gums and occasionally to thrust its tongue into the parent's mouth. This conspicuous behavior pattern has been noted as early as day 6 postpartum and commonly occurs when mother and offspring are reunited after a brief absence (McFadyen-Ketchum & Porter, 1989). The length of time that pups engaged in maternal mouth licking increased significantly if the mother had eaten a novel food during the separation period. That weanlings actually acquire specific dietary information through such interactions is evident in their subsequent feeding behavior when they were allowed free access to two food items: (a) a fresh morsel of the same food that their mother had recently consumed and (b) an unfamiliar food item. The amount of a normally nonpreferred food item—i.e., fresh potato—consumed by pups who had investigated the mouth of their potato-fed mother was significantly greater than that of control weanlings whose mother had eaten a different novel food immediately prior to her nose–mouth interactions with those pups.

Responses of Mothers to Pups' Odors

Initiation of Maternal Responsiveness. At parturition, mother rats engage in a sequence of species-typical behavior patterns that heighten their exposure to chemosensory stimuli associated with their newborn offspring. Rosenblatt and Lehrman (1963) describe in detail the increased self-licking by laboratory rats during parturition, including licking of birth fluids at the vaginal opening, followed by that of "the protruding birth membranes, and eventually the fetus;" (p. 12 see also Holloway, Dollinger, & Denenberg, 1980). After the fetus has emerged, the female licks and eats the placenta. The membrane is then torn from the newborn pup and also consumed. The mother continues to clean the pup—progressing from the head and body, to the limbs, and finally the anogenital region. Birth fluids that have spread onto the nesting material and the female's body are also licked. Maternal licking of offspring continues throughout the suckling period, with male pups being licked for longer periods of time than females (Moore, 1981). Overall maternal licking was reduced when pups' odors were masked and did not differ for male and female young. More recent experiments have implicated preputial glands in the anogenital region as likely sources of the chemical cues by which male and female pups are discriminated (Brouette-Lahlou, Vernet-Maury, & Chanel, 1991; Vernet-Maurey, Brouette-Lahlou, & Chanel, 1987). Male and female pups show different rates of production of specific compounds isolated from preputial gland secretions from the day of birth through weaning. The majority of pups whose heads were anointed with these same secretions, and whose anogenital areas were cleaned, were licked (on the head region) by lactating females. Control pups untreated with preputial gland secretions did not elicit head licking.

As pointed out by Leon (1983, p. 41), while the odor of newborn pups may play a role in early maternal responsiveness by parturient female rats, "it is probably not critical for its onset." This conclusion follows from the behavior of parturient females that suffered experimentally induced anosmia (reviewed by Elwood & McCauley, 1983; Leon, 1983; Rosenblatt & Siegel, 1983; Rosenblatt, Siegel, & Mayer, 1979). Holloway et al. (1980, p. 19), for example, observed that females bulbectomized on day 10 of gestation subsequently engaged in "a much higher incidence of non-pup-oriented behavior" than did sham-operated controls. These authors were not able to determine whether the inappropriate maternal behavior following bulbectomy was a function of olfactory deficits per se or due to nonsensory effects of the surgical manipulation. In support of the latter interpretation, the anomalous maternal responsiveness and pup development produced by olfactory bulbectomy (2 weeks before mating) was not mimicked when females were rendered anosmic by peripheral application of zinc sulfate (Benuck & Rowe, 1975). Furthermore, females that had been bulbectomized early in life appeared to behave normally during later interactions with their own offspring (e.g., Pollack & Sachs, 1975).

Data from related studies indicate that the odor of neonatal rats may actually be aversive to nonparturient, nonpregnant females (summarized by Leon, 1983; see also, Fleming & Rosenblatt, 1974a, 1974b; Mayer & Rosenblatt, 1977). Whereas intact virgin females tend initially to avoid contact with pups, bulbectomized virgins either cannibalize foster neonates or respond maternally to them with reduced latencies relative to control females. Anosmia resulting from peripheral application of zinc sulfate also elicits rapid onset of maternal behavior by virgin females, but with no concomitant increase in cannibalism. Heightened cannibalism rates among bulbectomized females is believed to be a function of general "irritability" following the surgical procedure (e.g., Rosenblatt et al., 1979).

Obviously, females who have just given birth do not avoid the odor of their neonates. The basis for the differential reactions to pups' odors by virgin versus parturient females is not understood fully, but it has been hypothesized that mothers may become familiarized with odors associated with their newborn litter while grooming their own anogenital region throughout pregnancy (Noirot, 1972; Rosenblatt & Siegel, 1980). Rosenblatt and Siegel (1980) have additionally suggested that hormonal changes during pregnancy may affect females' olfactory perception or their responsiveness to pups' odors.

Discrimination Between Own Versus Alien Young.   Until weaning, mammalian young are entirely dependent upon their mother (or an appropriate conspecific surrogate) as a source of nourishment and, in some species, warmth, shelter, and protection from predators. Because maternal resources are limited, mothers who care indiscriminately for their own and other neonates would risk depriving their offspring of essential nutrients while expending metabolic energy to benefit unrelated young, thereby lowering their own genetic fitness. It follows, therefore, that natural selection would favor the evolution of mechanisms that would facilitate discriminative nepotistic parental investment. One solution to this problem would be for mothers to be capable of recognizing their own offspring and distribute maternal resources to them alone.

The advantages associated with maternal recognition of offspring would increase with the degree of dependence of neonates on their own biological mother and the potential for costly misdirected parental investment (Hamilton, 1964). One would predict that mechanisms for accurate recognition of offspring would be most likely to evolve in contexts in which mothers' own and alien young intermingle or co-occur in the same area prior to weaning (for a further discussion of this issue, see Holmes, 1990). Exceptions to this prediction would include animals that engage in truly reciprocal communal nursing. Under these circumstances, it may be more critical for females to recognize one another rather than their young. By excluding alien adult females, the communal mothers could ensure that any suckling neonates that are present were born to members of their own group.

Beach and Jaynes (1956) observed that recently parturient laboratory rats accept both their own and alien pups, but they nonetheless more rapidly retrieve their own offspring. Preferential retrieval of own offspring is no longer evident among bulbectomized females, suggesting an olfactory basis for pup discrimination. Acceptance of foster young despite an ability to discriminate between them and one's own offspring is consistent with the belief that wild-living mothers keep their newborn litters in individual nests isolated from other conspecifics. In this context, caring for any young in the nest would be a viable maternal strategy since those young should indeed be the mother's own offspring. It is also possible, of course, that ready acceptance of foster young is an artifact of domestication or laboratory rearing conditions.

This latter caveat is likewise applicable when interpreting the responses of laboratory-housed spiny mice to alien conspecific neonates. When two females and their newborn litters were housed together in a large enclosure beginning shortly after parturition, those mothers were observed nursing the alien young as frequently as their own (Porter & Doane, 1978). Females also indiscriminately retrieved their own and alien newborns in tests conducted on day 2 postpartum. By the 8th day after giving birth, mothers interact preferentially with their offspring in comparison to unfamiliar pups of the same age, even though they will still accept and nurse newborn alien pups (less than 24 hours old) (Porter et al., 1980).

All spiny mouse mothers in the previously mentioned experiments had been maintained on the same laboratory diet. A different pattern of results was obtained, however, in similar studies conducted with mothers whose diets were systematically varied. Lactating females more rapidly retrieved alien 1-day-old pups whose mothers had been fed the same diet as the subject females than pups from mothers on a distinctly different diet (Doane & Porter, 1978). Cannibalism rates by foster mothers also differed reliably for pups from own-diet versus unfamiliar-diet females. Pups that had been housed with their own mother for 1 day before fostering were more likely to be cannibalized by the foster dam if her diet was not the same as that of the biological mother.

The olfactory phenotype of stimulus pups in the previous experiments apparently reflected the particular diet fed to their mothers. Dietary-dependent odors could be deposited directly onto the pups as their mother licks or otherwise interacts with them, or possibly transferred to the pups through her milk. In any event, standard laboratory practice of feeding all animals an identical diet could have the effect of masking subtle differences in pups' odors and also preclude offspring recognition mediated by dietary variability between mothers.

RABBITS

The European rabbit (*Oryctolagus cuniculus*) has spread, with human assistance, throughout much of the world (Mykytowycz, 1985). Wild rabbits inhabit "warrens" containing a system of burrows constructed by the colony members (Denenberg, Zarrow, & Ross, 1969). Within a warren, small subgroups establish individual territories that are protected against intrusion by others (Ewer, 1968; Mykytowycz, 1985). Birth takes place in a separate burrow dug by the mother in which she constructs a nest lined with her own fur (Ross, Sawin, Zarrow, & Denenberg, 1963). These nursery chambers have only a single entrance that the mother blocks with soil and marks with feces and urine (presumably to ward off conspecifics) (Mykytowycz & Dudzinski, 1972).

Altricial rabbit pups (sometimes referred to as *kittens*) are born following a 31-day gestation period and remain confined to the nest until approximately 13–18 days of age (e.g., Gottlieb, 1971; Hudson & Distel, 1982). There is no evidence of maternal retrieval of young, even when they are placed outside of the nest (Ross et al., 1963). Unlike most mammalian mothers, female rabbits leave their pups alone in the nest and return only for a single brief nursing period each day—typically lasting only 2–4 minutes (e.g., Denenberg et al., 1969; Hudson & Distel, 1982). Hudson and Distel (1982, 1983) noted that does remain "almost motionless" over their sucking pups and do not otherwise assist them in locating the nipples. Nursing females actively eject milk, and the pups in turn are capable of consuming as much as 25% of their body weight during a single feeding bout.

Several authors have suggested that the unique form of intermittent maternal care found in rabbits is an adaptation to heavy predatory pressure (e.g., Hudson & Distel, 1982, 1983; Ross et al., 1963). By blocking their young in an underground chamber and only visiting them for a short period once a day, mothers reduce the risk of attracting any of the numerous animals that prey upon rabbits to the secluded nest.

The Role of Odors in Mother–Young Interactions

Given the brevity of the mother rabbit's daily visits to the nest, pups must rapidly locate her nipples and begin sucking, or risk starvation. The critical dependence of pups on olfactory cues for successful nipple localization has been elucidated in a series of reports by Hudson and Distel (1983, 1984; Distel & Hudson, 1984, 1985), on which the following discussion is based.

The return of the mother to the nest elicits characteristic rearing behavior by the pups. Once the doe positions herself over the litter, such rearing brings the functionally blind pups into contact with her ventrum. Pups then proceed to probe through the dam's fur with lateral head movements until locating and attaching to a nipple. During their short feeding sessions, pups routinely switch nipples several times, necessitating further searching behavior. Covering the nipples per se or the surrounding area with a thin rubber film, thereby masking (at least partially) localized odor cues, interferes with nipple attachment and sucking. Effective sucking is also eliminated by bilateral olfactory bulbectomy. Pups suffering such surgical interventions do not exhibit the normal stereotyped nipple-searching behavior when placed on the belly of a lactating doe and fail to attach to a nipple if they come into contact with one.

Emission of rabbit *nipple-search pheromone* appears to be under the influence of reproductive hormones. Thus, although pups are most responsive to such chemical signals emanating from pregnant or lactating females (including alien dams), this same *pheromone* is produced by nonbreeding does on a seasonal basis, that is, peaking in late spring and early summer (Hudson & Distel, 1984). Rapid *initial* nipple attachment by caesarian-delivered neonates, and by pups that had been hand-raised for the first 5 days postpartum, argues against the need for postnatal learning of the odors that direct such behavior (Hudson, 1985). Finally, it has been determined that chemical cues found in mother's milk are sufficient to elicit searching movements by newborn pups (Keil, von Stralendorff, & Hudson, 1990). When presented with a glass rod coated with fresh milk, pups displayed "vigorous side-to-side" head movements and grasped the stimulus rod on 70% of the trials. Similar, but less consistent responses were evoked by milk diluted as much as 1:10,000.

Research on the possible influences of the odor of rabbit pups on maternal behavior seems to have been limited primarily to the question of offspring recognition. Mykytowycz and Dudzinski (1972) observed the responses of captive does to three categories of pups that were introduced into their home pens: The female's own offspring, alien pups born in the same captive breeding colony, and wild-caught aliens. Mothers more often sniffed their own pups than either category of aliens, especially at the head and posterior regions (sites of specialized scent glands). Aggressive attacks of pups, in the form of biting and ripping with the claws, were frequently directed towards aliens, but only rarely to the does' own offspring.

Over the course of the experiment, female aggression resulted in the death of 21% of the wild-caught aliens, while own pups were never killed. Pup killing by does is not an artifact of captivity—adult aggression toward young has been reported for wild populations and may be, "in certain circumstances, responsible for the death of a proportion of the immature members of the species" (Mykytowycz & Dudzinski, 1972, p. 97; see also Southern, 1948). As additional evidence that females rely on odor cues for offspring recognition, mothers attack their own pups that have been smeared with glandular secretions or urine from a strange lactating female (Mykytowycz, 1985; Mykytowycz & Dudzinski, 1972).

SHEEP

Domestication of sheep is believed to have begun in the Middle East several thousand years B.C. (e.g., Hafez, Cairns, Hulet, & Scott, 1969). The large number of currently existing races of wild sheep (estimated at about 40) are found in open habitats in a wide variety of climatic regions, ranging from desert to tropical and subpolar (Geist, 1971). Sheep can subsist on an array of plant material, including dry forage of a poor quality as found on high plateaus and mountain slopes. Like many ungulates, sheep spend a large portion of the daylight hours grazing. Peaks of grazing activity tend to occur early in the morning and during the late afternoon. Nighttime grazing is most likely to be observed during the warmest seasons and when flies are especially abundant (Hafez et al., 1969).

Wild and feral sheep, or domesticated sheep living in free-ranging conditions, establish home-range groups in which females and juveniles share the use of a common area. Adult males associate in bachelor groups whose areas cut across those of the ewes (Grubb & Jewell, 1966). The basic social unit is the female and her offspring, but closely related animals may also exist within the same home range (e.g., yearling offspring or the mothers of adult ewes).

Newborn lambs are highly precocial, and single and twin births the most common (Hersher, Richmond, & Moore, 1963; Gubernick, 1981). Ewes and their suckling lambs form large flocks. Rather than remaining in a particular site when their mother leaves them to graze, young lambs often wander away and aggregate in peer groups (Nowak, 1990; Hersher et al., 1963). Mother and offspring regularly reunite, enabling the lambs to feed.

The first behavioral signs of parturition are increasing restlessness and a tendency to seek isolation from the flock. At this time, ewes show a strong attraction to birth fluids and may sniff and lick the genital region of other females in the process of lambing. The ground where the waterbag has ruptured is also sniffed and licked, and birth usually takes place at this same site. Immediately after expulsion, the mother avidly licks her newborn that is covered with amniotic fluid (AF). Maternal licking often continues until the lamb is dry and much of the birth fluids and membranes is ingested. This behavior is associated with the emission of low-pitched bleats (produced only by maternal females) and pawing, which stimulates the activity of the neonate. As the lamb stands and searches for the udder, the mother responds by arching her body in such a way that the teats become accessible. Sniffing of the lamb's anogenital region by the mother may help push it in the direction of the udder. In this manner, suckling usually occurs within the first 2 hours after birth. Nursing behavior is progressively organized into well-defined patterns (Poindron, 1974), with the young usually sucking in a parallel-inverse position that is very common among ungulates. As the lamb passes near the head of its mother to reach the udder, the ewe smells the trunk, then the anogenital region, and continues to frequently sniff the latter area during suckling.

Maternal responsiveness is maximal at parturition but fades after a few hours in the absence of a newborn lamb (Poindron & Le Neindre, 1980). Within this initial *sensitive period*, any alien newborn exchanged for the mother's own neonate will elicit the characteristic sequence of maternal behaviors. However, if mother–young contact is maintained for at least 2 hours, a selective bond is formed between the ewe and lamb. The mother then will suckle only her own lamb and reject, often with threats and butts, any alien young attempting to approach the udder. This second phase of maternal responsiveness (i.e., the period of *maternal selectivity*) lasts throughout the remainder of the lactation period.

Conspicuous behavior patterns that obviously facilitate the exchange of olfactory information occur frequently during both stages of the establishment of mother–young interactions—especially on the part of the mother. In fact, as explicated later, olfaction is the major sensory channel involved in the regulation of maternal behavior. Not only are olfactory cues implicated in the attractiveness of the newborn during the sensitive period for maternal responsiveness, but selective bonding and suckling are also heavily reliant on olfaction.

Olfactory Regulation of Maternal Responsiveness

The Influence of Amniotic Fluid (AF).   As mentioned earlier, within a brief postpartum interval, parturient females will readily accept and care for any alien newborn exchanged for their own neonate. In contrast, more than 50% of ewes rejected 12- to 24-hour-old lambs substituted for their own at parturition (Poindron & Le Neindre, 1980). A series of experiments was undertaken to test the hypothesis that AF on the newborn's coat is responsible for the heightened attractiveness of lambs immediately after birth.

Initially, multiparous ewes were tested for their preferences for food that was either treated or not with AF (Lévy, Poindron, & Le Neindre, 1983). Females appeared to be strongly repelled by AF throughout their oestrus cycle and gestation, but at the moment of parturition (i.e., the first visible contractions) they became immediately attracted to AF (see Figure 2.1). Similar results were obtained for primiparous parturient ewes, indicating that the attraction to AF is not acquired through previous lambing experience (Figure 2.2) (Poindron, Le Neindre, & Lévy, 1984). Positive responsiveness to AF persisted after expulsion of the neonate but faded within 4 hrs if the mother was separated from her lamb during that time.

FIGURE 2.1.   Variations in ewes' responsiveness to AF according to experimental conditions. (Adapted from Lévy, 1985.)

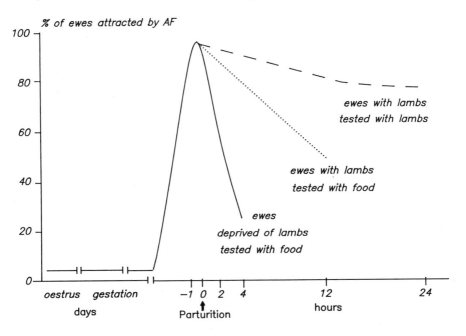

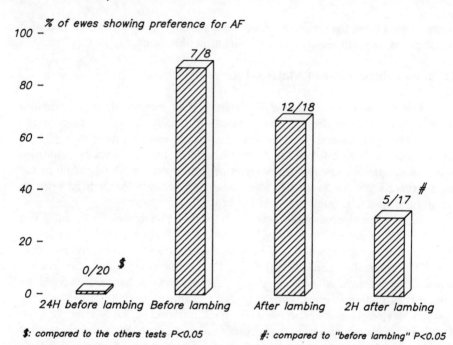

FIGURE 2.2. Responses to AF by primiparous parturient ewes. (Adapted from Lévy, 1985.)

However, when mother–young contact was allowed, half of the ewes were still attracted to AF 12-hrs after parturition (see Figure 1.1). Duration of AF attractiveness therefore is a function of the mother's motivational state (Lévy, 1985) but also varies according to the type of behavioral test used. Thus, attraction to AF 24 hrs after parturition was still evident in the amount of time that females licked a stimulus lamb treated with AF (Lévy, 1985). These results are supported by a study by Vince, Lynch, Mottershead, Green, and Elwin (1985) concerning the responses of parturient ewes to a model made of toweling covering a plastic bottle. More time was spent investigating a bottle containing AF than one without AF.

Related experiments confirm that the attraction–repulsion responses to AF are mediated by olfactory cues. Ewes rendered anosmic by irrigating the nasal mucosa with zinc sulfate were neither repelled nor clearly attracted to AF (Lévy et al., 1983). To determine whether the zinc sulfate treatment might have interferred with the functioning of the vomeronasal system as well as the main olfactory system, an anterograde tracer was injected into the vomeronasal organ (Lévy, unpublished data). The presence of fluorescent dye in the accessory olfactory bulb was evidence of the integrity of the vomeronasal system, therefore implicating the involvement of the main olfactory system in ewe's reaction to AF.

In an attempt to test the assumption that attraction to AF is a necessary step for the normal development of maternal responsiveness, the behavioral consequences of removing AF from the newborn's coat were evaluated (Lévy & Poindron, 1987). Washing the neonate with water or soap before introducing it to its multiparous dam had significant effects on her latency and duration of licking, whereas other parameters of maternal acceptance were not affected. Fourteen of 18 multiparous ewes accepted their washed young at the udder. By contrast, this same treatment completely disrupted maternal responsiveness of primiparous females. Not only was the ewes' licking behavior dramatically affected, but there was also a high incidence of aggressive behavior directed to the lambs, and only one mother allowed her newborn to suck. Thus the presence of AF is necessary to ensure appropriate maternal behavior by naive ewes. Experienced (multiparous) females, however, are able to compensate for the loss of olfactory information by relying on other cues associated with newborns—primarily auditory and visual.

The next question was whether the presence of AF alone is sufficient to induce maternal care in a context wherein multiparous females typically reject young. Parturient multiparous ewes were tested with 1-day-old alien lambs whose coats were treated with AF (Lévy & Poindron, 1984). Two lambs were presented to each female shortly after she gave birth. In the experimental group, one of the stimulus lambs had been rubbed with AF collected from either the tested ewe or from an alien ewe, and the second lamb was kept dry. Ewes in the control condition were tested with two dry lambs. AF treatment resulted in significantly enhanced maternal acceptance of alien lambs, including increased licking durations. Overall, 82% of the alien lambs coated with AF were accepted at the udder, as compared to 45% in the control group. These results were corroborated by a related study in which fostering of alien lambs onto parturient ewes was facilitated by covering the lambs in jackets soaked in AF (Basiouni & Gonyou, 1988).

The origin of AF had no reliable effect on maternal acceptance. Nevertheless, ewes were much more aggressive toward a lamb coated with alien AF than one treated with their own AF. It is interesting in this context that twin-bearing ewes licked their own second-born neonate more than a newborn alien lamb, but final acceptance rates were similar for these two categories of neonates (Poindron, LeNeindre, Raksanyi, Trillat, & Orgeur, 1980). Moreover, parturient ewes respond more positively to their twin that had been isolated at birth than to an alien isolated newborn (Porter, Lévy, Poindron, Litterio, Schaal, & Beyer, 1991). This suggests that members of the same newborn litter may share characteristic AF-borne odors. Thus, AF would contain olfactory cues responsible for general attractiveness, as well as particular molecules imparting distinctive litter odors.

The final point from this experiment is that the acceptance of dry alien lambs was facilitated by the presence of AF on the other stimulus lamb's coat. Dry lambs introduced with an AF-treated partner elicited more licking by the subject ewes than did paired dry lambs in the control group. Therefore, not only is AF sufficient to induce maternal care of lambs bearing that substance, but it also has a generalized arousing effect on maternal responsiveness.

Maintenance of Maternal Behavior.   During the sensitive period, the neonate provides the mother with olfactory cues that are important for the continued maintenance of maternal responsiveness. To demonstrate this point, two sets of experiments were designed in which ewes were allowed only limited interactions with, or exposure to, their lambs within the first 8–12 hrs postpartum. In the first study, depriving ewes of the opportunity to lick and suckle their lambs did not disturb subsequent maternal acceptance (Poindron & Le Neindre, 1980). On the other hand, ewes that were prevented from smelling their newborn had acceptance rates as low as mothers totally deprived of young. The second experiment (Poindron, Lévy, & Krehbiel, 1988) confirmed the primacy of olfactory information for the development of appropriate maternal behavior. For the first 8 hrs after birth, lambs were placed individually in a box allowing the selective elimination of either their olfactory or visual cues, or both. Mothers that could only smell and hear their lambs behaved later (after 8 hrs) like ewes that were exposed to all of the cues emanating from their young. In contrast, there was a significant decrease in acceptance by ewes when lambs' olfactory cues had been suppressed. Furthermore, the proportion of mothers in this latter condition that displayed maternal responsiveness was similar to that for ewes totally deprived of their young.

Deprivation of odors from the lamb thus has a drastic effect on the maintenance of maternal behavior, while elimination of visual cues appears to be of little consequence. At present, the nature of the salient olfactory cues is not known. Nonetheless, since the neonates in the previously mentioned deprivation experiments were still covered with AF, and given the previously discussed attraction of parturient females to that same substance, the odor of AF is also likely to be salient in the present context. Accordingly, aside from being a key stimulus for the onset of maternal behavior, AF could also contribute to its maintenance beyond the sensitive period.

Sensory Mediation of Maternal Selectivity

Once a selective bond is formed between a ewe and her lamb(s), two types of maternal discrimination of offspring may be observed. Recognition at a distance permits the ewe to locate her young, while recognition at close quarters is necessary before the young is allowed to suckle. Whereas the latter sort of recognition becomes evident within the first hours after parturition, the acquisition of distance recognition has not been studied.

The sensory basis of distal recognition of lambs differs from that mediating proximal recognition. Indiscriminate acceptance of alien lambs at suckling is found among females suffering olfactory deficits as a result of bulbectomy (Baldwin & Shillito, 1974; Bouissou, 1968), severing the olfactory nerves (Morgan, Boundy, Arnold, & Lindsay, 1975), irrigation of the olfactory mucosa with zinc sulfate (Poindron, 1976), or impairment of olfactory bulb functioning with neurotoxic agents (Lévy, Gervais, Kindermann, Orgeur, & Piketty, 1990; Pissonnier, Thiery, Fabre-Nys, Poindron, & Keverne, 1985). Deprivation of olfactory identity by washing the young, however, leads to rejection of both familiar and alien lambs that approach the udder (Alexander & Stevens, 1981; Alexander, Stevens, & Bradley, 1983). These finding are not contradictory but indicate that if the ewe is rendered anosmic before lambing, she is unable to associate suckling with the distinctive odor of one particular lamb and will therefore accept any young. On the other hand, once she has become familiar with a lamb's odor through suckling experience, the absence of that odor precludes recognition and elicits rejection of that same lamb or aliens. This interpretation may also explain why olfactory deficits introduced two weeks after parturition affected ewe's acceptance of their own lambs, even though visual and acoustic recognition are possible at this time (Poindron & Le Neindre, 1980).

Ewes' localization of their lambs at a distance primarily involves vision and audition (Lindsay & Fletcher, 1968; Morgan et al., 1975; Poindron & Carrick, 1976; Shillito & Alexander, 1975), but olfactory cues may also be salient to a lesser extent. Morgan et al. (1975) found that for distances up to 4.5 m, olfactory cues were sufficient to assist the ewe in finding her lamb. On the other hand, recognition was greater for separation distances of .25 m or less by ewes that could smell and hear or see their lambs than for ewes who could only smell their offspring (Alexander & Shillito, 1977). The importance of visual cues is further evident from a study by Martin, Price, Wallach, and Dally (1987) showing that attempts to foster lambs by odor transfer were unsuccessful when the alien was not similar in facial coloration to the ewe's own young. Compensatory reliance on audition and vision for recognition within close distances can even be observed when ewes are deprived of lambs' olfactory cues (Alexander & Stevens, 1981). Ewes tested with washed lambs correctly selected their own lambs at distances up to .25 m. When those same washed lambs were allowed access to the mother to suckle, however, 50% were rejected, emphasizing the fact that odors are the determinant cues for suckling.

The origin and chemical nature of the odors involved in lamb recognition are not precisely known. It appears that regions of the tail, trunk, and head of the lamb are of equal marked interest to the mother (Alexander, 1978; Alexander & Stevens, 1983). The lamb's distinctive odor signature does not originate from either its feces or urine (Alexander & Stevens, 1981, 1983), thus suggesting the possible involvement of sebaceous gland secretions.

Related experiments with goats point out that kids' olfactory signatures may not emanate from the young themselves but could be transferred from the doe to her newborn through licking or via her milk (Gubernick, 1981). Does more readily accepted unlicked alien kids that had been fed an artificial milk substitute (thus, presumably unlabeled) than alien kids that had been licked and/or fed by an alien ewe. Alexander, Stevens, and Bradley (1989) reported data suggesting that a similar process may contribute to lamb recognition by parturient sheep. Artificially fed alien lambs were eventually more frequently accepted than were mother-fed alien lambs, even though such differential acceptances did not seem statistically reliable during the initial acceptance tests. The results of additional experiments, including those conducted by some of the authors of the previous study, do not support the labeling hypothesis, however. Thus, Alexander and Stevens (1983) found that ewes show no more interest in swabs containing their own milk, inguinal wax, saliva, feces, urine, or wool than similar swabs from alien ewes. Also, selective maternal behavior can develop in the absence of licking, suckling, or other forms of physical contact, when lambs are confined in double-wire cages for the first several hours postpartum (Alexander et al., 1986; Poindron & Le Neindre, 1980). While studying the effects of postpartum mother–young separation, we determined that selective ewes (i.e., those that respond preferentially to their own offspring), rejected alien lambs that had fed on milk from the test ewes themselves, as well as aliens who fed from other sources (Lévy et al., 1991). Similarly, nonselective mothers did not accept preferentially alien lambs that had suckled from them.

Finally, alien lambs were equally rejected regardless of whether they had remained with their own mother (thereby having the opportunity to acquire a foreign label) or in isolation prior to testing (Porter et al., 1991). These conflicting results are likely to be a function of methodological differences between the cited experiments and do not rule out the possibility that recognizable lamb odors could originate both from the lamb itself and through maternal labeling. An acquired olfactory label could add to the distinctive individual odor of each lamb and thereby provide a powerful recognition signature for the mother.

Olfactory Regulation of Suckling Behavior

As discussed earlier, the preferred pattern of suckling is a parallel-inverse position in which the ewe is able to smell the hind region of its lamb (Poindron, 1974). Sniffing and olfactory identification of the lamb before taking up the suckling position favor the success of the feeding attempt by the mother's own offspring and rejection of aliens. Consequently, lambs that try to gain access to the udder of alien ewes adopt progressively (over a 2- to 3-week period) a rear approach that prevents the ewe from sniffing and rejecting them (Poindron, 1976).

The importance of maternal olfaction for suckling is further evident in the interactions between lambs and bulbectomized ewes (Poindron, 1976). In this treatment condition, there was no preferred suckling pattern between lambs and their nonselective mothers. The lambs also sucked less frequently from their own mother, and more from alien dams, than did lambs of intact control ewes. When sucking from alien anosmic ewes, lambs commonly adopted a parallel inverse position (Figure 2.3), because there was no need to avoid that pattern (i.e., that position would not contribute to olfactory discrimination and rejection in this context). From these results it appears that the ewe's postural orientation facilitates sampling of the odors of lambs attempting to suckle from her. In turn, the

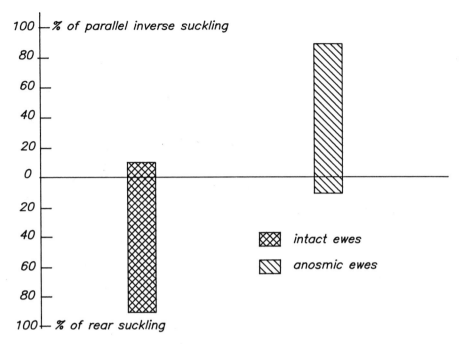

FIGURE 2.3.   Proportion of parallel inverse and rear sucking patterns
observed in intact or anosmic ewes tested with an alien lamb
(Adapted from Poindron, P. [1976]. Mother–young relationships
in intact or anosmic ewes at the time of suckling. *Biology of Behavior,*
2, 161–177. Reprinted by permission of Masson S. A., Paris.)

behavior of the lamb at suckling is strongly influenced by the ewe's sense of
smell.

Olfaction and the Behavior of Newborn Lambs

From a very early age, lambs actively contribute to the process of reciprocal attachment with their mother. Based upon the limited number of directly relevant investigations, however, it appears that the sense of smell is not as essential for the
lamb's interactions with its mother as it is for maternal responsiveness and selectivity. Indeed, newborn lambs rendered anosmic with an anesthetic spray did not
differ from controls in getting onto their feet, approaching the udder, and time of
first sucking (Vince, Lynch, Mottershead, Green, & Elwin, 1987). In comparison,
the lambs' behavior was adversely affected by blindfolding or loss of sensitivity
in the upper lip—suggesting that visual and tactile stimulation are of relatively
more important than olfaction for teat-seeking activity. Similarly, recognition of
ewes by their lambs did not involve the sense of smell, either at close or long distances (Nowak, 1991). Lambs suffering olfactory impairment recognized their own
mothers as well as control lambs did, whereas those that could not see or hear

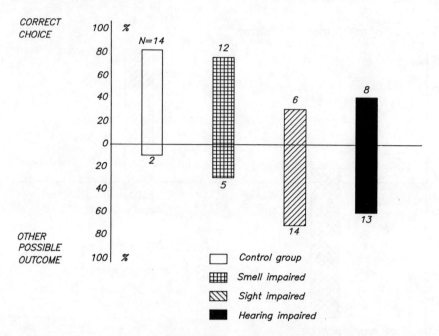

FIGURE 2.4. Proportions of lambs with various sensory deficits that
recognized (i.e., responded discriminatively to) their own mother.
(Adapted from Nowak, R. [1991]. Senses involved in discrimination
of merino ewes at close contact and from a distance by their newborn
lambs. *Animal Behaviour, 42,* 357–366. Used with permission
of Academic Press Inc. [London] Ltd.)

were less successful in locating their dams (Figure 2.4). Despite the apparent lack
of involvement of olfaction in lambs' responsiveness to their dam, they can
nonetheless perceive maternal chemical cues soon after birth and are also capable
of discriminating between maternal and alien odors. Changes in heart and respiration rates, as well as in teat-seeking activity, were reported to be more marked
when lambs were presented with the smell of dams' wax rather than milk or wool
(Vince & Ward, 1984). The odor of maternal wax elicited greater increases in these
same response measures than did wax from an alien dam. A similar pattern of results was obtained for lambs that had been separated from their dams soon after
birth and tested with wax and AF from their own versus alien mothers, suggesting
that such early olfactory discrimination may be mediated by prenatal experience.

    In light of these data, it seems reasonable to conclude that even though
lambs' sense of smell is well developed at birth and they are capable of discriminating between specific odors, olfaction may play only a minor role in the organization of their social interactions. At present, however, this remains a rather tentative conclusion, because the testing situations that have been employed thus far

may not have been adequate to detect more subtle involvement of the olfactory sense in lambs' responsiveness to their mothers.

CONCLUSIONS

The previous overview of reciprocal mother–newborn olfactory communication in rats, spiny mice, rabbits, and sheep illustrates the unique contribution of this sensory modality to offspring survival and development among terrestrial mammals. Chemical substances associated with parturition and the perinatal period provide the basis for discrete olfactory signals characteristic of particular classes of conspecifics. Accordingly, the initial responses of recently parturient females (e.g., ewes and rats) to their newborn offspring may be influenced by the presence of amniotic and birth fluids. For newborn rats and rabbits, nipple localization and suckling are dependent upon odors emanating from lactating females. Maternal olfactory signals also function to keep spiny mouse and rat pups from wandering away from the home area or nest and may provide information about appropriate dietary choices. Moreover, chemical cues may reflect the source individual's identity and thereby function as olfactory signatures mediating mother–offspring recognition.

In comparison to communication through visual and auditory channels, olfaction has several distinct advantages for coordinating early mother–infant interactions. Olfactory cues are equally available in the light and dark; therefore, they are effective during the night, in nests, or in underground burrows (e.g., Doty, 1986). Such signals are continuously accessible regardless of whether the stimulus animals are awake or sleeping and can be perceived by altricial neonates before their eyes open (i.e., while they are still functionally blind). Long-lasting chemical signals can be deposited onto a substrate and continue to influence the recipients' behavior even though the stimulus individual may no longer be present at that location. To the extent that individual odor signatures are genetically influenced, they should remain relatively invariant over the animal's lifetime and thus serve as reliable indicants of identity. In addition, exposure to particular odors may begin in utero, providing the opportunity for fetal learning and familiarization and continuity between the prenatal and postnatal environments (Schaal, 1988b).

The functions and ontogenetic patterning of olfactory signals exchanged between mothers and infants are reflections of complex interactions with the environment throughout the species' evolutionary history. Comparisons among the four species discussed in this chapter can nonetheless afford tentative insights into the correlation between ecological/life history variables and particular parameters of mother–infant olfactory communication. For example, precocial newborn lambs and spiny mice are not confined to a nest and, from a very early age, are capable of wandering away from the mother or home area. Attraction of neonates to maternal cues is one mechanism for ensuring necessary periodic mother–infant reunions. For spiny mouse pups, maternal olfactory signals serve as "beacons" or "tethers" that remain functional in rocky shelters and throughout the day and night. Maternal odors would provide a less adequate means for lambs to maintain contact with their mother, because ewes leave the birth site soon after parturition and frequently change their location while grazing. Visual cues, however, allow these large diurnal mammals inhabiting open grasslands to maintain social contact over relatively long distances.

Attraction to maternal odors also keeps rat pups in the vicinity of the nest. The age at which rat pups begin to orient reliably to such chemical signals and the timing of maximal production of maternal pheromone coincide with the developing motor capabilities of the altricial young and are therefore delayed in comparison with precocial spiny mice.

The omnivorous, opportunistic feeding habits of rats and spiny mice have enabled these species to exploit a range of habitats. Olfactory signals from the mother (as well as from other adult conspecifics in the case of rats) may facilitate initial choice of appropriate food items from among the wide array of substances available to weanlings.

As mentioned previously, the functional significance of individual mother–infant recognition, and its temporal development, also vary with the species' ecology and life history. As the opportunity for erroneous maternal investment in alien young increases, or when neonates would put themselves in jeopardy by approaching alien females, enhanced individual discrimination would be expected. To illustrate this point, lambs that indiscriminately approach alien females could experience delays in becoming reunited with their own mothers (and therefore delays in feeding) and also risk physical attacks. On the other hand, discriminative responsiveness to their own mothers versus alien females would be of little adaptive value to newborn rabbits. The young pups are unable to leave the nest chamber, and their survival is entirely dependent upon the mother's brief daily visits. In order to take in an adequate supply of nutrients, the functionally blind pups must locate a nipple and begin sucking as soon as the mother returns. This is accomplished by stereotyped, rapid, inborn responses to odors emanating from the mother's milk and nipple region.

Because ewes and their newborn lambs congregate in large flocks, early offspring recognition enhances the mother's reproductive fitness by allowing her to invest her limited resources in her own young alone rather than wasting nurturance on alien lambs. Similarly, rejection of conspecific pups labeled with the odors of alien females is a generally adaptive strategy for mother rabbits because pups carrying such foreign labels would normally not be the dam's own offspring. The weak evidence for mother–infant recognition in laboratory investigations of rats and spiny mice suggests that mothers and their newborn of these species may remain isolated from conspecifics, or possibly in communal nursery groups. Alternatively, standard laboratory housing conditions, especially feeding all members of a breeding colony the same diet, may eliminate salient sources of odor variability necessary for individual discrimination. These gaps in our current level of knowledge point out that assessments of the validity of functional interpretations of laboratory studies of animal behavior ultimately require relevant data concerning the species' life history and ecology.

REFERENCES

Alexander, G. (1978). Odour, and the recognition of lambs by Merino ewes. *Applied Animal Ethology, 4*, 153–158.
Alexander, G., Poindron, P., Le Neindre, P., Stevens, D., Lévy, F., & Bradley, L. (1986). Importance of the first hour postpartum for exclusive maternal bonding in sheep. *Applied Animal Behaviour Science, 16*, 295–300.
Alexander, G., & Shillito, E. (1977). The importance of odour, appearance and voice in maternal recognition of the young in Merino sheep. *Applied Animal Ethology, 3*, 127–135.
Alexander, G., & Stevens, D. (1981). Recognition of washed lambs by merino ewes. *Applied Animal Ethology, 7*, 77–86.
Alexander, G., & Stevens, D. (1983). Odor cues to maternal recognition of lambs: An investigation of some possible sources. *Applied Animal Ethology, 9*, 165–175.
Alexander, G., Stevens, D., & Bradley, L. R. (1983). Washing lambs and confinement as aids to fostering. *Applied Animal Ethology, 10*, 251–261.
Alexander, G., Stevens, D. & Bradley, L. R. (1989). Maternal acceptance of alien lambs in ewes treated and untreated with oestrogen at birth. *Australian Journal of Experimental Agriculture, 29*, 173–178.
Baldwin, B. A., & Shillito, E. (1974). The effects of ablation of the olfactory bulbs on parturition and maternal behaviour in Soay sheep. *Animal Behaviour, 22*, 220–223.
Barnett, S. A. (1958). Social behaviour in wild rats. *Proceedings of the Zoological Society of London, 130*, 107–152.
Basiouni, G. F., & Gonyou, H. W. (1988). Use of birth fluids and cervical stimulation in lamb fostering. *Journal of Animal Science, 66*, 872–879.
Beach, F. A., & Jaynes, J. (1956). Studies of maternal retrieving in rats: I. Recognition of young. *Journal of Mammalogy, 37*, 175–185.
Benuck, I., & Rowe, F. A. (1975). Centrally and peripherally induced anosmia: Influences on maternal behavior in lactating female rats. *Physiology & Behavior, 14*, 439–447.
Birke, L. I. A., & Sadler, D. (1987). Effects of odor familiarity on the development of systematic exploration in the spiny mouse, *Acomys cahirinus*. *Developmental Psychobiology, 20*, 627–640.
Blass, E. M., & Teicher, M. H. (1980). Suckling. *Science, 210*, 15–22.
Blass, E. M., Teicher, M. H., Cramer, C. P., Bruno, J. P., & Hall, W. G. (1977). Olfactory, thermal, and tactile controls of suckling in preauditory and previsual rats. *Journal of Comparative and Physiological Psychology, 91*, 1248–1260.
Bouissou, M. F. (1968). Effets de l'ablation des bulbes olfactifs sur la reconnaissance du jeune par sa mere chez les Ovins. *Revue du Comportement Animal, 2*, 77–83.
Brouette-Lahlou, I., Vernet-Maury, E., & Chanel, J. (1991). Is rat dam licking behavior regulated by pups' preputial gland secretion? *Animal Learning and Behavior, 19*, 177–184.
Brown, R. E., & Elrick, D. (1983).Preferences of pre-weanling Long-Evans rats for anal excreta of adult males and females. *Physiology & Behavior, 30*, 567–571.
Brunjes, P. C. (1990). The precocial mouse, *Acomys cahirinus*. *Psychobiology, 18*, 339–350.
Bruno, J. P., Teicher, M. H., & Blass, E. M. (1980). Sensory determinants of suckling behavior in weanling rats. *Journal of Comparative and Psychological Psychology, 94*, 115–127.
Calhoun, J. B. (1962). *The ecology and sociology of the Norway Rat*. Washington, DC: USDHW, PHS.
Campbell, B. A., & Raskin, L. A. (1978). Ontogeny of behavioral arousal: The role of environmental stimuli. *Journal of Comparative and Physiological Psychology, 92*, 176–184.
Clegg, F., & Williams, D. I. (1983). Maternal pheromone in *Rattus norvegicus*. *Behavioral and Neural Biology, 37*, 223–236.

Cornwell-Jones, C., & Sobrian, S. K. (1977). Development of odor-guided behavior in Wistar and Sprague-Dawley rat pups. *Physiology & Behavior, 19*, 685–688.

Degen, A. A., Kam, M., Hazan, A., & Nagy, K. A. (1986). Energy expenditure and water flux in three sympatric desert rodents. *Journal of Animal Ecology, 55*, 421–429.

Denenberg, V. H., Zarrow, M. X., & Ross, S. (1969). The behaviour of rabbits. In E. S. E. Hafez (Ed.), *The behavior of domestic animals* (2nd ed., pp. 417–437). Baltimore: Williams & Wilkins.

Dewsbury, D. A., & Hodges, A. W. (1987). Copulatory behavior and related phenomena in spiny mice (*Acomys cahirinus*) and hopping mice (*Notomys alexis*). *Journal of Mammalogy, 68*, 49–57.

Dieterlen, F. (1962). Geburt und Geburtshilfe bei der Stachelmaus, *Acomys cahirinus*. *Zeitschrift fur Tierpsychologie, 19*, 191–222.

Distel, H., & Hudson, R. (1984). Nipple-search performance by rabbit pups: Changes with age and time of day. *Animal Behaviour, 32*, 501–507.

Distel, H., & Hudson, R. (1985). The contribution of the olfactory and tactile modalities to the nipple-search behaviour of newborn rabbits. *Journal of Comparative Physiology, A., 157*, 599–605.

Doane, H. M., & Porter, R. H. (1978). The role of diet in mother–infant reciprocity in the spiny mouse. *Developmental Psychobiology, 11*, 271–277.

Doty, R. L. (1986). Odor-guided behavior in mammals. *Experientia, 42*, 257–271.

Eisenberg, J. F. (1981). *The mammalian radiations*. Chicago: University of Chicago Press.

Elwood, R. W., & McCauley, P. J. (1983). Communication in rodents: Infants to adults. In R. W. Elwood (Ed.), *Parental behaviour of rodents* (pp. 127–149). Chichester: John Wiley & Sons.

Ewer, R. F. (1968). *Ethology of mammals*. London: Logos Press.

Fleming, A. S., & Rosenblatt, J. S. (1974a). Olfactory regulation of maternal behavior in rats: I. Effects of olfactory bulb removal in experienced and inexperienced lactating and cycling females. *Journal of Comparative and Physiological Psychology, 86*, 221–232.

Fleming, A. S., & Rosenblatt, J. S. (1974b). Olfactory regulation of maternal behavior in rats: Effects of peripherally induced anosmia and lesions of the lateral olfactory tract in pup-induced virgins. *Journal of Comparative and Physiological Psychology, 86*, 233–246.

Galef, B. G. (1981). Development of olfactory control of feeding-site selection in rat pups. *Journal of Comparative and Physiological Psychology, 95*, 615–622.

Galef, B. G. (1986). Olfactory communication among rats: Information concerning diet. In D. Duvall, D. Muller-Schwarze, & R. M. Silverstein (Eds.), *Chemical signals in vertebrates, 4* (pp. 487–505). New York: Plenum Press.

Galef, B. G., & Clark, M. M. (1972). Mother's milk and adult presence: Two factors determining initial dietary selection by weanling rats. *Journal of Comparative and Physiological Psychology, 78*, 220–225.

Galef, B. G., & Heiber, L. (1976). Role of residual olfactory cues in the determination of feeding site selection and exploration patterns of domestic rats. *Journal of Comparative and Physiological Psychology, 90*, 727–739.

Galef, B. G., & Henderson, P. W. (1972). Mother's milk: A determinant of the feeding preferences of weaning rat pups. *Journal of Comparative and Physiological Psychology, 78*, 213–219.

Galef, B. G., Mason, J. R., Preti, G., & Bean, N. J. (1988). Carbon disulfide: A semiochemical mediating socially-induced diet choice in rats. *Physiology & Behavior, 42*, 119–124.

Galef, B. G., & Muskus, P. A. (1979). Olfactory mediation of mother–young contact in Long-Evans rats. *Journal of Comparative and Physiological Psychology, 93*, 708–716.

Galef, B. G., & Sherry, D. F. (1973). Mother's milk: A medium for transmission of cues reflecting the flavor of mother's diet. *Journal of Comparative and Physiological Psychology, 83*, 374–378.

Galef, B. G., & Stein, M. (1985). Demonstrator influence on observer diet preference: Analyses of critical social interactions and olfactory signals. *Animal Learning and Behavior, 13*, 31–38.

Geist, V. (1971). *Mountain sheep*. Chicago: University of Chicago Press.

Gottlieb, G. (1971). Ontogenesis of sensory function in birds and mammals. In E. Tobach, L. R. Aronson, & E. Shaw (Eds.), *The biopsychology of development* (pp. 67–128). New York: Academic Press.

Gregory, E. H., & Pfaff, D. W. (1971). Development of olfactory-guided behavior in infant rats. *Physiology & Behavior, 6*, 573–576.

Grubb, P., & Jewell, P. A. (1966). Social grouping and home range in feral Soay sheep. *Symposium of the Zoological Society of London, 18*, 179–210.

Gubernick, D. J. (1981). Parent and infant attachment in mammals. In D. J. Gubernick & P. H. Klopfer (Eds.), *Parental care in mammals* (pp. 243–305). New York: Plenum Press.

Hafez, E. S. E., Cairns, R. B., Hulet, C. V., & Scott, J. P. (1969). The behaviour of sheep and goats. In E. S. E. Hafez (Ed.), *The behavior of domestic animals* (2nd ed., pp. 269–348). Baltimore: Williams & Wilkins.

Haim, A., & Tchernov, E. (1974). The distribution of myomorph rodents in the Sinai Peninsula. *Mammalia, 38*, 201–223.

Hamilton, W. D. (1964). The genetical evolution of social behaviour: II. *Journal of Theoretical Biology, 7*, 17–51.

Harriman, A. E. (1980). Preferences by Egyptian spiny mice for solutions of sugars, salts, and acids in Richter-type drinking tests. *Perceptual and Motor Skills, 50*, 1075–1081.

Hersher, L., Richmond, J. B., & Moore, A. U. (1963). Maternal behavior in sheep and goats. In H. L. Rheingold (Ed.), *Maternal behavior in mammals* (pp. 203–232). New York: John Wiley & Sons.

Hill, D. L., & Almli, C. R. (1981). Olfactory bulbectomy in infant rats: Survival, growth and ingestive behaviors. *Physiology & Behavior, 27*, 811–817.

Hofer, M. A. (1976). Olfactory denervation: Its biological and behavioral effects in infant rats. *Journal of Comparative and Physiological Psychology, 90*, 829–838.

Hofer, M. A., Shair, H., & Singh, P. (1976). Evidence that maternal ventral skin substances promote suckling in infant rats. *Physiology & Behavior, 17*, 131–136.

Holinka, C. F., & Carlson, A. D. (1976). Pup attraction to lactating Sprague-Dawley rats. *Behavioral Biology, 16*, 489–505.

Holloway, W. R., Dollinger, M. J., & Denenberg, V. H. (1980). Parturition in the rat: Description and assessment. In R. W. Bell & W. P. Smotherman (Eds.), *Maternal influences and early behavior* (pp. 1–26). Jamaica, NY: Spectrum.

Holmes, W. G. (1990). Parent–offspring recognition in mammals: A proximate and ultimate perspective. In N. A. Krasnegor & R. S. Bridges (Eds.), *Mammalian parenting* (pp. 441–460). New York: Oxford University Press.

Hudson, R. (1985). Do newborn rabbits learn the odor stimuli releasing nipple-search behavior? *Developmental Psychobiology, 18*, 575–585.

Hudson, R., & Distel, H. (1982). The pattern of behaviour of rabbit pups in the nest. *Behaviour, 79*, 255–271.

Hudson, R., & Distel, H. (1983). Nipple location by newborn rabbits: Behavioural evidence for pheromonal guidance. *Behaviour, 85*, 260–275.

Hudson, R., & Distel, H. (1984) Nipple-search pheromone in rabbits: Dependence on season and reproductive state. *Journal of Comparative Physiology, A., 155*, 13–17.

Jans, J. E., & Leon, M. (1983). Determinants of mother–young contact in Norway rats. *Physiology & Behavior, 30*, 919–935.

Janus, C. (1988). The development of responses to naturally occurring odours in spiny mice *Acomys cahirinus. Animal Behaviour, 36*, 1400–1406.

Keil, W., von Stralendorff, F., & Hudson, R. (1990). A behavioral bioassay for analysis of rabbit nipple-search pheromone. *Physiology & Behavior, 47*, 525–529.

LeMagnen, J., & Tallon, S. (1968). Preference alimentaire du jeune rat induite par l'allaitement maternal. *Comptes Rendus des Seances de la Societe de Biologie, 162*, 387–390.

Lee, T. M., & Moltz, H. (1985). At what age do rat young stop responding to maternal pheromone? *Physiology & Behavior, 35*, 355–359.

Leon, M. (1975). Dietary control of maternal pheromone in the lactating rat. *Physiology & Behavior, 14*, 311–319.

Leon, M. (1983). Chemical communication in mother–young interactions. In J. G. Vandenbergh (Ed.), *Pheromones and reproduction in mammals* (pp. 39–77). New York: Academic Press.

Leon, M., & Moltz, H. (1971). Maternal pheromone: Discrimination by pre-weanling albino rats. *Physiology & Behavior, 7*, 265–267.

Leon, M., & Moltz, H. (1972). The development of the pheromonal bond in the albino rat. *Physiology & Behavior, 8*, 683–686.

Leslie, P. H., Venables, U. M., & Venables, L. S. V. (1952). The fertility and population structure of the brown rat (*Rattus norvegicus*) in corn ricks and some other habitats. *Proceedings of the Zoological Society of London, 122*, 187–238.

Lévy, F. (1985). *Contribution a l'analyse des mecanismes de mise en place du comportement mater-*

nal chez la brebis (Ovis aries): *etude de la repulsion et de l'attraction vis-a-vis du liquide amniotique, mise en evidence, determinisme, role.* These de Doctorat de l'Universite Paris VI.

Lévy, F., Gervais, R., Kindermann, U., Orgeur, P., & Piketty, V. (1990). Importance of B-Noradrenergic receptors in the olfactory bulb of sheep for recognition of lambs. *Behavioral Neuroscience, 104,* 464–469.

Lévy, F., Gervais, R., Kindermann, U., Litterio, M., Poindron, P., & Porter, R. (1991). Effects of early post-partum separation on maintenance of maternal responsiveness and selectivity in parturient ewes. *Applied Animal Behaviour Science, 31,* 101–110.

Lévy, F., & Poindron, P. (1984). Influence du liquide amniotique sur la manifestation du comportement maternal chez la brebis parturiente. *Biology of Behavior, 9,* 271–278.

Lévy, F., & Poindron, P. (1987). The importance of amniotic fluids for the establishment of maternal behaviour in experienced and inexperienced ewes. *Animal Behaviour, 35,* 1188–1192.

Lévy, F., Poindron, P., & Le Neindre, P. (1983). Attraction and repulsion by amniotic fluids and their olfactory control in the ewe around parturition. *Physiology & Behavior, 31,* 687–692.

Lindsay, D. R., & Fletcher, I. C. (1968). Sensory involvement in the recognition of lambs by their dams. *Animal Behaviour, 16,* 415–417.

Mainardi, M., Poli, M., & Valsecchi, P. (1989). Ontogeny of dietary selection in weaning mice: Effects of early experience and mother's milk. *Biology of Behavior, 14,* 185–194.

Martin, N. L., Price, E. O., Wallach, S. J. R., & Dally, M. R. (1987). Fostering lambs by odor transfer: The add-on experiment. *Journal of Animal Science, 64,* 1378–1383.

Mayer, A. D., & Rosenblatt, J. S. (1977). Effects of intranasal zinc sulfate on open field and maternal behavior in female rats. *Physiology & Behavior, 18,* 101–109.

McFadyen-Ketchum, S. A., & Porter, R. H. (1989). Transmission of food preferences in spiny mice (Acomys cahirinus) via nose-mouth interaction between mother and weanlings. *Behavioral Ecology and Sociobiology, 24,* 59–62.

Moore, C. L. (1981). An olfactory basis for maternal discrimination of sex of offspring in rats (Rattus norvegicus). *Animal Behaviour, 29,* 383–386.

Morgan, P. D., Boundy, C. A. P., Arnold, G. W., & Lindsay, D. (1975). The roles played by the senses of the ewe in the location and the recognition of lambs. *Applied Animal Ethology, 1,* 139–159.

Mykytowycz, R. (1985). Odour signals in the life of the wild rabbit. *Australian Science Magazine, 1,* 44–50.

Mykytowycz, R., & Dudzinski, M. L. (1972). Aggressive and protective behaviour of adult rabbits Oryctolagus cuniculus (L.) towards juveniles. *Behaviour, 43,* 97–120.

Noirot, E. (1972). The onset of maternal behavior in rats, hamsters and mice: A selective review. *Advances in the Study of Behavior, 4,* 107–145.

Nowak, R. (1990). Mother and sibling discrimination at a distance by three- to seven-day-old lambs. *Developmental Psychobiology, 23,* 285–295.

Nowak, R. (1991). Senses involved in discrimination of the mother at close contact and from a distance by their newborn lambs. *Animal Behaviour, 42,* 357–366.

Oswalt, G. L., & Meier, G. W. (1975). Olfactory, thermal, and tactile influences on infantile ultrasonic vocalization in rats. *Developmental Psychobiology, 8,* 129–135.

Pissonnier, D., Thiery, J. C., Fabre-Nys, C., Poindron, P., & Keverne, E. B. (1985). The importance of olfactory bulb noradrenalin for maternal recognition in sheep. *Physiology & Behavior, 35,* 361–364.

Poindron, P. (1974). Etude de la relation mere-jeune chez des brebis (*Ovis aries*) lors de l'allaitements. *Comptes Rendus de l'Academie des Sciences, Paris, Serie D, 278,* 2691–2694.

Poindron, P. (1976). Mother–young relationships in intact or anosmic ewes at the time of suckling. *Biology of Behavior, 2,* 161–177.

Poindron, P., & Carrick, M. J. (1976). Hearing recognition of the lamb by its mother. *Animal Behaviour, 24,* 600–602.

Poindron, P., & Le Neindre, P. (1980). Endocrine and sensory regulation of maternal behavior in the ewe. *Advances in the Study of Behavior, 11,* 75–119.

Poindron, P., Le Neindre, P., & Lévy, F. (1984). Maternal behaviour in sheep and its physiological control. In D. R. Lindsay & D. T. Pearce (Eds.), *Reproduction in sheep.* Canberra: Australian Wool Corp.

Poindron, P., Le Neindre, P., Raksanyi, I., Trillat, G., & Orgeur, P. (1980). Importance of the characteristics of the young in the manifestation and establishment of maternal behaviour in sheep. *Reproduction, Nutrition and Development, 20 (3B),* 817–826.

Poindron, P., Lévy, F., & Krehbiel, D. (1988). Genital, olfactory, and endocrine interactions in the development of maternal behaviour in the parturient ewe. *Psychoneuroendocrinology, 13*, 99–125.

Pollack, E. I., & Sachs, B. D. (1975). Male copulatory behavior and female maternal behavior in neonatally bulbectomized rats. *Physiology & Behavior, 14*, 337–343.

Porter, R. H. (1983). Communication in rodents: Adults to infants. In R. W. Elwood (Ed.), *Parental behaviour in rodents* (pp. 95–125). Chichester, UK: John Wiley & Sons.

Porter, R. H. (1991). Human reproduction and the mother–infant relationship: The role of odors. In T. V. Getchell, R. L. Doty, L. M. Bartoshuk, & J. B. Snow Jr. (Eds.), *Smell and taste in health and disease* (pp. 429–442). New York: Raven Press.

Porter, R. H., Cavallaro, S. A., & Moore, J. D. (1980). Developmental parameters of mother–offspring interactions in *Acomys cahirinus*. *Zeitschrift für Tierpsychologie, 53*, 153–170.

Porter, R. H., Deni, R., & Doane, H. M. (1977). Responses of *Acomys cahirinus* pups to chemical cues produced by a foster species. *Behavioral Biology, 20*, 244–251.

Porter, R. H., & Doane, H. M. (1976). Maternal pheromone in the spiny mouse (*Acomys cahirinus*). *Physiology & Behavior, 16*, 75–78.

Porter, R. H., & Doane, H. M. (1977). Dietary-dependent cross-species similarities in maternal chemical cues. *Physiology & Behavior, 19*, 129–131.

Porter, R. H., & Doane, H. M. (1978). Studies of maternal behavior in spiny mice (*Acomys cahirinus*). *Zeitschrift für Tierpsychologie, 47*, 225–235.

Porter, R. H., Doane, H. M., & Cavallaro, S. A. (1978). Temporal parameters of responsiveness to maternal pheromone in *Acomys cahirinus*. *Physiology & Behavior, 21*, 563–566.

Porter, R. H., Lévy, F., Poindron, P., Litterio, M., Schaal, B., & Beyer, C. (1991). Individual olfactory signatures as major determinants of early maternal discrimination in sheep. *Developmental Psychobiology, 24*, 151–158.

Porter, R. H., McFadyen-Ketchum, S. A., & King, G. A. (1990). The influence of maternal labels on dietary preferences of spiny mouse weanlings. *Physiology & Behavior, 48*, 103–106.

Porter, R. H., & Ruttle, K. (1975). The responses of one-day-old *Acomys cahirinus* pups to naturally occurring chemical stimuli. *Zeitschrift für Tierpsychologie, 38*, 154–162.

Porter, R. H., Sentell, S. W., & Makin, J. W. (1987). Effects of intranasal $ZnSO_4$ irrigation are mitigated by the presence of untreated littermates. *Physiology & Behavior, 40*, 97–102.

Porter, R. H., Tepper, V. J., Baumeister, A. A., Cernoch, J. M., & Matochik, J. A. (1982). Interactions among unfamiliar spiny mouse (*Acomys cahirinus*) weanlings. *Behavioral and Neural Biology, 34*, 190–200.

Raskin, L. A. (1982). Effect of olfactory bulbectomy on reactivity to environmental stimuli in the preweaning rat. *Behavioral and Neural Biology, 34*, 307–318.

Risser, J. M., & Slotnick, B. M. (1987). Nipple attachment and survival in neonatal olfactory bulbectomized rats. *Physiology & Behavior, 40*, 545–549.

Rosenblatt, J. S., (1983). Olfaction mediates developmental transition in the altricial newborn of selected species of mammals. *Developmental Psychobiology, 16*, 347–375.

Rosenblatt, J. S., & Lehrman, D. S. (1963). Maternal behavior of the laboratory rat. In H. L. Rheingold (Ed.), *Maternal behavior in mammals* (pp. 8–57). New York: John Wiley & Sons.

Rosenblatt, J. S., & Siegel, H. I. (1980). Maternal behavior in the laboratory rat. In R. W. Bell & W. P. Smotherman (Eds.), *Maternal influences and early behavior* (pp. 155–199). Jamaica, NY: Spectrum.

Rosenblatt, J. S., & Siegel, H. I. (1983). Physiological and behavioural changes during pregnancy and parturition underlying the onset of maternal behaviour in rodents. In R. W. Elwood (Ed.), *Parental behaviour of rodents* (pp. 23–66). Chichester, UK: John Wiley & Sons.

Rosenblatt, J. S., Siegel, H. I., & Mayer, A. D. (1979). Progress in the study of maternal behavior in the rat: Hormonal, nonhormonal, sensory, and developmental aspects. *Advances in the Study of Behavior, 10*, 225–311.

Ross, S., Sawin, P. B., Zarrow, M. X., & Denenberg, V. H. (1963). Maternal behavior in the rabbit. In H. L. Rheingold (Ed.), *Maternal behavior in mammals* (pp. 94–121). New York: John Wiley & Sons.

Rouger, Y., Tobach, E., & Schneirla, T. C. (1967). Development of olfactory function in the rat pup. *American Zoologist, 7*, 792–793.

Rozin, P. (1976). The selection of foods by rats, humans, and other animals. In J. S. Rosenblatt, R. A. Hinde, E. Shaw, & C. Beer (Eds.), *Advances in the study of behavior* (Vol. 6, pp. 21–76). New York: Academic Press.

Ruch, W. (1967). Die Implantationszeit und deren Beeinflussung durch die Laktation bei *Acomys cahirinus dimidiatus*. *Revue Suisse Zoologie, 74,* 566–569.

Schaal, B. (1988a). Olfaction in infants and children: Developmental and functional perspectives. *Chemical Senses, 13,* 145–190.

Schaal, B. (1988b). Discontinuite natale et continuite chimio-sensorielle: Modeles animaux et hypotheses pour l'homme. *Annee Biologique, 28,* 1–41.

Schapiro, S., & Salas, M. (1970). Behavioral response of infant rats to maternal odor. *Physiology & Behavior, 5,* 815–817.

Sczerzenie, V., & Hsiao, S. (1977). Development of locomotion toward home nesting material in neonatal rats. *Developmental Psychobiology, 10,* 315–321.

Shillito, E., & Alexander, G. (1975). Mutual recognition amongst ewes and lambs of four breeds of sheep. *Applied Animal Ethology, 1,* 151–165.

Singh, P. J., & Tobach, E. (1975). Olfactory bulbectomy and nursing behavior in rat pups (Wistar DAB). *Developmental Psychobiology, 8,* 151–164.

Singh, P. J., Tucker, A. M., & Hofer, M. A. (1976). Effects of nasal $ZnSO_4$ irrigation and olfactory bulbectomy on rat pups. *Physiology & Behavior, 17,* 373–382.

Southern, H. N. (1948). Sexual and aggressive behaviour in the wild rabbit. *Behaviour, 1,* 173–194.

Tchernov, E. (1975). Rodent faunas and environmental changes in the Pleistocene of Israel. In I. Prakash & P. K. Ghosh (Eds.), *Rodents in desert environments* (pp. 331–362). The Hague: Dr. W. Junk.

Teicher, M. H., & Blass, E. M. (1976). Suckling in newborn rats: Eliminated by nipple lavage, reinstated by pup saliva. *Science, 193,* 422–425.

Teicher, M. H., & Blass, E. M. (1977). First suckling response of the newborn albino rat: The roles of olfaction and amniotic fluid. *Science, 198,* 635–636.

Teicher, M. H., Flaum, L. E., Williams, M., Eckhert, S. J., & Lumia, A. R. (1978). Survival, growth and suckling behavior of neonatally bulbectomized rats. *Physiology & Behavior, 21,* 553–561.

Vernet-Maury, E., Brouette-Lahlou, I., & Chanel, J. (1987). Ontogenetic analysis of the rat pup pheromone implicated in perigenital licking. *Chemical Senses, 12,* 186.

Vince, M. A., Lynch, J. J., Mottershead, B., Green, G., & Elwin, R. (1985). Sensory factors involved in immediately postnatal ewe/lamb bonding. *Behaviour, 94,* 60–84.

Vince, M. A., Lynch, J. J., Mottershead, B., Green, G., & Elwin, R. (1987). Interactions between normal ewes and newly born lambs deprived of visual, olfactory and tactile sensory information. *Applied Animal Behaviour Science, 19,* 119–136.

Vince, M. A., & Ward, T. M. (1984). The responsiveness of newly born Clun forest lambs to odour sources in the ewe. *Behaviour, 89,* 117–127.

Wiesner, B. P., & Sheard, N. M. (1933). *Maternal behaviour in the rat.* Edinburgh: Oliver & Boyd.

Multiple Factors
Modulating Courtship,
Habituation, Attention,
and Other Motivated
and Motivating Behaviors

MARYLOU CHEAL
*University of Dayton Research Institute, Higley, AZ
and Arizona State University*

SYNOPSIS AND COMMENTS
Roderick Wong

The material in Cheal's chapter deals with her research in a number of diverse areas, the results of which indicate the role of multiple factors that motivate behavior and influence the direction of behavior development. This work reflects the intellectual influence of D. O. Hebb (1958), who proposed classes of factors that influence motivational aspects of behavior. These factors are very diverse, ranging from genes to physiological mechanisms and sensory input, as well as other behaviors that influence the subject being studied. Cheal draws upon her research in seemingly diverse areas to document the interaction of these classes of factors in influencing behavior and

Grateful acknowledgement is made to Drs. D. A. Dewsbury and R. Wong for comments on an earlier draft of this chapter. The gerbil work was conducted at McLean Hospital, Harvard Medical School, and at the Department of Psychology, Arizona State University. The human visual attention research, conducted in collaboration with Don R. Lyon, was done at University of Dayton Research Institute, at William Air Force Base, Arizona. This latter research was funded by the Air Force Office of Scientific Research (Life Sciences Task 2313T3) and the Air Force Human Resources Laboratory (Contracts F-33615-84-C-0066, F-33615-87-C-0012, and F-33615-90-C-0005).

motivational mechanisms underlying them. Her early work on courtship and spawning activity of the blue gourami reveals the influence of postnatal sensory stimuli on the modification of species-typical behaviors of these fish (Cheal & Davis, 1974).

Cheal's research on developmental changes over the life span of the Mongolian gerbil illustrates some very interesting interactions between environmental and genetic contributions to motivated behavior. She studied the impact of environmental variables on the developmental growth and the expression of behavior throughout the life span of these rodents by providing the experimental group with 1 hour a month of exposure to an enriched environment from the time they were 1 month to 28 months of age. During this exposure period the animals were given access to an outdoor pen in the Arizona desert that provided them with multiple stimuli. Within the aviary wire enclosure there were running water, rocks, sand, and desert vegetation. Although the animals were provided with a very brief period of environmental change and the interval between exposures was fairly long, the results indicate the effects of enrichment on behavior through modification of physiological/anatomical changes.

Gerbils are very prone to manifest spontaneous seizures, and normally this reaction is not seen until they are 2 months old. Cheal's results indicate that more male gerbils from the enriched group showed seizures at 2 months than those in the control group but that such an effect was not evident among females. This effect was still evident when the animals were tested at age 4 months, but the direction of the difference was reversed at later ages. In analyzing the pattern of results observed at various periods, Cheal concluded that the incidence of seizures reflects the interaction of many factors, including genetics, diet, and the environment.

Another species-typical behavior of gerbils that was influenced by the enrichment experience was their ventral gland marking. These animals mark items on various substrates by rubbing their abdominal sebaceous gland on these landmarks. Both marking behavior and the ventral gland are dependent on gonadal hormones. Cheal's study revealed an influence of enrichment on the size of the ventral gland and on behavior as well, but these effects occurred during different periods. Cheal (1986, 1987a) had suggested that the facilitation of ventral gland growth might signify earlier sexual maturation that would then result in greater reproductive capacity. Thiessen and Rice (1976) had noted that marking behavior is associated with territorial marking that may be important in control of social systems and with aggregation necessary for mating and reproduction. If marking provides an index of the male gerbil's potential reproductive performance, Cheal's results suggest that even a small amount of experience in a varied environment may lead to greater reproductive success. This suggestion should be tested in an experiment that would monitor the outcome of early experience on intermale competition, female mate choice, and offspring produced.

Differences in the response latencies of 24-month-old enriched and control gerbils in finding food in a novel apparatus also revealed interesting results. During the first test day the enriched gerbils took less time to reach the food than the control animals. During the subsequent test sessions both groups showed shorter response latencies but did differ from each other. Cheal suggests that the experience in moving about a larger environment may facilitate the animal's ability to observe its environment. This may enable the gerbil to focus or pay more attention to relevant cues in subsequent situations. Thus attentional as well as motivational variables are relevant in the analysis of instrumental behavior leading to food. Research from a different tradition, that concerning optimal foraging behavior, indicates that experience in larger ranges could lead to more successful encounters with a feeding source (Collier & Rovee-Collier, 1981).

An unexpected finding from Cheal's enrichment project was the effect of this variable on the growth of the gerbils' hind limb. This effect was evident when the animals were young. The age (12–14 days) during which the enriched gerbils showed rapid growth occurred about the same period when there was a great acceleration of their locomotory behavior. Cheal suggested that the large and topographically more varied environment of the enriched gerbils may have elicited more physical exercise that could have resulted in greater body and limb lengths. Research on hamsters has shown acceleration of growth in these rodents arising from increases in physical exercise (Borer & Kuhns, 1977).

Although it appears that brief periods of exposure to a natural environment produced many significant outcomes on morphology and behavior that may enhance the animals' fitness, Cheal was cautious about drawing strong implications about these results. One of the major limitation of these experiments is that of sample size, particularly as the animals aged. The effects that were reported reflect interactions of compound stimuli from all of the senses. It is possible that the mediating mechanism of these effects may arise from neural stimulation that, in turn, may affect endocrine functions. Unfortunately, Cheal was unable to directly assess these variables. Another consideration is that of the nature of the treatment variable. Would similar effects be obtained had the experimental group been exposed to "nonnatural" environments? Is it necessary to expose the gerbils to an outdoor desert pen? It is difficult to ascertain whether stimulus complexity, environmental change (sheer novelty effects), or removal from the laboratory environment is the critical variable.

Cheal's treatment of attention is an attempt to indicate some similarities between processes and mechanisms involved in human and gerbil reactions to various stimuli. Her theoretical position is that attentional facilitation of sensory information is the primary method by which motivational states guide behavior. This position was influenced by Hebb's (1972) contention that attention refers to "selectivity in what is responded to, or sensory selectivity." Her experiments with humans indicate that stimuli appearing suddenly in the peripheral visual field elicit rapid discriminations relative to those appearing at the fixation point. Stimuli such as sudden luminance changes and sudden movement that may be associated with life-threatening events elicit rapid attention. There is the question of whether the mechanism responsible for such rapid attention is reflexive or motivational. Hebb's analysis suggests that as long as a reflexive mechanism is adequate, so that the rest of the nervous system is not called into play, we do not consider the process to be motivational. However, if arousal is produced and the course of other behaviors is affected, then one may infer the influence of a motivational process.

In her work with gerbils, Cheal found that attention is dependent upon the type of stimulus, a finding that is consistent with her research on human attention. To investigate attentional processes in gerbils, Cheal developed the *stimulus-elicited investigation* task, which involves the animals' selective responses to novel stimuli and subsequent habituation with continued exposure. This task allowed Cheal to assess the effects of various brain lesions and drug administration.

A developmental analysis produced some interesting findings. Gerbils do not show selective responses to novel stimuli until they are 21 days old. The development of selective attention at this age is significant because it coincides with the time of weaning and movement away from the nest. Cheal points out that some of the developmental stages of attention in infants are analogous to behavior in other animals. Rothbart, Posner, and Boylan (1990) reported that 3-month-old babies make a number of head and eye movements in orienting toward a target. An earlier experiment by Ingle, Cheal, and Dizio (1979) also indicated that gerbils show a series of partial turns until they orient their head to a target.

In general, Cheal argues that her data with diverse species and tasks illustrate the ubiquity of interactions of factors that modulate motivated behavior. These factors affect the outward expression of behavior and some common central processes may be mediating these effects. In studying the effects of sensory stimuli on courtship behavior in fish and on investigatory behavior in gerbils, Cheal found more attentional behavior when all sensory stimuli are present than when sensory inputs are isolated.

Reference

Hebb, D. O. (1972). *Textbook of psychology* (3rd ed.). Philadelphia: Saunders.

INTRODUCTION

Proximal mechanisms for the motivation of behavior are very complex. Some behaviors are thought to be voluntary in that an organism must emit the behavior. If this is so, there must be predetermining factors that motivate the emission of the behavior. However, it may be impossible to separate each of these factors in normal behavior of humans and of other animals in a natural environment. It is possible, however, to separate various influential factors in laboratory situations where many variables can be controlled. As will be illustrated, factors that influence behavior are diverse, ranging from genes to other behaviors. Some studies on the question of behavioral motivation come from research with humans, but others derive from studies with animals. One importance of such comparative studies is the possibility of controlling many factors that cannot be controlled when working with humans.

The study of factors that motivate behavior is not new. From the early days of psychological research, motivation has intrigued the scientist. Hebb (1958) wrote of classes of factors that influence behavioral development and are important motivationally. As a simplification of all inputs that may be involved, Hebb listed six noninclusive factors: I. genetic, II. prenatal chemical, III. postnatal chemical, IV. sensory inputs that are variable within a species, V. sensory inputs that vary with individuals, and VI. traumatic events such as accidents and illness. A broad interpretation of these factors could include all inputs into an organism from before fertilization of the egg, through development, and the entire life span. Thus, Hebb's factors could influence all motivational aspects of behavior.

Furthermore, some of the factors that motivate behavior are other behaviors. Behavioral antecedents of behavior were demonstrated elegantly in the ring dove (Lehrman, 1965). The courtship behavior of the male ringdove leads to physiological changes in the female ringdove that result in nest building. Thus, such antecedent behaviors can be said to be motivating behaviors.

In this chapter, some specific examples of interactions of motivational factors will be discussed. The discussion will not include prenatal variables, although the fetus has been shown to be an active and interactive organism in its specialized intrauterine environment (Smotherman & Robinson, 1990). Neither will this discussion include genetic influences, although twin studies have shown that genetics can account for part of the phenotypic variance in particular aspects of behaviors such as intelligence and religion (Plomin, 1990; Waller, Kojetin, Bouchard, Lykken, & Tellegen, 1990). Most of the present discussion will be based on experimental manipulation of invariable and variable sensory inputs and postnatal, chemical factors and will include data from research on courtship behavior, changes over the life span, habituation, and attention.

EXPRESSION OF A SPECIES-TYPICAL BEHAVIOR

Many behaviors were considered to be instinctive in the past (Birney & Teevan, 1961). These behaviors seem very consistent within a species. For example, the courtship behavior of the blue gourami, a tropical, freshwater teleost fish of the suborder Anabantoidei, *Trichogaster trichopterus*, appears ritualistic. Mating, or spawning, is usually preceded by the blowing of a bubble nest at the surface of the water by the male (Cheal, 1973). Spawning is the culmination of a succession of responses in which the male clasps the female with the urogenital pores close together. The pair roll upside down, and eggs and sperm are simultaneously emitted. The eggs are fertilized as they float up into the nest. During the spawning act, the color of the male fish darkens from a light silver through an iridescent blue to black. These behaviors are very species specific; for instance, although other anabantoid fish exhibit similar clasps, the blue gourami is the only anabantoid known in which the male rubs the ventral surface of the female with its dorsum just prior to spawning (Hall, 1966; Miller, 1964).

Although these behaviors appear to be instinctive, it was possible to demonstrate the influence of particular sensory input in laboratory experiments (Cheal & Davis, 1974). Pairs of fish were introduced into divided aquaria in which (a) the two fish had no contact with each other (an opaque wall separated the pair); (b) visual cues were possible through the glass wall that separated the pair; (c) the center wall was opaque, but water was exchanged between the two compartments of the aquarium allowing the exchange of cues for the chemical senses; or (d) both visual and chemical sensory cues were provided. Visual cues from a potential partner had the most impact on increasing courtship behaviors. Chemical cues increased the effort that the male gourami expended in maintaining a nest but had no apparent effect on females.

In another experiment, the time to spawn after introducing a male and a female into an aquarium was measured. Male gouramis spawned on the first day if the female had been paired with other male fish on preceding days. Female gouramis, however, spawned only after several days in the aquarium with a male fish. The time for a female fish to spawn could be shortened by introducing a new strange male gourami each day or by placing a male gourami in a visual (but not tactile) proximity for 3 days prior to uniting them. These results suggest that the induction of spawning readiness in females is more susceptible to social and environmental variables than it is in males. More important to this chapter, both experiments provide support for the influence of postnatal sensory stimuli on the modification of species-typical behaviors.

DEVELOPMENTAL CHANGES OVER THE LIFE SPAN

Another interesting example of the interaction of environmental and genetic contributions to motivated behavior comes from a life-span study of the Mongolian gerbil, a small desert rodent, *Meriones unguiculatus*. Gerbils were selected for these studies because of their short life span and their low genetic variability (Cheal, 1986). All gerbils in the United States are descendants of 9 gerbils sent from Japan in 1954 (Schwentker, 1963). In this project, 70 gerbils were introduced into a longitudinal study on the day of birth. Of these, 31 male and 31 female gerbils survived until weaning and tests were conducted with them monthly throughout their natural life. The median life span for these animals was approximately 3 years, and the greatest age obtained was 49 months. Figure 3.1 shows the mortality curve for the study, both for all of the gerbils and separately by sex.

Concurrently with the longitudinal study, a cross-sectional study was conducted in which 5 male and 5 female naive gerbils were each tested only once. These gerbils were tested at the same ages as the testing of the gerbils in the longitudinal study from birth through 6 months of age and at 3-month intervals to 39 months of age. After 39 months of age, the number of gerbils in the cross-sectional study varied, because of availability of gerbils of the appropriate age. The cross-sectional study was included in order to prevent many problems of interpretation in aging research (Cheal, 1986; Elias & Elias, 1976; Sprott, 1975). Longitudinal studies eliminate behavioral variability that is due to differences in sampling at different ages. Stability of intraindividual behavior over time can be assessed, and parallels between behavioral changes and physical condition can be made. However, it is not possible to tell if a particular behavioral sequence is an effect of aging or whether it is a function of repeated testing. Also, only relatively noninvasive methods may be used, and pathology as reflected by organ condition or size cannot be monitored. Therefore, maximization of information can best be attained by combining longitudinal and cross-sectional studies.

A number of behavioral and somatic measurements were recorded from both

FIGURE 3.1. Number of gerbils living as a function of days of age for all gerbils in the study and separately by gender.

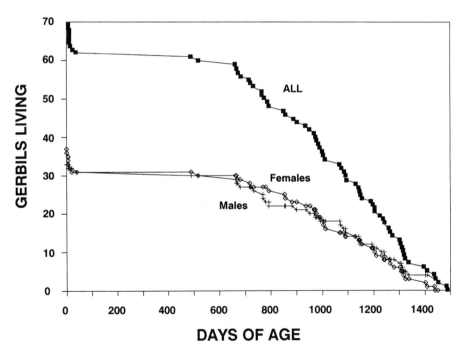

groups of gerbils, at first weekly, and then monthly after the first month. All the animals were reared in the same room, with all variables matched as closely as possible. In order to study the impact of environmental variables on the developmental growth and the expression of behavior throughout the life span, it was decided to give some of the gerbils an enrichment experience. The duration of this experience had to be limited for some practical reasons. Even in sunny Arizona, weather can drop to freezing at night in the winter and can be as high as 122° in the shade in the summer. Therefore, although gerbils are more tolerant of temperature extremes than most mammals, they could not be housed outdoors. Also, experimental time had to be realistic for repeated testing over several years by one or two experimenters with limited funding. Because the regular measures were to be repeated monthly, it was convenient to incorporate the enrichment experience into the regular testing sessions. Therefore, after the behavioral and somatic measures were recorded, half of the gerbils in the longitudinal study were exposed to an enriched environment for 1 hour a month from 1 month to 28 months of age. Control gerbils were exposed to a small indoor environment for an equal period of time.

At 1 month of age, the animals' small size and immature homeothermic mechanism necessitated a laboratory-housed enrichment environment. Starting at 2 months of age, the enriched environment was outdoors. The enrichment exposure was discontinued after 28 months of age for fear that changes in thermoregulation with age might result in premature death for those gerbils scheduled for exposure during extreme weather conditions (Cheal, 1986). Although the gerbils tolerated the conditions well, they might not have in old age.

During the hour a month from 2 to 28 months of age, the gerbils were allowed to run through an 8-foot-by-30-inches outdoor desert setting that provided multiple stimuli with natural meaning for the gerbils. These stimuli included "fresh air" and natural weather conditions in the desert southwest. During the course of the experiment, temperatures varied from 11°C to 41°C, wind velocity from 0 to 25 knots, visibility from 6 to 18 miles, humidity from 10% to 64%, and barometric pressure from 28.230 to 28.830 inches of mercury. There were running water, rocks, sand, and desert vegetation in the aviary wire enclosure (Cheal, Foley, & Kastenbaum, 1986). Although 1 hour a month is a very short exposure, the periods between environmental enrichment appeared to be short enough for accumulation of effects. Gerbils should remember these stimuli for at least 4 weeks in the same way that they remember novel objects and odors (Cheal, Klestzick, & Domesick, 1982). It was proposed that exposure to challenging enriching stimuli even for a brief period might prevent decreases in the ability to adapt to change in later life.

The early behavioral and somatic measurements that were recorded from both studies provided a more complete developmental description of this species than had been available previously (Cheal & Foley, 1985). The study also provided body weight and somatic measurements across the life span. In the male gerbils, body weight continued to increase until about 2 years of age and then began to decrease (Figure 3.2). The body weight of female gerbils reached asymptote at a younger age and exhibited no clear pattern of change at old age. There was much individual variation in old age, with some animals becoming very fat and others becoming very thin. Body length only increased through the first year of life. Body lengths through 36 months of age have been published (Cheal, 1987d). Statistical differences between enriched and control gerbils have been reported up to 18 months of age (Cheal et al., 1986; Cheal, 1987a). Statistical comparisons are difficult to make at older ages due to death of many of the gerbils. In this chapter, inferences based on individual data will be emphasized. Note that, although it required over 4 years to collect these data, there were relatively few gerbils in each condition, particularly at older ages. Therefore, in order to draw any strong conclusions, the work needs to be replicated.

Effects of Enrichment Experience

Of particular interest to this chapter was the effect of the brief enrichment experience on the gerbils in comparison to the control gerbils. The effects of this brief exposure to an outdoor environment are particularly surprising, considering not only the infrequency and short duration of the experience, but also that effects occurred well into adolescence and the comparison control group could not be con-

FIGURE 3.2. Body weight as a function of age for enriched (E) and control (C) gerbils with males (M) and females (F) presented separately.

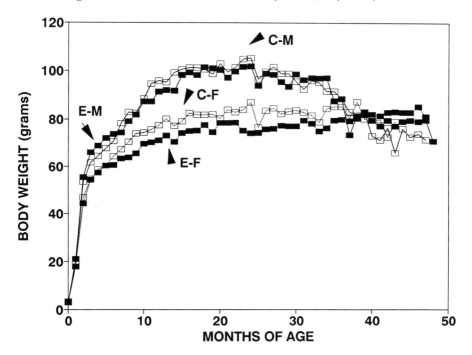

sidered impoverished. In fact, the living conditions for all of the gerbils in both studies were better than standard rodent conditions. These gerbils were maintained in same-sex groups and the home cages were 48 cm × 27 cm × 20 cm. Each cage contained aspen shavings, food (rabbit chow, millet, and cracked corn), and water bottles and had a climbing ladder made of 1/4-in hardware cloth.

In the sections that follow, several interesting effects of the enrichment experience will be described. Some of these effects were particularly surprising because they were shown in systems that are thought to be strongly dependent on genetics and/or diet. They are presented here because they offer the possibility that enrichment may affect behavior through modification of physiological/anatomical changes.

Life Span.   The effect that enrichment had on the life span cannot be determined with certainty in this study due to the small number of animals. Notwithstanding, two male enriched gerbils lived to an older age (49 months) than any animals of the other groups (Figure 3.3). However, there was a larger proportion of control male gerbils living to 40 months of age. In female gerbils, approximately the same proportion lived to 30 months of age, and then there was a larger proportion of enriched female gerbils living than control female gerbils.

FIGURE 3.3.   Proportion of gerbils living as a function of age for enriched (E) and control (C) male (M) and female (F) gerbils.

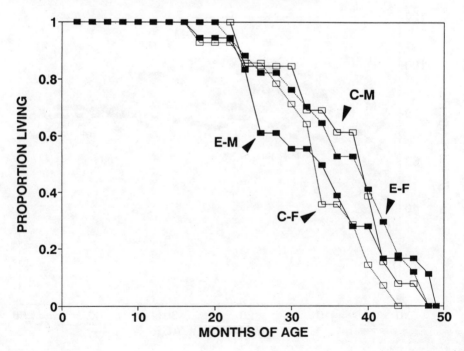

Body Weight. For male gerbils, the enriched group weighed slightly more than the control group from birth (enriched, 3.3 g; control, 3.2 g) to 6 months of age (see Figure 3.2). Then, from 7 to 17 months of age, the control male gerbils weighed 4% more than enriched male gerbils. At older ages there was considerable variability. The decrease in body weight at old ages did not differ significantly between the enriched and control male gerbils. The final body weight was 94% (4% SE) of the 39-month weight for enriched males and 86% (4% SE) of the 39-month weight for control males ($t[9] = 1.40$, NS).

For female gerbils, although enriched females weighed slightly more at birth (2.9 g in comparison to 2.8 g), the control females weighed a mean of 7.4% more from 1 month through 38 months of age. By 39 months of age, there were only three control female gerbils living. The range of weights for the enriched female gerbils was similar to the controls at this age (range: control, 65–95 g; enriched, 68–102 g). In the last few months, some female gerbils gained weight due to abdominal cysts. Thus, no inferences as to enrichment effects on body weight can be made at the late ages for female gerbils.

Smaller body weight of rodents given environmental enrichment in comparison to isolated animals has been reported frequently (Diamond, Rosenzweig, & Krech, 1965; Fiala, Snow, & Greenough, 1976; Morgan, 1973). It was suggested that the nonenriched animals were less active in a small cage and thus did not use as much energy. However, in the study described here, there was equal opportunity for activity in the home cages. The enriched gerbils had more space to explore for only 1 hour a month. It appears that this period of exploration may have influenced food intake (Fiala et al., 1976; Morgan, 1973) and/or metabolism in the home cage. Unfortunately, no home-cage observations were made, so there are no answers to this question from the study. It might be inferred, however, that the heavier body weight of control animals in enrichment studies is not a simple function of cage size. It is possible that the exposure to a more complex and varied environment changed behavior that resulted in a difference in body weight. It is even conceivable that the increased body weight of controls decreased activity in the home cage. This interaction of behavior and physiology within an animal is reminiscent of the interaction of behavior and physiology between male and female ring doves in the regulation of the reproductive cycle (Lehrman, 1965).

Seizures. Gerbils have spontaneous seizures during simple experimental manipulations (Loskota, Lomax, & Rich, 1974; Thiessen, Lindzey, & Friend, 1968). These seizures have made the gerbil an animal model of choice for research on epilepsy (Loskota et al., 1974). Seizures are not exhibited in gerbil pups but are first seen at 2 months of age (Cheal & Foley, 1985). In the life-span study, more enriched male gerbils had seizures during the testing procedures at 2 months of age than did male control gerbils (see Figure 3.4). Enriched exposure had little if any effect on the female gerbils' incidence of seizures. The same difference between enriched and control male gerbils was also found at 4 months of age, but thereafter the effect was reversed. Fewer of the enriched than of the control male

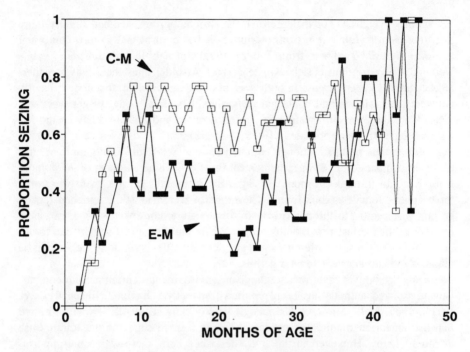

FIGURE 3.4. Proportion of enriched (E) and control (C) male (M) gerbils that had a seizure during the measurement session at each month of age.

gerbils had seizures from 5 months to 31 months of age relative to the male controls. The early pattern of more enriched gerbils seizing than controls could be due to a genetic influence on seizures inasmuch as gerbils can be bred for seizure-prone or seizure-resistant strains (Paul, Fried, Watanabe, Forsythe, & Scheibel, 1981). Because of the reversal of the relative proportion of gerbils seizing, however, the same genetics cannot explain the effect of fewer enriched than control gerbils having seizures at older ages.

The possible influence of multiple factors responsible for seizure incidence needs to be considered.

1. Daily gentle handling by the experimenter is known to reduce seizures in gerbils (Cheal, 1986). Handling cannot explain the enriched/control differences shown in the longitudinal study, however, because all of the gerbils in that study were handled similarly. The control gerbils were placed in a small holding cage in the laboratory for the same period as the outdoor enrichment experience.

2. Home caging also cannot explain the difference in frequency of seizures (Kaplan, 1983) because both groups lived in the same size cages with approximately the same number of gerbils per cage. Furthermore, the brief outdoor enrichment had a much smaller effect on seizure incidence than did housing gerbils in a complex environment (Kaplan, 1983). Another consideration is that the seizures in the life-span study were observed during experimental manipulations but were not specifically induced.

3. In spite of the fact that handling has been shown to reduce seizures, the particular handling used to take these measurements may have increased seizures. The fact that the incidence of seizures was relatively high in this study suggests that the gerbils may have been stressed (Cheal & Foley, 1985) inasmuch as stress has been associated with seizures (Kaplan, 1975). During the measurement procedures, the gerbils were held firmly in the experimenter's hand. Subjective observations suggested that this handling was somewhat stressful to the gerbils. However, such induced stress could not have been responsible for the differences between the enriched and control groups of the longitudinal study, because both groups were handled similarly.

4. Diet has been shown to affect the incidence of seizures (Harriman, 1980), but that probably cannot explain the group differences, because all of the gerbils in the colony were on the same diet for several generations. The only exception was the more varied diet available to the enriched gerbils for the 1 hour a month that they were in the large outdoor desert environment from 2 to 28 months of age. It seems unlikely that this variety offered for only an hour a month could make the difference. Furthermore, most of the choices were balanced laboratory feeds (prepared for rats, rabbits, dogs, etc.).

5. It seems most consistent with the data that the repeated experience in the outdoor environment resulted in fewer seizures for the enriched male gerbils in comparison with either the control males or the females. The cause of this difference is hard to determine. One might think that the opportunity to explore the large, natural environment made them less fearful in other situations. However, the enriched and control gerbils did not show differences in time to emerge from a small box when tested at 24 months of age. Such a test has been thought to represent fear responses for other rodents, but it is possible that the enclosure in a small box is so punishing to gerbils that escape is the preferred action. Gerbils do freeze on occasion, but flight is also a natural reaction to fear situations.

After 31 months of age, the incidence of seizures in the longitudinal study was highly variable (see Figure 3.4). The variability is partially explained because with decreasing numbers, proportions become less useful. However, the larger proportion of gerbils seizing during a test in old age may be attributed to at least two factors. First, enriched male gerbils that had a high incidence of seizures lived longer. The mean age of death was 41.0 months for those that seized on more than half of the sessions compared to a mean age of death of 28.6 months for those that seized on half or less than half of the sessions ($t[17] = 2.92$, $p < .01$). Second, four of the five male enriched gerbils with high seizure incidence that lived longer than 32 months had an increased incidence of seizure after 32 months (mean incidence $= .81$) as compared to the incidence of seizures prior to 32 months of age (mean $= .55$). Of control male gerbils, the seven that had high incidence of seizures did not show this increase. Most of them continued with approximately the same incidence of seizure and one gerbil decreased incidence. Note that all of these inferences are made on examination of individual data for each gerbil.

Several factors may have been responsible for the increased incidence of seizures in old male enriched gerbils. First, it is possible that the effects of the enrichment experience on this characteristic had worn off at this age inasmuch as the enrichment was not continued after 28 months of age. There also may have been some reason that those that survived had different genetic propensity to seize than those that died earlier. Other factors may also have contributed to the fact that the surviving enriched male gerbils all had a seizure during 5 of the 7 tests from 42 to 48 months of age. Although dietetic factors (Harriman, 1980) should not have influenced seizures in the younger gerbils because they were all on the same diet, it is possible that there were differences in nutritional intake due to pathology in the old animals.

In summary, the incidence of seizures expressed in this study most likely represents the interaction of several factors: (a) a genetic factor that may have determined the expression of seizures in young gerbils; (b) an environmentally induced reduction of seizures in gerbils from 5 to 31 months of age due to the enrichment experience; (c) a possible dietetic factor, particularly in old gerbils; and (d) additional unknown factors. Thus, multiple predisposing factors may be involved in the incidence of seizures.

Ventral Gland Marking.   Another intriguing effect of the enrichment experience relates to an interesting species-typical behavior of the gerbil. Gerbils have a sebaceous gland on the abdomen that they use to mark items on the substrate and to leave a sebum that has been shown to be important for communication (Roper & Polioudakis, 1977; Thiessen & Rice, 1976). Both males and females mark, but males do so much more than females. Both marking behavior and the ventral gland are dependent on gonadal hormones (Commins & Yahr, 1984; Swanson & Norman, 1978; Thiessen, 1973). There was no correlation between the size of the ventral gland and marking behavior in young or mature gerbils in the lifespan study (Cheal, 1987a; Cheal et al., 1986) however, and excision of the ventral gland does not eliminate marking (Baran & Glickman, 1970; Blum & Thiessen, 1970). Thus, a direct association between the gland and behavior in adults is hard to demonstrate.

In this study, however, there were effects of the enrichment experience on both the size of the ventral gland and on the frequency of marking behavior, but not necessarily at the same ages. Both male and female enriched gerbils had more rapid growth of the ventral gland in adolescence than did controls (Figure 3.5). At 3 months of age, the ventral glands of enriched female gerbils were 56.8% larger than glands of control females. At 4 months of age, the ventral glands of enriched males were 13% larger than control males.

As seen in Figure 3.5, the ventral glands of enriched female gerbils were again larger than controls from 15 to 35 months of age. This difference was not due to greater body size, because the enriched female gerbils weighed less than the control gerbils when they were 6 to 38 months of age (see Figure 3.2). The large increase in ventral gland size at 45 and 46 months of age for enriched females was mainly due to two females with ovarian cysts that caused an enlargement of the abdominal area. The rising curve for the control female gerbils after 40 months of age represents the one gerbil that lived past 41 months of age and

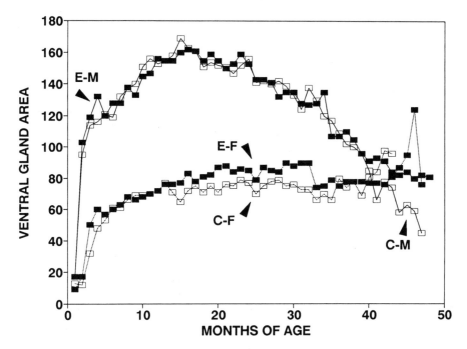

FIGURE 3.5.   Area of the ventral gland (cm^2) as a function of age for enriched (E) and control (C) gerbils with males (M) and females (F) presented separately. Area was calculated using the formula for an ellipse.

had an enlarged gland, although body weight decreased and no ovarian cyst was obvious.

In males, on the other hand, it was only after 3 years of age that enriched male gerbils again had ventral glands larger than those of controls. At this point it is necessary to look at the individual gerbils to determine the cause of the difference. Of the seven control male gerbils that lived to be 39 months of age, five developed large lesions of the ventral gland, so that it was possible to see little or no ventral gland by the last measurement day. The ventral glands of the other two gerbils also were considerably smaller on the last measurement than they had been in earlier months.

The ventral glands of enriched male gerbils had a gradual drop in size from the peak at 15 months, and only one developed a visible ventral gland lesion. The larger ventral glands in enriched male gerbils at old ages in comparison to old control gerbils may have been partially due to greater body weight. Enriched male gerbils were somewhat heavier than controls from 39 months of age, although both groups showed similar drops in body weight in their last few months.

Facilitative effects of enrichment on marking were much greater and more persistent than their effects on the ventral gland, particularly in male gerbils. These gerbils marked more frequently than control male gerbils in most of the tests from 2 to 48 months of age (Figure 3.6). Female enriched gerbils had more markings than controls for most of the tests from 6 to 26 months of age.

The ventral gland lesions that developed in old age did not prevent marking (see Figure 3.6). In fact, the peak in marking for control male gerbils at 37 months of age was partially due to two of the eight that were still living that had large lesions but marked much more than they had at younger ages. Marking may have served as a response to itching or irritation in these animals.

It is tempting to speculate on some possible interactions that may have determined the incidence of marking behavior. One speculation is that increased marking in enriched male gerbils resulted in more frequent rubbing of sebum from the ventral gland. It is possible that this increased rubbing helped to prevent development of ventral gland lesions if the lesions in control gerbils were due to impacting of the gland with sebum. Because the lesions became quite severe, they could have resulted in earlier death in these animals.

Another speculation is that facilitation of growth of the ventral gland in adolescence led to increased marking behavior in adulthood. Although there was no correlation between ventral gland size and amount of marking at any one age, there was a significant correlation in males between ventral gland size at 4 months

FIGURE 3.6. Number of markings with the ventral gland during a 3-minute test as a function of age for enriched (E) and control (C) gerbils with males (M) and females (F) presented separately.

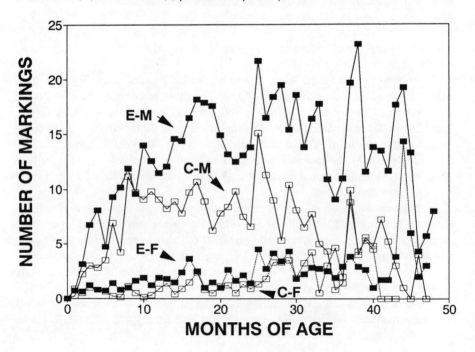

of age and the amount of marking at 18 months of age ($r[28] = .48, p < .01$). This correlation suggests that outdoor enrichment experience may result in increased levels of gonadal hormones during development and, in turn, adult marking may be partially dependent on the quantity of gonadal hormones present during puberty. The effects of enrichment experience appear to be persistent, because the large enrichment effect in male gerbils continued many months after the outdoor experience was discontinued.

I suggested earlier (Cheal, 1986, 1987a) that the facilitation of ventral gland growth could signify earlier sexual maturation that would then result in greater reproductive capacity. This suggestion is supported because marking behavior has been associated with territorial marking that may be important in control of social systems, and with aggregation necessary for mating and reproduction (Thiessen & Rice, 1976). In fact, male gerbils mark most if they are housed with fertile, pregnant, or lactating female gerbils (Pendergrass, Thiessen, & Friend, 1989). These authors suggest that marking may be a visible index of the male gerbils' potential reproductive performance. Thus, it appears that even a small amount of experience in a rich environment may lead to greater reproductive success. How these mechanisms work is of great interest.

Latency to Find Food.   There is another effect of enrichment that may shed some light on mechanisms (Cheal, 1987c). At 24 months of age, the enriched and control gerbils in the longitudinal study were tested for the latency to find food in a small novel enclosure (Figure 3.7). Each hungry gerbil was placed separately in the arena with its nose pointing to the position indicated by the arrow at the bottom of the figure. Latency was recorded from the time the gerbil was released until it found the food at cup "b." On the first day, the enriched gerbils found the food in less time than either the longitudinal control group or a naive control group of 8-month-old gerbils from the same colony (Figure 3.8A). The test was repeated on the second and third day to look for differential learning effects between the two groups. There were none. All three groups found the food more rapidly on subsequent days. The enriched group did not improve on the third day, but that may have been due to a basement effect.

The difference due to enrichment experience was a rather surprising effect. After all, the gerbils had had only 1 hour of enrichment a month for 24 months at this point. To support the results, two other groups of gerbils were tested in the same apparatus. These gerbils had been reared in large (35 cm × 45 cm × 66 cm) or small (18 cm × 20 cm × 25 cm) cages (see later discussion) and were tested for food searching at 8 months of age. It is obvious from Figure 3.8B that the same results were obtained.

Several factors that might have explained the results were eliminated: (a) These data cannot be explained as due to increases in general locomotor activity, because, in the longitudinal study, there were no differences between enriched gerbils or controls in the number of line crossings, in the amount of rearing on the hind legs, in latencies to jump down from a small platform, or in latencies to climb

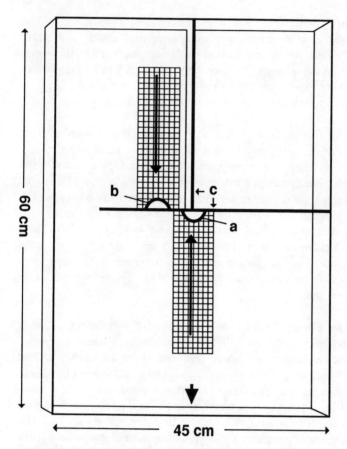

FIGURE 3.7. Apparatus for a food search test: "a," an empty aluminum food cup, and "b," a similar cup with food, are at the top of hardware cloth ladders, 14.2 cm from floor; "c" represents aluminum walls attached to aluminum floor; arrowhead marks start location. (Reprinted with permission from Cheal, M. L. [1987]. Environmental enrichment facilitates foraging behavior. *Physiology & Behavior, 39,* 281–283. Copyright 1987, Pergamon Press.)

down from a pole at the same age. There were also no differences between the groups in the latency to emerge from a small box or in attentional tasks at this age. (b) The differences were not due to experience with ladders, because the control longitudinal gerbils also had daily exposure to ladders. (c) Prior exposure to novel food cannot be responsible, because gerbils housed in both large and small cages had been exposed only to rabbit chow previously. (d) Fear of new experiences is not a likely explanation, because there were no differences between the groups in the latency to emerge from a small box; and the naive control group (with no prior handling or research experience) did not differ from the other control groups.

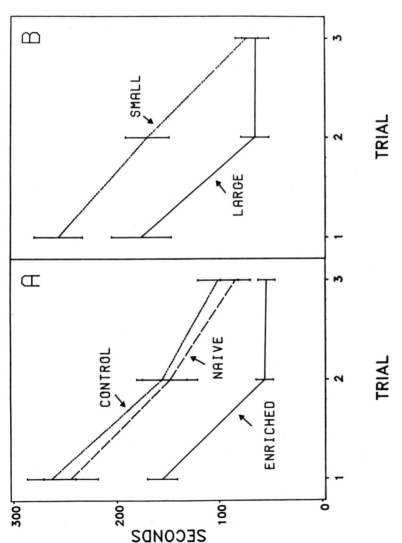

FIGURE 3.8. Latency (sec) for gerbils to place nose in cup with food on three trials on three consecutive days. A. Enriched and control gerbils from life-span study and a group of naive gerbils. B. Gerbils reared in small or large cages from growth study. (Reprinted with permission from Cheal, M. L. [1987]. Environmental enrichment facilitates foraging behavior. *Physiology & Behavior, 39*, pp. 281–283. Copyright 1987, Pergamon Press.)

(e) It is also unlikely that a greater motivation to investigate odors is responsible, because the longitudinal enriched group did not investigate conspecific odors in tests of odor-elicited investigation (described later) any more than the controls.

One possible explanation for these results is that experience of moving about a larger environment may facilitate the animal's ability to observe its environment. Perhaps the gerbil pays more attention to clues that are useful. These data suggest an interaction of genetic disposition (Gray, 1981), prior experiences, and foraging opportunities (Collier & Rovee-Collier, 1981) on the expression of efficient foraging. The data provide evidence that experience in larger ranges could lead to more successful encounters with a feeding source.

Limb Growth. Another interesting and unexpected finding was an acceleration of hind-limb growth during adolescence in the enriched male gerbils in comparison to the controls. From 4 to 7 months of age, the hind limb of enriched male gerbils was longer than that of the control male gerbils (Cheal et al., 1986). After this time, the control gerbils caught up and there were no differences between the groups in adulthood.

Surprising as these findings are, similar results were found in another study in my laboratory (conducted in collaboration with Dr. M. Marzke & S. Alongi; see Alongi, 1987). In this study, two groups of closely related gerbils were reared in separate environments. To produce the newborn pups for the study, a matched breeding design was used. Each two breeding pairs were chosen by mating two male littermates to two female littermates from another litter. One of each pair was housed in a large wire cage, 35 cm × 45 cm × 66 cm, where an enriched group was sired. Cages for these groups had tunnels for hiding, a river rock and pine shavings substrate, and a climbing apparatus made of hardware cloth. The other one of each breeding pair was housed in a standard rat cage, 18 cm × 20 cm × 25 cm, with pine shavings on the substrate, where a control group was sired. These environments differed in area and provision for exercise, exploration, and social contacts. All other conditions were the same for the two groups. Body size and shape measurements were made every other day from the day of birth until 60 days of age and again at 8 months of age.

In this study, there were two periods when body segment lengths of enriched gerbils were greater than those of controls. The first period was from approximately 14 days of age to 28 days of age, and the second period was from approximately 48 days of age to 58 days of age. During the earlier period, body weight, body length, foot length, forearm length, head length, and hind-limb length were larger for enriched than for control gerbils. During the later period, body length, forearm length, head length, and leg length were again larger in the enriched than in the control gerbils. Toward adulthood, the two groups converged in body and limb segment measurements, and the control gerbils exceeded the enriched group in body weight and head size as adults, consistent with findings from the longitudinal study and from other rodents (Diamond et al., 1965; Fiala et al., 1976; Morgan, 1973).

Because differences in body size may account for differences in shape, body size was analyzed for ages in which the two groups differed in limb segments relative to body length. During the later period of growth differences, 48–58 days of age, there were also differences in the ratio of forearm length and head length to body length. The differences in growth at particular periods during development were alleviated toward the end of these periods, in some cases by control group acceleration and in others by deceleration of the enriched group. It was interesting to note that the early age of rapid growth in the enriched gerbils began at approximately the same age that locomotor behavior accelerated dramatically (12 to 14 days of age).

It is possible that the large and topographically more varied environment of the enriched gerbils in both studies may have elicited a greater amount of physical exercise that could have resulted in greater body and limb lengths. This concept is consistent with data on growth acceleration in hamsters associated with an increase in physical exercise (Borer & Kuhns, 1977). Borer and Kuhns also found differential acceleration of body segments that resulted in a change in body shape.

Mechanisms of Enrichment Effects.   Mechanisms of the facilitatory effects of environmental enrichment on either behavioral or brain changes have not been determined. It is likely that effects due to environmental experience, similar to expression of other behaviors such as attention (Cheal et al., 1982), courtship (Cheal & Davis, 1974), and sexual behavior (Beach, 1948; Lehrman, 1965) are the result of interactions of compound stimuli from all of the senses. The stimuli impinging on the gerbils in this treatment are heterogeneous, and the present method does not separate effects of such diverse stimuli as bright light, motor exercise, and novel objects and odors. The mediation of these enrichment effects may be due to neural stimulation resulting in altered endocrine events, such as growth hormone. Such events could continue in the home cage after enrichment experience, thus, greatly extending the effects of 1 hour of experience.

Whatever the mechanism, our results are consistent with other behavioral changes found after brief environmental manipulations. Clark and Galef (1977) found changes in reactivity of gerbils to a "face" after they spent one 24-hour period in an environment with a natural tunnel system. These gerbils, as did those reared in a tunnel environment, ran more quickly to a shelter and were slower to emerge. Such research suggests that the opportunity to partake of a natural environment even for brief periods improves the animal's ability to extract and process information that leads to adaptive behavior. The modified behavior can be, for example, food finding or escaping from predators, dependent on the environmental experience and on the testing situation.

Lifetime Continuity of Behavior

It has been said that "the fundamental question for developmental research is the nature of the . . . interplay between change and preservation of sameness over the lifespan" (Haan, & Day, 1974, p. 11). After a 40-year study of the human life span, Haan and Day classified traits as follows: (a) those that have "unaltered sameness"—that is, traits do not change much through the lifetime, and each person stays relatively the same in comparison to others; (b) those that have "ordered transposition"—the group of people change on the measurements, but each individual keeps the same relative position; (c) those that show "experiential change"—the group of people change and the relative positions of individuals also change; (d) those that are "unclassifiable"—they neither maintain sameness nor is there systematic change.

In order to control conditions and thus see their effect on behavioral stability and change within a moderate length of time, the longitudinal and cross-sectional studies of the gerbil described earlier were used. In the cross-sectional study, each gerbil was tested only once at ages up to 39 months of age. These animals allowed the possibility of observing histopathology and organ growth or change, as well as the allometric and behavioral noninvasive measures that were used in the longitudinal study. These multiple measures of behavior, body and organ growth, and incidence of seizures were used in order to specify (a) developmental sequences of behavioral and biological systems, (b) developmental sequences of behavior that are dependent on experience with the testing situation, (c) "ordered transposition"—stability of behavior, and (d) sex differences in ontogeny of physical growth and behavior.

Developmental Sequences of Behavioral and Biological Systems. Developmental sequences showed that there was very little influence of prior handling on the behaviors expressed in gerbils prior to 2 months of age. Also, seizures did not occur at these early ages. Thus, growth and development during the first month of age might be considered to reflect developmental processes that resulted from internal maturation and experience in the home cage. Perhaps the brains of rodents must mature to some degree before seizures occur, or the animals are able to use the information gained from experience a week or more earlier (Bronstein & Hirsch, 1976; Cheal & Foley, 1985).

Developmental Sequences of Behavior That Are Dependent on Experience with the Testing Situation. After 2 months of age, gerbils without prior testing displayed more locomotor activity (Figure 3.9), more rearing on the hindlegs (Figure 3.10), and less marking with the ventral gland (Figure 3.11) and were slower to descend a pole covered with hardware cloth than gerbils given repeated tests. These effects all may be related to higher levels of stress or fear in gerbils that had no laboratory experience previously. These effects were shown throughout most of the life span.

The same results were not obtained for all of the behaviors. For marking with the ventral gland, which is a sexually dichotomous behavior, there was a large effect of testing experience for males, less for females (see Figure 3.11). A similar difference was seen in the size of the ventral glands. The longitudinal male gerbils had larger ventral glands than did the cross-sectional male gerbils (Figure 3.12). There were no consistent differences in the size of the female ventral glands. For some behaviors, such as jumping down from a platform and climbing down a wire mesh pole, there was a large effect of experience during the early months, but there was no consistent effect in adults. In a test of the ability to cling to a wire, there was no effect of experience and little stability of the rank order of the gerbils (see later discussion).

"Ordered Transposition": Stability of Behavior. In order to address the question of whether individual variations of behavior were stable over time, two separate analyses were computed: (a) Kendall's coefficient of concordance, *(w, tau)*, in which gerbils were rank ordered at each age from 6 to 18 months and then tested for consistency in the rank across ages. This coefficient was calculated by summing each gerbil's rank at each age in which the behavior was greater than zero. (b) Split half correlation, in which each gerbil's scores for even months from 6 to 18 months were correlated with the same gerbil's scores for odd months. These measures of stability showed that gerbils that were most active at a very

FIGURE 3.9. Number of times male (M) and female (F) gerbils from the longitudinal (L) and cross-sectional (CR) studies crossed lines of grid in a 1-minute test as a function of age.

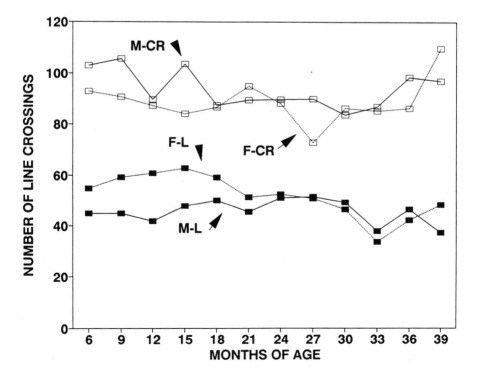

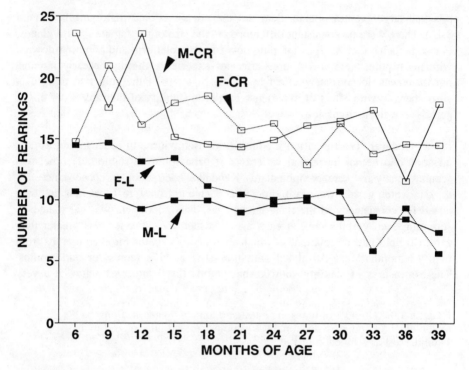

FIGURE 3.10. Number of rearings on the hind legs in the same
1-minute trial for male (M) and female (F) gerbils from the longitudinal
(L) and cross-sectional (CR) studies as a function of age.

young age were also most active at later ages (Table 3.1, p. 137). Thus, there was
considerable stability of some of the behaviors (i.e., marking, jump down, rearing,
and line crossing) in addition to the susceptibility to change induced by prior experience in the laboratory testing situation.

A profile score was calculated by transforming each behavioral score to a
standard score and then looking at the ratio of locomotor activity and rearing to
jumpdown and marking. This score was very stable in adult gerbils in both concordance and in split half correlations. Also, when a complete correlation matrix
for each age from 6 to 18 months was calculated, 68 of 78 possible comparisons
were significant for male gerbils (Table 3.2, p. 138). For female gerbils, there was
no significant correlation between profile scores at 6 months and other ages, but
at 7 to 18 months of age, 61 of 67 possible comparisons were significant.

Thus, the relative quantity of the same simple behavior is highly stable for
an individual gerbil even when that quantity changes as a result of life experiences.
In other words, those animals that are most active continue to be the most active
animals in that group even though the group as a whole may be less active due to
repeated testing.

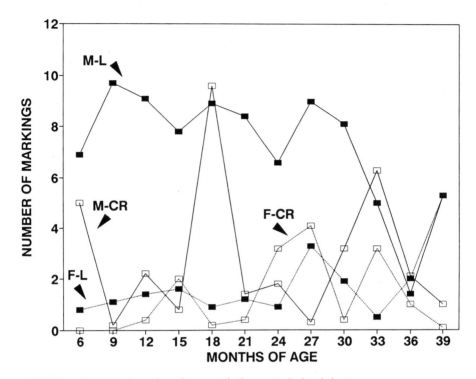

FIGURE 3.11. Number of markings with the ventral gland during a
3-minute test as a function of age for male (M) and female (F) gerbils
from the longitudinal (L) and cross-sectional (CR) studies.

In terms of change, there was ordered change in locomotor activity during
early development, but little change in adulthood. For rearing on the hind legs,
there was stability with change during early development, but there was also stability with change in adulthood: fewer rearings with age, particularly in female
gerbils. Along with change occurring with increasing age and differences due to
experience, there was very strong intraindividual stability of the behavior.

Sex Differences in Ontogeny of Growth and Behavior.   Behavioral and
biological differences between male and female gerbils in this study were consistent with those reported earlier (Cheal, 1986, 1987a; Thiessen & Rice, 1976).
Many of the measurements reflect the larger adult size of the male in comparison
to the female.

Conclusions from the Life-Span Study

The most interesting outcome of this study was the effect of brief periods of enrichment experience. Some of the effects of enrichment were modest and short
lived, but there were other effects that lasted throughout the life span. Effects were

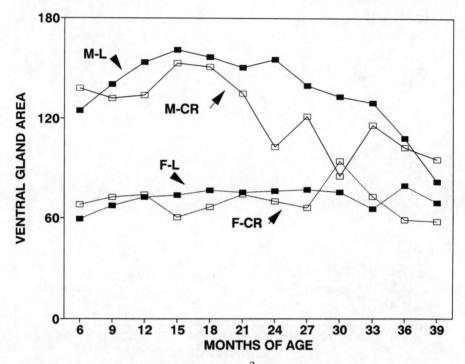

FIGURE 3.12.   Area of the ventral gland (cm^2) as a function of age for male (M) and female (F) gerbils from the longitudinal (L) and cross-sectional (CR) studies. Area was calculated using the formula for an ellipse.

found on growth rates in development, on particular behaviors, and on the latency to find food. Further inferences may be possible when the histopathology study is completed by Roderick Bronson and his colleagues.

This life-span study produced considerable data and the results suggest hypotheses of changes over the life span and speculations about their mechanisms. However, conclusions about the meaning of these changes are not readily apparent. The number of animals was relatively small, and, with deaths, sample size of older subjects becomes even smaller. A larger study was planned, but unfortunately the grant application reviewers thought the enriched animals should not be taken outside for fear that bacteria would result in early deaths in the enriched group. The data show that this did not occur. The study was completed without additional funding, which meant that much of the planned data collection could not be completed. It did show, however, that the outdoor environment did not appear to have aversive effects on the gerbils (the two longest living gerbils were in the enriched group), and that this exposure to natural stimuli can have long-lasting effects.

TABLE 3.1.   Stability of Individual Gerbil Behavior

			r	
Behavior	n	Tau	Males (n = 31)	Females (n = 31)
Marking	58	.65**	.94**	.88**
Jump Down	58	.53**	.93**	.78**
Rearing	60	.49**	.91**	.88**
Line Crossings	60	.43**	.81**	.89**
Climb Down	60	.28**	.19	.69**
Clinging	60	.17**	.17	.41*
Profile Score	60	.52**	.91**	.90**

Note. Tau: Kendall's coefficient of concordance; *r:* split half correlation coefficient. Profile score is a ratio of activity and rearing to marking and jumpdown; described in text.
* *p* < .05, ** *p* < .0001.
Reprinted with permission from Cheal, M.L. (1987). Adult development: Plasticity of stable behavior. *Experimental Aging Research, 13.* Copyright 1986, Beech Hill Enterprises, Inc.

ATTENTION

Motivational factors will now be examined from a different perspective. It has been suggested that attentional facilitation of sensory information is the primary method by which motivational states guide behavior (Derryberry, 1989). However, attention works in various ways. It is a ubiquitous part of life and is essential to survival. In fact, it is part of most behaviors. Without attention to relevant stimuli in the environment, we would not find food, sexual partners, jobs, or other necessities of life. There is evidence for attention early in evolution (i.e., frogs; Traub & Elepfandt, 1990) as well as in many advanced mammals, including humans. In spite of its importance, attention has received relatively little research effort in comparison to other behaviors, such as learning and memory, feeding regulation, or other life essential behavioral processes.

Early psychologists, such as William James (1890), found the study of attention of much interest. Later, with the advent of more experimental rigor, attention was considered to be too "mental" to study objectively (LaBerge, 1990b). Another problem for research on attention may have been the difficulty in defining this process. Although attention is a word that we all know and use frequently, there seems to be much variability in definitions and in experimental paradigms. This may reflect the study of different processes in different research paradigms. In other words, I suggest that there is a composite of behaviors that are known collectively as *attention.* In the next paragraphs, I will attempt to provide a framework for different types of attention and how they have been studied.

First of all, *attention* is not the same thing as *arousal.* Although some re-

TABLE 3.2. Correlation Matrix for Profile Scores at Each Month of Age

Ages	6	7	8	9	10	11	12	13	14	15	16	17	18
6	*	.42	.58	.69	.50	.58	.42	.69	.44	.50	.54	.55	.45
7	.34	*	.36	.26	.50	.46	.34	.56	.50	.44	.46	.65	.23
8	-.01	.49	*	.64	.68	.56	.67	.64	.52	.32	.40	.46	.32
9	.06	.59	.74	*	.56	.46	.44	.51	.41	.45	.55	.43	.60
10	.08	.58	.66	.79	*	.52	.52	.70	.58	.48	.50	.53	.33
11	.06	.41	.64	.70	.66	*	.59	.70	.69	.56	.51	.56	.27
12	.12	.19	.61	.47	.48	.51	*	.72	.48	.32	.45	.47	.33
13	.04	.43	.78	.62	.65	.73	.60	*	.70	.58	.61	.73	.38
14	-.17	.41	.57	.68	.57	.56	.40	.55	*	.68	.70	.76	.25
15	-.05	.07	.41	.27	.26	.40	.51	.54	.51	*	.80	.83	.51
16	.03	.44	.61	.67	.67	.58	.36	.54	.67	.46	*	.81	.55
17	.16	.33	.52	.51	.51	.29	.46	.59	.47	.57	.49	*	.55
18	-.11	.23	.75	.56	.51	.56	.43	.64	.62	.56	.60	.52	*

Females →   Males →

Note. Data for male gerbils in the upper right and data for female gerbils in the lower left. Correlations > .39, $p < .05$; > .45, $p < .01$; > .56, $p < .001$; > .64, $p < .0001$. Age in months.

Reprinted with permission from Cheal, M.L. (1987). Adult development: Plasticity of stable behavior. *Experimental Aging Research, 13.* Copyright 1986, Beech Hill Enterprises, Inc.

searchers seem to include arousal as a part of attention, I prefer to think of them as separate concepts. It is possible to show that arousal is distinct from attention, although they are related, as illustrated by the direct effects of changes in the level of arousal on tasks of *vigilance*: the ability to wait for an infrequent event to occur (Parasuraman, 1984). Although a certain level of arousal is necessary for attention to occur, arousal by itself is not attention. Arousal pertains to the state of the organism alone, whereas attention assumes a stimulus in relation to the organism. One must attend to something—either a stimulus in the environment, such as a sound, an odor, or an object; or an internal stimulus, such as a rumbling stomach or a sore thumb. These impinging stimuli compete for our attention, and we learn through experience to ignore those stimuli that are not relevant. As a simple example, in a familiar environment, such as your own desk, an unfamiliar bright red stapler will be readily apparent upon entrance to the room. After one has become familiar with it, the stapler is no longer noticed unless there is a need for it. We say that we have adapted to it. This does not imply receptor adaptation, but only behavioral adaptation.

In addition, attention can be directed to either the onset or the offset of a stimulus. For instance, when a symphony begins, it grasps our attention. But in a familiar environment, perhaps your own home, you will not notice the motor of the refrigerator, or an air conditioner unit, but when it stops operating, you will notice the lack of the noise.

The concept that attention may not be a unitary process has been suggested previously. William James described two aspects of the attentive process: accommodation, or adjustment of the sensory organs, and anticipatory preparation for the object of attention, including "an efflux of blood" for the latter (described in LaBerge, 1990a). Since then, attention has been classified variously by different researchers who work in very different paradigms. For instance, from his work with primate and human populations, Mirsky and his associates (Mirsky, 1987) have developed a battery of tests for diagnosis of attentional problems in psychiatric patients. These tests were based on the results of factor analysis of ten measures derived from eight frequently-used tests of attention. Mirsky suggested that the four resulting factors might represent focus/execute, sustain, encode, and shift of attention. Data recorded from normal adults, normal eight-year-old children, and people with disordered attention due to mental illness and brain lesions produced consistent results (Mirsky, Anthony, Duncan, Ahearn, & Kellam, 1991). From another laboratory, it was suggested that those working with psychiatric patients should chose tasks that measure particular types of attention, such as alertness, vigilance, sustained, shift, or maintenance of selective attention (Spring, 1980). The classifications from these two laboratories are very similar to those described in an animal model of attention in which the division was into selective attention, maintenance of attention, and shift of attention (Cheal, 1987b). This model will be discussed further later.

Another classification of attention includes a selective process, a laborious process, an alerting and sustaining process, and vigilance/maintenance (Umilta, 1988). These processes are defined differently than are similar-sounding processes described earlier. In Umilta's definition, the *selective process* occurs when information is perceived consciously, whereas information may also be analyzed unconsciously or may be filtered out. The *laborious process* occurs with processing resources that are voluntarily allocated to a particular task or activity, thus neglecting other tasks or activities. The *alerting process* heightens vigilance for a short time or allows it to be maintained for a longer period. Umilta further divides the selective process into the specific attention to a modality, a location, an attribute such as shape or color, and a particular class or category.

Other separation of types of attention have been suggested. For example, LaBerge (1973), working on human visual attention, suggested that attention not only must be switched to a target, but it must also be switched away from a previous target. Later, it was proposed that there are three mental operations involved in orienting attention to a visual stimulus without eye movements (Posner, Walker, Friedrich, & Rafal, 1984). It is necessary to first disengage attention from the current focus of attention, then move attention to a new stimulus, and finally engage attention on that stimulus. Disengagement has been divided further into (a) the time to perceive the cue and location and (b) the latency to initiate attentional relocation (Eriksen & Murphy, 1987).

Thus, it is apparent that currently there is no consensus on how attention should be defined. On the other hand, there is consistency in that researchers recognize that attention as a unitary concept is inadequate. It is not possible here to attempt to present a complete balanced analysis of all studies of attention, but a selection will be given to make particular points. Recognizing the complexities in the study of attention, we will examine how attention affects motivated behaviors. To illustrate some of the range of research on attention, examples will be given from my laboratory. These will include some work that examines the effects of attention on visual perception in humans and data from the gerbil model of attention. By using human and animal data for examples, it will be possible to illustrate how methods can be modified to fit the behavioral repertoire of the organism. Although visual discrimination in humans and exploratory behavior of gerbils appear to be very different, there are commonalities in the effects of spatial location and of the type of stimuli used.

Reflexive Versus Voluntary Attention in Human Visual Attention

Attention cannot be measured directly in the way that something like marking behavior is measured. Therefore, it must be inferred from its effect on something that can be measured. In humans, one task that relies on a manipulation of attention is location-cuing, in which the target location is precued in order to facilitate visual discrimination. In these tasks, the observer is asked to fixate on a point in the center of a computer screen (Figure 3.13A) and respond on the computer keyboard

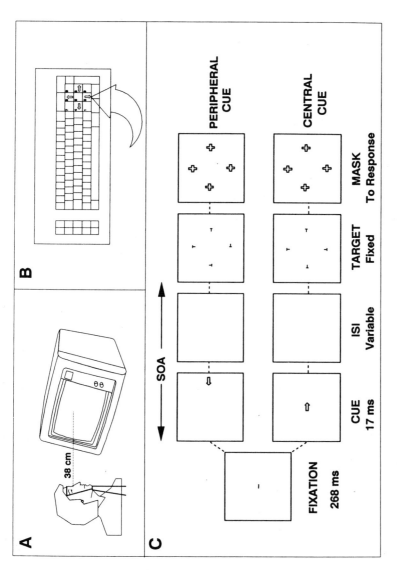

FIGURE 3.13. Method for conducting the visual attention studies. A. An observer watches a computer monitor. B. Responses are made on the arrow keys of the computer keyboard. C. For testing the effects of cue location, trials are blocked by cue type. Following fixation, for the peripheral cue, one cue is presented at one of four possible locations; for the central cue, the cue arrow is presented at fixation and points toward one of the four possible locations. Stimuli are presented in all four locations after a variable interval. The target is the stimulus in the location that was cued. After a brief period, stimuli are masked.

141

arrow keys (Figure 3.13B). Following a fixation bar of light, the cue comes on the computer screen (Figure 3.13C). The cue can occur in the peripheral field near where the target will be presented (a peripheral cue) or it can occur at fixation (a central cue). When the cue is peripheral, any bright onset of light will elicit attention reflexively to that location. In contrast, central cues are symbolic and must be interpreted. For instance, such a cue may be an arrow pointing toward the target location or letters or numbers that designate preestablished locations. The cue screen is followed by a variable interval blank screen prior to the target screen. The target is presented briefly (target duration is varied according to task difficulty in order to obtain 65% to 70% overall correct) and then masked to minimize further visual processing of the target. Observers are instructed to maintain their eyes at the fixation bar but to move attention to the target location as soon as the cue appears. The blank interval provides a variable period in which to move attention prior to target onset. Thus, the time course of the effects of attention allows a measure of the amount of improvement in discrimination as a function of the amount of time allowed for attention to concentrate at the target location.

In several studies on the perceptual effects of attention on a peripheral location, important differences were reported between the presentation of a peripheral precue and the presentation of a central precue. Although either cue facilitated performance, there appeared to be a difference in the time course of attentional facilitation of performance dependent on whether attention was voluntarily directed to a stimulus by a central cue or whether it was reflexively directed to a stimulus by a peripheral cue. Dependent on the type of task, reaction time was shorter, or accuracy was better, at short intervals between cue onset and target onset following a peripheral cue than following a central cue (Cheal & Lyon, 1989; Cheal, Lyon, & Hubbard, 1991; Jonides, 1981; Müller & Rabbitt, 1989).

In our laboratory, we made a direct test of how the time course for discrimination of visual stimuli is affected by attention if it is elicited or if it is voluntarily directed (Cheal & Lyon, 1991). Our investigation addressed several questions: (a) Does facilitation of performance require the same amount of time to move attention to the target location when the cue is peripheral as when it is central? (b) Is there equal facilitation by the two types of cues if sufficient time is allowed? And (c) what evidence is there for multiple mechanisms of attention in this task?

We wanted to determine the complete time course of the effects of attention for the two conditions. Therefore, a wide range of cue-target intervals was used from 0 to 500 msec. Because with the longest intervals eye movements could occur, eye movement was monitored with an EYE-TRAC infrared monitor. All trials with eye movements were discarded from the analysis and were repeated at the end of each block of trials. The number of eye movements was low and was similar for all cue-target intervals for both conditions (mean number of eye movements: peripheral cue, 4.3%; central cue, 4.6%).

In examining Figure 3.14, note that the only difference within a cue type for the various cue-target intervals was the time period between the onset of the cue and the onset of the target. These intervals were randomized within blocks of trials and all other aspects of the trials were identical. Thus, any differences as a function of the cue-target interval for one cue type occurred prior to onset of the target. Our interpretation of these data is that allowing time for attention to concentrate on the target location prior to target presentation improved four-alternative forced-choice discrimination of T-like characters in comparison to simultaneous cue and target presentation. As the interval between the precue and the target lengthened, there was a rapid rise in accuracy with a peripheral precue that reached asymptote at an interval around 100 msec. For a central precue, on the other hand, there was a gradual increase in accuracy with cue-target interval so that asymptote was delayed to intervals of approximately 300 msec. At long intervals (300 to 500 msec), there was as much or more facilitation of discrimination by central cues as by peripheral cues.

These data suggest that stimuli appearing suddenly in the peripheral visual field provide an advantage in reflexively eliciting attention so that discriminations can be made very rapidly in such locations. These mechanisms would be very advantageous when the discriminatory stimuli represented danger or a food source. Stimuli that elicit attention include sudden luminance changes and sudden move-

FIGURE 3.14. Proportion correct for trials cued peripherally (solid symbol) and centrally (open symbol) as a function of the interval between the onset of the cue and the onset of the target. The lower two curves show the proportion of trials with eye movements that were discarded from the analysis. Redrawn from Cheal and Lyon (1991).

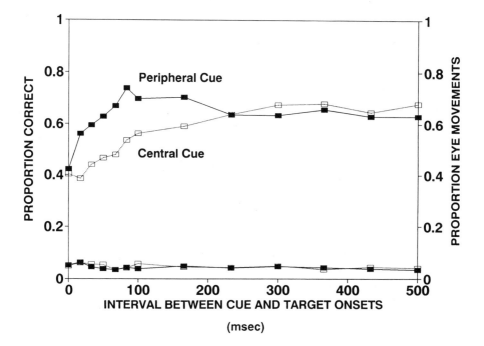

ment. Either of these may be associated with life-threatening events. Although a peripheral cue results in more rapid orientation of attention to a target than does a central cue, it appears that there is equal facilitation of discrimination by central and peripheral cues provided there is a long enough interval between the cue and the target.

The question of whether multiple processes of attention can be inferred is more difficult to answer. In the peripheral cue condition, there was a transient peak at 83–100 msec, followed by a longer sustained curve. It has been suggested that these represent separate mechanisms (Nakayama & Mackaben, 1989). In the central cue condition, the facilitation of discrimination was delayed in comparison to the peripheral cue condition, but the asymptote was sustained through the longest interval used. One reason for the delay is that time may be necessary to decode the symbolic central cue and determine the target location.

These experiments established clear differences in the time course between peripheral and central cuing conditions in discrimination of T-like characters. The differences that were found suggest that the two cue types involve at least some different mechanisms, such as a decoding process needed by a central cue. There may also be differences in the quantity of facilitation available when attention must be sustained at the target location for long cue-target intervals.

Different Use of Attention Dependent on the Target

In addition to the different effects of attention depending on the location of the precue, attention effects in this paradigm can also differ dependent on the type of discrimination to be made. For instance, in an experiment in which a comparison was made between discrimination of (a) a right- and a left-slanted line and (b) a left- and a right-facing T, the discrimination of lines (Figure 3.15) was much more accurate at 50 msec than was the discrimination of Ts (Figure 3.16) at the same target duration. In this experiment, we obtained approximately the same overall proportion correct by using three different target durations for each target type.

There were two other important findings from this experiment. First, there were differences in the time course of the effects of attention on discrimination dependent on the type of stimulus that was precued (Cheal et al., 1991). For the T-discrimination (differences in line arrangement), there was a big improvement with time to shift attention prior to target onset (see Figure 3.16). In contrast, with the line-discrimination (differences in line orientation), there was only a small facilitation by attention (see Figure 3.15). Since this experiment, we have tested other targets and find that the shape of the curve depends on the nature of the target. Our interpretation of these findings is that some discriminations have little need for attention, while for others, when attention is focused on the target, discrimination is facilitated.

Another question that could be considered is whether the differences between the curves in Figures 3.15 and 3.16 are due to a difference in difficulty of

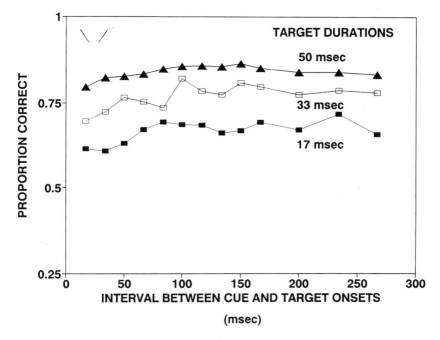

FIGURE 3.15. Proportion correct as a function of the interval between the onset of the cue and the onset of the target for discrimination of left or right slanted lines presented for different durations. Redrawn from Cheal et al. (1991).

the task. Does a more difficult task require more focus of attention? The answer to that is no. First, when we increased the target duration for Ts, thus making the task easier, there was little difference in the amount of improvement with cue-target interval (see Figure 3.16). Likewise, decreasing the target duration for the lines did not increase the need for attention greatly (see Figure 3.15).

We now have additional data that address this question (Cheal & Lyon, 1992). When the discrimination is between two colors (red/green, red/yellow, or green/yellow) there is a small amount of improvement with cue-target interval. This is true even though there are significant differences in the difficulty of the task. With our equipment green/yellow discrimination is much harder than are the other two discriminations. Therefore, the green/yellow targets were presented for longer durations. In spite of the differences in difficulty, the shape of the curves for the three conditions were approximately the same.

In another experiment, we tested the difference in discrimination of targets with different numbers of line endings (Cheal & Lyon, 1992). Here again there was a large difference in difficulty of the task. Targets that had the same number of line endings were much easier to discriminate than those with a different num-

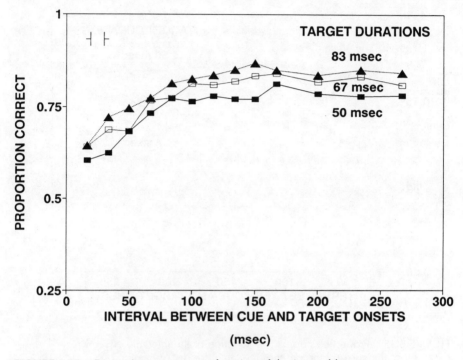

FIGURE 3.16. Proportion correct as a function of the interval between the onset of the cue and the onset of the target for discrimination of left or right Ts presented for different durations. Redrawn from Cheal et al. (1991).

ber of line endings. There were similar amounts of improvement with increase in the duration of the cue-target intervals for the two types of targets, however.

In one other experiment, we tested the effect of task difficulty directly (Cheal & Lyon, 1992). The targets were circles with a gap in either the top, the bottom, the right, or the left side. Observers had to indicate the location of the gap. To vary task difficulty, the gap was made various sizes; 1/2, 3/8, 1/4, or 1/8 of the circle was open. When the same target duration was used for all four gap sizes, there were differences in asymptote, but there was more improvement with cue-target interval for the larger gaps than for the smaller gaps (see Figure 3.17). This is the opposite of what would be expected if improvement is related to task difficulty. When different target durations were used so that overall proportions correct were about the same, there were no differences in the amount of improvement with cue-target interval (Figure 3.18). Therefore, in addition to differences in ability to discriminate dependent on how attention is directed (voluntarily or reflexively), rapidity of discrimination is also affected by the type of stimulus and is not dependent solely on task difficulty.

Behavior can also be affected by a recent prior event. In another precuing

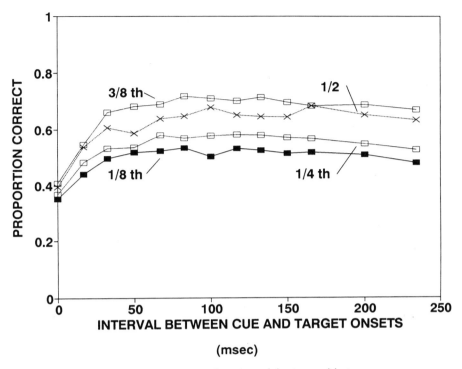

FIGURE 3.17. Proportion correct as a function of the interval between the onset of the cue and the onset of the target for discrimination of a gap on top, bottom, left, or right of a circle. Gap encompassed one-eighth, one-fourth, three-eighths, or one-half of the circle.

study (Derryberry, 1989), there were incentives for positive trials (points were earned) and costs for negative trials (points were lost). There was no evidence of general attentional biases for positive or negative incentives, but there was an interaction between the incentive value of the current trial and the outcome of the previous trial. If the prior trial was unsuccessful, there were greater costs for positive than negative incentives, but when the prior trial was successful, costs were larger for negative than for positive cues. Thus, the immediately prior event affected the behavior on the subsequent event.

These studies of human visual attention suggest several factors that interact to determine responses to perceptual stimuli. (a) The location of a precue that signals the location of a target affects the time course of attentional facilitation of discrimination; (b) prior knowledge, whether due to the outcome of a prior trial or to knowledge of the expected target provides "top-down" facilitation; and (c) the type of information available from the target provides "bottom-up" facilitation. These three processes interact to determine subsequent discrimination. Obviously, there are other factors that could also help to determine the behavioral outcome.

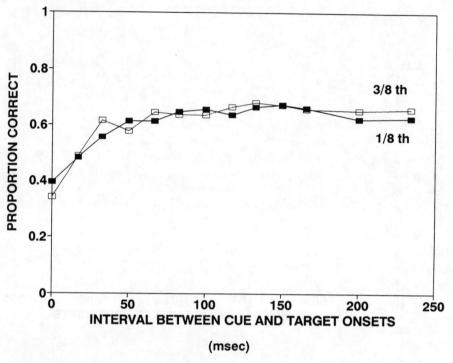

FIGURE 3.18. Proportion correct as a function of the interval between the onset of the cue and the onset of the target for discrimination of a gap on top, bottom, left, or right of a circle. Targets with gaps encompassing one-eighth or three-eighths of the circle were presented for different durations in order to equate the overall proportion correct.

The Gerbil Model of Attention

In this section, the gerbil model of attention will be described, and evidence will be presented to infer the separation of different forms of attention.

Stimuli Elicit Attention.   As stated earlier, in humans, a cue near the target location elicits attention reflexively. Gerbils, of course, cannot be told to attend to something, but when a novel stimulus is placed in a familiar environment, it will elicit attention from a gerbil. Attention in a gerbil is defined by the frequency of going to the stimulus and the duration of time spent licking, sniffing, and biting it. Thus, the behavior is voluntarily emitted, but it is also elicited by the stimulus.

Based on these phenomena, I developed a task that used the gerbils' natural behavior in order to study attention and habituation. This work was begun in order to develop an animal model for the dopamine theory of schizophrenia that was prevalent in the 1970s. Many similarities had been described between human amphetamine psychosis and schizophrenia (Bell, 1965; Ellinwood, 1967). Therefore, it was hoped that giving moderate doses of amphetamine would elicit changes in the behaviors measured that would be analogous to attentional changes in schizophrenia. It was found, however, that at low and moderate doses of amphetamine, there was no change in habituation or of the derived measures that would infer changes in attention in the animal model (Cheal, 1978a). The only significant effect of amphetamine was to decrease all behavior at high doses in what appeared to be a sedative effect. Other associates lost interest in the model at that point, but I found the reliability of the behavior to be intriguing.

The task is called *stimulus-elicited investigation*, primarily to indicate that it is a very specific, carefully controlled test. If the adaptation and handling procedures are not followed, then the reliable results that I have described (Cheal, 1978b; Cheal et al., 1982) do not occur. I will briefly describe the task and give a brief summary of treatments that allow inferences to habituation and attention. This summary is based on extensive data. In 1982, I reported that, with students in my laboratory, we had tested over 3,000 gerbils on this task (Cheal, 1982b).

Gerbils are usually given only one experimental treatment to avoid the interactions of repeated drug treatment. The only exceptions are made in order to specifically test for interactions or to test for chronic effects of a drug. In preparation for the task, naive gerbils are first handled daily for 5 days. The experimenter picks up one gerbil at a time, holds it for 1 minute, and places it in a holding cage. After all the gerbils from one living group are in the holding cage, each gerbil is again picked up, handled for 1 minute, and returned to the home cage. After these 5 days, on the next 3 days, the gerbils are placed in the empty apparatus (Figure 3.19) and allowed to run freely in and out of the arena for several minutes. Only after 8 days of this preliminary handling and adaptation are tests conducted.

The test consists of three 1-minute trials in an empty arena and six 1-minute trials with a stimulus, either an object held firmly in place with a magnet on the outside of the arena wall or an odor hidden under one of two or five holes in the floor. The trials with an empty arena provide further adaptation. The first five trials with a stimulus give measures of habituation, and on the sixth trial a change is made (usually moving an object to a new location) that allows dishabituation in the normal adult gerbil. For each trial, each gerbil is placed separately in the outer compartment of the rectangular glass apparatus. The door into the arena is opened, the gerbil allowed to run in, and the door again is closed. On the first stimulus trial, the normal gerbil reliably runs to a novel object and licks, sniffs, and bites the object. After 1 minute, the door is opened and the gerbil can run out. After 30–60 seconds, the door is again opened for a subsequent trial. On subsequent trials, the gerbil habituates and responds less on each trial. On the last trial, when the object is moved to a new location, the gerbil again increases responding (dishabituates). The six trials can be run in sequence within one session, or sometimes they are spaced to compare short-term with long-term habituation.

The dependent measures consist of the number of times (frequency) and the

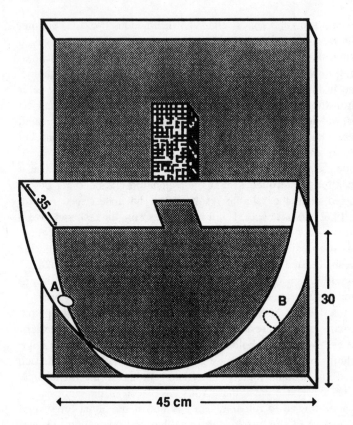

FIGURE 3.19. Apparatus for testing the object version of stimulus-elicited investigation. Gerbils start in the outer area (at the top of figure) and run through the tunnel for each trial. An object is held in place at A with a magnet placed outside the wall. The stimulus is moved to B for the last trial. Redrawn from Cheal (1978b).

total duration of time that the gerbil spends investigating the stimulus. Inferences as to attention are made based on the changes in these measures over trials and in the ratio of frequency to duration of investigation. Using these measures, attention has been separated into components of selective attention, maintenance of attention, and shift of attention (Cheal, 1981, 1983, 1987b). Evidence that these types of attention represent different processes comes from tests in which the gerbils were treated pharmacologically or surgically and from developmental studies.

Amount of Attention Depends on the Target.   In gerbils as in humans, attention is dependent on the type of stimulus (Cheal, 1978b). First of all, the total amount of investigation depends on the amount of affect of the stimulus. For instance, an ordinary magic marker elicits about 10 sec of investigation in the first 1-minute trial. A cup, on the other hand, elicits about 20 sec of investigation in the same type of trial. When an odor of soiled bedding from a group of male gerbils that are strangers to the subject is used, gerbils respond for about 10 seconds in the first 1-minute trial.

There is a reduction in the amount of investigation of either an object or an odor on subsequent trials (habituation). However, reaction to these types of stimuli differs on the sixth trial, when the stimulus is moved across the arena. For a cup, a marker, or other object, responding is increased (dishabituated) by having the stimulus in a new location (if it is moved 22.5°, 45°, or 90°, but not if it is moved 11.25°). Interestingly enough, there is no dishabituation if a habituated object is moved to a location that was habituated previously with a different object, although a novel object introduced on the sixth trial also increases investigation (Cheal, 1978b). These results indicate that there is generalization from one habituated object in a particular location to another object habituated in a different location.

For an odor, there is no increase in investigation after moving a stimulus. The gerbils can localize the odor, as shown by the fact that they spend more time investigating a hole with an odor in comparison to a hole without an odor, but apparently the location of the odor is not a salient feature of the stimulus. It is possible to demonstrate dishabituation by changing the odor from that of strange gerbils to that of the gerbil's own home bedding (Cheal et al., 1982). The context of the task seems to be specific for the odor, however. If gerbils are given four 1-minute exposures to the odor in a holding cage instead of four 1-minute trials, and then are given a test with the odor in the arena, they respond just as much as gerbils that had no preexposure. Thus, habituation is not due to receptor adaptation. The difference between objects and odors in the saliency of location may be because location is reflected by the area of the retina that is stimulated visually, whereas odor localization is only reflected by the concentration of the stimulus on the receptors. In this task, the distance of the odor from the entryway is the same for each location and, thus, odor concentration would not vary at different locations.

Evidence for Different Processes of Attention. In stimulus-elicited investigation, behavioral measurements are used to infer separate processes of selective attention, maintenance of attention, and shift of attention. *Selective attention* has been defined as the differential processing of simultaneous sources of information (Johnston & Dark, 1986). In the tests described here, the selective response is to a target that is novel. When it is no longer novel, responses are made to other, competing stimuli. These responses are not measured but can be observed (such as scratching in a corner). Maintenance and shift of attention are inferred from the relationship between the frequency of approaching a stimulus and the duration of time spent investigating it.

Disruption of different forms of attention was tested by preinjection of different drugs that alter neurotransmission. The drugs used alone and in combination are listed in Table 3.3, along with a simplistic description of their neural actions. More complete descriptions are included in the references to the drug actions on attentional behaviors that are cited later. The effects of olfactory bulbectomy, castration, and development were investigated in additional experiments.

Selective attention is defined by the normal pattern of attention to a stimulus. Thus, there is a large amount of investigation on the first trial, followed by normal habituation, and dishabituation to an appropriate change in stimulus. Habituation is shown when the second trial follows the first by 1 minute, but it is also evident after long intervals of 1 to 28 days (Cheal et al., 1982). The long-term memory in this task is useful in studying neural mediation of the behavior because it is possible to give a drug treatment and either test for habituation immediately or wait and test for habituation after the acute effects of the drug are past.

Disruptions of the normal pattern of habituation followed by dishabituation can be considered to be disruptions of selective attention. Such disruptions are not found following injections of amphetamine (Cheal, 1978a) or of piribedil (Cheal, 1983); but they are seen in gerbils given low doses of apomorphine (Cheal, 1979, 1980) or 100 mg/kg L-DOPA (Cheal, 1983) even though all four drugs are dopamine (DA) agonists (see Table 3.3). The effects of apomorphine can be blocked by the neuroleptics pimozide or haloperidol, but not by the atypical neuroleptic clozapine (Cheal, 1980, 1984), which suggests a role for DA in the mediation of selective attention. In addition, an interaction with norepinephrine (NE) is suggested because a concurrent injection of clonidine prevented the disruption by apomorphine (Cheal, 1982a). This interaction with NE mechanisms may explain why amphetamine and piribedil do not interfere with selective attention. Both of these drugs act via NE systems as well as DA, whereas apomorphine and L-DOPA have more specific action on the DA system. The interaction of DA and NE in the mediation of these motivated behaviors is particularly interesting in light of reports of other DA–NE interactions in survival-related behavior (Antelman & Caggiula, 1977).

Habituation to novel objects is much delayed in gerbils with complete removal of the olfactory bulbs (Cheal & Domesick, 1979). This delay is not due solely to a lack of olfactory input because gerbils that are peripherally anosmized show only slight delay in habituation. Bulbectomized gerbils and those with peripheral anosmia habituate similarly in a behavior of poking the nose into holes and in general activity. This difference in habituation dependent on the task gives support to the concepts that olfactory bulbs have central functions in addition to their role as sensory structures (Herrick, 1933; Wenzel, 1974) and that separate mechanisms subserve habituation in different behavioral tasks. It is possible that impairment of motivation caused by the surgery may contribute to changes in attention that contribute to delay in habituation to particular stimuli (Wenzel & Rausch, 1977).

Additionally, selective responses to novelty are not present in very young gerbils (Cheal, 1987b). By 21 days of age, responses are selective to a novel object and to a change in location of the object. At 28 days of age, gerbils are also selective to odors of conspecifics and durations of investigation are similar to

TABLE 3.3. Evidence for Different Processes of Attention

Treatment	Neural Action	Effects on		
		Selective Attention	Maintenance of Attention	Shift of Attention
Amphetamine	DA & NE agonist	—	—	—
Apomorphine	DA agonist	→	—	→
L-DOPA	DA agonist	→	—	→
Piribedil	DA & NE agonist	—	—	—
Pimozide	DA blocker	—	—	—
Haloperidol	DA blocker	—	→	—
Clozapine	DA blocker	—	—	—
Apomorphine + Pimozide		—	—	—
Apomorphine + Haloperidol		→	—	—
Apomorphine + Clozapine		—	—	—
Apomorphine + Clonidine		→	—	—
Clonidine	NE agonist	—	—	—
Desmethylimipramine	NE agonist	—	→	—
Scopolamine	ACh blocker	—	—	—
Methylscopolamine	Peripheral ACh blocker	—	—	—
Physostigmine	Indirect ACh agonist	→	—	—
Olfactory bulbectomy		—	—	→
Castration		→	—	→
Castration + L-DOPA		→	—	⇉
Less than 3 weeks old		→	—	—

— = no effect

Arrow indicates disruption

those of adults. The development of selective attention at about 3 weeks of age has adaptive significance in that this is the age when gerbils begin to wean themselves from the mother and show considerable movement away from the nest. It is not surprising that certain forms of attention need to develop.

Development of attention in humans has also been suggested (Skoczenski & Aslin, 1990). In recent work, an early attentional system was shown to develop between 3 and 6 months of age, whereas another system did not appear until later (Rothbart, Posner, & Boylan, 1990). It is possible that some of the developmental stages of attention in infants are analogous to behavior in other animals. For example, Rothbart et al. report that 3-month-old babies make a number of head and eye movements in orienting toward a target. Similarly, gerbils make a series of partial turns until they orient their head to a target (Ingle, Cheal, & Dizio, 1979). In discussing the antecedents of attention in infants, Rothbart et al. (1990) state that "the problem of attentional development is neither purely biological nor purely social" (p 3).

Maintenance of attention can be considered to be the relationship between the duration of responding and the number of approaches to the stimulus. Scopolamine (Cheal, 1981) and clozapine (Cheal, 1984) reduce the duration of each visit to the stimulus, even though the gerbils approach the stimulus frequently. Gerbils given scopolamine can choose appropriate stimuli but are unable to maintain attention long enough to do so when the selection requires more than a minimal amount of time and effort. No effect on maintenance of attention is shown when ACh is blocked peripherally with methylscopolamine or when it is increased with physostigmine (Cheal, 1981). None of the other treatments (see Table 3.3) affect maintenance of attention, nor do responses of young gerbils resemble those of scopolamine-treated gerbils.

Shift of attention is also inferred from the relationship between the number of visits and the duration of investigation. Gerbils given lower doses of L-DOPA or piribedil (Cheal, 1983) perseverate in their responses as if they cannot shift attention normally. This effect is not seen in gerbils treated with amphetamine or apomorphine. A similar effect is seen in castrated gerbils, and the effects of L-DOPA and castration are additive (Cheal, Johnson, Ellingboe, & Skupny, 1984). Thus, shift of attention may be mediated by an interaction of hormonal systems with catecholinergic mechanisms.

It is important to note the selective action of the drugs tested. Many of the drugs when used alone have little specific effect on the behaviors (such as amphetamine, pimozide, haloperidol, clonidine, desmethylimipramine, physostigmine), whereas other drugs (apomorphine, L-DOPA, piribedil, clozapine, scopolamine) affect only particular aspects of the behavior and not others at the appropriate low to moderate doses. If high doses are used, they are not as informative because all drugs have sedative and/or toxic effects at high doses and thus disrupt all the behavior.

The data summarized in Table 3.3 lend support to the concept that there are different forms of attention that can be distinguished by the neural circuits involved in the specific mediation of a particular type of attention. These data combined with inferences from human visual attention suggest some of the complexities in the study of attention.

Neural Networks of Attention. The research presented in the previous section should not be taken to mean that we now have a firm understanding of attention. As stated earlier, there have been various attempts to define different components or types of attention and several researchers have attempted to relate these components with particular neural structures. A complete analysis of the proposed neural networks is beyond the scope of this chapter, but two neural models of attention will be compared in order to illustrate the similarities and differences that presently exist in the literature. First of all, it should be emphasized that no one believes that any of the behaviors listed are solely dependent on a single neural structure, but rather that the structures listed in Table 3.4 are parts of networks that mediate behavior.

Posner and Petersen (1990), using a location-cuing paradigm, proposed that attention is mediated through a network that defines three attentional functions: (a) orienting to sensory events, (b) detecting signals for focal (conscious) processing, and (c) maintaining a vigilant state. A particular set of neural structures was suggested for each of these functions. The anterior system (responsible for detection of signals) is connected to the posterior system (responsible for orienting) by pathways between the posterior parietal lobe and areas of the lateral and medial frontal

TABLE 3.4. Neural Mechanisms of Attention

	Behavior[b]	
Neural Structure[a]	Posner & Petersen (1990)	Mirsky et al. (1991)
Prefrontal cortex		Shift
Midfrontal cortex	Detecting signals for focal processing	Shift
Anterior cingulate gyrus	Selective target detection	Shift
Superior temporal cortex		Focus
Corpus striatum		Focus/Execute
Inferior parietal cortex		Focus/Execute
Posterior parietal cortex	Orienting: Disengagement	
Midline thalamic nuclei		Sustain
Riticular thalamic nucleus		Sustain
Lateral pulvinar nucleus	Orienting: Engagement	
Hippocampus		Encode
Tectum	Orienting: Shift Orienting: Inhibition of return	Sustain
Mesopontine areas of reticular formation	Alertness or vigilance	Sustain

[a]Some of the neural structures implicated in attention

[b]Behaviors reported to be associated with particular neural structures

cortex, and the anterior cingulate which also projects to the dorsolateral prefrontal cortex. This model is based on what Posner (1985) has called a "hierarchical distributed attentional network." His concept is consistent with much current thinking of brain organization. That is, behaviors do not reside in one neural structure, but are mediated by pathways that include multiple structures (Cheal, 1981).

Posner and Petersen's model is based on a large amount of data obtained from people and primates by a variety of experimental techniques, such as lesions, positron emission tomography, and infant development (see Posner & Petersen, 1990, for details). Much progress has been made on the study of attention, but the inadequacy of our present state of knowledge is revealed when one tries to integrate the findings from Posner's laboratory with those from another laboratory, such as Mirsky's.

Mirsky and his colleagues (Mirsky et al., 1991) have also amassed a large quantity of data with the use of a neuropsychological approach. They have used several behavioral measures, segregated by factor analysis to arrive at four attentional processes: focus/execute, shift, sustain, and encode. Different human populations, such as those with absence, affective disease, anorexia, bulimia, epilepsy, head injuries, and schizophrenia, as well as normal adults and children have been assessed with this battery of tests. The data obtained are consistent with the separation of these four processes and their association with particular brain areas. Although there is overlap of behavioral descriptions and anatomical mechanisms between Posner's and Mirsky's models, there is no overall congruence (see Table 3.4). The reasons for the differences may be diverse (and nonexclusive):

1. Different behavioral tests are used by these researchers. For instance, even the simple concept of shift of attention may actually infer different behaviors. For Mirsky, shift is suggested by the ability to shift from one rule to another while sorting cards. For Posner, shift is associated with the change in the spatial locus of focal attention and is considered to be part of the orienting system. Thus, it is not surprising that these behaviors, although both are designated as shift, are mediated by different pathways.

2. As these complex behaviors are most likely mediated by networks in the brain, and there are many interconnected pathways, the neural areas identified in one laboratory may not include all of the structures active in a particular network.

3. It is possible that complete identification of the attentional network will never be defined, because of the great complexity of the brain (Uttal, 1990). This does not mean that such an attempt is not a useful endeavor. In fact, much useful information has already been learned, both for knowledge of basic concepts and for inference toward therapeutic applications.

I have based these comments on a comparison of work from only two laboratories. At this stage of the work, a more complete analysis might only add more to the inconsistencies and thereby mask the many congruencies. As further knowledge is amassed, it may be possible that there will be a convergence of thinking on how the brain mediates attention. It will certainly be necessary for researchers to address these issues before their work is complete. For instance, is the ability to sustain attention (wait for a target to appear) the same as the ability to maintain attention on a target?

DISCUSSION

Data from a number of very disparate research paradigms are presented in this chapter (some of the paradigms are listed in Table 3.5). These brief descriptions of different types of behavior demonstrated in organisms as distinct as fish and humans are given in order to show the ubiquity of interactions of factors that modulate behavior. The overall connecting theme is that each behavioral paradigm is dependent on an interaction of factors for the expression of motivated behaviors. For illustration, examples of the effects of various sensory stimuli on behaviors that might be considered to be "instinctual," or species specific, in fish, gerbils, and humans are described. In some cases, these stimuli have transitory effects, such as increasing the amount of courtship behavior in a male gourami during the period of the stimulus, and in other cases, there are long-lasting effects, such as the effects of short periods of outdoor stimulation on the ventral marking of a male gerbil. In each case, it is obvious that a number of different variables can affect the behavior.

These variables, or factors, affect the outward expression of behavior and, in addition, inferences can be made to central processes (see Tables 3.3 and 3.4). Several of the behavioral changes suggest the same change in a central process, which supports the suggestion that there are analogous concepts involved in the different paradigms. For instance, the mesopontine areas of the reticular formation have been implicated in vigilance in visual attention (Posner & Petersen, 1990) and in the ability to sustain attention (Mirsky et al., 1991). Other examples are the effects of sensory stimuli on courtship behavior in fish and on investigatory behavior in gerbils. In both cases, there is more attentional behavior when all sensory stimuli are present than when sensory inputs are isolated (such as only vision or only olfaction). Because of these wide-ranging interactions, Hebb's factors are as important today as when they were first published.

Much has been written on the nature–nuture question, and one would think that the matter could be laid to rest. Unfortunately, methods currently being used tend to emphasize precise contributions of genetic or environmental influences. For instance, in studies of twins reared apart, genetic contributions to intelligence (at least what is measured by IQ tests) and other behavioral measures are inferred (Bouchard, Lykken, McGue, Segal, & Tellegen, 1990). The problem is that researchers want to assign specific proportions to different contributions. Bouchard et al. state that approximately 70% of the variability in IQ is due to genetics. They arrive at this figure, however, by simply looking at the correlation between scores of twins reared apart. But all of the genetics are determined at conception. A great deal happens to the organism between conception and birth as well as afterwards. The twins in their study were together for as long as 4 years with the mean greater

TABLE 3.5. Experimental Paradigms and Inferences for Motivation

Research Paradigm	Independent Variable	Results	Inferences
Courtship behavior	Changes in sensory input	Visual cues increase courtship behavior	Elicits more attention
		Olfactory cues increase nesting	Increases motivation
		Presence of mate promotes spawning	Increases motivation
Lifespan Study	Enrichment	Rapid hindlimb growth	Greater reproductive success
		Increased marking	Improves evolutionary advantage
		Find food more quickly	Improves evolutionary advantage
		Stability of behavior	Stability with change
Short-term growth study	Repeated testing	Decreased activity	Reduces stress or fear
	Enrichment	Periods of rapid limb growth	Greater reproductive success
		Find food more quickly	Improves evolutionary advantage
Tests of attention in humans	Use of different types of cues	Change in accuracy/cue-target interval curve with type of cue	Attention elicited by stimulus has advantage over voluntarily directed attention
	Use of different types of targets	Change in accuracy/cue-target interval curve with type of target	Different need for attention
Tests of attention in gerbils	Use of different stimuli	Greater investigation of those of more interest	Elicits different amounts of attention
	Amphetamine	No specific behavioral changes	Attention is intact
	Apomorphine L-DOPA	Loss of typical behavioral pattern	Impaired selective attention
		No odor preference	
		No long-term habituation	
	Piribedil	Increased duration of investigation, with no increase in frequency	Impaired shift of attention
	Scopolamine Clozapine	Increased frequency of investigation with no change in duration	Impaired maintenance of attention
		Loss of typical pattern	
		No odor preference	
		No long-term habituation	
	Development		Selective attention must develop

than 5 months. Surely the nutrients, traumas, and other events that occurred during this 9 to 53 months (conception to 4 years of age) made a contribution. There is considerable research that demonstrates particular vulnerability to change in immature organisms (i.e., Beach & Jaynes, 1954; Clark & Galef, 1977; Greenough, Madden, & Fleischmann, 1972; Hebb, 1947; Takai & Wilkie, 1985). It has been reported that only 40 minutes of enrichment early in life had facilitative effects in rats (Rosenzweig, 1984). In fact, even Bouchard et al. (1990) state that "the proximal cause of most psychological variance probably involves learning through experience" (p. 227). They also note that "heritability of cognitive ability increases with age" (p. 224). If this is so, then their "heritability" measure is not solely a measure of the genetic contribution. The genetics do not change with age, only the measurements. It may be impossible, therefore, to determine the exact contribution of genetics and environment to behavior, and stating a specific proportion as due to heritability is misleading.

In the research paradigms described in this chapter, it was possible to demonstrate interacting factors that are responsible for behavior. It is quite likely that most behaviors, if studied carefully, could be shown to be mediated by multiple factors. In complex behaviors, it is not always possible to study such factors, but considering the ubiquity of interactions in disparate species and in disparate paradigms, it is not unreasonable to suggest that real world behaviors are also dependent on multiple factors. Thus, it is time to stop asking the nature/nurture question, but rather to determine the optimal conditions for optimal behavior for the activity under consideration.

REFERENCES

Alongi, C. A. (1987). *The effects of caging and environmental enrichment on body size and shape in the Mongolian gerbil, Meriones unguiculatus.* Unpublished masters thesis, Arizona State University.
Antelman, S. M., & Caggiula, A. R. (1977). Norepinephrine-dopamine interactions and behavior. *Science, 195,* 646–653.
Baran, D., & Glickman, S. (1970). "Territorial marking" in the Mongolian gerbil: A study of sensory control and function. *Journal of Comparative and Physiological Psychology, 71,* 237–245.
Beach, F. A. (1948). *Hormones and behavior.* New York: Paul B. Hoeber.
Beach, F. A., & Jaynes, J. (1954). Effects of early experience upon the behavior of animals. *Psychological Bulletin, 51,* 239–263.
Bell, D. S. (1965). Comparison of amphetamine psychosis and schizophrenia. *British Journal of Psychiatry, 111,* 701–707.
Birney, R. C., & Teevan, R. C. (1961). *Instinct.* Princeton, NJ: Van Nostrand.
Blum, S. L., & Thiessen, D. D. (1970). Effect of ventral gland excision on scent marking in the male Mongolian gerbil. *Journal of Comparative and Physiological Psychology, 73,* 461–464.
Borer, K. T., & Kuhns, L. R. (1977). Radiographic evidence for acceleration of skeletal growth in adult hamsters by exercise. *Growth, 41,* 1–13.
Bouchard, T. J., Lykken, D. T., McGue, M., Segal, N. L., & Tellegen, A. (1990). Sources of human psychological differences: The Minnesota study of twins reared apart. *Science, 250,* 223–228.
Bronstein, P. M., & Hirsch, S. M. (1976). Ontogeny of defensive reactions in Norway rats. *Journal of Comparative and Physiological Psychology, 90,* 620–629.
Cheal, M. L. (1973). Reproduction in the blue gourami. *Journal of Biological Psychology, 15,* 5–11.

Cheal, M. L. (1978a). Amphetamine effects on stimulus-elicited investigation in the Mongolian gerbil. *Physiology & Behavior, 21,* 299–305.

Cheal, M. (1978b). Stimulus-elicited investigation in the Mongolian gerbil *(Meriones unguiculatus). Journal of Biological Psychology, 20,* 26–32.

Cheal, M. L. (1979). Stimulus-elicited investigation in apomorphine-treated gerbils. *Behavioral and Neural Biology, 27,* 157–174.

Cheal, M. L. (1980). Disruption of selective attention by apomorphine, but not amphetamine, in the Mongolian gerbil. *Psychopharmacology, 69,* 93–100.

Cheal, M. L. (1981). Scopolamine disrupts maintenance of attention rather than memory processes. *Behavioral and Neural Biology, 33,* 163–187.

Cheal, M. L. (1982a). Attention and habituation: Catecholamine interactions and sex differences. *Pharmacology Biochemistry & Behavior, 16,* 377–385.

Cheal, M. L. (1982b). Separate mediation of different components of attention. *Society for Neuroscience Abstracts, 8,* 147.

Cheal, M. L. (1983). L-DOPA and piribedil alter different components of attentional behavior dependent on dose. *Psychopharmacology, 80,* 345–350.

Cheal, M. L. (1984). Differential effects of haloperidol and clozapine on attention. *Psychopharmacology, 84,* 268–273.

Cheal, M. (1986). The gerbil: A unique model for research on aging. *Experimental Aging Research, 13,* 3–21.

Cheal, M. L. (1987a). Adult development: Plasticity of stable behavior. *Experimental Aging Research, 13,* 29–37.

Cheal, M. L. (1987b). Attention and habituation: Separation of specific components in development. *Physiology & Behavior, 41,* 415–425.

Cheal, M. L. (1987c). Environmental enrichment facilitates foraging behavior. *Physiology & Behavior, 39,* 281–283.

Cheal, M. L. (1987d). Lifespan environmental influences on species typical behavior of *Meriones unguiculatus.* In A. D. Woodhead & K. H. Thompson (Eds.), *Evolution of longevity in animals* (pp. 145–159). New York: Plenum.

Cheal, M. L., & Davis, R. E. (1974). Sexual behavior: Social and ecological influences in the Anabantid fish. *Trichogaster trichopterus. Behavioral Biology, 10,* 435–445.

Cheal, M. L., & Domesick, V. B. (1979). Habituation of stimulus-elicited investigation in gerbils after olfactory bulbectomy. *Physiology & Behavior, 23,* 309–315.

Cheal, M. L., & Foley, K. (1985). Developmental and experiential influences on ontogeny: The gerbil *(Meriones unguiculatus)* as a model. *Journal of Comparative Psychology, 99,* 289–305.

Cheal, M. L., Foley, K., & Kastenbaum, R. (1986). Brief periods of environmental enrichment facilitate adolescent growth of gerbils. *Physiology & Behavior, 36,* 1047–1051.

Cheal, M. L., Johnson, M. O., Ellingboe, J., & Skupny, A. S. T. (1984). Perseveration of attention to conspecific odors and novel objects in castrated gerbils. *Physiology & Behavior, 33,* 563–570.

Cheal, M. L., Klestzick, J., & Domesick, V. B. (1982). Attention and habituation: Odor preferences, long-term memory, and minimal sensory cues of novel stimuli. *Journal of Comparative and Physiological Psychology, 96,* 47–60.

Cheal, M. L., & Lyon, D. (1989). Attention effects on form discrimination at different eccentricities. *Quarterly Journal of Experimental Psychology: A. Human Experimental Psychology, 41A,* 719–746.

Cheal, M. L., & Lyon, D. (1991). Central and peripheral precuing of forced-choice discrimination. *Quarterly Journal of Experimental Psychology: A. Human Experimental Psychology, 43A,* 859–880.

Cheal, M. L., & Lyon, D. R. (1992). Benefits from attention depend on the target type in location-precued discrimination. *Acta Psychologica, 81,* 243–267.

Cheal, M. L., Lyon, D., & Hubbard, D. C. (1991). Attention differentially affects discrimination of line orientation and line arrangement. *Quarterly Journal of Experimental Psychology: A. Human Experimental Psychology, 43A,* 825–857.

Clark, M. M., & Galef, B. G. (1977). The role of the physical rearing environment in the domestication of the Mongolian gerbil *(Meriones unguiculatus). Animal Behaviour, 25,* 298–316.

Collier, G. H., & Rovee-Collier, C. K. (1981). A comparative analysis of optimal foraging behavior: Laboratory simulations. In A. Kamil & T. Sargent, (Eds.), *Foraging behavior: Ecological, ethological, and psychological approaches* (pp. 39–76). New York: Garland GTPM Press.

Commins, D., & Yahr, P. (1984). Lesions of the sexually dimorphic area disrupt mating and marking in male gerbils. *Brain Research Bulletin, 13,* 185–193.

Derryberry, D. (1989). Effects of goal-related motivational states on the orienting of spatial attention. *Acta Psychological, 72*, 199–220.

Diamond, M. C., Rosenzweig, M. R., & Krech, D. (1965). Relationships between body weight and skull development in rats raised in enriched and impoverished conditions. *Journal of Experimental Zoology, 160*, 29–36.

Elias, P. K., & Elias, M. F. (1976). Effects of aging on learning ability: Contributions from the animal literature. *Experimental Aging Research, 2*, 165–186.

Ellinwood, E. H. (1967). Amphetamine psychosis: I. Description of the individuals and process. *Journal of Nervous and Mental Disease, 144*, 273–283.

Eriksen, C. W., & Murphy, T. D. (1987). Movement of attentional focus across the visual field: A critical look at the evidence. *Perception & Psychophysics, 42*, 299–305.

Fiala, B., Snow, F. M., & Greenough, W. T. (1976). "Impoverished" rats weigh more than "enriched" rats because they eat more. *Developmental Psychobiology, 10*, 537–541.

Gray, L. (1981). Genetic and experiential differences affecting foraging behavior. In A. Kamil & T. Sargent (Eds.), *Foraging behavior: Ecological, ethological, and psychological approaches* (pp. 455–473). New York: Garland GTPM Press.

Greenough, W., Madden, T., & Fleischmann, T. (1972). Effects of isolation, daily handling, and enriched rearing on maze learning. *Psychonomic Science, 27*, 279–280.

Haan, N., & Day, D. (1974). A longitudinal study of change and sameness in personality development: Adolescence to later adulthood. *International Journal of Aging and Human Development, 5*, 11–39.

Hall, D. D. (1966). An ethological study of three species of anabantoid fishes. (University Microfilms No. 67-7226).

Harriman, A. E. (1980). Seizure episodes during open-field tests among Mongolian gerbils fed different combinations of minerals. *Physiological Psychology, 8*, 61–64.

Hebb, D. (1947). The effects of early experience on problem-solving at maturity. *The American Psychologist, 2*, 306–307.

Hebb, D. O. (1958). *A textbook of psychology*. Philadelphia: Saunders.

Herrick, C. J. (1933). The functions of the olfactory parts of the cerebral cortex. *Proceedings of the National Academy of Science, 19*, 7–14.

Ingle, D., Cheal, M. L., & Dizio, P. (1979). Cine analysis of visual orientation and pursuit by the Mongolian gerbil. *Journal of Comparative and Physiological Psychology, 93*, 919–928.

James, W. (1890). *Principles of psychology*. New York: Holt.

Johnston, W., & Dark, V. (1986). Selective attention. *Annual Review of Psychology, 37*, 43–75.

Jonides, J. (1981). Voluntary versus automatic control over the mind's eye's movement. In J. Long & A. Baddeley (Eds.), *Attention and Performance IX* (pp. 187–203). Hillsdale, NJ: Erlbaum.

Kaplan, H. (1975). What triggers seizures in the gerbil, *Meriones unguiculatus? Life Science, 17*, 693–698.

Kaplan, H. (1983). Housing condition and seizure susceptibility in Mongolian gerbils. *Physiological Psychology, 11*, 191–194.

LaBerge, D. (1973). Identification of two components of the time to switch attention: A test of a serial and a parallel model of attention. In S. Kornblum (Ed.), *Attention and Performance IV* (pp. 71–85). New York: Academic Press.

LaBerge, D. L. (1990a). Thalamic and cortical mechanisms of attention suggested by recent positron emission tomographic experiments. *Journal of Cognitive Neuroscience, 2*, 358–372.

LaBerge, D. L. (1990b). William James Symposium: Attention. *Psychological Science, 1*, 156–162.

Lehrman, D. S. (1965). Interaction between internal and external environments in the regulation of the reproductive cycle of the ring dove. In F. A. Beach (Ed.), *Sex and behavior* (pp. 355–380). New York: John Wiley.

Loskota, W. J., Lomax, P., & Rich, S. T. (1974). The gerbil as a model for study of the epilepsies. *Epilepsia, 15*, 109–119.

Miller, R. J. (1964). Studies on the social behavior of the blue gourami, *Trichogaster trichopterus (Pisces, Belontiidae). Copeia*, pp. 469–496.

Mirsky, A. (1987). Behavioral and psychophysiological markers of disordered attention. *Environmental Health Perspectives, 74*, 191–199.

Mirsky, A. F., Anthony, B. J., Duncan, C. C., Ahearn, M. B., & Kellam, S. G. (1991). Analysis of the elements of attention: A neuropsychological approach. *Neuropsychology Review, 2*, 109–145.

Morgan, M. (1973). Effects of post-weaning environment on learning in the rat. *Animal Behaviour, 21*, 429–442.

162   *Cheal*

Müller, H. J., & Rabbitt, P. M. A. (1989). Spatial cuing and the relation between the accuracy of "where" and "what" decisions in visual search. *Quarterly Journal of Experimental Psychology, 41A*, 747–773.
Nakayama, K., & Mackeben, M. (1989). Sustained and transient components of focal visual attention. *Vision Research, 29*, 1631–1647.
Parasuraman, R. (1984). Sustained attention in detection and discrimination. In R. Parasuraman, R. Davies, & J. Beatty (Eds.), *Varieties of attention* (pp. 243–271). New York: Academic Press.
Paul, L. A., Fried, I., Watanabe, K., Forsythe, A. B., & Scheibel, A. B. (1981). Structural correlates of seizure behavior in the Mongolian gerbil. *Science, 213*, 924–926.
Pendergrass, M., Thiessen, D., & Friend, P. (1989). Ventral marking in the male Mongolian gerbil reflects present and future reproductive investments. *Perceptual and Motor Skills, 69*, 355–367.
Plomin, R. (1990). The role of inheritance in behavior. *Science, 248*, 183–188.
Posner, M. I. (1985). *Hierarchical distributed networks in the neuropsychology of selective attention.* (Report No. 85-1). Eugene: University of Oregon.
Posner, M. I., & Petersen, S. E. (1990). The attention system of the human brain. *Annual Review of Neuroscience, 13*, 25–42.
Posner, M. I., Walker, J. A., Friedrich, F. J., & Rafal, R. D. (1984). Effects of parietal injury on covert orienting of attention. *Journal of Neuroscience, 4*, 1863–1874.
Roper, T. J., & Polioudakis, E. (1977). The behaviour of Mongolian gerbils in a semi-natural environment, with special reference to ventral marking, dominance and sociability. *Behaviour, 61*, 207–237.
Rosenzweig, M. (1984). Experience, memory, and the brain. *American Psychologist, 39*, 365–376.
Rothbart, M. K., Posner, M. I., & Boylan, A. (1990). *Regulatory mechanisms in infant development* (Report No. 90-1, 1–24). Eugene: University of Oregon.
Schwentker, V. (1963). The gerbil: A new laboratory animal. *Illinois Veterinarian, 6*, 5–9.
Skoczenski, A. M., & Aslin, R. N. (1990). Infant "hyperacuity": What develops? *Investigative Ophthalmology & Visual Science, 31*, 9.
Smotherman, W. P., & Robinson, S. R. (1990). The prenatal origins of behavioral organization. *Psychological Science, 1*, 97–106.
Spring, B. J. (1980). Shift of attention in schizophrenics, depressed patients, and siblings of schizophrenics. *Journal of Nervous Mental Disease, 168*, 133–140.
Sprott, R. L. (1975). Behavioral characteristics of C57BL/6J, DBA/6J, and B6D2F1 mice which are potentially useful for gerontological research. *Experimental Aging Research, 1*, 313–323.
Swanson, H. H., & Norman, M. E. (1978). Central and peripheral action of testosterone proprionate on scent gland morphology and marking behaviour in the Mongolian gerbil. *Behavioral Processes, 3*, 9–19.
Takai, R., & Wilkie, D. (1985). Foraging experience affects gerbils' (*Meriones unguiculatus*) radial arm maze performance. *Journal of Comparative Psychology, 99*, 361–364.
Thiessen, D. (1973). Footholds for survival. *American Scientist, 61*, 346–351.
Thiessen, D. D., Lindzey, G., & Friend, H. C. (1968). Spontaneous seizures in the Mongolian gerbil. *Psychonomic Science, 11*, 227–228.
Thiessen, D. D., & Rice, M. (1976). Mammalian scent gland marking and social behavior. *Psychological Bulletin, 83*, 505–539.
Traub, B., & Elepfandt, A. (1990). Sensory neglect in a frog: Evidence for early evolution of attentional processes in vertebrates. *Brain Research, 530*, 105–107.
Umilta, C. (1988). Orienting of attention. In F. Boller & J. Grafman (Eds.), *Handbook of neuropsychology* (pp. 175–193). Amsterdam: Elsevier.
Uttal, W. R. (1990). On some two-way barriers between models and mechanisms. *Perception & Psychophysics, 48*, 188–203.
Waller, N. G., Kojetin, B. A., Bouchard, T. J., Lykken, D. T., & Tellegen, A. (1990). Genetic and environmental influences on religious interests, attitudes, and values: A study of twins reared apart and together. *Psychological Science, 1*, 138–142.
Wenzel, B. M. (1974). The olfactory system and behavior. In L. V. DiCara (Ed.), *Limbic and autonomic systems research* (pp. 1–40). New York: Plenum.
Wenzel, B. M., & Rausch, L. J. (1977). Does the olfactory system modulate affective behavior in the pigeon? *Annals of the New York Academy of Science, 290*, 314–330.

Part III

MOTIVATION OF INGESTIVE BEHAVIOR

chapter 4

The Biopsychology of Feeding Behavior in Rodents
An attempt at integration

LYN H. RAIBLE
Kalamazoo College

SYNOPSIS AND COMMENTS
Roderick Wong and Neil V. Watson

In this extensive review of research on the biopsychology of feeding in rodents, Raible has taken on a challenging task, given that it is one of the most popular areas of motivational research. The unique feature of this chapter is its integration of causal factors at many levels with its possibilities for a coherent analysis of feeding mechanisms. As Raible aptly points out, most reviews on feeding seem to regard the behavior as a mere endpoint for the evaluation of the effectiveness of physiological manipulations. To correct that deficiency, she presents a synthesis of information on physiological and psychological as well as ecological aspects of the feeding system. In this system, she considers not only food intake but also foraging and hoarding behavior. To facilitate this analysis, Raible organized her material in terms of control functions of three interacting regulatory systems. The emergency system consists of physiological and behavioral mechanisms that are activated when the organism experiences prolonged food restriction. The functions of this system are to disinhibit mechanisms that keep the animal from displaying risky feeding behaviors and to activate mechanisms of fuel conservation. The short-term system is involved in the initiation and termination of daily feedings as well as food preferences. The long-term system involves mechanisms that regulate fat deposits and may include mechanisms related to foraging strategies and behavior. Its main function is the regulation of energy stores.

A valuable contribution of this chapter is its discussion of the interplay of energy depletion/repletion cycles and the role of environmental/psychological factors in the regulation of feeding. The role of the emergency system is to increase food seeking under adverse deprivation conditions. Raible reviewed the literature demonstrating the effects of increasing levels of deprivation on the animals' frequency of high-cost (i.e., "risky") foraging behaviors. Experiments by Cabanac and his associates have shown that when rats were required to enter a −15° environment for food, there were a greater number of deprived than nondeprived rats venturing into that region. Also, deprived rats ate more frequent and larger meals in that situation than did the nondeprived ones. Glucoreceptors in the CNS that respond to glucose availability may be the "inhibitors" and "disinhibitors" of such behavior. Raible suggests that LH activity during glucoprivation activates neural mechanisms mediating foraging behavior, while decreasing activity in the VMH might disinhibit such behaviors. The emergency system may specifically act to increase carbohydrate ingestion and thus facilitate glucose utilization.

The primary role of the short-term system is the regulation of meal patterns and food intake over an 1–2-day period. Psychological and environmental factors have a greater effect on this system than they do on the emergency system. The physiological bases of the short-term regulation of feeding involves noradrenergic and serotonergic neurotransmitter systems that act in opposition to each other. Activation of the noradrenergic system specifically increases carbohydrate ingestion while activation of the serotonergic system decreases it. Signals from "nutrient monitors" in the liver and in the CNS are translated into changes in norepinephrine and serotonin release that act through the PVN and other brain areas to alter food intake. Raible also indicates how hormones influence feeding activity because of mediation through neurotransmitter systems. For example, the inhibiting influence of estrogen on feeding in rats may be mediated, in part, through its interaction with the serotonergic system. Alternatively, estrogen may decrease feeding in female rats by decreasing the level of dopamine-β-hydroxylase, thereby interfering with the conversion of DA to NE. These results were obtained with rats and are not necessarily generalizable to other rodents. Gerbils show a facilitation of feeding when treated with estrogen.

Opioid substances activate feeding, possibly because of their role in the reward mechanisms in the brain. Opioid antagonists suppress feeding in most rodents with relatively low-energy demands and are less effective with hamsters, presumably because of their high-energy demands. Raible suggests that opioids may exert their influence on food intake via the dopaminergic and/or serotonergic system. This relationship is complicated by findings indicating that sex steroids regulate both opioid production and opioid recep- tors within the CNS. In the rat, chronic estradiol treatment lowers hypothal- amic β-endorphin content, a finding consonant with the suppressing effects of estrodiol on food intake.

The primary role on the long-term system is the regulation of the ani- mals' buffers against privation. This can be achieved through the regulation of fat deposits as well as through food-hoarding behavior. Raible regards this system as being more flexible and less influenced by immediate envi- ronmental factors than the other two systems. Mechanisms of the long-term system may alter food intake indirectly through changes in the body weight "set point" (discussed in Schulze's chapter) through modifications in the an- imals' willingness to work for food or through modifying the palatability of food.

Although it is helpful to conceptualize feeding behavior as reflecting the control functions of three interacting regulatory systems, we wonder to what extent these are really separable mechanisms. The observation that estradiol benzoate (EB) decreases feeding is a relation between physiological and be- havioral variables. The overt behavior, *feeding*, however, is simply more eas- ily quantified than the psychological effects such as palatability, motivation, and so on that Raible would like to approach. It seems probable that all of these measurements are simply metrics of the functioning of a single under- lying mechanism or adaptation. That is, EB effects, NE effects, and palata- bility effects may all be measures of one adaptation. It is not necessary to infer that they are different factors; instead, they may be viewed as the re- sult of a single specialized information-processing device.

In her summary of physiological mechanisms of feeding behavior, Raible suggested that every neurotransmitter, sex steroid, and peptide that has been found to influence food intake appears to do so by acting in the PVN, VMH, and/or LH. This is a very bold sweeping statement, given the prevalence of many alternative models, but the coherence and elegance of this analysis is very attractive. Raible admits, however, that there are problems in specify- ing physiological mechanisms when considering more behaviorally oriented studies dealing with meal patterns, diet selection, foraging behavior, and food hoarding. Although several factors influence the intermeal interval, a good case could be made for the decline in blood glucose level as a con- tributor to meal onset. However, the facts that a drop in blood glucose pre- cedes meal onset and that glucose infusions delay meal onset do not mean that CNS glucoreceptors are involved. Raible relegates the latter mechanism to the hypothesized emergency system.

Diet selection is mediated by learning mechanisms in which animals avoid deficient diets and rapidly learn to ingest those substances necessary to restore the deficiency. In other words, animals acquire knowledge about the substances they ingest and use it to select appropriate diets. Thus they adopt feeding strategies that help compensate for deprivation of specific macronutrients. However, as the cost of a specific macronutrient increases, animals become less selective. They will adjust the composition of their diet if the preferred item is too "expensive." Such results indicate the role of interacting systems, which may be dependent on information regarding nutrient availability sent from the stomach and liver back to the CNS.

Foraging for food entails specific acts such as searching, identifying, procuring, and handling of food. Effective foraging is facilitated by processes involving spatial memory, temporal memory, and temporal integration. The most salient variable that influences such behavior, however, is response cost. Increases in procurement cost lead to decreases in foraging frequency and increases in meal size. Raible hypothesizes that during "times of plenty," animals forage, eat, and hoard in "anticipation" of need. When animals are depleted because of diminishing food and fat stores, short-term and long-term physiological changes will influence the extent to which they engage in foraging behavior under "risky" conditions. With increasing energy depletion, signals from the emegency system would increase in strength and thereby inhibit nonforaging activities as well as disinhibit high-cost foraging behavior. Although learning and memory may be the primary forces guiding foraging behavior, mechanisms dealing with energy regulation also exert an influence.

Hoarding behavior may be regarded as part of the long-term regulatory system because stored food provides a buffer against short-term deprivation. It may also be regarded as a natural and final element of day-to-day feeding behavior. The variation in propensity to hoard may reflect evolutionary adaptations to different environments. The Syrian golden hamster provides an example of an animal with an interesting strategy for dealing with the relative paucity of food in its environment. Material in R. Wong's chapter indicates how and why this rodent does not compensate for food restriction by increasing its food intake when diets are available. The absence of postfast compensation may reflect the animal's strong tendency to hoard, an activity whose consequence is a food store that precludes the experience of deprivation because the hamster has access to this supply. As the costs of procurement of food goes up, however, hamsters consume more of their hoard and decrease the amount that they add to the hoard. Thus, these animals act proactively to prevent food shortage from occurring and reduce the amount of time and energy spent foraging when food is scarce. Raible suggests that rats are more reactive, altering meal size and frequency when experiencing food shortages. Mongolian gerbils fall in the middle of this continuum. They show postfast compensation in their intake, but they also increase their hoarding activity in response to deprivation.

Hoarding behavior in the rat is directly related to body weight loss. This activity is inhibited by a serotonin agonist, and it has been hypothesized that this occurs because of a lowering of body weight set point. Because fluctuations in body weight are related to fluctuations in fat stores, hoarding in the rat may be regulated systems regulating the latter. The hoarding system in hamsters is regulated by other systems because these animals hoard regardless of body fat levels.

In general, Raible's chapter clearly indicates the impossibility of determining the relevance of factors by studying their effects in isolation from each other. For example, an animal may overeat or hoard food in excess of its physiological requirement because it is easy to obtain or because it is highly palatable. It is a truism that feeding and other motivated activities reflect the interaction of several systems. Raible's review provides us with concrete suggestions about the specifics of such interactions. The marked species and sex-dependent variability in the effects of steroids and peptides on feeding may have evolutionary implications. Do these effects reflect different adaptations, or are they "downstream" reflections of physiological preparations for different reproductive strategies?

INTRODUCTION

I recently decided that it was time to switch biopsychology texts. As I read through the chapters on "motivated" behaviors (e.g., sexual behavior, feeding behavior, aggression), I was reminded of a thought I'd first had as a graduate student: Where's the behavior? The chapters seemed to focus on the physiological mechanisms underlying the behavior, with little information about other potentially influential factors (e.g., environment, learning, individual preference). Behavior was understood in a physiological context, but not in a more global context that integrated the contributions of internal as well as external factors. It was as if behavior had become a mere endpoint for the evaluation of the effectiveness of physiological manipulations. Information on "psychological" and environmental factors was contained in other texts that dealt with behavioral ecology, not biopsychology.

The tendency of biopsychologists to study either physiology and behavior or environment and behavior is not new and is probably a consequence of the large number of factors controlling any single category of behavior; one individual cannot hope to study them all. Therefore, by necessity, we specialize. Nonetheless, one of the goals of biopsychology is the integration of all these factors in a manner that helps us to understand behavior. Review articles give us the opportunity to take this more global view. With this in mind, this chapter will attempt to synthesize information on the physiological, psychological, and environmental aspects of feeding behaviors (e.g., foraging, food intake, hoarding).

An examination of the rather vast literature on feeding behaviors suggests that it may be helpful to conceptualize feeding behaviors as falling under the control of three interacting regulatory systems: emergency, short term, and long term. For the purposes of this review, the *emergency* system will encompass physiological mechanisms and behaviors that may be of great importance during conditions of prolonged deprivation or food restriction. Two possible functions of this system are (a) the disinhibition of mechanisms that normally keep an animal from displaying risky feeding behaviors (e.g., foraging in very open areas or during very cold temperatures) and (b) the activation of mechanisms of fuel conservation. There has been relatively little research investigating mechanisms that might be involved in such a system, particularly with regard to the behavioral aspects.

The *short-term* system will encompass mechanisms that appear to be involved in food preference and in the initiation and termination of daily meals. This system is presumed to interact with systems monitoring food availability and other environmental factors. The probable function of this system is the regulation of the daily feeding strategy and/or the regulation of feeding strategy over periods of a few days. The majority of the existing research seems to fall under the functions served by the short-term system.

The *long-term* system will encompass mechanisms that regulate fat deposits (and thus influence feeding behavior on a short- and long-term basis) and may include mechanisms related to foraging strategy and behavior. Thus, this system would function to regulate energy stores and defend those stores through interactions with the short-term system. A moderate amount of research seems to pertain to this system.

Each system may utilize some (or all) of the same neurological/physiological mechanisms, although the importance of a given mechanism may vary between each system. For example, glucoreceptors monitoring the levels of blood glucose may be very important to the emergency system, less so to the short-term system, and unimportant to the long-term system. It is difficult to determine if perceived differences in these systems represent quantitative differences or qualitative differences. The mechanisms involved in the emergency system are more easily separated from those mechanisms that appear to be involved in regulating short- and long-term feeding. This separation may reflect qualitative differences between the emergency system and the short- and long-term systems. The mechanisms involved in regulating short- and long-term feeding behaviors, however, seem inextricably intertwined, and few attempts are made to declare a particular mechanism as the exclusive domain of one system. For these reasons, the emergency system is treated in a section separate from that covering short- and long-term regulation.

An examination of the literature relevant to these proposed systems reveals that each is influenced by a number of variables. Those that currently appear most important to the regulation of feeding behavior include physiological variables (e.g., neurotransmitters, hormones, peptides), psychological variables (e.g., palatability, motivation), and environmental variables (e.g., food availability, predators, climate). Although we often know a great deal about the role of one particular variable, we often have very little idea of how factors interact to regulate feeding behaviors. This is particularly true for interactions between physiological and psychological or environmental factors. For example, we know that in the female rat, chronic estradiol benzoate (EB; a physiological factor) will decrease food intake in a laboratory setting (Wade, 1976). Furthermore, this may be due to an EB-induced decrease in norepinephrine activity (Simpson & Dicara, 1973), which relates two physiological factors. We do not know how this might relate to psychological factors (e.g., does EB decrease food intake by decreasing palatability and/or motivation in general?).

There are ample excellent reviews of the feeding literature, particularly as it pertains to physiological mechanisms. For this reason, the physiological elements will be reviewed briefly while the focus of the review will be on possible relationships between physiological, psychological, and environmental factors that work to regulate feeding under emergency conditions, and in the short and long term.

This review will also attempt to address some of the controversies in the area of feeding regulation. One important debate concerns whether feeding behaviors are controlled primarily by cycles of depletion/repletion or by learned feeding strategies. It seems likely that the answer to this question is that the method of primary control depends upon the situation. Certainly it makes evolutionary sense for animals to forage and hoard, if not eat, in an anticipatory fashion. On the other hand, if these mechanisms fail, for one reason or another, it also seems reasonable that other mechanisms, based on physiological depletion, would come into play and strengthen responses that would lead to repletion.

Related to the depletion/repletion controversy are debates about which elements, glucose, free fatty acids, or their common currency, high-energy phosphate compounds (adenosine triphosphate, guanosine triphosphate), are the sources for signals about depletion/repletion (see commentary on Le Magnen, 1981, for examples). Although these debates have waned in recent years, it is worth noting that some of the theories (e.g., carbohydrostatic, glucostatic, energostatic) simply reflected different levels of analysis. For example, high-energy phosphate compounds are the source of cellular energy. However, they are not, in a more global sense, what are ingested and taken into the cell. Carbohydrates, fats, and proteins are ingested; glucose, fatty acids, and amino acids are absorbed (see Grossman, 1986, for a review). A theory that is correct at one level may seem unimportant or even incorrect at another level, but each is relevant to the global understanding of feeding behavior. Glucose, not carbohydrates, enters cells. Thus, the ingestion of carbohydrates would not make sense unless one also understood that they are broken down into glucose. But even this does not make sense unless one further understands that glucose provides the ATP needed by the cell. This review will focus on behavioral and global physiological levels of analysis rather than cellular and biochemical levels of analysis.

An additional general problem with studies of feeding behavior concerns the mechanisms underlying observed effects. It can be extremely difficult to exactly determine which aspects of feeding behavior have been influenced by an experimental treatment. For example, peptide X decreases food intake. Does it do so via a "satiety" signal, a decrease in palatability, an impairment of mouth movements, induction of nausea, a decrease in motivation to work for food, or via some other mechanism? Lesion Y decreases hoarding behavior. Is this due to the destruction of an area that initiates hoarding behavior in response to appropriate internal and/or external signals or to the destruction of an area that mediates motor movements, attention, or willingness to work for food? In some cases, investigators have eliminated many of these possibilities, but this is not always possible. For example, it is relatively easy to determine if taste aversions or gross motor deficiencies could account for changes in food intake. It can be more difficult to determine if general changes in motivation, palatability, or in macronutrient preference have influenced macronutrient selection. Such a determination is nonetheless vital to our understanding of the regulation of feeding behaviors. It is important to recognize these limitations and difficulties from the outset, because it would be unwieldy to attempt to discuss each one as it relates to the physiological, environmental, and behavioral variables discussed. Furthermore, it is essential that research on feeding behaviors is designed in such a way that these confounds are minimized.

THE EMERGENCY SYSTEM

Conceptually, this system is one that encompasses those mechanisms that are activated when an animal is in a severely depleted state. However, such depletion may be part of a continuum that moves from a nondepleted state, through one of normal depletion, to one of abnormal depletion. Presumably, then, physiological mechanisms of importance will be those that allow the animal to utilize available food stores as well as those that override factors such as low palatability and high-risk foraging that can inhibit feeding when the animal is in a less depleted state. Additionally, the emergency system may have some elements, such as those that "release" certain feeding behaviors, that are peculiar to a state of rather severe deprivation. As indicated earlier, there is relatively little data available on mechanisms involved in this type of feeding regulation. Most that is available is based on physiological mechanisms, although some environmental/behavioral research also exists.

Summary of Physiological Mechanisms: Emergency System

The primary source of energy for the CNS is glucose. During the absorptive (feeding) phase, glucose is readily derived from carbohydrates or, if necessary, from other macronutrients. During the fasting phase of the feeding cycle, however, glucose must be obtained from endogenous energy stores (fats and glycogen). Thus, during the fasting phase, insulin secretion decreases (insulin facilitates storage of fuel derived from glucose) and glucagon secretion increases (glucagon promotes gluconeogenesis by facilitating the release of fatty acids and glycogen). Grossman (1986) points out that during starvation, nearly half of the endogenously produced glucose is produced through gluconeogenesis in the kidney. However, during severe glucoprivation, ketone bodies (β-hydroxybutyrate, acetoacetate) are produced and may provide energy for the CNS (Owen, Morgan, & Kemp, 1967; Owen, Reichart, Boden, & Shuman, 1974). Most research indicates that utilization of ketones occurs only after prolonged glucoprivation, resulting in prolonged exposure to ketones (e.g., Corddry, Rapoport, & London, 1982; Gjedde, 1983; Gjedde & Crone, 1975). The research of Rowland, Bellush, and Carlton (1985) confirms that ketones are not an acute source of fuel for the CNS during times of severe depletion. Thus, even during glucoprivation, glucose is an important source of energy for the CNS. It should be noted that mechanisms within the CNS appear to monitor free fatty acids and glycerol (Friedman, Tordoff, & Ramirez, 1986; Oomura, 1976), but they must be converted to glucose or ketones to be used as fuel by the CNS.

Availability of glucose in the CNS appears to be monitored by glucoreceptors in the ventromedial hypothalamus (VMH) and the lateral hypothalamus (LH) (Anand, Chhina, Sharma, Dua, & Singh, 1964; Anand, Subberwal, Manchanda, & Singh, 1961; Mayer & Marshall, 1956, Oomura, 1976; Smith, 1972; Steffens, 1969a, 1969b). Glucose applied to the VMH stimulates the firing of VMH neurons, while glucose applied to the LH tends to inhibit the firing of LH neurons. Furthermore, the responsiveness of VMH neurons to glucose is enhanced by insulin while LH neurons, like most CNS neurons, are unaffected by the ability of insulin to facilitate the entry of glucose into cells (Oomura, 1976; Smith, 1972). Smith (1972) suggested that during glucoprivation, the VMH glucoreceptors are inactive (little insulin and little glucose) while the LH neurons are active (little glucose). Thus, the LH neurons would produce a "feed" signal. As the animal begins eating and insulin is secreted, the VMH glucoreceptors become more active, the LH glucoreceptors less active, and eventually the VMH would actively inhibit the LH neurons, sending a "satiety" signal (Smith, 1972).

An addition to this glucostatic theory is derived from the work of Louis-Sylvestre and Le Magnen (1980) and Larue-Achagiotis and Le Magnen (1985), which suggests that 3–5 min prior to the onset of a meal, rats show a pronounced decline in the level of blood glucose. This decline always preceded meal onset, always resulted in the initiation of a meal, and continued for about 3 min after meal onset (Louis-Sylvestre & Le Magnen, 1980). Are these the changes in glucose levels to which LH and VMH glucoreceptors or some other CNS system are responding? The drop in blood glucose observed by these investigators is considerably smaller than that found to elicit eating after insulin injection (e.g., Booth & Brookover, 1968; Brandes, 1977). Campfield, Brandon, and Smith (1985), however, found that when they administered a small amount of glucose into the blood supply as blood glucose levels began to decline, they could delay meal onset. This implies that the premeal drop in blood glucose causes meal initiation. Additional studies are needed to clarify the significance of the premeal drop in blood glucose.

The role of VMH and LH glucoreceptors in feeding behavior remains a matter of debate (see, for example, Grossman, 1986). However, I would like to suggest that their importance may be connected to feeding behaviors associated with more extreme deprivation rather than in the day-to-day regulation of food intake. It is possible that during prolonged deprivation signals from LH glucoreceptors may be of sufficient strength to override other signals that compete with signals to feed. Deprived animals are more tolerant of unfavorable feeding conditions than are their nondeprived counterparts. Although there are many way in which to analyze this finding, the conclusion that deprivation "inhibits" some behaviors and "releases" others seems inescapable. Perhaps CNS glucoreceptors are the inhibitors and disinhibitors of such behaviors. CNS glucoreceptors may still play an active role in regulating feeding in the nondeprived animal, but other factors (e.g., levels of fatty acids, hormones, environmental variables) also contribute and may be more important to the regulation of feeding in nondeprived situations.

Assuming that glucose and glucoreceptors play some role in the regulation of feeding, it seems fairly natural that the CNS areas that appear to respond to glucose availability would also influence the release of insulin and glucagon. The dorsal motor nucleus of the vagus (DMNV) influences the secretion of insulin (and glucagon) from the pancreas. Although the glucoreceptors in the VMH and LH may or may not send axons directly to the DMNV, neurons of the paraventricular nuclei (PVN) do send axons to this region (Gold & Simson, 1982; Kirchgessner & Sclafani, 1988). Research indicates that noradrenergic input to this area inhibits firing of the paraventricular axons synapsing within the DMNV, resulting in increased insulin secretion and eating (Leibowitz, 1978; Leibowitz & Brown, 1980a; Moss, Urban, & Cross, 1972). It appears that glucoreceptors in the tongue and liver send information to the PVN (Novin, Robinson, Culbreth, & Tordoff, 1983) and it is possible that glucoreceptors within the VMH and LH do the same.

It is clear from additional research (e.g., Friedman et al., 1986; Novin, VanderWeele, & Rezek, 1973; Oomura, 1976; Shimizu, Oomura, Novin, Grijalva, & Cooper, 1983) that available nutrients as well as glucose are monitored by the brain and by the liver. Glucose level is clearly an important signal in the regulation of feeding, however. Thus, I would suggest that glucoreceptors comprise an important element of the emergency regulatory system.

During the absorptive phase, glucose is the primary and most readily utilized source of energy for the body (see Grossman, 1986, for a review). Carbohydrates provide the most immediate source of glucose. Therefore, one might expect that an emergency system would be one that specifically enhances the ingestion of carbohydrates, because this will most rapidly increase glucose levels. Clearly, there are mechanisms within the CNS that appear to specifically regulate carbohydrate ingestion. Damage to neurons within the PVN, which are thought to produce a "satiety" signal, results in a chronic elevation in carbohydrate intake (Sclafani & Aravich, 1983; Shor-Posner, Azar, & Leibowitz, 1984). Injections of norepinephrine (NE) that inhibit PVN firing also increase food intake by preferentially increasing carbohydrate ingestion (Leibowitz, Weiss, Yee, & Tretter, 1985). Furthermore, it is clear that neuropeptide Y (NPY), particularly when administered to the PVN, increases feeding and, notably, carbohydrate ingestion (Leibowitz, 1978; Leibowitz

& Brown, 1980b; Morley, Levine, Gosnell, & Krahn, 1985; Stanley, Chin, & Leibowitz, 1985; Stanley, Daniel, Chin, & Leibowitz, 1985). Thus, the PVN, by regulating carbohydrate ingestion, may be an essential component of a system that regulates glucose levels. It is possible that LH and/or VMH glucoreceptors are located on neurons that synapse upon PVN neurons, thereby providing a means by which changes in glucose levels can produce changes in carbohydrate ingestion. To the best of my knowledge, studies examining PVN firing after the application of glucose to the LH or VMH have not been published.

The precise role of NE and NPY during severe depletion is unclear. However, NPY may be most important to the emergency system, NE to the short-term system. The work of Leibowitz (see Leibowitz, 1990, for a review) and of Morley and co-workers (e.g., Morley et al., 1985) indicates that despite the similarity in effects of NPY and NE on food intake, the two substances act via separate receptor systems. Furthermore, Leibowitz (1990) cites evidence indicating that when NE and NPY are co-localized, NPY tends to be released under conditions of high-frequency stimulation. Leibowitz (1990) points out that such high-frequency stimulation would occur when energy stores are depleted, and she goes on to suggest that the effects of NPY on food intake may be most specific to a depleted condition (Leibowitz, 1990). Thus, increased feeding due to NPY injection may be most relevant to an emergency feeding system, while increased feeding due to NE administration may be more important to short-term regulation of feeding. The latter possibility is discussed in more detail in the section on short-term regulation of feeding behaviors.

Outside of the possible involvement of CNS glucoreceptors, NPY, and NE in the initiation of feeding in deprived animals, little information exists on systems that may play an important role in an animal's response to deprivation. Furthermore, there are few studies that investigate how the physiological changes associated with depletion interact with physiological mechanisms that appear relevant to short- and long-term regulation. There are intriguing hints about these interactions, however, from studies examining the effects of hormones or neurotransmitters on feeding behaviors in deprived and nondeprived rats. For example, Cabanac, Ferber, and Fantino (1989) found that if animals had fallen below 90% of their original body weight, dexfenfluramine (a serotonin agonist) no longer inhibited foraging and food intake. Sieck, Nance, and Gorski (1978) found that food deprivation attenuated the anorectic effects of estrogen on food intake. Thus, the effects of neurotransmitters and hormones on food intake are modified by other physiological events, but which ones?

Using a purely physiological approach to study interactions between different CNS mechanisms can be quite difficult because one must know where to look for the interaction. The benefit of behavioral studies such as the two discussed earlier is that alterations in behavior may be the clearest indication that an interaction is taking place. Unfortunately, studies examining the behavioral effects of various substances on feeding behavior in severely deprived and nondeprived rats (and other rodents) are relatively scarce.

Behavioral and Physiological Factors: Emergency System

Because it is difficult to determine exactly when food deprivation departs from normal abstinence and becomes a more severe form of deprivation, it is also difficult to determine which feeding behaviors belong to each of these categories. Indeed, there may be no behavior that is qualitatively specific to a state of severe deprivation. Rather, behaviors may change in a quantitative fashion: As deprivation increases, the frequency of high-cost ("risky") foraging behaviors also increases.

In rats deprived for 22 hr or longer, the number of rats venturing out to forage in a −15°C environment was greater than that seen in nondeprived rats. In addition, deprived animals ate more frequent and larger meals than did nondeprived animals (Cabanac, 1985). In a similar study, Cabanac and Swiergiel (1989) found that food deprivation increases the amount of food hoarded. Indeed, research indicates that many species show increases in food hoarding in response to food deprivation/weight loss (e.g., Cabanac & Swiergiel, 1989, rats; DiBattista & Bedard, 1987; Fantino & Cabanac, 1980; Lea & Tarpy, 1986; Wong, 1984, hamsters; Nyby & Thiessen, 1980, gerbils). This seems a natural response to deprivation, because hoarding serves as a buffer against times of food scarcity. There are also limits to changes in foraging and hoarding behaviors, however. For example, as food becomes scarce, deer mice and voles will extend their foraging ranges if cover is available but tend not to venture into areas that are lacking in cover (Anderson, 1986). In the study by Anderson (1986), it is possible that animals would begin to venture into areas with little cover as their body weight decreased; for at some point in time, the costs of starvation will exceed the costs of risky feeding.

The studies by Cabanac et al. (1989) and Sieck et al. (1978), as well as those studies cited in the previous paragraph, suggest that at least some changes in feeding behaviors are mediated by, or reflect, neurophysiological changes. What neurophysiological mechanisms might be producing this behavioral change? There appears to be relatively little direct information on which to base an answer to this question. If we assume that LH and VMH glucoreceptors do play a role in the body's response to abnormal levels of food deprivation, these nuclei represent one possible neurophysiological mechanism that could produce behavior change. Perhaps increased activity in the LH during glucoprivation activates neural mechanisms mediating foraging behaviors. Alternatively, decreasing activity within the VMH might disinhibit foraging behaviors. In either case, it should be possible to block increases in risky foraging behavior in deprived animals by interfering with the "forage" message generated by changes in the activity of LH and/or VMH glucoreceptors. Alternatively, one might be able to induce risky foraging behavior in nondeprived animals by artifically creating the message to forage. A particularly interesting question is whether one can induce risky foraging without increasing food intake. If not, it would suggest that the two behaviors are subserved by the same mechanism but represent different points on a continuum. To further our understanding of a possible emergency system, additional studies examining the effects of experimental manipulations on foraging and feeding under conditions of risk and deprivation are essential.

SHORT-TERM AND LONG-TERM REGULATION

Physiological Mechanisms

Neurotransmitters. Although there are many neurotransmitters, there are two, NE and serotonin, that appear particularly important in the regulation of feeding behavior. Some evidence (e.g., Heffner, Vosmer, & Seiden, 1984; Hoebel, 1977; Stricker & Zigmond, 1974, 1976) does suggest that dopamine exerts a facilitatory action on feeding. The evidence however, is neither as abundant nor as consistent as that for NE and for serotonin. Thus, the discussion will focus on the latter two neurotransmitters. Little research has dealt with the role of neurotransmitters in foraging and hoarding. Therefore, the focus will be on food intake itself. Finally, there have been relatively few studies investigating how these neurotransmitters influence feeding in rodents other than rats. As a result, this section is primarily a discussion of how these neurotransmitters influence food intake in the rat. There are reasons to believe that these findings are not generalizable to all rodents.

Norepinephrine. In general, the administration of NE and NE agonists has been found to stimulate food intake, while the administration of NE antagonists has been found to decrease food intake in the rat (e.g., Leibowitz, Roossin, & Rosenn, 1984; Leibowitz et al., 1985; Matthews, Booth, & Stolerman, 1978). The facilitatory action of NE and NE agonists of food intake appears to be mediated by α-adrenergic receptors located within the PVN (e.g., Booth 1968; Goldman, Marino, & Leibowitz, 1985; Leibowitz, 1975). NE and NE agonists such as amphetamine, however, have been found by some (e.g., Grossman, 1962; Leibowitz, 1976; Margules, 1970) to decrease food intake. This "satiety" effect may be mediated by β-adrenergic receptors that are located within the LH because injections to this location produce the effect (Leibowitz, 1976). In general, the β-noradrenergic system in the LH does not appear to be of major importance in the regulation of feeding. Instead, the α-noradrenergic system and PVN appear to be of primary importance in regulating feeding and, as such, have been studied fairly extensively.

Research indicates that increases in food intake seen after the administration of NE to the PVN are dependent upon an intact hypothalamo-pituitary-adrenal axis; hypophysectomy or adrenalectomy abolishes the response (Leibowitz, Roland, Hor, & Squillari, 1984; McLean & Hoebel, 1982; Roland, Oppenheimer, Chang, & Leibowitz, 1985). NE-induced increases in feeding can be restored by the administration of corticosterone to hypophysectomized or adrenalectomized rats (Leibowitz, Roland et al., 1984). These effects appear to be due to an adrenalectomy-induced down-regulation of α_2-adrenergic receptors within the PVN that can be reversed by corticosterone in a rapid and dose-dependent fashion (Bhakthavatsalam & Leibowitz, 1986; Leibowitz et al., 1985; Roland, Bhakthavatsalam, & Leibowitz, 1986). These findings have led Leibowitz and co-workers (e.g., Leibowitz et al., 1985) to suggest that corticosterone, a glucocorticoid with a critical role in the regulation of blood glucose, permits NE within the PVN to regulate meal size relative to energy reserves. Given the role of corticosterone in regulating blood glucose, one might ask if the corticosterone-NE-PVN system initiates a generalized feeding response or if it initiates increased ingestion of specific macronutrients.

The work of Leibowitz et al. (1985) indicates that increases in food intake observed after the administration of NE to the PVN (which decreases PVN activity and increases DMNV activity) are due primarily to increases in carbohydrate ingestion. Furthermore, lesions of the PVN (which increase DMNV activity) produce chronic elevation of carbohydrate intake (Scalfani & Aravich 1983; Shor-Posner et al., 1984), while destruction of NE-containing neurons within the PVN (which decrease DMNV activity) inhibits the spontaneous ingestion of carbohydrates (Azar, Shor-Posner, Filart, & Leibowitz, 1984). Thus, at least part of the PVN system regulating food intake may be designed to regulate carbohydrate ingestion. One might ask what, then, might be the role of LH and VMH glucoreceptors?

Carbohydrates provide one of our most important sources of glucose (Grossman, 1986). However, carbohydrates must be broken down into simple sugars, notably glucose, in order to be utilized. It is also important to note that during the absorptive phase, glucose rather than protein or lipids is the primary source of energy for the body (Grossman, 1986). During the fasting phase, the absence of insulin prevents the use of glucose by body tissues, which then depend primarily on glycogen and fatty acids for energy (Grossman, 1986). Thus, it seems reasonable that the system involved in regulating meal-to-meal/short-term food intake would monitor the energy source that is important on a short-term basis—glucose. Because animals gain much of their glucose by ingesting carbohydrates, however, the signal that glucose is low needs to be translated into a signal to ingest carbohydrates. This may be the function of the VMH/LH-PVN system and the noradrenergic neurons within this system. To place this into the framework developed earlier: Glucose increases VMH activity and VMH glucoreceptors are insulin sensitive. Glucose decreases LH activity, and LH glucoreceptors are insulin insensitive. Thus, when glucose and insulin levels are low, neurons within the VMH are relatively inactive and may have little effect on the PVN. Neurons within LH would be active, however, particularly as depletion became more severe. These neurons, possibly noradrenergic, may send axons to the PVN that inhibit PVN activity, thereby increasing food intake (the DMNV may or may not be involved in this effect), or at least increasing the motivation to eat food. When glucose levels are high, the LH neurons would be inactive (low noradrenergic activity), and this signal would not be sent. Increased VMH activity may also engage some mechanism (possibly serotonergic; see Leibowitz, Weiss, & Shor-Posner, 1988) that serves to increase activity in the PVN, thereby decreasing food intake. The VMH might also increase β-noradrenergic activity within the LH, which could inhibit feeding. Such a "satiety" mechanism is not essential to the system, however. It would be of interest to investigate these possibilities.

Serotonin. Unlike NE, which usually stimulates food intake, serotonin has been found, in most circumstances, to inhibit food intake. Both centrally and peripherally administered serotonergic drugs can produce anorexia (Fletcher & Burton, 1984; Souquet & Rowland, 1990; and see Blundell, 1984, for a review). This complicates the interpretation of studies employing peripheral routes of drug administration because it is difficult to determine which effects might be peripherally mediated and which might be centrally mediated.

To further complicate matters, the relatively large number of serotonin receptor subtypes, some of which act in opposition to each other, make difficult the interpretation of effects observed even when serotonergic drugs are administered directly to the CNS. Given these complications, the clearest information on the role of serotonin in feeding comes from studies utilizing neurochemical depletions. In general, these studies indicate that 5,7-dihydroxytryptamine (5,7-DHT)-induced serotonin depletions lead to increases in food intake and body weight (e.g., Carlton & Rowland, 1984; Waldbillig, Bartness, & Stanley, 1981). In general, studies administering serotonergic drugs directly to the CNS support the conclusion that serotonin inhibits feeding (e.g., Kruk, 1973; Massi & Marini, 1987; Shor-Posner, Grinker, Mainescu, Brown, & Leibowitz, 1986; Weiss, Papadakos, Knudson, & Leibowitz, 1986). It is of particular interest to note that the administration of serotonin to the PVN produced a suppression of feeding, even in food-deprived rats (Weiss et al., 1986). However, research also suggests that as may be the case with β-noradrenergic versus α-noradrenergic receptors, serotonin type I_B receptors may mediate the inhibitory action of serotonin on food intake, while serotonin type I_A receptors may mediate a somewhat weaker hyperphagic response (e.g., Aulakh et al., 1988; and see Dourish, Hutson, & Curzon, 1985; Garattini, Bizzi, Caccia, Mennini, & Samanin, 1988; Leibowitz et al., 1988, for reviews). Thus, studies employing direct administration of serotonergic drugs indicate that central serotonin administration generally decreases food intake, an effect mediated predominantly by the serotonin type I_B receptor. A secondary facilitatory action may be observed if serotonin type I_A receptors are stimulated.

Peripheral manipulations of serotonin also suggest that serotonin usually inhibits food intake (e.g., Aulakh et al., 1988; Carlton & Rowland, 1984; Davies, Rossi, Panksepp, Bean, & Zolovick, 1983; Fletcher & Burton, 1984; Pollack & Rowland, 1981; Rowland & Carlton, 1988). At least some of these effects are peripherally rather than centrally mediated. Carlton and Rowland (1984) found that tolerance to the anorectic actions of quipazine (a serotonin type II receptor agonist) and fenfluramine (also a serotonin agonist) could be observed even after destruction of serotonergic systems within the CNS by 5,7-DHT. In addition, they found that the anorectic effects of quipazine in control animals and in 5,7-DHT-treated subjects were not significantly different (Carlton & Rowland, 1984). Furthermore, in agreement with Hoebel, Zemlan, Trulson, Mackenzie, DuCret, and Norelli (1978), Carlton and Rowland (1984) found that serotonin depletion within the CNS can actually enhance the anorectic action of peripherally administered fenfluramine. Thus, it is clear that manipulations of peripheral serotonin can influence food intake, but the mechanisms through which this is accomplished are far from clear. This is particularly the case for fenfluramine.

It has been reported that fenfluramine produces pronounced inhibition of feeding only in free-feeding animals (e.g., Davies et al., 1983; Rowland & Carlton, 1988). Carlton and Rowland (1984) did find that in rats treated with 5,7-DHT, 2 and 5 mg/kg fenfluramine increased anorexia while 10 mg/kg decreased observed anorexia, suggesting that the effect observed may depend upon the dose and paradigm used. To further complicate matters, even relatively low doses (3 mg/kg) of fenfluramine can produce conditioned taste aversions (Fletcher & Burton, 1984). Thus, some of the anorexia observed after fenfluramine administration may be due to general malaise rather than to a specific effect of serotonin. Nonetheless, fenfluramine also exerts specific effects that may account for some of the anorexia it induces. Hoebel (1977) suggests that fenfluramine may induce anorexia by increasing lipolysis and/or the utilization of glucose. Fletcher and Burton (1984) suggest that fenfluramine could induce anorexia by altering peristalsis. Others (e.g., Davies et al., 1983) suggest that fenfluramine-induced anorexia is due to delayed gastric emptying. At present, the peripheral mechanisms by which serotonin can decrease food intake remain undetermined.

The most important effect of serotonin on feeding appears to be a suppression of food intake. Thus, a reasonable question is whether or not the serotonergic feeding system acts in direct opposition to the noradrenergic system. Leibowitz et al. (1988) suggest that such an interaction occurs within the medial hypothalamus (i.e., the PVN), citing a variety of evidence to support this contention. Specifically, Leibowitz et al. (1988) point out that while NE increases body weight; food intake; and the size, duration, and speed of eating, serotonin decreases each of these. Meal frequency is changed by neither and PVN lesions block the effects of both (Leibowitz et al., 1988). These findings strongly suggest that serotonin and NE act in opposition to each other in the short-term regulation of feeding.

NE is also known to specifically increase carbohydrate ingestion and perhaps decrease protein ingestion. Does serotonin decrease carbohydrate ingestion and increase protein ingestion as one would expect if these systems worked in opposition? The review by Leibowitz et al. (1988), as well as numerous later studies (e.g., Luo & Li, 1990), suggests that this is indeed the case. An article by Fernstrom (1987) and the accompanying commentaries (e.g., Blundell & Hill, 1987; Booth, 1987; Peters & Harper, 1987), however, indicate that the role of serotonin in macronutrient selection is far from resolved, particularly with regard to protein ingestion.

This raises an important general question, however. When would an animal be expected to regulate protein ingestion? As Fernstrom (1987) suggests, it may only be in times when the animal is experiencing an actual protein deficiency. But there are good reasons to regulate carbohydrate ingestion from a meal-to-meal, day-to-day basis, because this provides the most readily available source of energy. The short-term regulation of fat intake also seems unnecessary. Thus, a model in which NE is proposed to increase food intake, and specifically carbohydrate ingestion, but in which serotonin is seen as a more general inhibitor of feeding is simple but may approximate the roles played by these two neurotransmitters.

Another important question concerns what aspects of feeding (or a lack thereof) lead to the release of these two neurotransmitters. This too is a matter of debate. For the purposes of this review, it seems safe to assume that signals from the liver, and perhaps the CNS, regarding nutrient levels are eventually translated into changes in NE and serotonin release that act through the PVN and other brain areas to alter food intake. Naturally, a number of other factors (e.g., hormones, peptides, environment) can modify these messages through direct and indirect actions.

Sex Steroids. The influence of sex steroids (specifically, 17β-estradiol, progesterone, testosterone) on food intake has been well documented for the rat and hamster, with little information available for the gerbil. Perhaps because the rat is not an avid hoarder of food, studies examining the effects of sex steroids on hoarding have generally employed the hamster. Unfortunately, there are relatively few studies of this nature. The consequence is that we do not have a very complete understanding of the role sex steroids play in the regulation of hoarding as it relates to food intake. Nonetheless, we do have a respectable understanding of the role sex steroids play in regulating food intake in the rat.

Estrogens. The effects of 17β-estradiol benzoate (EB) on food intake and body weight is sex and species dependent. Ovariectomy increases and treatment with EB decreases both food intake and body weight in the female rat (e.g., Gentry & Wade, 1976a; Landau & Zucker, 1976; McElroy & Wade, 1987; Tarttelin & Gorski, 1973; Wade, 1975), mouse (Blaustein, Gentry, Roy, & Wade, 1976; Wright & Turner, 1973), and guinea pig (Czaja, 1984; Czaja & Goy, 1975). EB has a less pronounced effect in male rats and guinea pigs (e.g., Czaja, 1984; Gentry & Wade, 1976a). Early research using the female golden (Syrian) hamster suggested that the effects of EB on food intake and body weight were similar to, but less pronounced than, those observed in the rat, mouse, and guinea pig (Gerall & Thiel, 1975; Miceli & Fleming, 1983; Morin & Fleming, 1978). More recent research suggests that though EB produces only mild effects on food intake and body weight in the golden hamster, EB given in conjunction with P produces an increase in food intake and a pronounced increase in body weight (Schneider, Palmer, & Wade, 1986). Thus, the effect of EB is similar to that observed in rats, mice, and guinea pigs, but the action of P with EB goes beyond a simple attenuation of estradiol's anorectic effect. EB has no significant effect in the male hamster (Kowaleski, 1969; Zucker, Wade, & Ziegler, 1972).

In the Mongolian gerbil, effects opposite to those seen in the rat are observed. Ovariectomy decreases food intake and body weight in female gerbils (Raible & Gorzalka, 1985), while EB increases food intake and body weight in both male (Raible & Gorzalka, 1985) and female gerbils (Maass & Wade, 1977; Raible & Gorzalka, 1985). It is worth noting that in both the rat and the gerbil, the antiestrogen MER-25 acts like estrogen, decreasing food intake in the rat (Roy & Wade, 1976) and increasing it in the gerbil (Roy, Maass, & Wade, 1977). As with the rat, the effects in the male gerbil are less pronounced than those observed in the female gerbil (Raible & Gorzalka, 1985). Thus, estrogen would appear to exert opposite effects on food intake in the rat and the gerbil, while exerting relatively weak effects in the golden hamster. Effects in the mouse and guinea pig appear similar to those observed in the rat.

Although Kanarek and Beck (1980) found that macronutrient selection was not significantly altered by ovariectomy, others (e.g., Bartness & Waldbillig, 1984; Wurtman & Baum, 1980) have found macronutrient selection to be influenced by ovariectomy, EB treatment, and the estrous cycle. Specifically, ovariectomy led to the selection of a more calorically dense diet, while EB treatment attenuated this effect. Furthermore, ovariectomy increased the consumption of protein and carbohydrate while decreasing the consumption of fat, while estradiol exerted the opposite effects (Bartness & Waldbillig, 1984). Thus, suppressant effects of estradiol on food intake and body weight in the female rat may specifically reflect a decreased consumption of carbohydrates. Increases in fat consumption in response to estradiol may well decrease the weight-reducing effects of reduced carbohydrate consumption. Given some of the parallels between the effects of EB and the effects of serotonin of food intake, it is possible that EB-induced changes in feeding are mediated, at least in part, through the serotonergic system.

Ovarian steroid-induced changes in body weight may not be due entirely to changes in food intake. In the rat, gerbil, and golden hamster, EB and/or P can influence body weight even without changes in food intake (Hervey & Hervey, 1968; Landau & Zucker, 1976; Raible & Gorzalka, 1985; Roy & Wade, 1977; Schneider et al., 1986), suggesting a metabolic action. Furthermore, although 17β-estradiol decreases both food intake and body weight in rats, 17α-estradiol has been found to decrease food intake without altering body weight (Donohoe, Stevens, Johnson, & Barker, 1984). Kanarek and Beck (1980) found that ovariectomized rats gained almost twice as much weight per kilocalorie consumed as did their sham-operated counterparts. Some of these metabolic actions of ovarian steroids may reflect a regulatory action on fat stores and energy utilization more than they reflect a regulatory action on short-term food intake and body weight. Indeed, it has been suggested (e.g., Fantino & Brinnel, 1986; Redick, Nussbaum, & Mook, 1973) that the modification of food intake produced by estradiol is a consequence of an estradiol-induced decrease in defended body weight, and that estradiol shifts the regulation of feeding to long-term factors (e.g., Nance & Gorski, 1977; Sieck et al., 1978).

Wade and others (e.g., Bartness & Wade, 1984; Edens & Wade, 1983; Galletti & Klopper, 1964; Leshner & Collier, 1973; Wade & Bartness, 1984; Wade & Gray, 1979) have investigated the effects of estradiol on brown adipose tissue (BAT) thermogenesis and deposition. Data indicate that in species where EB decreases food intake and body weight, EB decreases carcass fat content by increasing BAT thermogenesis (e.g., Bartness & Wade, 1984; Edens & Wade, 1983; Wade & Gray, 1979). Furthermore, the bilateral denervation of interscapular BAT eliminates EB-induced increases in interscapular BAT thermogenesis and leads to weight gain (Bartness & Wade, 1984). This suggests that the weight-reducing effects of EB may be due to increases in BAT thermogenesis as well as to decreases in food intake. The effects of estradiol on food intake may be of greatest importance in the short-term regulation of food intake, with the effects of estradiol on BAT thermogenesis being most relevant to the long-term regulation of fat stores.

By what mechanisms might estrogens act to alter food intake in a relatively short-term fashion? Implants of EB into areas such as the VMH and PVN of rats and guinea pigs suppress food intake (Beatty, O'Briant, & Vilberg, 1974; Butera & Czaja, 1984; Nunez, Gray, & Wade, 1980; Wade & Zucker, 1970). Given the roles of neurotransmitters such as NE and serotonin on food intake, and the findings that hormones can influence neurotransmitters and vice versa (e.g., Blaustein & Letcher, 1987; Blaustein & Turcotte, 1987; Luine & Rhodes, 1983; Renner, Gerhardt, & Quadagno, 1984; Sar & Stumpf, 1981; Wise, Rance, & Barraclough, 1981), one mechanism by which estrogen could alter food intake is through estrogen-induced changes in neurotransmitter activity or in neurotransmitter receptors. For example, Simpson and Dicara (1973) suggested that EB inhibited food intake in the rat by decreasing the activity of dopamine-β-hydroxylase, thereby interfering with the conversion of DA to NE. As NE normally increases food intake, this could result in a relative decrease in feeding. Their finding that DA increased eating only when levels of estradiol or EB were low (i.e., the DA could be converted to NE) supports their proposal. It is also possible that EB decreases food intake via an interaction with the opiate system. This possibility is discussed in the section on opiates and feeding.

Although there is a fair amount of evidence that α-noradrenergic activity may regulate the level of estrogen receptors (e.g., Blaustein, 1986; Blaustein & Letcher, 1986), there is less information on how estradiol might alter NE activity or NE receptors, particularly α_2-noradrenergic receptors. Research in these areas would provide valuable information on the mechanisms by which both NE and estradiol influence feeding behaviors. Furthermore, an investigation of these relationships in nonrat rodent species is essential to the understanding of feeding behavior. For example, the facilitatory action of EB on food intake in the gerbil may reflect a difference in the action of EB on the noradrenergic feeding system, or it may reflect a difference in the action of NE on feeding. The weaker action of EB on food intake in the golden hamster could reflect several species differences: a reduced influence of estrogen on NE activity or receptors, a reduced influence of NE on food intake, and/or an increased importance of androgenic actions on NE or other neurotransmitters.

If EB influences food intake, might it not also influence the amount of food hoarded? Research using female rats generally indicates that, like food intake, hoarding decreases in response to estradiol (e.g., Coling & Herberg, 1982; Fantino & Brinnel, 1986; Herberg, Pye, & Blundell, 1972; but see Donohoe et al., 1984). This decrease may be due to the same mechanisms that act to inhibit food intake, or it may be a natural consequence of a reduction in defended body weight. Food deprivation induces hoarding in male rats and increases hoarding in female rats (e.g., Blundell & Herberg, 1973; Morgan, Stellar, & Johnson, 1943), presumably because hoarded food provides the rat with a buffer against future deprivation. If estradiol does decrease defended body weight in the female rat, then the relative state of deprivation would also decrease during EB treatment, discouraging hoarding behavior.

Data on the effects of EB on hoarding in the golden hamster and the gerbil are relatively scarce. In the female golden hamster, the high level of hoarding and the weak effects of EB on food intake may make any effects of EB on hoarding difficult to detect. One would predict, however, that effects would be similar to, but less pronounced than, effects observed in the female rat. The lower level of hoarding in the female gerbil, and the facilitatory action of EB on food intake in this species, suggests that EB would facilitate hoarding and that this should be detectable. Wong and Raible (unpublished observations) were unable to confirm this prediction.

Given the potential interaction between estradiol and NE in the regulation of food intake in the rat, it seems reasonable to ask if this same system plays a role in hoarding behavior. At the present time, this question cannot be answered. Research in this area could help us determine if food intake and hoarding behavior are regulated by the same or by different mechanisms. Strong evidence for a shared system of regulation would be gained if it were found that virtually all manipulations that alter food intake alter hoarding in a similar direction. Evidence that one can be significantly altered without the alteration of the other could indicate independent regulation. At present, it seems that the hamster or gerbil would be the most appropriate species for such investigations because the rat is not a strong hoarder.

Progesterone and estrogen plus progesterone. In most rodent species tested, the administration of progesterone (P) in the absence of EB produces no significant effect on food intake or body weight (Blaustein & Wade, 1977; Czaja & Goy, 1975; Galletti & Klopper, 1964; Hervey & Hervey, 1967; Ross & Zucker, 1974; Wade, 1975). One possible exception to this is the Mongolian gerbil. Raible and Gorzalka (1985) found that in gonadectomized male and female gerbils, P may decrease body weight without substantially altering food intake, implying a metabolic action of P in this species. Maass and Wade (1977), however, did not observe any P-induced alterations in food intake or body weight in ovariectomized gerbils. Differences in experimental design might account for the contrasting results of these studies. Further investigation would serve to clarify the role of P in the regulation of food intake and body weight in this species.

In contrast to the lack of effects seen when P is administered alone, P administered in conjunction with estradiol can alter food intake and body weight. In the rat (e.g., Gentry & Wade, 1976a; Roberts, Kenny, & Mook, 1972; Wade, 1975), the administration of P in conjunction with EB attenuates the suppressant effects of EB on food intake and body weight. In the female golden hamster, the administration of P with EB not only abolishes the anorectic action of EB on food intake and body weight, it also stimulates food intake and weight gain (Schneider et al., 1986). In the gerbil (Maass & Wade, 1977; Raible & Gorzalka, 1985), the administration of P in conjunction with EB appears to enhance the stimulatory action of EB on food intake and body weight in the female. This was not observed in the male, where the effects on food intake of EB, P, or EB plus P appeared to be the same (Raible & Gorzalka, 1985).

These findings present us with very different and species-dependent actions of P, particularly in the female: In the rat, P appears to have little effect on its own but serves to block the inhibitory actions of EB on food intake and body weight. In the golden hamster, P blocks the action of EB and may have strong metabolic effects. In the gerbil, P enhances the actions of EB on food intake and body weight and may alter body weight through metabolic change. These contrasting effects imply that the mechanisms through which EB and P produce their actions may be quite different in these species, perhaps due to evolutionary changes associated with their habitat. Because little is known about neurotransmitter–hormone interactions within rodents other than the rat, discussions of possible mechanisms of progesterone action will focus on the rat.

One possible mechanism by which P may act to block the action of EB on food intake and body weight in the rat is by inhibiting the activation of the α_2-noradrenergic system by estradiol. The finding that P alone has no effect on food intake and body weight suggests that the observed effects are dependent upon the presence of estrogens. Thus, the effects may be mediated by estrogen-induced progestin receptors. The work of Blaustein & Turcotte (1988) indicates that, at least within the regions of the hypothalamus studied, estrogen-induced progestin receptors occur only within neurons also containing estrogen receptors. Thus, it is possible that the binding of progesterone to progestin receptors blocks or reverses the neuronal changes produced by the binding of estradiol to estrogen receptors. This, in turn, attenuates estradiol-induced decreases in food intake.

In species such as the gerbil, this is clearly not the case. P alone may activate systems that increase metabolic rate. Furthermore, P appears to facilitate the action of EB on food intake. As with estradiol alone, these species differences may reflect differences in the effects of P on neurotransmitters important to food intake and body weight, or they could reflect differences in the action of the neurotransmitter itself. It is also possible that the interaction between estradiol and P is different from that observed in the rat. The gerbil is much more dependent on the presence of P from induction of maximal receptivity than is the rat (Raible & Gorzalka, 1985, 1986). These species differences in hormonal sensitivity may be reflected in many behaviors influenced by ovarian hormones, including food intake and body weight.

Androgens. In male rats and guinea pigs, castration results in increased food intake and body weight, while the administration of moderate doses of testosterone propionate (TP) reduces food intake and body weight to precastration levels (Czaja, 1984; Gentry & Wade, 1976b; Kakolewski, Cox, & Valenstein, 1968). In male rats, it has been found that 5α-dihydrotestosterone (DHT), DHT propionate (DHTP), and androstenedione (AD) have less pronounced attenuating effects on castration-induced increases in food intake and body weight (Gentry & Wade, 1976b; Rowland, Perrings, & Thommes, 1980). It is of interest to note that high doses of TP can reduce food intake and body weight below precastration levels, an effect that has been attributed to estradiol derived from testosterone (Gentry & Wade, 1976b; Wade, 1976). The findings (Gentry & Wade, 1976b) that P can attenuate the inhibitory effects on food intake and body weight of high doses of TP and that high doses of DHTP do not inhibit food intake further support this hypothesis. It should be noted that female rats and guinea pigs also show increased food intake and weight in response to TP and DHT injections. In general, however, these effects appear less pronounced that those observed in males or after treatment of females with EB (Czaja, 1984; and see Wade, 1976, for a review).

Unlike the decrease in food intake and body weight seen after castration in the rat and guinea pig, increases in food intake and body weight are seen after castration in the golden hamster (Kowaleski, 1969; Zucker et al., 1972). These increases in food intake and body weight can be attenuated by the administration of TP (Kowaleski, 1969; Zucker et al., 1972). The male gerbil also shows an increase in body weight after castration; however, this is not immediately accompanied by a significant increase in food intake (Maass & Wade, 1977; Raible & Gorzalka, 1985). Castration was found to significantly increase hoarding behavior in the male gerbil (Nyby, Wallace, Owen, & Thiessen, 1973). The administration to castrated male gerbils of TP or DHTP did not produce any significant effects on food intake or body weight, although the withdrawal of these treatments produced the same facilitatory effects as did the initial castration (Maass & Wade, 1977). This facilitatory effect of steroid withdrawal on food intake and body weight in male gerbils was also seen after the cessation of treatment with ovarian steroids (Raible & Gorzalka, 1985). Thus, castration may produce more gradual changes in food intake and body weight in this species than it does in the rat and hamster. The administration of TP was found to reduce hoarding in castrated male gerbils (Nyby et al., 1973).

It is clear from the relative paucity of studies examining the role of androgens on food intake that further work is needed in this area. If we hope to integrate knowledge about hormone–neurotransmitter interactions with knowledge of food intake and hoarding patterns, the hamster or gerbil again seems to offer the greatest latitude for integration.

Peptides That Increase Food Intake

Opioids. Before the discovery of endorphins and enkephalins, research had indicated that morphine altered feeding behavior (Barbour, Gregg, & Hunter, 1930; Flowers, Dunham, & Barbour, 1929). Since that time, the administration of β-endorphin has been shown to increase food intake (Grandison & Guidotti, 1977). Numerous additional studies (e.g., Jaloweic, Panksepp, Zolovick, Najam, & Herman, 1981; Kirkham & Blundell, 1987; Lowy, Maickel, & Yim, 1980; McLaughlin & Baile, 1984; Morley, Levine, Murray, & Kneip, 1982; Robert, Orosco, Rouch, Jacquot, & Cohen, 1989) have demonstrated that the administration of opioid antagonists such as naloxone and naltrexone decrease food intake under a variety of conditions in a variety of species. The role of opiates in reward mechanisms of the brain suggests that opiates may play a particularly important role in the motivational/rewarding aspects of eating.

It should be noted that some rodent species do not show a suppression of feeding in response to the administration of opioid blockers. For example, although opiate antagonists suppress food intake in rats, mice, and the Siberian hamster, they fail to significantly alter food intake in the golden hamster or the Chinese hamster (Levine, Morley, Gosnell, Billington, & Bartness, 1985). After reviewing information on seasonal feeders, hibernators, and species with relatively stable food intake throughout the year, Levine, Morley, Gosnell et al. (1985) conclude that there is no single and simple explanation that accounts for the varied degree of food intake suppression in response to opiate blockers that is seen in different species. However, some of the species differences may reflect differences in metabolic rate. Levine, Morley, Gosnell et al. (1985) noted that opioid antagonists were usually, but not always, less effective in species with high energy demands than in those with low energy demands.

In the rodent species where opioids do suppress food intake, research indicates that both peripherally and centrally administered opioid agonists and antagonists influence food intake by acting within the CNS (Levine, Morley, Gosnell et al., 1985). Indeed, opiate agonists (e.g., β-endorphin, D-Ala-metenkephalinamide) administered to the VMH, PVN, and LH increase food intake (e.g., Leibowitz & Hor, 1982; McLean & Hoebel, 1982, 1983; Stanley, Lanthier, & Leibowitz, 1984) while naloxone to the PVN and VMH decreases food intake (e.g., Gosnell, Morley, & Levine, 1984). Studies utilizing lesions combined with naloxone or ketocyclazocine administration further suggest that both hypothalamic and nonhypothalamic sites (e.g., globus pallidus, striatum) are important to opioid-induced changes in food intake (see Levine, Morley, Gosnell et al., 1985, for a review). Although nonhypothalamic sites in the basal ganglia may be involved in regulating food intake per se, it seems more likely that they are involved in the production of the motor movements necessary for feeding.

Opioids have several types of receptors within the CNS, and it appears that at least two may play an important role in food intake. The effects of opioids on feeding appear to be greatest with drugs that act on kappa receptors (see Levine, Morley, Gosnell et al., 1985, for a review). Sigma receptors also appear important, while mu and epsilon receptors appear to play less important or indirect roles (Levine, Morley, Gosnell et al., 1985).

If opioids play an important role in modulating food intake, there should be specific, feeding-related signals that activate relevant branches of the opioid feeding system. Research suggests that glucose levels may alter β-endorphin levels and/or opioid receptors. Hypoglycemic and diabetic rats and mice show many signs, such as increased tail-flick latencies (e.g., Levine, Morley, Wilcox, Brown, & Handwerger, 1982) and decreased sensitivity to the antinociceptive effects of morphine (e.g., Simon & Dewey, 1981), indicative of elevated levels of endogenous opiates. In addition, during normal feeding and during feeding induced by deprivation, or insulin or 2-deoxy-D-glucose (2-DG) injection in the rat, plasma β-endorphin levels are also elevated (Davis, Lowy, Yim, Lamb, & Malven, 1983). Furthermore, naloxone can suppress food intake in response to an injection of 2-DG (Lowy et al., 1980; Ostrowski, Rowland, Foley, Nelson, & Reid, 1981; Sewell, & Jawaharlal, 1980). This research suggests that glucoprivic feeding may be mediated, in part, by the opioid system. The relationship may not be as simple as suggested by preliminary results, however. For example, it is not clear that naloxone suppresses feeding in response to insulin-induced hypoglycemia (see Levine & Morley, 1981a; Rowland & Bartness, 1982). Furthermore, opioids may exert their effects on food intake via the dopaminergic and/or serotonergic system, though the role of these neurotransmitters in opioid-induced feeding may depend on the rat's fat stores (see, for example, Robert et al., 1989). It also appears that an animal's environment may further modify feeding behavior modulated by glucose-opioid interactions (e.g., Levine, Morley, Kneip, Grace, & Brown, 1985; Rowland & Bartness, 1982). Finally, some research (e.g., Marks-Kaufman & Kanarek, 1980) suggests that opiates may act specifically to regulate fat and carbohydrate intake. Further research is needed to explore these possible effects and the interrelationship(s) of palatability, insulin/glucose levels, the opioid and reward systems, the environment, and food intake.

A further factor complicating our understanding of the role of opioids in modulating food intake comes from evidence that sex steroids can regulate both opioid production and opioid receptors within the CNS (e.g., Dupont et al., 1980; Hahn & Fishman, 1979; Lee, Panerai, Bellabara, & Friesen, 1980; Wardlaw, Wang, & Frantz, 1985). Indeed, in the rat chronic estradiol treatment lowers hypothalamic β-endorphin content (Wardlaw et al., 1985), a finding consonant with the suppressant action of EB on food intake in this species. Research also indicates that chronic estradiol treatment results in rats that are less sensitive to the suppressant action of naloxone on food intake (Morley, Levine, Grace, Kneip, & Gosnell, 1984), suggesting that the suppressant action of estradiol on food intake may be mediated through a decrease in opiate receptor sensitivity or a decrease in circulating endogenous opiates.

If, in the female rat, EB decreases food intake by decreasing opiate receptor concentrations, opiate sensitivity, and/or opiate production and release, does EB increase food intake in the gerbil by doing the opposite? To the best of my knowledge, studies examining the role of opiates in feeding in gerbils have not been published. A few such studies have been done in the golden hamster, however. Recall that in the golden hamster, androgens appear to play a more important role than estrogens in the regulation of feeding. Of interest is the finding that naloxone does not affect food intake in this species (Lowy & Yim, 1982, 1983). Could the weak effect of EB in the golden hamster reflect the weak role of the opioid system in the regulation of feeding in this species? Is this because androgens, rather than estrogens, are the sex hormone most important to changes in food intake in the hamster? Are some of the gender differences in food intake due to gender differences in estrogen and androgen levels and the effects that this has on the opioid system? A partial answer to these questions might be gained by further study of hormonal and opioid effects on food intake in the Siberian hamster, which does decrease food intake in response to opiate antagonists, and the Chinese hamster, which is insensitive to opiates (Levine, Morley, Gosnell et al., 1985).

The potential role of opioids in mediating the effects of estradiol on food intake in rats also suggests that this relationship should be examined in the female gerbil (and in the male, which shows no clear changes in food intake in response to sex steroids). Research is needed to determine if changes in opioid activity alter food intake in the gerbil and, if so, whether sex steroids can act through such a mechanism to alter food intake. The answers to these questions will certainly help to clarify the role of opiates in feeding.

Neuropeptide Y. Neuropeptide Y (NPY) is found in high concentrations within the rat CNS, particularly the hypothalamus (Allen et al., 1983; Emson & DeQuidt, 1984; Wahlestedt et al., 1987) and has a large concentration of binding sites within the PVN (Martel, St. Pierre, & Quirion, 1986). Peripheral injections of NPY are without effect on food intake; however, injections of NPY to the third ventricle (Clark, Kalra, Crowley, & Kalra, 1984) or to the VMH, LH, and PVN (Morley et al., 1985; Stanley & Leibowitz, 1984; Stanley, 1985a, Chin, & Leibowitz, 1985; Stanley, Daniel et al., 1985) produce a strong increase in food intake in both male (e.g., Morley & Levine, 1984, 1985) and female rats (Clark et al., 1984). This effect can last for over 4 hr (Morley et al., 1985; Tempel, Nicholas, & Leibowitz, 1988) and is seen most strongly during nighttime feeding, although daytime feeding is also increased (Morley et al., 1985; Tempel et al., 1988). NPY appears to increase food intake by increasing both the speed and the duration of feeding (Clark, Kalra, & Kalra, 1985; Stanley & Leibowitz, 1984).

When several macronutrients (i.e., fat, carbohydrate, and protein) are made available, NPY appears to specifically increase carbohydrate ingestion (Morley, Levine, Gosnell, Kneip, & Grace, 1987; Stanley, Daniel et al., 1985). NPY also appears to stimulate the release of corticosterone (and insulin and vasopressin) (Wahlestedt et al., 1987), which plays an important role in carbohydrate, and thus glucose, metabolism. More detailed information about NPY, corticosterone, insulin, vasopressin, glucose, and NE interactions in the regulation of feeding can be found in an excellent summary by Leibowitz (1990). What the information suggests is that NPY is part of a system designed to initiate carbohydrate ingestion and regulate carbohydrate storage and metabolism. This system clearly comes into play in short-term regulation and, as indicated earlier, the NPY component of this system may play a particularly important role during times of extreme deprivation.

Peptides That Decrease Food Intake. Before embarking on a discussion of peptides decreasing food intake, it is necessary to discuss the difficulty in separating issues of satiety, palatability, and illness. Of these possible contributors to decreased food intake, illness is the easiest to test for. For the purposes of this review, substances known to produce conditioned taste aversions have been assumed to decrease food intake predominantly through this mechanism and will not be discussed. Determining if decreases in food intake are due to decreases in palatability and to satiety is a more difficult problem. Indeed, palatability changes with satiety—the Key lime pie that was highly palatable before ingestion may become quite unpalatable as its consumption nears completion. The fact that animals will become sated with one flavor but consume a new flavor, if offered, also indicates that satiety and palatability are interrelated. In fact, a decrease in palatability may be one of the mechanisms involved in producing satiety. For this reason, changes in preference that are presumed to reflect changes in palatability are also assumed to reflect changes in satiety.

Cholecystokinin. Since the finding that cholecystokinin (CCK) produces behavioral signs of satiety (Antin, Gibbs, Holt, Young, & Smith, 1975; Gibbs, Young, & Smith, 1973a), a great deal of research has been conducted in an effort to elucidate the nature of this effect. Both peripherally (e.g., Ettinger, Thompson, & Staddon, 1986; Maddison, 1977; Smith et al., 1989; VanderWeele, Oetting, Jones, & Deems, 1985) and centrally (e.g., Maddison, 1977; McCaleb & Myers, 1980) administered CCK inhibit feeding and, as might be expected, they appear to do so through different mechanisms.

Studies of the centrally mediated inhibitory effect of CCK (and CCK-8, which is often the peptide actually used in CCK studies) on food intake have probably yielded the clearest results. When injected into the PVN, CCK-8 has been found to inhibit food intake in a dose-dependent fashion (e.g., McCaleb & Myers, 1980). It should be noted that others (e.g., Mori, Nagai, Nakagawa, & Yanaihara, 1986) have found that CCK-8, when injected into the VMH, did not inhibit food intake in free-feeding rats. These investigators did find that the administration of CCK-8 analogs to the VMH did suppress feeding (e.g., Thibault, Nagai, Hashida, Yanaihara, & Nakagawa, 1990; Mori et al., 1986). Furthermore, the majority of evidence indicates that CCK and its analogs inhibit feeding. Thus, the question has become, How does it do so?

The ability of CCK administered to the PVN (and VMH) to inhibit feeding suggests that CCK is part of the system that relays information from glucorecep-tors within the PVN (and VMH) to the DMNV, which in turn influences glucose levels by regulating insulin and glucagon secretion by the pancreas. The sugges-tion that CCK ties into this system is supported by research indicating that CCK inhibits tail-pinch-induced eating by producing hyperglycemia (Levine & Morley, 1981b). This hyperglycemia is probably mediated by the PVN-pancreatic axis and may involve the antagonism of opioids that are released in response to tail pinch. These opioids appear to be responsible for the eating observed in the tail-pinch paradigm (Morley & Levine, 1980). That CCK could antagonize opioid effects is supported by previous research indicating CCK can antagonize the analgesic ac-tions of opioids (Faris, Komisaruk, Watkins, & Mayer, 1983). Thus, centrally ad-ministered CCK may act in opposition to opioids, which normally increase food intake. These findings also suggest that CCK may work with the opioid system in the modulation of glucose levels. This modulation may involve regulating the ac-tivity within the PVN-pancreatic axis.

Research suggests that the effects of CNS CCK may be macronutrient spe-cific. Thibault et al. (1990) found that the administration of a CCK-8 analogue to the VMH led to a specific suppression of carbohydrate intake with a lesser sup-pression of lipid intake. The work of Leibowitz and co-workers (e.g., Leibowitz et al., 1985) suggests that increases in PVN NE specifically stimulate the ingestion of carbohydrates. Thus, centrally administered CCK may decrease carbohydrate intake by decreasing PVN NE activity as well as by opposing the effects of opi-ates on food intake. It would certainly be of interest to determine if central CCK administration alters NE activity in the PVN. To the best of my knowledge, this has not been been determined.

Peripherally administered CCK-8 clearly inhibits food intake and appears to do so by altering palatability/satiety rather than by inducing illness (e.g., Ettinger et al., 1986; Gibbs, Young, & Smith, 1973b; VanderWeele, Deems, & Gibbs, 1984; VanderWeele et al., 1985; West, Greenwood, Marshall, & Woods, 1987). Further-more, as with CNS CCK, the effects of peripherally administered CCK-8 may be macronutrient specific. Avery and Livosky (1986) found that single injections of 6, 9, or 12 µg/kg of CCK-8 (approximately) decreased fat ingestion, with the two higher doses also decreasing protein ingestion. VanderWeele and co-workers (1984, 1985) found that three injections of 4 µg/kg of CCK-8 spaced 90 min apart significantly reduced the intake of fats and carbohydrates. It might be argued that any substance that inhibits food intake will decrease carbohydrate and fat con-sumption; however, LiCl and bombesin appear to decrease food intake by de-creasing the intake of proteins (Avery & Livosky, 1986; Vanderweele et al., 1984, 1985). Furthermore, a review of the literature (and the effects of presumed non-physiological doses of peptides) suggests that illness may inhibit the ingestion of protein more easily than the ingestion of fats or carbohydrates, an occurrence also noted by Bernstein, Goehler, and Fenner (1984) and VanderWeele et al. (1985). Given the results of Liebowitz et al. (1985), Thibault et al. (1990), and Vander-Weele et al. (1984, 1985), it seems reasonable to suggest that one action of peripherally administered CCK is the inhibition of carbohydrate ingestion, with a potential additional action on fat ingestion.

The mechanisms by which peripherally administered CCK-8 decreases food intake are not entirely clear. It appears that peripherally administered CCK-8 can decrease feeding by causing the constriction of the pyloric sphincter leading from the stomach to the small intestine (Moran & McHugh, 1982). This could explain why CCK decreases meal size (West et al., 1987). It is difficult to see, however, how constriction of the pyloric sphincter would specifically affect carbohydrate and fat ingestion, but not protein ingestion. Nutrient-specific effects may, instead, be the result of CCK activating ascending vagal fibers.

Research (Garlicki, Konturek, Majka, Kwiecien, & Konturek, 1990) utilizing peripheral injections of .5–10 nmol/kg CCK-8 15 min before feeding indicated a dose-dependent suppression of feeding that could be abolished by vagotomy at all but the highest dose (which probably induced illness). Vagotomy also abolished the facilitation of food intake observed after the administration of the CCK receptor antagonist L-364,718 (Garlicki et al., 1990). These findings suggest that if CCK induces satiety to specific macronutrients, it may do so via ascending vagal fibers. This raises the possibility that CCK is released in response to the presence of specific macronutrients (i.e., carbohydrates and possibly fats). This possibility gains some strength from the finding that CCK receptors are located in pancreatic tissue (e.g., Philpott & Petersen, 1979). Endogenous CCK increases the release of pancreatic amylase, lipase, and nucleases in response to a meal, a response blocked by antibodies to CCK-8 (Reidelberger, Liehr, Varga, Wong, & Walsh, 1990). It is possible that it is macronutrients released by these enzymes that activate vagal afferents, leading to satiety for these macronutrients, but this does not seem to explain why injected CCK decreases ingestion of specific macronutrients and does so at meal *onset.*

If CCK activation of vagal fibers is one mechanism by which CCK decreases food intake, then endogenous CCK, released in response to appropriate stimuli, should also decrease food intake. Smith et al. (1989) used soybean trypsin inhibitor (STI) to induce CCK release in food-deprived rats and found that although there was up to a ninefold increase in plasma CCK, there was no decrease in food intake or gastric emptying. This contrasts with the findings of Garlicki et al. (1990). These investigators used an equivalent or smaller dose of STI (or a food preload) to stimulate CCK release in food deprived rats. Their data indicated at least a twelvefold (sixfold with the food preload) increase in plasma CCK and significant decreases in food intake. It is difficult to fully account for the contrasting findings of these two research groups. The results of Reidelberger and O'Rourke (1989) suggest that the use of food-deprived rats for such studies could mask effects of interest. Given the pronounced and well-documented effects of peripherally administered CCK on food intake, it seems likely that endogenous, intestinal CCK serves some inhibitory function. Perhaps the extraneous effects of food deprivation simply masked these actions in the Smith et al. (1989) study. Further investigations should clarify this issue.

To summarize, research utilizing CCK indicates that both central and peripheral administration of CCK decreases food intake, although by different means. Central CCK may decrease food intake by opposing NE and/or opioid activity, perhaps in the LH, VMH, or PVN. Further investigation of CCK–opioid and CCK–NE interactions within the hypothalamus could provide valuable information about the CNS mechanisms through which CCK influences food intake. Peripheral CCK may decrease food intake by slowing stomach emptying and by activating vagal afferents. The possible role of vagal afferents in modulating other CNS factors involved in feeding also warrants investigation.

Bombesin. In 1979, Gibbs et al. reported that peripherally administered bombesin (BBS) inhibited feeding in rats. This finding was quickly verified by other researchers for both peripheral (e.g., Kulkosky, Gibbs, & Smith, 1982; Stein & Woods, 1981) and central injections of BBS (e.g., ventricles—Avery & Calisher, 1982; Flynn, 1989; Morley & Levine, 1981; LH—Stuckey & Gibbs, 1982; PVN, VMH—Kyrkouli, Stanley, & Leibowitz, 1984). Like CCK, the suppressant effects of BBS may be macronutrient specific. VanderWeele et al. (1985) found that BBS (3 injections of 4 or 8 μg/kg given 90 min apart) predominantly inhibited protein intake, although fat intake was also decreased in animals receiving the higher dose of BBS. Avery and Livosky (1986) found that BBS (approximately 24, 40, 56, or 64 μg/kg) had a rapid (30 min) inhibitory effect on fat ingestion and a somewhat slower (60 min) inhibitory effect on protein intake. Thus, it appears that BBS may act primarily to decrease protein ingestion, with a weaker action on fat ingestion.

The nature of the effects of centrally and peripherally administered BBS on feeding, as well as the mechanisms mediating these effects, has received relatively little attention. That peripherally administered BBS appears to inhibit feeding primarily by suppressing protein intake leads one to question if the effect of peripherally administered BBS is truly specific or if it is producing a general malaise that is inhibiting protein intake. The answer to this question remains unclear; however, there appear to be mechanisms in place in the periphery through which BBS could act to alter food intake.

Peripheral BBS can cause the release of CCK from the gut (Banks, 1980; Konturek, Krol, & Tasler, 1976). Furthermore, the CCK receptor antagonist L-364718 can partially block the suppressant action of BBS, suggesting that the BBS-induced release of CCK is responsible for some of the inhibition of food intake that is observed (Garlicki et al., 1990). L-364718, however, did not completely block the suppressant effects of bombesin. This, as well as the somewhat different effects of BBS and CCK on macronutrient selection, suggests some independence in effects.

Like CCK, BBS has a stimulatory effect on pancreatic secretions; but this action of BBS appears to be produced by the binding of BBS to receptors on pancreatic cells rather than to a BBS-induced release of CCK (Dembinski, Jaworek, Konturek, Konturek, & Warzecha, 1989; Garlicki et al., 1990; Philpott & Petersen,

1979; Wisnar, Ozawa, & Renner, 1988). As with CCK, the release of pancreatic enzymes may play a role in the inhibition of food intake by BBS. Stuckey, Gibbs, and Smith (1985) found that BBS-induced decreases in meal size were blocked by peripheral deafferation (although extended intermeal intervals were not). This suggests that BBS-induced decreases in meal size are related to specific visceral signals, perhaps dependent upon macronutrient levels in the gut. The role of BBS in the regulation of feeding remains unclear. The inhibitory effects of both peripheral and central BBS administration on feeding, however, indicate that further investigation is warranted.

Corticotropin releasing factor. Although peripherally administered corticotropin releasing factor (CRF) decreases food intake, this effect may be due to general malaise (Gosnell, Morley, & Levine, 1983). Centrally administered CRF also inhibits feeding and may do so by binding to receptors in the PVN (Insel et al., 1984), thereby increasing the firing rate of cells within the PVN (Morley et al., 1985). Presumably, this increase in PVN activity would then inhibit firing in the DMNV, thereby decreasing food intake. Recall that the administration of NE to the PVN has the opposite effect; NE decreases PVN firing and, ultimately, increases food intake (e.g., Leibowitz, 1978; Leibowitz & Hor, 1982). Could CRF inhibit feeding by blocking this action of NE?

Morley et al. (1985) report that the administration of CRF to the PVN can block increases in food intake produced by the administration of NE to this region (Morley et al., 1985). Furthermore, these investigators also report that CRF specifically inhibits the ingestion of carbohydrates (Morley et al., 1985) while NE facilitates ingestion of carbohydrates (Leibowitz et al., 1985; Morley et al., 1987). Thus, endogenous, central CRF may act directly through its receptors in the PVN to block the stimulatory effects of NE on food intake, particularly carbohydrate intake.

Morley et al. (1985) provide another possible link in this chain of events. They point out that Buckingham (1980) found that NE inhibited the release of CRF from the hypothalamus while serotonin facilitated its release (note, however, that Fehm, Voight, Lang, & Pfeiffer, 1980, found NE led to CRF release in an in vitro assay). Morley et al. (1985) suggest that NE initiates feeding by inhibiting the release of CRF, thereby preventing CRF's inhibition of food intake. Although Morley and co-workers are not as specific about the role of serotonin, one assumes that a serotonin-induced release of CRF from the hypothalamus (an occurrence confirmed by other researchers—e.g., Holmes, Di Renzo, Beckford, Gillham, & Jones, 1982; Nakagami et al., 1986) would act in the PVN to block the stimulatory action of NE, thereby producing the inhibition of food intake generally seen after serotonin administration (e.g., Aulakh et al., 1988; Carlton & Rowland, 1984; Fletcher & Burton, 1984).

One possible difficulty with this hypotheses is that CRF does not appear to decrease food intake in female rats. If the effects of NE and serotonin on food intake were mediated exclusively through CRF, then CRF should be effective in altering food intake in female rats because NE is effective. Rivest, Deshaies, and Richard (1989) found that chronic intracerbroventricular (ICV) CRF decreased food intake, body weight, and body protein and fat gain in male but not female rats. Serum corticosterone levels were reduced in both sexes and serum testosterone levels decreased in male rats while serum estradiol levels decreased in females. Rivest et al. (1989) suggest that in intact female rats, CRF-induced decreases in serum estradiol (which would serve to increase food intake in female rats) may have attenuated the anorectic effects of CRF. Because it has been suggested that estradiol itself may act through the noradrenergic system, it is possible that the increase in NE activity that would be seen with decreased estradiol decreases the release of endogenous CRF in an amount sufficient to mask the effects of exogenous CRF. Alternatively, the increase in NE activity due to decreased estradiol may itself act in the PVN to block the action of CRF. Additional studies, particularly in species where EB and/or NE appear to play a less prominent role in regulating food intake, would provide information essential to determining if CRF plays a significant role in the regulation of food intake.

Insulin and glucagon.   Insulin and glucagon are released by the pancreas during the absorptive and fasting phases, respectively, and act in opposition to each other. Insulin facilitates the transport of glucose into cells as well as facilitating the process of converting glucose into a storable form of energy. Glucagon facilitates the breakdown of stored energy into forms that can be utilized by the body (e.g., glucose). Because peripheral insulin increases the rate of stomach emptying and decreases plasma glucose and free fatty acid levels (e.g., DiBattista, 1984a; Friedman, Ramirez, Wade, Siegel, & Granneman, 1982; Grossman, 1986), it is not surprising that peripherally administered insulin leads to increases in food intake in a number of species (Czech, Prince, & Jackson, 1990, spiny mouse; DeBattista, 1983, 1984b, hamster; Ritter & Balch, 1978, hamster; Rowland, 1978, hamster and gerbil; Steffens, 1969b, rat). The extent of these insulin-induced effects is species dependent, but the end result of peripheral insulin administration is an increase in food intake. It is worth noting that the effects of peripheral insulin on food intake appear to be unaffected by vagotomy or sympathectomy (see Grossman, 1986, for a review).

In contrast to the increases in food intake often seen after peripheral administration, central administration of insulin has generally been found to inhibit food intake (e.g., Arase, Fisler, Shargill, York, & Bray, 1988; Brief & Davis, 1984; Hatfield, Millard, & Smith, 1974; Ikeda et al., 1986; Ikeda, West, Pustek, & Woods, 1983; but see Tsujii & Bray, 1990). In most published studies, the effective doses of insulin appear to be in the pharmacological dose range, rather than the physiological range. Strubbe and Mein (1977), however, found that very small doses of antibodies to insulin, when administered to the VMH, increased food intake. Furthermore, Oomura's work (e.g., Oomura, 1976; Oomura & Kita, 1981) indicates that small doses of insulin can modify neuronal activity in the hypothalamus. Thus, centrally administered insulin may decrease food intake by a direct action on hypothalamic neurons. A second possibility is that centrally administered insulin further increases the level of glucose that can bind to glucoreceptors in the VMH (recall that they appear to be insulin sensitive), thereby producing a "satiety" signal. A third possibility was suggested by Morley et al. (1985). After reviewing evidence that suggested only pharmacological doses of insulin alter food intake as well as evidence for the cross-reactivity of insulin with receptors for somatomedins, Morley et al. (1985) suggested that the central actions of insulin may actually be mediated through somatomedins. Each of these alternatives warrants additional investigation.

Both peripherally (e.g., Geary & Smith, 1983) and centrally (e.g., Inokuchi, Oomura, & Nishimura, 1984; Oomura, Ooyama, Yamamoto, Ono, & Kobayashi, 1969) administered glucagon has been found to inhibit food intake in the rat. The peripheral action of glucagon appears to be mediated by vagal afferents because vagotomy blocks the suppressive effects of glucagon (Geary & Smith, 1983). The central action of glucagon may be mediated by glucoreceptors in the LH. Oomura et al. (1969) found that the administration of glucagon to the LH suppressed the activity of glucoreceptors in the region. Furthermore, Marubashi et al. (1985) found that ICV glucagon led to hyperglycemia, possibly accounting for the decreased activity in LH glucoreceptors (recall that glucose decreases the activity of these neurons). Further work is needed to elucidate both mechanisms of action.

Other peptides.   A variety of other peptides have also been found to inhibit feeding when administered peripherally and/or centrally. Calcitonin produces a strong suppression of food intake that can last more than 24 hr and may be mediated through calcitonin-induced changes in calcium uptake by hypothalamic tissue (see Morley et al., 1985, for a review). Neurotensin, thyrotropin releasing hormone (TRH), and the cyclic derivative of TRH, cyclo-histidyl-proline-diketopiperazine, are also peptides that have been found to inhibit food intake in what may be a specific fashion (Morley et al., 1985). Further research should provide interesting information on the specific roles that these, and other, peptides play in the regulation of feeding behaviors.

Brief Summary of Physiological Mechanisms.   The wealth of research on physiological mechanisms that may be involved in the regulation of feeding behavior makes a concise summary difficult. It is clear that virtually every neurotransmitter, sex steroid, and peptide that has been found to significantly influence food intake appears to do so by acting in the PVN, VMH, and/or LH. In some cases, we can see that substances regulating food intake interact in some way within and outside of these nuclei (e.g., CCK, EB, and glucose decrease opioid activity; NE decreases CRF release while serotonin increases it; corticosterone increases α-noradrenergic receptors). In most cases, however, studies of these substances and how they interact to regulate feeding are in their infancy. This is particularly true of studies examining the role of these substances in rodents other than the laboratory rat and for studies that look at components of feeding other than food intake. In addition to studies dealing with these issues, other areas where particularly fruitful information could be acquired include (a) the role of serotonin in feeding, particularly in relation to NE; (b) the role of EB, P, and androgens in relation to the noradrenergic system and CRF; (c) the role of neurotransmitters and peptides in hoarding; (d) the role of sex–steroid–opioid interactions in feeding and hoarding, particularly in hamsters and gerbils.

The lack of an organized and fairly complete body of knowledge on the physiological factors regulating feeding also makes the integration of the more purely physiological studies with the more purely behavioral studies difficult. This is particularly so when the physiological studies focus on simple food intake, while the behavioral studies focus on meal patterns, diet selection, foraging behavior, and hoarding. For this reason, models or theories of feeding behaviors have tended to be either physiologically based models or environmentally/behaviorally based models. The difficulty with this is that the use of one seems to lead to the neglect of the other. For example, *physiological* models seem to lead to the tendency to begin to view feeding in terms of specific brain areas that respond to depletion by initiating repletion, without regard to external influences. *Environmental* models, however, while evaluating environmental influences, sometimes appear to relegate physiological mechanisms to black-box status. These are not requirements of either category of model; one could easily postulate a variety of internal and external signals related to both physical and environmental states that would ultimately be integrated within the CNS to produce the observed feeding behaviors. What this integration requires, however, is a knowledge of how environmental factors influence the systems with which we are already familiar, and this knowledge is relatively limited at this time. The next section will examine behavioral aspects of three components of feeding: foraging, food intake, and hoarding. When possible, suggestions will be made regarding the possible roles in mediating feeding behaviors of the physiological mechanisms already discussed.

Behavioral Mechanisms and Possible Physiological Correlates

Foraging.   Research indicates that in most if not all rodents studied, optimal foraging behavior (searching, identifying, procuring, and handling food, cf. Collier, 1980) probably depends heavily upon spatial memory (e.g., Batson, Best, Phillips, Patel, & Gilliland, 1986; Ilersich, Mazmanian, & Roberts, 1988; Jones, McGhee, & Wilkie, 1990; Melcer & Timberlake, 1985; Roberts & Ilersich, 1989). Furthermore, it appears that temporal memory and temporal integration may play a key role in foraging effectively (e.g., Killeen, Smith, & Hanson, 1981; Timberlake, 1984; Timberlake, Gawley, & Lucas, 1987). In addition, rearing environment (e.g., Takai & Wilkie, 1985), as well as more recent experience with environmental cues (e.g., de Jong, Wilkie, & Willson, 1988) and conspecifics (e.g., Galef, 1980; Galef & Wigmore, 1983; Laland & Plotkin, 1990), can also influence the morphology and efficiency of foraging behavior. Although some of these elements may be influenced by the neurochemical systems discussed in this review, it seems likely that the processes involved in learning and memory are more directly involved in mediating these behaviors than are specific neuromodulators and neurotransmitters. However, the costs of foraging also have a large impact on foraging behavior. Because increased costs generally mean increased energy expenditure, it does seem likely that the neurochemical systems discussed in this review may, because of their role in regulating energy intake/expenditure, be involved in mediating the effects that increased costs of foraging have on foraging behavior.

The costs of foraging can be increased in a number of ways. Some investigators (e.g., Collier, 1980; Collier, Hirsch, & Hamlin, 1972; Collier, Johnson, Cy-Bulski, & McHale, 1990; Collier & Rovee-Collier, 1980; Gannon, Smith, & Tierney, 1983) have used an operant-like paradigm to conduct studies examining the effects on foraging patterns of search, identification, procurement, and/or handling costs; others (e.g., Anderson, 1986; Cabanac & Johnson, 1983; Johnson, Ackroff, Collier, & Plescia 1984; Johnson & Cabanac, 1982a, 1982b; Mellgren, Misasi, & Brown, 1984) have examined the effects of factors such as diet, temperature, palatability, predation risk, and prey density on foraging behavior. Each of these factors has been found to influence foraging strategy.

Effects of meal cost on foraging. The work of Collier and others (e.g., Collier, 1980; Collier & Rovee-Collier, 1980; Collier et al., 1972, 1990; Gannon et al., 1983; Morgan & Price, 1989) indicates that, in general, increasing the cost of searching for food increases the likelihood that food, once found, will be consumed. Furthermore, increasing the cost of procuring food (acquiring the food once it is found) decreases the frequency of eating but increases the size of the meal consumed. Finally, rodents may also compensate for the increased demands on time spent foraging (produced by increased bar-press requirements) by eating and/or bar-pressing more rapidly. The responses of rodents to changes in the costs of the components of foraging varies with the species examined, however, indicating the importance of environmental factors and evolutionary constraints (e.g., Hirsch & Collier, 1974a, 1974b; Collier & Rovee-Collier, 1981). Nonetheless, it is clear that all species examined have behavioral strategies that allow them to compensate for changes in food availability in their environment. What might be the physiological underpinnings of such behavioral changes?

Unfortunately, this question is virtually impossible to answer now because there is little data on the physiological changes that occur in situations where the animal is not food deprived and is able to forage at will. Indeed, it is currently difficult to determine if (or when) animals anticipate their energy needs or if they forage in response to some level of depletion. Furthermore, we have little information on the effects of neurotransmitters, hormones, and peptides on foraging responses in such environments. The research cited earlier, however, does provide some suggestions about what mechanisms might be involved.

Increases in procurement cost lead to decreases in foraging frequency and increases in meal size. Such alterations may reflect learned adjustments to environmental conditions. However, an animal's ability to tolerate such changes will also be determined by the animal's current physiological state. Although purely speculative, it is possible that during "times of plenty" (food stored, optimal fat deposits) animals forage, eat, and hoard in "anticipation" of need. When food stores are lacking and fat stores are decreasing, animals may be driven by depletion as well as by anticipation. Learning and memory may be the primary forces guiding foraging strategy; however, the time devoted to foraging may be influenced by short- and long-term physiological changes. For example, an animal with no food stores and little fat stores (i.e., a depleted animal) would presumably spend a great deal more time foraging because the risk of death due to deprivation is increasing. As the level of depletion increased, one would expect that signals from the "emergency" system could increase in strength, eventually inhibiting nonforaging activities and disinhibiting high-cost and risky foraging behaviors. Indeed, it is possible that increased activity of LH glucoreceptors, through increases in α-noradrenergic activity or decreases in serotonergic activity, disinhibit the mechanisms that normally prevent high-cost and risky foraging behaviors. Furthermore, the stress of severe depletion may cause the release of opioids and NPY, which could further strengthen the signal to forage, regardless of cost. In this manner, elements of both the emergency (e.g., glucoreceptors, NPY, and possibly NE) and the short-term (e.g., opiates, NE) systems could contribute to deprivation-induced increases in costly foraging behaviors. Thus, in times of need, physiological mechanisms such as these may send a strong signal to forage while learning and memory may determine where and how the foraging takes place.

It is interesting to note that in times of plenty, animals appear to eat until a certain level of fat storage is reached and then maintain that level (Hoebel & Teitelbaum, 1966; Liebelt, Bordelon, & Liebelt, 1973; Steffens, 1975). It is possible that when a particular level of fat is reached, there occur physiological changes that tend to reduce overall foraging levels and alter meal patterns, preventing additional long-term fat storage and reducing long-term anticipatory foraging and feeding. The physiological mechanisms involved remain to be determined. Given the role of fat as an internal buffer for periods of deprivation, however, it is not surprising that changes in fat stores can produce changes in food intake and, presumably, in foraging and hoarding behaviors as well. It seems reasonable to suppose that at least some of these changes are mediated by the CNS mechanisms altering food intake that were discussed earlier. Further investigation of their effects is essential if we are to understand the role of physiology and environment in the regulation of feeding behavior.

The difficulties presented by our relatively scarce knowledge of the neurochemistry of foraging behavior can be seen in our studies of the effects of EB on food intake. Although we know the effects of EB on food intake in most rodents, we do not know if EB alters food intake by making the animal less (or more, for gerbils) willing to work for food or perhaps by making food less (or more) palatable. We also do not know how other neurochemicals important in the regulation of food intake (e.g., opioids, NPY, CCK, NE) influence foraging patterns. Yet an understanding of the systems and substances regulating feeding requires examining all components of feeding as well as understanding the systems that influence how and when an animal searches for food in the first place. Paradigms such as Collier's, where effort expended in foraging and eating can be manipulated in a systematic fashion, are particularly well suited for these types of studies and would undoubtedly provide important and enlightening information on the biopsychology of feeding. Some speculations that could be tested using such a paradigm include the following:

1. Substances that increase carbohydrate ingestion should lead to increased tolerance of high costs of searching for, identifying, procuring, and handling food (assuming that substances initiating carbohydrate ingestion play a role in assuring an animal meets immediate energy needs).
2. For similar reasons, substances decreasing carbohydrate ingestion may decrease tolerance for high costs of feeding.
3. Some of these substances may decrease carbohydrate consumption so that other macronutrients are ingested. Thus, with some neurochemicals, one might see a shift in the type of food the animal is willing to procure.
4. Some substances that decrease food intake may actually lead to an increase in hoarding behavior because they may signal that immediate needs are taken care of, leaving the option of external food storage to take care of future needs.

Effects of other environmental factors on foraging.   It would be overly simplistic to view foraging behavior as a simple function of physiological need and environmental availability. Clearly, a number of additional factors also determine the pattern of foraging behavior. For example, temperature can have a profound impact on meal size, meal frequency, and foraging behavior. Davies (1977) and Kraly and Blass (1976) have found that rats will increase their meal size and/or frequency when ambient temperature is lowered. Decreasing temperature outside the home area also increases meal size during foraging, but, as one might expect, meal frequency decreases in this situation. For example, Johnson and Cabanac (1982a) found that rats required to forage in cold (5 or −15°C) environments decreased meal duration but increased food intake and speed of ingestion. Increasing the palatability of the food offered further increased food intake and speed of ingestion. In a related experiment, Johnson and Cabanac (1982b) found that increasing the distance that rats must travel to acquire food in a −15°C environment decreased the number of foraging expeditions and increased meal duration but did not alter speed of ingestion. Finally, Cabanac and Johnson (1983) found that even when chow was available in the home cage, rats would run the 16-M distance at −15°C in order to obtain highly palatable foods (i.e., shortcake, Coca-cola, peanut butter, or all of these). Indeed, Cabanac and Johnson (1983) found that highly palatable food could comprise up to half of a rat's nutrient intake. When ordinary chow was found 16 M away, rats made few excursions to the site and ate very little when they did go to the site (Cabanac & Johnson, 1983). Clearly, foraging behavior in the rat, and presumably other rodents as well, is influenced not only by the amount of effort expended in finding the food, but also by the palatability of the food and by more global environmental factors such as temperature.

An additional environmental factor that has been found to influence foraging patterns in rats is prey density. Mellgren et al. (1984) found that the amount of time rats spent foraging in a patch before moving on was closely related to "prey" (.12-g pieces of chow) density. Furthermore, as cost of procuring the food increased, rats foraged more efficiently. Thus, the density of available food in a particular food patch, as well as the number of patches available, influenced foraging strategy. When combined with the studies on foraging in unfavorable temperatures, these results compare nicely with those of Anderson (1986), who examined foraging behavior in mice (*Peromyscus maniculatus*) and two species of voles. Anderson (1986) found that foraging behaviors were influenced by travel distance and snowfall (search and procurement costs), ambient temperature, food supply/density, and available cover.

As with research on the effects of meal cost on foraging behavior, there seems to be relatively little information about the physiological mechanisms that could alter foraging strategy in response to environmental changes. Changes in temperature can alter metabolic rate and, thus, probably alter a number of physiological variables involved in feeding. However, changes in foraging strategy due to changes in prey density may reflect learned strategies. Studies examining the role of substances such as CCK, NE, and NPY in foraging that are similar to those suggested in the previous section on meal cost would again provide valuable information. For example, if NE is part of an emergency, or short-term glucose-monitoring mechanism, it would presumably increase the frequency of foraging in a cold or low food-density environment and these changes should be particularly noticeable when carbohydrate-rich (rapid glucose availability) foods are available. Other substances may increase food intake by increasing the palatability of particular food items rather than providing a more direct physiological signal to eat. In these cases, the effects of the substance on food intake may not be observed when foraging under highly unfavorable conditions or when foraging for nonaffected food items. That is, as environmental conditions become more unfavorable, foraging for palatable but unnecessary foods might be expected to decline more rapidly than foraging for necessary foods. If this is the case, substances signaling deprivation would be expected to increase foraging in unfavorable conditions to a greater extent than substances that simply increase palatability (and vice versa).

Food Intake

Nycthemeral meal patterns. Rats consume most of their food during the dark portion of the light:dark cycle (Le Magnen, 1981; Le Magnen & Tallon, 1963, 1966; Richter, 1927). When activity is relatively restricted, energy expenditure and the ad lib intake of chow is relatively constant from day to day (Le Magnen & Devos, 1980). When activity is not greatly restricted, however, energy expenditure and ad lib intake of chow can vary considerably from day to day (Niko-letseas, 1980). Nonetheless, rats are primarily nocturnal eaters.

What physiological factors might be involved in modulating a nycthemeral feeding pattern? Le Magnen (1981, pp. 568–569) discusses evidence for a 24-hr liporegulatory cycle and suggests that such a cycle could explain the observed nyc-themeral feeding pattern in rats. Evidence for such a cycle is taken from a num-ber of studies indicating that lipogenesis (fat synthesis) occurs primarily during the dark portion of the cycle, while lipolysis (fat utilization) occurs primarily during the light portion of the cycle. Le Magnen (1981, pp. 571–572) goes on to suggest that this liporegulatory cycle may be related to alterations in insulin levels, citing evidence that levels of insulin as well as tissue sensitivity to insulin are greater during the dark phase of the cycle than they are during the light phase. This in-creased level of insulin would not only encourage lipogenesis, it would also, by depleting blood glucose, encourage feeding. During daylight, lower insulin would encourage lipolysis and decrease absorption of glucose from the blood, perhaps de-creasing food intake. Le Magnen (1981, pp. 572–573) goes on to suggest that the VMH may be involved in the 24-hr liporegulatory cycle.

Many elements of Le Magnen's argument are subject to debate and alterna-tive interpretation. Nonetheless, there is evidence that the VMH (or noradrenergic output from the VMH) plays some role in insulin secretion, thereby influencing li-pogenesis. Indeed, the obesity associated with "VMH syndrome" may well be due to lesions of the noradrenergic terminals that synapse in the PVN (e.g., Gold, 1973; Gold, Jones, Sawchenko, & Kapatos, 1977). By removing the inhibitory ac-tion of NE on the PVN (Moss et al., 1972), the lesions increase PVN activity, thereby decreasing DMNV activity, resulting in increased insulin secretion, hyper-phagia, and lipogenesis (Gold & Simson, 1982). What is not clear is which CNS mechanisms are involved in producing the actual 24-hr cycle. The physiological mechanisms discussed previously suggest at least two possibilities, one strongly physiological, the other more cognitive/behavioral.

Nocturnal feeding might be induced by a relatively pronounced decline in blood glucose, which would increase the activity of glucoreceptors in the LH. This, in turn, could increase the activity of α_2-noradrenergic neurons synapsing within the PVN, which would inhibit PVN firing on neurons in the DMNV, thereby increasing DMNV activity. Increased DMNV activity could, by increasing insulin and decreasing glucagon secretion, lead to increased food ingestion and fat deposition. That noradrenergic activity may specifically increase carbohydrate in-gestion could explain why meals at the onset of the dark phase tend to be pre-dominantly carbohydrate in content. Meals later in the nocturnal period tend to have increased fat and protein content (Brennan et al., 1988; Shor-Posner, Bren-nan, Jasaitis, Leibowitz, & Leibowitz, 1988; Tempel, Shor-Posner, Dwyer, & Lei-bowitz, 1989), suggesting other physiological mechanisms may become active as the dark phase of the feeding cycle progresses. As daylight approaches, feedback from a variety of systems monitoring insulin and nutrient levels (e.g., glucose, free fatty acids, amino acids), including systems utilizing glucoreceptors, may act to increase VMH activity. This increase in VMH activity would, according to Smith (1972), inhibit feeding by inhibiting LH activity. Alternatively, systems monitoring nutrient levels might decrease food intake by increasing serotonin activity, or perhaps by altering other systems. Indeed, peptides such as NPY and β-endorphin may also be involved in producing a nycthemeral feeding pattern. In light of the longer term, neuromodulatory action of many peptides, studies carefully examining the secretion patterns of peptides and the correlation between these secretion patterns and feeding patterns could provide very valuable information.

A less physiologically "driven" explanation of the nycthemeral feeding pattern in the rat is that due to predation and/or food availability, rats evolved mechanisms that inhibit foraging, and therefore food intake, during daylight. To avoid depletion, rats simply "overeat" in anticipation of the period of relatively low caloric intake. It might be argued that they "overeat" as a consequence of daytime deprivation, but this seems unlikely, because rats quickly learn to alter intake in *anticipation* of periods of caloric reduction (see later sections of this chapter). Thus, high nocturnal feeding would serve as a buffer until the next nocturnal feeding period, rather than as a means of compensating for prior deprivation. The observed elevation of nocturnal insulin levels, even when food is not forthcoming, may be of evolutionary significance and/or it may reflect the animals anticipation of food. If food is ingested, elevated insulin levels and increased tissue sensitivity to insulin insure that the rat is able to store energy to use as a buffer. If food is not ingested, elevated insulin levels and/or the accompanying depletions of blood glucose may eventually serve to activate/disinhibit/permit more active foraging mechanisms as well as initiate metabolic changes to conserve energy.

To fully understand the evolutionary and physiological significance of the nycthemeral meal pattern that exists in some rodents, additional studies in non rat species are clearly needed. Between-species similarities and differences can provide an additional source of knowledge that can aid in the integration of physiological and environmental factors involved in the regulation of overall meal patterns. For example, although golden hamsters are nocturnal, they feed relatively evenly throughout the 24-hr cycle (e.g., Borer, Rowland, Mirow, Borer, & Kelch, 1979; Zucker & Stephan, 1973). Mongolian gerbils, on the other hand, show about the same level of activity and food intake throughout the 24-hr period (Kanarek, Ogilby, & Mayer, 1977), as do guinea pigs (Hirsch, 1973). The finding that golden hamsters feed rather evenly throughout the 24-hr cycle despite greater nocturnal activity may relate to their strong tendency to hoard; why have an internal buffer when you have an external buffer? The tendency to hoard may also relate to the inability of the golden hamster to compensate for food deprivation by increasing intake (Borer et al., 1979; Silverman & Zucker, 1976; Wong, 1984; Wong & Jones, 1985), something rats and gerbils do quite readily (e.g., Kutscher, 1969; Wong, 1984; Wong & Jones, 1985). The relatively even activity and feeding of Mongolian gerbils suggests that, at least in the short term, internal and external buffering mechanisms would be less important in this species. Unfortunately, relatively little work has been done on the physiological mechanisms that may underlie these feeding patterns in the hamster and gerbil. Thus, it is difficult to determine which physiological mechanisms are most relevant to the feeding patterns of each species and how these mechanisms are influenced by environmental constraints.

Meal-to-meal intake patterns. Le Magnen and co-workers (e.g., Le Magnen, 1981; Le Magnen & Tallon, 1963, 1966) found evidence for meal-to-meal regulation of food intake within the nycthemeral feeding pattern of the rat. However, prandial correlations, or the lack thereof, have been the source of a fair amount of debate. Although many investigators have found postprandial correlations (e.g., Davies, 1977; de Castro, 1975, 1978; Le Magnen & Devos, 1970; Thomas & Mayer, 1968), many have also failed to find such correlations (e.g., Collier, Hirsch, & Hamlin, 1972; Kanarek, 1976; Kenny & Mook, 1974; Levitsky & Collier, 1968; Panksepp, 1973). However, de Castro (1981) points out that the intermeal interval may be best predicted by stomach energy content at the termination of a meal rather than the actual size of the meal or the energy content at the start of the meal. When energy content rather than meal size is examined, stronger correlation coefficients are observed (De Castro, 1981, 1989).

Assuming that stomach energy content at the end of the meal is a fairly reliable predictor of intermeal interval, what mechanisms might mediate such an effect? It seems reasonable to suggest that substances (e.g., glucose, insulin, free fatty acids) that are released in response to nutrient ingestion may be more important in regulating meal-to-meal feeding patterns than are peptides, which tend to be slower and longer lasting in their actions. Many have argued against lipostatic, glucostatic, and related theories of food intake regulation, in part because such theories clearly oversimplify a complex regulatory process. Yet the physiological evidence discussed in previous sections suggests that levels of available glucose and other nutrients (e.g., free fatty acids) are monitored. Furthermore, de Castro's (1981, 1989) finding that stomach energy content is a good predictor of intermeal interval also suggests that mechanisms monitoring energy availability are involved in regulating meal patterns, although they most certainly share this task with other systems.

At the risk of sounding as if I am resurrecting the glucostatic theory of food intake, I will point out that evidence discussed earlier does suggest that a decline in glucose levels may contribute to the onset of a meal (Campfield et al., 1985; Larue-Achagiotis & Le Magnen, 1985; Louis-Sylvestre & Le Magnen, 1980). Recall that a drop in blood glucose has been found to precede meal onset, and that glucose infusions that delay this decline in blood glucose also delay meal onset. Note that this does not necessarily mean that CNS *glucoreceptors* are involved in this mechanism. Indeed, their role may be relegated to the hypothesized emergency system; vagal afferents, which appear to convey information about nutrient levels in general, may play a more important role in meal onset due to low blood glucose.

That initial meals are generally high in carbohydrates also suggests that increasing blood glucose may be an important purpose of early meals. However, the findings that later meals have lower carbohydrate and higher fat and protein content (Brennan et al., 1988; Shor-Posner et al., 1988; Temple et al., 1989) and that nutrients other than glucose are also monitored indicate that several factors probably contribute to meal onset and intermeal interval. Indeed, the change in meal composition over the nocturnal period suggests that reaching a particular level of blood glucose could allow mechanisms directed toward tissue building and energy storage to become more active. If this is the case, one should be able to increase the proportion of predominantly carbohydrate meals by increasing the amount of energy expended during the nocturnal period. Additional research is needed to examine this possibility and to examine the relationship between premeal declines in blood glucose and the type of macronutrient ingested. Also essential to understanding the physiological mechanisms regulating meal-to-meal intake are studies examining the physiological changes that accompany changes in food intake when caloric density, palatability, macronutrients, and cost of food are varied. Each of these factors can dramatically alter meal patterns, yet there are few investigations focusing on the physiological mechanisms mediating such changes.

Effects of caloric density on food intake. If mechanisms regulating meal size and/or meal initiation depend, in part, on feedback concerning levels of available nutrients, then altering the caloric density of the food should alter the size of the meal and/or the intermeal interval. In rats, if the caloric density of the diet is increased, rats decrease the number and/or size of daily meals; when caloric density is decreased, the number and/or size of meals increases (e.g., Adolph, 1947; Carlisle & Stellar, 1969; Janowitz & Grossman, 1949; Johnson, Ackroff, Peters, & Collier, 1986; Kanarek, 1976; Levitsky & Collier, 1968; Snowdon, 1969; Treit, Spetch, & Deutsch, 1984). Whether meal size and/or meal frequency is altered may depend on the paradigm and diets utilized. For example, Johnson et al. (1986) found that rats tended to regulate daily caloric intake by eating larger *and* more frequent meals (powdered or granulated food) as caloric density decreased. Kanarek (1976), altering both the cost and the caloric density of the chow, found that rats primarily changed meal frequency when costs were low but also increased meal size as costs increased. Snowdon (1969), using a liquid diet, found that rats compensated for caloric dilution primarily by increasing meal size rather than meal frequency. The one clear finding from these studies is that rats easily compensate for changes in the caloric composition of their diets. Indeed, the findings of Treit et al. (1984) and of Prabhakar and Rao (1985, 1989) indicate that the rat can respond quite rapidly to the caloric value of ingested substances. It appears that this monitoring is dependent upon both calorie metering by the stomach and on learned associations between sweet tastes and caloric consequences. Information regarding caloric content is presumably sent to the CNS, where it could then act to alter the activity of noradrenergic, opioid, and other systems involved in the regulation of feeding.

The gerbil also compensates for caloric dilution by increasing food intake (meal size and frequency were not examined) (Kanarek et al., 1977). However, gerbils appeared to be more precise than rats in their compensatory increases. Kanarek et al. (1977) suggest that this may reflect species differences in food/flavor preferences, noting that rats find acid and bitter solutions to be more aversive than do gerbils. Kanarek et al. (1977) suggest that dilution of diets with cellulose is less aversive to gerbils than to rats, and thus that gerbils would continue to compensate for the dilution at a point where rats would find the diet too unpalatable. Increasing the fat content of the diet could increase the palatability of the diet for rats, but not gerbils, causing rats, but not gerbils, to "overeat" calorically.

The guinea pig does not appear to defend caloric intake. Rather, the guinea pig appears to regulate the amount ingested and compensate for changes in caloric density by altering energy demands (Hirsch, 1973). Thus, even when powdered chow was diluted by 50% with celluflour, guinea pigs lost only 6% of their initial body weight, even though their food intake dropped to about 65% of its original value and their caloric intake dropped to about 40% of its original value (Hirsch, 1973). Although it is possible that guinea pigs are able to utilize cellulose (i.e., celluflour), this could not completely account for the ability of guinea pigs to maintain their weight at 6% below its original value. Hirsch (1973) suggests a variety of additional mechanisms that may account for his remarkable finding, one of which is a reduction in energy expenditure. This is certainly a possibility, given recent findings in other rodents suggesting that food deprivation can, but does not necessarily, lead to more efficient utilization of food (e.g., Archambault, Czyzewski, Cordura y Cruz, Foreyt, & Mariotto, 1989; Brownell, Greenwood, Stellar, & Shrager, 1986; Graham, Chang, Lin, Yakubu, & Hill, 1990; Gray, Fisler, & Bray, G.A., 1988; Hill, Anderson, Lin, & Yakubu, 1988; Hill, Thacker, Newby, Sykes, & Digirolamo, 1988).

Changes in caloric density may relate to "real-world" events such as the seasonal variation of available foodstuffs. It is thus not surprising to find that there are species-specific responses to the caloric dilution of food, which probably relate to differences in species habitat. Studies of these differences between species, their habitats, and their evolutionary histories are necessary if we are to gain a full understanding of the physiological mechanisms behind observed feeding behaviors. For example, one can suggest that rats increase food intake in response to caloric dilution because various nutrient monitors indicate that an inadequate amount of nutrient has been ingested. Such an explanation may fit the data obtained in studies using the rat and the gerbil. But such an explanation does not seem to account for data from the hamster or the guinea pig. Unfortunately, when compared to data for the rat, relatively little is known about the physiological mechanisms that may control feeding in other rodents and how this may relate to the animal's niche.

Diet selection and macronutrient preference. Closely related to an animal's response to changes in caloric content of a diet is an animal's response to changes in the nutritional composition of a diet. A number of studies indicate that, given the choice, rats allowed to "assemble" their diet by selecting from fats, carbohydrates, protein, and sometimes vitamins and minerals are able to select appropriate diets to maintain health and growth (e.g., Collier, Leshner, & Squibb, 1969; Leshner, Collier, & Squibb, 1971; Richter, 1942–1943; Young, 1944). Furthermore, rats learn to avoid deficient diets and will rapidly learn to ingest those substances necessary to supplement deficient diets or, if given the opportunity, will switch to a nondeficient diet (e.g., Arbour & Wilkie, 1988; Bolles, Hayward, & Crandall, 1981; Booth, 1985; Harper, Benevenga, & Wohlheuter, 1970; Harris, Clay, Hargreaves, & Ward, 1933; Rozin & Kalat, 1971). Rats will also show preferences for solutions associated with calories even when the caloric consequence of that solution is delayed (Capaldi, Campbell, Sheffer, & Bradford, 1987). Thus, on a day-to-day basis, rats (and other rodents; cf. Arbour & Wilkie, 1988) acquire knowledge about the substances they ingest and use it to select appropriate diets.

There are difficulties associated with interpreting results from studies of macronutrient preference, even in purely behavioral studies. For example, the texture of macronutrients (e.g., granular, powder, and gelled powder) can influence preference for that macronutrient (McArthur & Blundell, 1986). It is also possible that the ingestion of a substance decreases over time because the animal becomes "bored" with the taste of the substance. However, the number of studies indicating preference shifts in response to prefeeding, deprivation, increased cost, and administration of peptides and neurotransmitters indicate that animals do show preference shifts that are probably attributable to more than the texture of, or "boredom" with, the macronutrient in question. Nonetheless, one must interpret such studies with caution.

Recall that Leibowitz and co-workers found that rats show differential ingestion of macronutrients during the dark phase of the light:dark cycle. Early in the dark phase, rats show a preference for carbohydrates that declines over the dark cycle (Brennan et al., 1988; Shor-Posner et al., 1988; Temple et al., 1989). Indeed, for most rats, carbohydrates compose the majority of the first meal after onset of the dark phase. As the dark phase progresses, however, preference for protein and, to a lesser extent, fat, increase (Brennan et al., 1988; Shor-Posner et al., 1988; Temple et al., 1989). Leibowitz (1990) suggests that the preference for carbohydrates during the early portion of the dark phase may reflect the physiological need to increase available energy (i.e., blood glucose). Preference for other macronutrients later in the dark phase may reflect the need for amino acids and fats for protein synthesis and energy storage. The behavioral findings suggest that, at least during the dark portion of the light:dark cycle, there might be a physiological and/or neurological signal that permits increased ingestion of protein and fat once immediate energy needs have been met. Leibowitz and co-workers found that α_2-noradrenergic inhibition of PVN activity increases carbohydrate ingestion. NPY may also be involved, although its effects appear to be separable from those of NE. It is possible that decreases in blood glucose, as well as changes in circulating levels of insulin, glucagon, and somatostatin, act upon a variety of CNS mechanisms, including LH and possibly VMH glucoreceptors, that increase α_2-noradrenergic activity to the PVN, thereby initiating carbohydrate ingestion. But what might lead to the observed change in macronutrient preference over the dark portion of the cycle?

Experiments examining macronutrient preference may provide answers as to why we have not found the neurotransmitters and peptides involved in regulating protein and fat intake. Perhaps the actions of these substances on ingestion of fat and protein are masked by systems regulating carbohydrate intake. Several factors appear to initiate, and possibly terminate, carbohydrate ingestion. The activity of these components could inhibit systems that lead to protein and fat ingestion. During the course of the nocturnal period, any number of signals (e.g., release of various "gut" hormones, changes in pancreatic hormones, increased conversion of glucose to fats) could serve to gradually inhibit the "carbohydrate" system or increase the activity of mechanisms leading to the intake of other macronutrients. Nonetheless, there should be situations in which a "carbohydrate" system could be overridden by other dietary needs. For example, one might predict that an animal suffering from a protein deficiency (not simply short-term deprivation) would initially consume predominantly protein rather than carbohydrate meals. As far as I know, this prediction has not specifically been examined. Research does indicate, however, that rats readily adopt feeding strategies that help compensate for deprivation of specific macronutrients. Furthermore, rats alter their food intake to compensate for increasing costs of specific macronutrients. In general, as costs increase, rats become less selective (Ackroff, Schwartz, & Collier, 1986). When the costs of specific macronutrients are altered, rats will adjust the composition of their diet if a preferred macronutrient becomes too "expensive" (Johnson, Ackroff, Collier, & Plescia, 1984). These findings suggest that interacting systems are responsible for the ingestion of different macronutrients. These systems may be dependent primarily on information regarding nutrient availability that is sent from the stomach and liver back to the CNS.

Social learning and food selection.   A great deal of evidence suggests that although overall health is the final determinant of diet selection, conspecifics also play an important role in feeding behavior. Work by Beck and Galef (1989) indicates that rats allowed to interact with conspecifics that ate a protein-rich diet also learned to eat that diet while rats not given this opportunity failed to discover which of the four diets was protein rich. Research also indicates that rats will show an increased preference for foods eaten by "demonstrator" rats (Galef, Attenborough, & Whiskin, 1990; Galef & Wigmore, 1983; Posadas-Andrews & Roper, 1983; Richard, Grover, & Davis, 1987; Strupp & Levitsky, 1984). Indeed, the one situation in which this does not appear to work to the advantage of the "observer" rat is when the demonstrator rat has ingested toxic bait. In this situation, the observer rat still shows an increased preference for food consumed by the demonstrator rat (Galef, McQuoid, & Whiskin, 1990). Thus, rats are capable of selecting appropriate diets and observation of conspecifics may help in this selection, but rats do not appear to be able to learn what foods to avoid by observing conspecifics.

In summary, in a traditional laboratory environment, rats eat most of their meals at night, showing an initially high preference for carbohydrates that decreases over the nocturnal period as preference for fats and protein rises. Energy content within the stomach may determine intermeal interval and meal size. It was suggested that the nycthemeral meal pattern may be more dependent upon the influence of neuromodulators, particularly those showing circadian fluctuations, while meal-to-meal regulation may be more dependent upon substances, including nutrients, released in response to food ingestion. Existant research suggests that a complex interplay of several variables, including environmenal factors (e.g., food availability, caloric density, behavior of conspecifics), physiological factors (e.g., peptides, hormones, neurotransmitters), and psychological factors (e.g., learning, memory, palatability), will determine the pattern of food intake. Additional research examining the correlation between secretions of substances such as NPY and endorphin, and feeding will help clarify the role of neuromodulators on food intake, particularly if comparative data are collected.

Hoarding. In many ways, hoarding behavior can be thought of as part of the long-term regulatory system, because stored food provides a buffer against short-term deprivation. It may also be thought of as part of the emergency system for the same reason. It is included at the end of this section however, because it seems a natural and final element of day-to-day feeding behavior.

There is a relatively large variation in the propensity of rodents to hoard food; rats and some mice hoard very little, hamsters hoard quite extensively, and gerbils and some mice hoard to a moderate degree (e.g., Fantino & Cabanac, 1980; Herberg & Stephens, 1977; Lanier, Estep, & Dewsbury, 1974; Lea & Tarpy, 1986; Manosevitz, 1970; Nyby & Thiessen, 1980; Rowland, 1982; Wong, 1984; Wong & Jones, 1985). These differences may well reflect evolutionary adaptations to different environments (cf. Silverman & Zucker, 1976; Wong, 1984).

The majority of studies on hoarding behavior per se appear to have employed a deprivation paradigm, as this generally increases hoarding behavior. Indeed, it can be difficult to observe any hoarding behavior in the rat unless deprivation is used (e.g., Bindra, 1948; Fantino, Boucher, Faion, & Mathiot, 1988; Fantino & Cabanac, 1980; Herberg & Blundell, 1970; Herberg & Stephens, 1977; Morgan et al., 1943; Stellar & Morgan, 1943; Wolfe, 1939). However, nondeprived rats will, if given the opportunity, hoard food that is not normally part of their diet (Bindra, 1948; Raible, unpublished observation, 1991). In species such as the hamster and gerbil, hoarding increases with deprivation but is usually observable without deprivation (Lea & Tarpy, 1986; Nyby & Thiessen, 1980; Wong, 1984; Wong & Jones, 1985). These findings suggest that (a) hoarding behavior serves as a buffer against times of food scarcity, and (b) deprivation somehow enhances the activity of those systems that initiate hoarding behavior.

The importance of hoarding behavior as a strategy for dealing with a relative paucity of food in the environment is perhaps best illustrated by the hamster. The hamster does not compensate for food restriction/deprivation by increasing food intake during food access times (Borer et al., 1979; DiBattista, 1983; DiBattista & Bedard, 1987; Kutscher, 1969; Lea & Tarpy, 1986; Rowland, 1982; Silverman & Zucker, 1976). Several investigators (e.g., Silverman & Zucker, 1976; Wong, 1984; Wong & Jones, 1985) have suggested that the absence of postfast food compensation in the hamster may be a consequence of the hamster's strong tendency to hoard, which would normally preclude periods of food deprivation because the hamster would simply eat from its stored supply. Indeed, Lea and Tarpy (1986) found that as the costs of procuring food increase, hamsters consume more of their hoard and decrease the amount that they add to the hoard. Complete food deprivation, on the other hand, increases hoarding (Lea & Tarpy, 1986). Thus, hamsters act proactively to prevent food shortage from actually occurring and, by doing so, can reduce the amount of time and energy spent foraging when food is scarce. It would appear that rats are more reactive, altering meal size and frequency in times of shortage or deprivation. Rodents such as the gerbil may fall in the middle of this continuum. They clearly compensate for deprivation by increasing food consumption during food access but may also show an increase in hoarding activity (Wong, 1984).

What mechanisms might serve to initiate hoarding behavior? Considering the amount of behavioral information we have on hoarding and the amount of physiological information we have on food intake, there is surprisingly little information about physiological mechanisms that might be involved in hoarding. Research indicates that, in rodents such as the rat, hoarding behavior seems to be tied to body weight; as body weight decreases, the tendency to hoard increases (e.g., Fantino & Cabanac, 1980; Herberg & Stephens, 1977; Morgan et al., 1943; Stephens, 1982). Fantino and co-workers (e.g., Fantino et al., 1988; Fantino, Faion, & Rolland, 1986) have suggested that dexfenfluramine (serotonin agonist) inhibits hoarding behavior by decreasing body weight "set point," thereby increasing the level of deprivation a rat will tolerate before beginning to hoard. Because fluctuations in body weight are generally related to fluctuations in fat stores, hoarding behavior in the rat may be tied most directly to those systems that regulate fat stores. It is possible that systems regulating fat stores also comprise one element of the system regulating hoarding behavior in species that normally hoard at high levels (e.g., hamsters). Given the pervasive tendency to hoard, however, it seems unlikely that systems regulating fat stores are of primary importance in regulating hoarding in species such as the hamster.

It is worth noting that sex steroids may play an important role in hoarding behavior in the laboratory rodent, although surprisingly little information actually exists on this topic. In the wild, seasonal changes in reproductive status due to hormonal changes have been linked to changes in hoarding behavior, with increased hoarding often associated with testicular regression in the fall. Recall that most laboratory studies examining the effects of sex steroids on hoarding behavior (see section on hormones and food intake) have not, as a rule, revealed robust effects of sex steroids on hoarding. It is possible that like the effects of castration on food intake and weight in male gerbils, the effects of sex steroids on hoarding are manifested gradually. Such an occurrence is consonant with a neuromodulatory role of sex steroids. Indeed, an examination of the actions of sex steroids on food intake in most rodent species generally reveals the clearest effects are observed after several days of hormone administration. Perhaps manipulations of substances that produce more immediate effects on food intake (e.g., NE, NPY, opioids, bombesin) would also produce more immediate effects on hoarding behavior. Further studies examining the effects of such substances on food intake and hoarding in the hamster and the gerbil will help clarify the physiological systems regulating hoarding and their relationship to the systems regulating food intake.

Brief Summary of Feeding Behaviors

Research on the behavioral aspects of foraging, food intake, and hoarding suggests that a number of environmental, physiological, and psychological factors interact to determine the pattern of feeding exhibited by an organism. Learning appears to play an important role in some aspects of feeding behavior such as foraging strategy, while physiological factors appear to be more important to other aspects of feeding such as food intake. Psychological factors such as palatability add an additional influence that can modify feeding behaviors.

In general, relatively little is known about the physiological factors regulating foraging, hoarding, and actual meal patterns, while a relatively great amount of information in known about the physiological factors influencing actual food intake. Thus, although we know that NE, NPY, and opioids increase food intake and that serotonin, CCK, bombesin, and CRF decrease food intake, we have almost no information on how these substances affect foraging and hoarding behaviors. An animal's ability to quickly learn to compensate for changes in caloric density, macronutrient availability, and increases in meal and macronutrient costs suggests that foraging and feeding strategy is influenced by some form of feedback between systems in the periphery that monitor the availability of nutrients and CNS systems regulating feeding.

It is probably impossible to determine the importance of each relevant factor in isolation. For example, although the release of neurochemicals (e.g., NE and NPY) in the PVN may increase carbohydrate ingestion, learning undoubtedly plays a role in the animal's foraging for, and selection of, carbohydrate-rich foods. Even a "carbohydrate-deplete" animal may reject a carbohydrate-rich food if it is connected to a high procurement cost or if it occurs in a highly unpalatable form. Similarly, an animal may overeat (or hoard) "unneeded" food because it was easy to obtain and/or was highly palatable. Thus, the final form of feeding behavior seen reflects the interaction of several systems. Although this can make difficult the study of physiological and neurochemical factors influencing foraging and hoarding behaviors, such studies are vital to our understanding of feeding. Yet, as can be seen in this section, such studies are in short supply.

The problem generated by the relative paucity of information on potential physiological underpinnings of foraging and hoarding behavior is compounded by the fact that the vast majority of studies on the physiological and neurochemical mechanisms involved in food intake utilize rats while many of the behavioral studies on foraging and hoarding utilize hamsters and gerbils. Thus, extant physiological and neurochemical data on food intake cannot be directly applied to behavioral data on hoarding and foraging. We are badly in need of studies examining the physiological and neurochemical mechanisms underlying all feeding behaviors in nonrat rodents.

SUMMARY AND FUTURE DIRECTIONS

A review of the literature suggested that conceptualizing the regulation of feeding as being achieved by three interacting systems (emergency, short-term, and long-term) could help to highlight areas in need of further study. It was suggested that the primary role of the emergency system is to increase food-seeking behaviors during periods of prolonged food deprivation. Although there are studies examining the effects of mild to moderate deprivation on food intake and willingness to forage under adverse conditions, it is difficult to relate these behavioral studies to physiological studies examining factors that may initiate meals after a period of mild to moderate deprivation. Physiological studies suggest that glucose deprivation and activation of LH glucoreceptors may be an important component of the emergency system. Other components of this system include the noradrenergic and NPY inputs to the PVN, inhibitory connections from the PVN to the DMNV, and pancreatic responses to changes in DMNV activity. It was additionally suggested that the emergency system may specifically act to increase carbohydrate ingestion because carbohydrates are quickly converted to utilizable glucose. The role of NPY, NE, and the pancreatic hormones (insulin and glucagon) in altering behavior itself remains unclear. Thus, there is a need to enhance our understanding of the physiological and neurochemical mechanisms that may alter feeding behaviors in moderately to severely deprived animals. Because many of the existing studies have utilized the rat, there is a particularly strong need to conduct behavioral and physiological studies in other rodent species.

The primary role of the short-term system was envisioned to be the regulation of meal patterns and food intake over periods of 1 or 2 days. The literature suggests that this system is modified by psychological and environmental factors to a greater extent than is the emergency system, which is presumed capable of overriding these influences. Foraging behavior, as part of the daily routine in the wild, is included as part of this system. There is an enormous base of literature on neurochemical factors influencing food intake in nondeprived and mildly deprived rats. The role of NE in regulating short-term food intake is perhaps the best understood of these factors, and the work of Leibowitz and co-workers should serve as a model for future research into neurochemical correlates of feeding. The work in Collier's laboratory provides an excellent model for future research on many aspects of feeding behavior. Indeed, the wealth of literature on feeding behaviors is quite impressive in its quality, its breadth, and, on occasion, its depth. Yet, this research base, as a whole, remains unsatisfying.

First, there are too few data on the neurochemistry of feeding in nonrat rodents. Fully understanding the regulation of feeding behaviors requires fully understanding what underlies species differences in feeding behaviors.

Second, although there exists a relatively long list of neurotransmitters, hormones, and peptides that can influence food intake in the rat, there exists relatively little knowledge of the circumstances under which they might be secreted for this purpose. Thus, the actual significance or purpose of their action on food intake is unclear. Although investigations utilizing traditional feeding paradigms (12- to 24-hr deprivation followed by 1-hr free access to food) can be useful in providing clues to which substances might regulate feeding, they have not proved particularly useful in revealing when, in the "normal" animal, these substances would influence food intake.

Third, the neurochemical data that do exist relate almost exclusively to effects on food intake; the neurochemistry of foraging and hoarding behaviors has, for the most part, been ignored. Related to this is a fourth problem: Studies on the behavioral aspects of foraging and hoarding often use hamsters and gerbils. Because these species can differ greatly in the morphology of feeding behaviors and in the effects of neurochemicals on food intake, this species split may preclude the integration of data on the neurochemistry of food intake with data on foraging and feeding behaviors.

A global statement of the type of information needed to enhance our understanding of factors influencing the short-term regulation of feeding is that we need more studies of rat foraging and hoarding behaviors and the effects various neurochemicals have on these behaviors. Furthermore, we need more studies that examine the effects of neurochemicals on foraging, food intake, and hoarding behavior in rodents such as the hamster and gerbil.

The primary role of the long-term system was suggested to be the regulation of the animal's buffers against food deprivation. Thus, the regulation of fat deposits and perhaps also the regulation of hoarding behavior would come under the control of this system. The long-term system is viewed as being the most flexible and least influenced by immediate environmental factors. Furthermore, it may alter food intake in a global manner by modifying an animal's willingness to work for food or by modifying the palatability of food. In this manner, the system could increase and decrease daily intake to prevent severe obesity. The current review did not provide extensive coverage of the literature on the regulation of fat stores because it seems indirectly (and at this time, largely hypothetically) related to the regulation of feeding. Nonetheless, as we gain additional knowledge about those factors that more immediately influence feeding behaviors, we should also begin to work toward an understanding of factors that may, in subtle but important ways, regulate global feeding patterns.

This review attempted to summarize and integrate the rather disparate data on various physiological, psychological, and environmental influences on feeding behaviors. It seems that this attempt was not entirely successful, perhaps attesting to the limitations of the author, perhaps attesting to the limitations of our existing knowledge. Certainly, I have gained a greater understanding of why most texts do not attempt to integrate the information. Nonetheless, I believe that the effort to integrate the information should be made; for not only does this increase our current understanding, it also indicates which avenues of research are likely to advance our understanding beyond its current level.

REFERENCES

Ackroff, K., Schwartz, D., & Collier, G. (1986). Macronutrient selection by foraging rats. *Physiology and Behavior, 38,* 71–80.

Adolph, E. F. (1947). Urges to eat and drink in rats. *American Journal of Physiology, 151,* 110–125.

Allen, Y. S., Adrian, T. E., Allen, J. M., Tatemoto, K., Crown, T. J., Bloom, S. R., & Polak, J. M. (1983). Neuropeptide Y distribution in the rat brain. *Science, 221,* 877–879.

Anand, B. K., China, G. S., Sharma, K. N., Dua, S., & Singh, B. (1964). Activity of single neurons in the hypothalamic feeding centers: Effect of glucose. *American Journal of Physiology, 207,* 1146–1154.

Anand, B. K., Subberwal, U., Manchanda, S. K., & Singh, B. (1961). Glucoreceptor mechanism in the hypothalamic feeding centres. *Indian Journal of Medical Research, 49,* 717–724.

Anderson, P. K. (1986). Foraging range in mice and voles: The role of risk. *Canadian Journal of Zoology, 64,* 2645–2653.

Antin, J., Gibbs, H., Holt, J., Young, R. C., & Smith, G. P. (1975). Cholecystokinin elicits the complete behavioral sequence of satiety in rat. *Journal of Comparative and Physiological Psychology, 89,* 784–790.

Arase, K., Fisler, J. S., Shargill, N. S., York, D. A., & Bray, G. A. (1988). Intracerebroventricular infusion of 3-hydroxybutrate and insulin in a rat model of dietary obesity. *American Journal of Physiology, 255,* R974–R981.

Arbour, K. J., & Wilkie, D. M. (1988). Rodents' (*Rattus, Mesocricetus,* and *Meriones*) use of learned caloric information in diet source. *Journal of Comparative Psychology, 102,* 177–181.

Archembault, C. M., Czyzewski, D., Cordura y Cruz, G. D., Foreyt, P., & Mariotto, M. J. (1989). Effects of weight cycling in female rats. *Physiology and Behavior, 46,* 417–421.

Aulakh, C. S., Wozniak, K. M., Haas, M., Hill, J. L., Zohar, J., & Murphy, D. L. (1988). Food intake, neuroendocrine and temperature effects of 8-OHDPAT in the rat. *European Journal of Pharmacology, 146,* 253–259.

Avery, D. D., & Calisher, S. B. (1982). The effects of injections of bombesin into the cerebral ventricles on food intake and body temperature in food-deprived rats. *Neuropharmacology, 21,* 1059–1063.

Avery, D. D., & Livosky, M. (1986). Peripheral injections of bombesin and cholecystokinin affect dietary self-selection in rats. *Pharmacology, Biochemistry and Behavior, 25,* 7–11.

Azar, A. P., Shor-Posner, G., Filart, R., & Leibowitz, S. F. (1984). Impact of medial hypothalamic 6-hydroxydopamine injections on daily food intake, diet selection, and body weight in freely-feeding and food-restricted rats. *Proceedings of the Eastern Psychological Association, 55,* 106.

Banks, W. A. (1980). Evidence for a CCK gut-brain axis with modulation by BBS. *Peptides, 1,* 347–351.

Barbour, H. G., Gregg, D. E., & Hunter, L. G. (1930). The calorigenic action of morphine as revealed by addiction studies. *Journal of Pharmacology and Experimental Therapeutics, 40,* 433–465.

Bartness, T. J., & Wade, G. N. (1984). Effect of interscapular brown adipose tissue denervation on body weight and energy metabolism in ovariectomized and estradiol-treated rats. *Behavioral Neuroscience, 98,* 674–685.

Bartness, T. J., & Waldbillig, R. J. (1984). Dietary self-selection in intact, ovariectomized, and estradiol-treated female rats. *Behavioral Neuroscience, 1,* 125–137.

Batson, J. D., Best, M. R., Phillips, D. L., Patel, H., & Gilliland, K. R. (1986). Foraging on the radial-arm maze: Effects of altering the reward at a target location. *Animal Learning and Behavior, 14*, 241–248.

Beatty, W. W., O'Briant, D. A., & Vilberg, T. R. (1974). Suppression of feeding by intrahypothalamic implants of estradiol in male and female rats. *Bulletin of the Psychonomic Society, 3*, 273–274.

Beck, M., & Galef, B. G., Jr. (1989). Social influences on the selection of a protein-sufficient diet by Norway rats (*Rattus norvegicus*). *Journal of Comparative Psychology, 103*, 132–139.

Berstein, I. L., Goehler, L. E., & Fenner, D. P. (1984). Learned aversions to proteins in rats on a dietary self-selection regimen. *Behavioral Neuroscience, 96*, 1065–1072.

Bhakthavatsalam, P., & Leibowitz, S. F. (1986). α_2-Noradrenergic feeding rhythm in paraventricular nucleus: Relation to corticosterone. *American Journal of Physiology, 250*, R83–R88.

Bindra, D. (1948). The nature of motivation for hoarding food. *Journal of Comparative and Physiological Psychology, 41*, 211–218.

Blaustein, J. D. (1986). The noradrenergic antagonist prozosin decreases the concentration of estrogen receptors in the female rat hypothalamus. *Brain Research, 404*, 39–50.

Blaustein, J. D., Gentry, R. T., Roy, E. J., & Wade, G. N. (1976). Effects of ovariectomy and estradiol on body weight and food intake in gold-thioglucose-treated mice. *Physiology and Behavior, 17*, 1027–1030.

Blaustein, J. D., & Letcher, B. (1986). Noradrenergic regulation of cytosol estrogen receptors in female rat hypothalamus: Possible role of noradrenergic receptors. *Brain Research, 404*, 51–57.

Blaustein, J. D., & Turcotte, J. (1988). Estradiol-induced progestin receptors-immunoreactivity is found only in estrogen receptor-immunoreactive cells in guinea pig brain. *Society for Neuroscience Abstracts, 14*, 511.

Blaustein, J. D., & Wade, G. N. (1977). Ovarian hormones and meal patterns in rat: Effects of progesterone and role of gastrointestinal transit. *Physiology and Behavior, 19*, 23–27.

Blundell, J. E. (1971). Possible mechanism for the effect of anorexic agents on feeding and hoarding in rats. *Psychopharmacologia, 22*, 224–229.

Blundell, J. E. (1984). Serotonin and appetite. *Neuropharmacology, 23*, 1537–1551.

Blundell, J. E., & Herberg, L. J. (1973). Effectiveness of lateral hypothalamic stimulation, arousal, and food deprivation in the initation of hoarding behavior in naive rats. *Physiology and Behavior, 10*, 763–767.

Blundell, J. E., & Hill, A. J. (1987). Nutrition, serotonin, and appetite: Case study in the evolution of a scientific idea. *Appetite, 8*, 183–194.

Bolles, R. C., Hayward, L., & Crandall, C. (1981). Conditioned taste preferences based on caloric density. *Journal of Experimental Psychology: Animal Behavior Processes, 7*, 59–69.

Booth, D. A. (1968). Mechanism of action of norepinephrine in eliciting an eating response on injection into the rat hypothalamus. *Journal of Pharmacology and Experimental Therapeutics, 160*, 336–348.

Booth, D. A. (1985). Food-conditioned eating preferences and aversions with interoceptive elements: Conditioned appetites and satieties. *Annals of the New York Academy of Sciences, 433*, 22–41.

Booth, D. A. (1987). Central dietary "feedback onto nutrient selection": Not even a scientific hypothesis. *Appetite, 8*, 195–201.

Booth, D. A., & Brookover, T. (1968). Hunger elicited in the rat by a single injection of bovine crystalline insulin. *Physiology and Behavior, 3*, 439–446.

Borer, K. T., Rowland, N., Mirow, A., Borer, R. C., Jr., & Kelch, R. P. (1979). Physiological and behavioral responses to starvation in the Golden hamster. *American Journal of Physiology, 236*, E105–E112.

Brandes, J. S. (1977). Insulin induced overeating in the rat. *Physiology and Behavior, 18*, 1095–1102.

Brennan, G., Shor-Posner, G., Ian, C., Jasaitis, P., Eyith, P., Madhu, K., & Leibowitz, S. F. (1988). Nutrient composition: Effects on temporal patterns of feeding. *Society for Neuroscience Abstracts, 14*, 531.

Brief, D. J., & Davis, J. D. (1984). Regulation of food intake and body weight by chronic intraventricular insulin infusion. *Brain Research Bulletin, 12*, 571–575.

Brownell, K. D., Greenwood, M. R. C., Stellar, E., & Shrager, E. E. (1986). The effects of repeated cycles of weight loss and regain in rats. *Physiology and Behavior, 38*, 459–464.

Buckingham, J. C. (1980). Corticotropin releasing factor. *Pharmacology Reviews, 31*, 253–274.

Butera, P. C., & Czaja, J. A. (1984). Intracranial estradiol in ovariectomized guinea pigs: Effects on ingestive behaviors and body weight. *Brain Research, 322*, 41–48.

Cabanac, M. (1985). Influence of food and water deprivation on the behavior of the white rat foraging in a hostile environment. *Physiology and Behavior, 35*, 701–709.

Cabanac, M., Ferber, F., & Fantino, M. (1989). Effects of dexfenfluramine on the feeding behavior of rats foraging in the cold for palatable bait. *Pharmacology, Biochemistry and Behavior, 32*, 1025–1031.

Cabanac, M., & Johnson, K. G. (1983). Analysis of a conflict between palatability and cold exposure in rats. *Physiology and Behavior, 31*, 249–253.

Cabanac, M., & Swiergiel, A. H. (1989). Rats eating and hoarding as a function of body weight and cost of foraging. *American Journal of Physiology, 257*, R952–R957.

Campfield, L. A., Brandon, P., & Smith, F. J. (1985). On-line continuous measurement of blood glucose and meal pattern in free-feeding rats: The role of glucose in meal initiation. *Brain Research Bulletin, 14*, 605–617.

Capaldi, E. D., Campbell, D. H., Sheffer, J. D., & Bradford, J. P. (1987). Conditioned flavor preference based on delayed caloric consequences. *Journal of Experimental Psychology: Animal Behavior Processes, 13*, 150–155.

Carlisle, H. J., & Stellar, E. (1969). Caloric regulation and food preferences in normal, hyperphagic, and aphagic rats. *Journal of Comparative and Physiological Psychology, 69*, 107–114.

Carlton, J., & Rowland, N. (1984). Anorexia and brain serotonin: Development of tolerance to the effects of fenfluramine and quipazine in rats with serotonin-depleting lesions. *Pharmacology, Biochemistry and Behavior, 20*, 739–745.

Clark, J. J., Kalra, P. S., Crowley, W. R., & Kalra, S. P. (1984). Neuropeptide Y and human pancreatic polypeptide stimulate feeding behavior in rats. *Endocrinology, 115*, 427–429.

Clark, J. T., Kalra, P. S., & Kalra, S. P. (1985). Nueropeptide Y stimulates feeding but inhibits sexual behavior in rats. *Endocrinology, 117*, 2435–2442.

Coling, J. G., & Herberg, L. J. (1982). Effect of ovarian and exogenous hormones on defended body weight, actual body weight, and the paradoxical hoarding of food by female rats. *Physiology and Behavior, 29*, 687–691.

Collier, G. H. (1980). An ecological analysis of motivation. In F. M. Toates & T. R. Halliday (Eds.), *Analysis of motivational processes* (pp. 125–151). New York: Academic Press.

Collier, G. H., Hirsch, E., & Hamlin, P. (1972). The ecological determinant of reinforcement in the rat. *Physiology and Behavior, 9*, 705–716.

Collier, G. H., Johnson, D. F., CyBulski, K. A., & McHale, C. A. (1990). Activity patterns in rats (*Rattus norvegicus*) as a function of the cost of access to four resources. *Journal of Comparative Psychology, 104*, 53–65.

Collier, G. H., Leshner, A. I., & Squibb, R. L. (1969). Dietary self-selection in active and non-active rats. *Physiology and Behavior, 4*, 79–82.

Collier, G. H., & Rovee-Collier, C. K. (1980). A comparative analysis of optimal foraging behavior: Laboratory simulations. In A. C. Kamil & T. Sargent (Eds.), *Foraging behavior: Ecological, ethological, and psychological approaches* (pp. 39–76). New York: Garland Press.

Corddry, D. H., Rapoport, S. I., & London, E. D. (1982). No effect of hyperketonemia on local cerebral glucose utilization in conscious rats. *Journal of Neurochemistry, 38*, 1637–1641.

Czaja, J. A. (1984). Sex differences in the activational effects of gonadal hormones on food intake and body weight. *Physiology and Behavior, 33*, 553–558.

Czaja, J. A., & Goy, R. W. (1975). Ovarian hormones and food intake in female guinea pigs and rhesus monkeys. *Hormones and Behavior, 6*, 329–349.

Czech, D. A., Prince, R. J., & Jackson, V. A. (1990). Effect of exogenous insulin on meal patterns and stomach emptying in the spiny mouse. *Physiology and Behavior, 47*, 899–902.

Davies, R. F. (1977). Long- and short-term regulation of feeding patterns in the rat. *Journal of Physiological and Comparative Psychology, 91*, 574–585.

Davies, R. F., Rossi, J. R., Panksepp, J., Bean, N. J., & Zolovick, A. J. (1983). Fenfluramine anorexia: A peripheral locus of action. *Physiology and Behavior, 30*, 723–730.

Davis, J. M., Lowy, M. T., Yim, G. K. W., Lamb, D. R., & Malven, P. V. (1983). Relationship between plasma concentration of immunoreactive beta-endorphin and food intake in rats. *Peptides, 4*, 79–83.

de Castro, J. M. (1975). Meal pattern correlations: Facts and artifacts. *Physiology and Behavior, 15*, 13–15.

de Castro, J. M. (1978). An analysis of the variance in meal patterns. *Neuroscience and Biobehavioral Reviews, 2*, 301–309.

de Castro, J. M. (1981). The stomach energy content governs meal patterning. in the rat. *Physiology and Behavior, 26*, 795–798.

de Castro, J. M. (1989). The interactions of fluid and food intake in the spontaneous feeding and drinking patterns of rats. *Physiology and Behavior, 45,* 861–870.

de Jong, J., Wilkie, D. W., & Willson, R. J. (1988). Signals for food facilitate gerbils' foraging behavior. *Behavioural Processes, 16,* 1–9.

Dembinski, A., Jaworek, J., Konturek, P. K., Konturek, S. J., & Warzecha, Z. (1989). Cholecystokinin receptor antagonism by peptidergic and non-peptidergic agents in rt pancreas. *Journal of Physiology, 411,* 419–435.

DiBattista, D. (1983). Food deprivation and insulin-induced feeding in the hamster. *Physiology and Behavior, 30,* 683–687.

DiBattista, D. (1984a). Food consumption, plasma glucose and stomach emptying in insulin-injected hamsters. *Physiology and Behavior, 33,* 13–20.

DiBattista, D. (1984b). Characteristics of insulin-induced hyperphagia in the golden hamster. *Physiology and Behavior, 32,* 381–387.

DiBattista, D., & Bedard, M. (1987). Effects of food deprivation on hunger motivation in golden hamsters (*Mesocricetus auratus*). *Journal of Comparative Psychology, 101,* 183–189.

Donohoe, T. P., Stevens, R., Johnson, N. J., & Barker, S. (1984). Effects of sterioisomers of estradiol on food intake, body weight and hoarding behavior in female rats. *Physiology and Behavior, 32,* 589–592.

Dourish, C. T., Hutson, P. H., & Curzon, G. (1985). Low doses of the putative serotonin agonist 8-hydroxy-2-(di-n-propylamino)tetralin (8-OH-DPAT) elicit feeding in the rat. *Psychopharmacology, 86,* 197–204.

Dupont, A., Barden, N., Cusan, C., Merand, Y., Labrie, F., & Vaudry, H. (1980). β-Endorphin and met-enkephaline: Their distribution, modulation by estrogens and haloperidol, and role in neuroendocrine control. *Federation Proceedings, 39,* 2544.

Edens, N. K., & Wade, G. N. (1983). Effects of estradiol on tissue distribution of newly-synthesized fatty acids in rats and hamsters. *Physiology and Behavior, 31,* 703–309.

Emson, P. C., & DeQuidt, M. E. (1984). NPY—A new member of the pancreatic polypeptide family. *Trends in Neuroscience, 7,* 31–35.

Ettinger, R. H., Thompson, S., & Staddon, J. E. R. (1986). Cholecystokinin, diet palatability, and feeding regulation in rats. *Physiology and Behavior, 36,* 801–809.

Fantino, M., Boucher, H., Faion, F., & Mathiot, P. (1988). Dexfenfluramine and body weight regulation: Experimental study with hoarding behavior. *Clinical Neuropharmacology, 11* (suppl. 1), S97–S104.

Fantino, M., & Brinnel, H. (1986). Body weight set-point changes during the ovarian cycle: Experimental study of rats using hoarding behavior. *Physiology and Behavior, 36,* 991–996.

Fantino, M., & Cabanac, M. (1980). Body weight regulation with a proportional hoarding response. *Physiology and Behavior, 24,* 939–942.

Fantino, M., & Cabanac, M. (1984). Effect of a cold ambient temperature on the rat's food hoarding behavior. *Physiology and Behavior, 32,* 183–190.

Fantino, M., Faion, F., & Rolland, Y. (1986). Effect of dexfenfluramine on body weight set-point: Study in the rat with hoarding behavior. *Appetite, 7,* 115–126.

Faris, P. I., Komisaruk, B. R., Watkins, L. R., & Mayer, D. J. (1983). Evidence for the neuropeptide, cholecystokinin, as an antagonist or opiate analgesia. *Science, 219,* 310–312.

Fehm, H. L., Voigt, K. H., Lang, R. E., & Pfeiffer, E. F. (1980). Effects of neurotransmitters on the release of corticotropin releasing hormone (CRH) by rat hypothalamic tissue in vitro. *Experimental Brain Research, 39,* 229–234.

Fernstrom, J. D. (1987). Food-induced changes in brain serotonin synthesis: Is there a relationship to appetite for specific macronutrients? *Appetite, 8,* 161–182.

Fletcher, P. J., & Burton, M. J. (1984). Effects of manipulations of peripheral serotonin on feeding and drinking in the rat. *Pharmacology, Biochemistry and Behavior, 20,* 835–840.

Flowers, S. H., Dunham, E. S., & Barbour, H. G. (1929). Addiction edema and withdrawal edema in morphinized rats. *Proceedings of the National Academy of Sciences, USA, 79,* 5435–5437.

Flynn, F. W. (1989). Fourth ventricle bombesin injection suppresses ingestive behaviors in rats. *American Journal of Physiology, 256,* R590–R596.

Friedman, M. I., Ramirez, I., George, G. N., Siegel, L. I., & Granneman, J. (1982). Metabolic and physiologic effects of a hunger-inducing injection of insulin. *Physiology and Behavior, 29,* 515–518.

Friedman, M. I., Tordoff, M. G., & Ramirez, I. (1986). Integrated metabolic control of food intake. *Brain Research Bulletin, 17,* 855–859.

Galef, B. G., Jr. (1980). Diving for food: Analysis of a possible case of social learning in wild rats (*Rattus norvegicus*). *Journal of Comparative and Physiological Psychology, 94*, 416–425.

Galef, B. G., Jr., Attenborough, K. S., & Whiskin, E. E. (1990). Responses of observer rats (*Rattus norvegicus*) to complex, diet-related signals emitted by demonstrator rats. *Journal of Comparative Psychology, 104*, 11–19.

Galef, B. G., Jr., McQuoid, L. M., & Whiskin, E. E. (1990). Further evidence that Norway rats do not socially transmit learned aversions to toxic baits. *Animal Learning and Behavior, 18*, 199–205.

Galef, B. G., Jr., & Wigmore, S. W. (1983). Transfer of information concerning distant foods: A laboratory investigation of the "information-centre" hypothesis. *Animal Behaviour, 31*, 748–758.

Galletti, F., & Klopper, A. (1964). The effect of progesterone on the quantity and distribution of body fat in the female rat. *Acta Endocrinologica, 46*, 379–386.

Gannon, K. N., Smith, H. V., & Tierney, K. J. (1983). Effects of procurement cost on food consumption in rats. *Physiology and Behavior, 31*, 331–337.

Garattini, S., Bizzi, A., Caccia, S., Mennini, T., & Samanin, R. (1988) Progress in assessing the role of serotonin in the control of food intake. *Clinical Neuropharmacology, 11* (suppl 1), S8–S32.

Garlicki, J., Konturek, P. K., Majka, J., Kwiecien, N., & Konturek, S. J. (1990). Cholecystokinin receptors and vagal nerves in control of food intake in rat. *American Journal of Physiology, 258*, E40–E45.

Geary, N., & Smith, G. P. (1983). Selective hepatic vagotomy blocks pancreatic glucagon's satiety effect. *Physiology and Behavior, 31*, 391–394.

Gentry, R. T., & Wade, G. N. (1976a). Sex differences in sensitivity of food intake, body weight, and running-wheel activity to ovarian steroids in rats. *Journal of Comparative and Physiological Psychology, 90*, 747–754.

Gentry, R. T., & Wade, G. N. (1976b). Androgenic control of food intake and body weight in male rats. *Journal of Comparative and Physiological Psychology, 90*, 18–25.

Gerall, A. A., & Thiel, A. R. (1975). Effects of perinatal gonadal secretions on parameters of receptivity and weight gain in hamsters. *Journal of Comparative and Physiological Psychology, 89*, 580–589.

Gjedde, A. (1983). Modulation of substrate transport to the brain. *Acta Neurologica Scandinavica, 67*, 3–25.

Gjedde, A., & Crone, C. (1975). Induction processes in blood–brain transfer of ketone bodies during starvation. *American Journal of Physiology, 229*, 1165–1169.

Gibbs, J., Fauser, D. J., Rowe, E. A., Rolls, B. J., Rolls, E. T., & Maddison, S. P. (1979). Bombesin suppresses feeding in rats. *Nature, 282*, 208–210.

Gibbs, J., Young, R. C., & Smith, G. P. (1973a). Cholecystokinin decreases food intake in rat. *Journal of Comparative and Physiological Psychology, 84*, 488–495.

Gibbs, J., Young, R. C., & Smith, G. P. (1973b). Cholecystokinin elicits satiety in rats with open gastric fistulas. *Nature, 245*, 323–325.

Gold, R. M. (1973). Hypothalamic obesity: The myth of the ventromedial nucleus. *Science, 182*, 488–490.

Gold, R. M., Jones, A. P., Sawchenko, P. E., & Kapatos, G. (1977). Paraventricular area: Critical focus of a longitudinal neurocircuitry mediating food intake. *Physiology and Behavior, 18*, 1111–1119.

Gold, R. M., & Simson, E. L. (1982). Perturbations of serum insulin, glucagon, somatostatin, epinephrine, norepinephrine and glucose after obesifying hypothalamic knife-cuts. In B. G. Hoebel & D. Novin, *The neural basis of feeding and reward*. Brunswick, ME: Haer Institute.

Goldman, C. K., Marino, L., & Liebowitz, S. F. (1985). Postsynaptic α_2-noradrenergic receptors mediate feeding induced by paraventricular nucleus injection of norepinephrine and clonidine. *European Journal of Pharmacology, 115*, 11–19.

Gosnell, B. A., Morley, J. E., & Levine, A. S. (1983). A comparison of the effects of corticotropin releasing factor and sauvagine on food intake. *Pharmacology, Biochemistry and Behavior, 19*, 771–775.

Gosnell, B. A., Morley, J. E., & Levine, A. S. (1984). Localization of naloxone-sensitive brain areas in relation to food intake. *Society for Neuroscience Abstracts, 10*, 306.

Graham, B., Chang, S., Lin, D., Yakubu, F., & Hill, J. O. (1990). Effect of weight cycling on susceptibility to dietary obesity. *American Journal of Physiology, 259*, R1096–1102.

Grandison, L., & Guidotti, A. (1977). Stimulation of food intake by muscimol and beta-endorphin. *Neuropharmacology, 16*, 533–536.

Gray, D. S., Fisler, J. S., & Bray, G. A. (1988). Effects of repeated weight loss and regain on body composition in obese rats. *American Journal of Clinical Nutrition, 47,* 393–399.

Grossman, S. P. (1962). Direct adrenergic and cholinergic stimulation of hypothalamic mechanisms. *American Journal of Physiology, 202,* 872–882.

Grossman, S. P. (1986). The role of glucose, insulin and glucagon in the regulation of food intake and body weight. *Neuroscience and Biobehavioral Reviews, 10,* 295–315.

Hahn, E. F., & Fishman, J. (1979). Changes in rat brain opiate receptor content upon castration and testosterone replacement. *Biochemical Biophysical Research Communications, 90,* 819–823.

Harper, A. E., Benevenga, N. J., & Wohlheuter, R. M. (1970). Effects of ingestion of disproportionate amounts of amino acids. *Physiological Reviews, 50,* 428–458.

Harris, L. J., Clay, J., Hargreaves, F. J., & Ward, A. (1933). Appetite and choice of diet. The ability of the vitamin B-deficient rat to discriminate between diets containing and lacking the vitamin. *Proceedings of the Royal Society of London, Series B, 113,* 161–190.

Hatfield, J. S., Millard, W. J., & Smith, C. J. V. (1974). Short-term influence on intraventromedial hypothalamic administration of insulin on feeding in normal and diabetic rats. *Pharmacology, Biochemistry and Behavior, 2,* 223–225.

Heffner, T. G., Hartman, J. A., & Seiden, L. S. (1980). Feeding increases dopamine metabolism in the rat brain. *Science, 208,* 1168–1170.

Heffner, T. G., Vosmer, G., & Seiden, L. S. (1984). Time-dependent changes in hypothalamic dopamine metabolism during feeding in the rat. *Pharmacology, Biochemistry and Behavior, 20,* 947–949.

Herberg, L. J., & Blundell, J. E. (1970). Non-interaction of ventromedial and lateral hypothalamic mechanisms in the regulation of feeding and hoarding behavior in the rat. *Quarterly Journal of experimental Psychology, 22,* 133–141.

Herberg, L. J., Pye, J. G., & Blundell, J. E. (1972). Sex differences in the hypothalamic regulation of food hoarding: Hormones versus calories. *Animal Behavior, 20,* 186"191.

Herberg, L. J., & Stephens, D. N. (1977). Interaction of hunger and thirst in the motivational arousal underlying hoarding behavior in the rat. *Journal of Comparative and Physiological Psychology, 91,* 359–364.

Hervey, E., & Hervey, G. R. (1967). The relationship between the effects of ovariectomy and of progesterone treatment on body weight and composition in the female rat. *Journal of Physiology, 187,* 44P–45P.

Hervey, E., & Hervey, G. R. (1968). Energy storage in female rats treated with progesterone in the absence of increased food intake. *Journal of Physiology, 200,* 118P–119P.

Hill, J. O., Anderson, J. C., Lin, D., & Yakubu, F. (1988). Effects of meal frequency on energy utilization in rats. *American Journal of Physiology, 255,* R616–R621.

Hill, J. O., Thacker, S., Newby, D., Sykes, M. N., & Digirolamo, M. (1988). Influence of food restriction coupled with weight cycling on carcass energy restoration during ad-libitum feeding. *International Journal of Obesity, 12,* 547–555.

Hirsch, E. (1973). Some determinants of intake and patterns of feeding in the Guinea pig. *Physiology and Behavior, 11,* 687–704.

Hirsch, E., & Collier, G. H. (1974a). The ecological determinants of reinforcement in the Guinea pig. *Physiology and Behavior, 12,* 239–249.

Hirsch, E., & Collier, G. H. (1974b). Effort as determinant of intake and patterns of drinking in the Guinea pig. *Physiology and Behavior, 12,* 647–655.

Hoebel, B. G. (1977). Pharmacologic control of feeding. *Annual Review of Pharmacology and Toxicology, 17,* 605–621.

Hoebel, B. G., & Teitelbaum, P. (1966). Weight regulation in normal and hypothalamic hyperphagic rats. *Journal of Comparative and Physiological Psychology, 61,* 189–193.

Hoebel, B. G., Zemlan, F., Trulson, M., Mackenzie, R., DuCret, R., & Norelli, C. (1978). Differential effects of p-chlorophenylalanine and 5, 7 dihydroxytryptamine on feeding in rats. *Annals of the New York Academy of Science, 305,* 590–594.

Holmes, M. C., Di Renzo, G., Beckford, U., Gillham, B., & Jones, M. T. (1982). Role of serotonin in the control of secretion of corticotropin releasing factor. *Journal of Endocrinology, 93,* 151–160.

Ikeda, H., West, D. B., Pustek, J. J., Figlwicz, D. P., Greenwood, M. R., Porte, D., & Woods, S. C. (1986). Intraventricular insulin reduces food intake of lean but not obese Zucker rats. *Appetite, 7,* 381–386.

Ikeda, H., West, D. B., Pustek, J. J., & Woods, S. C. (1983). Insulin infused intraventricularly reduces food intake and body weight of lean but not obese (fa/fa) Zucker rats. *Diabetes, 32* (suppl 1), 61A.

Ilersich, T. J., Mazmanian, D. S., & Roberts, W. A. (1988). Foraging for covered and uncovered food on a radial maze. *Animal Learning and Behavior, 16,* 388–394.

Inokuchi, A., Oomura, Y., & Nishimura, H. (1984). Effect of intracerebroventricularly infused glucagon on feeding behavior. *Physiology and Behavior, 33,* 397–400.

Insel, T. R., DeSouza, E. B., Perrin, M., Rivier, J., Vale, W., & Kuhar, M. J. (1984). Corticotropin-releasing factor (CRF) receptors: Identification in brain by autoradiography. *Society for Neuroscience Abstracts, 10,* 217.

Jaloweic, J. E., Panksepp, A. J., Zolovick, A. J., Najam, N. & Herman, B. (1981). Opioid modulation of ingestive behaviors. *Pharmacology, Biochemistry and Behavior, 15,* 477–484.

Janowitz, H. D., & Grossman, S. P. (1949). Effects of variations in nutritive density on intake of food of dogs and rats. *American Journal of Physiology, 158,* 184–193.

Johnson, D. F., Ackroff, K. M., Collier, G. H., & Plescia, L. (1984). Effects of dietary nutrients and foraging costs on meal patterns of rats. *Physiology and Behavior, 33,* 465–471.

Johnson, D. F., Ackroff, K., Peters, J., & Collier, G. H. (1986). Changes in rats' meal patterns as a function of the caloric density of the diet. *Physiology and Behavior, 36,* 929–936.

Johnson, K. G., & Cabanac, M. (1982a). Homeostatic competition between food intake and temperature regulation in rats. *Physiology and Behavior, 28,* 675–679.

Johnson, K. G., & Cabanac, M. (1982b). Homeostatic competition in rats fed at varying distances from a thermoneutral refuge. *Physiology and Behavior, 29,* 715–720.

Jones, C. H., McGhee, R., & Wilkie, D. M. (1990). Hamsters (*Mesocricetus auratus*) use spatial memory in foraging for food to hoard. *Behavioural Processes, 21,* 179–187.

Kakolewski, J. W., Cox, V. C., & Valenstein, E. S. (1968). Sex differences in body weight changes following gonadectomy of rats. *Psychological Reports, 22,* 547–554.

Kanarek, R. B. (1976). Energies of meal patterns in rats. *Physiology and Behavior, 17,* 395–399.

Kanarek, R. B., & Beck, J. M. (1980). Role of gonadal hormones in diet selection and food utilization in female rats. *Physiology and Behavior, 24,* 381–386.

Kanarek, R. B., Ogilby, J. D., & Mayer, J. (1977). Effects of dietary caloric density on feeding behavior in Mongolian gerbils (*Meriones unguiculatus*). *Physiology and Behavior, 19,* 497–501.

Kenny, M. J., & Mook, D. G. (1974). Effects of ovariectomy on meal patterns in the albino rat. *Journal of Comparative and Physiological Psychology, 87,* 302–309.

Killeen, P. R., Smith, J. P., & Hanson, S. J. (1981). Central place foraging in *Rattus norvegicus*. *Animal Behavior, 29,* 64–70.

Kirchgessner, A. L., & Sclafani, A. (1988). PVN-hindbrain pathway involved in hypothalamic hyperphagia-obesity syndrome. *Physiology and Behavior, 42,* 517–528.

Kirkham, T. C., & Blundell, J. E. (1987). Effects of naloxone and naltrexone on meal patterns of freely-feeding rats. *Pharmacology, Biochemistry and Behavior, 26,* 515–520.

Konturek, S. J., Krol, R., & Tasler, J. (1976). Effect of BBS and related peptides on the release and action of intestinal hormones on pancreatic secretion. *Journal of Physiology, 257,* 663–672.

Kowaleski, K. (1969). Effect of pre-pubertal gonadectomy and treatment with sex hormones on body growth, weight of organs and skin collagen of hamsters. *Acta Endocrinologica, 61,* 48–56.

Kraly, F. S., & Blass, E. M. (1976). Mechanisms for enhanced feeding in the cold in rats. *Journal of Comparative and Physiological Psychology, 90,* 714–746.

Kruk, Z. L. (1973) Dopamine and 5-hydroxytryptamine inhibit feeding in rats. *Nature, 246,* 52–53.

Kulkosky, P. J., Gibbs, J., & Smith, G. P. (1982). Behavioral effects of bombesin administration in rats. *Physiology and Behavior, 28,* 502–512.

Kutscher, C. L. (1969). Species differences in the interaction of feeding and drinking. *Annals of the New York Academy of Sciences, 157,* 539–551.

Kyrkouli, S. E., Stanley, B. G., & Leibowitz, S. F. (1984). Suppression of feeding by bombesin: Sites of action in the rat brain. In *The neural and metabolic bases of feeding* (p. 25) (abstracts). Davis: University of California.

Laland, K. N., & Plotkin, H. C. (1990). Social learning and social transmission of foraging information in Norway rats (*Rattus norvegicus*). *Animal Learning and Behavior, 18,* 246–251.

Landau, I. T., & Zucker, I. (1976). Estrogenic regulation of body weight in the female rat. *Hormones and Behavior, 7,* 29–39.

Lanier, D. L., Estep, D. Q., & Dewsbury, D. A. (1974). Food hoarding in muroid rodents. *Behavioral Biology, 11,* 117–187.

Larue-Achagiotis, C., & Le Magnen, J. (1985). Feeding rate and responses to food-deprivation as a function of fast-induced hypoglycemia. *Behavioral Neuroscience, 99,* 1176–1180.

Lea, S. E., & Tarpy, R. M. (1986). Hamsters' demand for food to eat and hoard as a function of deprivation and cost. *Animal Behavior, 34,* 1759–1768.

Lee, S., Panerai, A. E., Bellabara, D., & Friesen, H. G. (1980). Effect of endocrine modifications and pharmacological treatments on brain and pituitary concentrations of β-endorphin. *Endocrinology, 107,* 245–248.

Leibowitz, S. F. (1975). Ingestion in the statiated rat: Role of alpha and beta receptors in mediating effects of hypothalamic adrenergic stimulation. *Physiology and Behavior, 14,* 743–754.

Leibowitz, S. F. (1976). Brain catecholamine mechanisms for controlling hunger. In D. Novin, W. Wyrwicka, & G. Bray (Eds.), *Hunger: Basic mechanisms and clinical implications* (pp. 1–18). New York: Raven Press.

Leibowitz, S. F. (1978). Paraventricular nucleus: A primary site mediating adrenergic stimulation of feeding and drinking. *Pharmacology, Biochemistry and Behavior, 8,* 163–175.

Leibowitz, S. F. (1990). Hypothalamic neuropeptide Y in relation to energy balance. *Annals of the New York Academy of Science, 611,* 284–301.

Leibowitz, S. F., & Brown, L. L. (1980a). Analysis of behavioral deficits produced by lesions in the dorsal and ventral midbrain tegmentum. *Physiology and Behavior, 25,* 829–843.

Leibowitz, S. F., & Brown, L. L. (1980b). Histochemical and pharmacology analysis of noradrenergic projections to the paraventricular hypothalamus in relation to feeding stimulation. *Brain Research, 201,* 289–314.

Leibowitz, S. F., & Hor, L. (1982). Endorphinergic and α-noradrenergic systems in the paraventricular nucleus: Effects on eating behavior. *Peptides, 3,* 421–428.

Leibowitz, S. F., Roland, C. R., Hor, L., & Squillari, V. (1984). Noradrenergic feeding elicited via the paraventricular nucleus is dependent upon circulating corticosterone. *Physiology and Behavior, 32,* 857–864.

Leibowitz, S. F., Roossin, P., & Rosenn, M. (1984). Chronic norepinephrine injection into the hypothalamic paraventricular nucleus produces hyperphagia and increased body weight in the rat. *Pharmacology, Biochemistry and Behavior, 21,* 801–808.

Leibowitz, S. F., Weiss, G. F., & Shor-Posner, G. (1988). Hypothalamic serotonin: Pharmacologic, biochemical and behavioral analyses of its feeding-suppressant action. *Clinical Neuropharmacology, 11* (suppl. 1), S51–S71.

Leibowitz, S. F., Weiss, G. F., Yee, F., & Tretter, J. B. (1985). Noradrenergic innervation of the paraventricular nucleus: Specific role in control of carbohydrate ingestion. *Brain Research Bulletin, 14,* 561–567.

Le Magnen, J. (1981). The metabolic basis of dual periodicity of feeding in rats. *The Behavioral and Brain Sciences, 4,* 561–607.

Le Magnen, J., & Devos, M. (1970). Metabolic correlates of the meal onset in the free food intake of rats. *Physiology and Behavior, 5,* 805–814.

Le Magnen, J., & Devos, M. (1980). Parameters of the meal pattern in rats: Their assessment and physiological significance. *Neuroscience and Biobehavior Reviews, 4* (suppl. 1), 1–11.

Le Magnen, J., & Tallon, S. (1963). Enregistrement et analuse preliminaire de la "periodicite alimentaire spontanee" chez le rat blanc. *Journal de Physiologie, 55,* 286–297.

Le Magnen, J., & Tallon, S. (1966). La periodicite spontanee de la prise d'ailments ad libitum du rat blanc. *Journal de Physiologie, 58,* 323–349.

Leshner, A. I., & Collier, G. (1973). The effects of gonadectomy on the sex differences in dietary self-selection patterns and carcass composistion of rats. *Physiology and Behavior, 11,* 671–676.

Leshner, A. I., Collier, G., & Squibb, R. L. (1971). Dietary self-selection at cold temperatures. *Physiology and Behavior, 6,* 1–3.

Levine, A. S., & Morley, J. E. (1981a). Peptidergic control of insulin-induced feeding. *Peptides, 2,* 261–264.

Levine, A. S., & Morley, J. E. (1981b). Cholecystokinin-octapeptide suppresses stress-induced eating by inducing hyperglycemia. *Regulatory Peptides, 2,* 353–357.

Levine, A. S., Morley, J. E., Gosnell, B. A., Billington, C. J., & Bartness, T. J. (1985). Opioids and consummatory behavior. *Brain Research Bulletin, 14,* 663–672.

Levine, A. S., Morley, J. E., Kneip, J., Grace, M., & Brown, D. M. (1985). Environment modulates naloxone's suppressive effect on feeding in diabetic and non-diabetic rats. *Physiology and Behavior, 34,* 391–393.

Levine, A. S., Morley, J. E., Wilcox, G., Brown, D. M., & Handwerger, B. S. (1982). Tail pinch behavior and analgesia in diabetic mice. *Physiology and Behavior, 28*, 39–43.

Levitsky, D. A., & Collier, G. (1968). Effects of diet and deprivation on meal eating behavior in rats. *Physiology and Behavior, 3*, 137–140.

Liebelt, R. A., Bordelon, C. B., & Liebelt, A. G. (1973). The adipose tissue system and food intake. In E. Steelar & J. M. Sprague (Eds.), *Progress in physiological psychology.* New York: Academic Press.

Louis-Sylvestre, J., & Le Magnen, J. (1980). A fall in blood glucose level precedes meal onset in free-feeding rats. *Neuroscience and Biobehavioral Reviews, 4* (suppl. 1), 13–16.

Lowy, M. T., Maickel, R. P., & Yim, G. K. W. (1980). Naloxone reduction of stress-related feeding. *Life Sciences, 26*, 2113–2118.

Lowy, M. T., & Yim, G. K. W. (1982). Drinking, but not feeding is opiate sensitive in hamsters. *Life Science, 30*, 1639–1644.

Lowy, M. T., & Yim, G. K. W. (1983). Stimulation of food intake following opiate agonists in rats but not hamsters. *Psychopharmacology, 81*, 28–32.

Luine, V. N., & Rhodes, J. C. (1983). Gonadal hormone regulation of MAO and other enzymes in hypothalamic areas. *Neuroendocrinology, 36*, 235–241.

Luo, S. & Li, E. T. S. (1990). Food intake and selection pattern of rats treated with dexfenfluramine, fluoxetine and RU24969. *Brain Research Bulletin, 24*, 729–733.

Maass, C. A., & Wade, G. N. (1977). Effects of gonadal hormones on eating and body weight in Mongolian gerbils (*Meriones unguiculatus*). *Hormones and Behavior, 9*, 178–187.

Maddison, S. (1977). Intraperitoneal and intracranial cholecystokinin depress operant responding for food. *Physiology and Behavior, 19*, 819–824.

Manosevitz, M. (1970). Prolonged aperiodic feeding and adult hoarding in mice. *Journal of Comparative and Physiological Psychology, 70*, 228–234.

Margules, D. L. (1970). Alpha-adrenergic receptors in hypothalamus for the suppression of feeding behavior by satiety. *Journal of Comparative and Physiological Psychology, 73*, 1–12.

Marks-Kaufman, R., & Kanarek, R. B. (1980). Morphine selectively influences macronutrient intake in the rat. *Pharmacology, Biochemistry and Behavior, 12*, 427–430.

Martel, J.-C., St. Pierre, S., & Quirion, R. (1986). Neuropeptide Y receptors in rat brain: An autoradiographic localization. *Peptides, 7*, 55–60.

Marubashi, S., Tominaga, M., Katagiri, T., Yamatani, K., Yawata, Y., Hara, M., & Sasaki, H. (1985). Hypoglycemic effect of glucagon administered intracerebroventricularly in the rat. *Acta Endocrinologica, 108*, 6–10.

Massi, M., & Marini, S. (1987). Effect of the 5-HT$_2$ antagonist ritanserin on food intake and on 5-HT-induced anorexia in the rat. *Pharmacology, Biochemistry and Behavior, 26*, 333–340.

Matthews, J. W., Booth, D. A., & Stolerman, I. P. (1978). Factors influencing feeding elicted by intracranial noradrenaline in rats. *Brain Research, 141*, 119–128.

Mayer, J., & Marshall, N. B. (1956). Specificity of goldthioglucose for ventromedial hypothalamic lesions and obesity. *Nature, 178*, 1399–1400.

McArthur, R. A., & Blundell, J. E. (1986). Dietary self-selection and intake of protein and energy is altered by the form of the diets. *Physiology and Behavior, 38*, 315–319.

McCaleb, M. L., & Myers, R. D. (1980). Cholecystokinin acts on the hypothalamic "noradrenergic system" involved in feeding. *Peptides, 1*, 47–49.

McElroy, J. F., & Wade, G. N. (1988). Short- and long-term effects of ovariectomy on food intake, body weight, carcass composition, and brown adipose tissue in rats. *Physiology and Behavior, 39*, 361–365.

McLaughlin, C. L., & Baile, C. A. (1984). Feeding behavior responses of Zucker rats to naloxone. *Physiology and Behavior, 32*, 755–761.

McLean, S., & Hoebel, B. G. (1982). Opiate and norepinephrine-induced feeding from the paraventricular nucleus of the hypothalamus are dissociable. *Life Science, 31*, 2379–2382.

McLean, S., & Hoebel, B. G. (1983). Feeding induced by opiates injected into the paraventricular hypothalamus. *Peptides, 4*, 287–292.

Melcer, E. W., & Timberlake, W. (1985). Poison avoidance and patch location selection in rats. *Animal Learning and Behavior, 13*, 60–68.

Mellgren, R. L., Misasi, L., & Brown, S. W. (1984). Optimal foraging theory: Prey density and travel requirements in *Rattus norvegicus*. *Journal of Comparative Psychology, 98*, 142–153.

Miceli, M. O., & Fleming, A. S. (1983). Variation of fat intake with estrous cycle, ovariectomy and estradiol replacement in hamsters (*Mesocricetus auratus*) eating a fractionated diet. *Physiology and Behavior, 30*, 415–420.

Moran, T. H., & McHugh, P. R. (1982). Cholecystokinin suppresses food intake by inhibiting gastric emptying. *American Journal of Physiology, 242*, R491–R497.

Morgan, C. T., Stellar, E., & Johnson, O. (1943). Food deprivation and hoarding in rats. *Journal of Comparative Psychology, 35*, 275–295.

Morgan, K. R., & Price, M. V. (1989). Foraging in heteromyid rodents: The energy cost of scratch-digging. *American Zoologist, 29*, 167A.

Mori, T., Nagai, K., Nakagawa, H., & Yanaihara, N. (1986). Intracranial infusion of CCK-8 derivatives suppresses food intake in rats. *American Journal of Physiology, 251*, R718–R723.

Morin, L. P., & Fleming, A. S. (1978). Variation of food intake and body weight with estrous cycle, ovariectomy, and estradiol benzoate treatment in hamsters (*Mesocricetus auratus*). *Journal of Comparative and Physiological Psychology, 92*, 1–6.

Morley, J. E., & Levine, A. S. (1980). Stress induced eating is mediated through endogenous opiates. *Science, 209*, 1259–1261.

Morley, J. E., & Levine, A. S. (1981). Bombesin inhibits stress-induced eating. *Pharmacology, Biochemistry and Behavior, 14*, 149–151.

Morley, J. E., & Levine, A. S. (1984). Neuropeptide Y potently induces ingestive behaviors after central administration. *Digestive Diseases and Sciences, 29*, 538.

Morley, J. E., & Levine, A. S. (1985). Pharmacology of eating behavior. *Annual Review of Pharmacology and Toxicology, 25*, 127–146.

Morley, J. E., Levine, A. S., Grace, M., Kneip, J., & Gosnell, B. A. (1984). The effect of ovariectomy, estradiol and progesterone on opioid modulation of feeding. *Physiology and Behavior, 33*, 237–241.

Morley, J. E., Levine, A. S., Gosnell, B. A., Kneip, J., & Grace, M. (1987). Effect of neuropeptide Y on ingestive behaviors in the rat. *American Journal of Physiology, 252*, R599–R609.

Morley, J. E., Levine, A. S., Gosnell, B. A., & Krahn, D. D. (1985). Peptides as central regulators of feeding. *Brain Research Bulletin, 14*, 511–519.

Morley, J. E., Levine, A. S., Murray, S. S., & Kneip, J. (1982). Peptidergic regulation of norepinephrine induced feeding. *Pharmacology, Biochemistry and Behavior, 6*, 225–228.

Moss, R. L., Urban, I., & Cross, A. B. (1972). Microelectrophoresis of cholinergic and aminergic drugs on paraventricular neurons. *American Journal of Physiology, 223*, 310–318.

Nakagami, Y., Suda, T., Yajima, F., Shiyama, T., Tomori, N., Sumitomo, T., Demura, H., & Shizumi, K. (1986). Effects of serotonin, cyproheptadine and reserpine on corticotropin-releasing factor release from the hypothalamus in vitro. *Brain Research, 386*, 232–236.

Nance, D. M., & Gorski, R. A. (1977). Sex hormone dependent alterations in responsiveness to caloric dilution. *Physiology and Behavior, 19*, 679–683.

Nikoletseas, M. M. (1980). Food intake in the exercising rat: A brief review. *Neuroscience and Biobehavioral Reviews, 4*, 265–268.

Novin, D., Robinson, B. A., Culbreth, L. A., & Tordoff, M. G. (1983). Is there a role for the liver in the control of food intake? *American Journal of Clinical Nutrition, 9*, 233–246.

Novin, D., VanderWeele, D. A., & Rezek, M. (1973). Hepatic-portal 2-deoxy-D-glucose infusion causes eating: Evidence for peripheral glucoreceptors. *Science, 181*, 858–860.

Nunez, A. A., Gray, J. M., & Wade, G. N. (1980). Food intake and adipose tissue lipoprotein lipase activity after hypothalamic estradiol benzoate implants in rats. *Physiology and Behavior, 25*, 595–598.

Nyby, J., & Thiessen, D. D. (1980). Food hoarding in the Mongolian gerbil (*Meriones unguiculatus*): Effects of food deprivation. *Behavioral and Neural Biology, 30*, 39–48.

Nyby, J., Wallace, P., Owen, K., & Thiessen, D. D. (1973). An influence of hormones on hoarding behavior in the Mongolian gerbil (*Meriones unguiculatus*). *Hormones and Behavior, 4*, 283–288.

Oomura, Y. (1976). Significance of glucose, insulin, and free fatty acid on the hypothalamic feeding and satiety neurons. In D. Novin, W. Wywricka, & G. A. Bray (Eds.), *Hunger: Basic mechanisms and clinical implications*. New York: Raven Press.

Oomura, Y., Ooyama, H., Yamamoto, T., Ono, T., & Kobayashi, N. (1969). Behavior of hypothalamic unit activity during electrophoretic application of drugs. *Annals of the New York Academy of Science, 157*, 642–665.

Oomura, Y., & Kita, H. (1981). Insulin acting as a neuromodulator through the hypothalamus. *Diabetologia, 20* (suppl.), 290–298.

Ostrowski, N. L., Rowland, N., Foley, T. L., Nelson, J. L., & Reid, L. D. (1981). Morphine antagonists and consummatory behaviors. *Pharmacology, Biochemistry and Behavior, 14*, 549–559.

224   *Raible*

Owen, O. E., Morgan, A. P., & Kemp, H. G. (1967). Brain metabolism during fasting. *Journal of Clinical Investigation, 46*, 1589–1595.

Owen, O. E., Reichart, G. A., Jr., Boden, G., & Shuman, C. R. (1974). Comparative measurements of glucose, beta-hydroxybutyrate, acetoacetate, and insulin in blood and cerbrospinal fluid during starvation. *Metabolism, 23*, 7–14.

Panksepp, J. (1973). Reanalysis of feeding patterns in the rat. *Journal of Comparative and Physiological Psychology, 82*, 78–94.

Peters, J. C., & Harper, A. E. (1987). A skeptical view of the role of central serotonin in the selection and intake of protein. *Appetite, 8*, 206–210.

Philpott, H. G., & Petersen, O. H. (1979). Separate activation sites for CCK and BBS on pancreatic acini: An electrophysiological study employing a competitive antagonist for the action of CCK. *European Journal of Physiology, 382*, 263–268.

Pollock, J. D., & Rowland, N. (1981). Peripherally administerered serotonin decreases food intake in rats. *Pharmacology Biochemistry and Behavior, 15*, 179–183.

Posadas-Andrews, A., & Roper, T. F. (1983). Social transmission of food preferences in adult rats. *Animal Behaviour, 31*, 265–271.

Prabhakar, E., & Rao, B. S. (1985). Rapid calorie metering in ad lib rats. *Journal of Bioscience, 9*, 41–45.

Prabhakar, E., & Rao, B. S. (1989). Effects of gustation and gastric loading on rapid calorie metering in rats. *Physiology and Behavior, 45*, 685–688.

Raible, L. H., & Gorzalka, B. B. (1985). Food intake, body weight and lordosis in male and female Mongolian gerbils: Effects of ovarian steroids. *Physiology and Behavior, 35*, 767–774.

Raible, L. H., & Gorzalka, B. B. (1986). Receptivity in gerbils: Dose and temporal parameters of estrogen and progesterone administration. *Laboratory Animals, 20*, 109–113.

Redick, J. H., Nussbaum, A. I., & Mook, D. G. (1973). Estradiol induced suppression of feeding in the female rat: Dependence on body weight. *Physiology and Behavior, 10*, 543–547.

Reidelberger, R. D., Liehr, R.-M., Varga, G., Wong, H., & Walsh, J. H. (1990). Effects of a cholecystokinin (CCK) monoclonal antibody on the pancreatic exocrine response to CCK-8 and food intake in rats. *Gastroenterology, 98*(suppl.), A519.

Reidelberger, R. D., & O'Rouke, M. F. (1989). Potent cholecystokinin antagonist L 364718 stimulates food intake in rats. *American Journal of Physiology, 257*, R1512–R1518.

Renner, K. J., Gerhardt, G. A., & Quadagno, D. M. (1984). Brain catecholamine content during the estrous cycle and in seroid-primed rats. *Brain Research Bulletin, 12*, 363–368.

Richard, M. M., Grover, C. A., & Davis, S. F. (1987). Galef's transfer of information effect occurs in a free-foraging situation. *Psychological Record, 37*, 79–87.

Richter, C. P. (1927). Animal behavior and internal drives. *Quarterly Review of Biology, 2*, 307–343.

Richter, C. P. (1942–1943). Total self-regulatory functions in animals and human beings. *Harvey Lecture Series, 38*, 63–103.

Ritter, R. C., & Balch, O. K. (1978). Feeding in response to insulin but not to 2-deoxy-D-glucose in the hamster. *American Journal of Physiology, 234*, E20–E24.

Rivest, S., Deshaies, Y., & Richard, D. (1989). Effects of corticotropin-releasing factor on energy balance in rats are sex dependant. *American Journal of Physiology, 26*, R1417–R1422.

Robert, J. J., Orosco, M., Rouch, C., Jacquot, C., & Cohen, Y. (1989). Effects of opiate agonists and an antagonist on food intake and brain neurotransmitters in normophagic and obese "cafeteria" rats. *Pharmacology, Biochemistry and Behavior, 34*, 577–583.

Roberts, S., Kenny, N. J., & Mook, D. G. (1972). Overeating induced by progesterone in the ovariectomized, adrenalectomized rat. *Hormones and Behavior, 3*, 267–276.

Roberts, W. A., & Ilersich, T. J. (1989). Foraging on the radial maze: The role of travel time, food accessibility, and the predictability of food location. *Journal of Experimental Psychology: Animal Behavior Processes, 15*, 274–285.

Roland, C. R., Bhakthavatsalam, P., & Leibowitz, S. F. (1986). Interaction between corticosterone and alpha-z-noradrenergic system of the paraventricular nucleus in relation to feeding behavior. *Neuroendocrinology, 42*, 296–305.

Roland, C. R., Oppenheimer, R. L., Chang, K., & Leibowitz, S. F. (1985). Hypophysectomy disturbs noradrenergic feeding system of the paraventricular nucleus. *Psychneuroendocrinology, 10*, 109–120.

Ross, G. E., & Zucker, I. (1974). Progesterone and the ovarian-adrenal modulation of energy balance in rats. *Hormones and Behavior, 5*, 43–62.

Rowland, D. L., Perrings, T. S., & Thommes, J. A. (1980). Comparison of androgenic effects on food intake and body weight in adult rats. *Physiology and Behavior, 24*, 205–209.

Rowland, N. (1978). Effects of insulin and 2-deoxy-D-glucose on feeding in hamsters and gerbils. *Physiology and Behavior, 21,* 291–294.

Rowland, N. (1982). Failure by deprived hamsters to increase food intake: Some behavioral and physiological determinants. *Journal of Comparative and Physiological Psychology, 96,* 591–603.

Rowland, N. E., & Bartness, T. J. (1982). Naloxone supresses insulin-induced feeding in novel and familiar environments, but does not affect hypoglycemia. *Pharmacology, Biochemistry and Behavior, 16,* 1001–1003.

Rowland, N. E., Bellush, L. L., & Carlton, J. (1985). Metabolic and neurochemical correlates of gucoprivic feeding. *Brain Research Bulletin, 14,* 617–624.

Rowland, N. E., & Carlton, J. (1988). Dexfenfluramine: Effects on food intake in various animal models. *Clinical Neuropharmacology, 11* (suppl.), S33–S50.

Roy, E. J., Maass, C. A., & Wade, G. N. (1977). Estrogenic effect of an antiestrogen on eating and body weight: Species comparison and central action. *Physiology and Behavior, 18,* 137–140.

Roy, E. J., & Wade, G. N. (1976). Estrogenic effects of an antiestrogen, MER-25, on eating and body weight in rats. *Journal of Comparative and Physiological Psychology, 90,* 156–166.

Roy, E. J., & Wade, G. N. (1977). Role of food intake in estradiol-induced body weight changes in female rats. *Hormones and Behavior, 8,* 265–274.

Rozin, P., & Kalat, J. W. (1971). Specific hungers and poison avoidance as adaptive specializations of learning. *Psychological Reviews, 6,* 459–486.

Sar, M., & Stumpf, W. E. (1981). Central noradrenergic neurones concentrate ^{3}H-oestradiol. *Nature, 289,* 500–502.

Scalfani, A., & Aravich, P. F. (1983). Macronutrient self-selection in three forms of hypothalamic obesity. *American Journal of Physiology, 244,* R686–R694.

Schneider, J. E., Palmer, L. A., & Wade, G. N. (1986). Effects of estrous cycles and ovarian steroids on body weight and energy expenditure in Syrian hamsters. *Physiology and Behavior, 38,* 119–126.

Sewell, R. D. E., & Jawaharlal, K. (1980). Antagonism of 2-deoxy-d-glucose induced hyperphagia by naloxone: Possible involvement of endorphins. *Journal of Pharmacy and Pharmacology, 32,* 148–149.

Shimizu, N., Oomura, Y., Novin, D., Grijalva, C., & Cooper, D. H. (1983). Functional correlations between lateral hypothalamic glucose-sensitive neurons and hepatic portal glucose-sensitive units in the rat. *Brain Research, 265,* 49–54.

Shor-Posner, G., Azar, A. P., & Leibowitz, S. F. (1984). Electrolytic paraventricular nucleus (PVN) lesions and feeding behavior: Relation to food restriction, drugs and corticosterone. *Society for Neuroscience Abstracts, 10,* 302.

Shor-Posner, G., Brennan, G., Jasaitis, R., Leibowitz, B., & Leibowitz, S. F. (1988). Feeding patterns in young animals in relation to body weight and sex. *Society for Neuroscience Abstracts, 14,* 760.

Shor-Posner, G., Grinker, J. A., Marinescu, C., Brown, O., & Leibowitz, S. F. (1986). Hypothalamic serotonin in the control of meal patterns and macronutrient selection. *Brain Research Bulletin, 17,* 663–671.

Sieck, G. C., Nance, D. M., & Gorski, R. A. (1978). Estrogen modification of feeding behavior in the female rat: Influence of metabolic state. *Physiology and Behavior, 21,* 893–897.

Silverman, H. J., & Zucker, I. (1976). Absence of post–fast food compensation in the golden hamster (*Mesocricetus auratus*). *Physiology and Behavior, 17,* 271–285.

Simon, G. S., & Dewey, W. L. (1981). Narcotics and diabetes: I. The effects of streptozotocin-induced diabetes on the antinoa, C., & Cooper, D. H. (1983). Functional correlations between lateral hypothalamic glucose-sensitive neurons and hepatic portal glucose-sensitive units in the rat. *Brain Research, 265,* 49–54.

Shor-Posner, G., Azar, A. P., & Leibowitz, S. F. (1984). Electrolytic paraventricular nucleus (PVN) lesions and feeding behavior: Relation to food restriction, drugs and corticosterone. *Society for Neuroscience Abstracts, 10,* 302.

Shor-Posner, G., Brennan, G., Jasaitis, R., Leibowitz, B., & Leibowitz, S. F. (1988). Feeding patterns in young animals in relation to body weight and sex. *Society for Neuroscience Abstracts, 14,* 760.

Shor-Posner, G., Grinker, J. A., Marinescu, C., Brown, O., & Leibowitz, S. F. (1986). Hypothalamic serotonin in the control of meal patterns and macronutrient selection. *Brain Research Bulletin, 17,* 663–671.

Sieck, G. C., Nance, D. M., & Gorski, R. A. (1978). Estrogen modification of feeding behavior in the female rat: Influence of metabolic state. *Physiology and Behavior, 21,* 893–897.

226   Raible

Silverman, H. J., & Zucker, I. (1976). Absence of post–fast food compensation in the golden hamster (*Mesocricetus auratus*). *Physiology and Behavior, 17*, 271–285.

Simon, G. S., & Dewey, W. L. (1981). Narcotics and diabetes: I. The effects of streptozotocin-induced diabetes on the antinociceptive potency of morphine. *Journal of Pharmacoloy and Experimental Therapeutics, 218*, 324–329.

Simpson, C. W., & Dicara, L. V. (1973). Estradiol inhibition of catecholamine elicited eating in the female rat. *Pharmacology, Biochemistry and Behavior, 1*, 413–419.

Smith, C. J. V. (1972). Hypothalamic glucoreceptors: The influence of goldthioglucose implants in the ventromedial and lateral hypothalamic areas of normal and diabetic rats. *Physiology and Behavior, 9*, 391–396.

Smith, G. P., Greenberg, D., Falasco, J. D., Avilion, A. A., Gibbs, J., Liddle, R. A., & Williams, J. A. (1989). Endogenous cholycystokinin does not decrease food intake or gastric emptying in fasted rats. *American Journal of Physiology, 257*, R1462–R1466.

Snowdon, C. T. (1969). Motivation, regulation and the control of meal patterns with oral and intragastric feeding. *Journal of Comparative and Physiological Psychology, 69*, 91–100.

Souquet, A. M., & Rowland, N. E. (1990). Dexfenfluramine: Action with estradiol on food intake and body weight in ovariectomized rats. *American Journal of Physiology, 258*, R211–R215.

Stanley, B. G., Chin, A. S., & Leibowitz, S. F. (1985). Feeding and drinking elicited by central injection of neuropeptide Y: Evidence for a hypothalamic site(s) of action. *Brain Research Bulletin, 14*, 521–524.

Stanley, B. G., Daniel, A. S., Chin, A. S., & Leibowitz, S. F. (1985). Paraventricular nucleus injections of peptide YY and neuropeptide Y selectively enhance carbohydrate ingestion. *Peptides, 6*, 1205–1211.

Stanley, B. G., Lanthier, D., & Leibowitz, S. F. (1984). Feeding elicited by the opiate peptide D-ala-2-met enkephaliniamine: Sites of action in the brain. *Society for Neuroscience Abstracts, 10*, 1103.

Stanley, B. G., & Leibowitz, S. F. (1984). Neuropeptide Y: Stimulation of feeding and drinking by injection into the paraventricular nucleus. *Life Sciences, 35*, 2635–2642.

Stanley, B. G., & Leibowitz, S. F. (1985). Neuropeptide Y injected in the paraventricular hypothalamus: A powerful stimulant of feeding behavior. *Proceedings of the National Academy of Sciences USA, 82*, 3940–3943.

Steffens, A. B. (1969a). Blood glucose and FFA levels in relation to the meal pattern in the normal rat and the ventromedial hypothalamic lesioned rat. *Physiology and Behavior, 4*, 215–225.

Steffens, A. B. (1969b). The influence of insulin injections and infusions on eating and blood glucose level in the rat. *Physiology and Behavior, 4*, 823–828.

Steffens, A. B. (1975). Influence of reversible obesity on eating behavior, blood glucose, and insulin in the rat. *American Journal of Physiology, 228*, 1738–1744.

Stein, L. G., & Woods, S. C. (1981). Cholecystokinin and bombesin act independently to decrease food intake in the rat. *Peptides, 2*, 431–436.

Stellar, E., & Morgan, C. T. (1943). The role of experience and deprivation in the onset of hoarding behavior in the rat. *Journal of Comparative Psychology, 36*, 47–55.

Stephens, D. N. (1982). Hoarding behavior and the defence of body weight in adult rats, following undernutrition during different periods of early development. *Quarterly Journal of Experimental Psychology, 34B*, 183–194.

Stricker, E. M., & Zigmond, M. J. (1974). Effects on homeostasis of intraventricular injection of 6-hydroxydopamine in rats. *Journal of Comparative and Physiological Psychology, 86*, 973–995.

Stricker, E. M., & Zigmond, M. J. (1976). Recovery of function after damage to central catecholamine-containing neurons: A neurochemical model for the lateral hypothalamic syndrome. In J. M. Sprague & A. N. Epstein (Eds.), *Progress in psychobiology and physiological psychology* (Vol. 6, pp. 121–188). New York: Academic Press.

Strubbe, J. H., & Mein, C. G. (1977). Increased feeding in response to bilateral injections of insulin antibodies in the VMH. *Physiology and Behavior, 19*, 301–313.

Strupp, B. J., & Levitsky, D. A. (1984). Social transmission of food preferences in adult hooded rats (*Rattus norvegicus*). *Journal of Comparative Psychology, 98*, 257–266.

Stuckey, J. A., & Gibbs, J. (1982). Lateral hypothalamic injection of bombesin decreases food intake in rats. *Brain Research Bulletin, 8*, 617–621.

Stuckey, J. A., Gibbs, J., & Smith, G. R. (1985). Neural disconnection of gut from brain blocks bombesin-induced satiety. *Peptides, 6*, 1249–1252.

Swanson, H. H. (1967). Effects of pre- and post-pubertal gonadectomy on sex differences in growth, adrenal and pituitary weight of hamsters. *Journal of Endocrinology, 39*, 555–564.

Takai, R. M., & Wilkie, D. W. (1985). Foraging experience affects gerbils' (*Meriones unguiculatus*) radial arm maze performance. *Journal of Comparative Psychology, 99*, 361–364.

Tarttelin, M. F., & Gorski, R. A. (1973). The effects of ovarian steroids on food and water intake and body weight in the female rat. *Acta Endocrinologica, 72*, 551–568.

Tempel, D., Nicholas, L., & Leibowitz, S. F. (1988). *Proceedings of the Eastern Psychological Association, 59*, 55.

Tempel, D. L., Shor-Posner, G., Dwyer, D., & Leibowitz, S. F. (1989). Nocturnal patterns of macronutrient intake in freely feeding and food-deprived rats. *American Journal of Physiology, 256*, R541–R548.

Thibault, L., Nagai, K., Hashida, A., Yanaihara, N., & Nakagawa, H. (1990). Satiation due to CCK-8 derivative infusion into VMH is related to a specific macronutrient selection. *Physiology and Behavior, 47*, 911–915.

Thomas, D. W., & Mayer, J. (1968). Meal taking and regulation of food intakes by normal and hypothalamic hyperphagic rats. *Journal of Comparative and Physiological Psychology, 66*, 642–653.

Timberlake, W. (1984). A temporal limit on the effect of future food on current performance in an analogue of foraging and welfare. *Journal of the Experimental Analysis of Behavior, 41*, 117–124.

Timberlake, W., Gawley, D. J., & Lucas, G. A. (1987). Time horizons in rats foraging for food in temporally separated patches. *Journal of Experimental Psychology: Animal Behavior Processes, 13*, 302–309.

Treit, D., Spetch, M. L., & Deutsch, J. A. (1984). Caloric regulation in the rat: Evidence for a calibration mechanism. *Physiology and Behavior, 32*, 883–886.

Tsujii, S., & Bray, G. A. (1990). Effects of glucose, 2-deoxyglucose, phlorizin, and insulin on food intake of lean and fatty rats. *American Journal of Physiology, 258*, E476–E481.

VanderWeele, D. A., Deems, D. A., & Gibbs, J. (1984). Cholecystokinin, lithium, and diet self-selection in the rat: Lithium-chloride decreases protein, while cholecystokinin lowers fat and carbohydrate ingestion. *Nutrition and Behavior, 2*, 127–135.

VanderWeele, D. A., Oetting, R. L., Jones, R. E., & Deems, D. A. (1985). Sham feeding, flavor associations, and diet self-selection as indicators of feeding satiety or aversive effects of peptide hormones. *Brain Research Bulletin, 14*, 529–535.

Wade, G. N. (1975). Some effects of ovarian hormones on food intake and body weight in female rats. *Journal of Comparative and Physiological Psychology, 88*, 183–193.

Wade, G. N. (1976). Sex hormones, regulatory behaviors, and body weight. In J. Rosenblatt, R. Hinde, E. Shaw, & C. G. Beer (Eds.), *Advances in the study of behavior* (pp. 201–279). New York: Academic Press.

Wade, G. N., & Bartness, T. J. (1984). Effects of photoperiod and gonadectomy on food intake, body weight, and body composition in Siberian hamsters. *American Journal of Physiology, 246*, R26–R30.

Wade, G. N., & Gray, J. M. (1979). Gonadal effects on food intake and adiposity: A metabolic hypothesis. *Physiology and Behavior, 22*, 583–593.

Wade, G. N., & Zucker, I. (1970). Modulation of food intake and locomotor activity in female rats by diencephalic hormone implants. *Journal of Comparative and Physiological Psychology, 72*, 328–336.

Waldbillig, R. J., Bartness, T. J., & Stanley, B. G. (1981). Increased food intake, body weight, and adiposity in rats after retinal neurochemical depletion of serotonin. *Journal of Comparative and Physiological Psychology, 95*, 391–405.

Wahlestedt, C., Skagerberg, G., Ekman, R., Heilig, M., Sundler, F., & Håkanson, R. (1987). Neuropeptide Y (NPY) in the area of the hypothalamic paraventricular nucleus activates the pituitary-adrenocortical axis in the rat. *Brain Research, 417*, 33–38.

Wardlaw, S. L., Wang, P. J., & Frantz, A. G. (1985). Regulation of b-endorphin and ACTH in brain by estradiol. *Life Sciences, 37*, 1941–1947.

Weiss, G. F., Papadakos, P., Knudson, K., & Leibowitz, S. F. (1986). Medial hypothalamic serotonin: Effects on deprivation and norepinephrine-induced eating. *Pharmacology, Biochemistry and Behavior, 25*, 1223–1230.

West, D. B., Greenwood, M. R. C., Marshall, K. A., & Woods, S. C. (1987). Lithium chloride, cholecystokinin and meal patterns: Evidence that cholecystokinin suppresses meal size in rats without causing malaise. *Appetite, 8*, 221–227.

Wise, P. M., Rance, N., & Barraclough, C. A. (1981). Effects of estradiol and progesterone on catecholamine turnover rates in discrete hypothalamic regions in ovariectomized rats. *Endocrinology, 108*, 2186–2193.

Wisnar, J. R., Ozawa, S., & Renner, I. G. (1988). Evidence against cholecystokinin mediation of basal and bombesin-stimulated pancreatic secretion in rats. *Gastroenterology, 95*, 151–155.

Wolfe, J. B. (1939). An exploratory study of food storing in rats. *Journal of Comparative Psychology, 28*, 97–108.

Wong, R. (1984). Hoarding versus the immediate consumption of food among hamsters and gerbils. *Behavioural Processes, 9*, 3–11.

Wong, R., & Jones, C. H. (1985). A comparative analysis of feeding and hoarding in hamsters and gerbils. *Behavioural Processes, 11*, 301–308.

Wright, P., & Turner, C. (1973). Sex differences in body weight following gonadectomy and goldthioglucose injections in mice. *Physiology and Behavior, 11*, 155–159.

Wurtman, J. J., & Baum, M. J. (1980). Estrogen reduces total food and carbohydrate intake, but not protein intake, in female rats. *Physiology and Behavior, 24*, 823–827.

Young, P. T. (1944). Studies of food preference, appetite and dietary habit: II. Groups self-selection maintenance as a method in the study of food preferences. *Journal of Comparative Psychology, 37*, 371–391.

Zucker, I., & Stephan, F. K. (1973). Light–dark rhythms in hamster eating, drinking and locomotor behaviors. *Physiology and Behavior, 11*, 239–250.

Zucker, I., Wade, G. N., & Ziegler, R. (1972). Sexual and hormonal influences on eating, taste preferences, and body weight of hamsters. *Physiology and Behavior, 8*, 101–111.

chapter 5

Flavor Neophobia in Selected Rodent Species

RODERICK WONG
University of British Columbia

COMMENTS

Georg Schulze and Neil V. Watson

In this provocative chapter, Roderick Wong introduces the reader to issues related to flavor neophobia and taste aversion, and their interrelationships. These processes are discussed with reference to the experiments conducted in his laboratory on flavor neophobia in some rodent species, and the chapter concludes with thoughts on the mechanisms and significance of flavor neophobia and taste aversion. The chapter raises some intriguing questions. These may be divided into one of two broad (and related) categories: The first concerns the adaptive significance of flavor neophobia, while the second relates to the amount of functional overlap between flavor neophobia and taste aversion.

When considering flavor neophobia from an evolutionary perspective, a key concern is what the ecological significance of flavor neophobia might be. Because tastes and flavors are likely to be immediate and potent environmental markers, it seems plausible that flavor neophobia and taste aver-

The experiments were supported by a grant from NSERC of Canada. Two years have intervened since the completion of this chapter and the production of this book. During the interim period all the experiments described in this chapter have been submitted and published in journals. Because of feedback from journal referees there are differences in the presentation and analysis of the data as well in their interpretation. These papers by Wong and McBride (1993), Wong, McBride, and Owen (1994) and Wong (1994) were added to the references in this chapter.

I thank C. B, McBride, Carol Goddard, Jacqueline McLure, Georg Schulz, and Neil V. Watson for their generous help in offering critical comments on this chapter.

sion may be mechanisms allowing an animal to "lock in" on and track its environmental niche. This perspective raises some important issues. First, it emphasizes the need to consider a species' ethogram in designing experiments—the use of natural behaviors and stimuli may yield data of greater clarity. The experiments reported in this chapter, where flavor neophobia was investigated using solid food instead of liquids, provide an example of the usefulness of such an ecologically guided approach. Second, the toxicity and hedonic value of food may have to be interpreted in terms of an animal's metabolism. Bitter-tasting substances are likely to be toxic to humans but not necessarily gerbils and hamsters, which may have adapted metabolically to an environment where bitter-tasting substances are more plentiful. This is addressed in Wong's discussion of the relative lack of flavor neophobia shown by gerbils and hamsters in his experiments. Third, in order to engage in comparative studies of flavor neophobia, one needs to sample cognitive adaptations using qualitatively similar variables. That is, the same absolute stimulus may not be comparable in its effects across species. This cannot be done without reference to the different species' ethograms. Once again, the use of solid food instead of flavored liquids in the experiments presented here facilitates a comparative approach, because these stimuli are more likely to be ecologically valid.

The same evolutionary approach also suggests a way to relate neophobia and taste aversion. It seems plausible that the neonate is given safe access to its gustatory environment by virtue of taste imprinting. Commensurate with taste imprinting, taste neophobia should operate to keep the organism's taste preferences from straying from the original imprinted taste(s). The opposing poles of taste imprinting and taste neophobia should then operate to keep the organism's feeding behavior locked in on a safe track. Many environments are not stable, however, and such a locking in of taste preferences could be disastrous should food sources with the imprinted taste(s) suddenly become scarce. Therefore, an additional mechanism is needed to enable adaptation to a changing environment.

This could be supplied by a taste-learning mechanism. Here, taste avoidance and taste preference are opposing poles; movement from an intermediate position toward taste avoidance could be termed *taste aversion*, and movement toward taste preference could be termed *taste acquisition*. In other words, the gradual process of taste acquisition eventually leads to taste preference, and the gradual process of increasing taste aversion leads to taste avoidance. To summarize, the taste imprinting/neophobia mechanism locks an organism into a gustatory channel, subject to modification by the taste aversion/acquisition mechanism. These mechanisms can presumably operate concurrently, but it is likely that the former will be more salient in neonates.

Figure 5I.1a illustrates the "taste space" of a neonate animal. At the center of this space is the imprinted taste. Radiating from the imprinted taste are

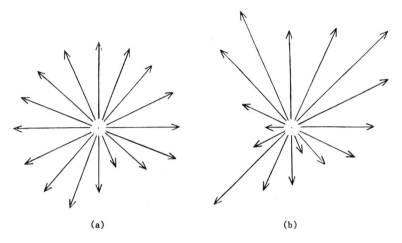

(a)   (b)

FIGURE 5I.1. This figure shows the "taste space" of a neonate animal (a) and an animal with considerable taste experience (b).

various other tastes. The length of the radius of the sphere indicates the innate degree of neophobia and can be expressed in various ways (e.g., latency to consume a food item). The more similar a taste is to the imprinted taste, the shorter the distance between the center and that particular taste. Figure 5I.1b illustrates the taste space of an adult animal. The occurrence of taste aversion generated particularly long distances between origin and taste to which aversion was developed, while taste acquisition shortened the distance between acquired taste and imprinted taste.

This structuring of mechanisms allows the conceptual reinterpretation of several factors associated with neophobia and taste aversion and their mutual relationships. First, contrary to Miller and Holzman's (1981a, 1981b) view, as discussed by Wong, it suggests that neophobia should not directly vary with the flavors of toxic substances. If it did, an unnecessary duplication seems to result: Either neophobia by itself or taste aversion conditioning should suffice to protect an organism from maladaptive feeding behavior. Neophobia should not be equated with (unconditioned) taste aversion—in a sense, it is independent of any particular taste. Support for this view seems to be provided by Braveman and Jarvis's (1978) experiments.

Second, neonates may have an innate degree of neophobia. The degree of innate neophobia of a particular species may reflect that species' habitat. It is postulated that a stable habitat would foster a high degree of neophobia, because adaptation is already complete and presumably optimal for that habitat. An unstable habitat would foster a lesser degree of neophobia because more emphasis is placed on continued adaptation, which would be impeded by a high degree of innate neophobia.

Third, the innate degree of neophobia extant in an organism could be augmented by aversive taste experiences and attenuated by beneficial taste experiences. The feedback processes of augmentation and attenuation of neophobia reflect some form of stimulus generalization, which is primarily across the dimension of novel/familiar tastes and perhaps secondarily across dimensions of individual taste categories. This is deemed consistent with the findings of Miller and Holzman (1981a) and Braveman and Jarvis (1978), as discussed by Wong.

Fourth, it is expected that neophobia is less likely to operate on taste categories similar to those of the imprinted tastes. An inspection of Table 5I.1, composed from Wong's chapter on flavor neophobia in selected rodent species, suggests that imprinted tastes in rats are more likely to be sourish, and imprinted tastes in gerbils, hamsters, and guinea pigs bitterish.

Fifth, it makes no sense to have the taste of a substance that is toxic or hard to metabolize imprinted on a neonate. This suggests that the usefulness of foodstuffs may vary from species to species, depending on their metabolisms, which in turn would reflect their habitats. Thus, a bitter taste may not universally signify food that had better be avoided; for instance, unadulterated nuts are more likely to be slightly bitter than sweet. Conversely, if sweet tastes generally indicated useful foods, one should expect all animals to be primarily frugivores! Although it makes sense to interpret tastes in terms of their adaptive value to an organism, consideration should be given to the contexts in which these tastes should have adaptive value.

Finally, stimulus salience should be equated before inferences can be drawn about neophobia of different flavors. It is likely that the more foreign tastes are likely to be more salient. Therefore, higher intensities of the familiar (imprinted) taste category need to be used in comparison to the unfamiliar categories.

Wong's discussion of possible neural mechanisms of flavor neophobia suggests that both flavor neophobia and taste aversion be seen in the broader context of anxiety and stress-modulated behaviors. The availability of new nonsedating anxiolytics (such as buspirone) might be of use in evaluating stress-hypotheses in flavor neophobia and neophobia in general. It would also be interesting to see whether flavor neophobia and taste aversion are dependent on the same neural mechanisms. In this respect the dopamine hy-

TABLE 5I.1. Flavor Neophobia

Rodent	Salt	Sweet	Sour	Bitter
Rat	1	1	0	1
Gerbil	1	1	1	0
Hamster	1	1	1	0
Guinea pig	1	1	1	0

pothesis of reward may provide a useful source for generating the appropriate experimental hypotheses.

In conclusion, this chapter provides much material for thought and further investigation: what the adaptive significance of flavor neophobia is; what the roles of flavor neophobia and taste aversion are; and which neural mechanisms mediate these processes.

INTRODUCTION

In their review of ethological studies on rodents, Barnett and Cowan (1976) described the animal's tendency to explore a new place when given access to it and called this tendency *neophilia*. Sudden access to a new place provokes entry and increased movement, an observation that led these authors to suggest that the function or survival value of such activity is to promote dispersion. Thus, the animals' chances of finding necessities are believed to be enhanced. In addition, commensal species (i.e., pests that are dependent upon humans for food) manifest a new object avoidance, which the authors called *neophobia*. Because pests are continually subjected to the selective pressures of human predation, Barnett and Cowan hypothesized that these rodents have undergone behavioral changes that may protect them from the consequences of neophilia.

Neophobic reactions are believed to be responsible for the difficulties of farmers in trapping rats or getting them to eat poison bait (Chitty, 1954). These field observations on rats were also substantiated among two species of Indian gerbils (Prakash & Jain, 1971). Researchers have postulated dual neophilic–neophobic processes to explain the animals' reactions to new places or new objects. Mitchell (1976) has studied neophobia in wild and laboratory rats from this perspective. In the present chapter, I consider another aspect of neophobia: the effects of a change in the flavor or taste of the food, rather than a change in the setting in which food is embedded. This consideration was inspired by the work of Miller and Holzman (1981a, 1981b), who were the first to suggest that neophobia is greatly influenced by (a) the flavor of toxic substances in the natural habitat of a species, and (b) the flavors of required nutrients in this habitat.

The perspective taken in this chapter regards neophobia as an inherent wariness of novel food exhibited by animals, and more specifically, the avoidance of novel foods compared to familiar foods. Flavor neophobia involves unconditioned aversions manifested during the animal's exposure to novel flavors or tastes that may or may not have inherent negative effects. The early studies on neophobia involved wild, food-deprived rats and their reactions when presented with a new food or a familiar one in a novel container (Richter, 1953; Rzoska, 1953, 1954). Their daily food intake was suppressed for several days, and they remained in the back of their cages for up to 7 hours before approaching the food. Subsequent experiments by Barnett (1956, 1958) indicated that domestic rats did not exhibit the same manifestations of neophobia as their feral counterparts. The former approached and consumed the novel food without any hesitation. For a detailed discussion and explanation of emotional differences between wild and domestic rats, see Mitchell (1976).

ENHANCED NEOPHOBIA

Although the results of the earlier studies led researchers to regard neophobia as a reaction shown only in wild rats, subsequent experimenters attempted to demonstrate this phenomenon in domestic rats under specific test conditions. In general, these efforts met with mild success, and the results were equivocal. The clearest demonstration involved a procedure in which rats were poisoned 24 hours prior to the presentation of a novel food (Rozin, 1968). In this experiment the rats were tested in a three-choice preference test (a familiar safe food vs. a novel food vs. a familiar food that was associated with poisoning). The latter condition caused an increase in the rats' neophobic reactions and was referred to as *enhanced neophobia* or *illness-induced neophobia*. Notice an important procedural difference between enhanced neophobia and conditioned taste aversion. In contrast to the procedure in which the aversive agent is administered to the animals after they are exposed to the food (taste aversion learning), in this case, the poison is administered to them before they are exposed to the food (enhanced neophobia). Corey (1978) suggested that the illness experience sensitizes the animal to novel events such that its usual neophobic response is enhanced. However, the effective interval between the the time of poisoning and the test for neophobia may vary according to other test conditions. Domjan (1977) found that toxicosis in the absence of edibles results in enhanced neophobia if the rats were tested within several hours after the injection. Although Brackbill, Rosenbush, and Brookshire (1971) failed to observe manifestation of enhanced neophobia among rats in a 3-hr three-choice preference test, Rozin's study revealed an effect. The former attributed these discrepant findings to procedural differences, the major one being that Rozin gave his rats the initial test for neophobia while they were still ill.

Another critical variable that may influence the manifestation of enhanced neophobia is the length of the test sessions. Carroll, Dinc, Levy, and Smith (1975) pointed out that because neophobia is most effectively measured in a brief test, it is possible that enhanced neophobia is a short-lived event. This phenomenon could appear and then be overcome during the course of an hour's contact with the novel taste substance. If measurements were made only at the end of the hour, enhanced neophobia may not be evident. In a series of experiments involving fluid intake, Carroll et al. demonstrated neophobia and enhanced neophobia in the albino rat when it was tested during a 10-min test period with a 0.1% saccharin solution for the first time. The animals drinking this solution for the first time showed a significant decrement in consumption when compared with either the previous day's water consumption or the following day's saccharin consumption. These experimenters also found that the magnitude of the neophobia was enhanced when the rat was either X-irradiated or given LiCl injection on the previous day. In addition, they demonstrated that interposing 2 days of water drinking between LiCl poisoning and the first saccharin exposure eliminated enhanced neophobia in a 10-min test. Thus, these results indicate that neophobia and enhanced neophobia are short-lived phenomena and experimental tests should take this fact into account. Short-term dependent measures would provide a more sensitive method of demonstrating neophobia.

INDEPENDENCE OF NEOPHOBIA AND TASTE AVERSION LEARNING

Carroll et al. (1975) suggested another implication of their findings. They predicted that the degree of neophobia resulting from the initial presentation of a taste solution, when measured by short-term tests, would reflect subsequent taste aversion resulting from the pairing of that taste with an aversive stimulus. Earlier studies, however, had already demonstrated that rats acquire taste aversion more readily to a solution that evokes a neophobic response than to a solution that does not (Kalat & Rozin, 1973; Nachmann & Jones, 1974; Revusky & Bedarf, 1967). Braveman and Jarvis (1978), therefore, pursued this issue in further detail in their attempt to demonstrate the independence of neophobia and taste aversion learning. They followed up previous findings indicating the reduction of neophobia by familiarizing animals with a solution whose taste is different from that of the test solution. Siegel (1974) had found that rats preexposed to one solution drank more of a second solution than animals not preexposed to a novel tasting solution. Similar results were obtained when immature rats that received a series of distinctively flavored novel solutions were compared with those that had not been previously exposed to the variable series of solutions (Capretta, Petersik, & Stewart, 1975). Corey (1978) interpreted these results as indicating that early experience with only one diet produces an imprinting-like attachment to that diet that can be disrupted if a large number of foods (i.e., a mixed diet) have been experienced later.

These considerations led Braveman and Jarvis (1978) to conduct experiments to determine whether or not animals that were familiarized with either one distinctively flavored solution or a set of solutions would exhibit reduced neophobia and, in addition, form weaker taste aversions to another, distinctively different, flavored solution. In their first experiment, they found that familiarization with the taste of a solution can reduce neophobia to another solution without interfering with associations between the taste of the latter solution and the aversive aftereffects of a LiCl injection. They thus concluded that animals may learn that a particular solution is a safe one even though they have not previously tasted it, and that such learning does not disrupt associations between the taste of that solution and the aversive aftereffects of LiCl injections. In the other Braveman and Jarvis experiments, the results were similar. They again found that when rats received a solution or a series of solutions whose flavors differed from that of the test solution, neophobia was reduced but conditioned aversions were unaffected.

In general, the results of the Braveman and Jarvis (1978) study indicate that the processes involved in neophobia and conditioned taste aversions need not be coupled. They also found that neophobia quickly dissipates, a conclusion consonant with the views of Carroll et al. (1975). These findings may be interpreted within a framework that views avoidance of novel or unfamiliar tastes as a reaction to the potentially aversive properties of novel stimuli. From this perspective, Braveman and Jarvis proposed that neophobia is influenced by the characteristics of the solution(s) that the rats experience prior to tests for neophobia. As long as a novel test solution is not perceived as being too unusual, and therefore not as aversive, animals will ingest it readily. One way to reduce the aversiveness of novelty is to preexpose the animals to other novel solutions. Thus, the novelty's aversiveness can be reduced rather quickly following the presentation of even a single solution. They suggest, however, that reducing the aversiveness of one novel solution has no effect on associations between ingestion of the now nonaversive novel solution and the noxious effects of a LiCl injection.

If the reduction of neophobia with prior diverse taste experience and the dissociation of neophobia from the conditioned taste aversion propensity are reliably demonstrated, the original views of Barnett and Cowan (1976) could be questioned. They held that flavor neophobia is prominent among rats because of their varied diets and because of the high likelihood of toxins occurring in novel, untried substances. They also contended that neophobia and conditioned taste aversion are merely different points on a common dimension of aversiveness, a ground of common function. This position was challenged by Miller and Holzman (1981a) in the following manner: In the previous experiments in which rats were exposed to various flavors, such as the one by Braveman and Jarvis (1978), a stimulus generalization gradient may have influenced the results. The tendency of rats to generalize across flavors that humans would judge to be dissimilar indicates the importance of the choice of the particular flavor used for pretraining and training. This possibility prompted Miller and Holzman to minimize generalization between the novel treatment substances and the test substance by restricting their studies to the use of one that was sweet (sucrose), sour (hydrochloric acid), bitter (quinine), and salty (saline). By using one flavor for testing, the three remaining flavors could be used as novel substances.

The design of Miller and Holzman's (1981a) first experiment was similar to that of Braveman and Jarvis's (1978) except for the choice of flavors that minimized stimulus generalization between them. The former obtained the same basic effects as the latter and thus concluded that the observed reduction in neophobia was not due to stimulus generalization. The ease with which neophobia was reduced without previous exposure to the flavor in question raises questions about Barnett and Cowan's (1976) hypothesized protective role of neophobia. Miller and Holzman found that the capacity to form conditioned taste aversions was unaffected by previous flavor exposure and concluded that neophobia and conditioned taste aversions have different bases.

Further experiments by Miller and Holzman (1981a) indicated that although neophobia to NaCl and HCl was attentuated by prior diverse taste experiences maximally dissimilar to the test substance, such effects were not obtained when the rats were tested with sucrose and quinine. These prior taste experiences also did not affect the acquisition of conditioned taste aversions. As a consequence of these results, the authors proposed that the primary function of neophobia may not be to minimize intake of poisons; rather, alternative functions should be considered. In this regard, they suggested that this apparent dilemma may be a manifestation of one of nature's imperfections. Natural selection averages over situations and does not yield an optimal fit to each and every ecological problem (Cosmides & Tooby, 1987, this volume).

The effects of dissimilar flavor exposure upon neophobia to NaCl and HCl in contrast to that to sucrose and quinine eludes a convincing interpretation. Sweet and bitter flavors may be inherently more salient to rats because sweetness often connotes high caloric food stuffs and bitterness frequently indicates toxic substances in the natural habitat of the rat. This suggestion was based on the assumption that, owing to the high correlation of bitter substances with both naturally occurring and manufactured toxins, bitter flavors such as that of quinine had been identified through natural selection as being highly relevant or salient. Similarly, sweet substances such as sucrose were assumed to possess an inherently high relevance due to their consistent association with sources of nourishment in the rat's natural habitat. In contrast, salty and sour flavors may be less highly correlated with specific outcomes of ingestion in the rat. This does not imply, however, that sour or salty tastes are necessarily of little consequence to rats. This line of reasoning led Miller and Holzman (1981b) to probe the relationship between neophobia to specific flavors and the ecological role of a particular flavor across species from diverse ecological niches. A comparative perspective is particularly important because the majority of experiments on neophobia have been limited to the domestic rat.

COMPARATIVE ANALYSIS OF FLAVOR NEOPHOBIA

In the Miller and Holzman (1981b) project, the differential neophobic reactions of rats (*Rattus norvegicus*, Sprague Dawley strain), guinea pigs (*Cavia porcellus*), and gerbils (*Meriones unguiculatus*) were the basis of tests with four highly dissimilar flavors. The experiment with rats indicated neophobia to solutions of sucrose, NaCl, and quinine, but not to 1% citric acid. The authors rejected the argument that the concentration of the latter was too weak to taste or was unpalatable. The rats' 5-ml average consumption of citric acid was much lower than that of water yet was large enough to indicate that it was not unpalatable. The failure of citric acid solutions to evoke neophobia suggests the possibility that sour is a basic flavor that is less meaningful to the animals than the others. An exception is the sour taste of foods that are in decay. Although highly acidic substances are potentially toxic to animals, such substances are rarely encountered in the natural habitat of rats. Such theorizing is congruent with the adaptive–evolutionary analysis by Rozin and Kalat (1971).

In order to probe the validity of their analysis, Miller and Holzman (1981b) used the same procedure to study the reactions of guinea pigs, which have different nutritional requirement than rats. The former are unusual among rodents because they require exogenous ascorbic acid. Because this substance is sour and highly similar in taste to citric acid, the experimenters predicted that guinea pigs would display pronounced neophobia to citric acid. Given that herbivores with the natural diet of guinea pigs must independently regulate salt and caloric intake, neophobia to salty and sweet tastes was also predicted. The results indicated an appreciable neophobia to citric acid, sucrose, and NaCl, but marginal reactions to quinine. On the basis of their differential intake of these solutions, it was assumed that these animals were able to discriminate between the bottles containing quinine and water.

The weak neophobia of guinea pigs to quinine is consistent with Jacobs's (1978) finding that these animals show a low rejection in preference tests of quinine as well as another bitter-tasting substance, sucrose octa-acetate (SOA). Indifference to SOA has been found in various strains of mice (Warren, 1963; Warren & Lewis, 1970). The guinea pig's insensitivity to bitter stimuli seems to be incongruous with its herbivorous mode of feeding. Many plants contain chemicals that are toxic and frequently have bitter tastes associated with them. Jacobs suggested that a priori rejections of bitter substances may severely limit the quantity of food available to the herbivore that may have also evolved some degree of tolerance for the alkaloids and other toxicants in the plants of its native habitat. Schneider (1987) proposed that even if most secondary plant substances were in principle "invented" by the plant against herbivores, one would also expect that some plant feeders "learn" to cope with such plants by metabolizing the bitter and/or toxic substances or storing them in an inert form. This is clearly documented in insect herbivores such as the larvae of some noctuid moth species. Alternatively, guinea pigs may reject toxic alkaloid plants on the bases of their complex flavors or their nongustatory cues. These animals have been shown to easily acquire color-toxin associations (Braveman, 1974).

The view that neophobias and conditioned taste aversions reflect, respectively, unlearned and learned tendencies to minimize consumption of potentially toxic substances suggests that it should be easier for an animal to acquire an aversion to a flavor that the animal is initially highly reluctant to ingest than a flavor evoking less neophobia. Thus Miller and Holzman (1981b) examined the tendency of rats and guinea pigs to form conditioned aversions to ascorbic acid, a substance that evokes different degrees of neophobia in these two species. Their results indicate that guinea pigs display greater neophobia than rats to ascorbic acid, but that the two species did not differ in propensity to form conditioned taste aversions. These results do not support Carroll et al.'s (1975) view that the degree of neophobia is correlated with propensity to form conditioned taste aversions. According to their prediction, the greater sensitivity of guinea pigs arising from their need of ascorbic acid should produce both heightened neophobia and a greater propensity to form conditioned taste aversions to this substance. It should be noted that Brackbill et al. (1971) were unable to condition rats to show aversions to citric acid, even though NaCl and saccharin served as effective CSs. They theorized that palatable stimuli are more conditionable than less palatable ones.

To test their views of biological relevance with other species, Miller and Holzman (1981b) studied gerbils, rodents that synthesize ascorbic acid. Because they do not require exogenous ascorbic acid and there is no evidence that a regular part of their natural diet tastes sour, the experiments predicted little neophobia to sour flavors. A high degree of neophobia to bitter flavors was predicted because many varieties of desert plants produce toxins, particularly alkaloids that are bitter in taste. Miller and Holzman (1981b) also predicted that gerbils should resemble rats and guinea pigs in manifesting neophobia to both sweet and salty solutions, given the biological relevance of these substances. Much to their surprise, the authors observed a lack of neophobia to all of the test fluids. Initially, they hypothesized that these results reflected a high gustatory threshold for these substances rather than an absence of neophobic defense mechanisms in the gerbils. Thus, they tested the gerbils for neophobia with quinine on a range of concentrations and also used these solutions as CSs in a test for conditioned taste aversions. Again, the gerbils failed to show neophobia to any of the quinine solutions despite their ability to detect the novel solutions and a readiness to form conditioned taste aversions to them. The authors suggested that gerbils may be devoid of neophobia because of their strong exploratory tendency relative to rats (Osborne, 1977; Riddell, Galvani, & Foster, 1976). Alternatively, in their natural habitat gerbils obtain much of their water through the moistness of food rather than the consumption of free water. It is, therefore, possible that neophobia in gerbils or any other species that obtain water via the metabolism of solid foods might be more evident in the consumption of novel food than in the drinking of novel liquids. Support for this prediction may be derived from theoretical and experimental arguments developed by Bernstein and Goehler (1983) in their discussion of research on conditioned taste aversions.

There are differences in the intensity or concentration of the flavor chemicals in solid and liquid diets. Bernstein and Goehler (1983) have argued that food stimuli are more intense or "salient" than liquid stimuli, and that food aversions are consistently more robust and immune to interference than liquid aversions. In their experiments, they found that foods interfered with liquid aversions, but that liquids did not interfere with food aversions. In analyzing the features of food stimuli that are responsible for the robustness of food aversions, these experimenters considered differences in the intensity of the flavors as well as in the nutrient or energy content of liquid versus solid diets. Bernstein and Goehler examined the contribution of these parameters as targets for aversions by comparing aversions to sucrose solutions that differed in concentrations. They found that although concentrated and dilute sucrose solutions differed in their resistance to interference effects, these results were not as clear-cut as the food–liquid differences obtained in their preceding experiment. This led them to conclude that differential effectiveness of foods and liquids as interfering agents are mainly due to their differences along the dimensionality of "intensity." The authors also suggest that foods (and not drinks) are the likely targets for which learned taste aversions evolved—both in terms of toxin avoidance and nutrient selection. Their experimental results indicate that "dilute solutions appear to be but a pale imitation of foods" (p. 148).

FLAVOR NEOPHOBIA TO SOLID FOOD

Neophobia to Sweet and Sour Flavors in Food-Deprived Hamsters

Given the difficulties experienced by Miller and Holzman (1981b) in demonstrating flavor neophobia with liquid substances in gerbils, and the findings by Bernstein and Goehler (1983) on "intensity" differences between food and liquid stimuli in conditioned aversion studies, I reconsidered the appropriate methodology for experiments on flavor neophobia. There is greater ecological validity in the use of solid foods in neophobia studies because animals are more likely to experience taste differences in the foods that they encounter than in the liquids they consume. For seed and nut eaters such as gerbils and hamsters, the choice of nuts as test material may be more appropriate, because these rodents readily approach such food items.

I began my series of experiments (with Vivien Yee) on flavor neophobia by studying the Syrian golden hamster (*Mesocricetus auratus*) because of their invariant species-typical reactions to nuts and seeds. These rodents readily approach nuts (especially when they are in their shell) and react to them by pouching rather than by eating them. The tendency for hamsters to hoard rather than consume food pellets has been documented in many studies (e.g., DiBattista & Bedard, 1987; Rowland, 1982; Silverman & Zucker, 1976; Wong, 1984; Wong & Jones, 1985). The hoarding–pouching behavior sequence of these animals lends itself to a clear and simple procedure for testing flavor neophobia. I used the latency of the hamster's pouching response as a means of assessing its reactions to new flavors. When offered nuts, a hamster typically picks up and deposits each nut in its cheek pouch, one at a time.

During the experiment, one unflavored roasted peanut was placed in the corner of the cage opposite to the area where the animal built its sleeping nest. The nut was dropped into the corner, and a timer was used to record the response latency of the hamster in placing the nut in its cheek pouch after it sniffed the nut. This test was continued until the animals showed asymptotic response latency.

Then the animals were randomly assigned to either a group in which they were tested with a nut coated with sugar in a cornstarch base or one in which they continued to be tested on the unflavored nut. The animals were tested for 10 daily sessions. The animals switched to the sugar-coated nut took a much longer time (M = 80 sec) to pouch the nut than those tested with the unflavored nut (M = 3 sec). These results indicate that hamsters exhibit neophobia upon their initial encounter with a familiar food adulterated with a novel (sweet) flavor. This neophobic is consistent with Miller and Holzman's (1981b) results with rats tested on sucrose-flavored fluids. This finding is particularly interesting because sweet-tasting foods evoke pleasure (positive affective reactions) and generally elicit greater consumption than foods that are either of neutral or negative hedonic value (Blass, 1987; Young, 1959). Because sweet-tasting substances are generally associated with sources of nourishment in the animal's habitat (Rozin, 1987), one may not expect inherent wariness toward such a flavor although it may be novel. However, Miller and Holzman (1981b) suggested that animals are highly sensitive or attentive to sweets that identify necessary nutrients, and this sensitivity may enhance neophobic reactions.

In the same experiment, Miller and Holzman (1981b) also found that rats showed little neophobia to sour solutions, whereas guinea pigs did. In order to determine whether or not hamsters would display the neophobic reaction to sour solutions, I conducted another experiment using nuts flavored with 2% citric acid. The results of Experiment 2 indicate that, unlike rats, hamsters exhibit flavor neophobia to citric-acid flavored nuts. Aside from possible differences due to species' reactions to tastes, these results probably reflect effects arising from the medium in which the flavor was embedded (i.e., food vs. solution). The results obtained in this experiment indicate the value in the use of solid food rather than fluid in flavor neophobia studies because animals are more likely to experience taste differences in the foods that they encounter than in the liquids they consume. Given the fact that highly acidic and sour-tasting substances are potentially toxic to animals, it is reasonable to expect a neophobic reaction to such a citric-acid based nut. Miller and Holzman (1981b), however, proposed that although highly acidic substances are potentially toxic to animals, such substances rarely occur in the natural habitat of rats and other rodents. Thus, there should be a relatively low degree of inattentiveness to sour substances and consequently little neophobia to them relative to sweet substances. Our results with hamsters tested on citric-flavored nuts indicate the contrary, however. It is possible, though, that rats, that are adapted to a mesic (moist) habitat and also parasitic on humans may encounter toxic liquids; this is not the case with rodents adapted to a semiarid habitat.

In my and Yee's experiments, the hamsters were tested under conditions of food deprivation and were maintained at 85% of their normal body weight. There were a number of factors that led me to reconsider the appropriateness of this procedure. Hamsters who are living on lab chow will eat seeds and nuts avidly, regardless of food deprivation, once they overcome their initial neophobic reactions to them. The difficulty with which hamsters recover from body weight loss (Borer,

Rowland, Mirew, Bores, & Kelch, 1979), along with ethical considerations, would also lead one to test these animals under nondeprived conditions. Because it is likely that hamsters in natural conditions hardly ever experience body weight loss because of access to the food larder arising from their hoarding behavior, it may be more appropriate to test them for neophobia when they are maintained at normal body weight. Earlier, Berstein and Goehler (1983, p. 134) pointed out that "the vast majority of studies have employed a conditioned taste-aversion paradigm with water-deprived rats as subjects and flavored liquids as conditioned stimuli (CSs). The degree to which the results of such studies generalize to nondeprived animals and/or animals consuming solid foods merits investigation." Thus, Chris McBride and I embarked on a series of experiments on hamsters with these considerations in mind.

Neophobia to Salty, Sweet, Sour, but Not Bitter Flavors Among Nondeprived Hamsters

Aside from testing the hamsters under nondeprived conditions, McBride and I instituted another procedural change in the present experiments. In the initial project with Yee, I studied the effects of quinine-flavored nuts on the hamsters' latency to pouch and failed to observe any difference between the control animals tested with unflavored nuts and ones roasted with quinine mixed in a cornstarch base. In order to ensure that the lack of an effect was not due to an inadequate concentration of quinine, McBride and I conducted Experiment 3, in which the nut was rolled in a dish of quinine powder to ensure that this food item was absorbed with the substance. The animals were tested with unflavored nuts until they showed a stable baseline response latency. Then those in the experimental condition were shifted to a quinine-saturated nut while those in the control condition continued to receive an unflavored nut during the test trials. Again, the results indicated that the response latency to pouch the nut during the three test sessions was unaffected by quinine ($M = 5.4$ sec) relative to that of the control condition ($M = 4.7$ sec).

This led us to conduct Experiment 4, in which the hamsters' response latency to pouch nuts saturated with NaCl crystals was assessed. Despite the fact that both salty and sweet tastes elicit positive hedonic reactions (Grill & Berridge, 1985), previous results with rats indicate substantial neophobic reactions to fluids flavored with these substances (Miller & Holzman, 1981b). When tested with a nut flavored with NaCl, hamsters took a significantly longer period of time before pouching the nut than those tested with an unflavored nut, $F(1, 18) = 24.36$, $p < .0002$. There was also a significant group by trials interaction, $F(5, 90) = 6.50$, $p < .0001$. An inspection of Figure 5.1 reveals that although the hamsters were neophobic to the salted nut during the first few days of exposure to this novel flavor, they pouched the nut within the same period of time as the control animals by the fourth test session.

Given the previous findings indicating neophobic reactions to salty but not bitter-tasting nuts among hamsters with a procedure in which the nuts were fla-

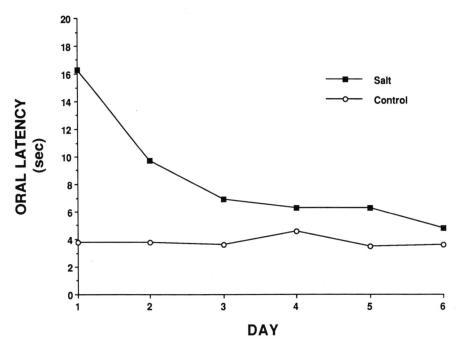

FIGURE 5.1. Latency of hamsters to pouch a NaCl-flavored or unflavored nut.

vored with the test substance, McBride and I used the same procedure to replicate Experiments 1 and 2, where the effects of sucrose and citric acid flavors roasted on a cornstarch base were demonstrated. In Experiment 5, following a baseline period where both groups were tested with an unflavored nut, the experimental group was given 6 successive daily trials with a nut rolled in sucrose crystals while the control group continued to be tested with the unflavored nut. Again, there was a significant effect of sucrose-coated nuts on the hamsters' pouching latency relative to the control group, $F(1, 18) = 76.58$, $p < .0001$ as well as a significant group by trials interaction, $F(5, 90) = 51.75$, $p < .0001$. These results are depicted graphically in Figure 5.2.

Although Experiment 2 indicated that hamsters show neophobic tendencies in pouching a nut roasted with a cornstarch and 2% citric acid base, Miller and Holzman (1981b) reported the failure of rats and gerbils to show a neophobic reaction to a sour-tasting fluid. The latter predicted that rats and other rodents would show little neophobia to sour tastes, because highly acidic substances rarely occur in their habitat. In order to ensure that the results with hamsters in Experiment 2 were not spurious or specific to particular test conditions, we conducted Experiment 6 to determine whether nondeprived hamsters tested with nuts flavored with citric acid crystals would show neophobia. The results are graphically depicted in

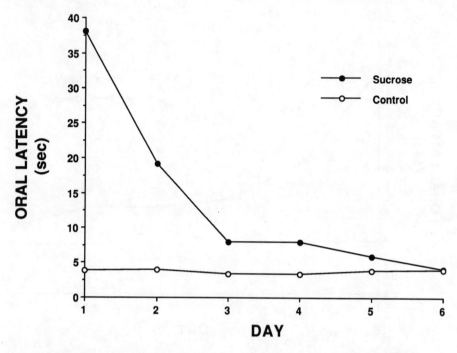

FIGURE 5.2.   Latency of hamsters to pouch a sucrose-flavored or unflavored nut.

Figure 5.3. It is obvious that the hamsters showed a much longer latency to pouch a nut adulterated with citric acid crystals than a familiar nonadulterated one. Unlike the results with salty and sweetened nuts, there was slower habituation to the sour-tasting nut. Although the animals in the experimental group showed a decline in response latency over the 10 test sessions, they still showed a longer latency up to the fifth test session than those in the control group. This is similar to the results by Miller and Holzman when citric acid consumption was compared to water intake.

In general, the results of these experiments with hamsters clearly indicate that these rodents show strong neophobic reactions to sweet, salty, and sour flavors in a peanut adulterated with these chemicals. These findings replicate the effects observed by Miller and Holzman (1981b) with rats tested with sweetened and salted fluids. Thus, it appears that flavors that generally elicit a positive hedonic reaction also produce initial hesitancy when these animals encounter foods or fluids conveying such flavors. Our results when the hamsters were tested with citric acid–flavored nuts contrast with those observed by Miller and Holzman in rats tested with hydrochloric acid–flavored fluids. We believe that embedding a solid food with a sour flavor is a more sensitive method of revealing neophobia than embedding this flavor in a fluid. Therefore, we are confident that there are reliable differences between the hamster's latency to pouch a plain familiar nut and one

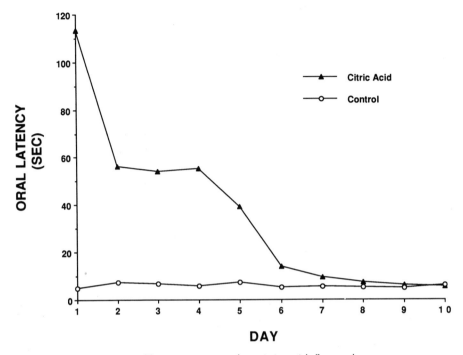

FIGURE 5.3.   Latency of hamsters to pouch a citric acid–flavored or unflavored nut.

that is novel and sour tasting. One may argue, however, that the hamsters may have taken a longer time to pouch the sour-tasting nut, not because of neophobia, but because such a taste is of negative hedonic value (i.e., has aversive properties). The observation that latency differences between the experimental and control groups continued to be evident for 5 days of testing may indicate the presence of possible aversive effects of the citric acid flavor. Yet the results of Experiment 3 indicate the failure of hamsters to manifest neophobia to bitter-tasting quinine, which generally inhibits food intake (Garcia & Hankins, 1975). Thus, we conclude that it is the neophobic factors that play a role in influencing the hamsters' initial encounters with a sour-tasting nut.

Flavor Neophobia to Sweet, Salty, Sour, but Not Bitter Flavors in Nondeprived Mongolian Gerbils

The experiments in the preceding section indicate the effectiveness of the hamster's response latency in handling a food item as a measure of neophobia. Although Miller and Holzman (1981b) did not observe neophobic reactions among gerbils tested with fluids of various flavors, it is very possible that these animals may reveal neophobic tendencies if tested with the method developed to study neophobia in hamsters. However, the test method must be modified to deal with obvious species differences in the way the animals respond to the nut. Hamsters pouch their food because of the morphological characteristics of their cheek pouches. Although gerbils have also been known to hoard food (Nyby & Thiessen, 1980), they do not pouch it. Instead, gerbils often consume any single item of food that is presented to them. In the following experiments we dropped a nut in their cage, started the timer when the animals first sniffed the nut, and stopped it when they ate it. This response measure was referred to as *oral latency*.

In Experiment 7 the gerbils were tested for 5 days with an unflavored nut. By the end of this period all the animals showed a stable oral latency baseline. Then 10 of the gerbils were tested for 4 consecutive days with a sugar-coated nut, while the other 10 continued to be tested with the plain nut. The results indicated that those switched to the sweetened nut showed a greater oral latency than the control animals, $F(1, 18) = 15.11$ $p < .001$. There was also a significant groups by trials interaction, $F(3, 54) = 12.34$, $p < .001$. These results are depicted in Figure 5.4 and they suggest that neophobic reactions were manifested by the gerbils to the sweet flavor. Such a finding indicates Miller and Holzman's (1981b) negative results with gerbils may be due to the nature of their test procedure. In order to ascertain whether our present results with this method are specific only to foods flavored with sucrose, we conducted another experiment in which the gerbils' reactions to a peanut flavored with NaCl was compared to their oral latency to a fa-

FIGURE 5.4.   Latency of gerbils to ingest a sucrose-flavored or unflavored nut.

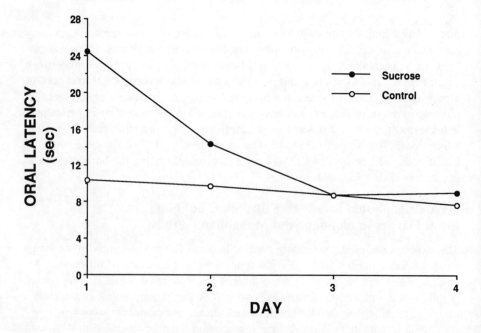

miliar nut. In Experiment 8 the animals' reactions, when switched to a salted nut, were compared with that of the control animals over a 5-day test period. Again, the results indicated that the gerbils showed a longer oral latency to the flavored nut than the unflavored nut, $F(1, 18) = 11.17$, $p < .001$ and a significant group by trials interaction, $F(4, 72) = 7.16$, $p < .001$. The results are displayed in Figures 5.4 and 5.5.

The results of Experiments 7 and 8 demonstrate that Mongolian gerbils are capable of showing neophobic reactions to novel flavors that are hedonically positive. The next step we took was to study the effects of novel flavors regarded as hedonically negative on the gerbil's oral latency. Theoretically, one might expect that animals would take a longer time to investigate and manipulate foods that contain flavors considered aversive than those conveying pleasant tastes. Yet our results with hamsters indicated that nuts adulterated with quinine crystals did not increase these animals' pouching latency relative to the control animals. Thus, we performed a comparable experiment (Experiment 9) with gerbils and found no significant difference between the oral latency of those tested with quinine ($M = 10.5$ sec) and the controls ($M = 9.6$ sec). Such results produce difficulties for the notion that bitter flavors such as quinine have been selected as ecologically relevant to animals and should therefore elicit cautious, if not neophobic, reactions. Simi-

FIGURE 5.5. Latency of gerbils to ingest a NaCl-flavored or unflavored nut.

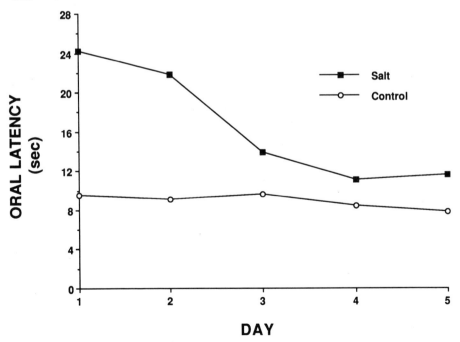

lar results were obtained when neophobia among gerbils and guinea pigs was assessed via changes in fluid consumption (Miller & Holzman, 1981b). The failure of these animals to show a negative reaction to quinine appears to be a behavioral anomaly in view of the presumed correlation between bitter-tasting substances and plants with high levels of alkaloid poisons. Would these animals fail to react to nuts flavored with other bitter-tasting chemicals? This question will be answered in a later section in this chapter.

Our final experiment on gerbils in this series (Experiment 10) concerned their reactions to nuts flavored with citric acid. Although Miller and Holzman (1981b) did not observe any effects of citric acid relative to unflavored water on the fluid consumption of gerbils and rats, our results indicated that hamsters showed a substantially delayed latency to pouch nuts laced with citric acid crystals upon initial encounter with them. In the final experiment, we tested the effects of nuts flavored with citric acid on the gerbils' oral latency relative to their reactions to unflavored nuts. The animals were tested for 3 days, and there was a significant group by trials effect, $F(1, 18) = 6.44$, $p < .02$. An examination of this interaction indicated that the citric acid group displayed a longer oral latency on Day 1 but soon showed the short latency of the control group on Day 2 (Figure 5.6). Again, these results contradict those reported by Miller and Holzman. Although the gerbils, like hamsters, showed neophobia to citric acid flavored nuts,

FIGURE 5.6.   Latency of gerbils to ingest a citric acid–flavored or unflavored nut.

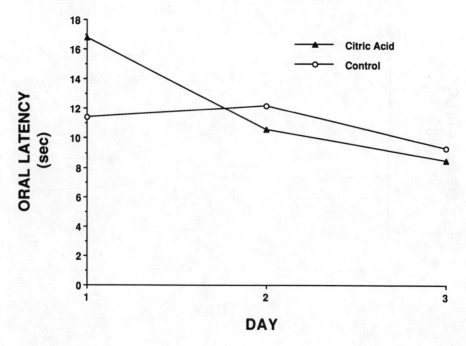

they differed from hamsters with respect to rate and degree of habituation to the substance.

Flavor Neophobia to Bitrex in Gerbils

Because natural plant toxins, which are often bitter in taste, occur in the natural environment of Mongolian gerbils, the presence of a selection for mechanisms that would protect these animals from foods conveying this taste would seem likely. Yet we did not observe neophobic reactions to nuts highly adulterated with quinine powder. This failure to demonstrate neophobia may reflect the particular bitter substance that we had chosen rather than an absence of neophobic defense mechanisms toward bitter flavors. For this reason we conducted an experiment using two substances that also evoke an intense bitter taste.

Psychophysical studies on human taste function have indicated that the compound sucrose octa acetate (SOA) evokes as high a rating of bitterness as the quinine salts (McBurney, 1969). Rats show a lower consumption of a solution containing .0005 M SOA than that of water (Warren, 1963). We also chose a compound, denatonium benzoate, which is described in the Merck Index (10th ed.) as "the most bitter substance known to man." This product, produced by McFarlan Smith Ltd in Edinburgh, Scotland, is known commercially as Bitrex. A study on children between 2 and 4 years old drinking orange juice containing 10 parts per million of Bitrex showed that these subjects rejected the juice after the first taste (Berning, Griffith, & Wild, 1982). The extremely bitter taste of the denatonium ion makes it an effective deterrent to ingestion.

Kathryn Koehler and I conducted an experiment with gerbils (Experiment 11) in which we compared the effects of SOA and Bitrex on their oral latency. The test procedure was similar to one developed in the previous experiments. The animals were given 3 days of testing with a plain, unflavored nut and then were subdivided into three groups. The control group continued to be tested with the unflavored nut, the second group with a nut adulterated with SOA crystals, and the third group with a nut dusted with Bitrex powder. The animals were given six test trials under their respective conditions and then given three trials with an unflavored nut. The results indicated an overall difference among the treatment groups, $F(2, 27) = 13.55$, $p < .0002$, but the groups by trials interaction was not statistically significant. The Newman-Keuls test was performed on the data collapsed across the trials and the results ($p < .05$) revealed that the Bitrex group took a much longer period of time to eat the nut ($M = 48.85$ sec) than those tested with a SOA-flavored ($M = 8.63$ sec) or an unflavored nut ($M = 5.55$ sec). There were no significant differences between the SOA and control groups, however.

There are at least two very interesting findings from Experiment 10. Although psychophysical studies on humans indicate that the magnitude of the bitterness rating for SOA is as great as that for the quinine salts, neither of these compounds increased the gerbils' latency to ingest a nut coated with them. There may be species differences in animals' reactions to SOA. Kare (1976) reported that

SOA at levels aversive to rats and humans is accepted by dogs and horses. Comparable findings were documented by Brindley (1965) on reactions of herring gulls and chicken to SOA. Similarly, Jacobs's (1978) results described earlier indicate the guinea pig's indifference to SOA in fluid concentrations approaching the limits of solubility. Perhaps Mongolian gerbils can be added to the list of SOA nontasters.

In contrast to SOA, however, Bitrex did attenuate (but not block) the gerbils' oral reactions to a nut flavored with it. This substance is extremely bitter to humans, to the extent that the experimenters were required to wear two sets of rubber gloves and a filter respirator to avoid the aversive effects of the extremely bitter and unpleasant sensations arising from contact with traces of Bitrex. Even with such precautions, the experimenters found that they could taste a bitter flavor on their lips and tongue for hours following the initial handling of Bitrex. While there were indications that the gerbils found the nut coated with Bitrex to be distasteful (i.e., they would run away from the nut or chew on a piece of the Sanicel corn bedding after tasting the nut), they nevertheless ate it eventually. A report by Mason (1987) also indicated acceptance of Bitrex by red-winged blackbirds. Because of the correlation between bitter tastes and alkaloids in poisonous plants, one would expect selection for protective mechanisms against the ingestion of foods conveying such flavors. Yet the nondeprived gerbils in this experiment ingested the bitter-tasting nut.

Although the gerbils took a longer period of time to initiate ingestion of a Bitrex-coated nut than an unflavored one, thus demonstrating neophobia, the fact that they ingested it at all is rather puzzling. With less potent sources of bitter flavors such as quinine and SOA (which inhibit ingestion in rats and most other rodents), the gerbils showed no impedance relative to their latency to ingest an unflavored nut. Since results by Carroll et al. (1975) indicated that neophobia is most effectively measured by short-term dependent measures, we had adopted the use of the latency measure in all of our experiments on flavor neophobia. Had we based our analysis on consumption rather than latency measures of intake, we may have observed a more dramatic effect of Bitrex on food intake. The fact that different chemical forms of bitter substances can elicit different reactions lends support to Grill, Spector, Schwartz, Kaplan, and Flynn's (1987) call for the use of a broader range of stimuli in the flavor research.

Conditioned Aversions to Bitter Tastes

Although we were able to demonstrate an unconditioned aversion to a Bitrex-coated nut, such an effect was not observed when the gerbils were tested with two other bitter-tasting substances, quinine and SOA. Earlier studies by Karanek, Adams, and Mayer (1975) and Miller and Holzman (1981b) demonstrated that gerbils can acquire an aversion to quinine solutions that have been paired with LiCl injections. Expanding on these studies, Brenda Leung and I conducted an experiment to ascertain whether similar results would be obtained with nuts flavored with quinine or SOA. In this experiment (Experiment 12) we assessed the effects of a single injection of .15 M LiCl (3 ml/100 g body weight) paired with the ingestion of either a nut flavored with quinine or with SOA. We gave these animals six daily test trials following this injection. We also ran control conditions in which one group of gerbils received the LiCl injection 10–15 min after the animals had ingested a plain nut, as well as groups that received an isotonic saline injection 10–15 min after eating an unflavored nut or one flavored with quinine or SOA. The results indicated an overall difference in oral latency among the groups, $F(2, 23) = 5.58$, $p < .05$, but there were no significant effects due to trials nor the groups by trials interaction. Multiple comparisons with the Newman-Keuls test of the data collapsed across trials indicated that the group tested with a quinine-flavored nut following the LiCl injection differed from all the other groups ($p < .01$), and that none of the other comparisons was statistically significant. These results are depicted in Figure 5.7.

The results of Experiment 12 indicate that quinine can serve as an effective CS and, thus, can elicit a conditioned taste aversion in gerbils. In contrast, sucrose octa acetate, which elicits an equivalent magnitude of bitterness in human judgment ratings (McBurney, 1969), did not produce an aversion in gerbils, even though it had been paired with an LiCl injection. Similarly, Jacobs's group (Jacobs, 1978; Jacobs & Labows, 1979) reported nonsignificant effects of SOA paired

FIGURE 5.7.   Latency of gerbils to ingest a nut flavored with quinine, sucrose octa acetate (SOA) or nothing following .15M LiCl injection.

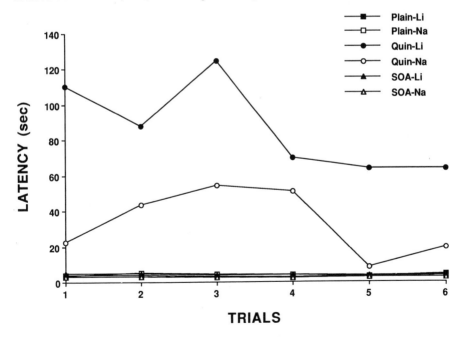

with LiCl on guinea pigs' subsequent intake. His experiments involved tests of fluid consumption so it appears that similar results are obtained whether or not one embeds SOA in a liquid or in solid food.

Our results with quinine-embedded nuts serving as a CS replicate the findings by Karanek, Adams, and Mayer (1975) and Miller and Holzman (1981b) on gerbils tested with liquids. The next question we asked was whether hamsters would acquire an aversion to nuts flavored with either quinine or SOA when these flavors are paired with a LiCl injection. We conducted Experiment 13 to study the effects of these flavors as CSs on the pouching latency of these animals. Following a period of baseline assessment to an unflavored nut, the animals were assigned to groups as either those tested with quinine or SOA. These groups in turn were subdivided into those receiving 0.15M LiCl or isotonic NaCl injection 10 min after they had pouched the nut. The day after the injection, the animals' latency times to pouch the nut were recorded and this test was carried on for 12 consecutive days. The results are plotted in Figure 5.8, and a visual inspection of it suggests that conditioned aversion occurred only among hamsters injected with LiCl following exposure to the quinine-flavored nut. An analysis of variance and the Newman-Keuls test of the data collapsed across trials substantiated this observation ($p \leq .01$).

The results with hamsters on the conditioned aversion paradigm are consistent with those with gerbils. Animals of both species showed an aversion to qui-

FIGURE 5.8.   Latency of hamsters to pouch a nut flavored with quinine, sucrose octa acetate (SOA), or nothing following .15M LiCl injection.

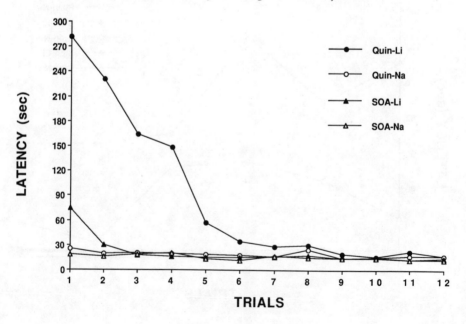

nine when it was paired with LiCl but fail to show a conditioned response to SOA. These animals' relative indifference to bitter-tasting substances such as SOA, either as an unconditioned or as a conditioned stimulus, is similar to results involving the fluid intake of cavies (Jacobs, 1978; Jacobs & Labows, 1979). Unfortunately, Jacobs did not test the guinea pigs' reactions in a conditioned taste aversion experiment using quinine as the CS. The reactions of hamsters, gerbils, and guinea pigs contrast with those of rats that were given a brief two-choice preference test involving 0.1% quinine and 1.0% SOA mixed in food powder. Rats (nonlesioned as well as VMH-lesioned ones) found a 0.1% quinine diet more acceptable, and presumably less bitter than a 1.0% SOA diet (Sclafani, Aravich, & Schwartz, 1979). Although hamsters and gerbils did not show any unconditioned aversion to either of these agents, they acquired an aversion to quinine but not to SOA when these substances were associated with the effects of LiCl injection. The conditionability of quinine as an aversive agent may be due to the postingestive effects of this substance. Quinine is known to have widespread systemic and central actions. In particular, quinine is a local irritant that, when taken orally, can produce gastric pain, nausea, and vomiting in humans (Rollo, 1975). Sucrose octa acetate, although more bitter tasting, appears to be free of toxic effects (Green, 1942; Linegar, 1943) and can be ingested in large amounts by rats (Sclafani et al., 1979, Experiment 3).

In interpreting their findings of conditioned aversion to sacacharin but not to SOA solutions in guinea pigs, Jacobs and Labows (1979) suggested that the salience of the gustatory stimulus is a critical variable. They presented the conjecture that these animals have evolved tolerance of many bitter-tasting toxicants that they encounter in nature. Consequently, the importance of the bitter taste as a discriminative cue in regard to the safety of food may have been diminished. The validity of this hypothesis is dependent upon data indicating that guinea pigs show an inability to form aversions to quinine as a result of conditioning. However, although this condition has not yet been assessed in cavies, our results for hamsters and gerbils indicate the conditionability of quinine to LiCl effects. For this reason, one may question the premise of Jacobs and Labows's explanation of their results with SOA. There still remains the question of how wild cavies are able to avoid poisoning themselves.

Jacobs and Labows (1979) suggested that cavies must rely on mechanisms other than sensitive innate or acquired aversions to bitter tastes similar to those inherent in SOA or quinine. They conducted an experiment indicating the rapid acquisition of an aversion to toxic substances contained in a plant such as the Japanese honeysuckle. When offered this plant and others that were nontoxic, the cavies showed rapid rejection of the honeysuckle but not of the others. Their immediate rejection of honeysuckle indicates that sensory factors, such as taste, smell, or fuzzy texture, could account for the animals' responses to it. It is also possible that the cavies rapidly acquired an aversion to the physiological effects arising from the toxic compound saponin, found in this plant. Thus, these results suggest that these animals possess the ability to avoid self-poisoning despite their relative insensitivity to bitter tastes. Alternatively, or in addition, some herbivorous animals could develop detoxifying mechanisms. Insects have developed such a strategy, and perhaps plant–insect interactions have led the way to the bitter-rejection system in some invertebrates. The tissues of the Monarch butterfly (*Danaus plexippus*) contain toxic cardiac glycosides that are bitter and deter most predators (Brower, 1984). Of the many species of mice living in the Monarch butterfly's wintering ground in Mexico, only one (*P. melanotis*) preys upon this insect, eats enough of them to gain weight in a laboratory study, and selectively eats the least toxic parts (Glendinning & Brower, 1990). When tested in the laboratory, these mice were found to be less sensitive to the taste of cardiac glycosides, were able to withstand high levels of toxic compounds, and did not show well-developed behavioral techniques for assessing the nutritive value of foods (i.e., the ability to form conditioned aversions).

PREFERENCE–AVERSION FUNCTIONS AND NEOPHOBIA

It is commonly assumed that animals universally show acceptance of sweet- and salty-tasting diets and rejection of sour- and bitter-tasting substances. This premise is based on the model curves for the preference–aversion functions of animals (typically rats) presented with such stimuli (Catalanotta, Frank, & Contreras, 1986; Pfaffman, 1960). Similar outcomes are evident with the taste reactivity method, which analyzes the effects of brief oral infusions on oral motor behavior. This general method was pioneered by Jacobs, Smutz, and DuBose (1977) in their comparative observations on the ontogeny of taste preference in neonatal humans, rats, and hamsters. Since that work, Grill and Berridge (1985) have developed an extremely comprehensive technology and behavioral taxonomy for analyzing facial reactions to taste stimuli. The outcome of this analysis indicates that salty and sweet solutions elicit a positive affective (ingestive) reaction, while sour and bitter substances elicit a negative (aversive) reaction. Such results appear to be obvious, given the adaptive consequences of such reactions. The rejection of sour and bitter taste stimuli is a protective reaction against the ingestion of substances that may induce illness. For this reason, researchers interested in controlling food intake and body weight of animals typically use acids and quinine as dietary adulterants (Peters, Wellman, Gunion, & Luttmers, 1979). Such agents are effective in decreasing diet palatability and consumption in most species, including rabbits (Ganchrow, 1979). Foods and liquids flavored with sour-tasting acids induce concentration-dependent undereating and weight loss in rats (Peters et al., 1979). However, these researchers found that wet mash diets containing quinine in various concentrations induced initial undereating and weight loss but that the rats showed adaptation to the food, as evidenced by weight gain after the 10th day. In our experiments on flavor neophobia with quinine, we found that the latency to ingest/hoard nuts flavored with this substance did not differ from that to unflavored nuts. Similarly, Jacobs (1978) observed absence of bitter rejection to quinine-flavored fluids in cavies, although fluids containing citric acid were rejected.

In their extensive review of the literature, Garcia and Hankins (1975) summarized the data on protozoan, invertebrate, and vertebrate species and concluded that "the rejection of bitter may represent a phylogenetically ancient natural response tendency" (p. 39). They suggested that "natural aversions to bitter have been acquired by a wide variety of species through natural selection" (p. 39). Similarly, Brower (1984) stated that "virtually all compounds of biological origin which are toxic are also bitter tasting to humans" (p. 117). Garcia and Hankins cite the rapidity with which organisms acquired conditioned aversions to any flavor that is followed by toxicosis. However, Bernays and Chapman (1987) suggest that the relationship between deterrent responses and bitterness/toxicity may not be as tight as commonly presumed. Scott and Mark (1987) also observed that although there is a rough correlation between bitterness and toxicity, it is not perfect. Our findings with hamsters and gerbils, as well as Jacobs's (1978) data on cavies, are congruent with these suggestions.

In his chapter in this volume, Cabanac proposed that there is a relationship between pleasure and usefulness and between displeasure and harm or danger. Earlier, Cabanac (1971) indicated that in the commerce of a subject with incentives, the wisdom of the body leads the organism to seek pleasure and avoid displeasure and manifest behaviors that are beneficial to its physiology. Thus, the affective dimension of a sensation depends directly on the usefulness of the stimulus to the subject. From this perspective, an innate preference for sweet and salty tastes and avoidance of bitter and sour tastes in many generalist species has a sound ecological basis (Rozin, 1987). In nature, fruits are the most common items that produce the sweet sensation, which is associated with energy-producing sugars. Similarly, organisms show a preference for foods and fluids containing sodium chloride. Exogneous NaCl is critical for normal electrolyte balance and therefore has consequences for cellular regulation. Thus, it is "useful" for the organisms to react to salty-tasting items with positive affect. This consideration is relevant to Cabanac's proposition that the seeking of pleasure and the avoidance of displeasure leads to behaviors with useful (i.e., positive) homeostatic consequences. From this perspective, is the indifference of hamsters, gerbils, and guinea pigs to bitter-tasting substances such as quinine and SOA an indication that they have evolved tolerance of some bitter-tasting substances that they encounter in their habitat?

In our experiments on flavor neophobia we have plied the animals with a nut that was either sweetened, salted, soured, or embittered and compared their latency to ingest/pouch this nut with one that was familiar and unflavored. It might be expected that these animals would take a longer time to accept a nut flavored with a stimulus endowed with negative hedonic value (e.g., sour or bitter) than a neutral one. It might also be assumed that a flavor that elicits a positive affective reaction would be ingested/hoarded in a shorter period of time than one of neutral hedonic value. Our results, however, indicated that sweetened and salted substances evoked longer response latencies than bitter nuts. Although it can be argued that the longer response latency to a sour nut relative to a plain one may reflect the effects of the negative hedonic value of the sour taste as well as neophobia, this is not the case with sweetened and salted nuts. The fact that the gerbils' response latencies to the latter flavors were greater than those to the sour one indicates the salience of neophobic tendencies. The animals' response latency to the bitter-tasting nut was not different from that to an unflavored one. Yet most measures of intake and choice of nutrients lead one to conclude that bitter flavors elicit negative affect, thus acting as aversive stimuli.

MECHANISMS OF FLAVOR NEOPHOBIA

There have not been many systematic attempts to uncover the mechanisms of flavor neophobia. In his review of determinants of exploration and neophobia, Corey (1978) regarded neophobia as a specific instance of *neotic behavior*. This term refers to the entire range of responses to novel stimuli, including exploration, aggression, orientation, and of course, neophobia. Novelty is a function of the discrepancy between past experience and the present sensation; the greater the discrepancy, the greater the novelty. Arousal level is influenced by the degree of novelty, and aversive effects may ensue from highly arousing novel stimuli. More specifically, Domjan (1977) interpreted the rodents' avoidance of novel or unfamiliar tastes as a reaction to the assumed aversive properties of such stimuli. Preexposure of the rodent to the test or related stimuli reduces the aversiveness of novelty and thus the neophobic reaction is thereby attenuated. Although this interpretation appears to be reasonable, it lacks details about the physiological mechanisms responsible for the aversiveness of novel stimuli.

Katz (1988) suggested that rodents encountering novel stimuli experience a stress reaction and that the hormones released during this stress response mediate the neotic behavior. Exploratory behavior is evoked by novel stimuli and consists of behaviors that allow information about the object to be collated (van Abeleen, 1989). Van Abeleen proposed that the behaviors occurring when the rodent encounters new situations may involve a certain degree of fearfulness. Katz suggested that exploratory behavior and opiate activity may covary, and van Abeleen pointed out the impossibility of empirically separating unique effect of novelty from that of stress. When rodents are tested with novel stimuli, they experience some degree of stress, and opiates may be released as a result. However, the effects of novelty on exploratory behavior may be secondary to their effects on stress. The intake of novel foods is suppressed because such foods increase arousal above an optimal level (Domjan, 1977). These effects may be reflected by increased stress indicated by β-endorphin release.

Novel foods are approached with hesitation (Rozin, 1977), and this might be interpreted as indicating the effects of stress on exploratory behavior of the novel food item. When rats are exposed to novel flavored solutions, they show numerous approach and withdrawal tendencies to and from the fluids. Such responses decrease over time, and the attenuation of neophobic reactions to the fluid may constitute part of the normal voluntary ingestion pattern of the rats (Domjan, 1977). With increasing number of exposures to the novel food, the degree of neophobia decreases (Nachman, Rauschenberger, & Ashe, 1977; Testa & Ternes, 1977). Such an attenuation of neophobia may reflect lowered stress as the test food item becomes more familiar.

If neophobia is mediated by stress, opiates may play a role in this process. Endogenous opiates may somehow act to counteract the stress associated with a novel stimulus, therefore promoting exploratory behavior. Normally, rats explore new surroundings when placed in that setting. If they are administered naloxone, an opiate antagonist, they show a decrease in their exploratory activity (File, 1980). Another possible mechanism influencing neotic behavior involves the hypothalamic peptide corticotrophin releasing factor (CRF). This factor induces the release of the adrenocorticotropic hormone (ACTH) and β-endorphin. In turn, ACTH regulates the release of corticosterone from the adrenal glands. Administration of CRF into the brains of rats (which increases the stress-induced hormonal response) has been found to decrease the amount of food eaten in the open field and the number of approaches to the food (Britton, Koob, River, & Kale, 1982). These researchers also found that anxiolytic drugs increase the amount of food eaten in the test apparatus as well as the mean amount eaten per approach to the food. These findings provide further suggestions that the neophobic response may be mediated by variables that influence stress.

It follows from the preceding discussion that various stress-reducing agents that influence an animal's exploratory behavior in a novel environment would also reduce their reactivity in a flavor neophobia experiment. In the analysis of mechanisms mediating flavor neophobia in hamsters, antiopioid treatments may not be appropriate because of the presence of an endorphin-mediated hibernation system in these animals. Opiate antagonists have little effect on the feeding and locomotory activity of nonhibernating hamsters (Lowy, Sangiah, & Yim, 1985). Any attempt to test the stress-mediation of neophobia hypothesis via manipulation of the endorphin system is also inappropriate for the following reasons. Material in Raible's chapter on feeding systems indicates that opiate agonists and antagonists facilitate and inhibit feeding, respectively, through their actions within the CNS. For this reason, any effects of such agents on an animal's latency to ingest or pouch a novel food item may reflect their direct influence on the feeding system as much as their action on the stress system.

Instead of manipulating the hamster's reactions to stress-eliciting stimuli via the administration of antiopioid drugs, we consider the use of a synthetic glucocorticoid dexamethasone (DEX). This substance binds to corticosterone receptors in the pituitary and prevents the release of ACTH and β-endorphin (Guillemin et al., 1977). Although DEX does not cause a reduction of food intake in nonstressed hamsters (Lowy & Yim, 1982), it suppresses the adrenal reaction to stress of pregnant hamsters (Pratt & Lisk, 1990). DEX was administered to them via drinking water at a dosage of 1.0 ug/ml. The effects of DEX on these hamsters were likely due to its inhibition of ACTH. From this perspective, it may be possible to test the stress-mediated flavor neophobia hypothesis with hamsters by comparing DEX-treated animals with controls. Currently this hypothesis is being tested in my laboratory by Chris McBride and Marne Owen.

Another approach to the study of the effects of pituitary–adrenal responsiveness on neophobia was taken by Weinberg, Smotherland, and Levine (1978). They argued that because infantile handling alters the rats' responses to novelty and handled rats show less elevation of plasma corticosterone in response to novel stimuli than controls (Levine, Haltmeyer, Kavas, & Deneberg, 1967), flavor neophobic responses would be attenuated by infantile handling. The results supported this prediction. When presented with a pleasant (sweet) novel solution, handled rats drank more of it than the nonhandled ones. These results are consistent with Domjan's (1976) contention (presented earlier) that exposure increases subsequent intake because it reduces the novelty of the substance and thereby attenuates the neophobic or aversive responses elicited by novelty. Unfortunately, the infantile handling treatment is effective mainly in rats and some strains of mice, and there are doubts whether emotional reactivity can be attenuated in hamsters or gerbils through early stimulation. Another method to study the relationship between emotional reactivity and neophobia is to administer CRF, which has been shown to induce stress-related behaviors in rats (Britton et al., 1982). Assuming that this peptide has the same physiological effects on gerbils and hamsters, we predict that it would produce greater neophobic reactions in them than in control animals. Lesion studies may be another viable approach to the study of mechanisms underlying flavor neophobia. Brain structures such as the hippocampus and amygdala have been implicated in novelty-induced responding (van Abeleen, 1989; Nachmann et al., 1977), and it is possible that manipulations of these regions will influence flavor neophobic responses.

SYNOPSIS

I began this chapter with a consideration of the possible adaptive function of neophobic reactions in rodents and, after describing research on conditions that elicit it, presented some conjectures about possible proximate (physiological) mechanisms mediating this inherent wariness of novel-tasting foods. The earlier experiments in various laboratories were conducted to demonstrate the existence of this phenomenon in the laboratory with deprived domestic rats. Most of these experiments involved tests in which the rat's consumption of novel-tasting fluids was compared with that of an unflavored and therefore familiar fluid (water). In these studies the nature of the novel flavor was not considered of great importance. The main consideration was that the solutions had to be novel, and the flavor of the particular test stimulus seemed almost arbitrarily chosen. These tests involved substances such as saccharin, vinegar, sucrose, coffee, and others containing complex flavors. The hedonic reaction evoked by these flavors was not considered in the design of such experiments. In general, these experiments indicated the manifestation of flavor neophobia, although the phenomenon was enhanced when illness-inducing toxic injections were administered to the animals prior to their exposure to the novel-tasting edible. It was assumed that the degree of neophobia resulting from the initial presentation of the test substance would reflect the subsequent conditionability of that flavor in a taste aversion experiment. Subsequent studies by a number of investigators indicated that the processes involved in neophobia and conditioned taste aversions do not necessarily overlap. If this proposition were true, there is the possibility that neophobic reactions have not neccessarily been selected as a primary defense against poisoning as suggested by Barnett (1958) and Barnett and Cowan (1976). Instead, it may be more probable that learned aversions are the primary defense against the ingestion of toxins (Miller & Holzman, 1981a).

An alternative perspective on the relationship between neophobia and conditioned taste aversions is to consider the ontogeny of these processes. The neonate is able to select "safe" foods or fluids as a result of imprinting-type mechanisms—for instance, Porter and Levy's discussion in this volume on development of dietary preferences of rodents, in which they indicate that mothers may deposit chemical labels onto food items suitable for feeding. These labels may then be used by the pups to select safe foods. Commensurate with flavor imprinting, flavor neophobia might operate to keep the organism's flavor preference from straying away from the original imprinted flavor. The interplay of flavor imprinting and flavor neophobic processes would direct the organism's feeding behavior to appropriate substances. Given that many environments are unstable, however, rigidity of flavor preferences would not be adaptive in the event that food sources with the imprinted flavor(s) become scarce. An additional mechanism is therefore necessary to ensure adaptation to a changing habitat. Thus enters into the scenario the role of acquired taste or flavor aversions. An elaboration of this perspective is presented in Schulze and Watson's commentary on the present chapter.

The perspective of Schulze and Watson's formulation suggests that neophobia should not vary directly with the flavor of toxic substances as argued by Miller and Holzman (1981b). If this were the case, there would be duplication of function between neophobic processes and those of conditioned taste aversions. The extent to which a neonate manifests innate neophobic reactions depends upon its habitat. Those living in a stable habitat would be more likely to show neophobia than those adapted to a unstable habitat. This is a likely possibility because adaptation is complete and optimum for the former habitat while an unstable one would favor adaptations requiring flexibility.

The preceding discussion certainly indicates the necessity of a comparative approach to the analysis of flavor neophobia. The Miller and Holzman (1981b) project on rats, gerbils, and guinea pigs is interesting and useful from that perspective. Although some of their results were congruent with expectations derived from an evolutionary perspective, there were many puzzling aspects about the reactions of these animals to various experimental conditions. For one thing, rats did not show neophobic reactions to sour-tasting fluids and guinea pigs showed weak neophobia to bitter-tasting fluids. Most surprising of all was the failure of gerbils to react with neophobia to any of the basic flavors, sweet, salty, sour, or bitter. I attributed these results to the methodology of the studies. Intake measures were taken of fluids offered these animals, and I argued that latency measures of the animals' reactions to a food containing a novel flavor are more appropriate in neophobia studies. This led me into a series of experiments on hamsters and gerbils that indicated the manifestation of neophobia to a sweet, salty, and sour-tasting nut, but not to one saturated with quinine. The findings with the first three flavors confirmed my hypothesis about appropriate test conditions for these animals, but their failure to react to quinine posed another puzzle.

The observation that the animals' response latencies to a novel bitter-tasting nut were similar to those to a familiar unflavored one indicated that neither neophobia nor unconditioned aversion to a bitter taste was evident. Such an observation is contrary to that commonly reported in rats (Miller & Holzman, 1981b). Although hamsters and gerbils are capable of detecting and discriminating the taste of either quinine or SOA when these agents are used as a CS in a conditioned taste aversion experiment, they do not find it as unpalatable as do rats. When we conducted an experiment using Bitrex, "the most bitter substance known to man" (Merck Index, 10th ed.), however, we found that although gerbils took a long time in inspecting the flavored nut, they did eventually ingest it. These results suggest that extremely bitter-tasting substances may inhibit ingestion in gerbils but not enough to initiate a protective defensive reaction against them. Perhaps, like guinea pigs that may have evolved tolerance for the alkaloids of plants in their habitat (Jacobs, 1978), gerbils may have developed similar adaptations. This line of reasoning suggests that a priori rejection of bitter but nontoxic foods may limit the quantity of food available to a herbiviore or granivore. A similar argument might be made for the Syrian golden hamster but not for omnivores such as rats.

There has been little work on the physiological mechanisms underlying flavor neophobia. Reactions to novel stimuli involve the organism's detection of the discrepancy between past stimuli and the present sensation (Corey, 1978). Large discrepancies result in a state of high arousal that is aversive to the organism. On the basis of Katz's (1988) work indicating stress reactions when rats encounter novel stimuli and the release of endorphins that mediate exploratory behavior, I suggested that similar mechanisms may be mediating reactions to novel flavors. At present there are insufficient data to assess the validity of this proposal.

Earlier in this discussion I alluded to the possible effects of early experience resulting in flavor imprinting and how this process interacts with that of flavor neophobia to guide the organism to appropriate foods. Acquired flavor aversions enter into the situation later to ensure adaptive food selection in a changing habitat where the imprinting flavor(s) may become scarce. These processes are examples of adaptive specializations or behavioral phenotypes that have specifically evolved in response to environmental pressures. The demands of the natural situation provide a framework for the types of domain-specific psychological mechanisms suggested in the Cosmides and Tooby chapter in this volume. Presumably, natural selection resulted in rearrangement of patterns in tissues and molecules in the food processing machinery of hamsters and gerbils that resulted in their indifference to bitter-tasting chemicals such as quinine and SOA for the reasons discussed earlier. Selection processes shaped the taste preferences of these animals to produce the specific behavioral reactions indicated in our experiments, and these may correlate to some degree with their fitness.

REFERENCES

Barnett, S. A. (1956). Behaviour components in the feeding of wild and laboratory rats. *Behaviour, 9*, 24–43.

Barnett, S. A. (1958). Experiments in "neophobia" in wild and laboratory rats. *British Journal of Psychology, 49*, 195–201.

Barnett, S. A., & Cowan, P. E. (1976). Activity, exploration, curiosity and fear: An ethological study. *Interdisciplinary Science Reviews 1*, 43–62.

Berning, C. K., Griffith, J. F., & Wild, J. E. (1982). Research on the effectiveness of denatonium benzoate as a deterrent to liquid ingestion by children. *Fundamental and Applied Toxicology, 2*, 44.

Bernays, E., & Chapman, R. (1987). The evolution of deterrent responses in plant-feeding insects. In R. F. Chapman, E. A. Bernays, & J. G. Stoffolano Jr. (Eds.), *Perspectives in chemoreception and behavior*. New York: Springer-Verlag.

Bernstein, I. L., & Goehler, L. E. (1983). Relative potency of foods and drinks as targets in aversion conditioning. *Behavioral and Neural Biology, 37*, 134–148.

Blass, E. M. (1987). Opioids, sweets and a mechanism for positive affect: Broad motivational implications. In J. Dobbing (Ed.), *Sweetness*. New York: Springer-Verlag.

Borer, K. T., Rowland, N., Mirow, A., Borer, R. C., & Kelch, R. P. (1979). Physiological and behavioral responses to starvation in the golden hamster. *American Journal of Physiology, 236*, E105–E112.

Brackbill, R. M., Rosenbush, S. N., & Brookshire, K. H. (1971). Acquisition and rentention of conditioned taste aversions as a function of the taste quality of the CS. *Learning and Motivation, 2*, 341–350.

Braveman, N. S. (1974). Poison-based avoidance learning with flavored or colored water in guinea pigs (*Cavia procellus*). *Behavioral Biology, 14*, 189–199.

Braveman, N. S. (1978). Preexposure to feeding-related stimuli reduces neophobia. *Animal Learning and Behavior, 6*, 417–422.

Braveman, N. S., & Jarvis, P. S. (1978). Independence of neophobia and taste aversion learning. *Animal Learning and Behavior, 6*, 406–412.

Brindley, L. D. (1965). Taste discrimination in bobwhite and Japanese quail. *Behavioral Biology, 13*, 507–512.

Britton, D. R., Koob, G. F., River, J., & Vale, W. (1982). Intraventricular corticotropin-releasing factor enhances behavioral effects of novelty. *Life Science, 31*, 363–367.

Brower, L. P. (1984). Chemical defense in butterflies. In R. I. Vane-Wright & P. R., Ackery (Eds.), *The biology of butterflies*. London: Academic Press.

Cabanac, M. (1971). Physiological role of pleasure. *Science, 173*, 1103–1107.

Capretta, P. J., Petersik, J. T., & Stewart, D. J. (1975). Acceptancy of novel flavours is increased after early experience with diverse tastes. *Nature, 254*, 689–691.

Carroll, M. E., Dinc, H. I., Levy, C. J., & Smith, S. C. (1975). Determinants of neophobia and enhanced neophobia in the albino rat. *Journal of Comparative and Physiological Psychology, 89*, 457–467.

Catalanotto, F. A., Frank, M. E., & Contreras, R. J. (1986). Animal models of taste alteration. In H. L. Meiselman & R. S. Rivlin (Eds.), *Clinical measurement of taste and smell*. New York: Macmillan.

Chitty, D. (Ed.). (1954). *Control of rats and mice* (Vols. I–II). London/New York: Oxford University Press (Clarendon).

Corey, D. T. (1978). The determinants of exploration and neophobia. *Neuroscience and Biobehavioral Reviews, 2*, 235–253.

DiBattista, D., & Bedard, M. (1987). Effects of food deprivation and hunger motivation in golden hamsters. *Journal of Comparative Physiological Psychology, 101*, 183–189.

Domjan, M. (1976). Determinants of the enhancement of flavor-water intake by prior exposure. *Journal of Experimental Psychology, 2*, 17–27.

Domjan, M. (1977). Attenuation and enhancement of neophobia for edible substances. In L. M. Barker, M. R. Best, & M. Domjan (Eds.), *Learning mechanisms in food selection*. Waco, TX: Baylor University Press.

File, S. E. (1980). Naloxone reduces social and exploratory activity in the rat. *Psychopharmacology, 71*, 41–44.

Ganchrow, J. R. (1979). Taste preferences in rabbits for acids, sucrose, saccharin and quinine. *Physiology and Behavior, 22*, 457–460.

Garcia, J., & Hankins, W. G. (1975). The evolution of bitter and the acquisition of toxiphobia. In D. A. Denton & J. P. Coughlin (Eds.), *Olfaction and taste: Fifth International Symposium*. New York: Academic Press.

Glendenning, J. I., & Brower, L. P. (1990). Feeding and breeding responses of five mice species to overwintering aggregations of the Monarch butterfly. *Journal of Animal Ecology, 59*, 1091–1112.

Green, M. W. (1942). Sucrose octa acetate as a possible bitter stomachic. *Bulletin of the National Formulary Committee of the American Pharmacological Association, 10*, 131–133.

Grill, H. J., & Berridge, K. C. (1985). Taste reactivity as a measure of the neural control of palatability. *Progress in Psychobiology and Physiological Psychology, 11*, 1–61.

Grill, H. J., Spector, A. C., Schwartz, G. J., Kaplan, J. M., & Flynn, F. W. (1987). Evaluating taste effects on ingestive behavior. In F. Toates & N. Rowland (Eds.), *Feeding and drinking*. Amsterdam, The Netherlands: Elsevier.

Guillemin, R., Vargo, T., Rossier, J., Minick, S., Ling, N., Rivier, C., Vale, W., & Bloom, F. (1977). Beta-endorphin and adrenocorticopin are secreted concomitantly by the pituitary gland. *Science, 197*, 1367–1369.

Jacobs, H. L., Smutz, E. R., & DuBose, C. N. (1977). Comparative observations on the ontogeny of taste preference. In J. M. Weiffenbach (Ed.), *Taste and development: The genesis of sweet preference*. Bethesda, MD: U.S. Department of Health, Education and Welfare.

Jacobs, W. W. (1978). Taste responses in wild and domestic guinea pigs. *Physiology and Behavior, 20*, 579–588.

Jacobs, W. W., & Labows, J. N. (1979). Conditioned taste aversion, bitter taste and the avoidance of natural toxicants in wild guinea pigs. *Physiology and Behavior, 22*, 173–178.

Kalat, J. W. (1977). Status of "learned safety" or "learned non correlation" as a mechanism in in taste-aversion learning. In L. M. Barker, M. R. Best, & M. Domjan (Eds.), *Learning mechanisms in food selection*. Waco, TX: Baylor University Press.

Kalat, J. W., & Rozin, P. (1971). Role of interference in taste-aversion learning. *Journal of Comparative and Physiological Psychology, 77*, 53–58.

Kalat, J. W., & Rozin, P. (1973). "Learned safety" as a mechanism in long-delay taste-aversion learning in rats. *Journal of Comparative and Physiological Psychology, 83*, 198–207.

Karanek, R., Adams, K. S., & Mayer, J. (1975). Conditioned taste aversion in the Mongolian gerbil (*Meriones unguiculatus*). *Bulletin of the Psychonomics Society, 6*, 303–305.

Kare, M. (1976). Comparative study of taste. In L. Beidler (Ed.), *Handbook of sensory physiology*: Vol. 4. *Chemical senses, Part 2, Taste* (pp. 278–292). Berlin: Springer-Verlag.

Katz, R. J. (1988). Endorphins, exploration and activity. In R. J. Rodgers & S. J. Cooper (Eds.), *Endorphins, opiates and behavioural processes*. Chichester, UK: Wiley.

Levine, S., Haltmeyer, G. C., Karas, G., & Deneberg, V. (1967). Physiological and behavioral effects of infantile stimulation. *Physiology and Behavior, 2*, 55–59.

Linegar, C. R. (1943). Acute and chronic studies on sucrose octa acetate by the oral method. *Bulletin of the National Formulary Committee of the American Pharmacological Association, 11*, 59–63.

Lowy, M. T., Sangiah, S., & Yim, G. K. W. (1985). Naltrexone fails to suppress spontaneous locomotor activity in hamsters. *Pharmacology, Biochemistry and Behavior, 22*, 399–401.

Lowy, M. T., & Yim, G. K. W. (1982). Drinking, but not feeding, is opiate sensitive in hamsters. *Life Sciences, 30*, 1639–1644.

Mason, J. R. (1987). Ro-Pel efficiency: Evaluation of active ingredients under optimum conditions with red-winged blackbirds (*Angelaius phoericens*). Denver Wildlife Research Center Bird Damage Report No. 384.

Flavor Neophobia 263

McBurney, D. H. (1969). Effects of adaptation on human taste function. In C. Pfaffmann (Ed.), *Olfaction and taste: Proceedings of the Third International Symposium*. New York: Rockefeller University Press.
Merck Index of Chemicals and Drugs, Tenth Edition. (1963). Rahway, NJ: Merck & Co.
Miller, R. S., & Holzman, A. D. (1981a). Neophobias and conditioned taste aversions in rats following exposure to novel flavors. *Animal Learning and Behavior, 9*, 89–100.
Miller, R. S., & Holzman, A. D. (1981b). Neophobia: Generality and function. *Behavioral and Neural Biology, 33*, 17–44.
Mitchell, D. (1976). Experiments on neophobia in wild and laboratory rats: A reevaluation. *Journal of Comparative and Physiological Psychology, 90*, 190–197.
Nachmann, M., & Jones, D. R. (1974). Learned taste aversions over long delays in the rat: Behavioral assessment of noxious drug effects. *Journal of Comparative and Physiological Psychology, 86*, 949–956.
Nachmann, M., Rauschenberger, J., & Ashe, J. H. (1977). Stimulus characteristics and food aversion learning. In N. W. Milgram, L. Krames, & T. M. Alloway (Eds.), *Food aversion learning*. New York: Plenum Press.
Nyby, J., & Thiessen, D. D. (1980). Food hoarding in the Mongolian gerbil (*Meriones unguiculatus*): Effects of food deprivation. *Behavioral and Neural Biology, 30*, 39–48.
Osborne, G. L. (1977). Differences in locomotory activity between rats and gerbils. *Behavioral Biology, 19*, 548–553.
Peters, R. H., Wellman, P. J., Gunion, M. W., & Luttmers, L. L. (1979). Acids and quinine as dietary adulterants. *Physiology and Behavior, 22*, 1055–1059.
Pfaffmann, C. (1960). The pleasures of sensation. *Psychological Review, 67*, 253–268.
Prakash, I., & Jain, A. P. (1971). Bait shyness of two gerbils, *Tatera indica* and *Meriones hurricane Jerdon*. *Annals of Applied Biology, 69*, 169–172.
Pratt, N. C., & Lisk, R. D. (1990). Dexamethasone can prevent stress-related litter deficits in the golden hamster. *Behavioral and Neural Biology, 54*, 1–12.
Revusky, S., & Bedarf, E. W. (1967). Association of illness with ingestion of novel foods. *Science, 155*, 219–220.
Riddell, W. J., Galvani., P. F., & Foster, K. M. (1976). The role of escape-motivated behavior in aversive conditioning in rats and gerbils. *Behavioral Biology, 17*, 485–494.
Richter, C. P. (1953). Experimentally produced behavior reactions to food poisoning in wild and domesticated rats. *Annals of the New York Academy of Sciences, 56*, 225–239.
Rollo, I. M. (1975). Drugs used in the chemotherapy of malaria. In L. S. Goodman & A. Gilman (Eds.), *The pharmacological basis of therapeutics*. New York: Macmillan.
Rowland, N. (1982). Failure by deprived hamsters to increase food intake: Some behavioral and physiological determinants. *Journal of Comparative and Physiological Psychology, 96*, 591–603.
Rozin, P. (1968). Specific aversions and neophobia resulting from vitamin deficiency or poisoning in half-wild and domestic rats. *Journal of Comparative and Physiological Psychology, 66*, 82–88.
Rozin, P. (1977). The significance of learning mechanisms in food selection: Some biology, psychology, and sociology of science. In L. M. Barker, M. R., & Domjan, M. (Eds.), *Learning mechanisms in food selection*. Waco, TX: Baylor University Press.
Rozin, P. (1987). Sweetness, sensuality, sin, safety, and socialization: Some speculations. In J. Dobbing (Ed.), *Sweetness*. New York: Springer-Verlag.
Rozin, P., & Kalat, J. W. (1971). Specific hungers and poison avoidance as adaptive specializations. *Psychological Review, 78*, 459–486.
Rzoska, J. (1953). Bait shyness, a study in rat behavior. *British Journal of Animal Behaviour, 1*, 128–135.
Rzoska, J. (1954). The behavior of white rats towards poison baits. In D. Chitty (Ed.), *Control of rats and mice* (Vol. 2). Oxford: Clarendon Press.
Sclafani, A., Aravich, P. F., & Schwartz, J. (1979). Hypothalamic hyperphagic rats overeat bitter sucrose octa acetate diets but not quinine diets. *Physiology and Behavior, 22*, 759–766.
Schneider, D. (1987). The strange fate of pyrrolizidine alkaloids. In R. F. Chapman & E. A. Bernays (Eds.), *Perspectives in chemoreception and behavior*. New York: Springer-Verlag.
Scott, T. R., & Mark, G. P. (1987). The taste system encodes stimulus toxicity. *Brain Research, 414*, 197–203.
Siegel, S. (1974). Flavor pre-exposure and "learned safety." *Journal of Comparative and Physiological Psychology, 87*, 1078–1082.

Silverman, H. J., & Zucker, I. (1976). Absence of post-fast food compensation in the golden hamster (*Mesocricetus auratus*). *Physiology and Behavior, 17,* 271–285.

Testa, T. J., & Ternes, J. W. (1977). Specificity of conditioning mechanisms in the modification of food preferences. In L. M. Barker, M. R. Best, & M. Domjan (Eds.), *Learning mechanisms in food selection.* Waco, TX: Baylor University Press.

van Abeleen, J. H. F. (1989). Genetic control of hippocampal and dynophinergic mechanisms regulating novelty-induced exploratory behavior in house mice. *Expericntia, 45,* 839–845.

Warren, R. P. (1963). Preference aversion in mice to bitter substance. *Science, 140,* 808–809.

Warren, R. P., & Lewis, R. C. (1970). Taste polymorphism in mice involving a bitter sugar derivative. *Nature, 227,* 77–78.

Weinberg, J., Smotherland, W. P., & Levine, S. (1978). Early handling effects on neophobia and conditioned taste aversion. *Physiology and Behavior, 20,* 589–596.

Wong, R. (1984). Hoarding versus the immediate consumption of food among hamsters and gerbils. *Behavioural Processes, 9,* 3–11.

Wong, R. (1994). Response latency of gerbils and hamsters to nuts flavored with bitter-tasting substances. *The Quarterly Journal of Experimental Pscyhology, 47B,* 173–186.

Wong, R., & Jones, C. H. (1985). A comparative analysis of feeding and hoarding in hamsters and gerbils. *Behavioural Processes, 11,* 301–308.

Wong, R., & McBride, C. B. (1993). Flavour neophobia in gerbils (*Meriones unguiculatus*). *The Quarterly Journal of Experimental Psychology, 46B,* 129–143.

Wong, R., McBride, C. B., & Owen, M. (1994). Dexamethasone and flavor neophobia in hamsters. *Psychobiology, 55,* 203–208.

Young, P. T. (1959). The role of affective processes in learning and motivation. *Psychological Review, 66,* 104–125.

_____ chapter 6 _____

Motivation
Homeostatic mechanisms
may instigate and shape
adaptive behaviors
through the generation
of hedonic states

GEORG SCHULZE
University of British Columbia

SYNOPSIS AND COMMENTS
Roderick Wong

In this chapter Schulze provides the framework for a general theory of motivation that regards the proximal mechanism of homeostasis as the basis for motivated activities that affect the organism's fitness. Hedonic states are associated with these homeostatic mechanisms (HM), and these states provide feedback about the consequences of the organism's behavior. Although there have been criticisms of the application of homeostatic theory to motivation because of its apparent simplicity and seeming inability to account for the complexities of motivated behavior, Schulze's analysis is more difficult to discount. To accomplish this task, he presents a detailed description of different ways in which a homeostatic system operates. His elaboration on the components of a HM, the character of its operation, and the arrangement of these components relative to one another indicates the complexity as well as the utility of such a system. Although it may appear protracted, the discussion of alternative ways in which water temperature in an aquarium can be

I wish to express my sincere gratitude to Roderick Wong, Stephen Bowlsby, and Neil V. Watson for their constructive comments.

regulated via different kinds of control loops, the arrangement and types of heating and cooling coils, serves as a model of how motivated behavior may be regulated.

Cosmides and Tooby (this volume) viewed the psychology of an organism as the total set of proximate mechanisms that cause behavior. Because adaptive behavior is predicated on adaptive thought, these authors regard cognitive programs as the most important aspect of proximate causation, because the cognitive level is specified in a psychological mechanism's function. Schulze's presentation adds homeostatic mechanisms to the list and argues for their importance, because they regulate the consequences of behavior. These mechanisms function by triggering behaviors to counteract environmental stimuli that may affect the physical integrity of the organism. When the current value of the regulated variable (CP) is moved away from the set point (SP) by these stimuli, this deviation may be counteracted in two ways. Internal physiological-compensatory processes or external behavioral processes may be activated to attain this goal. These processes may be linked in a hierarchical order. Schulze suggests that the operation of a particular HM can influence more than one type of behavior, and that the same behavior can be affected by more than one HM. This leads us to the phenomenon of adjunctive behavior (Falk, 1977), which is also discussed in the commentary on P. Wong's chapter.

When rats are allowed access to small pellets of food under intermittent schedules of delivery and are given concurrent free access to water, they drink regularly and almost continuously after each pellet. Because water intake is well in excess of that required to maintain the homeostatic balance of the hydrational system, such behavior appears to be anomalous. Falk (1971) regarded this polydipsic behavior as "absurd," because it is not in the interests of a food-restricted animal to heat water to body temperature only to lose it as urine and also risk water intoxication in the process. Falk (1977) coined the term *adjunctive behavior* to describe such behavior maintained under such circumstances. Water takes on a reinforcing property to a nonthirsty animal because of a schedule relevant to hunger. His analysis of adjunctive activities suggests that in the natural habitat, adaptive value is served by the animal's switching to an alternative behavior when the ongoing activity is in some way thwarted. This polydipsia is an exaggeration of a natural switching mechanism operating in the unnaturally restrictive environment of the test chamber.

It is adaptive for animals to avoid situations when they learn that reward no longer occurs there. This is one of the coping strategies in dealing with frustrative stress that is discussed in P. Wong's chapter in this volume. Staddon and Simmelhag (1971) suggested that subdominant motivational states may be elevated when the animal is thwarted from responses appropriate to the relevant state. In the wild, such facilitation will usually ensure that the animal leaves the situation to seek other reinforcers. Schulze attempts to analyze these issues in terms of homeostatic control. In some ways, his analysis parallels the explanations put forth by Falk (1977) and Staddon and Simmelhag (1971) regarding the switching of activities but differs in its interpretation of reasons for such a switch. It occurs as an attempt to maintain the positive hedonic state experienced during eating, and it is selected because it is controlled by the same HM mechanism. Water is consumed until the negative hedonic state generated by overconsumption of water exceeds the masking effect generated by the same behavior.

It is obvious from the preceding discussion that the concept of hedonic state is defined in relation to the position of the current stimulus with respect to some hypothetical set point (SP) for a given variable. A pleasant hedonic state is attained when the stimulus moves in the direction of the SP; and when it moves away from the SP, an aversive hedonic state is generated. An organism reacts to a stimulus on the basis of the hedonic state produced by the stimulus, which, in turn, is also influenced by the internal state of the organism. Cabanac's research on the pleasantness ratings of various temperature stimuli applied to the skin, as well as on the effects of glucose gastric preloads on ingestive behavior in rats, documents this point fairly clearly.

Adaptive behavior arises from the hedonic state resulting from a response to a stimulus. From this premise Schulze discusses the relation between the current stimulus and SP as the basis of the hedonic state experienced. He concedes difficulties in determining how the value of a SP is established by the organism but speculates that it may have been determined through evolution as a means of maintaining the integrity of the organism. Following Cosmides and Tooby's contention that evolution selects for mechanisms that represent the manifestation of adaptive design at the psychological level, Schulze views HMs and their associated hedonic states as other products of such selection. He uses the results of Cabanac's work on alliesthesia to define SP. It is represented by the point at which an organism fails to express affect in reponse to a stimulus.

In response to criticisms of set point theory, by Bolles (1979), Pinel (1990), and Wirtshafter and Davis (1977), Schulze argues that their alternative explanations deal with comparisons between a signal indicating the current state of the system and some input reference signal. This is true whether the input signal and system signal are directly related or are transformed before comparison. It may be possible to design a system that does not explicitly contain a SP, but its function may emerge under a different guise.

In general, innate psychological mechanisms that process information in ways that lead to adaptive behavior may be regulated by HMs. Concepts in motivation such as arousal, incentive, reinforcement, punishment, and so on may be defined more precisely to reflect the relationships between stimuli, regulated variables, set point, and hedonic state. Mrosovsky (1990) presented an extensive analysis dealing with regulation around shifting set points. He uses the term *rheostasis* to refer to the condition or state involving change in set points. In that respect, Schulze's analysis is congruent with the more extensive theory presented by Mrosovsky.

References

Falk, J. L. (1971). The nature and determinants of adjunctive behavior. *Physiology and Behavior, 6,* 577–588.
Mrosovsky, N. (1990). *Rheostasis: The physiology of change.* New York: Oxford University Press.
Staddon, J. E., & Simmelhag, V. L. (1971). The "superstition" experiment: A reexamination of its implications for the principles of adaptive behavior. *Psychological Review, 78,* 3–43.

INTRODUCTION

Given that the behavior of an organism in an environment may play a major role in the outcome of natural selection (Aboitiz, 1989; Manning, 1971; Tooby & DeVore, 1987), it is assumed that organisms are motivated to engage in behaviors that would, on balance, have the result of maximizing their inclusive fitness (Hamilton, 1964). It is therefore of interest to know how this is accomplished. I propose that homeostasis is involved in the proximal mechanisms influencing many motivated behaviors that are adaptively shaped by hedonic states associated with these homeostatic mechanisms.

Although the concept of homeostasis has been featured prominently in many discussions of motivated behaviors and related research strategies (e.g., Adolph, 1943; Cabanac, Duclaux, & Spector, 1971; Nisbett, 1972; Richter, 1927; Rowland, 1987; Stellar & Stellar, 1985; Toates, 1986), this approach has frequently been considered as being too limited to account for the complexity of behavior (e.g., Apter, 1989; Colgan, 1989; Deutsch, 1971; Dewey & Humber, 1951; Evans, 1989; McFarland, 1989; Young, 1961). This attitude or viewpoint may be the result of an inadequate understanding or a superficial application of homeostatic theory to motivated behaviors. Hence hypotheses used are likely to be too coarse grained for the data, with ensuing confusion (Toates & Evans, 1987). A more in-depth understanding of the organization of homeostatic systems, how they regulate important variables, how they may give rise to hedonic states and determine behaviors, the role they may play in learning and memory, as well as how they can be investigated by psychologists, may allow the terminology of motivation to be stated in more unambiguous terms. The clarity of terminology contributes to the clarity of theories (Cabanac, this volume; Toates & Evans, 1987). It may consequently be useful to reconsider the analysis of motivation in the context of homeostasis and new developments in the field.

HOMEOSTATIC MECHANISMS

Since the introduction of "le milieu interieur" by Claude Bernard (see Langley, 1973, for a historical review), the concept of *homeostasis* has played an important role in the understanding of many physiological processes (Colgan, 1989; Dilman, 1981; Hardy, 1983; Kupfermann, 1985b; Smith, 1987). A *homeostatic mechanism* (HM) can be described as a mechanism that operates to keep a variable within a certain range of values (however small the range) by counteracting, in one or a variety of ways, perturbations that may move the variable out of this range. A HM consists of several key components and the character of its operation crucially depends on the arrangement of these components relative to one another. A brief discussion of a HM, its components, and the manner in which their arrangement may influence the operation of the HM follows.

Probably the most familiar type of HM is the thermostat or air conditioner used to regulate the internal temperature of a building. Such an arrangement usually involves a source of heat and/or cold (the effector), a temperature gauge (the sensor), and a switch (the controller). If the ambient temperature in the building as registered by the temperature sensor falls below a certain value (the set point), the switch controlling the heat source is switched on. This will result in an increase in the ambient temperature. When the temperature has risen to equal the set point temperature, the switch to the heat source is switched off. An air conditioner works on the same principle, except that the air is cooled instead of heated. This sequence of events will repeat itself over and over again, and in the process the ambient temperature will stay relatively close to the set point temperature irrespective of the outside temperature.

The arrangement of these components relative to one another can have very important consequences for the operation of the mechanism. Consider a homeostatic system consisting of a mixing tank that can hold a certain volume of water. The tank provides water to an aquarium, and proper regulation of the water temperature entering the aquarium is critical. Water is pumped into the tank from outside, and the incoming water temperature can fluctuate considerably depending on the season and the time of day. The tank is equipped with two effectors: a heating element and a cooling element. There is also a sensor, a temperature gauge, added to this arrangement.

The Effect of Sensor Position

Before this tank can be put into operation, the temperature sensor needs to be installed. This is not as trivial as it may seem. The sensor can be installed in the pipe that leads from the tank to the aquarium. From the sensor a connection leads to the controller, which will switch the heating coil on when the temperature drops below the set point and off when the temperature rises above the set point. The controller will also switch the cooling coil on when the temperature rises above the set point and off when it drops below the set point.

If the water coming out of the tank is too cold, the temperature sensor will cause the heating coil to be switched on. This will lead to an increase in the water temperature coming from the tank. Such an arrangement forms a feedback control loop: The outcome of the heating or cooling process is fed back to control the on-going activity of the process. If the water coming out of the tank is too cold, however, it does not matter whether the water will subsequently be heated; it is too late to affect the temperature of the water entering the aquarium. Therefore, installing the temperature sensor in the pipe leading from the tank to the aquarium may not be advisable.

The sensor can be installed in the pipe feeding water into the tank from outside. This would allow the mechanism to respond to changes in the temperature of the water before the water reaches the tank by switching the heating or cooling coils on and off. This arrangement constitutes a feedforward control loop and allows the system to anticipate the temperature of the water that will enter the tank: If cold water is headed for the tank, the heating element can be activated to heat the incoming cold water, and vice versa for hot water entering the tank. Since there is no temperature sensor monitoring the temperature of the water leaving the tank, however, it cannot be ascertained whether the temperature adjustments have been adequate. In response to cold water coming into the tank, the water in the tank could be overheated, and thus the water fed to the aquarium would be too hot. A similar problem could result from hot water entering the tank. Consequently, installing the temperature sensor in the pipe feeding into the tank may also be ill advised.

This leaves one more option: The temperature sensor could be installed in the tank itself. But such a solution may incorporate the worst elements of the previous two. The mechanism can now neither anticipate the temperature of incoming water nor can it verify the temperature of the outgoing water.

The existence of control loops, that is, feedforward and feedback loops, is an essential feature of homeostatic systems (Colgan, 1989; Evans, 1989; Hardy, 1983; Smith, 1987), and both may be incorporated into the same HM. There are two types of control loops: positive and negative. In the preceding examples, negative control loops have been discussed. These generally counteract disturbances to the system, while positive feedback will tend to magnify disturbances. It should also be kept in mind that the signal fed from the sensor to the controller need not be proportional to the magnitude of the variable measured but can be damped or amplified by signals from other homeostatic systems.

Finally, the arrangement of the heating and cooling coils would also affect the operation of the system, and their placement should be taken into consideration.

The Effect of Controller Type

In addition to the arrangements of the components of the HM, the nature of these components can dramatically affect the operation of the mechanism. This is perhaps especially true for the controller. There are four basic types of controller, each with a characteristic effect on variable regulation. This typically concerns the ways in which the controllers control the operation of the effectors. For instance, if the electrical current that flows through the heating coil can be regulated and control can be exerted over the amount of cooling fluid flowing through the cooling coil, a considerable amount of control can be exercised over the temperature of the water leaving the tank.

The simplest way to regulate the temperature of the water in the tank is by merely switching the appropriate coil, say the heating coil, on or off. That is, when the heating coil is switched on, the maximum amount of current flows through the coil to heat it. If there is a small drop in the tank temperature, just sufficient to let the water temperature fall below the set point (SP) and so trigger activation of the heating coil, there may be an overheating of the water in the tank that is likely to activate the cooling coil causing undercooling of the water. This in turn will activate the heating coil and thus precipitate a "temperature war" between the heating and cooling coils—an event that is likely to be unnecessarily costly because, in addition to temperature fluctuations from outside, the system now generates its own fluctuations. If this does not result from a simple on–off controller, then there will still be a certain amount of fluctuation in the tank temperature. In other words, an on–off controller that works in an all-or-nothing manner causes by its very nature oscillations in the water temperature (Smith, 1987).

If, instead of the on–off controller, a proportional controller is used, then the temperature of the water in the tank can be much more smoothly regulated. For instance, if there is only a small drop in the temperature of the water, then a small current can be allowed to pass through the heating coil, causing a small heating effect. On the other hand, a sudden large drop in the temperature of the water can be countered by maximal activation of the heating coil. Thus, the amount of heating or cooling effected is in proportion to the extent to which the temperature of the water deviates from the set point temperature.

Another way in which control can be exerted is through rate control. If the water in the tank is initially at the desired temperature and starts to change gradually, getting progressively colder, the heating coil needs to be activated in a manner that reflects the change in incoming water temperature and opposes it. A rate controller is sensitive to the rate at which the water temperature changes and will increase the flow of current through the heating coil at the same rate at which it is cooled by the incoming water. These opposing processes should then balance each other out. A rate controller allows the process to take corrective action at the rate at which it is needed: Fast action results from fast occurring changes, and slower action occurs in response to more gradual changes.

There is one more type of control to consider, namely integral or reset control. Reset control causes heating or cooling for as long as an error (a difference between the temperature of the water in the tank and the set point temperature) exists. Controller action is based on cumulative error, and thus even very small constant errors will eventually activate the controller enough to reduce the error to zero. In other words, if an error exists that is too small to activate the controller, it will eventually do so if the error is accumulated. Thus, if the temperature in the tank is for some reason always constant and just slightly below the set point and it is imperative that the set point temperature be exactly maintained, integral control should be used.

The proportional, integral, and rate controllers can be used individually or in combination (in some form of hierarchy) to control a process. If one considers the fact that there are four different types of controller and three different positions where the temperature sensor can be installed, each with its own implications for temperature regulation, it is clear that there are several control options available for regulating the temperature of the water in the mixing tank.

HOMEOSTATIC MECHANISMS AND BEHAVIOR

An organism can be conceptualized as a collection of proximate mechanisms (Tooby & DeVore, 1987). Some of these proximate mechanisms could be HMs. Behaviors are the consequences of the functioning of these mechanisms. That is, a particular behavior is only expressed if one of its associated HMs is operating. The primary function of HMs may be the preservation of the physical integrity of the organism. This implies that HMs will function by triggering behaviors to counteract environmental stimuli likely to compromise the organism's physical integrity. Consequently, in a fairly stable environment, homeostatically triggered behaviors frequently show a periodicity that reflects the physiology of the organism (Richter, 1927).

It should be noted that the activation of a HM can result in two types of "behavior." Both physiological processes and behavioral acts can contribute to regulation (Adolph, 1943; Richter, 1927). When a HM is activated as a result of the current value or current point (CP) of the regulated variable being moved away from the SP by some stimulus, it attempts to counteract this deviation from the SP through the activation of internal processes (e.g., sweating) or external processes (e.g., moving to a shady spot). For instance, there is some dissociation of physiological and behavioral thermoregulation (see Stellar & Stellar, 1985). It is possible that physiological and behavioral regulation are linked in a hierarchical order such that one is triggered when the other can no longer maintain homeostatic balance. Thus, homeostatically triggered behavior serves to control the relationship between organism and external environment and so helps to regulate the stability of the internal environment (Adolph, 1943; Koshtoyants, 1960; Richter, 1927; Stellar & Stellar, 1985; Young, 1961).

Although properly functioning mechanisms are always triggered into operation by factors external to the mechanism—stimuli provided by the environment or by other mechanisms in the same organism—they are ultimately prompted by factors external to the organism. The behaviors expressed by the operation of HMs are consequently all "elicited" behaviors. If one HM is triggered by the operation of another, and the stimulus that triggered the first has not been noticed, the behavior expressed by the operation of the second HM may appear to be an "emitted" behavior.

It is possible that the operation of a particular HM can express or generate more than one type of behavior, and that more than one HM can express the same behavior. This can lead to confusion when interpreting homeostatically driven behaviors. Some investigators (e.g., Falk, 1977) have claimed that certain behaviors, such as adjunctive behaviors (e.g., schedule-induced polydipsia), are not under homeostatic control. This conclusion is likely to be drawn if two different behaviors are under control of the same HM, but not to the same extent or in the same ratio. This is illustrated in Figure 6.1.

FIGURE 6.1.   This figure illustrates two homeostatic mechanisms (HM 1 and HM 2) that are responsive to several stimuli and are individually or collectively responsible for various behaviors. The relationships between the components of these mechanisms and between the mechanisms themselves are indicated. Note that different homeostatic mechanisms can exert control over the same effector thus leading to the same behavior and that a single sensor can feed information to different homeostatic mechanisms (see text for greater detail). Legend: S = sensor, M = memory associated with a particular homeostatic system, C = controller, E = effector.

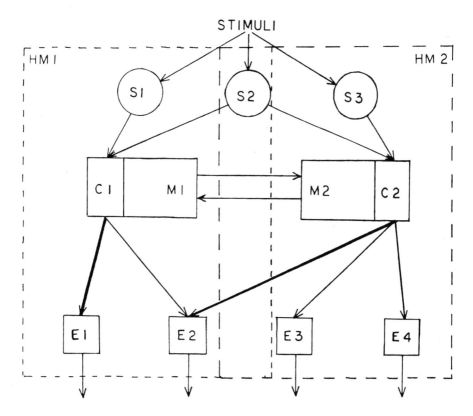

Under some conditions, a mechanism that normally expresses one behavior may express another. Because such behavior is unlikely to make sense when viewed in terms of the mechanism normally responsible for its expression, it may be considered not to be due to the functioning of that mechanism. However, to conclude that it is then not the consequence of the functioning of any HM is inappropriate. For instance, if the ingestion of fluids can affect the regulation of energy level, water balance, salt balance, and perhaps other systems, then it is to be expected that drinking behavior, the only normal way through which fluids are ingested, may be expressed by several different HMs. Normally, the mechanism responsible for the regulation of energy levels may express eating behavior when it is triggered, but in the absence of "edibles," drinking behavior may be expressed in spite of the fact that water balance does not need to be adjusted.

Roper (1983) considers the problems of potentiation (degree or extent of behavior) and selection (type of behavior) to be the most prominent problems of schedule-induced behavior. Both these problems may be tractable, given the present approach. A food-deprived animal experiences a negative hedonic state as a result of the displacement of the CP away from the SP of the relevant HM (see the next section). The consumption of a small food pellet generates a positive hedonic state because the CP is now moved toward the SP. This positive hedonic state is terminated upon consumption of the food pellet. Given that nourishment can be obtained by either eating or drinking, and that they are activated according to their hierarchical order and the stimulus qualities of the nourishment, the animal now switches to drinking. This switch occurs most likely in an attempt to maintain the positive hedonic state experienced during eating. This solves the problem of selection: It is most likely that another behavior will be selected that is controlled by the same HM as the thwarted behavior. If the substituted behavior is slightly hedonically positive or succeeds in masking the negative hedonic state of the animal, it will be pursued.

Given the fact that schedule-induced polydipsia shows an acquisition curve, it may be possible that the modification of the prevalent hedonic state is dependent on the amount of water consumed. That is, relatively little modification occurs with small volumes of water ingested, and more modification occurs with greater volumes consumed. These hedonic modifications occurring in response to drinking in a food-deprived animal may not be immediately obvious to the animal. Furthermore, because the consumption of water will affect the HM-regulating water balance, it is to be expected that the hedonic states set up by this mechanism will also influence the amount of water consumed. This may solve the problem of potentiation: Water is consumed until the negative hedonic state generated by overconsumption of water exceeds the masking effect generated by the same behavior. This type of interpretation may account for many aspects of adjunctive behaviors, although some factors, such as the abolition of schedule-induced drinking with some types of liquid reinforcers, may prove troublesome.

HOMEOSTATIC MECHANISMS
AND HEDONIC STATES

As indicated in the previous section, HMs are ultimately triggered by environmental stimuli, that is, those stimuli that are likely to compromise the physical integrity of the organism. The impingement of such a stimulus causes a variable or variables regulated by a HM to be affected. Thus, every stimulus impinging on an organism serves to move at least one variable in a constant direction along the dimension on which that variable is being regulated for as long as this stimulus impinges on the organism. Although this movement of a variable by a stimulus is unidirectional, it may be either toward or away from that variable's set point, depending on the original position of the variable relative to the SP when the stimulus first impinged. For instance, if an animal is initially dehydrated, its ratio of body fluid weight to total body weight is below an ideal ratio. If the animal now starts to ingest water, this ratio will start to increase until it reaches the ideal ratio, and if the animal continues to ingest water, this ratio will increase beyond the ideal ratio. The conservation laws of physics are reflected in this unidirectionality of movement of the regulated variable.

If more than one variable is influenced by the same stimulus, it must not be assumed that all of those variables are moved in the same direction relative to their set points, that is, either all toward or all away from their set points, but some can be moved toward and some away from their set points. It should also make intuitive sense that a stimulus causing the current value of a variable to move away from its relevant SP is likely to cause the organism distress, while movement toward the SP will not.

A stimulus that serves to move a CP toward the relevant SP for that variable sets up a positive hedonic state in the organism. Similarly, a stimulus that moves a CP away from its relevant SP causes a negative hedonic state. This is illustrated in Figure 6.2. The intensity of the hedonic state set up by an impinging stimulus is assumed to depend on both the degree of displacement of the CP away from (or toward) the SP and the rate at which such displacement is occurring. When a stimulus sets up a positive hedonic state, it is perceived as a "pleasant" stimulus, while it will be reacted to as an "aversive" stimulus when it sets up a negative hedonic state. An organism will react to a stimulus that it receives in such a way that if the stimulus is pleasant, it will continue to pursue it; if the stimulus is aversive, it will not seek contact with it.

Because more than one variable can be affected by the same stimulus, or more than one stimulus can impinge on the organism, several variables are likely to be influenced at the same time and not necessarily in the same direction. Therefore, there may be a summation of hedonic states to yield a single positive or negative state and, thus, a net hedonic value for that stimulus.

It is important to realize that an organism reacts to a stimulus not on the basis of the nature of the stimulus, but on the basis of the hedonic state set up by this stimulus. By way of illustration, let the CP of a variable regulated by a

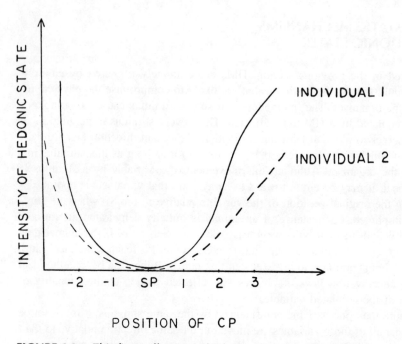

POSITION OF C P

FIGURE 6.2.   This figure illustrates "hedonic curves" for two different individuals. Individual 1 is likely to take stronger action in response to the same stimulus than individual 2 (see text for detail on the relation between hedonic states and behavior). Curves may be assymmetrical.

HM of an organism be such that for a given stimulus impinging on the organism, the CP is moved initially toward the SP. This sets up a positive hedonic state, and the organism will continue to receive the stimulus. If this stimulus impinges on the organism long enough, the CP would eventually reach and then pass and move away from the SP. When the CP starts moving away from the SP, a negative hedonic state will be set up and the organism will avoid the stimulus. Because the stimulus did not change but the hedonic state did, it is clear that the organism responded to the stimulus on the basis of the hedonic state set up by that stimulus and not on the basis of the inherent qualities of the stimulus itself.

One of the major consequences of this view is that stimuli cannot be considered to possess any intrinsic hedonic values, but that the organism, so to speak, assigns a hedonic value to a stimulus based on the internal state of the organism. If stimuli were given a consistent hedonic value, then responses to them should be consistent so that the resulting behavior is likely to be a reflex behavior (or perhaps a fixed action pattern) and not a motivated behavior. Under such conditions, hedonic states will essentially be superfluous.

Contrary to James's (1890/1950) view that pleasures and pains shape and modify behaviors but do not instigate them, hedonic states may serve to alert an organism and spur it into action—actions accompanied by feeling are actions accompanied by will (Spencer, 1870). Hedonic states typically do not arise when action is automatic (Spencer, 1870), but when the automatic or physiological regulatory mechanisms are not capable of counteracting a particular stimulus and the CP is being moved away from the SP by that stimulus.

There are several experimental findings to support the claim that an organism responds to the hedonic state set up by a stimulus as opposed to the qualities of the stimulus itself. It should be clear that the same stimulus can set up either a net positive or a net negative hedonic state, depending on the internal state(s) of the organism that are affected by a particular stimulus. This is characterized by the pleasantness ratings that subjects gave to temperature stimuli applied to the skin: Their indication of the hedonic value of a stimulus depended greatly on their present body temperatures (Cabanac, 1979). The phenomenon where the hedonic nature of a stimulus is changed when a reversal of movement of the CP relative to the SP occurs is called *alliesthesia*, and it has also been demonstrated in the rat (Cabanac & Lafrance, 1990). In this study glucose gastric preloads resulted in rats showing aversion to sweet stimuli, but ingestive consummatory behavior to the same stimuli after water gastric preloads.

The present homeostatically based view of motivated behaviors is also compatible with some theoretical positions, for instance the opponent-process model (Solomon, 1980; Solomon & Corbit, 1974). According to this theory, a stimulus causes a primary hedonic state to be established and, in addition, an opponent hedonic state as well, which is unmasked by withdrawal of the stimulus. At first, why the same stimulus should create two opponent processes may not make much sense, but once one interprets it in terms of homeostasis, these events become more intelligible. Consider the case in which a stimulus impinges on an organism and moves the CP away from the SP. This stimulus immediately sets up a negative hedonic state. Furthermore, the HM affected by this stimulus will try to counter the movement of the CP away from the SP and so activates the opponent process. This sequence of events is consistent with the claim that primary affect closely tracks stimulus intensity and that the opponent process has greater inertia (Solomon, 1980). As this opponent process takes effect, it may slow down and even reverse the effects of the initial stimulus. Whether the HM manages to slow, stop, or reverse the movement of the CP away from the SP will depend on the intensity of the stimulus and the robustness of the HM. At this stage, the CP has been displaced away from the SP, and it may still be moving further away from the SP while a negative hedonic state has been established in the organism. If the original stimulus was now removed, the opponent process would come to dominate and succeed in moving the CP toward the SP. In so doing, it would establish a positive hedonic state. Repeated presentation of a stimulus will allow the hedonic effect of the stimulus to be anticipated and the opponent process can be activated earlier.

HOMEOSTATIC MECHANISMS
AND ADAPTIVE BEHAVIORS

It may now be possible to address the question of how an organism determines what is "adaptive" in terms of its behaviors. In my opinion, the key to the answer lies in "guiding hedonism" (Evans, 1989): the built-in hedonic states set up in response to stimulus impingement. A behavior that causes an organism to be subjected to a stimulus that sets up a negative hedonic state is inappropriate because such a stimulus is likely to cause the organism physical harm if it persists. The hedonic state that follows a behavior signals the "appropriateness" of that behavior (Spencer, 1870), and an organism that is readily reinforced by such events will acquire highly efficient behavior (Skinner, 1953). Therefore, behaviors that generate pleasure and avoid displeasure have useful homeostatic consequences (see Cabanac, this volume) and thus adaptive value.

The behavioral response to a stimulus is hypothesized to be proportional to the intensity of the hedonic state set up by that stimulus and should indicate the rate at and degree to which this behavioral response should occur. The term *rate* may include both latency to activate a behavior and speed of execution of that behavior.

These considerations may allow some predictions to be made about an organism's behavior:

1. The further the CP has been displaced from the SP, the more drastic or intense (greater in amplitude) the behavior will be; that is, the extent of behavior will be commensurate with the extent of displacement of the CP. For instance, an animal could be expected to consume a greater volume of water in response to a challenge of hypertonic saline of higher concentration than one of lower concentration given in equal volumes.

2. The faster the CP is moving away from the SP, the faster consequent behavior will be executed; that is, the speed (and perhaps latency) of behavior will reflect the speed at which the CP is being displaced—for example, the acute administration of hypertonic saline is likely to induce drinking behavior sooner and at a faster rate than the administration of exactly the same solution over a much longer period.

3. The behavior that reduces the intensity of a negative hedonic state or produces a positive hedonic state the fastest and to the greatest extent will be preferred; that is, an animal that received a challenge of hypertonic saline is likely to consume water rather than sucrose solution, provided that the HM regulating blood glucose level is not active.

A hedonic state is generated proportional to the displacement of the CP from the SP and the relative motion of the CP with regard to the SP. The intensity of a negative hedonic state may be correlated with the degree of physical stress induced in the organism and the intensity of a positive hedonic state correlated with the degree to which stress is relieved. It is not clear how the value of a set point is established by the organism, or what the precise physiological significance of a set point is. I suggest that they are not mental representations of goals that an organism wishes to achieve (see McFarland, 1989) but that they are ultimately linked to the physical properties of those materials that make up an organism under a certain set of environmental conditions. Set points may have been determined through evolution as a means of safeguarding the "building materials" of the organism from undue and perhaps catastrophic stress and so allow an organism to maintain its physical integrity in a particular environment. It is therefore likely that set points reflect, directly or indirectly, some state of the environment when environment and system are in balance. Interesting ideas about homeostatic regulation have been expressed by Bolles (1979), and one could speculate that set points result from a particular juxtaposition of floor and ceiling effects. Set point control may be an artificial means of introducing a floor or ceiling effect into a mechanical system.

The reference signal (set point signal) indicating the state of the environment is incorporated into the organism. In the case of the thermostat, the set point directly reflects the state of a major component of the thermostat's environment, namely, the state of its owner. Furthermore, a set point determines the strength of the reference stimulus. Because set points in some way reflect the state of the environment, they are likely to be "independent" signals, even though they are mediated by the nervous system of the organism. The strength of these independent signals is determined by trial-and-error evolutionary processes. The "dependent" signal indicates the current internal state of the organism and is compared to the set point and action taken based on the difference between these two signals (see also the discussion of set points in the last section of this chapter). It can be expected that such comparisons will involve neural events such as temporal and spatial summation of postsynaptic potentials.

Hedonic states are mediated by nerve impulses and may be activated by the peripheral nervous system (see Stellar & Stellar, 1985, for a discussion of neural mechanisms of reward). This can be expected to result in the automatic and rapid generation of hedonic states and frees the organism from cogitation about the inclusive fitness consequences of its behaviors (see also Cabanac, this volume). The manner of hedonic state generation, and the types of hedonic states generated, are likely to be the result of evolutionary processes. Natural selection selects for mechanisms (Cosmides & Tooby, 1987) that represent the manifestation of adaptive design at the psychological level (Symons, 1989), and HMs and their associated hedonic states may reflect such selection.

Hedonic states, then, are set up when stimuli impinge on the organism and serve to activate and direct the organism's behavior in adaptive ways. The behavior of an organism causes changes in the stimuli that impinge on it (Manning, 1971) and so provides feedback in terms of hedonic states. It should be kept in mind that there may be time lags between the alteration of internal states and hedonic states.

HOMEOSTATIC MECHANISMS AND LEARNING AND MEMORY

Learning is a ubiquitous and important phenomenon (Toates & Evans, 1987) and may also be manifest in biological homeostatic systems, especially in the controller. It may be hypothesized that some memory is incorporated in the controller of every HM. Learning may cause the controller function to be modified in ways that would optimize regulation and so improve the efficiency of the system. A more efficient operation of a particular HM will result in fewer deviations from the setpoint, and, consequently, fewer and less intense hedonic states will be experienced. It implies that as learning progresses, behaviors triggered by a HM are more likely to be anticipatory behaviors, although ultimately they are still hedonically driven: Learned behaviors are responses to expected hedonic states rather than presently experienced hedonic states. This interpretation of the relationship between HMs and learning may bear on the debate regarding the control of feeding behavior (Raible, this volume). Learning is likely to play a more important role in the feeding strategies of more experienced animals, while inexperienced animals are more likely to feed based on their level of energy depletion. Also relevant here may be Valle's (this volume) analysis of drinking behavior and his conclusion that drinking reflects hedonic processes rather than learning.

The physiological correlates of hedonic states evoked by stimuli acting on an organism may have a twofold function: They set up hedonic states that direct the responses of the organism in adaptive ways and they may simultaneously facilitate the association of stimuli, responses and hedonic states. This facilitation of learning by (the physiological consequences of) hedonic states is supported by two lines of evidence. First, some hormones play a role in memory formation (Kupfermann, 1985a), and endocrine levels may be sensitive indices of emotional responses to social and physical stimuli (Mason & Brady, 1964). Second, there are experimental findings indicating that recall may be state dependent (Singer & Salovey, 1988), that attention may be biased by emotional stimuli (Williams, Watts, MacLeod, & Matthews, 1988), and that hormones activate certain behaviors (Kupfermann, 1985a). These considerations may bring a different perspective to the study of attention. Attention is frequently considered to facilitate sensory pathways and to play a role in directing an organism to appropriate stimuli (e.g., Cheal, this volume). However, it is not clear how an organism would know what to pay attention to. From a homeostatic perspective, this problem would not arise. A deviation of a variable from its set point would set up a negative hedonic state. This hedonic state will in turn have several physiological (e.g., biochemical) effects, some of which may involve the modulation of the animal's hormone levels. As pointed out earlier, hormones can activate certain behavioral pathways and memory processes, and presumably sensory pathways as well. In other words, a specific deficit may result, via hormone adjustments, in the activation of sensory pathways needed for the registration of stimuli pertinent to the generated deficit. Attention is thus much more likely to be seen as an effect or consequence of homeostatic regulation than as a cause of sensory activation or stimulus selection.

If one postulates that ease of learning depends on the intensity of the hedonic state evoked, it can be concluded that salient stimuli, that is, those that have pertinent survival consequences, will be learned rather more rapidly than other stimuli because they are more likely to produce strong hedonic states. Furthermore, if recall is state dependent, the hedonic state set up by a stumulus may not only facilitate learning, but also recall. The hedonic state functions here as a cue in memory retrieval. A combination of endocrine response to and neural activation by a stimulus could cause the sensitization of the relevant behavioral circuitry.

HOMEOSTATIC MECHANISMS AND COMPLEX BEHAVIORS

An organism typically has more than one HM incorporated into its set of proximal mechanisms. This coexistence of HMs may have several implications.

Conflicts may arise due to the simultaneous activation of some of these mechanisms. If the behavior or part of the behavior expressed by the operation of one mechanism is incompatible with the behavior or part of the behavior of another mechanism, both the mechanisms generally should not be activated concurrently. This logic suggests the existence of a hierarchy of HMs or a protocol for their activation. For instance, if incompatible HMs are neurally integrated to ensure lateral inhibition, the activation of one HM will inhibit the simultaneous activation of other incompatible HMs. If a stimulus or several stimuli displace several regulated variables from their set points, the HM associated with the regulated variable producing the most intense hedonic state will be activated.

The sequential activation of HMs due to such a hierarchy or protocol may give rise to specific behavior patterns. The HMs contributing to a stable behavior pattern (foraging, day journey) can be investigated by some form of multivariate analysis analogous to the determination of factors influencing body weight in baboons (Dunbar, 1989). Because the activation of two different HMs may result in the same behavior, the latency, speed, and intensity with which this behavior will be executed may be very complex. This could complicate the analysis of behavior patterns, and it may necessitate an investigation to identify those HMs contributing to a single behavior first.

THE USE OF THE CONCEPT *HOMEOSTATIC MECHANISM* AS A RESEARCH TOOL

It is one thing to claim that biological organisms incorporate HMs but quite another to investigate whether this is so. Here I wish to discuss ways in which hypotheses regarding biological HMs can be empirically tested.

In order to fully demonstrate that a certain behavior results from the operation of a HM, it has to be shown that the essential complement of homeostatic components is present. These components are sensors, effectors, a variable being regulated around a set point, and also a controller.

It should be kept in mind that various HMs can interact with each other (Colgan, 1989; Davis, 1979; Haussinger, Meijer, Gerok, & Sies, 1988; Smith, 1987; Toates & Evans, 1987). Raible (this volume) discusses the control of feeding behavior by three interacting regulatory systems: the emergency system, the short-term system, and the long-term system. The interaction between various HMs can be direct in the sense that components are shared between two systems in a manner analogous to the interaction between motor systems and speech (Kimura, 1982; Watson & Kimura, 1989) and may occur at the level of the hypothalamus, brain stem, or spinal cord (Stellar & Stellar, 1985); or it can be indirect in the sense that the operation of one mechanism may activate another (e.g., the ingestion of cold water in the process of water balance regulation may have an effect on the thermoregulatory mechanism). Interactions or competition between different systems (Stellar & Stellar, 1985) are frequently used to induce behavioral "cost," such as foraging in a hostile environment (Cabanac, 1985) or crossing an electrified grid to gain some reward. It is therefore rather important to isolate systems through appropriate experimental manipulation to avoid ambiguity in interpretation.

The Regulated Variable

The most salient aspect of a homeostatic system is that a certain value of a variable will be defended. This suggests ways in which such a regulated variable can be investigated. For instance, body weight may be directly regulated or may be the result of the regulation of other factors, for example, fat levels (Mrosovsky & Powley, 1977). If body weight were directly regulated by a HM, then an experimental manipulation of body weight, in ways that did not affect other HMs, should result in a change in the organism's behaviors responsible for effecting changes in body weight. This can perhaps be accomplished by the implantation of silicon pads under the skin of an experimental animal. Because the body weight of the animal has now been increased relative to its baseline value, it is to be expected that the animal's food intake may be reduced until the baseline value is reached. In this case, the body weight baseline value serves as a first approximation of the set point value for body weight. If, given that the increased energy expenditures due to increased body weight are corrected for, there is no effect on food intake of such manipulation of body weight, then one has to conclude that body weight per se is not regulated by any HM.

It should be kept in mind that not every stable or defended physiological factor is necessarily under direct control of a HM. For instance, although body weight may appear to be regulated, it may also be the product of other homeostatically regulated variables such as water balance and fat level.

The Set Point

The notion of a set point can be problematic (Booth, Fuller, & Lewis, 1981; Mrosovsky & Powley, 1977) and may not be an essential feature of a control system (Wirtshafter & Davis, 1977). The latter view can be applied to the leaky-barrel model (Pinel, 1990); however, the set point appears to be merely implicit or concealed rather than absent. In this model, the difference between the force of a partially filled barrel pressing down on the hose and that of water pressure in the hose pushing the barrel up is equivalent to the error signal generated in a set point mechanism. From a conceptual point of view, the set point mechanism performs a comparison between a signal indicating the current state of the system (water level in the barrel) and some input reference or set point signal (water pressure in the hose—which can be set via the tap); and on the basis of such a comparison, controlling occurs. This is true whether the input signal is directly related to the system signal or whether the input signal and system signal are transformed (transduced) before comparison. Wirtshafter and Davis (1977) have proposed a model for the control of body weight that does not contain a set point. However, it appears that their system also implicitly contains a set point embodied in the input signal "S." Similarly, in the feeding system of the fly discussed by Bolles (1979), the input reference signal appears to be the gustatory stimulus "G." The intensity of this signal is compared to the intensity of the satiety signal and eating occurs on the basis of the extent in difference between these two signals: That is, only if the gustatory stimulus is stronger than the satiety signal will food be ingested. If the intensity of the gustatory signal in response to a specific stimulus is changed, the regulation of food intake would change. For instance, if the gustatory signal is amplified but the satiety signal remains operating as before, the maximum level attained by the satiety signal may not be adequate to cancel the gustatory signal and so to suppress eating—with disastrous consequences. Presumably then, through evolutionary processes, the correct intensity of the gustatory stimulus (set point) relative to the satiety signal has been determined. As discussed in a previous section, the input signal is an independent signal indicating the state of the environment and analogous to the set point of a thermoregulatory system. According to Bolles (1979), the feeding system of the fly is not homeostatic because there is nothing that is being held constant. This interpretation renders a thermostat with an on–off controller, which by its nature causes fluctuations in ambient temperature, not homeostatic. It may be as difficult doing completely away with the notion of a set point as it may be to interpret it in biological terms. It is useful, therefore, to heed the caution expressed by Davis (1979) when applying control theory to biological mechanisms. In this way, maximum use could be made of the conceptual framework provided by control theories.

For the present approach, though, a set point is defined in the strict sense (Mrosovsky & Powley, 1977). Stimuli, hedonic states, and set points have been related in previous sections. These relations should provide ways in which the values of set points can be determined. If a stimulus is experimentally provided that moves a regulated variable away from its set point, the organism experiencing this manipulation will perceive the stimulus as being hedonically negative and is likely to express aversion to it. If, on the other hand, a stimulus is experimentally provided and serves to move the variable toward the set point value, it would set up a positive hedonic state, and an organism is likely to express pleasure in response to this stimulus. This is borne out well by the phenomenon of alliesthesia (e.g., Cabanac & Lafrance, 1990). The point at which an organism fails to express affect in response to a stimulus is likely to be that value that represents the set point. Experimental procedures such as that used by Cabanac and co-workers (e.g., Cabanac, 1979; Cabanac & Lafrance, 1990) are well suited to the determination of set point values. Furthermore, because an organism regulates the variable in question around the set point for that particular variable, the baseline value for that variable in an unstressed organism can be taken as a good first approximation of the set point value.

If a variable (e.g., body weight) is not directly regulated, but its stability is the result of contributing factors that are being regulated (e.g., water balance and fat level), it is not useful to talk about a set point for that variable. In other words, body weight may be stable, not because it is being regulated, but because other factors contributing to body weight are. If body weight per se is not regulated, there will be no sensors and effectors and thus no HM associated with body weight. It may not be correct, however, to claim that body weight is nonhomeostatically regulated. Therefore, care should be exercised before discarding the notion of homeostasis altogether, if experimental data do not conform to a simple interpretation of homeostasis.

The Sensors

A HM cannot function without appropriate sensors. It may rely on only one type of sensor, but it is far more likely that several different types of sensors at one or various locations are involved. The reader may find it useful to refer to Figure 6.1. For instance, opioids may exert their effects on food intake through kappa and sigma receptors, while glucoreceptors in the tongue, liver, and ventromedial hypothalamus may play a role in the regulation of glucose levels (see the review by Raible). It is also possible that a single type of sensor may feed information to two or more different HMs. An example here is provided by Raible's (this volume) discussion of the effects of cholecystokinin (presumably acting on its receptors) on both carbohydrate and fat ingestion. It is therefore necessary to establish (a) how many different sensor types are associated with a specific HM and (b) which other HMs are being subserved by a particular sensor type. Experimental stimulation or inhibition of sensor function should have an effect on the HM(s) that this sensor type is associated with. Disabling or inhibition of a sensor type should render the mechanism less sensitive to particular stimuli, while artificial stimulation of a sensor type should result in a hypersensitivity to specific stimuli.

The Effectors

Considerations applying to sensors are equally likely to apply to effectors. That is, one HM may exert control over several different effector types or several different HMs may exert control over a single effector type (see Figure 6.1). For instance, the operation of the same HM may express several different behaviors: The operation of the mechanism regulating blood glucose level may express behavior that results in the ingestion of solid sources of glucose (eating behavior) or liquid sources of glucose (drinking behavior). Another example may be provided by the activation of both feeding and hoarding behaviors in food-deprived rodents (Raible, this volume). Likewise, the same behavior may be expressed upon the activation of different HMs: The ingestion of liquid sources of glucose may affect both water balance and glucose balance; thus drinking behavior can be expressed by the glucose level regulating mechanism as well as by the water balance regulating mechanism.

If a particular effector (type) is associated with a particular HM, experimental activation or inactivation of the effector should have an effect on the level of the variable being regulated by that mechanism. It is therefore necessary to establish for effectors, too, (a) how many different effector types are associated with a specific HM, and (b) which other HMs are being subserved by a particular effector type.

The Controller

The final and potentially the most complex component of a HM that has to be investigated is the controller. The various types of controllers have been discussed in a previous section and it is suggested that they be investigated in the order mentioned, that is, from the more simple to the more complex. If a HM incorporates an on–off controller, then the behavior expressed when this mechanism is in operation is likely to be fairly constant: It is either present at a certain level or it is not. For instance, if the controller controlling drinking behavior is of the on–off type, then the rate of drinking, once the behavior is initiated, will be the same irrespective of how long the animal has been water deprived. If the rate of drinking is proportional to the length of water deprivation, then drinking behavior is likely to be controlled by either a proportional or a rate controller. Methods to differentiate between these two types of controller, as well as for investigating combinations such as rate and reset (PI) control, can be obtained from texts on process control (e.g., Balchen & Mumme, 1988). Manipulating "signals" to biological controllers or perturbing biological processes in a tightly controlled manner may not be as easy as doing the same in engineering type processes, but psychologists can in a variety of ways still perform analyses on biological control systems (see Fitzsimons, 1987, for a discussion of some techniques). Finally, it should be kept in mind that controller action may be mediated by hedonic states.

The characterization of the components mentioned should satisfy even the most dubious that a HM is responsible for a certain behavior. For a complete description of the mechanism in question, however, the nature of its control loops have to be elucidated: whether feedforward or feedback or a combination is used by the process and, perhaps the most daunting, how the control loops of one HM may interface or connect to the control loops of other HMs.

CONCLUSIONS

Homeostatic mechanisms may be innate psychological mechanisms that process information in ways that lead to adaptive behavior (Cosmides & Tooby, 1987). They are likely to be more domain general than reflex behaviors but too domain specific to deal with poorly defined information-processing problems. It is not clear whether the entire information-processing problem set can be partitioned into subsets representing specific and well-defined information-processing problems, or whether some subsets will always represent ill-defined information-processing problems and problems of an intermediate nature. If the latter is the case, one should expect reflexes to represent psychological mechanisms dealing with well-defined information-processing problems, homeostatic mechanisms to represent psychological mechanisms dealing with information-processing problems of an intermediate kind, and a third type of psychological mechanism, perhaps some type of servo-mechanism, to represent psychological mechanisms dealing with more ill-defined information-processing problems. All of these psychological mechanisms can then be seen as regulatory devices that extend the range of conditions over which the system is viable (Bolles, 1979).

The view of homeostatic mechanisms espoused here may prove useful in achieving a coherent reevaluation of many widely held concepts about motivated behaviors and motivational states—for example, arousal, incentive, reinforcement, reward, and punishment. These terms should perhaps be reformulated to reflect the relationships between stimulus, regulated variable, set point, and hedonic state. Less ambiguous and more precise terminology may contribute to an appropriate framework for the investigation of issues such as the relationship between emotion and cognition. Also in need of analysis is the relationship between emotion and motivation (Toates, 1988). In the present context, emotion could perhaps be seen as an amalgam of factors involving stimuli, behaviors, and hedonic states. This would imply that every emotion has an associated hedonic state, and, moreover, that hedonic states are primary and emotions secondary. The relationship between hedonic states and personality factors could also be investigated. For instance, the nature in which different individuals generate hedonic states may have a bearing on personality traits. For example, individuals in whom hedonic states with steep gradients are generated in response to deviations from the set point are more likely to be spurred into, and take, strong action in response to a particular stimulus than those individuals in whom hedonic states with less steep gradients are generated in response to an equivalent stimulus. It is therefore more likely that the former individuals will be seen as expressive and dominant. (See Figure 6.2.)

It may also be possible to interpret drug abuse in the current context. Normally a positive hedonic state is generated when the CP moves toward the SP. HMs can be bypassed by drug action to directly influence the hedonic mechanisms. For instance, a particular drug can generate a signal that would be interpreted by a hedonic mechanism as indicating a movement of the CP toward the SP. A positive hedonic state would then be generated.

A solid theoretical framework may also provide a springboard to approach much wider issues: the relationship between esthetics and hedonic states, humor and hedonic states; the nature of subjective experiences for humans and other animals; and perhaps issues related to learned helplessness and depression.

Finally a word of caution: Biological systems tend to be supremely economical, and it may be impossible to identify discrete homeostatic mechanisms. If that is the case, a novel approach to motivated behaviors may have to be synthesized.

REFERENCES

Aboitiz, F. (1989). Behavior, archetypes and the irreversibility of evolution. *Medical Hypotheses, 30*, 87–94.

Adolph, E. F. (1943). *Physiological regulations*. Lancaster, PA: Jacques Cottell Press.

Apter, M. J. (1989). *Reversal theory: Motivation, emotion and personality*. London: Routledge.

Balchen, J. G., & Mumme, K. I. (1988). *Process control*. New York: Van Nostrand Reinhold.

Bolles, R. C. (1979). Some functionalistic thoughts about regulation. In F. M. Toates & T. R. Halliday (Eds.), *Analysis of motivational processes* (pp. 63–75). London: Academic Press.

Booth, D. A., Fuller, J., & Lewis, V. (1981). Human control of body weight: Cognitive or physiological? Some energy-related perceptions and misperceptions. In L. A. Cioffi, W. P. T. James, & T. B. Van Itallie (Eds.), *The body weight regulatory system: Normal and disturbed mechanisms* (pp. 305–314). New York: Raven.

Cabanac, M. (1979). Sensory pleasure. *Quarterly Review of Biology, 54*, 1–29.

Cabanac, M. (1985). Influence of food and water deprivation on the behavior of the white rat foraging in a hostile environment. *Physiology and Behavior, 35*, 701–709.

Cabanac, M., & Lafrance, L. (1990). Postingestive alliesthesia: The rat tells the same story. *Physiology and Behavior, 47*, 539–543.

Cabanac, M., Duclaux, R., & Spector, N. H. (1971). Sensory feedback regulation of body weight: Is there a ponderostat? *Nature, 229*, 125–127.

Colgan, P. (1989). *Animal motivation*. London: Chapman and Hall.

Cosmides, L., & Tooby, J. (1987). From evolution to behavior: Evolutionary psychology as the missing link. In J. Dupre (Ed.), *The latest on the best: Essays on evolution and optimality* (pp. 277–306). Cambridge, MA: MIT Press.

Davis, J. D. (1979). Homeostasis, feedback and motivation. In F. M. Toates & T. R. Halliday (Eds.), *Analysis of motivational processes* (pp. 23–37). London: Academic Press.

Deutsch, J. A. (1971). Appetitive motivation. In J. L. McGaugh (Ed.), *Psychobiology: Behavior from a biological perspective* (pp. 99–128). New York: Academic Press.

Dewey, R., & Humber, W. J. (1951). *The development of human behavior*. New York: Macmillan.

Dilman, V. M. (1981). *The law of deviation of homeostasis and diseases of aging*. H. T. Blumenthal (Ed.). Boston: John Wright PSG Inc.

Dunbar, R. I. M. (1989). Ecological modelling in an evolutionary context. *Folia Primatologica, 53*, 235–246.

Evans, P. (1989). *Motivation and emotion*. London: Routledge.

Falk, J. L. (1977). The origin and functions of adjunctive behavior. *Animal Learning and Behavior, 5*, 325–334.

Fitzsimons, J. T. (1987). Some methods for investigating thirst and sodium appetite. In F. M. Toates & N. E. Rowland (Eds.), *Feeding and drinking* (pp. 393–428). Amsterdam: Elsevier.

Hamilton, W. D. (1964). The genetical evolution of social behavior. *Journal of Theoretical Biology, 7*, 1–52.

Hardy, R. N. (1983). *Homeostasis*. London: Edward Arnold.

Haussinger, D., Meijer, A. J., Gerok, W., & Sies, H. (1988). Hepatic nitrogen metabolism and acid-base homeostasis. In D. Haussinger (Ed.), *pH Homeostasis: Mechanisms and control* (pp. 337–377). London: Academic Press.

James, W. (1950). *The principles of psychology*. New York: Dover. (Original work published 1890)

Kimura, D. (1982). Left-hemisphere control of oral and brachial movements and their relation to communication. *Philosophical Transactions of the Royal Society of London, B298*, 135–149.

Koshtoyants, C. S. (1960). Some facts and conclusions of comparative physiology as related to the problem of homeostasis. In E. F. Adolph (Ed.), *The development of homeostasis with special reference to factors of the environment* (pp. 13–20). London: Academic Press.

Kupfermann, I. (1985a). Hypothalamus and limbic system: I. Peptidergic neurons, homeostasis, and emotional behavior. In E. R. Kandel & J. H. Schwartz (Eds.), *Principles of neural science* (pp. 611–625). New York: Elsevier.

Kupfermann, I. (1985b). Hypothalamus and limbic system: II. Motivation. In E. R. Kandel & J. H. Schwartz (Eds.), *Principles of neural science* (pp. 626–635). New York: Elsevier.

Langley, L. L. (1973). Homeostasis origins of the concept. In L. L. Langley (Series Ed.), *Benchmark papers in human physiology*. Stroudsburg, PA: Dowden, Hutchinson and Ross.

Manning, A. (1971). Evolution of behavior. In J. L. McGaugh (Ed.), *Psychobiology: Behavior from a biological perspective* (pp. 1–52). New York: Academic Press.

Mason, J. W., & Brady, J. V. (1964). The sensitivity of psychoendocrine systems to social and physical environment. In P. H. Leiderman & D. Shapiro (Eds.), *Psychobiological approaches to social behavior* (pp. 4–23). Palo Alto, CA: Stanford University Press.

McFarland, D. J. (1989). *Problems of animal behaviour*. New York: Longman Scientific and Technical.

Mrosovsky, N., & Powley, T. L. (1977). Set points for body weight and fat. *Behavioral Biology, 20*, 205–223.

Nisbett, R. E. (1972). Hunger, obesity and the ventromedial hypothalamus. *Psychological Review, 79*, 433–453.

Pinel, J. P. J. (1990). *Biopsychology*. Boston, MA: Allyn & Bacon.

Richter, C. P. (1927). Animal behavior and internal drives. *Quarterly Review of Biology, 2*, 307–343.

Roper, T. J. (1983). Schedule-induced behaviour. In R. L. Mellgren (Ed.), *Animal cognition and behavior* (pp. 127–164). Amsterdam: North-Holland.

Rowland, N. E. (1987). The study of ingestive behavior: General issues. In F. M. Toates & N. E. Rowland (Eds.), *Feeding and drinking* (pp. 1–18). Amsterdam: Elsevier.

Singer, A. J., & Salovey, P. (1988). Mood and memory: Evaluating the network theory of affect. *Clinical Psychology Review, 8*, 211–251.

Skinner, B. F. (1953). *Science and human behavior*. New York: Macmillan.

Smith, R. E. (1987). Mammalian homeostasis. In J. J. Head (Series Ed.), *Carolina biology readers*. Burlington, NC: Carolina Biological Supply Company (Scientific Publications Department).

Solomon, R. L. (1980). The opponent-process theory of acquired motivation. *American Psychologist, 35*, 691–712.

Solomon, R. L., & Corbit, J. D. (1974). An opponent-process theory of motivation: I. Temporal dynamics of affect. *Psychological Review, 81*, 119–145.

Spencer, H. (1870). *The principles of psychology*. London: Williams and Norgate.

Stellar, J. R., & Stellar, E. (1985). *The neurobiology of motivation and reward*. New York: Springer.

Symons, D. (1989). A critique of Darwinian anthropology. *Ethology and Sociobiology, 10*, 131–144.

Toates, F. M. (1986). *Motivational systems*. Cambridge, UK: Cambridge University Press.

Toates, F. M. (1988). Motivation and emotion from a biological perspective. In V. Hamilton, G. H. Bower, & N. Frijda (Eds.), *Cognitive perspectives on emotion and motivation* (pp. 3–35). Dordrecht: Kluwer Academic Publishers.

Toates, F. M., & Evans, R. A. S. (1987). The application of theory, modelling and simulation to feeding and drinking. In F. M. Toates & N. E. Rowland (Eds.), *Feeding and drinking* (pp. 531–562). Amsterdam: Elsevier.

Tooby, J., & DeVore, I. (1987). The reconstruction of hominid behavioral evolution through strategic modelling. In W. G. Kinzey (Ed.), *The evolution of human behavior: Primate models* (pp. 183–237). Albany, NY: State University of New York Press.

Watson, N. V., & Kimura, D. (1989). Right-hand superiority for throwing but not for intercepting. *Neuropsychologia, 27*, 1399–1414.

Williams, J. M., Watts, F. V., MacLeod, L., & Matthews, A. (1988). *Cognitive psychology and emotional disorders*. New York: Wiley.

Wirtshafter, D., & Davis, J. D. (1977). Set points, settling points, and the control of body weight. *Physiology and Behavior, 19*, 75–78.

Young, P. T. (1961). *Motivation and emotion: A survey of the determinants of human and animal activity*. New York: Wiley.

chapter 7

A Reexamination of the Role of Associative Factors in the Control of "Normal Drinking" in the Rat

FRED P. VALLE
University of British Columbia

SYNOPSIS AND COMMENTS
Roderick Wong and Georg Schulze

In his detailed and scholarly analysis of the basic mechanisms regulating "normal" drinking when rats are given free access to food and water, Valle reviews the status of alternative explanations and, in doing so, covers territory encountered in previous chapters. Although this chapter was written without knowledge of the contents of other contributors, it articulates with concepts and analyses developed in the chapters by Schulze, Raible, and Cabanac. Valle's chapter presents a thorough and comprehensive evaluation

I would like to thank Craig Jones, Stephanie Shepard, and Lynne Krefting, who assisted in Experiments 1, 2, and 3, respectively. They were supported by student summer research grants from the Province of British Columbia.

I would also like to thank my colleagues in the Psychology Department, especially Lucille Hoover, who have been consistently generous in sharing animals and equipment. Funds to maintain an animal colony, along with encouragement to pursue this research, were provided by the department head, Richard C. Tees, for which I am grateful.

Finally, I would like to thank Rod Wong for 25 years of delightful conversations about jazz, evolution, motivation, movies, and the challenges of child rearing.

of a commonly held position that "normal" drinking occurs in the absence of fluid deficits and "anticipates" imminent deficits (Epstein, 1982; Fitzsimons, 1972; Rolls & Rolls, 1982). He raised the question, If water is freely available in such a situation, why is there any reason for the rat to avoid impending water deficit? It could drink later, when the deficit arises. Possible benefits arising from combining feeding and drinking under a foraging bout could include conservation of time and energy along with reduction of exposure to predation. This might favor the selection for associative/motivational mechanisms that results in secondary drinking. From this perspective, feeding is regarded as a major determinant of future water needs, and the extent of these needs reflects the nature of the food consumed.

In questioning whether normal drinking in the rat is really geared to the anticipation of future deficits, Valle went through a detailed review of the procedure and results of the Fitzsimons and Le Magnen (1969) experiments from which this notion was derived. Their first three experiments showed a causal connection between feeding and drinking and that the former was a motivational determinant of the latter. Their fourth experiment, which Valle regarded as crucial for their hypothesis, dealt with the effects of switches of low- and high-protein diets on water consumption over the course of the day. Because of the theoretical importance of these effects, Valle conducted experiments that were designed to probe, in greater detail, associative processes that were indicated in the diet switch operation. In these studies he used a procedure in which the rats were given access to food for a limited period, and, because it resulted in substantial daily food intake, he believed that such feeding habits would maximize the impact of feeding on body fluid loss and facilitate associations between the two consummatory activities.

In general, Valle's experiments showed that under meal-feeding conditions when animals were switched from a high- to a low-protein diet, water consumption dropped immediately to a value characteristic of low-protein diets, a change that did not appear to involve a learning process. When the animals were switched from a low- to high-protein diet, their water intake during the meals increased immediately to a level characteristic of high-protein meals, an effect evident within the first 30 min of the rat's first encounter with the food. Again, there was no evidence that the animals' water intake during meals was influenced by a learned anticipation of subsequent changes in its water economy. Valle argued that although normal meal-related drinking in the rat does not reflect the influence of existing fluid deficit, the motivating force behind this secondary drinking has little to do with anticipation of a subsequent fluid deficit. Instead, water intake during the meals is controlled by the oropharyngeal properties of the food. The rats' water intake is influenced by some hedonic factor that is related to its difficulty in chewing and swallowing particular foods The greater the difficulty in processing the food, the greater is the positive hedonic value of the accompanying drink. Thus, meal-related drinking is primarily a hedonically driven option for the animal.

Valle also tested whether an arbitrary flavor embedded in a high-protein diet could acquire the ability to motivate excess drinking when it is transferred to a new low-protein diet. These comparisons were made in order to evaluate the associative processes hypothesis. Despite experiments that were designed to optimize the conditioning of various flavors with a high-protein diet, there was no indication that such flavors acquired the ability to motivate water consumption. Although one may argue that the parameters of this flavor-conditioning procedure were not sensitive enough to detect the effects of associative processes, this possibility is unlikely.

In order to be assured that associative mechanisms are not involved in the control of normal drinking, Valle reviewed a number of experiments designed to tap this process with different methodologies. The consensus view is that rats are unable to use circadian rhythms to anticipate the availability of water, even though this is a possibility with food cues (Bolles, 1968). In addition, exposure to food cues increases not only anticipatory responding, but also the rat's urge to eat when food is made available (Valle, 1968; Weingarten, 1985). However, there is no experimental evidence indicating an associative mechanism regulating the rat's adjustment to a water-deprivation schedule (Beck, 1964). Manipulations that appear to produce conditioned drinking (e.g., Zamble, Baxter, & Baxter, 1980) do so indirectly as a consequence of their direct effect on feeding behavior.

The final question raised in this chapter concerns whether rats can learn to anticipate a water-free meal. It is known that rats show a substantial reduction of food intake when they are totally deprived of water. This reaction reflects a mechanism to defend the water balance (Collier & Knarr, 1967). Rats placed on a meal-feeding schedule, in which they have water available at all times except when food is available, also reduce their food intake. Jacobs (1963) hypothesized that they behave in this way because of the substantial impact of feeding on drawing water into the stomach, and so on. The rats automatically react as if they were in danger of dehydration. If this hypothesis were true, the rats should be able to learn to anticipate the food-produced dehydration and, as a consequence, learn to drink just prior to the meal period. This would enable them to eat adequate-sized meals, even in the absence of concurrent drinking water. Jacobs found no evidence to support this hypothesis, which led Valle to conduct an experiment using a more sensitive training procedure. The latter used the taste of food as a potential cue signifying the imminence of a water-free feeding interval. The results of this experiment indicated that water intake during meals is better explained in terms of hedonic than associative factors. The depressed food intake of animals denied drinking water during the meal reflects oropharyngeal conditions.

On the basis of the results of his experiments, Valle proposed that normal, feeding-related drinking in rats is controlled primarily by hedonic-related drinking engendered by the taste and texture of food. Although more recent work by Kraly (1990) suggests that histaminergic mechanisms may be involved in normal drinking, the influence of hedonic variables on fluid ingestion has been documented with a variety of methods. The addition of saccharin to the water of nondeprived rats produces increased intake which was not further affected by deprivation (Ernits & Corbit, 1973). Similarly, research by Rolls, Woods, and Rolls (1980) indicates that other palatable flavors such as orange or cherry enhance the fluid intake of nondeprived rats. Conversely, the addition of an unpalatable substance such as quinine reduces the fluid intake of rats (Nicolaidas & Rowland, 1975). The relationship between hedonic value and taste preference is discussed in further detail in R. Wong's chapter on flavor neophobia.

Additional support for a hedonic interpretation of normal drinking may be derived from experiments in which rats were given intravenous infusions of water and thus should show decreased intake of water. Rowland and Nicolaidis (1976) found that despite the infusion of 180 ml of water a day, which is six times normal intake, the rats persisted in 50% of their normal water intake. Drinking was abolished only when water was infused during the animals' feeding and when the tube carrying water to the stomach provided oropharyngeal cues similar to those provided by the actual ingestion of water. It seems that drinking is suppressed under conditions that mimic the stimulus consequences of fluid ingestion at those times when the animal would normally seek out water and drink.

In general, Valle's chapter demonstrates why the currently held associative processes hypothesis about food-related drinking has to be reconsidered. In doing so, Valle marshaled data that challenged the prevailing position. The outcome of Valle's experiments was persuasive and led us to raise the following questions and observations: It is possible that low- and high-protein diets may have an effect on the relationship between drinking and urination. In his review, Valle considers that on the output side water is lost through respiration, grooming, salivation, urine, and bolus formation. Thus, in addition to measuring food and water intake, experimenters would also benefit from taking measurements of urination and defecation. If a complete description of the water flow in and out of the animal were available as depicted in Figure 7.1, one may be able to ascertain whether normal drinking is primary or secondary.

We were also intrigued about possible differences in meal characteristics contingent upon the availability of water. Would rats eat shorter meals but more frequent ones if water were absent? If drinking were motivated by water balance factors rather than by oropharyngeal factors, the rats would not eat shorter and more frequent meals, because the water deficit remains the same. If drinking is only motivated by oropharyngeal factors, smaller but more frequent meals would be consumed. This would happen because a shorter meal allows time for the masticating processes to recover from the effects of the dry food, and the saliva stores would be replenished.

One may also wonder whether the differences in food-related consumption would occur if both high- and low-protein diets were dispersed over many short periods during which water was available. If differences in food-related water consumption between high- and low-protein diets occur because differential water deficits are generated by these diets, the differences in water consumption would persist regardless of whether one big or many small meals are consumed. If differences in food-related water consumption between high- and low-protein diets occur because of hedonic oropharyngeal processes, many small meals would tend to reduce the difference in water consumption because the hedonic differences between high- and low-protein diets would be less pronounced or would be ameliorated when eaten in small amounts.

We also wondered whether differences in diet are associated with differences in feeding patterns on variables such as number of bouts, duration, and size associated with differences in diet. If the hedonic quality of the high- and low-protein diets differ, one would expect that the rats' feeding pattern should differ accordingly. If drinking reflects the physical necessities of mastication, there are interesting implications regarding taxonomy. Would this effect be considered as primary or secondary drinking? From a comparative perspective, we wonder whether Valle's results are specific to rats or would other rodents such as gerbils and hamsters manifest behaviors reflecting the control of different types of domain-specific adaptive mechanisms?

Through his thorough, and sometimes painstakingly detailed, considerations of a reasonable-sounding and commonly held hypothesis of mechanisms of normal drinking, Valle indicates how easy it is to be trapped by one's assumptions. As a result of his pursuit of the logical implications of assumptions of the associative cues explanation and his experiments designed to test predictions arising from it, Valle was led to reconsider the assumptions that led to his experiments. His notion that meal-related drinking is hedonically driven had arisen as the result of his findings, not of his original assumptions. The role of hedonic factors in motivated behavior has been discussed in the chapters on homeostatic mechanism, feeding, and flavor neophobia, as well as Cabanac's essay. It is interesting that this theme recurs in the present chapter, even though it was not the original intention of Valle to do so.

Reference

Collier, G. H., & Knarr, F. (1967). Defense of water balance in the rat. *Journal of Comparative and Physiological Psychology, 61*, 5–10.

THE PROBLEM

When rats are given continuous access to food and water, their drinking behavior, like their eating behavior, is organized into discrete bouts. Thus, under essentially constant external conditions (constant except for the transition from light to dark), the onset and offset of drinking behavior must reflect dynamic internal events. The issue I would like to explore in this chapter is the nature of those internal events. Specifically, I would like to examine in detail the proposition that the most important determinant of "normal" (i.e., unrestricted) drinking in the rat is an associatively based memorial process in which information regarding future water deficits is retrieved on the basis of taste/odor cues produced by the food the animal consumes.

Primary and Secondary Drinking

For the past three decades, research into the determinants of drinking behavior has been guided by two motivational taxonomies. The first—more inclusive—taxonomy is the distinction between *primary* and *secondary* drinking (Fitzsimons, 1966, 1972, 1979). Primary drinking is drinking that occurs in response to an existing fluid deficit—it is homeostatic in the classic sense. Secondary drinking is drinking that occurs for any other reason.

The Double Depletion Hypothesis

The second motivational taxonomy (sometimes called the *double depletion hypothesis*—see, e.g., Epstein, Kissileff, & Stellar, 1973) is nested under primary drinking. Total body water is conceptualized as being partitioned into two compartments that are separated by a semipermeable membrane, the cell walls. *Intracellular* water is that proportion (estimated at approximately two-thirds) of total body water that is confined within the cells of the body; *extracellular* water is the fraction that exists outside the cells, either as interstitial fluid or as blood plasma.

   Corresponding to this distribution of total body water are two different thirst mechanisms. *Extracellular*, or *hypovolemic*, thirst arises when there is a deficit in the extracellular compartment. Such a deficit—which inevitably occurs in the absence of water intake—results in a change in blood pressure. That change is monitored by special baroreceptors whose output motivates drinking behavior. *Intracellular*, or *osmotic*, thirst arises when there is a deficit in intracellular water. Such a deficit—which will occur as water moves out of the cells in response to an extracellular deficit or if the concentration of solutes in the extracellular fluid increases for any other reason—results in an increase in osmotic pressure (reflecting the increased concentration of ions inside the cells). That increase is detected by special receptors whose output also motivates drinking behavior.

   It seems reasonable to ask, then, whether the dynamics of normal drinking in the rat can be reduced to some corresponding cycle in intra- or extracellular water levels. Figure 7.1 presents a simplified summary of the avenues by which

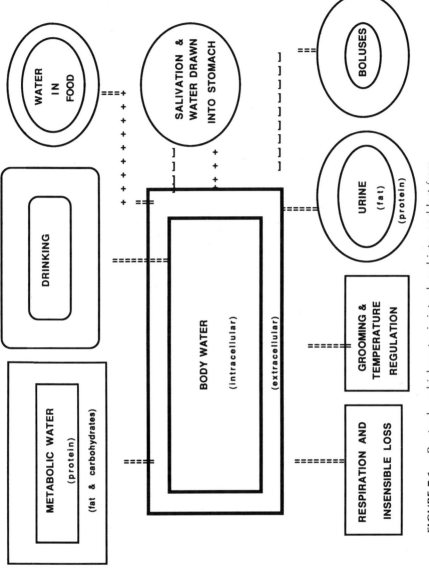

FIGURE 7.1. Routes by which water is introduced into, and lost from, the internal environment.

water is introduced into or removed from the extracellular compartment (and by temporal extension, into or out of the intracellular compartment). Rectangles represent events or processes that are more or less continuous over time (or at least have a cycle that, for our purposes, can be considered independent of the drinking cycle). On the input side, the water of metabolism represents such a process. Relative to caloric yield, carbohydrate metabolism is the most "efficient" source of metabolic water, yielding 0.133 g of water per kcal, while fat yields 0.113 g of water per kcal, and protein yields 0.092 g of water per kcal (Chew, 1963).

On the output side, (a) water lost through respiration and insensible water loss (i.e., water lost via diffusion through the skin) and (b) water lost through normal grooming and through grooming used for thermoregulation have been represented as more or less continuous processes. There are some avenues of water loss however, that are at least potentially cyclic in nature, and these have been represented by somewhat flattened circles in Figure 7.1. First, there is the water lost in urine formation. Because urine is used, in part, to excrete metabolic by-products, it is possible that urine production could be tied to food intake. If food intake is cyclic, as it is in rats with food freely available, then urine production (and the resultant drop in extracellular fluid) could show feeding-related cyclicity. Second, there is the water lost in the formation of boluses, which again will be temporally tied to food intake. Third, there is the water "lost" as saliva, the water that is drawn into the stomach by hypertonic foods, and the water that is drawn into dry food itself during the process of digestion.

On the input side are also two sources that are cyclic in nature. The first is water present in the food itself (e.g., lettuce vs. Purina Chow). To the extent that the food contains water that is released during digestion, and to the extent that food intake is cyclic, water will enter the extracellular compartment on a cyclic basis. Finally, of course, is the water obtained by drinking. This is the cycle we are trying to account for. And, from all of the foregoing, we might be inclined to speculate that normal drinking occurs on a cyclic basis because deficits in the extra- and intracellular compartments occur on a cyclic basis due to the cyclicity of food intake. In other words, normal drinking is primary drinking that occurs because of the efflux of extracellular water (lost in urine or feces, or temporarily diverted to the digestive tract), occasioned by cyclic bouts of eating. From the earliest statements of the distinction between primary and secondary drinking, however, this conclusion has been rejected.

Normal Drinking as Secondary Drinking

In one of the seminal articles propounding the primary/secondary distinction, Fitzsimons, wrote that

> It is important to realize at the outset that secondary drinking is the normal way whereby water is introduced into the body. Thus when environmental conditions are constant from one day to the next, the pattern of drinking and the amount of water taken are determined by circadian factors, including feeding habits and activity, by

the nature of the diet ... but not by an existing need for water. Such drinking is therefore secondary. What is particularly interesting is that it enables the animal to anticipate its future water requirements quite accurately. (Fitzsimons, 1972, p. 477)

This conclusion that normal drinking occurs in the absence of fluid deficits and "anticipates" imminent deficits is one that appears to have been accepted by most authorities.

There are controls of drinking that appear to operate in the absence of significant water loss. In the typical adult mammal, they may be the dominant controls of spontaneous drinking behavior ... ingestive behavior is preceded by expectations and is accompanied by feelings. It is the anticipation of water intake that begins an episode of drinking behavior. (Epstein, 1982, pp. 200–201)

When organisms have free access to a variety of palatable fluids ... it is possible that fluid deficits occur only rarely and that fluid intake is usually in excess of actual requirements and in anticipation of deficits. (Rolls & Rolls, 1982, p. 161)

Why, one might speculate, does the animal "bother" to avoid the impending deficit, when water is freely available? Why not simply drink later, when the deficit arises? The answer could be that, under natural conditions, there are benefits to be gained from combining, when circumstances permit, feeding and drinking into one foraging bout. If that assumption is tenable, and if feeding is indeed a major determinant of future water needs, and if the extent of those needs reflects *the nature of the food consumed*, then the stage is set for the evolution of the associative/motivational components that underlie normal, secondary drinking, given that the genetic potential for such components is present in the population. Of course, until we are convinced that normal drinking in the rat is truly geared to the anticipation of future deficits, such speculation is premature.

The primary source of evidence for the conclusion that normal drinking in the rat *anticipates* (i.e., is geared to, is regulated by) *future water deficits* is a set of experiments by Fitzsimons and Le Magnen (1969). Because much of what follows is an attempt to clarify and extend their findings, it is necessary to examine in some detail Fitzsimons and Le Magnen's assumptions, procedures, results, and conclusions.

THE FITZSIMONS–LE MAGNEN EXPERIMENTS

The Relationship Between Feeding and Drinking

The starting point for the experiments reported by Fitzsimons and Le Magnen (1969) is the observation that there is a close relationship between feeding and drinking in rats when food and water are freely available, (e.g., both tend to occur primarily during the dark part of the day/night cycle; Siegel & Stuckey, 1947). Fitzsimons and Le Magnen suggest three possible explanations for that relationship. First, the relationship could arise fortuitously, as a consequence of the rat's circadian cycle of general activity. Because most activities occur at night, feeding and drinking could show a temporal coincidence, even if they were completely independent activities. Second, as we noted earlier, perhaps food ingestion leads to immediate losses in extracellular fluid (e.g., extracellular water diverted to the digestive tract) that are sufficiently large so as to activate the extracellular thirst mechanism. Feeding would thus be seen as a cause of primary drinking. Third, the animal may have *learned* that food ingestion leads to a subsequent fluid deficit (as water is lost via urine and feces) and the "taste of food, its smell, or its presence in the mouth or stomach could cause an anticipatory intake of water in amounts appropriate to the future needs of the animal" (Fitzsimons & Le Magnen, 1969, p. 273). Thus, according to the first hypothesis, feeding and drinking are motivationally independent events. According to the second, feeding is a motivational determinant of drinking, with food ingestion leading to an immediate change in the motivational foundation of primary drinking (an immediate loss of extracellular fluid). According to the third, feeding is a motivational determinant of drinking, but one that depends on an associative mechanism: The animal learns that feeding is followed sometime later by a fluid deficit; the taste of the food then serves as a retrieval cue for that information, and the animal then engages in secondary drinking (while feeding) in anticipation of (i.e., in avoidance of) that fluid deficit. The experiments that followed were an attempt to determine which of those three hypotheses best explains the relationship between feeding and drinking.

Evidence That Feeding Is a Motivational Determinant of Drinking

In Experiment 1, Fitzsimons and Le Magnen continuously monitored feeding and drinking behavior throughout the diurnal cycle so as to obtain precise, quantitative information about the relationship between the two activities. A meal was defined as a bout of feeding behavior separated by 40 minutes or more from other such bouts. And water taken (a) in the 10 minutes prior to the onset of a meal, (b) during a meal, or (c) in the 30 minutes following a meal was regarded as being directly associated with that meal. Using those criteria, Fitzsimons and Le Magnen found that at least 70% of the rats' total water intake was associated with meals. Furthermore, there was a sizeable positive correlation associated between the grams of food consumed during a meal and the milliliters of water consumed with that meal (the mean Pearson r for 10 rats was +0.80). The fact that over 70% of water intake was associated with meals argues against the hypothesis that the relationship between the two activities is merely fortuitous; the fact that amount of water consumed during a meal was strongly correlated with the amount of food ingested suggests that feeding is somehow acting as a motivational determinant of drinking.

In their second experiment, Fitzsimons and Le Magnen provided additional support for the conclusion that there is a causal connection between feeding and drinking. The animals were placed on feeding schedules that confined their food intake to the daylight hours, with water available *ad libitum*. It was found that drinking behavior changed (from being primarily a nocturnal activity) in accordance with the change in the temporal location of feeding behavior. In their third experiment, Fitzsimons and Le Magnen found that when food was withheld completely from these animals, drinking behavior again reverted to being a primarily nocturnal activity.

The first three experiments show that feeding does indeed appear to be a motivational determinant of drinking. It is the fourth experiment, however, that provides the critical evidence for choosing between the primary- versus secondary-drinking interpretations of meal-associated drinking.

Evidence for a Secondary, Associative Basis for Normal Drinking

Fitzsimons and Le Magnen's (1969) fourth experiment was an extension of results (reported in French) by Le Magnen and Tallon (1966). Le Magnen and Tallon (1966) found that rats establish a ratio of water intake to food intake that is determined by the nature of the food. That ratio is higher for high-protein diets than for high-carbohydrate or high-fat diets. In other words, rats drink more grams of water per gram of food eaten when they are eating a high-protein diet than when they are eating a high-carbohydrate or high-fat diet. Thus, the causal connection between feeding and drinking is made even stronger: Not only does the temporal location of drinking behavior change to follow that of feeding behavior, and not only is there a correlation between *quantity* of food eaten during any particular meal and the quantity of water consumed during that meal, but there is a strong relationship between the *type* of food eaten during the course of the day and the total amount of water consumed over the course of the day.

According to Fitzsimons and Le Magnen (1969), high-protein diets cause the animals to produce a greater *volume* of urine, in order to excrete the nitrogenous by-products of protein metabolism. That increased output of water in urine, coupled with the smaller amount of water produced by protein metabolism, leads to a greater water loss with high-protein diets. That greater water loss is compensated for by an increase in drinking behavior, which results in a greater ratio between water intake and food intake on high-protein diets. The question is, Should that additional drinking behavior be classified as primary or secondary drinking?

An initial answer to this question is suggested by results Le Magnen and Tallon (1966) obtained when they *switched* animals from a low- to a high-protein diet. The animals showed an *immediate increase* in the ratio between daily water intake and daily food intake. Doesn't the fact that the increase is immediate suggest that learning mechanisms are *not* playing a role and that the increased water consumption caused by protein ingestion must be a result of unlearned, primary drinking, which occurs in response to the increased urine production?

Fitzsimons and Le Magnen (1969), however, were hesitant to reject a role for an associative process in this situation. Their hesitation stemmed from the results Le Magnen and Tallon (1966) obtained from the opposite type of diet shift.

When animals were switched from a high- to a low-protein diet, their water to food ratio fell "with a degree of inertia which suggests that the rat has to *relearn* the optimal intake of water for the new regime" (Fitzsimons & Le Magnen, 1969, p. 279, emphasis added).

Given the fact that at least some of Le Magnen and Tallon's (1966) data point to the operation of an associative mechanism in the control of normal drinking, Fitzsimons and Le Magnen (1969) believed that a closer examination of the effects of diet change on drinking behavior was warranted. Le Magnen and Tallon (1966) had only recorded total daily intake data. Fitzsimons and Le Magnen used their continuous-recording procedure to monitor the fine-grain effects on water consumption of changes from low- to high-protein diets and vice versa. Specifically of interest was the impact of diet changes on (a) drinking behavior associated with meals and (b) drinking behavior that occurs between meals. *If* the increased water intake that occurs following a switch to a high-protein diet represents primary drinking that is elicited by a loss in body fluid caused by urine production, *then* that increased water intake should occur, primarily, between meals, when the protein from the previous meal is being metabolized.

In other words, switching an animal from a low- to a high-protein diet should *disrupt* the normal temporal association between feeding and drinking, because the major new impact of the high-protein diet on fluid economy would occur sometime after the meal. If primary drinking were the only process at work, then the disjunction of feeding and drinking should continue as long as the high-protein diet continued.

However, if a learning mechanism enables an animal to anticipate fluid deficits, and if the animal is motivated to avoid such deficits, then the normal temporal association between feeding and drinking might be gradually reestablished over the course of several consecutive high-protein meals. In other words, while total daily fluid intake would remain constant and elevated following the switch to high-protein food, the dynamics of the drinking behavior responsible for that increased daily intake might change from elicited (*primary*) on the initial day(s) to anticipatory (*secondary*) on the subsequent days.

In short, there are two independent sources of evidence in the diet-switch paradigm that might reveal the operation of an associative mechanism in the regulation of normal drinking. (a) The first source involves the water/food ratio. A gradual decline in that ratio, following a switch from high- to low-protein food, would be consistent with the operation of associative mechanism. This is the effect obtained by Le Magnen and Tallon (1966) and cited (in English) by Fitzsimons and Le Magnen (1969). (b) The second source involves the proportion of total daily water that is consumed during meals. An abrupt decrease in that proportion, followed by a gradual recovery, following a shift from low- to high-protein food, would be consistent with the operation of an associative mechanism.

The Design and Results of Fitzsimons and Le Magnen's Fourth Experiment. The rats in Experiment 4 were maintained on a low- or high-protein diet for at least a week, prior to the collection of data. Feeding and drinking bouts were monitored for 2 days prior to the change in diets and for at least 3 days following the change. The high-protein diet contained 30% protein, 60% carbohydrates, and 8% fats. The low-protein diet contained 2% protein, 88% carbohydrates, and 8% fat.

At first glance, the results of the experiment appear entirely consistent with the secondary drinking hypothesis. First of all, the rats did indeed consume more water per gram of food when receiving the high-protein diet (the water/food ratio was approximately 1.50) than when receiving the low-protein diet (the ratio was approximately 1.00). This replicates Le Magnen and Tallon's (1966) finding and shows that the diet manipulation was having the intended effect on total water intake. Furthermore, when the animals were switched from the high- to the low-protein diet,

> Total water intake fell, usually quite gently over a period of days and with it the water associated with meals. . . . However, the proportion of total water associated with meals remained high and associated water continued to be positively correlated with meal size during the transition. (Fitzsimons & Le Magnen, 1969, p. 281)

Two aspects of this first finding are, in retrospect, perplexing. First, the critical evidence in Le Magnen and Tallon (1966) that initially suggested the presence of a learning mechanism in the control of normal drinking was the gradual decline in the water/food *ratio* that occurred following a shift from high- to low-protein food. Such ratio data are not presented for Fitzsimon and Le Magnen's fourth experiment; instead, changes in total water intake are described; and in the absence of information about possible concurrent changes in food intake, such data are open to alternative interpretations. Second, a description (quoted earlier) is all that is provided: No descriptive or inferential statistics are supplied. Instead, Fitzsimons and Le Magnen direct the reader to three graphs of data from individual rats (Fitzsimons & Le Magnen, 1969, Figure 9 d, e, and f, p. 281), which show (a) total daily water intake and (b) water intake associated with meals for 2 days prior to the shift and 3 days following the shift. For two of the three animals shown, both total water intake and water intake during meals drop precipitously on the first day with the low-protein diet. We are left, therefore, with little visible evidence of an inertial effect in water intake following the high- to low-protein shift (i.e., with little visible evidence for the operation of an associative mechanism).

Fortunately, the data from the low- to high-protein switch appear to offer much firmer support for the associative interpretation, although, once again, statistical analyses are not provided. Data from three individual subjects are provided (Fitzsimons & Le Magnen, 1969, Figure 9 a, b, and c, p. 281), and in all three cases, two things are apparent: (a) Total water intake increases immediately and thereafter remains relatively constant, following the transition to the high-protein diet; (b) the amount of water consumed during meals gradually increases over successive high-protein days. Thus it appears to be the case that immediately following the shift to the high-protein diet, the increased water consumption occurred between meals (primary drinking), but, over days, a greater and greater proportion of that increased intake was taken during meals (secondary drinking). It is these latter data that provide the real foundation for the current consensus described earlier—that normal drinking in the rat is regulated by an associative mechanism that allows the animal to associate the flavor or odor of a particular diet with the subsequent consequences of that diet on the animal's water economy. The animal then consumes an amount of water, while eating, that anticipates the fluid deficit (or excess) that would otherwise occur.

Because of the theoretical weight borne by these data, I thought it would be valuable to examine in more detail the effects of diet shifts on water intake, the goal being to characterize more completely the functional properties of the associative mechanism underlying normal drinking. I thought it would be valuable, specifically, to examine more closely the change in water intake following a high- to low-protein shift, to determine the extent of the inertial effect described by Fitzsimons and Le Magnen, but not apparent in their data.

Additionally, I thought it would be worthwhile to attempt to condition the "water-deficit" association to an arbitrary flavor cue embedded in the high-protein diet. If such conditioning were successful, one could then embed the flavor cue in a new, low-protein diet and show that an animal that had received such conditioning would drink more water in conjunction with that diet than would an animal that had not received such conditioning to the flavor. The advantage here is that both animals would be eating exactly the same test diet, and one could then be sure that differences in water intake between the two animals reflect the presumed association and not some gustatory property of the diet itself. After all, perhaps part of the reason rats consume more water when fed a high-protein diet is that such diets are simply harder to chew and swallow.

Ludlow's Critique of the Fitzsimons–Le Magnen Data; Meal-Feeding as a Methodological Alternative. Although eager to explore further the Fitzsimons–Le Magnen diet-shift effects on water consumption, I did not have access to the type of equipment that permits continuous monitoring of feeding and drinking behavior. As an alternative, I decided to use a meal-feeding procedure. In meal-feeding, rats are given access to food for a limited amount of time each day (in this instance, 2 hours). The animals quickly adjust to such a schedule and, after a week or so, are able to eat enough in 2 hours so as to gain weight at essentially normal rates. Using such a procedure, it is relatively easy to determine (a) the amount of food eaten each day, (b) the amount of water consumed during the meal, and (c) the amount of water consumed following the meal, the basic types of data necessary to address the Fitzsimons–Le Magnen hypothesis. Furthermore, because a meal-feeding schedule results in a large amount of food being ingested in a relatively brief period of time each day, such feeding habits should maximize the impact of feeding on body fluid loss and hence maximize the likelihood of the kind of learning postulated by Fitzsimons and Le Magnen (1969).

After the research was underway, the appearance of an article by Ludlow (1982) provided an additional empirical justification of the use of the meal-feeding procedure in the study of feeding/drinking relationships. Ludlow (1982) suggested that the gradual increase in meal-associated drinking that occurred following the low- to high-protein shift in Fitzsimons and Le Magnen's (1969) fourth experiment—the strongest evidence, as we have seen, for the operation of an associative mechanism in the control of normal drinking—may have been an artifact resulting from (a) a novelty effect involving the new, high-protein diet; (b) the greater water requirements associated with high-protein meals; and (c) Fitzsimons and Le Magnen's liberal definition of "meal-associated" drinking.

The novelty effect referred to by Ludlow (1982) was the observation that the rats in Experiment 4 ate more on day 1 of the new diet than on day 2. This increase took the form of larger *but less frequent* meals (a larger meal is usually followed by a longer intermeal interval—hence, any variable that produces an increase in the size of meals is likely to result in a decrease in the frequency of meals). At the same time, of course, drinking became more frequent to compensate for the increased water loss. As a result there were fewer meals, but more frequent drinks. As the novelty of the diet diminished on day 2, meals once again became smaller and more frequent. With the shorter gaps between meals, there was inevitably more water drunk within 10 min of the start or 30 min of the end of a meal, that is, an increase in the proportion of daily water consumed with meals. Ludlow's hypothesis, then, is that this increase in meal-related drinking was not a learned adjustment to the proteinaceous nature of the diet; it was simply an inevitable consequence of the changes in (a) meal frequency and (b) drink frequency produced, in the first instance, by the novel nature of the new diet, and, in the second instance, by the proteinaceous nature of that novel diet.

In light of Ludlow's (1982) criticism, it can be seen that the meal-feeding procedure offers one distinct advantage over the free-feeding situation: The frequency and pattern of meals are under experimental control. Therefore, if the same results could be obtained under meal-feeding conditions as Fitzsimons and Le Magnen obtained under free-feeding conditions, the plausibility of the secondary drinking hypothesis would be considerably strengthened. If Fitzsimons and Le Magnen's results could not be replicated using the meal-feeding procedure, then, in light of Ludlow's critique, the associatively based, secondary drinking analysis of normal drinking would have to be given a much more tentative status than it currently enjoys. The first experiment, described next, investigated the effects of low- and high-protein diets on water consumption, within the meal-feeding paradigm.

EXPERIMENT 1

Design

In Experiment 1, 20 sixty day old male Wistar rats were placed on a 2 h/day meal-feeding schedule, using a standard diet composed of 1000 g of Purina Chow and 450 g of commercial Canola oil, for 10 days. Then, the type of diet was manipulated over four blocks of eight meals (i.e., days) each.

In the first and third blocks, a low-protein diet was used (3% protein, 65% carbohydrates, 29% fats) that was obtained by mixing 200 g Purina Chow, 800 g commercial sucrose, and 200 g oil. In the second and fourth blocks, a high-protein diet was used (52% protein, 24% carbohydrates, 16% fats) that was obtained by mixing 600 g Purina Chow, 600 g vitamin-free casein, and 200 g oil.

For half the animals (Group Consistent), the high-protein diet was always flavored with cinnamon powder (20 g were added to 1400 g of the diet). The low-protein diet was never flavored with cinnamon for Group Consistent. For the remaining animals (Group Inconsistent), both the low- and high-protein diets were flavored with cinnamon on half the days, using the sequence + − + − + −, where + means flavored. (The flavored and unflavored versions of the diets had noticeably different smells to the human nose.)

Finally, in a fifth block of meals, all animals received four meals with a cinnamon-flavored test diet that was 4% protein, 88% carbohydrates, and 6% fats. If Group Consistent has learned to anticipate a protein-induced water deficit, and if the flavor of cinnamon serves as an effective retrieval cue for that association, then Group Consistent ought to consume more water when eating the test diet than does Group Inconsistent.

Results

In the analysis of the first four blocks of meals, the data have been collapsed over groups. Figure 7.2 shows the total daily water/food ratios for the low- and high-

FIGURE 7.2. Mean daily ratio of total water intake to food intake as a function of type of food in Experiment 1. The data have been collapsed over groups and over blocks of meals. Vertical lines represent the standard error of the mean.

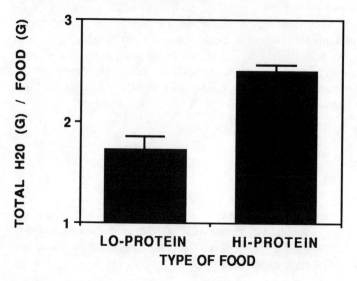

protein diets (collapsed over blocks and days). The ratio was significantly higher ($t = 6.70$, $p < .001$) for the high-protein diet. Thus, the diet manipulation had the desired effect on total water intake.

Effects of the High- to Low-Protein Switch. Having seen that the diet manipulation produced the required effect on total water/food ratios, we can now determine whether there is any evidence for the hypothesis that normal drinking in the rat is regulated by an associative process that functions to anticipate post-meal water deficits (or excesses) and that requires repeated experience with a particular diet to recalibrate following a change in diets. The first data to be examined are those from the last 4 days in Block 2 (the last 4 days of the first series of high-protein days) and the first 4 days in Block 3 (the first 4 days of the second series of low-protein days). The question is, Does water intake fall gradually following the change from high- to low-protein food?

Figure 7.3 presents the mean total water/food ratios for the last 4 days of Block 2 and the first 4 days of Block 3. It can be seen that the water/food ratio fell as soon as the diet was changed. The difference between the last high-protein day and the first low-protein day is significant ($t = 6.83$, $p < .01$). The elevated value for the second day of low-protein food reflects one very atypical score, as the size of the standard error lines would suggest.

An even more sensitive test of the associative hypothesis is the ratio between the amount of water drunk during a meal and the amount of food eaten during that

FIGURE 7.3.   Mean daily ratio of total water intake to food intake as a function of type of food in Experiment 1. Shown are the final 4 days of the first series of high-protein days and the immediately following first 4 days of the second series of low-protein days. The data have been collapsed over groups. Vertical lines represent the standard error of the mean.

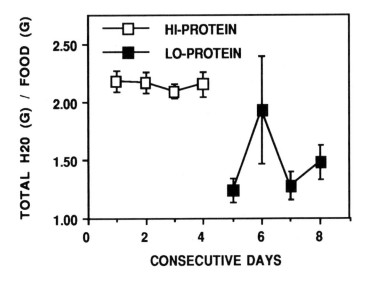

meal. Figure 7.4 shows these ratios for the last 4 days of Block 2 and the first 4 days of Block 3. It can be seen that water intake *during the meal* fell as soon as the diet was changed and remained relatively constant thereafter. The difference between the last high-protein day and the first low-protein day was significant ($t = 3.76$, $p < .01$), while the difference between the first low-protein day and the fourth low-protein day was not ($t = 1.07$). *In short, under meal-feeding conditions, there is no evidence of an inertial overconsumption of water following a shift from high- to low-protein food.*

It should be noted at this point that the animals did not find the low-protein diet very attractive. Over the course of the two series of low-protein meals, their intake declined approximately 60%. In the first block of low-protein meals their intake averaged 10.7 g on the first meal and 7.2 g on the 8th. On the second block, their intake averaged 11.6 g on the first meal and 6.2 on the 8th. The most immediate significance of this pattern is that the animals were inclined to eat atypically small meals, each time a block of high-protein meals began.

Effects of the Low- to High-Protein Switches. Fitzsimons and Le Magnen (1969) found that a low- to high-protein switch was accompanied by two changes in drinking behavior: an immediate overall increase in water intake and a gradual increase in the proportion of total water consumed during meals. We have

FIGURE 7.4. Mean daily ratio between water intake during meals and food intake, as a function of type of food, in Experiment 1. Shown are the final 4 days of the first series of high-protein days and the immediately following first 4 days of the second series of low-protein days. The data have been collapsed over groups. Vertical lines represent the standard error of the mean.

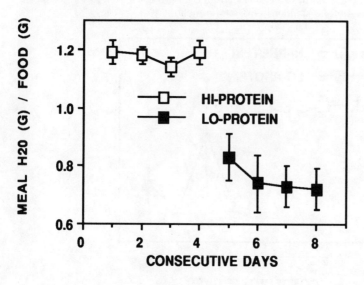

already seen (Figure 7.2) that high-protein diets resulted in more drinking behavior overall. Figure 7.5 shows the proportion of total daily water that was consumed during meals, over 2-day blocks of high-protein meals (collapsed over groups and over series). It can be seen that there is indeed a gradual and significant increase in the proportion of total daily water that was consumed during meals, exactly the type of pattern called for by the hypothesis that rats learn to associate subsequent body water levels with the flavor of the food they consume, and modify their drinking behavior, during meals, so as to anticipate those fluid changes. And, because of the meal-feeding procedure, this change in the proportion of total daily water consumed during meals cannot be an artifact of a change in meal frequency.

Unfortunately, although the meal-feeding procedure brings the frequency and pattern of meals under experimental control, it does not bring the amount eaten during any given meal under experimental control. Figure 7.6 shows mean food intake over 2-day blocks of high-protein meals, for both the first and second series of high-protein meals (collapsed over groups). It can be seen that there is a gradual and significant increase in the amount of food eaten over consecutive high-protein meals. In each series, the initial low-levels of intake appear to reflect the depressed intake associated with the immediately preceding low-protein meals.

The fact that food intake increased over consecutive high-protein meals complicates our interpretation of the increase in the ratio between meal water and total water that also occurred over days. The latter increase may have nothing to do

FIGURE 7.5.   Mean daily ratio between water intake during meals and total water intake, over 2-day blocks of high-protein days in Experiment 1. The data have been collapsed over groups and series of high-protein days. The vertical lines represent the standard error of the mean.

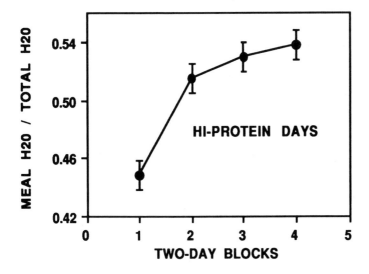

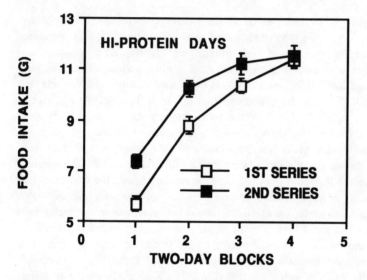

FIGURE 7.6.   Mean daily food intake over 2-day blocks of
high-protein meals for the 1st and 2nd series of high-protein
days in Experiment 1. The data have been collapsed over
groups. Vertical lines represent the standard error of the mean.

with the anticipation of fluid deficits and may simply reflect the necessity (or
pleasantness) of drinking more water while eating bigger meals.

If the increase in the ratio between meal water and total water does indeed
reflect, at least in part, a learned anticipation of food-dependent water deficits, then
there should still be an increase in the amount of water consumed during meals,
even when the effects of bigger meals per se have been removed. Figure 7.7 shows
the mean ratio between amount of water consumed during a meal and amount of
food consumed during that meal, over 2-day blocks of high-protein meals, collapsed over groups and over series of high-protein meals. It can be seen from Figure 7.7 that not only is there no increase, there is actually a decrease from the first
block to the remaining blocks.

Another way to illustrate the contrast between the two different interpretations of meal-associated drinking is to examine the absolute amounts of water consumed during meals and between meals, over blocks of high-protein meals. The
associative hypothesis leads one to expect a more or less reciprocal relationship
between the two. That is to say, as the animal learns to anticipate more and more
accurately the postmeal water requirements imposed by the food—and, as a consequence, drinks more and more during each meal—the amount of water consumed between meals ought to decline. And indeed, that appears to be what is
shown in Figure 7.5, which shows an increase in the proportion of total daily water
consumed during meals, over consecutive high-protein meals. However, the data
shown in Figure 7.5 could result from two quite different underlying patterns of
drinking. The first we have just described: The ratio between meal water and total

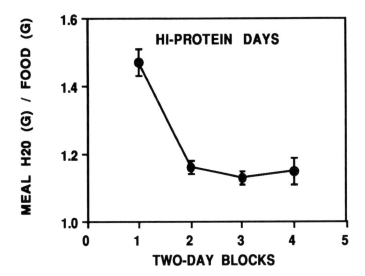

FIGURE 7.7. Mean daily ratio of water intake during meals to food intake, over 2-day blocks of high-protein meals in Experiment 1. The data have been collapsed over groups and over series of high-protein meals. Vertical lines represent the standard error of the mean.

water would increase over days if (a) amount of water consumed during meals increased and (b) amount of water consumed between meals decreased. The second pattern of results that would yield the same change in the meal water/total water ratio is if (a) amount of water consumed during meals increased over days while (b) the amount of water consumed between meals remained constant. The first pattern is what the associative hypothesis would lead one to expect. The second pattern is what would be expected if (a) water intake during meals is determined primarily by conditions during the meal and is not influenced by postmeal conditions (although it would certainly influence those postmeal conditions for a short time) and (b) water intake subsequent to meals reflects postmeal conditions. If water intake during the meal "automatically" increases as food intake increases (and hence automatically compensates for the increased urine and bolus production caused by the increased food consumption), then postmeal conditions would be relatively independent of the amount of food eaten during the meal and would be expected to remain relatively constant over meals, despite an increase in food intake over meals.

Figure 7.8 presents the amount of water (g) consumed during and following meals for the high-protein days, over blocks of 2 days, collapsed over groups and series. It can be seen that water consumption *during meals* increased over consecutive days. The animals drank significantly more water during the final two high-protein meals than they had during the initial two high-protein meals ($t = 13.20$, $p < .001$). Water consumption *following meals*, however, did not show a

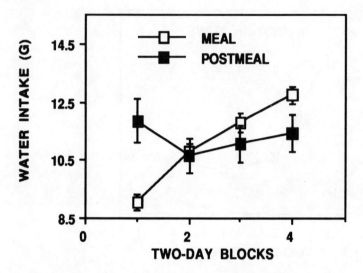

FIGURE 7.8.   Mean daily water intake during (a) the 2-h daily meal and (b) the 22-h following the meal, over 2-day blocks of high-protein meals in Experiment 1. The data have been collapsed over groups and over series of high-protein meals. Vertical lines represent the standard error of the mean.

consistent change over consecutive days, and the animals were not drinking significantly less postmeal water on the final 2 days of high-protein meals than they were on the initial 2 days of high-protein meals ($t = 0.68$). In short, the ratio between meal water and total water (Figure 7.5) increased over days, primarily because amount of water consumed during meals increased, while amount of water consumed subsequent to meals remained relatively constant.

It should also be noted at this point that the dipsogenic effect that high-protein food had during the meal period *was present from the very first encounter with high-protein food*. On the last day of the first series of low-protein meals, the mean ratio between amount drunk during the meal and amount eaten during the meal was 0.706. On the immediately following high-protein meal, which was the first encounter the subjects had with high-protein food, the mean water/food ratio for the meal was 1.514, a difference that is significant ($t = 7.33$, $p < .001$). Figure 7.9 shows the underlying bases for this difference in terms of absolute amounts of food and water ingested on these two meals. It can be seen that while food intake was less during the first high-protein meal than during the preceding low-protein meal ($t = 4.36$, $p < .001$), water intake was greater ($t = 6.26$, $p < .01$). These data suggest that the consumption of high-protein food itself (i.e., independent of subsequent changes in fluid economy) engenders increased water consumption.

Results of the 4 Test Days.   So far we have found no evidence from the training series to indicate that water consumption during a meal is regulated by

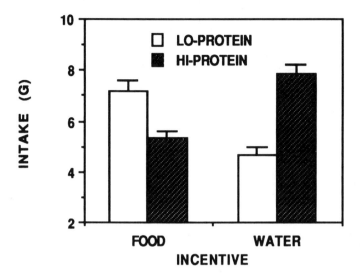

FIGURE 7.9. Mean amounts of food and water ingested on the last day of the first low-protein series and the first day of the first high-protein series, in Experiment 1. The data have been collapsed over groups. Vertical lines represent the standard error of the mean.

fluid requirements subsequent to the meal. Instead, the data seem to indicate that water consumption during a meal is determined by (a) some unknown oral property of the food and (b) the amount of that food that is eaten during the meal. On the series of 4 test days, which followed the final series of 8 high-protein meals, both groups ate the same new, low-protein diet, flavored with cinnamon. For Group Consistent, cinnamon had always been associated with high-protein meals; for Group Inconsistent, cinnamon had been associated with both high- and low-protein meals. If food flavor can serve as a cue for subsequent fluid deficits, and if the flavors that can serve in that manner are not restricted to the flavor of protein per se, then Group Consistent should (a) consume more water per gram of food eaten on the test days (or at least the first test day) than does Group Inconsistent, and (b) show a higher meal water/total water ratio than does Group Inconsistent. If, however, water intake during a meal reflects the gustatory properties of the food, independent of the impact of the food on fluid losses, then both groups should show similar water/food ratios and similar meal water/total water ratios on the test days, because both groups are eating the same food.

Figure 7.10 shows the mean ratio between water consumed during the meal and food consumed during the meal, over the 4 test days, for the two groups. The difference between the two groups over the 4 test days is not significant ($F < 1.00$), and, as can be seen, on the first test day the groups showed essentially identical water/food ratios. Figure 7.11 shows the mean meal water/total water ratios,

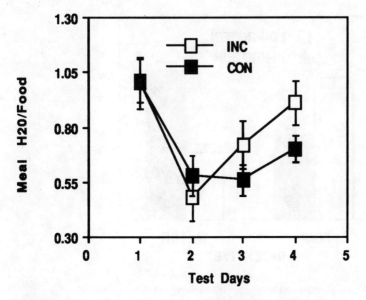

FIGURE 7.10.   Mean ratio between water intake (g) during a meal and food intake (g) during that meal, over 4 test days in Experiment 1. Vertical lines represent the standard error of the mean.

over the 4 test days, for the two groups. Again, the difference between the groups over the 4 days is not significant ($F < 1.00$), nor was there a significant difference present on the first test day. In short, there is no evidence that a flavor associated with high-protein food acquires the ability to increase water consumption during a meal.

Summary of Experiment 1 and Rationale for Experiment 2.   The results of the first experiment were a major disappointment for one who initiated the study with the intention of providing a more detailed picture of the associative process assumed to underlie normal drinking in rats. The high- to low-protein shift was accompanied by an immediate reduction in the amount of water consumed during the meal, and the low- to high-shifts were accompanied by an immediate increase in the amount of water consumed during the meal, suggesting that it is the immediate, oropharyngeal properties of the diet, rather than its delayed consequences for fluid economy, that determine water intake during a meal. Furthermore, the increase in the ratio between water consumed during the meal and total daily water intake appeared to reflect an increase in the amount eaten over consecutive meals, rather than a motivational shift from primary drinking to secondary drinking. And the results of the test trials were consistently negative: Water intake appeared to reflect the gustatory properties of the test diet itself, rather than the presence of an arbitrary flavor that had been paired with high-protein diets.

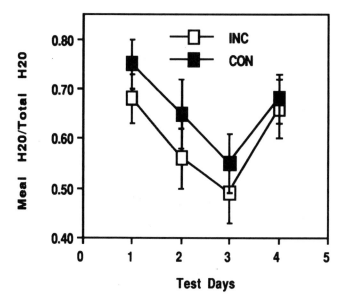

FIGURE 7.11. Mean ratio between water intake during meals (g) and total water intake (g), over 4 test days in Experiment 1. Vertical lines represent the standard error of the mean.

Nonetheless, a second study was undertaken with the following goals in mind: First, I hoped to establish a situation in which the switch to high-protein food would be followed by relatively stable meal sizes. In the first study, meal size fell over the course of low-protein meals, and hence the animals began the high-protein series with a depressed tendency to eat, which then recovered over the high-protein meals. Because the standard Purina Chow mixture supported large, stable meal sizes, it was decided to eliminate the low-protein meals in the second experiment and switch the animals directly from the Purina diet to the high-protein diet. If this change were successful in eliminating the increase in the size of the high-protein meals over days as a confounded variable, and if the high-protein meals were still accompanied by an increase, over days, in the amount of water consumed during meals, such an increase would provide much more satisfactory evidence for the associative hypothesis.

Second, having water available for the full 2-hour meal period, as was the case in Experiment 1, increases the likelihood that at least some of the drinking that occurred during that interval could be interpreted as primary drinking: Perhaps some of the water losses specific to high-protein diets would already be occurring within 2 hours of the initiation of the meal. Therefore, in the second experiment, water was available only for the initial 30 minutes of the meal; it was assumed that any increase in water intake during that interval caused by a switch to high-protein food would reflect either the sought-after associative process or the immediate oropharyngeal properties of the diet.

Third, in order to accentuate any impact the high-protein diet might have on the animal's internal water economy following the meal—and hence to strengthen, presumably, any learning process regarding that impact—water was withheld from the animal for 3 hours following the termination of the meal and was then given for only 15 minutes, before being withheld once again until the beginning of the next meal the following day. It was hoped that this procedure would (a) increase any disposition the animals might have to associate the ingestion of the high-protein diet with challenges to their fluid balance, and (b) encourage them to reveal that association via an increased consumption of water, while it was available during the meal.

Finally, the length of the meal itself was reduced from 2 hours to 1 hour. It was hoped this might encourage greater consistency in food intake.

EXPERIMENT 2

Design

The subjects were 16 adult, male, Charles River rats. One animal was dropped from the study for inability to adjust to the meal-feeding schedule. The animals were placed on a 1-h/day meal-feeding schedule, using the same Purina Chow + oil mixture that was used in the first part of Experiment 1 (a 15% protein diet) for 14 days. Then they were switched for 8 days to a 50% protein diet, which was composed of 500 g casein, 250 g Purina Chow, 300 g oil, and 50 g flavoring. For half the animals, the flavoring was vanilla food flavoring, for the other half, almond. (Commercial, liquid food flavorings from Safeway Canada Ltd. were used.) Thus, each animal had a distinctive flavor embedded in the high-protein diet. Finally, the animals were given 1 test day when they received a flavored, low-protein diet (100 g wheat flour, 100 g sugar, 100 g oil, 15 g flavoring): For half the animals, the flavoring was the same as that used with the high-protein diet; for the other half, the other flavor was used. As noted earlier, throughout the study, water was available only twice a day: For the first 30 minutes of the daily meal and for 15 minutes, 3 hours following the end of the meal.

Results

Food Intake. Figure 7.12 shows mean food intake over the last eight Purina meals and the eight high-protein meals, in 2-day blocks, collapsed over groups. It can be seen that the food intake dropped following the switch in diets but remained relatively constant thereafter; there was no significant effect of blocks on high-protein intake.

Total Water/Food Ratios. Figure 7.13 shows the mean daily ratio between total water intake and food intake, over last 8 days with the Purina diet and the 8 days with the high-protein diet, in blocks of 2 days. It can be seen that, overall,

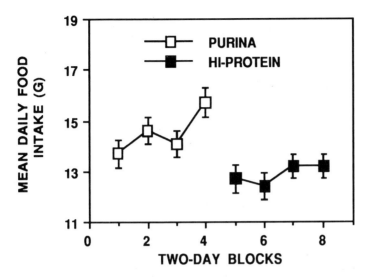

FIGURE 7.12.   Mean daily food intake, over 2-day blocks, as a function of type of diet in Experiment 2. The data have been collapsed over groups. Vertical lines represent the standard error of the mean.

total water intake per g of food eaten was substantially higher with the high-protein diet ($t = 16.21$, $p < .001$). Moreover, that ratio was significantly higher on the first high-protein day, compared with the immediately preceding Purina day ($t = 6.92$, $p < .001$).

It should be noted that the increase in the total water/food ratio is not simply a reflection of the reduction in food intake that occurred following the switch to high-protein food. Total water intake averaged 14.7 g/day over the last 8 Purina days and 18.2 g/day over the 8 high-protein days, a difference that is significant ($t = 15.10$, $p < .001$).

Meal Water/Food Ratios.   The question is then, When did that additional drinking take place, during meals or after meals? Figure 7.14 shows the mean daily ratio between water consumption during meals and food consumption during meals, over blocks of 2 days, for the last 8 Purina days and the 8 high-protein days. Overall, the ratio was significantly higher on high-protein days ($t = 11.28$, $p < .001$), and it was significantly higher on the first high-protein day than on the immediately preceding, last Purina day ($t = 3.92$, $p < .01$). It can be seen, however, that the results from the high-protein days present a definite saw-tooth profile. In other words, *initially* the greater water consumption associated with high-protein meals occurred *during* the meal; subsequently, however, on some days, the animals (for whatever reasons) drank relatively less during the meal, and on those days, the increased water intake occurred following the meal.

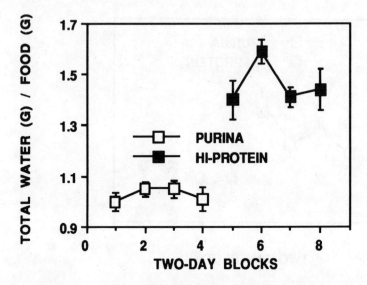

FIGURE 7.13. Mean daily ratio between total water intake and food intake, over the last 8 Purina days and the 8 high-protein days, in blocks of 2 days, in Experiment 2. The data have been collapsed over groups. Vertical lines represent the standard error of the mean.

FIGURE 7.14. Mean daily ratio between water consumption during meals and food consumption, for the last 8 Purina days and the 8 high-protein days, over 2 day blocks, in Experiment 2. The data have been collapsed over groups. Vertical lines represent the standard error of the mean.

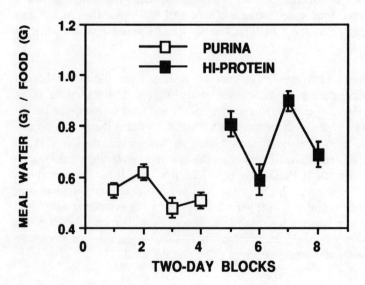

The increase in meal-time intake was present from the very first high-protein meal ($t = 1.95$, $p = .07$), although atypical data from one subject (who did not drink during the first high-protein meal—there may have been equipment problems) obscure the difference; if that subject is ignored, the remaining 14 subjects showed significantly greater water intake on the first high-protein meal ($t = 4.59$, $p < .001$). Furthermore, for those 14 subjects, postmeal water intake was significantly lower on the first high-protein day than on the preceding Purina day (t 2.42, $p < .05$).

Thus, the very first encounter with high-protein food led to an immediate elevation in water intake during the meal. Furthermore, there was no gradual increase over days in the ratio between water consumed during meals and total water intake, presumably because there was no increase over days in the amount of high-protein food eaten during meals. Instead, the ratio between meal water and total water showed the same saw-tooth pattern over days as is seen in Figure 7.14. In short, the most parsimonious way to describe the effects of high-protein food on water intake in Experiment 2 is to say that the high-protein food served as a dipsogenic stimulus from the very first encounter, and its dipsogenic properties did not increase over successive meals.

Test Trial. Finally, the results of the test trial were uniformly negative. Animals who had the test diet flavored with the same flavor as had been contained in the high-protein diet consumed no more water and showed the same meal-water/food ratio (and hence ate the same amount of food) as animals that encountered a novel flavor in the test diet. Once again, water intake during a meal appears to reflect the oropharyngeal properties of the diet, rather than an anticipation of signaled water deficits.

SYNOPSIS OF EXPERIMENTS 1 AND 2

Two things seem clear from the results of the studies just described. First, under meal-feeding conditions, when animals are switched from a high- to a low-protein diet, water consumption drops immediately to a value characteristic for low-protein diets. There is no suggestion in the data that the animals have to learn to readjust their water intake under such circumstances. Second, under meal-feeding conditions, when animals are switched to a high-protein diet, their water intake *during meals* increases immediately to a level characteristic of high-protein diets, the increase being evident in the first 30 minutes of the animals' very first encounter with high-protein food. Again, there is no evidence that an animal's water intake during meals is influenced by a learned anticipation of subsequent changes in its water economy. The results of the flavored-test trials in both experiments also failed to provide any evidence for associative control of water intake.

In short, the data from these experiments are consistent with the notion that normal, meal-related drinking in the rat is *secondary* in nature (i.e., is not in response to an existing fluid deficit) but are inconsistent with the notion that the motivating force behind that secondary drinking is an attempt to avoid a subsequent fluid deficit. Instead, these data appear to show that water intake during meals is controlled, for the most part, directly by the oropharyngeal properties of the food.

In other words, I am suggesting that the evolutionary scenario sketched out earlier—that natural selection favored rats who (a) could learn to associate future water deficits with current food flavors, (b) were motivated to avoid such deficits, and (c) as a consequence combined feeding and drinking into single foraging bouts, thus reducing risk of predation and conserving time and energy—may not have taken place, because it was unnecessary. All natural selection had to do was to produce rats that find drinking hedonically positive while eating, with hedonic value at least partly determined by the difficulty of chewing and swallowing the particular food being consumed. What then appears at first glance to be an adaptive bit of purposive behavior turns out to be the consequence of a fortuitous coincidence: the caloric component that produces the greatest challenge to fluid economy (dry protein) also is difficult to chew and swallow.

This latter explanation, as it stands, would probably not receive a passing mark in Professor Wong's Motivation course. Q: Why do rats drink during meals? A: Rats drink during meals because they like to. Q: How do we know they like to? A: Because they do it. As stated, the explanation is clearly circular. But how else do we explain the facts that (a) feeding-related drinking increased *immediately* upon the introduction of high-protein food, (b) increased as the amount of high-protein food eaten increased, and (c) fell as soon as a low-protein diet was substituted for the high-protein diet? If a dietary supplement could be found that (a) does not increase water intake during meals (compared to a standard diet) but (b) causes an increased water loss (compared to the standard diet), the "hedonic" hypothesis leads one to predict that the increased water intake ought to occur, persistently, between meals, with no increase in meal-associated drinking as a function of experience with the diet—exactly the opposite prediction that would be derived from Fitzsimons and Le Magnen's associative-anticipation hypothesis.

Some support for the "hedonic" hypothesis may be found in Rowland (1979). Rowland added salt (3%) to standard chow. A salt-enriched diet has the same effect on urine production as a protein-enriched diet does: More urine has to be produced, to excrete the excess salt. (We are assuming, in both cases, that the volume of urine increases because the solute or nitrogen load cannot be, or at least is not, excreted by an increase in the concentration of urine—see Radford, 1959.) Rowland found that the addition of salt to the animals' food increased the amount of water consumed daily, but that most of that increase was consumed between meals, with no increase in meal-related drinking over days, (i.e., no indication that the animals learned to anticipate the impending fluid deficit while they were eating the salty food). In short, if the gustatory properties of the food per se do not serve to motivate "excess" drinking, then meal-related drinking does not "anticipate" (i.e., obviate) food-induced water deficits.

CAN RATS LEARN TO ANTICIPATE THE OPPORTUNITY TO DRINK?

Other attempts have been made to determine if different experimental paradigms would reveal a possible associative component among the determinants of (more or less) normal drinking. A brief review of these experiments will show that, by and large, their results corroborate the conclusion reached earlier: Associative mechanisms do not appear to play a demonstrable role in the control of normal drinking in the rat.

Can Rats Use Circadian Cues to Anticipate the Availability of Water?

It has been known for some time that when rats are placed on a meal-feeding schedule in which food is made available at the same time every day, the rats learn to anticipate the availability of food, as long as they are maintained on a 24-hour diurnal cycle (Bolles & Stokes, 1965). The "anticipation" can take several forms, depending upon the particular environmental context. Bolles and Stokes (1965), for example, maintained rats in cages that contained both a lever (that had to be pressed in order to obtain small pellets of food, whenever food was available) and a running wheel. As the time of feeding approached, the rats both pressed the lever more and more frequently and ran in the running wheel more and more often. If, however, the animals are merely confined to their home cages, with food provided at a consistent time of day, the animals engage in more and more exploratory behavior as the time of feeding draws closer and closer (Mathews & Finger, 1966). In all of these instances, the behavioral symptoms of "anticipation" emerge only over successive days, and they only emerge if the rats are maintained on a 24-hour diurnal cycle. Apparently, the animals use circadian cues provided by the environment (or internal cues that they provide themselves) as signals as to when the food will arrive. If you place them on an artificially short or long "day," so that their internal circadian cues are no longer synchronized with the experimenter's definition of "time of day," and if the environment itself lacks time-correlated cues, the anticipatory behaviors do not emerge. This pattern of results points strongly to the operation of an associative mechanism: Rats can learn to anticipate when food will be available, using external and/or endogenous circadian cues.

Bolles (1968) extended this line of research to drinking behavior, using an experimental procedure similar to those used in the feeding studies just described. The animals were housed in cages that included an activity wheel. Water was then made available for 30 minutes a day at the same time every day. Contrary to the results obtained with hungry rats, however, most of the thirsty animals showed no increase in running activity as the time of watering approached, and those few animals that did exhibit increased activity showed relatively weak effects, compared to animals in the feeding experiments. Furthermore, as noted by Bolles, Riley,

Canter, and Duncan (1974), the weak anticipatory effects shown by those few animals probably reflected the anticipation of feeding (which occurred once water was made available) rather than the anticipation of drinking.

In a similar manner, Bolles et al. (1974) investigated whether rats could learn to anticipate an electric shock, given once a day. The rats were given a mild electric shock in the compartment in which they lived, at the same time every day. In order to terminate the shock, the animals had to perform a specific escape response. Again, no evidence for an anticipation of shock was found. Bolles et al. concluded:

> We are suggesting that perhaps the anticipation of events scheduled at the same time each day is a phenomenon which, at least in the rat, is restricted to the feeding system. (p. 366)

Do Cues That Predict the Availability of Water Acquire the Ability to Increase the Urge to Drink?

In the context of feeding, it has been found that cues that uniquely precede or accompany the opportunity to eat acquire the ability to increase hunger (Valle, 1968; Weingarten, 1985). In other words, exposure to such cues not only increases anticipatory responding related to feeding, as was shown in the previous section, it also increases the urge to eat when food is next made available. Presumably, this associative process is one of the factors that enable rats to adjust to meal-feeding schedules. When rats are placed on such schedules, their food consumption increases, over days, in a negatively accelerated manner that suggests a learning process. Moreover, adjustment to such schedules does not take place if the meals are scheduled irregularly (Valle, 1981). Furthermore, once an animal has adjusted to a regimen of regularly-scheduled meals, delaying the meal beyond the normal time results in a reduction in food intake (Bousfield & Elliott, 1934), a decrement that would be expected if hunger is at least partly under stimulus control. We can ask, then, whether analogous results are found with drinking behavior.

Beck (1964) was unable to find any evidence of an associative process in rats' adjustment to a water-deprivation schedule. Although Beck's animals did increase the amount of water they consumed over consecutive days, when they received water for 30 minutes a day at the same time every day, the actual occurrence of drinking behavior was not necessary for this change. If animals simply had the same amount of water intubed directly into their stomachs that they would have drunk on the initial days of the drinking schedule, they drank just as much, when next given an opportunity to drink, as did control animals that "practiced" drinking over the initial days. These results suggest that adaptation to drinking schedules involves a nonbehavioral physiological process that, in turn, determines subsequent drinking behavior.

Zamble, Baxter, and Baxter (1980) also looked for an associative component in adaptation to drinking schedules and, at first glance, the results of their somewhat complex study appear to demonstrate just such a mechanism. Zamble et al.

gave rats 30-minute opportunities to drink at irregular intervals that ranged from 6 to 30 hours, with food available *ad libitum*. For one group of animals, Group Forward, each drinking opportunity in the first phase of the study was preceded by a 15-minute visual cue: The colony lights were turned off. For the other group, Group Backward, the visual cue occurred following the opportunity to drink. I'll call this first phase of the experiment, 1st Original Conditions. In the next phase, 1st Reversal Conditions, the conditions for the two groups were reversed, so that the visual cue now predicted the opportunity to drink for Group Backward but not for Group Forward. In the third phase, 2nd Original Conditions, the groups were returned to their original conditions. And in the last phase, 2nd Reversal Conditions, the conditions of the groups were once again reversed. Zamble et al. found that although the effects were small in absolute terms, the animals did drink significantly more when the opportunity to drink was preceded by a distinctive cue. Zamble et al. concluded that these results are consistent with an associative hypothesis whereby cues that predict the opportunity to engage in the consummatory response acquire the ability to augment the consummatory response—a phenomenon for which there is substantial evidence within the feeding domain.

There is an alternative interpretation of Zamble et al.'s (1980) results, however, one that does not involve an associative mechanism. Given the consistently negative results obtained by other investigators, this alternative explanation must be given some consideration. Several features of the experiment play a role in generating this alternative hypothesis.

First, it should be noted that for both groups, water intake showed a substantial increase when the subjects were changed from the backward condition to the forward condition. Second, Zamble et al. (1980) report that each time the groups were placed in the backward condition, the animals lost weight, and that each time the groups were shifted to the forward condition, the animals gained weight. These changes in body weight must reflect differences in food intake under the backward and forward conditions. Third, although the article does not state so explicitly, because the visual cue used in the study was the termination of colony lighting for 15 minutes, the animals must have been maintained under constant light conditions at all other times. This means that, on the average, the animals were exposed to 18 hours of constant light before each 15-minute interval of darkness, and, half the time, they were exposed to even longer intervals (up to 30 hours) of constant light conditions.

The relevance of these procedural details is that when rats are maintained under natural diurnal conditions, they eat most of their food at night (e.g., Siegel & Stuckey, 1947). Furthermore, the *onset* of darkness precipitates catecholamine release in the hypothalamus that, in turn, triggers vigorous feeding behavior, especially carbohydrate consumption (Stanley, Schwartz, Hernandez, Hoebel, & Leibowitz, 1989). It is possible, therefore, that the main effect of the forward condition in the Zamble, Baxter, and Baxter experiment was to stimulate feeding behavior following the 15-minute exposure to darkness, and it was the increased feeding that resulted in the increased water intake. Under the backward condition, exposure to darkness would not result in nearly as much feeding behavior, because water was not available at the same time.

Once again, manipulations directed toward an associative aspect of drinking behavior appear to have produced indirect effects via their impact on feeding behavior. And we still lack any unambiguous evidence that an associative mechanism regulates water intake per se.

Can the Rapid Onset of Primary Drinking Be Conditioned?

An initially more promising set of results emerged from studies done by Seligman and associates. Seligman, Ives, Ames, and Mineka (1970) reported that subcutaneous injections of hypertonic saline solution (plus procaine to reduce the discomfort of the injections) led to (a) immediate copious unconditioned drinking (as a consequence of intracellular water loss as cellular water was drawn into the hypertonic extracellular space) and (b) conditioned drinking to a white box in which the animals were placed immediately following the injections. The only "discordant" note in the results was the fact that the conditioned drinking did not extinguish, even with 81 unreinforced exposures to the CS (the white box).

Seligman, Mineka, and Fillit (1971) attempted to isolate the factor(s) that might be responsible for this uncharacteristic (for Pavlovian CRs) resistance to extinction. First, they tried saline injections without the procaine anesthetic, varying the concentration of the saline solution. They found that as the concentration of the saline increased, the amount of unconditioned drinking elicited by the injection increased (the more hypertonic the solution, the greater the degree of primary, intracellular thirst that resulted). Only marginal evidence of conditioned drinking was obtained, however, and that bore no (or at best, an inverse) relationship to the concentration of saline that had been used to elicit the unconditioned drinking, an atypical state of affairs for Pavlovian conditioning preparations. Apparently, in the absence of procaine, saline injections—while precipitating copious "unconditioned" drinking—do not engage a reinforcement mechanism or process very effectively. This inference, based on Seligman et al.'s Pavlovian conditioning paradigm, is consistent with observations obtained with instrumental conditioning: saline-injection-induced drinking does not serve as a very effective instrumental reinforcer (O'Kelly & Heyer, 1951; Wayner & Emmers, 1959).

When Seligman et al. (1971) tried procaine injections without saline they found (a) "unconditioned" drinking that gradually increased over conditioning trials, and conditioned drinking (to the white box) that, again, was very resistant to extinction. Subsequent research (Mineka, Seligman, Hetrick, & Zuelzer, 1972) led to the conclusion that procaine acts as a poison, and that the conditioned drinking that is produced by procaine injections is really an avoidance response (to alleviate the anticipated malaise). Thus, while drinking behavior is clearly under the control of an associative process in this situation, the drinking is not part of the animal's normal drinking behavior.

Seligman et al. (1971, Experiment 4) did find that intracranial injections of angiotensin, a hormone produced in response to extracellular deficits, produced (a) robust unconditioned drinking and (b) weak and very transient conditioned drinking to the white box in which the animals were placed following the injections. Unfortunately, no controls for pseudoconditioning effects were included, and other investigators have found sizeable pseudoconditioning effects in situations in which unconditioned drinking is triggered by formalin injections (Weisenger, 1975). If we assume that the conditioned angiotensin (II) effects that Seligman et al. found were not due to pseudoconditioning, then we have evidence for an associative mechanism controlling water intake in rats. Two questions then remain to be answered in evaluating the implications of that effect for the phenomena we have been addressing. First, is the amount of angiotensin (II) used by Seligman et al. (1971) as a UCS, within the range of levels that exist when animals have *ad libitum* access to water? If not, then the putative associative mechanism would not contribute to normal drinking. Second, is there any way to relate angiotensin II levels to the abrupt changes in normal drinking that occur when the type of food is changed?

HISTAMINES AND NORMAL DRINKING

Evidence That Histamines and Angiotensin II Elicit Drinking in the Absence of Fluid Deficits

There is a substantial body of data, reviewed by Kraly (1990), that shows that water intake in rats can be elicited by histaminergic mechanisms and by naturally produced angiotensin II, with both effects occurring in the absence of concurrent fluid deficits. The case Kraly builds is as follows: First, subcutaneous, exogenous histamine precipitates drinking behavior, and that effect is abolished if histamine antagonists are administered. Second, gastrointestinal responses early in (or even in anticipation of) a meal involve histaminergic components. Third, histamine antagonists reduce meal-related drinking in rats than have *ad libitum* access to both food and water by 60%. Fourth, sham feeding results in (a) the activation of histaminergic responses and (b) increased water intake, and the latter can be abolished by the injection of histamine antagonists. Fifth, cues that regularly accompany sham feeding (and the resulting increased intake of water) *acquire* the ability (a) to increase the rate of synthesis of angiotensin II via sympathetic neurons and (b) to elicit drinking behavior. Such drinking is *not* abolished by histamine antagonists; it is, however, abolished by injections of captopril, a compound that prevents the synthesis of angiotensin II. Sixth, captopril injections also reduce meal-related drinking in rats that have *ad libitum* access to food and water (Kraly & Corneilson, 1990).

Thus, the total picture implied by this pattern of results might be described as follows: Even before rats begin to eat, exposure to cues associated with feeding activate the synthesis of angiotensin II, prior to any changes in extracellular fluid levels. The resulting angiotensin II elicits a small amount of drinking behavior before the meal begins. Then, once feeding begins, oral cues activate histaminergic mechanisms, and those mechanisms, in turn, engender substantial intakes of water, again before any change in extracellular fluid level occurs. Thus, we have two nicely isolated physiological mechanisms that, between them, appear to account for the bulk of normal, feeding-related drinking. And one of them—involving angiotensin II—is based on an associative process. Have we at last reached our goals of explaining the basis of normal drinking and describing the role that associative processes play in its operation?

Difficulties with the Histamine/Angiotensin Explanation of Normal Drinking

Despite the obvious appeal of having the occurrence of normal drinking linked to the presence of tangible chemical signals operating upon known neural mechanisms, there are difficulties that prevent one from concluding that Kraly's model offers a more or less complete explanation of normal, meal-related drinking in rats. For one thing, of course, we could ask how the model would explain those effects of high-protein food on meal-related drinking that we discussed earlier.

A second difficulty in accepting Kraly's model as an explanation of normal drinking is the obverse of his observation noted earlier: Histamine antagonists eliminated 60% of meal-related drinking under *ad libitum* conditions—that means 40% remains to be accounted for. Furthermore, as soon as a single food-free interval is inserted into the experimental procedure, so that subjects are 24-hours food deprived at the time food is once again made available, histamine antagonists reduce meal-related drinking by only 25%. Presumably, under the meal-feeding conditions used in the experiments we discussed earlier, histaminergic mechanisms make only a minor contribution to meal-related drinking. Kraly's model, therefore, offers a partial account of meal-related drinking under one specific set of conditions: completely *ad libitum* access to both food and water.

There are additional difficulties in evaluating the role that the associative, angiotensin II component uncovered by Kraly might play in the control of normal drinking. To appreciate the problem we have to take a closer look at the results of Kraly's sham-feeding experiments. First, there was no relationship between (a) how much *liquid* diet that animals sham fed and (b) how much water they drank during the meal. In other words, unlike the situation with normal eating and drinking, the animals did not drink more water as they consumed more food, a not surprising finding, you might say, given that the food was itself a liquid. In fact, you might anticipate that the amount of water consumed would be low and constant. It was indeed constant, but it was not low. Kraly's animals drank an average of 37 ml of water during the 2-hour sham-feeding period, and that was *in addition* to the 42 ml of liquid food they sham fed, on the average. To put those figures into perspective, in Experiment 1, described earlier, my animals drank an average of approximately 11 ml of water during the 2-hour periods when they were eating *dry, high-protein food*. Therefore, the set of causal factors driving water consumption during Kraly's sham-feeding procedure does not appear to be the same as the set of causal factors that drives water consumption during real feeding of dry food. Indeed, the polydipsia shown by Kraly's sham-feeding animals seems more similar to the phenomena described by Falk (e.g., 1971) than to the fluid intake shown by animals eating normal meals.

This then brings us to the difficulty involved in evaluating the significance of the associative process discovered by Kraly. Kraly obtained his conditioned drinking by pairing (a) handling cues (required to prepare the animals for sham-feeding and for measurements of stomach secretions) with (b) the copious drinking that occurred during sham feeding. Since, as we have seen, the latter does not appear to reflect the same set of controlling factors that operate during real feeding, it is difficult to assess the role that such conditioned drinking might play in the regulation of normal drinking. (And again, there were no controls to assess the contribution that pseudoconditioning might have made to the drinking that ultimately occurred to handling cues alone.)

It may be, of course, that additional research will resolve some of the concerns that I have expressed; normal, meal-related drinking in rats may well turn out to be primarily a "physiological" rather than a "psychological" phenomenon. For the time being, however, I think a case can still be made that at least a sizeable fraction of normal drinking in rats represents a hedonically driven behavioral option, rather than the consummatory component of a complex set of reflexes. The last studies to be examined touch upon this possibility.

CAN RATS LEARN TO ANTICIPATE A WATER-FREE MEAL?

It has been known for many years that rats substantially reduce their food intake when they are totally deprived of water (e.g., Verplanck & Hayes, 1953). From the point of view of survival, this is a sensible course of action, because, as we have seen, the digestion of food and the elimination of solutes acquired as a consequence result in the loss of body water. And, over the short run, an individual is much more likely to die from dehydration than from starvation. Thus, the rat that reduces its food intake to conserve body water lives to eat and drink another day.

More surprising, perhaps, is the finding that if rats are placed on a meal-feeding schedule in which they have water available at all times *except* when food is available, they also reduce their food intake, by about 25% (Verplanck & Hayes, 1953). Why should rats behave that way? They are in no danger of dying from dehydration, because they can drink as much as they wish or need to as soon as the meal period is over. Perhaps the immediate impact of feeding on body water (water drawn into the stomach, etc.) is substantial enough that, under the circumstances, the rats automatically react as if in danger of dehydration. If that were true, shouldn't rats be able to learn to *anticipate* the food-produced dehydration and, as a consequence, learn to drink just prior to the meal period? This would enable them to finesse the potential dehydrating consequences of eating and, as a consequence, enable them to eat adequate-sized meals, even in the absence of concurrent drinking water.

Rats Do Not Use Circadian Cues to Anticipate a Water-Free Meal

Such a question was asked by Jacobs (1963), and he could find no evidence that rats can learn to anticipate a water-free feeding. After 3 weeks of experience with such a schedule, his rats were still not drinking prior to the onset of the meal period and as a consequence, were still eating less than they otherwise would (if water were available with the meal). Similar results have apparently been obtained by Rowland (unpublished observations cited by Toates & Evans, 1987). Jacobs then went on to ask what he could do, in terms of artificially hydrating his animals, to enable them to eat normal-sized meals under nondrinking conditions. We will return to his observations and conclusions shortly, but first, I would like to discuss one final set of experimental results from my laboratory that address the same issue.

The Taste of Food as a Salient Predictor of Food-Induced Water Loss. Because we have already seen that rats cannot (or least, do not) use circadian cues to anticipate a daily opportunity to drink, perhaps we should not be surprised that Jacobs (1963) found that they cannot use such cues to anticipate a (presumed) fluid challenge imposed by having to ingest dry food in the absence of water at the same time every day. Maybe the potential to learn is present, but an inappropriate cue is being used. Maybe, as Fitzsimons and Le Magnen (1969) originally suggested, rats are disposed to use the taste of food as a cue to anticipate subsequent changes in their fluid economy. In the studies just discussed, the animals would be unable to reveal this capability, because by the time the taste of food occurs, the opportunity to drink is no longer present. In Experiment 3, therefore, the taste of food itself served as a potential cue that a water-free feeding interval was imminent.

EXPERIMENT 3

Design

Two groups of six adult, male Wistar rats were placed on the following meal-feeding schedule for 21 days: In order to accentuate the consequences of food consumption on body water, a 55% protein diet was used, obtained by adding casein to Purina Chow, vegetable oil, and sugar. Both groups received a 15-minute Premeal each day, during which both food and water were available. Then both groups received an immediately following meal, lasting 75 minutes. During the meal, Group Water had water available while Group NoWater did not. Following the meal, water was returned to Group NoWater and, 15 minutes later, water consumption for both groups was recorded: The data from this 15-minute interval are referred to as Immediate Postmeal Intake. Subsequently, water intake was measured again just prior to the beginning of the Premeal the following day: The data from this 22.25-hour interval are referred to as Subsequent Postmeal Intake.

Results

The first question to be asked of the results is, Did Group Water consume water during the 75-minute meal interval? Figure 7.15 shows the mean daily water intake for the two groups, collapsed over the last 7 days of the experiment, for the Premeal and meal intervals. It can be seen that Group Water did indeed take advantage of the availability of water during the meal. This finding indicates that Group NoWater was indeed deprived of something they would otherwise have consumed during the meal.

The next question to be addressed is, Did Group NoWater learn to anticipate the unavailability of water during the meal interval—did they learn to drink more during the Premeal interval? As can be seen in Figure 7.15, the answer is, no. Group NoWater actually drank less water during the Premeal interval than did Group Water, although the difference is not significant ($t = 1.78$).

FIGURE 7.15. Mean daily water intake during the 15-min Premeal interval and the immediately-following, 75-min meal interval for Groups Water and NoWater, collapsed over the last 7 days of Experiment 3. Only Group Water had water available during the meal interval. The data are expressed as grams of water consumed per 100 grams of body weight. Vertical lines represent the standard error of the mean.

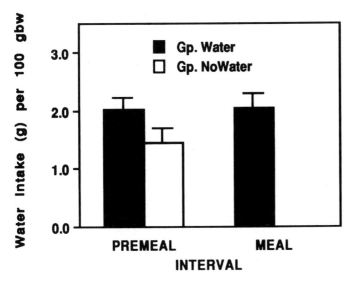

With respect to food intake, contrary to the results described earlier (Jacobs, 1963; Verplanck & Hayes, 1953), the lack of water during the meal interval did not adversely affect Group NoWater's food intake. Group NoWater actually ate more food than did Group Water during both the meal and the Premeal intervals, although the differences were not significant. Apparently, being able to drink some water during the Premeal interval enabled Group NoWater to eat normal amounts of food during their waterless meal.

If Group NoWater failed to compensate in advance for the water they were unable to drink during the meal, did they compensate following the meal? Figure 7.16 shows mean daily water intake for the two groups during the 15-minute interval immediately following the meal period (Immediate Postmeal Intake). It can be seen that Group NoWater consumed more water immediately following the meal than did Group Water, and the difference approached significance ($t = 2.03$, $p = .07$). Note, however, that the variability in Group NoWater was substantially greater than in Group Water (as revealed by the length of the standard error bars): Two of the six animals in Group NoWater did not show increased water intake (relative to Group Water) in the Immediate Postmeal interval. Once again we find evidence suggesting that normal water intake in rats is generally "facultative" rather than "obligatory." During the subsequent 22.25 interval (Subsequent Post-

FIGURE 7.16.   Water consumption during the 15 min immediately following the meal interval in Experiment 3, as a function of whether water had been available during the meal. The data have been expressed as grams of water consumed per 100 grams of body weight and have been collapsed over the last 7 days. Vertical lines represent the standard error of the mean.

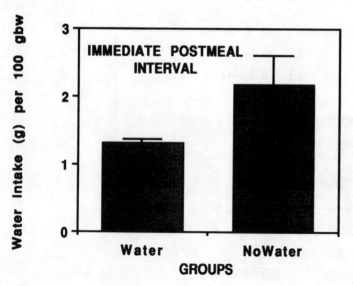

meal Intake), Group NoWater consumed slightly less water than did Group Water, but the difference was not significant ($t = 0.62$).

Having seen that Group NoWater compensated, to some extent, for the water they missed during the meal by drinking more during the 15-minute interval immediately subsequent to the meal, we can ask if, relative to food intake, they compensated completely. An analysis of total water/food ratios for the last 7 days of the experiment found that those ratios were significantly lower for Group NoWater than for Group Water ($t = 2.85$, $p = .02$). One way to interpret that difference is to assume that at least some of Group Water's water intake during the meal interval was in excess of the amount needed to maintain internal water balance.

Why Don't Rats Drink in Anticipation of a Waterless Meal?

In short, the results of Experiment 3 suggest, once again, that water intake during meals for rats is at least partly under the control of purely hedonic factors. Observations reported by Jacobs (1963) support this interpretation. Jacobs, it will be recalled, found that (a) in the absence of water, food intake in meal-feeding rats was significantly depressed, and (b) the animals showed no inclination to circumvent that problem by drinking excess water just prior to the meal. There are two different ways to interpret that pair of observations. One could say that (a) rats lack the ability to anticipate the demands on their body water that food consumption imposes, and (b) their depressed food intake when water is not available represents an attempt to avoid fluid deficits during the meal. Alternatively, one could propose that rats do not drink in anticipation of the water-free feeding interval because systemic water is not a motivational factor in this situation. In other words, their depressed feeding scores reflect oral hedonic factors during the meal period rather than internal fluid losses during the meal period. While drinking in anticipation of a water-free feeding interval would circumvent the consequences of food consumption on body water, it would not alleviate the unpleasant aspects of trying to eat dry food in the absence of water. These two explanations may be evaluated by assessing the impact of various hydrational manipulations on food intake under such circumstances, the strategy used by Jacobs.

Evidence for a Hedonic Basis of Normal Drinking from Jacobs's Hydrational Studies

Jacobs (1963) found that gastric infusion of 20 ml of water (the amount typically consumed during a 2-hour meal) either prior to or during a meal failed to result in normal levels of food intake, when drinking water was unavailable during the meal. Furthermore, 20 ml of saccharin solution consumed just prior to the meal also failed to enable the animals to eat normal-sized meals, in the absence of drinking water during the meal. However, 20 ml of water infused orally during the meal resulted in normal levels of food consumption (just as the opportunity to drink some water during the Premeal apparently enabled Group NoWater to eat normal quantities of food during the subsequent meal, in Experiment 3 described earlier).

Thus, the depressed food intake of animals that do not have drinking water available during the meal reflects oropharyngeal conditions and not, primarily, systemic conditions. This conclusion was supported by one final observation reported by Jacobs (1963). He devised a "wet" diet that had a low water content by adding fat to powdered chow. With this diet, the animals ate greater than usual amounts of food during 2-hour meals, even without drinking water available, and the animals' water/food ratios dropped in half. All in all, Jacobs's results support the assumption that rats drink during meals, primarily for hedonic reasons, and they reduce dry food intake when water is not immediately available primarily for hedonic reasons.

Other Types of Data Consistent with the Hedonic Hypothesis

Our working hypothesis is that normal, feeding-related drinking in rats is controlled, primarily, by hedonic factors engendered by the taste and texture of food (with histaminergic mechanisms contributing as well). This type of interpretation would be strengthened if it could be shown that fluid ingestion in rats is sensitive, in general, to other types of hedonic variables. To this end, relevant evidence can be cited from studies that have investigated both the positive and negative ends of the hedonic continuum.

The Effects of Pleasant and Unpleasant Flavors on Normal Drinking. For example, the fluid intake of nondeprived rats can be substantially increased by the addition of saccharin to their water, and making the animals thirsty has relatively little additional impact on their saccharin solution ingestion (Ernits & Corbit, 1973). Similarly, if hedonically attractive artificial flavors such as orange or cherry are added to the water, rats increase their fluid consumption, and they increase their consumption even more if they receive a variety of flavors in succession rather than just a single flavor (Rolls, Wood, & Rolls, 1980). In short, fluid intake in rats can be enhanced by the presence of pleasant flavors and by flavor variety.

On the negative side, the addition of quinine to water causes rats to reduce their fluid intake (Nicolaïdis & Rowland, 1975). Indeed, in this study, 20% of the animals (3/14) refused to ingest bitter water and, as a consequence, died.

The Effects of Supplying Large Amounts of Water via Infusions. Additional support for a hedonic interpretation of normal drinking is found in studies that have attempted to eliminate the need to engage in drinking behavior by infusing water through various routes into the internal environment. For example, Rowland and Nicolaïdis (1976) found that with a standard chow available *ad libitum*, their animals drank about 30 ml of water a day. The animals then received continuous intravenous infusions of water, with the amount infused manipulated across groups. Despite the infusion of substantially more water than they would normally drink, the animals continued to exhibit substantial amounts of drinking behavior. For example, a group that received 180 ml a day via infusion—six times its normal intake—still drank 16 ml per day—50% of its normal intake.

Interestingly enough, one infusion technique was successful in completely eliminating drinking behavior in most animals. Drinking was abolished when (a) water was infused only when the animals were eating, and (b) the tube carrying the water to the stomach provided oropharyngeal cues similar to those provided by the actual ingestion of water. In other words, drinking was suppressed under conditions that mimic the stimulus consequences of fluid ingestion at those times when the animal would normally seek out water and drink. Rowland and Nicolaïdis concluded "there may be an urge to drink through the mouth independent of need condition" (1976, p. 7).

The Consequences of Restricting Water Intake.   Evidence for water intake in excess of "needs" may also be found in studies that take an approach opposite to that just discussed. In other words, rather than attempting to circumvent the need to drink by infusing water into the internal environment, it is possible to examine the physiological consequences of *reducing* water intake below that normally maintained under *ad libitum* conditions.

Kutscher (1964), for example, placed rats on a 1/2-hour-a-day drinking schedule, with food available *ad libitum*. Under those conditions, after a few days of adaptation to the schedule, the animals were able to drink about 60% of their normal *ad libitum* water intake. However, their food intake (after adaptation to the schedule) equaled that achieved with *ad libitum* access to water. In a sense, the animals were drinking 40% more water than they "needed to," under *ad libitum* conditions. *Needed to* refers to the amount needed to maintain internal water balance, given normal levels of food intake.

The reason the animals were able to "sacrifice" 40% of their normal water intake, while still maintaining normal levels of food intake, is the same reason the animals in the Rowland and Nicolaïdis (1976) study were able to tolerate infusions of up to 500% of their normal water intake with no ill effects: the remarkable efficiency of the kidney. It is because of the physiological efficiency of the kidney (and hypothalamus and pituitary) in adjusting both the absolute amount and the concentration of urine produced that the behavioral mechanism of drinking can, under most circumstances, be uncoupled from physiological deficits or excesses and can be controlled, instead, by hedonic, "psychological" variables (Bolles, 1979).

Under normal circumstances, the rat's responsiveness to hedonic variables ensures that it will ingest enough water to remain in a physiological state that fluctuates between overhydration (following water intake) and euhydration (following action by the kidneys) (Rowland & Nicolaïdis, 1976). From this perspective, "primary drinking" represents an emergency response in which the normal determinants of drinking are supplanted by a set of controlling mechanisms that only become engaged under atypical conditions.

SUMMARY AND CONCLUSIONS

We began with two observations and a question regarding the relationship between them. The two observations are (a) rats drink more water when eating high-protein food than when eating low-protein food; and (b) if the concentration of urine does not increase, rats will need more water, in order to produce more urine, in order to excrete the by-products of metabolism, when eating a high-protein diet than when eating a low-protein diet. Most authorities, we discovered, believe there is a causal relationship between these two facts—a causal relationship that is mediated by an associative mechanism. The source of that interpretation is an experiment by Fitzsimons and Le Magnen (1969).

Fitzsimons and Le Magnen's (1969) interpretation of the relationship between these two facts is that rats drink more water while eating high-protein food *because* they have *learned* that the ingestion of such food is followed, some time later, by a loss of body water. Thus, the second, physiological fact stands as an explanation of the first, behavioral fact. The behavior is *regulatory* and *purposive* in the sense that its occurrence is contingent upon repeated experiences with the consequences on body water of ingesting a particular type of food and, concurrently, a given amount of water. Since most drinking behavior in rats occurs in the context of eating, it follows from Fitzsimons and Le Magnen's interpretation that most drinking behavior in rats is regulatory (i.e., modified by its impact on internal water balance) and is purposively controlled by associatively acquired information.

As evidence for the associative basis of meal-related drinking, Fitzsimons and Le Magnen (1969) investigated two changes in drinking behavior that occur when rats are switched from low- to high-protein diets, and vice versa. First, Fitzsimons and Le Magnen found that when rats are switched from high- to low-protein food, their water/food ratios fall gradually over successive days. That gradual decline suggests the rats are learning that low-protein food does not lead to as much urine being formed as does high-protein food, and hence the rats gradually adjust their fluid intake during meals in accordance with that information. Although the interpretation is clear and persuasive, the actual data it is based upon are not. At least some of Fitzsimons and Le Magnen's animals showed abrupt decreases in water intake following the shift from high- to low-protein food, and we are not given enough information to assess the typicality of those animals.

The second change in drinking behavior used by Fitzsimons and Le Magnen (1969) as evidence for the operation of an associative process in the control of normal drinking is the complex change in the proportion of total daily water drunk during meals that occurs following a switch from low- to high-protein food. While total water intake increases abruptly as soon as the diet is changed, the proportion of that total consumed during meals at first falls and then gradually recovers. It is this gradual recovery in meal-related drinking that Fitzsimons and Le Magnen offer as the second indication that meal-related drinking in rats is based on an associative mechanism: The rats gradually learn to associate the flavor of the food with the loss in body water and change their drinking behavior during meals as a consequence. Again, while the interpretation seems straightforward and persuasive, the data on which it is based contain ambiguities, in this instance stemming from changes in the frequency of meals that occurred following the change in diets (Ludlow, 1982).

In the experiments described in this report, three questions were asked: (a) How abrupt is the decline in water intake following a shift from high- to low-protein food? (b) How gradual is the increase in meal-related drinking following a shift from low- to high-protein food, when frequency of meals is controlled experimentally? (c) Will an arbitrary flavor embedded in a high-protein diet acquire the ability to motivate excess drinking behavior, if transferred to a new low-protein diet?

The results for the first two questions were quite clear. Under meal-feeding conditions (a) water intake falls abruptly and asymptotically on the very first low-protein meal, following a series of high-protein meals; and (b) water intake increases abruptly, within the first 30 minutes of an animal's first encounter with high-protein food, and, if care is taken to minimize changes in meal *size*, the change in the proportion of total daily water taken during meals is asymptotic on the first high-protein meal. Both of these findings are inconsistent with Fitzsimons and Le Magnen's (1969) hypothesis that meal-related drinking in rats is controlled by an associative process. Instead, meal-related drinking appears to be determined, ahistorically, by the gustatory or masticulatory properties of the current diet.

The results for the third question were also quite consistent but, given the impossibility of proving the null hypothesis, are not as decisive as one would like: (c) No evidence could be found that an arbitrary flavor associated with high-protein meals acquires the ability to signal water loss and motivate water consumption. This could mean that no such associative process exists, as the other two observations imply, or, that the parameters of the flavor-conditioning procedure were simply not sensitive to its existence.

A review of other attempts to demonstrate an associative basis for normal drinking in rats also led to consistently negative results. Along the way, the impression grew consistently stronger that water intake during meals in rats is controlled by nonregulatory, hedonic factors, engendered by the taste and texture of food. The conclusion was reached, reluctantly, that the relationship between the two observations we started with is entirely fortuitous: Rats drink more water when eating high-protein food because high-protein food has gustatory properties that promote drinking for purely hedonic reasons. That hedonically driven increase in water intake more than compensates for the water that will subsequently be lost as a consequence of increased urine production. The disposition to find drinking pleasurable while eating ensures that rats will almost always ingest more water than they need to meet daily water requirements. The rat's kidneys easily eliminate the daily excess.

It also appears to be the case that histamines, released at the start of a meal as a normal component of the digestive process, are capable of eliciting a certain amount of drinking behavior (Kraly, 1990). At the present time, there is no reason to believe that histamingeric mechanisms play any role in the different amounts of drinking engendered by high- versus low-protein meals.

Perhaps the most apt way to conclude is with the final sentence of Pfaffman's seminal paper on the hedonic control of behavior:

> Sensory stimulation "*qua* stimulation" plays a significant role in the motivation as well as the guidance of behavior—euphemistically we might say, in controlling behavior for the "pleasures of sensation." (1960, p. 265)

REFERENCES

Beck, R. C. (1964). Some effects of restricted water intake on consummatory behavior of the rat. In M. J. Wayner (Ed.), *Thirst* (pp. 305–315). Elmsford, NY: Pergamon.
Bolles, R. C. (1968). Anticipatory general activity in thirsty rats. *Journal of Comparative and Physiological Psychology, 65,* 511–513.
Bolles, R. C. (1979). Toy rats and real rats: Nonhomeostatic plasticity in drinking. *Behavioral and Brain Sciences, 2,* 103.
Bolles, R. C., Riley, A. L., Canter, M. B., & Duncan, P. M. (1974). The rat's failure to anticipate regularly scheduled shocks. *Behavioral Biology, 11,* 365–372.
Bolles, R. C., & Stokes, L. W. (1965). Rat's anticipation of diurnal and adiurnal feeding. *Journal of Comparative and Physiological Psychology, 60,* 290–294.
Bousfield, W. A., & Elliott, M. H. (1934). The effect of fasting on the eating behavior of rats. *Journal of Genetic Psychology, 45,* 227–237.
Chew, R. M. (1963). Water metabolism of mammals. In W. V. Mayer & R. G. Van Gelder (Eds.), *Physiological mammalogy: Vol 11. Mammalian reactions to stressful environments* (pp. 43–178). New York: Academic Press.
Epstein, A. N. (1982). The physiology of thirst. In D. W. Pfaff (Ed.), *The physiological mechanisms of motivation* (pp. 165–214). New York: Springer-Verlag.
Epstein, A. N., Kissileff, H. R., & Stellar, E. (Eds.). (1973). *The neuropsychology of thirst: New findings and advances in concepts.* Washington, DC: V. H. Winston & Sons.
Ernits, T., & Corbit, J. D. (1973). Taste as a dipsogenic stimulus. *Journal of Comparative and Physiological Psychology, 83,* 27–31.
Falk, J. L. (1971). The nature and determinants of adjunctive behavior. *Physiology and Behavior, 6,* 577–588.
Fitzsimons, J. T. (1966). The hypothalamus and drinking. *British Medical Bulletin, 22,* 232–237.
Fitzsimons, J. T. (1972). Thirst. *Physiological Reviews, 52,* 468–561.
Fitzsimons, J. T. (1979). *The physiology of thirst and sodium appetite.* London: Cambridge University Press.
Fitzsimons, J. T., & Le Magnen, J. (1969). Eating as a regulatory control of drinking in the rat. *Journal of Comparative and Physiological Psychology, 67,* 273–283.
Jacobs, H. L. (1963). The interaction of hunger and thirst: Experimental separation of osmotic and oral-gastric factors in regulating caloric intake. In M. J. Wayner (Ed.), *Thirst* (pp. 117–134). Elmsford, NY: Pergamon.
Kraly, F. S. (1990). Drinking elicited by eating. In A. N. Epstein & A. R. Morrison (Eds.), *Progress in psychobiology and physiological psychology* (Vol. 14, pp. 67–133). San Diego: Academic Press.

Kraly, F. S., & Corneilson, R. (1990). Angiotensin II mediates drinking elicited by eating in the rat. *American Journal of Physiology, 258*, R436–R442.

Kutscher, C. (1964). Some physiological correlates of adaptation to a water deprivation schedule. In M. J. Wayner (Ed.), *Thirst* (pp. 257–267). Elmsford, NY: Pergamon.

Le Magnen, J., & Tallon, S. (1966). La périodicité spontanée de la prise d'aliments ad libitum du Rat blanc. *Journal de Physiologie (Paris), 58*, 323–349.

Ludlow, A. R. (1982). Towards a theory of thresholds. *Animal Behavior, 30*, 253–267.

Mathews, S. R., Jr., & Finger, F. W. (1966). Direct observation of the rat's activity during food deprivation. *Physiology and Behavior, 1*, 85–88.

Mineka, S., Seligman, M. E. P., Hetrick, M., & Zuelzer, K. (1972). Poisoning and conditioned drinking. *Journal of Comparative and Physiological Psychology, 79*, 377–384.

Nicholaïdis, S., & Rowland, N. (1975) Regulatory drinking in rats with permanent access to a bitter fluid source. *Physiology and Behavior, 14*, 819–824.

O'Kelly, L. I., & Heyer, A. W., Jr. (1951). Studies in motivation and retention: V. The influences of need duration on retention of a maze habit. *Comparative Psychology Monographs, 20*(106), 287–301.

Pfaffman, C. (1960). The pleasures of sensation. *Psychological Review, 67*, 253–268.

Radford, E. P., Jr. (1959). Factors modifying water metabolism in rats fed dry diets. *American Journal of Physiology, 196*, 1098–1108.

Rolls, B. J., & Rolls, E. T. (1982). *Thirst.* Cambridge: Cambridge University Press.

Rolls, B. J., Wood, R. J., & Rolls, E. T. (1980). Thirst: The initiation, maintenance, and termination of drinking. In J. M. Sprague & A. N. Epstein (Eds.), *Progress in psychobiology and physiological psychology* (Vol. 9, pp. 263–321). New York: Academic Press.

Rowland, N. (1979). Natural drinking, interactions with feeding, and species differences-three data deserts. *Behavioral and Brain Sciences, 2*, 117–118.

Rowland, N., & Nicholaïdis, S. (1976). Metering of fluid intake and determinants of ad libitum drinking in rats. *Journal of Physiology, 231*, 1–8.

Seligman, M. E. P., Ives, C., Ames, H., & Mineka, S. (1970). Failure to extinguish conditioned drinking: Avoidance, preparedness, or functional autonomy? *Journal of Comparative and Physiological Psychology, 71*, 411–419.

Seligman, M. E. P., Mineka, S., & Fillit, H. (1971). Conditioned drinking produced by procaine, NaCl, and angiotensin. *Journal of Comparative and Physiological Psychology, 77*, 110–121.

Siegel, P. S., & Stuckey, H. L. (1947). The diurnal course of water and food intake in the normal mature rat. *Journal of Comparative and Physiological Psychology, 40*, 365–370.

Stanley, B. G., Schwartz, D. H., Hernandez, L., Hoebel, B. G., & Leibowitz, S. F. (1989). Patterns of extracellular norepinephrine in the paraventricular hypothalamus: Relationship to circadian rhythms and deprivation-induced eating behavior. *Life Sciences, 45*, 275–282.

Toates, F. M., & Evans, R. A. S. (1987). The application of theory, modeling and simulation to feeding and drinking. In F. M. Toates & N. E. Rowland (Eds.), *Feeding and drinking* (pp. 531–562). Amsterdam: Elsevier.

Valle, F. P. (1968). Effect of exposure to feeding-related stimuli on food consumption in rats. *Journal of Comparative and Physiological Psychology, 66*, 773–776.

Valle, F. P. (1981). Effects of irregular meals on rats' ability to adjust to meal feeding. *American Journal of Psychology, 94*, 3–11.

Verplanck, W. S., & Hayes, J. R. (1953). Eating and drinking as a function of maintenance schedule. *Journal of Comparative and Physiological Psychology, 46*, 327–333.

Wayner, M. J., & Emmers, R. (1959). A test of the thirst-deprivation trace hypothesis in the hooded rat. *Journal of Comparative and Physiological Psychology, 52*, 112–115.

Weingarten, H. P. (1985). Stimulus control of eating: Implications for a two-factor theory of hunger. *Appetite, 6*, 387–401.

Weisenger, R. S. (1975). Conditioned and pseudoconditioned thirst and sodium appetite. In G. Peters, J. T. Fitzsimons, & L. Peters-Haefeli (Eds.), *Control mechanisms of drinking* (pp. 148–154). New York: Springer-Verlag.

Zamble, E., Baxter, D. J., & Baxter, L. (1980). Influences of conditioned incentive stimuli on water intake. *Canadian Journal of Psychology, 34*, 82–85.

Part IV

AVERSIVE MOTIVATION

chapter 8

A Stage Model
of Coping
with Frustrative Stress

PAUL T.P. WONG
Trent University and University of Toronto

SYNOPSIS AND COMMENTS
Roderick Wong

Motivation is concerned with purposive and goal-achieving behavior, and with access to the appropriate goal-objects, such behavior is rewarded and consummated. When there are obstructions to an anticipated goal, instrumental behavior is thwarted, and other forms of activity occur. This change in behavior is assumed to be due to a hypothetical internal activating state such as frustration arising from the organism's reactions to nonreward. In contrast to traditional approaches, which focus on the adverse effects of frustration on behavior, Paul Wong offers a "competence" orientation. Wong's research and theorizing reflect a tradition common in the clinical sciences, in which "animal models" are developed to illuminate comparable processes operating in humans. Although the material in this chapter is less specifically evolutionarily oriented than that in most of the other chapters in this volume, there are interesting implications from it that are relevant to the theme of this book.

In his chapter, Wong elaborates on his stage model of coping with frustration in which the focus is on natural behavioral tendencies that serve adaptive functions. The notion of adaptation as used here is in the context of better "adjustment" of the individual to its environment. This notion signifies an ability to deal effectively with the varied demands of everyday living, including coping with stress. This usage of the term is not quite the same as the evolutionary process of adaptation in the Darwinian sense, which refers to evolved solutions to problems posed by the challenges of survival and reproduction. However, not all features of behavior or morphology are adaptations. In his chapter, Wong analyzes frustration in the general context of stress processes. *Stress* is defined as "a problematic internal or external condition that creates tension/upset in the individual and calls for some form of coping."

Wong argues that frustration is probably the most common source of stress and that it is important for humans to know how to cope with the former. Thus, he offers a model that posits an adaptation process involving three stages, of which each stage is characterized by dominant behavioral strategies. In the first stage, the organism deals with frustration by "trying harder," coupled with the mechanism of perseveration. If this strategy proves unsuccessful, the organism will explore all available coping options by "trying something else." Aggression most likely occurs during this stage because it is one of the instrumental options. The third stage of coping is called *resolution* and occurs when the organism ceases all efforts and becomes helpless or switches to a substitute goal, if one is available. Helplessness, according to this model, serves an adaptive function for the individual and may have fitness-enhancing potential. Resignation is more adaptive when the organism faces an unsolvable problem because it conserves energy as well as lessening distress. This state is nonadaptive only when it occurs prematurely or when it generalizes to situations involving solvable problems.

Wong conceptualizes the coping mechanisms in each stage as preprogrammed adaptive reactions that are generated in frustrating situations. In that respect, they may be regarded as adaptive specializations exhibited by individuals in a species. Although Wong did not deal with coping mechanisms from a comparative perspective, it is assumed that they are manifested only among species capable of forming expectancies and thus of experiencing frustration. These coping mechanisms enable the organism to survive in an environment where dwindling resources and intraspecific competition act to thwart its ability to attain relevant goals.

Support for the stage model comes from studies on experimental extinction by Wong's group in which rats were presented with a choice of various routes leading to different goal objects. At first, the animals perseverated in the habitual pattern for several trials before switching to alternative routes. Wong found that extinction increased both temporal and sequential variability such that the rats showed a gradual increase in hole exploration and biting behavior. Later in the series, the rats switched to a substitution activity of sand digging that Wong regarded as indicative of Stage 3 in his coping model. He also described data from other investigators that are congruent with the stage model.

A number of motivational phenomena can be explained by Wong's stage model of coping with frustration. When a response fails to enable an organism to attain its goal, it often explores new ways to deal with the situation.

The creative expansion of the animal's repertoire and the maintenance of goal persistence are adaptive consequences of frustration-induced exploration. Another reaction to frustration is aggression and such reactions often enable the organism to achieve important objects or goals. Thus, aggressive behavior may be instrumental to the animal's success in attaining its goal. According to the stage model analysis, when the alternatives to aggression involve dismal prospects, the organism resorts to aggressive behavior. Wong also considered the possibility that aggression may serve some cathartic function but conceded that this hypothesis has been challenged by contrary evidence.

Goal substitution is interpreted as an activity occurring during the third stage of coping with prolonged frustration. When the original goal is blocked, animals tend to substitute one incentive object for another. This phenomenon has been analyzed in a different theoretical context by Falk (1977) as "adjunctive behavior." One can also analyze goal substitution in terms of the ethological concept of "displacement activity." When the consummatory act appropriate to a motivational state (i.e., eating) is thwarted by the absence of a proper releasing stimulus (e.g., exteroceptive food cues), another act (e.g., drinking) will be secondarily activated by either an increase in its action specific energy or by a lowering of its reaction threshold. The secondarily activated behavior is referred to as either *appetitive* if it makes the occurrence of the blocked consummatory response possible, or *displacement* if it does not. From another ethological perspective, McFarland (1965) suggests that it makes functional sense for an animal to "switch attention" from a fruitless activity (trying to get food when none is available) to a fruitful one. Alternatively, Lucas, Timberlake, and Gawley (1988) view adjunctive behavior as part of a natural food-getting sequence in which rearing and drinking appear to be transition behaviors occurring between postfood focal search and more general search or withdrawal. Schulze's chapter in this volume suggests that there may be homeostatic mechanisms underlying adjunctive behavior.

P. Wong argues that helplessness/depression following repeated failure can be averted if substitution incentive objects are readily available. In contrast to Seligman's cognitive interpretation of helplessness that focuses on the presentation on noncontingent events (Seligman & Altenor, 1980), Wong posits that only prolonged frustration operations result in this state. Whereas the interpretation emphasizing cognition of response–outcome independence would lead one to predict ready transfer of reactions from one situation to the next, the frustration interpretation stipulates a more restrictive set of boundary conditions for the transfer of helplessness. Following the frustration experience, transfer will occur only when the initial helplessness treatment is long enough to trigger the resignation mechanism and when the test situation contains sufficient frustrative cues to instigate resignation prematurely. The evidence on the generality of learned helplessness, particularly that of cross-situational appetitive transfer, is very limited. Prior exposure to uncontrollable events in one task does not automatically result in transfer of helplessness in other situations.

From the applied perspective, factors that immunize the animal against the onset of helplessness are of great importance. While learned helplessnes theory points out the facilitating effects on prior exposure to consistent reinforcement, frustration theory differs in its predictions. Prior experience with consistent reinforcement may make the onset of the removal of response–outcome contingencies more disrupting. If the animal has previously been exposed to degraded reinforcement contingencies and has learned how to cope with frustration, then it is less likely to be helpless. More specifically, partial reinforcement should be more effective than continuous reinforcement as an immunization procedure against helplessness. The efficacy of partial reinforcement as immunization and a treatment against learned helplessness has been documented in many experiments.

In general, the stage model provides a means of conceptualizing the processes of behavioral adaptation consequent to the blocking of goal-directed behavior. Although organisms may have been selected with mechanisms that enable them to cope with chronic frustration in an adaptive manner, Wong's model indicates the specific conditions under which nonadaptive coping responses are acquired and generalized. This analysis allows us to understand how a diversity of effects such as response invigoration, aggression, exploration, and helplessness represents different aspects of the same coping process. Wong argues that if all animals manifest a similar sequence of behavior in reaction to different frustrating situations, this is a reflection of coping reactions that have been preprogrammed.

References

Falk, J. L. (1977). The origin and functions of adjunctive behavior. *Animal Learning and Behavior, 5,* 325–335.
Lucas, G. A., Timberlake, W., & Gawley, D. J. (1988). Adjunctive behavior of the rat under periodic food delivery in a 24-hr environment. *Animal Learning and Behavior, 16,* 19–30.
McFarland, D. J. (1965). Hunger, thirst and displacement behavior in the Barbary dove. *Animal Behavior, 13,* 292–300.

INTRODUCTION

Who has not been frustrated by unfulfilled ambition, unrequited love, or unsolvable problems? Who does not know the bitter taste of failure and rejection? Life is a continuous drama of how to narrow the gap between reality and aspiration. To be alive is to be acquainted with frustration and touched by its varied effects.

Dwindling resources and rising inequality are likely to make its presence more keenly felt individually and collectively (Clark, 1967). Given the prevalence of frustration, it is not surprising that there is a long and venerable tradition of frustration research. Many of the older findings have been summarized by Yates (1962) and Lawson (1965). More recent research is largely an outgrowth of Amsel's (1958, 1962, 1967) frustration theory which has exerted considerable impact on contemporary psychology (see Garfield, 1978). The present stage model is an extension and reformulation of Amsel's frustration theory.

Past research on frustration tends to focus on its adverse effect. A variety of pathological symptoms have been attributed to frustration (Freud, 1908/1959; Miller & Stevenson, 1936; Parker & Kleiner, 1966; Yates, 1962), and only the deleterious effects of frustration on learning and performance have been noted (Lazarus, Deese, & Osler, 1952; Postman & Bruner, 1948; Sears, 1942).

In contrast to this traditional deficit model, a competence orientation is favored here. The main thrust of the stage model of coping is that organisms are predisposed to exhibit qualitatively different response patterns in different stages of coping with frustration and that these natural behavioral tendencies serve an important adaptive function.

Frustration Defined

Frustration is typically defined in terms of the operations that produce it. Dollard, Doob, Miller, Mowrev, and Sears (1939) define frustration as "an interference with the occurrence of an instigated goal-response at its proper time in the behavior sequence" (p. 7). According to Amsel (1958, 1962), frustration occurs only when nonreward follows a history of reward in that particular situation. For Buss (1961), the blocking of any instrumental action leads to frustration. Yates (1962) proposes that "the term frustrating situation should be restricted to those situations in which an organism is prevented by a physical barrier from attaining a physical goal by the performance of responses which previously led to the attainment of the goal" (p. 176).

Other psychologists favor a broader definition. Rosenzweig (1934, 1944) recognizes that both obstruction to an anticipated goal and unfulfillment of a felt need may trigger frustration. In a similar vein, Maslow (1941) proposes that both deprivation of needs and threats to need fulfillment may occasion frustration; he also points out that human needs are not limited to biological ones (Maslow, 1943).

Berkowitz (1989) emphasizes expectancy as the necessary condition for triggering frustration reactions. In other words, blocking a person from some goal is frustrating only to the extent that this person anticipates the satisfaction of goal attainment. Such expectancy may be the result of prior success, instructional set, social norm, parental expectations, or personal aspirations. It makes sense to assume that any goal-directed activity implies some expectancy of success, because it is unlikely that anyone would pursue a goal that is totally unattainable.

Simply put, any operation that prevents an expected goal attainment occasions frustration. Such a definition is capable of encompassing a wide array of situations that engender frustration reactions. Lawson (1965) has identified the following operations that have been used in the laboratory to produce frustration: (a) nonreinforcement after a history of reinforcement, (b) preventing completion of a reinforced response sequence, (c) preventing a response aroused by goal stimuli, (d) delayed reinforcement, (e) unfavorable changes in incentive conditions, (f) failure, and (g) hypothetical or simulated frustrating situations.

Coleman and Hammen (1974) have identified five sources of frustration in real-life situations: (a) delay when time is valued, (b) lack of resources that are made attractive or necessary by advertising, (c) loss of friendship or loved ones through death, (d) failure in a competitive society that values individual success and achievement, and (e) difficulty in finding meaningful and fulfilling jobs.

All of these operations presuppose the existence of an expected goal object. Even the search for a life goal implies its existence. The presence of any goal, whether tangible or intangible, can be inferred from goal-directed or "persisting until" behavior (Tolman, 1932). It is only when a goal-directed behavior is blocked that frustration occurs.

Frustration typically accompanies the pursuit of goals, because there are always some obstacles that stand between where you are and where you want to be. These obstacles include unavailability of needed resources, lack of opportunities, social barriers, discrimination, and stiff competition. Personal characteristics can also prevent or delay goal attainment; these include insufficient effort, inadequate skills, or inappropriate strategies.

The present operational definition of frustration can even be extended to situations in which the expected goal is relief from pain or pressure. Maier and Ellen (1955, 1959) consider persistent, inescapable punishment as frustrating situations. Amsel (1967) has proposed a fourfold classification of unconditioned goal responses (reward, frustration, relief, and punishment) and has hypothesized that frustrative nonrelief from punishment may have similar properties as frustrative nonreward. This hypothesis has been supported in a number of studies (McAllister, McAllister, Brooks, & Goldman, 1972; Millard & Woods, 1975; Sgro, 1977; Woods, 1967).

So far, I have focused on the *stimulus* aspect of frustration and defined it as failure to attain an expected goal, be it a rewarding object or relief from punishment. Concerning the *response* aspect, frustration may be conceptualized as an emotive-motivational state, which predisposes the organism to certain patterns of reactions. For example, Yates (1962) has offered this definition: "Organisms placed in objectively defined frustrating situations will experience frustration to varying degrees and will manifest varying responses to this state of frustration" (p. 175).

A variety of responses have been linked to the organismic state of frustration. These include invigoration (Amsel & Roussel, 1952), aggression (Dollard et al., 1939), escape (Daly, 1969), fixation (Maier, 1949), and exploration (Wong,

1979). The present stage model attempts to specify the conditions under which various frustration reactions will likely occur.

In sum, frustration is treated as a hypothetical construct that is anchored to any operation that prevents the attainment of an expected goal, and a specific set of observable reactions to such operations.

Frustration and Stress

In this section, I attempt to place frustration within the larger context of stress research. It will be argued that frustration is stressful, and that most stressful situations involve frustration.

Stress is typically used as a catch-all term to cover conditions that involve aversive stimulation or excessive demands on the coping resources of an organism (e.g., Lazarus & Folkman, 1984; Mechanic, 1970; Selye, 1980). It is also used to refer to the internal state of the organism under stressful conditions. For the purpose of clarity, conditions that induce a state of stress will be called *stressors*.

Early stress research focused on various physical stressors, such as extreme heat, noise, or virus, although frustrations and conflict were also recognized as having similar effects on physiological processes (Selye, 1976). More recently, increasing attention has been given to psychological stressors, such as uncontrollability (Glass & Singer, 1972; Seligman, 1975; Weiss, 1971a, 1971b), frustration (Brown, 1980), life changes (Holmes & Rahe, 1967), and lack of meaning in life (Wong, 1989). In view of these diverse sources of stress, a more comprehensive definition of stress has been proposed by Wong (1990): "Life stress can be defined as a problematic internal or external condition that creates tension/upset in the individual and calls for some form of coping" (p. 70).

There is now considerable evidence that frustration per se can activate physiological responses known to be elicited by physical stressors. For example, several human studies have demonstrated that frustration increases physiological arousal as measured by various autonomic responses, such as galvanic skin reflex and pulse rate (Freeman, 1948; Hokanson & Burgess, 1964; Hokanson, Burgess, & Cohen, 1963; Thiesen & Meister, 1949). Frustration of the need for love and protection may lead to peptic ulcers (Alexander, 1950). In animal research, extinction induces changes in both testosterone and behavior in chicks (Archer, 1974) and frustrative nonreward increases pituitary–adrenal activity as measured by an elevation of plasma corticosterone (Coover, Goldman, & Levine, 1971; Davis, Mommott, MacFadden, & Levine, 1976; Levine, Goldman, & Coover, 1972). It should be noted that plasma corticosterone is also sensitive to other kinds of stressful situations, such as maternal separation (Coe & Levine, 1981), avoidance learning (Natelson, Krasnegor, & Holaday, 1976), and uncontrollable loud noise (Hanson, Larson, & Snowdon, 1976).

The aversive property of frustration has been established in behavioral studies as well. For instance, animals learn to escape from cues associated with frustrative nonreward (e.g., Daly, 1969; Terrace, 1971) and from the unbaited goalbox during extinction (Rosellini & Seligman, 1975; Wong, 1977a, 1978a). Pigeons and rats also give themselves time-out in a progressive ratio schedule when response requirement for reinforcement is progressively increased (Azrin, 1961; Dardano, 1973; Thompson, 1964). Generally, the degree of aversiveness of frustration is related to variables known to determine the amount of frustration. For example, the amount of urine excreted by rats, which is an index of aversive emotionality, is directly related to the number of reinforced trials prior to frustrative nonreward (McHenry, 1973).

A number of investigators have even proposed that frustration and fear share many similar properties (Gray, 1987; Wagner, 1967). Some similarities in the effects of discomfort and frustration have also been documented (Berkowitz, 1989); in his frustration-aggression reformulation, Berkowitz proposes that "frustrations are aversive events and generate aggressive inclinations only to the extent that they produce negative affect" (p. 71).

Frustration as a source of stress has long been recognized in the clinical literature. For example, Arieti (1959) listed failure in an important relationship and failure in achieving important life goals as among the major stressful situations that cause depression. Similarly, Brown (1980) has included a number of frustrating situations, such as chronic unemployment, socioeconomic impoverishment, and failure to fulfill one's aspirations as sources of stress. Kanner, Kafry, and Pines (1978) have also argued that the lack of positive conditions—the deprivation or unattainability of various rewarding goal events—is a major source of stress that demands closer attention.

Uncontrollability enjoys a great deal of vogue in stress research, thanks largely to the influential learned helplessness theory (e.g., Maier & Seligman, 1976; Seligman, 1975). This theory posits that the perception of noncontingency between response and outcome (uncontrollability) leads to expectancy of noncontingency, resulting in cognitive, emotional, and motivational deficits that interfere with subsequent instrumental learning. Shock is almost exclusively used in animal learned helplessness research. According to the present analysis, inescapable shock is more stressful than escapable shock, simply because the former involves the additional frustrative stress. Inescapable shock should be viewed as an unsolvable problem in which attempts at securing relief are repeatedly frustrated. It may be argued that it is the experience of frustrative nonrelief rather than perceived noncontingency that is responsible for the interference effects. A case may be made that uncontrollability per se does not necessarily lead to stress, and that uncontrollability is stressful only to the extent that one desires and anticipates gaining control but fails.

Another source of psychosocial stress is known as life events or life changes (Holmes & Rahe, 1967). An impressive amount of evidence has been collected to substantiate the linkage between life events and health outcomes (Dohrenwend & Dohrenwend, 1974). However, a number of investigators (Mueller, Edwards, & Yarvis, 1977; Sarason, Johnson, & Siegel, 1978) have shown that only undesirable life events, such as marital separation and job loss, have a negative impact on one's mental and physical health. Most of the undesirable life events involve failure and frustration. It can be argued that the detrimental effects of stressful life events may be mediated by extinction-related behavioral mechanisms.

More recently, everyday hassles have become recognized as a major source of stress. Lazarus and his associates have shown that the frequency and intensity of these hassles are positively related to both physical and mental health (De-Longis, Coyne, Dakof, Folkman, & Lazarus, 1982; Lazarus & Folkman, 1984). Some of the most frequently cited hassles include concerns over wasting time, anxiety over meeting high standards of performance, and various forms of interference. It does not require any stretch of imagination to recognize that most of these hassles are frustrating conditions that interfere with the pursuit and prosecution of life tasks.

The previous analysis serves to make the point that frustration is probably the most common source of stress. In the current social context, economic recession, rising unemployment, and spiraling rates of inflation all conspire to frustrate an individual's quest for security. On a global scale, inequality of wealth among nations, rising expectations brought about by education and television, population growth coupled with dwindling natural resources, all combine to escalate frustration and conflict between nations. As alluded to earlier, frustration is a two-edged sword—it either sharpens our wits or defeats us. Therefore, individually and collectively, it is important to know how to cope with frustration in a way that maximizes its benefits but minimizes its harms.

A STAGE MODEL OF COPING WITH FRUSTRATIVE STRESS

Coping covers a wide range of responses, both learned and unconditioned, that assist living organisms in adapting to demanding or stressful situations (Coelho, Hamburg, & Adams, 1974; Mechanic, 1970). In studying the physiological mechanisms of coping with stress, Selye (1976) discovered the general stress syndrome, which consists of three qualitatively different stages. The initial stage is called *alarm reaction*, which involves activation of the autonomic nervous system and discharge of norepinephrine and epinephrine from the adrenal gland. The organism is said to be in a state of shock or arousal. During the second stage, bodily resources are mobilized to cope with the stress at the expense of other bodily functions, such as sexual behavior. This is called the *resistance* stage. However, if stress is prolonged, *exhaustion* sets in, resulting in a general weakening of resistance to disease and other sources of stress. *Exhaustion* does not necessarily mean adrenal exhaustion to the point of nonfunctioning. It may mean a temporary depletion of physiological coping resources.

In this section, I describe the model of coping with frustration that is based on behavioral studies of coping reactions. Supporting evidence is presented in the following section. In its simplest terms, the stage model posits that the adaptation process involves four orderly stages, and each of these stages is characterized by certain dominant behavioral strategies. In the *initial habit stage*, when an individual first encounters a frustrating situation, the dominant strategy is *try harder*. Typically, the individual becomes aroused by the negative encounter and tries again with greater vigor the same behavior that has been successful. In a novel situation not associated with any particular habit, however, initial frustration will result in the invigoration of general activity of an ongoing behavior.

The coping mechanism of perseveration is often concommittant with invigoration. When a habitual way of responding runs into difficulty, rarely does the individual give up this habit immediately. The habitual response will perseverate for some time albeit with greater vigor. How long the response will persist depends on a number of factors, such as the strength of the habit, strength of competing habits, and so on.

At this point, it is important to bear in mind two kinds of persistence: response persistence and goal persistence (Wong, 1978a). The former refers to repetition of the same response, whereas the latter refers to continued pursuit of the same goal by whatever means. Throughout this chapter, perseveration of habit is equated with response persistence.

Habit mechanism operates in many life situations: We may continue to turn left even when our new address calls for a right turn; we tend to follow certain routines even though a change in our present practice may improve efficiency. Habits are perpetuated as long as they continue to serve our needs. The advantage of habit mechanism is quite apparent in terms of cognitive economy: It frees the individual to devote his or her attention to more pressing and more complex matters. In most frustrating situations, response repetition with enhanced vigor (i.e., "try harder") serves an adaptive function. It is only when perseveration becomes unduly prolonged in spite of repeated failure that it becomes unadaptive, and this sort of perseverative behavior has been regarded as an index of brain damage (Reitmen & Darison, 1974). In normal functioning organisms, the initial habit stage is typically transitory as it inevitably gives way to the more sustained trial-and-error stage.

When the habitual mode of responding proves to be ineffectual, the frustrated individual will mobilize his or her resources and explore all available coping options. During the *trial-and-error stage*, the organism adopts the strategy of "try something else." This may takes the form of exploring alternative means or attacking the obstacle. The availability of different coping options helps sustain goal striving.

A number of investigators have recognized the important role of *hope* in coping with stress (Reker & Wong, 1983; Scheier, Weintraub, & Carver, 1981; Stotland, 1969; Tiger, 1979). There are different conceptions of hope. For example, Farber (1967) views hope as jointly determined by one's sense of competence and perceived threat in a given situation. Mowrer (1960) considers hope as based on prior experience with reinforcement and equates hope with the mechanism of conditioned goal anticipatory responses, such as salivation in anticipation of food.

According to the present analysis, hope is simply a summary term for the expectancy of attaining a particular goal, and hope depends on the totality of coping resources available in a particular situation. Broadly speaking, there are internal and external coping resources. Internal resources include one's competence, knowledge, past experiences, response options, and the creative capacity of trying novel solutions. External resources include whatever opportunities and help are available. Hope is kept alive as long as there are still some coping options to be explored.

Aggression most likely occurs during the trial-and-error stage, not only because of the build-up of anger, but also because it is one of the instrumental options. Hostile display or actual attack is often effective in removing an obstacle. The distinction between instrumental and hostile aggression made by Feshbach (1964) has been widely accepted. Aggression tends to take precedent over other instrumental alternatives, when (a) all nonaggressive solutions have failed; (b) aggression has been reinforced in dealing with similar frustrating situations; (c) there are no nonaggressive outlets for pent-up emotions; (d) there is a ready target for aggression; and (e) the individual does not anticipate costly consequences for aggression.

The second stage is also called the conflict stage because two kinds of conflict take place during this state: response conflict and approach–avoidance conflict. Response conflict involves competition between various response tendencies directed toward the same goal, whereas approach–avoidance conflict involves competition between approach to or avoidance of the same goal. The former conflict tends to predominate in the early part of Stage 2, while the latter intensifies toward the latter part of Stage 2.

The final stage of coping is called *resolution*, because the approach–avoidance conflict is eventually resolved. When all instrumental efforts fail to secure the incentive object, the tendency of goal-substitution will increase. Failure to find an acceptable substitution goal should instigate the resignation mechanism, at which point the organism ceases from all efforts and becomes helpless.

A great deal of confusion now exists concerning the usage of various terms such as *helplessness* and *depression*. For example, cessation from instrumental activities and a low level of general activity have been taken as evidence of depression (Klinger, Kemble, & Barta, 1974). These behavioral patterns have also been referred to as evidence of learned helplessness (Maier & Seligman, 1976; Seligman, 1975). To clarify matters, the following definitions are proposed:

Helplessness is used to describe the result of an *unconditioned* resignation coping mechanism triggered by prolonged failure. An individual does not require any prior learning to become helpless. One automatically becomes helpless when one has exhausted all personal coping resources.

Learned helplessness, on the other hand, refers to the transfer to helplessness to a new situation in which the problem is soluble. If a person has failed repeatedly, and given up many times, he or she has learned to give up prematurely in the face of frustration in a new situation. Learned helplessness is a conditioned reaction, when the resignation mechanism is triggered prematurely and inappropriate by frustrative cues in a different situation. Therefore, *learned helplessness* means *generalized helplessness*. The extent of generalization depends on the similarities between situations as well as the strength of the learned tendency to become resigned.

The relationship between helplessness and depression also needs clarification. There are different kinds of depression (Friedman & Katz, 1974). Here, we are only concerned with reactive depression. Depression has been equated both helplessness (Klinger et al., 1974) as well as learned helplessness (Seligman, 1975). Seligman and his associates reformulated the learned helplessness theory and proposed that depression occurs only when an individual attributes uncontrollable events to internal, stable, and global causes (Abramson, Seligman, & Teasdale, 1978). Thus, depression depends on how a person explains events. It needs to be reiterated that neither helplessness nor learned helplessness is evidence of depression; one must take into account a variety of cognitive factors, such as hopelessness (Beck, 1967; Kovacs, Beck, & Weissman, 1975).

According to the stage model, helplessness serves an adaptive function (Engel, 1953, 1962; Klinger, 1975; Price, 1972). Although instrumental activity is generally more effective than passivity in reducing stress (Gal & Lazarus, 1975), resignation is obviously more adaptive when the problem is insolvable, not only because it conserves energy (Engel, 1953, 1962), but also because it lessens distress (Gatchel & Proctor, 1976). Helplessness become unadaptive only when it occurs prematurely or generalizes to situations in which the problem is solvable.

The response patterns associated with each stage are conceptualized as coping mechanisms in the sense that there are preprogrammed adaptive reactions that occur automatically in frustrating situations. It is difficult to imagine how any organism not endowed with these coping mechanisms can long survive in an environment in which dwindling resources, competition, and social barriers often frustrate one's basic needs. A summary of the stage model is shown in Table 8.1.

At this point, an astute reader may have detected a parallel between Selye's general stress syndrome and the present stage model of coping with frustrative stress. There is certainly some basis to speculate that the three stages of physiological reaction as outlined by Selye accompany or subserve the three stages of behavioral coping. The initial *alarm* stage seems to coincide with general arousal and behavioral invigoration observed in many frustrating situations. The second *resistance* stage seems compatible with the trial-and-error stage in which the frustrated organism mobilizes all its coping resources to remove frustrative stress. Finally, the *exhaustion* stage seems equally applicable to physiological exhaustion as well as the exhaustion of behavioral coping resources and the ensuing helplessness when goal substitution cannot be achieved.

It seems plausible that Selye's general stress syndrome and the present behavioral process of coping represent different levels of analysis of the same adaptational process. Health outcomes of coping may depend on the interaction between behavioral and physiological reactions. For example, the availability of

TABLE 8.1. Different stages of coping with frustration

Stages	Coping mechanisms	Motivation	Learning
Habit	Invigoration Perseveration	Increase in arousal and effort	Facilitates performance; interferes with new learning
Trial and error	Exploration Aggression	Increase in arousal and effort	Facilitates new learning
Resolution	Goal substitution Resignation	Decrease in arousal and effort	Interferes with performance and new learning

larger behavioral coping resources may also enhance one's physiological resistance to stress.

EMPIRICAL EVIDENCE FOR THE STAGE MODEL

It is not possible to document all the relevant evidence within the space of this chapter. Therefore, the review of the literature has to be selective. I will first report some of the results from my laboratory.

The paradigm that I have used extensively to study frustrative stress is experimental extinction—the procedure of discontinuing reward after various conditions of rewarded learning. Experimental extinction has much to recommend itself as a coping paradigm for the following reasons: (a) It represents the extreme case of delay of gratification (where delay is infinite), and it allows the psychologists to identify the maximum degree of delay tolerated by an individual. (b) It permits the study of the entire coping process in dealing with chronic frustrative stress. (c) It resembles many life situations in which one's wants and desires remain unfulfilled, no matter how hard and how long one strives.

Traditional studies of experimental extinction have not told us very much about coping, because these studies treat extinction as a measure of associative learning and pay little attention to the kind of coping behaviors that naturally occur in the course of extinction (Hall, 1989). In contrast, these coping behaviors have been the focus of my own investigation. Some of the preliminary results have already been published (Wong, 1977a, 1978a).

Different from the traditional simple straight alleyway for rats, the runway I have designed was partitioned into nine equal segments, which were numerically coded to specify the route taken by each rat. Three separate swinging doors separated the runway from the goalbox. Thus, the rat could choose any route and go through any one of these doors to enter the goalbox. One side of the runway had a hole leading to an enclosed box to measure exploratory activity. A furry model animal was mounted on the runway to record biting and aggressive behavior. A sand-digging platform was also made available in the startbox, so that rats might switch to sand digging as a substitution activity. A combination of naturalist observation and electromechanical reading devices were used to obtain various measures of the behavioral field during acquisition and extinction.

I will now briefly summarize the preliminary findings (Wong, 1977a, 1978a) to illustrate how well the stage model can account for extinction performance after different reinforcement conditions. During acquisition partially reinforced (PRF) rats chose a greater variety of routes than consistently reinforced rats (CRF), but most subjects settled on a particular route, which was in most cases a straight path. A more general statement of this finding is that ``instrumental learning involves a process of narrowing the behavioral field through dropping out inefficient response patterns (i.e., long routes) and unproductive instrumental activities'' (Wong, 1977a, p. 8).

It should be noted that the dominant response pattern that emerged in my complex runway is analogous to reinforcement-induced behavioral stereotypy in pigeons and humans (Schwartz, 1980, 1981, 1982). The paradigm used by Schwartz is as follows: The subject is shown a display of a matrix of light, with the light illuminated at the top left corner as the starting point. Responding on the left (L) key moves the light one step down, while responding on the right (R) key moves the light one step right. As soon as the light is moved to the bottom right corner which is the end point, reinforcement is delivered. Thus, there are many different routes for the light to travel from the start to the end of the matrix. In this situation, individuals tend to fixate on a particular sequence, such RRRRLLLL or LRLRLRLR. The dominant pattern is referred to by Schwartz as stereotyped behavior.

During extinction, rats typically perseverated in the habitual pattern for several trials before switching to alternative routes (Wong, 1977a, 1978a). As predicted, overtrained subjects persisted longer in the dominant route (Wong, 1978a, Experiment 2). Contrary to Wong's rat data, Schwartz (1981) reports that extinction has little effect on either sequence completion time or sequence variability in overtrained pigeons. In other words, the second stage of response variation does not occur if pigeons have developed a strong habit. This finding in fact questions the plasticity of learned behavior and equates overtrained sequential operant with species-specific stereotype. We have tested rats and humans using the same procedure as Schwartz (Peacock & Wong, 1984 a, 1984b; Wong & Peacock, 1986). Our consistent finding is that extinction increases both temporal and sequential variability regardless of the amount of overtraining!

It is interesting to note that consistent with the stage model, Wong (1978a) also observed a gradual increase in hole-exploration and biting behavior (indicative of the second trial-and-error stage), which peaked before switching to sand digging (indicative of Stage 3).

In the complex runway situation, I did not observe the invigoration effect, because of the discrete-trial procedure. Typically, rats were given extinction trials with a 30-minute intertrial interval. The invigoration effect is known to be a rather transitory reaction to frustrative nonreward, and it can be obtained in discrete-trial extinction only when the intertrial interval is relatively short (Jensen & Cotton, 1960).

In the free-operant situation, the testing chamber was equipped with six manipulanda: a panel, a lever, a pair of blades attached to the lever to measure biting and attack on the lever, and a platform for sand digging, as well as a drinking spout to detect time spent in drinking (Wong, 1977b). In this study, following baseline measures of these behaviors, panel pushing was first consistently reinforced with food reward and then extinguished. While reinforcement decreased alternative responses, extinction increased the complexity and variability of the behavioral field, as predicted by the stage model. Further, invigoration in panel pushing was evident only in the first two extinction sessions.

In another series of studies (Wong, 1978b) in which the Skinner box was only equipped with three pushing panels without the opportunity for substitution activities, more than 70% of all the subjects showed an increased rate of pushing the previously reinforced panel during the initial stage of extinction, tried alternative panels later on, and eventually showed signs of helplessness such as passivity, crouching, or sleeping. When reinforcement contingency was restored in the *same* situation, these rats remained passive and showed learning deficits as compared to rats that had not been exposed to prolonged periods of extinction. I have not been able to obtain evidence of generalized or learned helplessness, however, because when rats were tested in a different situation, such as running or a different Skinner box, following prolonged extinction, they did not show any learning deficit.

Similar patterns of results have been obtained in human subjects and some of these findings were reported in the Leuven Symposium on Cognitions in Human Motivation (Wong & Dimitroff, 1980a). In one of the experiments the subjects were tested in a complex finger maze. The surface of the maze was carved with three grooves that emanated from a common starting point. The nine intersections and the three end points were labeled with different alphabetical letters to identify the routes chosen on each trial. The goalbox was equipped with a small lightbulb and an incremental counter. To complete a trial, subjects used a finger to trace a route of their choice from the start point to one of the endpoints. They were told that a correct route would be automatically signaled by the light on the goalbox and the addition of a point to the counter. Each point was worth five cents.

This finger maze, like Wong's complex maze for rats, allows a variety of routes to be reinforced. Subjects were either consistently reinforced (CRF) or partially reinforced (PRF). Following acquisition training, they were given extinction training before the learned helplessness test. In addition to behavioral measures, we also obtained paper-and-pencil measures of perceived causes (i.e., attributions) of their performance outcomes and their effective states.

During acquisition, PRF subjects showed greater variability in routes and reported greater effort attribution (i.e., claimed that they tried harder) than their CRF counterparts. Both the variability data and effort attribution indicate that PRF subjects adopted a try strategy (Wong & Amsel, 1976).

During the first 10 extinction trials, there was a significant increase in response speed and in effort attribution as compared with the last 10 acquisition trials for both CRF and PRF subjects, providing evidence for the hypothesis that nonreward initially triggers the invigoration coping mechanism. We also obtained evidence of exploration in that during the second 10 extinction trials, response variation was greater than during terminal acquisition trials.

Prolonged extinction (two consecutive 10-minute sessions of repeated failure) resulted in a decrease in response speed, discontinuation of the task by some subjects, and an increase in feelings of anxiety and depression as measured by Zuckerman's affect checklist. However, when these subjects were given a learned helplessness test in which reinforcement was contingent on pushing a button for 99 times, their rate of reinforcement was not different from that of those who had not been exposed to prolonged extinction. We have also given the subjects other kinds of helplessness tests, such as a different kind of finger maze or anagram problems, but we were never able to obtain evidence of the transfer of helplessness.

To summarize, careful observations of both rats and humans in many extinction situations have produced results that are in basic agreement with the stage model. There is also considerable evidence from other laboratories, which I will discuss shortly. Meanwhile, we must consider two criticisms that may be leveled against the stage model. The first criticism is that the stage model is untestable, because it encompasses all possible outcomes of frustration manipulation—invigoration of the old responses (Stage 1), increase of alternate responses (Stage 2), and a cessation of instrumental responding (Stage 3). This criticism can be easily dismissed because the model does not cover all possible outcomes. For example, one of the possible outcomes of prolonged frustration is the gradual weakening of the previously reinforced criterion response without either the invigoration of the old response or the occurrence of competing responses. In other words, the criterion response simply becomes progressively slower in initiation and execution. This is what is predicted by most theories of extinction except the stage model. Further, the stage model can be rejected if the actual sequence of events differs from that hypothesized by the model. Thus, if response alternation occurs before invigoration, or if passivity occurs before response alternation, then the model is falsified.

A second criticism is that it is descriptive, rather than predictive. Although Hall (1989) has many positive things to say about the model, he nevertheless regards it as a descriptive analysis of experimental extinction. Generally speaking, a model or theory ceases to be descriptive when one can derive test implications. A number of testable hypotheses can be deduced from the stage model. The following are just some of the more obvious ones:

1. Amount of response repetition increases response persistence (the habit stage) but has no effect on goal persistence (the trial-and-error stage).

2. A change in stimulus complex from acquisition to extinction weakens response persistence, but has no effect on goal persistence.

3. Overtraining with large reward increases response persistence because of the habit strength associated with training trials but decreases goal persistence because of the magnitude of frustration associated with holding a large reward.

4. The number of instrumental coping options (such as additional manipulanda) decreases response persistence but increases goal persistence.

5. The greater the "attractiveness" of substitutions, the shorter the goal persistence.

We must now consider findings based on rather different paradigms and reported by other investigators to evaluate the stage model.

Frustration-Induced Invigoration-Perseveration

A classical demonstration of frustration-induced invigoration is the well-known Amsel's frustration effect (Amsel & Roussel, 1952). Amsel and many other investigators have found that when two straight alleyways are connected together (i.e., the double-runway), occasional omission of food reward in the first goalbox increases the speed of running to the second baited goalbox. This effect has been well documented (Amsel, 1958, 1962; Scull, 1973) and has been obtained in many species, ranging from planarians (Micklin & May, 1975) to humans (Ryan & Watson, 1968). It has also been demonstrated in double-lever situations (Marx, 1967; Marx & Tombaugh, 1967; Wookey & Strongman, 1974). As well, the energizing effect of frustration can be obtained when general activity level is measured in rats and children (Gallup & Altomari, 1969; Klinger et al., 1974; Ruiz, 1975).

The initial invigoration effect is also well established in free operant situations and is characterized by a burst of responding following the onset of extinction (Ferster & Skinner, 1957; Margulies, 1961; Notterman & Mintz, 1965). Because the invigoration effect is generally rather transitory, it is obtained in discrete-trial extinction only when the intertrial interval is relatively short (e.g., Jensen & Cotton, 1960). The extinction-induced invigoration effect has also been obtained in humans working on a finger maze for monetary reward (Wong & Dimitroff, 1980a). In some response systems, the initial invigoration effect can be of considerable magnitude and duration. For example, after rats have been reinforced for sand digging, they displaced almost twice as much sand during the first two extinction sessions (10 min per session) as during terminal acquisition (Wong & Dimitroff, 1980b).

Consistent with the frustration interpretation, the invigoration effect is related to parameters that are supposed to affect frustration, i.e., number of prior reinforced trials (Marx, 1967; Marx & Tombaugh, 1967) and drive level (Dunlap & Frates, 1970; McHose & Ludvigson, 1964). Available evidence suggests that invigoration is perhaps the most common and most robust coping mechanism.

The initial invigoration effect can also be predicted from Atkinson's theory of achievement motivation (Atkinson, 1957; Atkinson & Feather, 1966) and Brehm's reactance theory (Brehm, 1966; Wortman & Brehm, 1975). According to these alternative theories, the initial invigoration is derived from higher cognitive constructs. For example, reactance theory presumes the cognition of personal freedom, and the need for such freedom: Nonreward threatens one's freedom to obtain a desired outcome: invigoration is treated as an attempt to regain "outcome freedom." According to the present analysis, frustration of any anticipated need fulfillment should instigate a series of behavioral coping mechanisms, and invigoration tends to occur first. Thus, psychological reactance may be considered as a special case of a more general rule of frustration-induced invigoration.

A related mechanism that operates in the initial stage of coping is perseveration. The force of habit in regulating behavior has long been recognized by psychologists (e.g., Allport, 1957; James, 1890; Skinner, 1938). It has been variously called *habit strength, reflex reserve,* or *functional autonomy.* The basic idea is that if a behavior has been practiced or reinforced many times in a situation, it is likely to be repeated in the presence of similar cues. This habitual mode of responding has been described as automatic (Kimble & Perlmuter, 1970) and ballistic (Bindra, 1969). Once a habit is activated, it is assumed to run off to its completion in the absence of incentive (Logan, 1971), and "nothing external to the organism is necessary to ensure that continuation of the sequence, even though external factors are crucial for its initiation" (Mandler, 1964).

Perseveration, coupled with invigoration, is clearly very adaptive in simple instructional learning situations. To react to nonreward by repeating the same response with greater vigor tends to facilitate performance and increase the likelihood of success in such situations (see Scull, 1973, for a review). In complex learning tasks, however, perseveration-invigoration may have a deleterious effect. An interesting experiment by Schmeck and Brunning (1968) provides some support for this hypothesis. They used a modified double runway in which the second runway consisted of one short alley directly connected to a complex maze. There was one correct path in the linear maze leading to a baited goal cup. They reported that frustrative nonreward increased the speed in the short alley but also produced more errors in the complex maze. Serum (1973) obtained similar findings in humans when two complex tasks were used in a manner that was analogous to a double runway: Nonreward on the first task tended to increase errors on the second task.

Frustration-Induced Exploration

When a response fails, it is repeated with greater vigor; when the repetition fails, other responses are attempted. This sequence of coping actions accords well with everyday experience. Frustration-induced exploration of alternative responses has been demonstrated under many conditions and in several species (Wong, 1979). It has also been observed (Miller, 1971) that frustration increases perceptual exploration of incongruous stimuli. Thus, it may be concluded that frustration enhances exploration of both the frustration situation and coping options. In other words, frustration broadens the scope of stimulus selection (Sutherland, 1966), as well as response selection (Wong, 1979).

Hull's (1934) concept of habit-family hierarchy is relevant to the present discussion. According to Hull, a divergent excitatory mechanism gives rise to response variation, and competing multiple excitatory tendencies are the result of past associative learning. In coping with frustration, however, organisms not only attempt previously acquired alternative responses, but also explore new ways of responding. In other words, response selection is not only limited to the existing response repertoire, it may creatively expand the repertoire.

Another important adaptive function of frustration-induced exploration is the maintenance of goal persistence. Other things being equal, the degree of goal persistence should be positively related to the number of goal-oriented coping options. There is already some preliminary evidence (Wong, 1981) that during extinction, rats persisted longer in entering an unbaited goalbox in a multiple-route runway than in a single alley. Such a finding indicates that competition between goal-directed excitatory tendencies increases rather than decreases goal persistence.

Frustration-induced exploration can also be derived from the dynamic theory of achievement motivation (Atkinson & Birch, 1970, 1974; Kuhl & Blankenship, 1979a, 1979b). According to this view, blocking one of two functionally equivalent responses should increase the motivation to engage in the alternative response. If one considers approach–avoidance conflict also as response competition (Amsel, 1967), then there are actually two different kinds of response competitions with opposite effects on goal persistence. Conflict among instrumental possibilities increases goal-persistence, while approach–avoidance conflict decreases it. It is interesting to note that according to Brown and Farber (1951), both types of conflicts are in themselves sources of frustration. Thus, frustration should continue to build up throughout the second stage of coping until conflict is resolved.

Two explanations, which are not mutually exclusive, may be offered to account for goal persistence. First, a larger response repertoire should keep an organism persisting longer simply because it takes longer to exhaust the repertoire. If an organism has learned a number of instrumental responses, such as lever pressing, panel pushing, and so on, then all these responses will be attempted in a frustrating situation. A broader and more cognitive explanation is that the frustrated individual appraises his or her coping resources, which will include both internal instrumental options and external sources of help. "Hope" or the expectancy of goal attainment lives on, as long as coping resources are not yet exhausted. It is this hope that maintains goal persistence.

The present analysis of frustration-induced exploration seems to contradict the familiar frustration-regression hypothesis (e.g., Barker, Dembo, & Lewin, 1941; Mowrer, 1940). According to Barker et al. (1941), regression primarily consists of *primitation*, which refers to regression to an earlier stage of development or a less mature way of behaving. Primitation is evident in a decrease in behavioral variability and organization. In other words, behavior should become less variable and less organized under conditions of frustration. However, the authors did not quantify response variability and they only inferred regression from reduced constructiveness of play when children could not gain access to a set of attractive toys. A number of criticisms may be directed to the measure of constructiveness of play (see Yates, 1962). For example, this measure was subjective and the raters were not blind to the experimental manipulation. Further, alternative interpretations are available. Reduced constructiveness of play might be due to emotional responses and/or alternative instrumental activities. Child and Waterhouse (1952) were able to demonstrate a significant negative correlation between constructiveness of play and time spent in frustration-induced activities. Child and Waterhouse (1952) were able to demonstrate a significant negative correlation between constructiveness of play and time spent in frustration-induced activities, such as trying to reach the inaccessible toys and attempting to escape. In short, there is little unequivocal evidence of frustration-induced regression to an earlier stage of development.

From the present theoretical perspective, regression is only one facet of the trial-and-error stage of coping. As the organism explores alternative instrumental responses, it often returns to earlier patterns of responding that have been successful in coping with frustration. This kind of instrumental regression has been demonstrated in rats (Amsel, 1971; Martin, 1940; Mowrer, 1940) and humans (Barthol & Ku, 1959).

Another controversial issue is whether frustration leads to behavioral variability or unadaptive fixation. I have already documented frustration-induced response variability (Wong, 1979), which is clearly at variance with the well-known finding of frustration-induced abnormal fixation (N. Maier, 1949). How do we reconcile these two contradictory sets of findings? A close scrutiny of the experimental situation employed by Norman Maier may shed some light.

The procedure by Maier used to induce fixation typically involves the following features: (a) pressure or the threat of aversive stimulation from behind, (b) absence of escape routes, (c) an insolvable problem. For example, a rat is placed in the Lashley jumping-stand apparatus and required to jump into either one of two stimulus cards placed side by side. If it jumps on the correct side, the stimulus card will yield and the rat will land on a platform where it is rewarded with food. If it jumps to the incorrect side, the stimulus card is latched, and the rat will bump its nose and fall into a net. Under the insolvable condition, the stimulus cards are latched or unlatched according to a random sequence, and over many trials, the rat will be correct about 50% of the time regardless of which side it chooses. If the rat fails to jump within a certain time, it is punished by an air-blast. It should be noted that this situation is not unlike the coerced approach situation devised by Wong (1971a, 1971b) in which rats were coerced to approach an aversive goalbox by more aversive consequences for goal avoidance. Under such conditions, most rats develop position fixation, jumping consistently to one side. When the problem is subsequently made solvable, and the rat is rewarded for jumping to the alternative side, some rats continue to fixate for many trials, thus exhibiting "neurotic compulsions" or "abnormal fixation." This kind of stereotype does not readily generalize to other situations (Maier, 1949).

Such a phenomenon could be better understood in terms of coping and learning principles. Response fixation is perhaps the most adaptive coping strategy available when one is trapped in the impossible situation devised by Maier. Even Maier recognized that response fixation "gives the animal a way of responding to insolvable problem situations—a way without which such situations would have remained highly stressful" (Maier, 1949, p. 52). There are several sources of stress inherent in Maier's setup—punishment for failure to jump quickly, the threat of punishment, the approach–approach conflict of choosing between two stimulus cards, the frustration of not being able to solve the problem. These stressful factors should be reduced by a response fixation strategy, because such a strategy eliminates the need for deciding between two response alternatives that yield similar outcomes and, hence, increases the speed of execution and decreases the likelihood of punishment. To put it differently, response fixation predominates probably because this is the only coping strategy that is differentially reinforced by a reduction of various sources of stress.

The perseveration of a position fixation when a discrimination problem becomes solvable could also be accounted for in terms of learning principles. First of all, the stereotyped response has been partially reinforced and, therefore, should be very resistant to extinction. Second, even though the fixed response is no longer successful in landing on the safe platform, it is nevertheless consistently successful in avoiding the air-blast. If the air-blast is more aversive than bumping the nose against a latched stimulus card, differential negative reinforcement should work in favor of the continuation of a position fixation. Third, the rat might not be aware of the change in reinforcement contingency. If a cue is provided to indicate a contingency shift, the rat might not perseverate and might learn the discrimination problem as readily as if it were placed in a new discrimination learning situation. In short, what appears to be a symptom of an underlying pathology or neurosis, may be simply a coping strategy shaped and maintained by differential reinforcement. This line of reasoning suggests that if one removes the pressure (i.e., a penalty for not responding quickly) and provides salient cues regarding the change of contingency, rats and humans should no longer perseverate when the problem becomes solvable.

We have conducted a study (Quek & Wong, 1983) to test this coping interpretation. According to this coping view, fixation is not "behavior without a goal," as described by Norman Maier, but rather a goal-oriented instrumental coping response. More specifically, we predicted that frustration produces response variability, but fixation would eventually prevail as the subject learns that varying responses does not increase the pay-off, and that fixation is the most efficient strategy to cope with a partially reinforced insolvable problem.

Schwartz's (1982) paradigm was adapted to incorporate critical features of Norman Maier's fixation studies. Subjects were exposed to a 5 × 5 matrix of light and were required to manipulate two buttons to move the light from the upper left corner to the lower right corner. One press on the left (L) button moved the light across one step. One press on the right (R) button moved the light down one step. There are 70 different sequential patterns to move the light to the lower right corner. The diagonal between the upper left corner and the lower right corner divided the matrix into two equal triangles. For the Discrimination group, any sequential pattern that fell within one triangle was consistently reinforced; any sequential pattern that fell outside the triangle was not reinforced. For example, the sequence LLLLRRRR falls within the right triangle, while RRRRLLLL falls within the left triangle. For the Insolvable condition, reinforcement randomly occurred 50% of the time for each triangle; therefore, it was not possible for the subject to learn which triangle was correct. In this situation, reinforcement was partially contingent on completing 4 L responses and 4 R responses, but not contingent on which triangle the sequential pattern belongs. This is equivalent to Maier's Insolvable discrimination problem.

We also had a noncontingent condition in which subjects were yoked with Discrimination subjects in terms of reinforcement. In fact, noncontingent subjects could sit passively without pushing a single button and still received reinforcement whenever their yoked discrimination subjects made the correct response. This is equivalent to Seligman's learned helplessness condition, in which reinforcement is completely independent of the subject's behavior. Reinforcement occurred in the form of points accumulated on a counter, exchangeable for money. Half of the subjects in the discrimination and insolvable conditions were also subjected to time pressure such that if they failed to complete the response sequence (four presses on the L button and four on the R in any order), within 4 sec, they were penalized four points. This treatment is similar to Maier's procedure of administering an aversive air-blast to rats for failing to make the jumping response quickly.

As predicted, the PRF Insolvable group made more different sequences than the discrimination group, and 50% of the subjects in the Insolvable group stated that they sought to get as many points as possible by trying different responses, thus demonstrating the exploration strategy. Also consistent with prediction, fixation increased significantly over trials for the Insolvable subjects. Noncontingent subjects also exhibited more response variability than the discrimination group, although both groups received identical patterns of reinforcement. Noncontingent subjects might have been motivated to seek response contingency. In fact, 31% of these subjects thought that they had found the response rules for reinforcement.

Time pressure did not have the hypothesized effect of increasing response fixation in the PRF insolvable condition probably because frustration-induced exploration is stronger than anxiety-induced fixation. In a consistent reinforcement situation that did not involve discrimination learning, time pressure did have the hypothesized effect of increasing sequential stereotype.

During testing, when all subjects were given a solvable discrimination learning task in which the previously nonpreferred triangle was now associated with reinforcement, there was no evidence of abnormal fixation or learned helplessness because the Insolvable and Uncontrollable groups reached the same asymptote of learning as the Discrimination group.

In view of these findings, the discrepancy between Noman Maier's findings of abnormal fixation and frustration-induced exploration may be reconciled by the following hypotheses:

1. Exploration is the predominant coping strategy in a partially reinforced insolvable problem situation; fixation gradually emerges only when trying different responses fails to improve the payoff.
2. Fixation is the predominant coping strategy in situations of extreme pressure because it is faster and safer to repeat the same routine than to try out new ones. It is hypothesized that the tendency to use a fixation strategy is positively related to the amount of pressure, such as the severity of punishment for not responding fast enough. The dominant emotional response to threat of punishment is anxiety; therefore, fixation should be reinforced by anxiety reduction.
3. When a situation involves both frustration and anxiety, which coping strategy will have an upper hand depends on which emotional state is stronger.

In our paradigm, frustration should be stronger than anxiety because the penalty for losing four points or four pennies is really not that aversive. Therefore, frustration-induced exploration is the main coping strategy. In Maier's paradigm, anxiety should be stronger than frustration because punishment by air-blast should be more aversive than failure to receive food reward. Therefore, fixation should be the dominant coping strategy.

On the basis of interviews with our subjects, we found that consistent with our orientation that focuses on competence, they did employ appropriate coping strategies to handle the problem of noncontingency. The coping strategy of exploring different responses was widely used when they were exposed to a partially reinforced insolvable problem or noncontingent reinforcement. Contrary to deficit models such as learned helplessness theory, these subjects did not become helpless or abnormally fixated in subsequent discrimination learning.

Frustration-Induced Aggression

The frustration-aggression hypothesis, with slight variations, has been proposed by many psychologists (see Berkowitz, 1989, for a review). Initially, aggression was considered as an inevitable consequence of frustration, and "the occurrence of aggressive behavior always presupposed the existence of frustration" (Dollard et al., 1939, p. 1). More recently, aggression has been considered a heterogeneous phenomenon, having multiple causes and functions (Moyer, 1976). Further, several investigators have recognized that frustration-induced aggression is dependent on situational variables (Berkowitz, 1974; Geen, 1972).

There is now sufficient empirical evidence that extinction induces aggression in both humans and animals (Azrin, Hutchinson, & Hake, 1966; Frederiksen & Peterson, 1977; Hutchinson, Azrin, & Hunt, 1968; Kelly & Hake, 1970), but aggression does not always occur. Interestingly, it has been shown that consistent with the present stage analysis, aggression is an inverted-U function of extinction trials in animals and humans (Azrin et al., 1966; Nation & Cooney, 1982; Thompson & Bloom, 1966; Wong, 1978a). In other words, the highest frequency of aggression occurs neither at the beginning nor at the end of extinction trials, but somewhere in between. To underscore the importance of frustration, Nation and Cooney (1982) were able to demonstrate that reinforcement parameters known to affect frustration (e.g., schedule and number of reinforcement) actually determined when the highest frequency of aggression would occur. For instance, they reported that 30 reinforced trials as compared to 10 reinforced trials resulted in greater amount, as well as earlier peaking, of aggression, presumably because stronger expectancy of reward led to faster development and greater amount of frustration during extinction.

Frustration-induced aggression serves at least two adaptive functions: *instrumental* and *catharsis*. Aggression is essential to survival according to rules of the jungle, but does aggression "pay" in a civilized society? The answer seems to be yes. For example, an individual who is prepared to "destroy" anyone who impedes his or her progress is more likely to succeed in a competitive society than those who are submissive or passive. Such an individual is considered civilized as long as he or she does not resort to physical aggression. Further, for many unemployed minority youths in city ghettos, hamstrung by language, educational, and cultural disadvantages, aggression promises to be the only route to survival and self-respect. When the alternatives to aggression are deprivation and degradation, even gentle and peace-loving individuals are likely to turn into violent aggressors.

Although aggression serves an adaptive function in achieving important objects for individuals and groups under certain circumstances, it always poses a threat to other individuals and humanity as a whole. Rules of the jungle will continue to operate in civilized societies unless legitimate and basic needs of all people can be met without resorting to violence. From the perspective of the stage model, violence will remain a way of life for those whose fundamental needs and rights are denied, all attempts at a peaceful solution are frustrated, and aggression is reinforced some of the time. This hypothesis is applicable to both individuals and nations and sounds an ominous note concerning the potential danger of frustration when it cannot be reduced through nonviolent means.

The second function of aggression is *catharsis*. The adaptive value of catharsis has been observed in both clinical and laboratory settings. Baruch (1941) observed that children who were allowed to dissipate their frustration by mutilating clay models of their parents became better adjusted at home. Physiological arousal returned to prefrustration levels when human subjects were given the opportunity to display aggression (Hokanson & Burgess, 1963; Wells, 1970). All of us have experienced the cathartic effect of a variety of angry, aggressive outbursts, ranging from slamming a door to screaming at someone. Denying the expression of angry feelings may result in psychosomatic problems. Therefore, aggression during the second stage of coping is both an outlet of pent-up feelings of anger and frustration, and an instrumental attempt to resolve a problem.

The catharsis hypothesis has not gone unchallenged. Both Berkowitz (1989) and Tavris (1989) have questioned whether the expression of anger has the effect of reducing physiological arousal as well as further aggression. Available evidence seems to suggest that aggression may increase rather than decrease further aggression because it may become conditioned through reinforcement or practice to frustrating or aversive situations (Azrin, Hutchinson, & McLaughlin, 1965; Berkowitz, 1974; Feshbach, 1964; Tavris, 1989). According to the stage model, prior reinforcement of frustration-induced aggression makes it more likely to be employed as a coping option during the trial-and-error stage.

Frustration-Induced Goal Substitution

The importance of goal substitution as a coping mechanism has long been recognized. Dollard et al. (1939) point out that attainment of an alternative goal reduces the original goal response. Masserman (1961) has observed that individuals become increasingly inclined to accept alternative goals when blocking of the original goal is prolonged. Animals also have the tendency to substitute one incentive object for another (Rachlin, Battalio, Kagel, & Green, 1981). For example, Rachlin and Krasnoff (1983) report that external constraints of eating increase drinking, and vice versa. Wong (1977b) reports that spontaneous sand digging increases when rats are blocked from eating.

One can readily identify numerous instances of goal substitution in real life. The familiar "rebound" phenomenon in love relationships is a case in point. A frustrated, rejected lover may readily fall in love with a less desirable person, and wonder why he or she had not discovered that person earlier. Overeating as a way to cope with frustration is also a common observation.

According to the present analysis, the negative impact of failure is attenuated by the availability of alternative goals. One test implication is that the greater the incentive value of alternative goals, the faster the goal substitution under conditions of frustration.

The coping mechanism of goal substitution brings to the fore the importance of ecology. One cannot fully understand adaptation apart from the context in which it takes place. When substitution incentive objects are readily available, repeated failure does not pose a major threat, and helplessness/depression can be averted.

Frustration-Induced Helplessness

Yates (1962) observed that "under extreme and prolonged frustration, a subject may simply resign himself to his fate and refuses to perform any positive action" (p. 23). Maier (1949) considered resignation as the terminal state following prolonged frustration. Similarly, Klinger (1975) observed that "at some point during sustained unrelieved frustration, organisms begin to give up" (p. 10). According to the present analysis, giving up in favor of an alternative goal involves the mechanism of goal-substitution, whereas giving up in the absence of any substitution goal involves the mechanism of resignation.

In animal research, Klinger et al. (1974) reported that prolonged extinction reduced activity level in the runway. Wong (1978b) also observed an increase in passivity in a Skinner box following extended extinction, although different amounts of extinction might be needed to induced a high degree of passivity in different rats.

There is also a large body of evidence that prolonged failure leads to passivity, helplessness, and depression (e.g., Brown, 1972; Ellner, 1970; Klinger,

1975; Leff, Roatch, & Bunney, 1970; Seligman, 1975). It has also been observed that patients suffering from chronic renal failure show symptoms of helplessness and depression, such as passivity and negative self-concept (Shanan, Kaplan-De-Nour, & Garty, 1976). These symptoms may be attributed to prolonged frustrative stress associated with the unavoidable hemodialysis treatment and the endless waiting for a kidney transplant.

The literature of maternal separation is relevant to the present stage model. Separation-induced depression has been observed in both humans and primates (Bowlby, 1973; Kaufman & Rosenblum, 1967; Suomi & Harlow, 1977). Some have argued that this is due to the loss of control (Kaufman, 1973, 1977; Mineka & Suomi, 1978), but it could be easily argued that infants suffer not so much from loss of control, as from loss of reinforcement associated with mother. According to the present analysis, prolonged maternal separation is not different from experimental extinction.

It has been observed that monkey infants typically go through a stage of protest before the depression sets in (Mineka & Suomi, 1978; Seay, Hansen, & Harlow, 1962). The protest stage corresponds to the exploration–aggression stage, during which there is an increase in instrumental attempts to reestablish contact with mother as well as an increase in anger and aggression. The depressive stage during maternal separation is equivalent to the helplessness stage during prolonged extinction.

Once the resolution stage is reached, regardless of whether it is due to the mechanism of resignation or goal-substitution, there should be an immediate reduction of frustrative stress because of conflict resolution. In other words, frustration levels should be an inverted-U function of extinction trials. This prediction has been supported by a number of studies (Brooks & Goldman, 1971; Rosellini & Seligman, 1975; Wong, 1978b).

A FRUSTRATION ACCOUNT OF LEARNED COMPETENCE

So far, the focus of my analysis has been on the preprogrammed or unconditioned coping responses. In this and the next sections, I focus on the effects of conditioning different coping mechanisms to frustrative cues, and how an organism can learn to be competent or helpless in coping with new situations.

The concept of competence motive was first thrust to the forefront of motivational research by White's (1959) seminal paper. According to White, the competence or effectance motive is assumed to be global and intrinsic, giving rise to all kinds of behaviors that enable organisms to deal effectively with their environment. White also believes that the competence motive is maintained and enhanced by a feeling of efficacy or competence that comes from mastery over the environment. White's concept has been developed by a number of researchers (Bandura, 1977; deCharms, 1968; Harter, 1978). It is generally agreed that the competence motive depends on the belief that one can interact effectively with the environment, and that this belief is fostered by some success experience in coping. However, different views have been proposed as to what kinds of success experience are most effective in promoting the competence motive.

According to the *contingency* view, it is the personal experience of contingency of covariance between behavior and outcome that gives rise to the feeling of competence. This view is shared by many psychologists (e.g., deCharms, 1968; Seligman, 1975; Weiner, 1980). There is now some indirect evidence that experience of contingency may contribute to one's sense of competence. For example, Joffe, Rawson, and Mulick (1973) found that rats raised in a contingent environment where food, water, and ambient lighting were controllable by lever pressing were less emotional in an open field test than rats exposed to food, water, and lighting that were presented independently of their behavior. Wright and Katzer (1977) extended this finding and reported that rats exposed to contingent deliveries of food and water subsequently learned an avoidance response faster than rats exposed to noncontingently presented food and water.

The beneficial effects of exposure to contingent events have also been observed in humans (Dweck & Licht, 1980; Gunnar, 1980). For example, Watson and Ramey (1972) reported that infants who could make a mobile spin by pressing their heads against a pillow expressed more smiling and cooing and subsequently performed better in certain tasks than the no-control counterparts.

According to the *learned effort* view, it is not the experience of the contingency per se but the expenditure of effort that is important. Thus, it is effort–outcome covariance, rather than response–outcome contingency, that increases the persistence and vigor of goal-directed behavior. This view as developed by Eisenberger has been supported in numerous ingenious experiments (Eisenberger, Carlson, & Frank, 1979; Eisenberger, Carlson, Guile, & Shapiro, 1979; Eisenberger, Heerdt, Hamdi, Zimet, & Bruckmeir, 1979; Eisenberger, Park, & Frank, 1976; Eisenberger, Terberg, & Carlson, 1979). According to the learned effort hypothesis, effort involves the expenditure of energy and an organism is capable of learning the amount of effort involved in a task, independently of specific responses required to execute the task. The degree of effort necessary for reinforcement in one situation is positively related to the amount of effort expenditure in subsequent and different situations. Thus, transfer of persistence across different situations is attributed to the mechanism of learned effort.

There is little disagreement that exposure to contingent events reduces emotionality and facilitates learning as compared to exposure to noncontingent events. From the standpoint of frustration theory, however, degraded contingencies are better than a perfect contingency in promoting competence. To put it in a lay person's terms, when good work does not always lead to positive outcomes, people learn to tolerate and overcome frustration; their success experience in handling frustration should enable them to be more persistent and effective in coping with subsequent problems as compared to individuals who have never experienced failure.

There is now a well-established body of literature that partial reinforcement results in greater resistance to extinction than consistent reinforcement (Robbins, 1971). More recent research has also shown that the persistence effect of partial reinforcement is very resilient, capable of surviving prolonged extinction (Amsel, Wong, & Traupmann, 1971; Wong, Traupmann, & Brake, 1974) and increasing the persistence of another response (Wong & Amsel, 1976).

The learned effort hypothesis is correct in recognizing that it is the effort rather than specific response topographies that determines subsequent persistence. However, Eisenberger's conception of effort seems to be limited to the expenditure of physical energy, because he typically manipulates effort in terms of number of responses per reinforcement (Eisenberger, Carlson, & Frank, 1979), and amounts of force required (Eisenberger, Carlson, Guile, & Shapiro, 1979). From the perspective of frustration analysis, the amount of frustration involved is more important than the amount of physical effort spent in determining subsequent persistence. It is possible to manipulate physical effort and frustration independently, and to determine which factor is more important in determining subsequent persistence. For example, the task of carrying a heavy load or depressing a heavy lever definitely involves effort expenditure but not necessarily frustration. Delay of reinforcement, on the other hand, involves frustration but not effort expenditure. Furthermore, learned effort may be reformulated as the conditioning of "try harder" and "try something different" strategies to frustrative cues.

I have previously proposed that under partial reinforcement conditions, organisms acquire the "try" strategy (Wong, 1977a, 1978a; Wong & Amsel, 1976). In fact, organisms learn two kinds of "try" strategies. If reinforcement takes place during the first stage of coping, then the tendency of "try harder" is conditioned, and the organism learns to try harder in subsequent frustrating situations. However, if reinforcement takes place during the second phase, then the tendency of "try something different" is strengthened; the organism learns to explore various response options to solve subsequent problems.

Repeated reinforcement during the second stage of coping should produce greater persistence than reinforcement during the invigoration stage for the simple reasons that the former not only involves a longer period of frustrative nonreward, but also involves the reinforcement of more coping actions. Individuals who have learned to cope with difficulty with greater vigor and persistence are likely to be competent in problem solving.

It may be noticed that the present concept of the "try" strategy is similar to Eisenberger's learned effort hypothesis because both involve reinforcement of a high degree of energy expenditure. There is, however, one significant difference: in the former, effort or "try" is induced by the frustration; in the latter, effort is demanded by task characteristics (such as depressing a heavy lever) that may not involve frustration. My prediction is that reinforcement of frustration-induced effort should be more effective in enhancing persistence and competence than reinforcement of task-related effort apart from frustration.

According to the literature, a number of dependent variables have been used to measure the competence motive; these include emotionality, level of learning or performance, and goal persistence. A series of studies (Wong, 1981) have provided support not only for the construct validity of these measures, but also for the present frustration account of learned competence. In these studies, the only independent variable was whether maintenance feeding was frustrative or nonfrustrative. Under the frustrative condition, a mesh barrier separated the lab chow from young rats. Frustration occurs under this condition, because the barrier interfered with food consumption. Under the nonfrustrative condition, no barrier was inserted and the rats had ready access to food. In subsequent tests, the previously frustrated group showed less emotionality in an open field and faster rate of learning, as well as greater resistance to extinction. Thus, all three measures seem to be sensitive to the frustration manipulation designed to promote competence.

A FRUSTRATION ACCOUNT OF LEARNED HELPLESSNESS AND DEPRESSION

Learned helplessness is observed when an organism ceases instrumental activities prematurely in a new learning situation because of prolonged failure experience in the past. To put it simply, the organism learns to give up readily in a difficult or frustrating situation. Conditioned resignation is assumed to subserve learned helplessness.

When the unconditioned giving up mechanism is activated after prolonged failure, this mechanism may become conditioned to frustrative and situational cues. Subsequent encounter with these cues may trigger learned resignation, which operates like a conditioned response and does not necessarily depend on the perception of noncontingency.

Numerous investigators have already proposed that prolonged failure or frustration may lead to helplessness/depression (Boyd, 1982; Coyne, Metalsky, & Lavelle, 1980; Eastman, 1976; Ferster, 1973, 1974; Klinger, 1975; Lazarus, 1968; Lewinsohn, 1974, 1975). The present frustration account of learned helplessness is spelled out in greater detail so that differential predictions can be derived from the frustration account and Seligman's learned helplessness hypothesis. For example, according to the learned helplessness hypothesis, exposure to all uncontrollable or noncontingent events will produce learned helplessness. In other words, learned helplessness is a unitary phenomenon, produced by a single operation—the presentation of noncontingent events (Seligman & Altenor, 1980). In contrast to this view, the frustration hypothesis posits that only prolonged frustration operations result in learned helplessness, and these include experimental extinction, repeated failure, unnegotiable barriers, and inescapable shock.

Seligman has explicitly stated that "if learned helplessness is cognition of response-outcome independence, it should transfer widely" (Weinraub & Schulman, 1980, p. 482). In contrasts, frustration theory has a more restrictive set of boundary conditions for the transfer of helplessness. Following the frustration operation, transfer will occur only when the initial helplessness treatment is long enough to trigger the resignation mechanism, and when the test situation contains sufficient frustrative cues to instigate resignation prematurely.

The evidence on the generality of learned helplessness is not strong. The best evidence comes from studies that employ aversive-to-aversive transfer. For example, Altenor, Kay, and Richter (1977) reported that exposure to inescapable shock produced a deficit in learning to escape from water, and water immersion produced a deficit in shock escape learning. Weiss (1980) has suggested that such cross-situational transfer may be mediated by stress-induced depletion of norepinephrine. Because prolonged inescapable stress (be it shock or cold water) involves frustrative nonrelief, this transfer may be mediated by frustration instigated resignation.

The importance of frustration as a mediating factor can be inferred from the fact that following inescapable shock, rats will show learned helplessness only when the aversive test employs degraded contingencies that involve either frustrative nonrelief or delay of reinforcement (Maier & Testa, 1975; Maier, Albin, & Testa, 1973; Seligman & Beagley, 1975; Seligman, Rosellini, & Kozak, 1975).

So far, there has been no clear evidence of cross-situational appetitive-to-appetitive transfer. The evidence of appetitive-to-appetitive transfer is very limited and tenuous. For example, Goodkin (1976) reported that exposure to noncontingent food presentation interfered with a subsequent escape test only when noncontingent treatment and subsequent testing took place in the same context. The escape learning deficit may simply be due to competing responses and the competing drive related to food and may not involve the cognitive deficit of noncontingency. In another appetitive–aversive transfer study, Wright and Katzer (1977) found that exposure to noncontingent deliveries of food and water early in life resulted in poor escape/avoidance learning as compared to the contingent group that earned food and water through instrumental responding. This difference may be due to learned competence of the contingent group rather than learned helplessness of the noncontingent group. In the case of aversive–appetitive transfer, Rosellini (1978) found that exposure to inescapable shock produced a transient interference effect when rats learned to bar-press for food; however, interference was obtained only when the reinforcement contingency during testing involved delay of food reward.

In the human learned helplessness literature, the evidence of transfer is even more tenuous than in the animal literature. There is some evidence of transfer of helplessness to new tasks (Hiroto & Seligman, 1976; Roth & Kubal, 1975), but there are also numerous reports of failure of transfer (Douglas & Anisman, 1975; Klein, Fencil-Morse, & Seligman, 1976; Kuhl, 1981; Roth & Kubal, 1975). It is now clear that prior exposure to uncontrollable events in one task does not automatically result in transfer of helplessness to other tasks/situations. The difficulty in obtaining transfer of helplessness in animals and humans is contrary to the learned helplessness hypothesis, but it reaffirms the adaptiveness of living organisms. If exposure to uncontrollable events in one situation automatically renders an organism helpless in all subsequent situation, very few organisms would have survived.

According to frustration theory, all variables that are known to affect the level of frustration, such as number of nonreinforced trials, the incentive value of the goal object, and deprivation level, should affect the learned helplessness. From the perspective of Seligman's cognitive noncontingency view, these variables should not be important determinants. The literature again supports the frustration account. For example, perceived importance of the task is relevant to the development of learned helplessness (Roth & Kubal, 1975; Wortman & Brehmn, 1975). Several investigators have also reported a curvilinear relationship between number of helplessness treatment trials and the learned helplessness effect (Roth & Bootzin, 1974; Roth & Kubal, 1975; Wortman & Brehm, 1975). That is, short exposure to failure or uncontrollable events facilitates subsequent learning, while long exposure produces interferences. Such findings are clearly consistent with the present stage model of frustration coping, which posits that short exposure should activate the invigoration and exploration mechanisms, which generally facilitate learning, while prolonged failure should activate the resignation mechanism, which typically has a debilitating effect on learning. Consistent with the frustration analysis, Roth and Kubal (1975) have reported an increase in expressed feelings of frustration, helplessness, and incompetence from short to long exposures to failure.

Rather different approaches of immunization are dictated by Seligman's cognitive theory and the present frustration theory. From the perspective of learned helplessness theory, prior exposure to a perfect response–outcome contingency should immunize the organism against the onset of helplessness. According to the frustration theory, prior exposure to consistent reinforcement may make onset of extinction (i.e., loss of control) more upsetting than without such an exposure, because loss of control can be more frustrating than lack of control. However, if an organism has been exposed to degraded reinforcement contingencies and has learned how to cope with frustration, then it is less likely to become helpless. Therefore, partial reinforcement should be more effective than consistent reinforcement as an immunization procedure against helplessness. The efficacy of the partial reinforcement as immunization and treatment against learned helplessness has already been demonstrated in numerous studies (Jones, Nation, & Massad, 1977, 1978; Nation & Woods, 1980).

CONCLUSIONS

As a theory of coping with frustrative stress, the present stage model is an extension of Amsel's (1958, 1962, 1967) frustration theory and Klinger's (1975) incentive–disengagement cycles. The functional properties of frustration are more finely differentiated here. Active properties include invigoration, perseveration, exploration, and aggression, while inhibitory properties include goal avoidance and resignation.

The present stage model provides a very useful conceptual apparatus to study behavioral adaptation. It has been suggested that how one copes with blocking of a goal-directed behavior reflects one's adaptiveness or intelligence (Charlesworth, 1978a, 1978b). The present model directs our attention to qualitatively different behavioral patterns in the course of adaptation. For example, given a solvable problem, invigoration, exploration, and goal persistence are indices of adaptiveness, while response perseveration or premature resignation is unadaptive. Although the present theory posits that all organisms are predisposed to cope with chronic frustration in an adaptive manner, it also identifies conditions in which unadaptive coping responses are learned and generalized.

The stage model is capable of integrating a broad spectrum of frustration-related findings within a temporal sequence of adaptation. Thus, we know how a variety of frustration effects, such as invigoration, aggression, exploration, and helplessness, are related to one another as different aspects of the same coping process. The fact that both humans and animals exhibit the same behavioral sequence in very different frustration situation lends some credence to the proposition that the frustration coping behaviors are preprogrammed for survival.

The frustration account of various psychological phenomena, such as creativity, persistence, competence, fixation, and learned helplessness provides important insights regarding their etiology and transfer. Therefore, the theory provides a useful guide on effective coping with life's many frustrations—it indicates how we can promote and benefit from the positive aspects of frustration while reducing its negative effects. In the midst of conflicts and revolutions fueled by frustration, we can learn something from nature's way of managing unfulfilled aspiration as delineated in this chapter.

REFERENCES

Abramson, L. Y., Seligman, M. E. P., & Teasdale, J. D. (1978). Learned helplessness in humans: Critique and reformulation. *Journal of Abnormal Psychology, 87,* 49–74.

Alexander, F. (1950). *Psychosomatic medicine.* New York: Norton.

Allport, G. W. (1957). *Personality: A psychological interpretation.* New York: Holt.

Altenor, A., Kay, E., & Richter, M. (1977). The generality of learned helplessness in the rat. *Learning and Motivation, 8,* 54–61.

Amsel, A. (1958). The role of frustrative nonreward in noncontinuous reward situations. *Psychological Bulletin, 55,* 102–119.

Amsel, A. (1962). Frustrative nonreward in partial reinforcement and discriminatory learning: Some recent history and a theoretical extension. *Psychological Review, 69,* 306–328.

Amsel, A. (1967). Partial reinforcement effect on vigor and persistence. In K. W. Spence & J. T. Spence (Eds.), *The psychology of learning and motivation.* New York: Academic Press.

Amsel, A. (1971). Frustration, persistence, and regression. In H. D. Kimmel (Ed.), *Experimental psychopathology; Recent research and theory.* New York: Academic Press.

Amsel, A., & Roussel, J. (1952). Motivational properties of frustration: I. Effect on a running response of the addition of frustration to the motivational complex. *Journal of Experimental Psychology, 43,* 363–368.

Amsel, A., Wong, P. T. P., & Traupmann, K. L. (1971). Short-term and long-term factors in extinction and durable persistence. *Journal of Experimental Psychology, 90,* 90–95.

Archer, J. (1974). Testosterone and behaviour during extinction in chicks. *Animal Behaviour, 22,* 650–655.

Arieti, S. (1959). Manic-depressive psychosis. In S. Arieti (Ed.), *American handbook of psychiatry* (pp. 419–454). New York: Basic Books.

Atkinson, J. W. (1957). Motivational determinants of risk-taking behaviour. *Psychological Review, 64,* 359–372.

Atkinson, J. W., & Birch, D. (1970). *The dynamics of action.* New York: Wiley.

Atkinson, J. W., & Birch, D. (1974). The dynamics of achievement oriented activity. In J. W. Atkinson & J. O. Raynor (Eds.), *Motivation and achievement.* New York: Wiley.

Atkinson, J. W., & Feather, N. (Eds.) (1966). *A theory of achievement motivation.* New York: Wiley.

Azrin, N. H. (1961). Time-out from positive reinforcement. *Science, 133,* 382–383.

Azrin, N. H., Hutchinson, R. R., & Hake, D. F. (1966). Extinction-induced aggression. *Journal of the Experimental Analysis of Behaviour, 9,* 191–204.

Azrin, N. H., Hutchinson, R. R., and & McLaughlin, R. (1965). The opportunity for aggression as an operant reinforcer during aversive stimulation. *Journal of Experimental Analysis of Behavior, 8,* 171–180.

Bandura, A. (1977). Self-efficacy: Toward a unifying theory of behavioral change. *Psychological Review, 84,* 191–215.

Barker, R., Dembo, T., & Lewin, K. (1941). Frustration and regression: An experiment with young children. *University of Iowa Studies: Studies in Child Welfare, 18*(1).

Barthol, R. P., & Ku, N. D. (1959). Regression under stress to first learned behavior. *Journal of Abnormal Social Psychology, 59,* 134–136.

Baruch, D. W. (1941). Aggression during doll-play in a pre-school. *American Journal of Orthopsychiatry, 11,* 252–260.

Beck, A. T. (1967). *Depression: Clinical, experimental, and theoretical aspects.* New York: Hoeber.

Berkowitz, L. (1974). Some determinants of impulsive aggression: Role of mediated associations with reinforcements for aggression. *Psychological Review, 81*(2), 165–176.

Berkowitz, L. (1989). Frustration-aggression hypothesic: Examination and reformulation. *Psychological Bulletin, 106,* 59–73.

Bindra, D. (1969). The interrelated mechanisms of reinforcement and motivation, and the nature of their influence on response. In D. Levine (Ed.), *Nebraska Symposium on Motivation, 17,* 1–37.

Bowlby, J. (1973). *Separation: Anxiety and anger.* New York: Basic Books.

Boyd, T. L. (1982). Learned helplessness in humans: A frustration-produced response pattern. *Journal of Personality and Social Psychology, 89,* 738–752.

Brehmn, J. W. (1966). *A theory of psychological reactance.* New York: Academic Press.

Brooks, C. I., & Goldman, J. A. (1971). Changes in the intensity of primary frustration during continuous nonreward. *Journal of Experimental Psychology, 90,* 153–155.

Brown, B. (1974). Depression roundup. *Behavior Today, 5,* 117.

Brown, B. (1980). Perspectives on social stress. In H. Selye (Ed.), *Selye's guide to stress research* (Vol. 1, pp. 21–45). New York: Van Nostrand Reinhold.

Brown, G. W. (1972). Life-events and psychiatric illness: Some thoughts on methodology and causality. *Journal of Psychosomatic Research, 16,* 311–320.

Brown, J. S., & Farber, I. E. (1951). Emotions conceptualized as intervening variables—with suggestions toward a theory of frustration. *Psychological Bulletin,* 465–495.

Buss, A. (1961). *The psychology of aggression.* New York: Wiley.

Charlesworth, W. R. (1978a). Ethology: Understanding the other half of intelligence. *Social Sciences Information, 17,* 231–277.

Charlesworth, W. R. (1978b). Ethology: Its relevance for observational studies of human adaptation. In G. P. Sackett (Ed.), *Observing behavior.* Baltimore: University Park Press.

Child, I. L., & Waterhouse, I. K. (1952). Frustration and the quality of performance: I. A critique of the Barker, Dembo, and Lewin experiment. *Psychological Review, 59,* 351–362.

Clark, K. B. (1967). Explosion in the ghetto. *Psychology Today, 1*(5), 31–38, 62–66.

Coe, C., & Levine, S. (1981). Normal resposes to mother–infant separation in non-human primates. In D. Klein & J. Rabkin (Eds.), *Anxiety: New research and changing concepts.* New York: Raven.

Coelho, G., Hamburg, D., & Adams, J. (Eds.). (1974). *Coping and adaptation.* New York: Basic Books.

Coleman, J. C., & Hammen, C. L. (1974). *Contemporary psychology and effective behavior.* Glenview, IL: Scott, Foresman & Co.

Coover, G. D., Goldman, L., & Levine, S. (1971). Plasma corticosterone increases produced by extinction of operant behaviour in rats. *Journal of Comparative and Physiological Psychology, 6,* 261–263.

Coyne, J. C., Metalsky, G. L., & Lavelle, T. L. (1980). Learned helplessness as experimenter-induced failure and its alleviation with attentional redeployment. *Journal of Abnormal Psychology, 89,* 350–357.

Daly, H. B. (1969). Learning of a hurdle-jump response to escape cues paired with reduced reward or frustrative nonreward. *Journal of Experimental Psychology, 76,* 146–157.

Dardano, J. F. (1973). Self-imposed time-outs under increasing response requirements. *Journal of Experimental Analysis of Behavior, 19,* 269–287.

Davis, H., Mommott, J., MacFadden, L., & Levine, S. (1976). Pituitary-adrenal activity under different appetitive extinction procedures. *Physiology and Behaviour, 17,* 687–690.

deCharms, R. (1968). *Personal causation.* New York: Academic Press.

DeLongis, A., Coyne, J. C., Dakof, G., Folkman, S., & Lazarus, R. S. (1982). Relationship of daily hassles, uplifts, and major life events to health status. *Health Psychology, 1,* 119–136

Dohrenwend, B. S., & Dohrenwend, B. P. (Eds.). (1974). *Stressful life events: Their nature and effects.* New York: Wiley.

Dollard, J., Doob, L. W., Miller, N. E., Mowrer, D. H., & Sears, R. R. (1939). *Frustration and aggression.* New Haven, CT: Yale University Press.

Douglas, D., & Anisman, H. (1975). Helplessness or expectation incongruency: Effects of aversive stimulation on subsequent performance. *Journal of Experimental Psychology: Human Perception and Performance, 1,* 411–417.

Dunlap, W. P., & Frates, S. B. (1970). Influence of deprivation on the frustration effect. *Psychonomic Science, 21,* 1–2.

Dweck, C., & Licht, B. (1980). Learned helplessness and intellectual achievement. In J. Garber & M. E. P. Seligman (Eds.), *Human helplessness: Theory and applications.* New York: Academic Press.

Eastman, C. (1976). Behavioral formulations of depression. *Psychological Review, 83,* 277–291.

Eisenberger, R., Carlson, J., & Frank, M. (1979). Transfer of persistence to the acquisition of a new behavior. *Quarterly Journal of Experimental Psychology, 31,* 691–700.

Eisenberger, R., Carlson, J., Guile, M., & Shapiro, N. (1979). Transfer of effort across behaviors. *Learning and Motivation, 10,* 178–197.

Eisenberger, R., Heerdt, W. A., Hamdi, M., Zimet, S., & Bruckmeir, M. (1979). Transfer of persistence across behaviors. *Journal of Experimental Psychology: Human Learning and Memory, 5,* 522–530.

Eisenberger, R., Park, D. C., & Frank, M. (1976). Learned industriousness and social reinforcement. *Journal of Personality and Social Psychology, 33,* 716–722.

Eisenberger, R., Terberg, R., & Carlson, J. (1979). Transfer of persistence across reinforced behaviors. *Animal Learning and Behavior, 7,* 493–498.

Ellner, M. R. (1970). *The effects of experimentally inducted frustration on depressed and nondepressed college students.* Unpublished doctoral dissertation, City University of New York.

Engel, G. L. (1953). Homeostasis, behavioral adjustment and the concept of health and disease. In R. Grinker (Ed.), *Mid-century psychiatry.* Springfield, IL: Charles C Thomas.

Engel, G. L. (1962). *Psychological development in health and disease.* New York: Saunders.

Farber, M. L. (1967). Suicide and hope: A theoretical analysis. In N. L. Farberon (Ed.), *Proceedings of the Fourth International Conference on Suicide Prevention* (pp. 297–306). Los Angeles.

Ferster, C. B. (1973). A functional analysis of depression. *American Psychologist, 28,* 857–870.

Ferster, C. B. (1974). Behavioral approaches to depression. In R. J. Friedman & M. M. Katz (Eds.), *The psychology of depression: Contemporary theory and research.* Washington, DC: Winston-Wiley.

Ferster, C. B., & Skinner, B. F. (1957). *Schedules of reinforcement.* New York: Appleton-Century-Crofts.

Feshbach, S. (1964). The function of aggression and the regulation of aggressive drive. *Psychological Reviews, 71,* 257–272.

Fredericksen, L. W., & Peterson, G. L. (1977). Schedule-induced aggression in humans and animals: A comparative parametric review. *Aggressive Behavior, 3,* 57–75.

Freeman, G. I. (1948). *The energetics of human behavior.* Ithaca, NY: Cornell University Press.

Freud, S. (1959). "Civilized" sexual morality and modern nervous illness. In J. Strachey (Ed.), *The standard edition of the complete psychological works of Sigmund Freud.* London: The Hogarth Press. (Original work published 1908)

Friedman, R. J., & Katz, M. M. (Eds.). (1974). *The psychology of depression: Contemporary theory and research.* Washington, DC: Winston-Wiley.

Gal, R., & Lazarus, R. (1975). The role of activity in anticipating and confronting stressful situations. *Journal of Human Stress, 1,* 4–20.

Gallup, G. G., Jr., & Altomari, T. S. (1969). Activity as a post-situation measure of frustrative nonreward. *Journal of Comparative and Physiological Psychology, 68*, 382–384.

Garfield, E. (1978). The 100 articles most cited by social scientists, 1969–1977. *Current Contents, 32*, 5–14.

Gatchel, R., & Procter, J. D. (1976). Physiological correlates of learned helplessness in man. *Journal of Abnormal Psychology, 85*, 27–34.

Geen, R. G. (1972). *Aggression.* Morristown, NJ: General Learning Press.

Glass, D., & Singer, J. (1972). *Urban stress.* New York: Academic Press.

Goodkin, F. (1976). Rats learn the relationship between responding and environmental events: An expansion of the learned helplessness hypothesis. *Learning and Motivation, 7*, 382–393.

Gray, J. (1987). *The psychology of fear and stress* (2nd ed.) London: Cambridge University Press.

Gunnar, M. (1980). Contingent stimulation: A review of its role in early development. In S. Levine & H. Ursin (Eds.), *Coping and health.* New York: Plenum.

Hall, J. F. (1989). *Learning and memory* (2nd ed.). Boston: Allyn & Bacon.

Hanson, J. P., Larson, M. E., & Snowdon, C. T. (1976). The effects of control over high intensity noise on plasma cortisol levels in rhesus nomkeys. *Behavioral Biology, 16*, 333–340.

Harter, S. (1978). Effectance motivation reconsidered. *Human Development, 21*, 34–64.

Hiroto, D. S., & Seligman, M. E. P. (1975). Generality of learned helplessness in man. *Journal of Personality and Social Psychology, 31*, 311–327.

Hokanson, J. E., & Burgess, M. (1964). Effects of physiological arousal level, frustration and task complexity on performance. *Journal of Abnormal and Social Psychology, 68*(6), 698–702.

Hokanson, J. E., Burgess, M., & Cohen, M. F. (1963). Effect of displaced aggression on systolic blood pressure. *Journal of Abnormal and Social Psychology, 67*(3), 214–218.

Hokanson, J. E., DeGood, D. E., Forrest, M. S., & Brittain, T. M. (1971). Availability and avoidance behavior in modulating vascular-stress responses. *Journal of Personality and Social Psychology, 19*, 60–68.

Holmes, T. H., & Rahe, R. H. (1967). The Social Readjustment Rating Scale. *Journal of Psychomatic Research, 11*, 213–218.

Hull, C. L. (1934). The concept of the habit-family hierarchy and maze learning. *Psychological Review, 41*, 33–54.

Hutchinson, R. R., Azrin, N. H., & Hunt, G. M. (1968). Attack produced by intermittent reinforcement of a concurrent operant response. *Journal of the Experimental Analysis of Behavior, 11*, 489–495.

James, W. (1890). *The principles of psychology.* New York: Holt.

Jensen, G. D., & Cotton, J. W. (1960). Successive acquistions and extinctions as related to percentage of reinforcement. *Journal of Experimental Psychology, 60*, 41–49.

Joffe, J., Rawson, R., & Mulick, J. (1973). Control of their environment reduces emotionality in rats. *Science, 180*, 1383–1384.

Jones, S. L., Nation, J. R., & Massad, P. (1977). Immunization against learned helplessness in man. *Journal of Abnormal Psychology, 86*, 75–83.

Kanner, A. D., Kafry, D., & Pines, A. (1978, December). Conspicuous in its absence: The lack of positive conditions as a source of stress. *Journal of Human Stress*, pp. 33–39.

Kaufman, I. C. (1973). Mother–infant separation in monkeys: An experimental model. In J. P. Scott & I. Senay (Eds.), *Separation and depression: Clinical and research aspects* (Rep. No. 94) Washington, DC: American Association for the Advancement of Science.

Kaufman, I. C. (1977). Developmental considerations of anxiety and depression: Psychobiological studies in monkeys. In T. Shapiro (Ed.), *Psycholanalysis and contemporary science.* New York: International Universitites Press.

Kaufman, I. C., & Rosenblum, L. A. (1967). The reaction to separation in infant monkeys: Anaclitic depression and conservation-withdrawal. *Psychosomatic Medicine, 29*, 648–675.

Kelly, J. F., & Hake, D. F. (1970). An extinction-induced increase in an aggressive response with humans. *Journal of the Experimental Analysis of Behavior, 14*, 153–164.

Kimble, G. A., & Perimuter, L. C. (1970). The problem of volition. *Psychological Review, 77*, 361–384.

Klein, D. C., Fencil-Morse, E., & Seligman, M. E. P. (1976). Learned helplessness, depression and the attribution of failure. *Journal of Personality and Social Psychology, 33*, 508–516.

Klinger, E. (1975). Consequences of commitment to and disengagement from incentives. *Psychological Review, 82*, 1–25.

Klinger, E., Kemble, E. C., & Barta, S. G. (1974). Cyclic activity changes during extinction in rats: A potential model of depression. *Animal Learning and Behavior, 2,* 313–316.

Kovacs, M., Beck, A. T., & Weissman, A. (1975). Hopelessness: An indicator of suicidal risk. *Suicide,* pp. 95–103.

Kuhl, J. (1981). Motivational and functional helplessness: The moderating effect of state versus action orientation. *Journal of Personality and Social Psychology, 40,* 155–170.

Kuhl, J., & Blankenship, V. (1979a). The dynamic theory of achievement motivation: From episodic to dynamic thinking. *Psychological Review, 86,* 141–151.

Kuhl, J., & Blankenship, V. (1979b). Behavioral change in a constant environment: Shift to more difficult tasks with constant probability of success. *Journal of Personality and Social Psychology, 37,* 551–563.

Lawson, R. (1965). *Frustration: The development of a scientific concept.* New York: Macmillan.

Lazarus, A. P. (1968). Learning theory in the treatment of depression. *Behavior Research Therapy, 8,* 83–89.

Lazarus, R. S., & Folkman, S. (1984). *Stress, appraisal, and coping.* New York: Springer

Lazarus, R. S., Deese, J., & Osler, S. F. (1952). The effects of psychological stress upon performance. *Psychological Bulletin, 49,* 293–317.

Leff, M. J., Roatch, J. F., & Bunney, W. E., Jr. (1970). Environmental factors preceding the onset of severe depressions. *Psychiatry, 33,* 293–311.

Levine, S., Goldman, L., & Coover, G. D. (1972). Expectancy and the pituitary-adrenal system. In R. Porter & J. Knight (Eds.), *Physiology, emotion, and psychosomatic illness* (pp. 281–296). Amsterdam: Elsevier.

Lewinsohn, P. M. (1974). A behavioral approach to depression. In R. Friedman & M. Katz (Eds.), *The psychology of depression: Contemporary theory and research,* Washington, DC: Winston.

Lewinsohn, P. M. (1975). The behavioral study and treatment of depression. In M. Herson, M. M. Eisler, & P. M. Miller (Eds.), *Progress in behavior modification* (Vol. 1, pp. 19–64). New York: Academic Press.

Logan, F. A. (1971). Incentive theory, reinforcement and education. In F. Glaser (Ed.), *The nature of reinforcement* (pp. 45–61). New York: Academic Press.

Maier, N. R. F. (1949). *Frustration: The study of behavior without a goal.* New York: McGraw-Hill.

Maier, N. R. F., & Ellen, P. (1955). The effect of three reinforcement patterns on positional stereotypes. *American Journal of Psychology, 68,* 83–95.

Maier, N. R. F., & Ellen, P. (1959). The integrative value of concepts in frustration theory. *Journal of Consulting Psychology, 23,* 195–206.

Maier, S. F., Albin, R. W., & Testa, T. J. (1973). Failure to learn to escape in rats previously exposed to inescapable shock depends on nature of escape response. *Journal of Comparative and Physiological Psychology, 85,* 581–592.

Maier, S. F., & Seligman, M. E. P. (1976). Learned helplessness: Theory and evidence. *Journal of Experimental Psychology: General, 105,* 3–46.

Maier, S. F., & Testa, T. J. (1975). Failure to learn to escape by rats previously exposed to inescapable shock is partly produced by associative interference. *Journal of Comparative and Physiological Psychology, 88,* 554–564.

Mandler, G. (1964). The interruption of behavior. In D. Levine (Ed.), *Nebraska Symposium on Motivation.* Lincoln: University of Nebraska Press.

Margulies, S. (1961). Response duration in operant level, regular reinforcement, and extinction. *Journal of Experimental Analytical Behavior, 4,* 317–322.

Martin, R. F. (1940). "Native traits" and regression in rats. *Journal of Comparative Psychology, 30,* 1–16.

Marx, M. H. (1967). Non-reinforced response vigor as a function of number of training rewards. *Psychological Reports, 21,* 197–204.

Marx, M. H., & Tombaugh, J. W. (1967). The frustration vigor effect (TVE) as a function of number of rewarded barpress trials. *Psychonomic Science, 8,* 105–106.

Maslow, A. H. (1941). Deprivation, threat, and frustration. *Psychological Review, 48,* 364–366.

Maslow, A. H. (1943). A theory of human motivation. *Psychological Review, 50,* 370–396.

Masserman, J. H. (1961). *Principles of dynamic psychiatry* (2nd ed.). Philadelphia: W. B. Saunders.

McAllister, D. E., McAllister, W. R., Brooks, C. I., & Goldman, J. A. (1972). Magnitude and shift of reward in instrumental and aversive learning in rats. *Journal of Comparative and Physiological Psychology, 80,* 490–501.

McHenry, D. S. (1973). *Odor of frustration as it is related to the number of reinforced trials prior to frustrative nonreward.* Unpublished doctoral dissertation, Michigan State University, East Lansing.

McHose, J. H., & Ludvigson, H. W. (1964). Frustration effect as a function of drive. *Psychological Reports, 14,* 371–374.

Mechanic, D. (1970). Some problem in developing a social psychology of adaptation to stress. In J. McGrath (Ed.), *Social and psychological factors in stress.* New York: Holt, Rinehart and Winston.

Micklin, M. P., & May, J. G. (1975). An apparent frustration effect in planarians. *The Journal of Biological Psychology, 17,* 4–9.

Millard, W. J., & Woods, P. J. (1975). Frustrative nonrelief in instrumental escape conditioning. *Animal Learning and Behavior, 17,* 4–9.

Miller, C. F. (1971). *Frustration and curiosity in exploratory behavior.* Unpublished doctoral dissertation, Pennsylvania State University, University Park.

Miller, N. F., & Stevenson, S. S. (1936). Agitated behavior of rats during experimental extinction and a curve of spontaneous recovery. *Journal of Comparative Psychology, 21,* 205–231.

Mineka, S., & Suomi, S. J. (1978). Social separation in monkeys. *Psychological Bulletin, 85,* 1376–1400.

Mowrer, O. H. (1940). An experimental analogue of "regression" with incidental observations on "reaction formation." *Journal of Abnormal and Social Psychology, 35,* 56–87.

Mowrer, O. H. (1960). *Learning theory and behavior.* New York: Wiley.

Moyer, K. E. (1976). *The psychobiology of aggression.* New York: Harper & Row.

Mueller, D. P., Edwards, D. W., & Yarvis, R. M. (1977). Stressful life events and psychiatric symptomatology: Change or undesirability? *Journal of Health and Social Behavior, 18,* 307–317.

Natelson, B. H., Krasnegor, N., & Holaday, J. W. (1976). Relations between behavioral arousal and plasma cortisol levels in monkeys performing repeated free-operant avoidance sessions. *Journal of Comparative and Physiological Psychology, 90,* 958–965.

Nation, J. R., & Cooney, J. B. (1982). The time course extinction-induced aggressive behavior in humans: Evidence for a stage model of extinction. *Learning and Motivation, 13,* 95–112.

Nation, J. R., & Massad, P. (1978). Persistence training: A partial reinforcement procedure for reversing learned helplessness and depression. *Journal of Experimental Psychology: General, 107,* 436–451.

Nation, J. R., & Woods, D. J. (1980). Persistence: The role of partial reinforcement in psychotherapy. *Journal of Experimental Psychology: General, 109*(2), 175–207.

Notterman, J. V., & Mintz, D. E. (1965). *Dynamics of response.* New York: Wiley.

Parker, S. O., & Kleiner, R. (1966). *Mental illness in the urban Negro community.* New York: The Free Press.

Peacock, E. J., & Wong, P. T. P. (1984a, August). *Acquisition and extinction of over-trained stereotype in the rat.* Paper presented at the annual meeting of Canadian Psychological Association, Ottawa.

Peacock, E. J., & Wong, P. T. P. (1984b, August). *The effects of task demands on reinforcement-induced stereotype.* Paper presented at the annual meeting of American Psychological Association, Toronto.

Postman, L., & Bruner, J. S. (1948). Perception under stress. *Psychological Review, 55,* 314–323.

Price, J. S. (1972). Genetic and phylogenetic aspects of mood variation. *International Journal of Mental Health, 1,* 124–144.

Quek, T., & Wong, P. T. P. (1983). *Abnormal fixation and learned helplessness: A coping interpretation.* Paper presented at the annual meeting of the Canadian Psychological Association, Winnipeg.

Rachlin, H., & Krasnoff, J. (1983). Eating and drinking: An economic analysis. *Journal of the Experimental Analysis of Behavior, 39,* 385–404.

Rachlin, R., Battalio, R., Kagel, J., & Green, L. (1981). Maximization theory in behavioral psychology. *The Behavioral and Brain Sciences, 4,* 371–390.

Reitman, R. M., & Davison, L. A. (Eds.). (1974). *Clinical neuropsychology: Current status and applications.* New York: Halsted Press.

Reker, G. T., & Wong, P. T. P. (1984). Personal optimism, physical and mental health: The triumph of successful aging. In J. E. Birren & J. Livingstone (Eds.), *Cognition, stress and aging.* Englewood Cliffs, NJ: Prentice Hall.

Robbins, D. (1971). Partial reinforcement: A selective review of the alleyway literature since 1960. *Psychological Bulletin, 76*, 415–431.

Rosellini, R. A. (1978). Inescapable shock interferes with the acquisition of a free appetitive operant. *Animal Learning and Behavior, 6*, 155–159.

Rosellini, R. A., & Seligman, M. E. P. (1975). Frustration and learned helplessness. *Journal of Experimental Psychology: Animal Behavior Processes, 104*, 149–157.

Rosenzweig, S. (1934). Types of reaction to frustration: An heuristic classification. *Journal of Abnormal Social Psychology, 29*, 298–300.

Rosenzweig, S. (1944). An outline of frustration theory. In J. McV. Hunt (Ed.), *Personality and the behavior disorders*. New York: Ronald Press.

Roth, S., & Bootzin, R. R. (1974). Effects of experimentally induced expectancies of external control: An investigation of learned helplessness. *Journal of Personality and Social Psychology, 29*, 253–263.

Roth, S., & Kubal, L. (1975). Effects of noncontingent reinforcement on tasks of differing importance: Facilitation and learned helplessness. *Journal of Personality and Social Psychology, 29*, 253–263.

Ruiz, Z. R. (1975). *The frustration effect in children: Two methods for its measurement and study*. Unpublished doctoral dissertation, Tulane University, New Orleans, LA.

Ryan, T. J., & Watson, P. (1968). Frustrative nonreward theory applied to children's behavior. *Psychological Bulletin, 69*, 111–125.

Sarason, I. G., Johnson, J. H., & Siegel, J. M. (1978). Assessing the impact of life changes: Development of the Life Experiences Survey. *Journal of Consulting and Clinical Psychology, 46*, 932–946.

Scheier, M. F., Weintraub, J. K., Carver, C. F. (1981). Coping with stress: Divergent strategies of optimist and pessimist. *Journal of Personality and Social Psychology, 51*, 1257–1264.

Schmeck, R. R., & Bruning, J. L. (1968). Task difficulty and the frustration effect. *Journal of Experimental Psychology, 78*, 516–520.

Schwartz, B. (1980). Development of complex, stereotyped behavior in pigeons. *Journal of the Experimental Analysis of Behavior, 33*(2), 153–166.

Schwartz, B. (1981). Reinforcement creates behavioral units. *Behavior Analysis Letters, 1*, 33–41.

Schwartz, B. (1982). Reinforcement-induced behavioral stereotypy: How to teach people to discover rules. *Journal of Experimental Psychology: General, 111*(1), 23–59.

Scull, J. W. (1973). Amsel frustration effect: Interpretations and research. *Psychological Bulletin, 79*, 352–361.

Sears, R. R. (1942). Success and failure: A study of motility. In Q. McNemar & M. Merrill (Eds.), *Studies in personality*. New York: McGraw-Hill.

Seay, B. M., Hansen, E. W., & Harlow, H. F. (1962). Mother–infant separation in monkeys. *Journal of Child Psychology and Psychiatry, 3*, 123–132.

Seligman, M. E. P. (1975). *Helplessness: On depression, development, and death*. San Francisco: W. H. Freeman.

Seligman, M. E. P., & Altenor, A. (1980). Learned helplessness. *Behavioral Research and Therapy, 18*, 462–473.

Seligman, M. E. P., & Beagley, G. (1975). Learned helplessness in the rat. *Journal of Comparative and Physiological Psychology, 88*, 534–541.

Seligman, M. E. P., Rosellini, R. A., & Kozak, M. (1975). Learned helplessness in the rat: Time course, immunization and reversibility. *Journal of Comparative and Physiological Psychology, 88*, 542–547.

Selye, H. (1976). *The stress of life* (2nd ed.). New York: McGraw-Hill.

Selye, H. (Ed.). (1980). *Selye's guide to stress research* (Vol. 1). New York: Van Nostrand Reinhold.

Serum, C. S. (1973). *The interaction of locus of control of reinforcement as a personality variable and as an instructional set in a frustrative nonreward paradigm*. Unpublished doctoral dissertation, University of Alabama, University.

Sgro, J. A. (1977). The use of relief and nonrelief from shock in the double alleyway. *American Journal of Psychology, 90*, 243–251.

Shanan, J., Kaplan De-Nour, A., & Garty, I. (1976). Effects of prolonged stress on coping style in terminal renal failure patients. *Journal of Human Stress, 2*, 19–27.

Skinner, B. F. (1938). *The behavior of organisms: An experimental analysis*. New York: Appleton-Century.

Stotland, E. (1969). *The psychology of hope: An integration of experimental, clinical and social approaches.* San Francisco: Jossey-Bass.

Suomi, S. J., & Harlow, H. F. (1977). Production and alleviation of depressive behaviors in monkeys. In J. Maser & M. E. P. Seligman (Eds.), *Psychopathology: Experimental models.* San Francisco: W. H. Freeman.

Sutherland, N. S. (1966). Partial reinforcement and breadth of learning. *The Quarterly Journal of Experimental Psychology, 18,* 289–301.

Tavris, C. (1989). *Anger: The misunderstood emotion.* New York: Simon & Schuster.

Terrace, H. S. (1971). Escape from S-. *Learning and Motivation, 2,* 148–163.

Thiesen, J. W., & Meister, R. K. (1949). A laboratory investigation of frustration tolerance of preadolescent children. *Journal of Genetic Psychology, 75,* 277–291.

Thompson, D. M. (1964). Escape from S^D associated with fixed-ratio reinforcement. *Journal of the Experimental Analysis of Behavior, 7,* 1–8.

Thompson, T., & Bloom, W. (1966). Aggressive behavior and extinction-induced response rate increase. *Psychonomic Science, 5,* 335–336.

Tiger, L. (1979). *Optimism, the biology of hope.* New York: Simon & Schuster.

Tolman, E. C. (1932). *Purposive behavior in animals and men.* New York: Appleton-Century-Crofts.

Wagner, A. R. (1967). Frustration and punishment. In R. N. Harber (Ed.), *Current research in motivation* (pp. 229–239). New York: Holt, Rinehart and Winston.

Watson, J., & Ramey, C. (1972). Reaction to response-contingent stimulation in early infancy. *Merrill-Palmer Quarterly, 18,* 219–228.

Weiner, B. (1980). *Human motivation* New York: Holt, Rinehart and Winston.

Weinraub, M., & Schulman, A. (1980). Coping behavior: Learned helplessness, physiological change and learned inactivity: Interchange between Martin I. P. Seligman and Jay Weiss. *Behavior, Research, and Therapy, 18,* 459–512.

Weiss, J. M. (1971a). Effects of coping behavior in different warning signal conditions on stress pathology in rats. *Journal of Comparative and Physiological Psychology, 77,* 1–13.

Weiss, J. M. (1971b). Effects of punishing the coping response (conflict) on stress pathology in rats. *Journal of Comparative and Physiological Psychology, 77,* 14–21.

Weiss, J. M. (1980). Explaining behavioral depression following uncontrollable stressful events. *Behavior, Research, and Therapy, 18,* 485–504.

Wells, A. E. (1970). *Three responses to frustration and their effects upon subsequent aggression.* Unpublished doctoral dissertation, University of Florida, Gainsville.

White, R. W. (1959). Motivation reconsidered: The concept of competence. *Psychological Review, 66,* 297–333.

Wong, P. T. P. (1971a). Coerced approach to shock and resistance to punishment suppression and extinction in the rat. *Journal of Comparative and Physiological Psychology, 75,* 82–91.

Wong, P. T. P. (1971b). Coerced approach to shock, punishment of competing responses, and resistance to extinction in the rat. *Journal of Comparative and Physiological Psychology, 76,* 275–281.

Wong, P. T. P. (1977a). A behavioral field approach to instrumental learning in the rat: I. The partial reinforcement effects and sex differences. *Animal Learning and Behavior, 5,* 5–13.

Wong, P. T. P. (1977b). A behavioral field approach to operant conditioning: Extinction induced sand-digging. *Bulletin of the Psychonomic Society, 12,* 203–206.

Wong, P. T. P. (1978a). A behavioral field approach to instrumental learning in the rat: II. Training parameters and a stage model of extinction. *Animal Learning and Behavior, 6,* 82–93.

Wong, P. T. P. (1978b, August). *Extinction induced facilitation and helplessness.* Paper presented in a symposium on Learned Helplessness and Frustration in the XIXth International Congress of Applied Psychology, Munich.

Wong, P. T. P. (1979). Frustration, exploration and learning. *Canadian Psychological Review, 20,* 133–144.

Wong, P. T. P. (1981, November). *A stage model of coping with frustrative stress.* Paper presented at the Psychonomic Society Meeting, St. Louis.

Wong, P. T. P. (1989). Successful aging and personal meaning. *Canadian Psychology, 30,* 516–525.

Wong, P. T. P. (1990). Measuring life stress. *Stress Medicine, 6,* 69–70.

Wong, P. T. P., & Amsel, A. (1976). Prior fixed ratio training and durable persistence in rats. *Animal Learning and Behavior, 4,* 461–466.

Wong, P. T. P., & Dimitroff, G. (1980a, July). *Cognitive factors in coping with frustrative stress.* Paper presented in Leuven Symposium on Human Cognition and Motivation, Leuven.

Wong, P. T. P., & Dimitroff, G. (1980b, August). *Does food reinforcement reduce the intrinsic motivation of sand-digging?* Paper presented in the annual meeting of American Psychological Association, Montreal.

Wong, P. T. P., & Peacock, E. J. (1986). When does reinforcement induce stereotypy: A test of the differential reinforcement hypothesis. *Learning and Motivation, 17,* 139–160.

Wong, P. T. P., Traupmann, K. L., & Brake, S. (1974). Does delay of reinforcement produce durable persistence? *Quarterly Journal of Experimental Psychology, 26,* 218–228.

Woods, P. J. (1967). Performance changes in escape conditioning following shifts in the magnitude of reinforcement. *Journal of Experimental Psychology, 75,* 487–491.

Wookey, P. K., & Strongman, K. T. (1974). Frustration and elation effects in operant analogues of the double runway. *British Journal of Psychology, 65,* 305–313.

Wortman, C. B., & Brehmn, J. W. (1975). Responses to uncontrollable outcomes: An integration of reactance theory and the learned helplessness modes. In L. Berkowitz (Ed.), *Advances in experimental social psychology* (Vol. 8). New York: Academic Press.

Wright, M. T., & Katzer, R. D. (1977). Noncontingent positive reinforcers retard later escape/avoidance learning in rats. *Bulletin of the Psychonomic Society, 9,* 319–321.

Yates, A. J. (1962). *Frustration and conflict.* New York: John Wiley & Sons.

chapter 9

Stable and Chaotic Patterns of Fish Agonistic Activity

LINCOLN CHEW
University of Lethbridge
Lethbridge, Alberta

SYNOPSIS AND COMMENTS
Roderick Wong

All of the previous chapters have dealt with mammalian species. Yet approximately one-half of all vertebrates consist of fish, and it is fitting that at least one chapter deals with the behavior of this group. This is in keeping with the biological perspectives theme of the volume. Because I assume that many of the readers are not as familiar with research on fish as with that on mammalians, I encouraged Lincoln Chew to present his material in a manner that would elicit the interest of the reader. Thus, he wrote a chapter with a style and delivery that is inviting yet scholarly. I hope that you will find the material as well as the style of this chapter as delightful as I do.

The focus of Chew's chapter is the role of aggressive behavior in the establishment and maintenance of conspecific relationships among fish. Social interactions were discussed in previous chapters in this volume, namely, Raible's section on social learning and food selection and Porter and Lévy's on olfactory cues mediating parent–offspring interactions. The present chapter presents a fascinating account of another social behavior of adaptive significance—aggressive interactions. In general, animals fight in order to gain access to resources such as mates, food, or nest sites that may be in short supply. Individuals that fight readily and effectively would have a competitive edge over their rivals. Despite the obvious advantage to the animals in gaining limited resources, they do not always engage in all-out fights. There are intriguing differences in the pattern of agonistic behavior of the different groups of fish described in Chew's chapter. To make sense out of these data, Chew developed two models to account for these differences.

In studying the ontogeny of agonistic encounters among salmonid fry, Chew observed accidental collisions among them as they strike edible targets. From these inadvertent encounters, the fry learn to modify their feeding movements to ward off competitors for food. The lunging and snapping that was initially directed at food is now used in the context of intraspecific interactions. As with parent–offspring bonding, there is a sensitive period associated with feeding in these fry. If the fry are not fed within a few days after free-swimming in the tank, they will not feed later and also do not exhibit agonistic behavior. Thus, the manifestation of a "cognitive program" for agonistic behavior is dependent upon some other specific prior experience.

If food is available, the fry continue to feed, grow, and fight among themselves, and form dominant–nondominant relationships. Generally, the "winners" are larger and lighter colored than the "losers." Although there are differences in the influence of size and color among salmonids such as the brook charr and rainbow trout, their interactions are characterized by energetically costly initial physical encounters that are later replaced by less metabolically demanding, species-typical visual displays. Not only does the type of combat change with time, but there is a change in the frequency of agonistic encounters. Eventually, agonistic activity declines to a low level as relationships become established.

Species differences in agonistic behavior reflect the behavioral ecology of the fish. Highly aggressive trout tend to proliferate throughout a range, whereas the less aggressive charr tend to settle into despotic hierarchies. The relative success of the fry in intraspecific conflict is an important determinant of their habitat selection. They learn to use indices of size, color, and past experiences of victory or defeat to determine their subsequent behavior. The "standard" model of agonistic behavior was developed from such observations. According to this model, as relationships are established, territories are claimed and defended. Thus, the level of conflict declines and agonistic activities cease to be predominant in the lives of these fry.

The story on a specific cichlid, the White-Cloud Mountain Minnow, is very different. Chew's long-term study of these minnows reveals behaviors that do not conform with the standard model developed for salmonids and other fish. These minnows exhibit "flare-ups" in which their agonistic activity increased from 300% to 400% above baseline levels. These unstructured patterns appear to be independent of group size or availability of nesting sites. To analyze what seemed to be a chaotic pattern of interactions among these fish, Chew employed techniques from a branch of mathematics known as nonlinear dynamical analysis or "chaos theory." He found that population size per se is not critical in accounting for the observed rates of aggression.

Rather, it is the combined interaction of combatants and noncombatants in a population of a specific size and the inherent aggressiveness of these fish that determines the level of aggression. Chew acknowledges problems in ascertaining the "inherent" aggression of any population. A multifactor analysis of the type described in the chapters by Cheal, Porter and Lévy, and Raible would be useful. Indeed, Chew surmises that the confluence of physiological and psychological factors may influence this motivational tendency.

Although Chew's research indicates how salmonids and minnows differ in their social interactions, the question remains of why such startling differences occur in these fish. What were the selection pressures responsible for the evolution of the apparently anomalous social behavior of the White Cloud Mountain minnow? Are such behavior patterns manifested in other minnows? Chew alludes to the possibility that the "patternless pattern" observed in the White Cloud Mountain minnows may reflect the particular parameters analyzed in his experiment. Further experiments should attempt to establish the conditions that would produce the "standard" mode of agonistic behavior in these fish.

INTRODUCTION

Nearly one-half of all vertebrates on earth are fish. Much of what we know about them has necessarily been confined to those species that can be held in aquaria or in the wild where observation is possible. Nevertheless, there appear to be some commonalities across those species that have been studied in terms of their processes. Aggressive behavior is one such area that displays such class common properties.

In this chapter, I describe what role aggressive behavior plays in the establishment and maintenance of conspecific relationships. Drawing from experiments conducted in my laboratory on salmonids (i.e., salmon, trout, or charr), I present what I call the "standard model" of agonistic behavior in salmonids. This model describes the development of aggressive activity patterns for trout and charr and also offers theoretical predictions on their ecology. This model is discussed with reference to what is known about other fish species as well, such that I hope to portray this model not only as representative for salmonids but for teleosts in general.

I then proceed to the unusual case of the White Cloud Mountain Minnow, which challenges the standard model by virtue of the unorthodox patterns of interaction exhibited by members of this species. Finally, I attempt to reconcile the minnow puzzle with the standard model, using some techniques derived from the study of nonlinear dynamical, or chaotic, phenomena. By forging this partnership of fundamental empiricism with mathematics, I hope a fuller understanding of fish aggressive behavior will emerge.

THE "STANDARD MODEL" OF SALMONID AGGRESSION

Agonistic interactions in salmonids (i.e., salmon, trout, charr, grayling) begin soon after they become free-swimming (Dill, 1977). Following yolk-sac absorption, the fry feed voraciously and seemingly continuously, usually upon surface drift. They rove throughout the depths, striking at targets, learning what is edible and what is not. Antipredator systems come into play at this time, even as the population of fry is whittled down by fish of other species.

Upon this tableau of eat-or-be-eaten, intraspecific interactions also occur. These interactions appear to be random: Fry striking simultaneously or near simultaneously at the same target will collide from time to time. In such instances, the rapid closing upon, and the biting at, the target is inadvertently directed at the other fry. Initially, these interactions are no more than collisions—the initial movement is not directed, nor is there any directed response. Ironically, the outcome of such collisions is that the food particle "escapes" capture and drifts leisurely away from the fry.

Within days of becoming free-swimming, the fry learn to modify their feeding movements for use in warding off competitors for food. Agonistic activity is intimately linked with feeding in this way: The lunging and snapping that was initially solely directed at food now is used in the slightly more abstract context of intraspecific engagements.

There is a sensitive period associated with feeding. Laboratory-held fry, if not fed within a few days after free-swimming, never learn to strike at drift and will not feed even if copious amounts of food are introduced at a later time. In the absence of feeding, these fry exhibit no agonistic activity either. In such artificial conditions they swim until their natural body reserves are depleted and then die. This effect is as clear as it is dramatic.

Provided that food is available, the fry continue to feed, grow, and fight among themselves in the days and weeks following swim-up. The nature of the agonistic encounters begins to differentiate and elaborate throughout this time. In addition to the feeding-related biting and chasing, such behaviors as displacement (Cole & Noakes, 1980), tail beating (Noakes & Leatherland, 1977), body wagging (Chiszar, Drake, & Windell, 1975), fin erection, and opercular flaring (Stringer & Hoar, 1955) emerge in the arsenal of agonistic behaviors.

These new behaviors may be thought of as subtler, less energetically taxing forms of aggressive behavior (Rhijn & Vodegel, 1980). Chasing a conspecific from an area gives way to displacement, which only involves supplanting a fry from an area—there is no pursuit. Similarly, biting becomes less frequent over time, whereas ritualized body wags, fin, and opercular flaring become more prominent (see Figure 9.1).

There are victors and vanquished in these encounters. The fighting can be fierce with periods of severe strikes and counterstrikes lasting for minutes on end. The blows struck possess tremendous force, sufficient to literally bowl over an adversary. No prizefight or clash of ironclads displays more ferocity or tenacity.

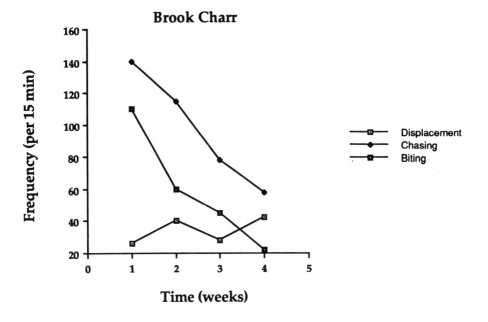

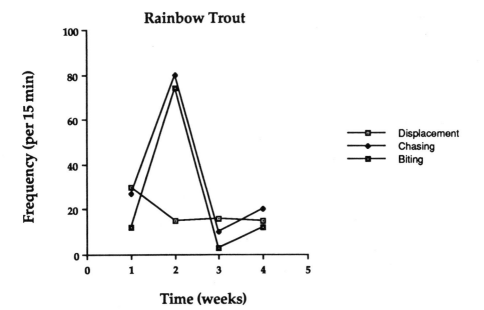

FIGURE 9.1. Aggressive activity in groups of *n* = 6. For both trout and charr, chasing and biting are initially high and then decline to the same frequency for displacement by the end of the first month of free-swimming.

Such interactions are typically dyadic although triadic interactions are occasionally observed. Why these triads are rarely seen or conversely, why they are seen at all, remains unknown (Jenkins, 1969). Suffice to say, during their early weeks as fry, the young trout and salmon pair off and, through rigorous combat, establish, quite literally, their standing relative to one another. Not surprisingly, the consistent winners tend to be larger than the losers. Even the slightest difference (usually of no more than half a head length) appears to figure in the resolution of any contest: Bigger fry simply have more physical resources to outlast their smaller adversaries.

To the victors goes the prize of space: territory. In the wild, the dominant fry tend to occupy and patrol preferred portions of the range, fending off interlopers with aggressive displays, although more energetic episodes of biting may be involved (Jenkins, 1969). In the laboratory, under ideal conditions of temperature and food access, this spatial imperative is undiminished. Dominant fish occupy the central portions of the tank, excluding less successful fry to the periphery. All may get access to food but the dominant ones feed first. The close association of feeding with aggression is affirmed yet again.

It is not a simple case of the haves and the have-nots, however. Interactions continue, particularly so when the territories are poorly defended or the issue of dominance is not clearly resolved due to the absence of a clear winner. Even in situations of well-defended territories, it is not unusual to find territories interdigitating such that fry will occasionally "stray" into neighboring territories to probe for weaknesses (Jenkins, 1969; Yamagishi, 1962). If the territory holder is vigilant, eviction is immediate. Intruders are chased out or, in the case of established territories, a face-to-face confrontation accompanied by gill flaring is sufficient to obtain results.

Given that territorial borders are rather plastic, Yamagishi (1962) advanced the notion of subterritories: areas of occupation in which defense is minimal relative to the defense of full territories (see also Heland, 1979). Alternatively, multiple subterritories within a large single territory have been observed (Jenkins, 1969: Moyle, 1976). In these cases, small fish will aid the dominant "overfish;" in the defense of the common territory against invaders.

Physiological changes accompany success or failure in combat. Dominant fish, who as pointed out earlier tend to be large, are also lighter than nondominant fish in coloration. *Nondominant* is generally preferred to the more traditional *subordinate* designation, because true submissive behavior is rarely seen: Nondominant fry are potentially dominant fry that lack the armamentarium and experience to succeed in status-raising duels.

Using a simple schema of "larger or smaller than" and "lighter or darker colored than," it is possible to conduct a simple, reliable taxonomy for evaluating the win–loss records of fry who have engaged in the territorial disputes. Large, lightcolored (LL) fry are the most aggressive and successful. They top the list, whereas small, dark-colored (SD) fry are the untouchables of the salmonid caste system. Two other combinations of size and color also are possible: large, dark-colored (LD) fry, and small, light-colored (SL) fry.

The question as to what is more important as a signal of success—size or color—can be answered by looking at these latter two intermediate categories. The answer is: It depends.

For rainbow trout, LD fry are dominant (win more encounters, have better and larger territories, are lighter colored) over SL fry, whereas, for brook charr, the reverse is true. That is, for rainbow trout, size is a better predictor of success than color; but in brook charr it is color that is a better predictor. Using analogous prizefighting terms, it is better to be a loser in the heavyweight division than a winner in a lower weight class if you are a trout, whereas the payoffs are greater if you are a successful middleweight charr rather than a heavyweight with a poor record.

Further, the fates of LL fry between the two species differ. In intruder experiments, where the dominant LL fry is removed from its home aquarium and placed into another environment with an extant hierarchy, a rainbow trout transplantees fare poorly.

They are attacked relentlessly following introduction by all residents, particularly so by the resident LL fry. Although responding gamely, the intruder is typically driven to the aquarium periphery and undergoes a darkening of body coloration—a clear marker of its loss of status.

If returned to its home range, the formerly dominant fry must contend with the fry that succeeded it in the hierarchy following its removal. Its previous status has no currency, and it must fight to regain its former position of prominence. Indeed, the ensuing conflict follows the same pattern as the initial period of establishment of group interrelationships: There are flurries of extensive biting and chasing that decline to posturing displays (body wagging, opercular flaring) as new relationships are established. This is true not only for the returnee and the usurper, but for all other fish in the tank as well. It is as if the return of the dominant fish destabilizes all relationships. As in the case of the initial establishment of group hierarchies, these displays, and the occasional episode of displacement without actual contact, become the predominant form of agonistic behavior as new dominance relationships are forged and the group becomes socially stable once again. Typically, rainbow trout returnees fail to regain their status, darken, and are banished to the periphery, as they were when they were intruders.

LL brook charr are much more successful as intruders and, later, as returnees. When transplanted as intruders, they are able to fend off the territorial forays of the residents and typically depose the LL defenders to assume the dominant position in their new environs, with the accompanying gains in territory and retention of the silvery coloration indicative of success in combat.

When these emigrants are returned home, the charr, like their trout cousins, must reestablish their dominance anew. But, unlike the trout, LL brook charr reacquire their previous status after engaging the residents in territorial encounters (see Figure 9.2).

Control experiments in which the dominant fry is removed from its home tank but is isolated rather than placed into an unfamiliar group environment address questions of the mechanisms underlying the differences between the two

Brook Charr Intruder Study

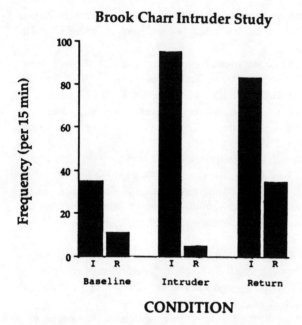

FIGURE 9.2.   Activity by LL brook charr. Their
aggressiveness as residents, intruders, and returnees is
clearly shown by the relative number of encounters
initiated (I) versus those received (R).

species. In these isolation studies, when the LL fry are returned to their home
tanks, the fry *regardless of species* regain their status after going through the
process of challenge, vigorous engagement, and resolution (Figure 9.3).

These isolation studies suggest that there is nothing inherently detrimental to
LL fry following removal from the home range. Rather, it is the experiences beyond the range that influence subsequent success or failure either in the home
range or in new ranges.

As a further comparison to the LL emigration scenario, nondominant SD fry
were transplanted from home tanks into tanks with established conspecific groups
(Figure 9.4). The fate of these individuals is an unhappy one. Hounded and beaten
in their home tanks, these transplantees of low status fare no better as emigrants
or as returnees. Alas, once a loser, always a loser.

Given that trout and charr have different success rates after leaving their
home territories for new ranges, it is possible to extrapolate these laboratory findings for LL and SD transplantees to natural settings.

Beginning with the lowliest first, the optimal strategy would appear to be to
stay put. Venturing outward from the initial home range is disastrous for both nondominant trout and charr in terms of the energy expended in defending themselves
against resident fish in new territories. By remaining at home, albeit under less

Rainbow Trout Isolate

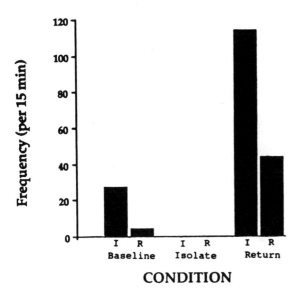

Brook Charr Isolate

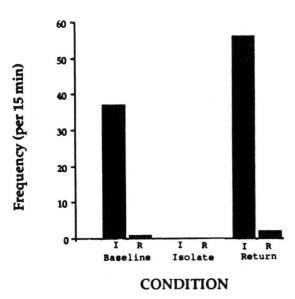

FIGURE 9.3. Activity by LL rainbow trout and brook charr isolates. Following isolation, dominant fry of both species continue to be the initiators (I) of aggressive episodes more often than they are the receipients (R).

Rainbow Nondominant

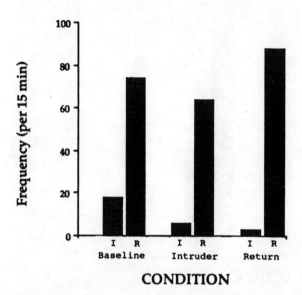

FIGURE 9.4. Activity by nondominant SD
rainbow trout transplantees. They receive (R) more
aggressive attacks as residents, intruders, or
returnees than they initiate (I).

than ideal social conditions, attacks by dominant individuals eventually decline. Emigration is best suited for fry hardier and more successful in combat than for nondominant ones.

Thus, for dominant rainbow trout fry, which seem unable to establish themselves in either new, occupied environments or in their home ranges upon their return, the optimal strategy is to keep moving outward from their range until they come into unoccupied but favorable reaches of their environment.

In contrast, dominant brook charr migrants are able to establish themselves readily in new, occupied areas. Any possible disadvantages of having to battle an ever-increasing number of conspecific challenges and defenders is offset by the advantage of expanding one's territory into areas that are demonstrated to contain resources favorable to the species as indicated by the very presence of conspecifics in that area.

Thus, brook charr expand their territories by a slow process of annexation through conflict whereas the optimal rainbow trout strategy would be to bypass all inhabited regions and seek out new areas. It follows from this that for populations of trout and charr, trout tend to proliferate faster through a region than charr that must take their time in consolidating their slowly expanding empires.

In fact, it is known that trout tend to occupy a variety of habitats within any water system, whereas brook charr tend to be more particular (McNicol & Noakes, 1981). For populations of a given size, charr tend to have one despot with many subordinates, whereas trout populations tend to form as many independent territories in which each owner is relatively unmolested by its neighbors. In the charr social system, the advantages are those conferred upon group association: mutual defense and the sharing of resources. The trout social system, in contrast, seems to have evolved so that the species rapidly proliferates through a habitat.

Given the well-known aggressiveness of trout against sympatric species (e.g., Hartman & Gill, 1968), it is ironic that if trout had been as successful in intraspecific combat as they are interspecifically, they might have evolved patterns of socialization more akin to charr. It is this very lack of success intraspecifically, however, that makes trout so successful in their ability to expand into, and occupy, the spectrum of riverine and lacustrine habitats.

Several aspects of fish agonistic behavior are now apparent. First, size and color are critical in salmonid behavior both as determinants of combative outcomes as well as badges of past success. Not surprisingly, larger individuals tend to prevail over smaller individuals of the same color: Large, light-colored fry are dominant over small, dark-colored fry. Size also determines success in encounters between trout fry of differing colors: Large fry dominate small fry. Brook charr are exceptional in that small but light-colored fry (i.e., those that are dominant in their "weight class") tend to dominate larger, dark-colored fry (i.e., those that are unsuccessful against fry of comparable size).

Size and color figure prominently in the interactions of other fish species. In most of these cases, the salmonid scenario is repeated—large fish tend to dominate smaller fish—and there are conspicuous color differences between winners and losers. Some of these species include bluegill sunfish (*Lepomis macrochirus*) (Henderson & Chiszar, 1977), Midas cichlids (*Ciclasoma citrinellum*) (Barlow & Ballin, 1976), brown bullheads (*Ictalurus nebulosus*) (Keen, 1982), Arctic charr (*Salvelinus alpinus*) (Jobling & Wandsvik, 1983), chum salmon (*Oncorhynchus keta*) (Chebanov, 1979), goby (*Coryphopterus nicholsi*) (Cole, 1982), pencilfish (*Nannostomus beckfordi*) (Kuenzer, 1982) and rainbow cichlids (*Herotilapia multispinosa*) (Wiley Driscoll & Welanko, 1981).

Second, interactions for both species are characterized by energetically costly initial physical encounters that are replaced by much less metabolically demanding, species-typical visual displays. This pattern is followed whether the situation involves the *de novo* establishment of relationships, the introduction of an intruder into established regions, or the reintroduction of a dominant fish in its home range after an absence.

Not only does the type of combat change with time but also the frequency of agonistic encounters changes: As relationships are established, agonistic activity declines to a low level. It is never wholly absent because there are periodic probes into neighboring territories. Such probes occur with rhythmic frequency but barring the introduction from external threats or the unlikely defeat of a dominant fish by a subordinate one, the long-term picture is a dynamic yet stable one.

This decline reflects the refining of intragroup relationships through the learning of the relative probabilities of success and failure of conflicting with other group members (Abbott, Dunbrack, & Orr, 1985; Kohda & Watanabe, 1982; Newman, 1956). Such patterns of declining interaction with time have also been found for other species including the pupfish (*Cyprinodon variegatus*) (Itzkowitz, 1979) and the bluegill sunfish (*Lepomis macrochirus*) (Henry & Atchison, 1979).

Third, species differences in agonistic behavior reflect what is known of this ecology of the trout and charr (Moyle, 1976). Highly aggressive trout tend to proliferate throughout a range, whereas somewhat less aggressive charr tend to settle into despotic hierarchies although hierarchies of various types are possible for each species (Jenkins, 1969; Lewis, 1969; McIntyre & Healy, 1978). Figuring prominently as a determinant in these differences in habitat selection is the relative success in intraspecific conflict. That is, learning is involved not only in the initial establishment of intragroup relationships, but also in later emigration when indices of size, color, and past experiences of victory or defeat in combat determine subsequent behavior.

The confluence of psychological and physical factors leading to the overt agonistic behavior so far seems to be a rather comfortable story. It is intuitively appealing that as relationships are established, territories claimed and defended, the level of conflict declines and, although it never completely disappears, ceases to be the predominant behavior in the lives of these fry, who must after all also forage and defend themselves against predators as well. It is a civilized, orderly, tractable, and therefore conceptually comforting view of salmonids and, with some variation, of teleosts in general.

But having established this view, I now present evidence from a species whose behavior is seemingly anomalous and runs counter to this model.

THE CHAOTIC WHITE CLOUD MOUNTAIN MINNOWS

In Guangzhou (formerly Kwangtung) province of southern China lies a range of low mountains. Placid, lush, and very ancient, this range is characterized by low clouds that graze along its peaks and give its picturesque name—the Mountains of the White Clouds.

Endemic to the streams and quiet waters of the range is a small, seemingly innocuous minnow-like fish known not surprisingly as the White Cloud Mountain Minnow (*Tanichthys albonubes*). Like most cyprinids, these minnows are not large, reaching a maximum length of about only 5 cm. The males are somewhat smaller than the females, but both are sleek with colorful trim along the body and fin margins. Known for their hardiness, ease of maintenance, and high-breeding success, they have become popular with aquarists the world over. They are also known among serious aquarists as "jitter fish" that never seem to settle down to become living ornaments, as is often the case with other aquarium species. It is this "jitteriness" that is the focus of the following discussion.

A casual study of these minnows reveals nothing out of the ordinary about them. When small groups of minnows are formed there is the familiar pattern of high initial periods of aggression, particularly biting and chasing, followed by a decline in activity with a concomitant shift to less energetically demanding displacement movements or opercular or fin displays. Somewhat more prolonged observations uncover occasional conflicts as territory holders probe the defenses of their neighbors. These patterns are entirely consistent with the "standard model."

However, long-term study of minnow groups reveals something startling: From time to time, agonistic activity soars dramatically, involving a 300% to 400% increase above baseline (Figure 9.5). These flare-ups occur too frequently to be considered happenstance, and yet they are irregular enough in frequency to be considered random. It is this chaotic fluctuation of activity, the aforementioned jitteriness, in supposedly established groups that brings the species into stark contrast with those species that exhibit the stately and comfortable standard model.

We have made some forays into solving the puzzle of minnow behavior. In a test of the hypothesis that territoriality might be affected by available space, 10 minnows were transplanted from a small, 23-gallon aquarium to a large, 300-gallon tank. After an initial period of exploration with no conspecific interactions, the minnows became aggressive such that activity waxed and waned in an apparent haphazard fashion over time just as it had in the smaller volume: The increase in available habitat had no effect on aggressiveness.

In a second experiment, the environment was further enhanced by providing more spawning sites than there were fish. A low population density of fish was again used (approximately one breeding pair per 50 liters). The pattern of low rates of interaction punctuated by periods of intense chasing and biting persisted, with the frequency of interaction at any time being unpredictable from one time period to the next.

These unstructured patterns, then, appear to be independent of absolute group size or spawning site availability even under ideal conditions of water quality, food availability, and the absence of predators. The usual approaches to understanding aggressive behavior in fish were apparently stymied by this species, and so investigations turned momentarily away from the study of the underlying causes of these activity patterns (e.g., motivation for food, mates, or territory) to an analysis of the patterns themselves.

Extensive and continuous observation of minnow interaction at first suggested time-series analysis might be the best method of characterizing the patterns detected. However, even a rudimentary pass through the data demonstrated the futility of this approach: No periodicities were found in the chaotic data. Or more correctly, so many underlying periodicities were needed to generate the irregular fluctuations that almost as many underlying oscillators were needed as there were data points. This result was so unwieldy that it was theoretically inelegant and lacked the ring of parsimony and truth.

Fortunately, the study of complex natural phenomena has also come under the scrutiny of a branch of mathematics known as nonlinear dynamical analysis, or more popularly, chaos theory (see Gleick, 1987, for a thorough yet refreshing

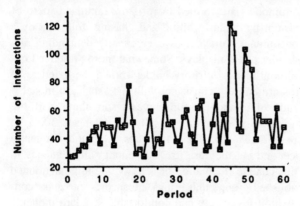

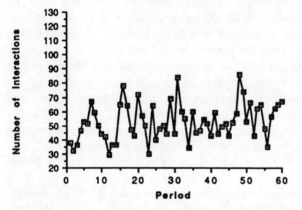

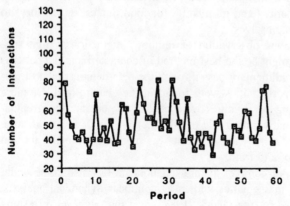

FIGURE 9.5. Activity of White Cloud Mountain Minnows during three 60-min periods with 1 month between each period.

general introduction to deterministic chaos). It has been used to address a number of biological problems ranging from cardiovascular arrhythmias to bird flocking, and it was this type of analysis that was brought to bear on the minnow problem.

Of particular relevance to the minnow puzzle was the early demonstration that very simple biological processes that behave in well-defined linear fashion became unstable and intractable following even the slightest modification of the initial parameters. It was through this new area of analysis that we attempted to find a simple yet feasible explanation for the observed nonlinearities in minnow aggressive behavior.

In the model proposed, we assumed that the observed level of interaction was dependent on three factors: (a) an inherent initial rate of group interaction, r, (b) the proportion of the population at any time involved in aggressive activity, x, and (c) the proportion of the population who are nonparticipants, $(1 - x)$. The number of interactions at any time is then:

$$f(x) = r\,(x)\,(1 - x).$$

That is, activity level is simply an expression of the baseline level of aggression in a population and the number of players and nonplayers. This rate equation may be more familiar to some readers in the characterization of population growth in which the population of each generation is a function of the starting or seed population, the birthrate, and the death rate. Here we have merely substituted reproductive activity with aggressive activity.

By taking the number of interactions at some time, t_1, and then using it as the seed value r for the very next time period, t_2, one can predict the value of $f(x)$ for t_2 given a fixed number of combatants and hence noncombatants. This value of $f(x)$ if fed back into the equation will, in turn, give a value for time, t_3, and so on. In this way the activity level for successive time periods can be calculated.

Nonuniqueness: Implications for Chaos in Minnow Society

What is interesting is that if the previously mentioned process of successive seeding is used, a unique solution is not always derived. In one set of scenarios, under certain conditions of r and x, the predicted levels of activity *do* stabilize. These asymptotic levels may be high or low depending on the specific values of r and x.

Under a different set of starting parameters, the process stabilizes at not one but two levels. In these cases, alternating high and low levels of activity are observed. That is, the population fluctuates between being relatively active and inactive and is said to be bifurcated. Trifurcation can also occur, wherein, not just one or two, but three levels of activity are observed over the long term.

Of the greatest interest is that, under other conditions, no stabilization of activity emerges: Activity levels cannot be predicted from one period to the next even though the parameters are known. This so-called deterministic chaos is possible even in simple, perfectly defined systems.

Although such modeling is still rudimentary and allegorical, a number of insights can be gleaned from a dynamical approach to the minnow puzzle. First, consideration of population size per se is insufficient in accounting for the observed rates of aggression. This is why considerations of absolute population size of fish density (fish per unit volume) have not told us much. Rather, it is the combined interaction of combatants and noncombatants in a population of a specific size and their inherent aggressiveness that contribute to overt behavior. That is, it appears necessary to consider these factors of initial activity level and population simultaneously.

Second, in terms of predictions based on the modeling, we can say that populations of similar size can have different activity levels if the number of combatants and noncombatants vary from population to population (i.e., have different r values). Moreover, in populations of different size, similar rates of interaction may be observed given appropriate differences in r and x.

A third prediction is that in large populations with a significant proportion of combatants, persistent regular fluctuations in activity would be observed. With still higher numbers of aggressive fish in such populations, irregular or chaotic fluctuations in activity will emerge. That is, too many aggressive individuals could destabilize a fish population.

Upon reflection, none of these findings or prognostications are surprising; indeed, they are conceptually sensible and empirically testable. It is doubtful, however, if such thinking could have been derived so readily without the use of a dynamical approach.

Several questions remain to be answered though. For example, what determines the "inherent" rate of aggressiveness (r) of any population remains unknown. A credible solution will doubtless incorporate the contribution of physiological factors such as the learning from interactions with conspecifics. Similarly, why fish choose to be aggressive or nonaggressive toward a neighbor at a specific time remains to be determined although such motivation doubtless involves the confluence of physiological and psychological factors.

Returning to the specific question of the White Cloud Mountain Minnow "patternless pattern" of interactions, the answer we have arrived at is that the chaos is only apparent—the observed departure from the standard model may be due to parametric shifts in an otherwise simple and orderly process. In the minnow case, this shift has led to a chaotic pattern whereas in other species, which may alternate between periods of high aggressive activity and periods of relative calm, the shift is not so extreme and so yields a bifurcated rather than a chaotic activity pattern.

It also follows that if this nonlinear dynamical view of White Cloud Mountain Minnow behavior is correct there should exist a set of r and x parameters in which no chaotic patterns are seen. That is, under the "proper" conditions the minnows should, like the other species discussed, also exhibit the standard mode. Further, it remains an article of faith that there are more parameters than just x and r. What they are and how they relate to the ones considered here will be revealed only through further experimentation and cogitation.

These methods, in concert with traditional hypothetico-deductive speculation obtained from the empirically based standard model, enable us to understand not only common patterns of fish aggressive behavior, but also seemingly intractable chaotic patterns. Refinement and rigorous application of these methods will doubtless reveal more of the mechanisms underlying aggression in fish and perhaps other vertebrate species.

SUMMARY

Evidence drawn from studies of salmonids and other species was presented in the form of a "standard model." The relative success of individuals following the model was examined in light of potential success as emigrants into new habitats. These predictions were then found to corroborate what is known about the ecology of these species.

The exceptional behavior of White Cloud Mountain Minnows was presented by virtue of their apparently chaotic and nonstandard patterns of conspecific agonistic behavior.

A possible explanation of minnow activity using a basic nonlinear dynamical approach was derived such that the observed patterns, although seemingly chaotic, could be accounted for by considerations of population composition and "inherent" aggression.

The utility of a dynamical approach was extended to making testable predictions of groups of differing or similar size. It is hoped that the continued co-application of mathematical methods and basic empiricism will lead to further understanding of the causes of aggression in fishes.

REFERENCES

Abbott, J. C., Dunbrack, R. L., & Orr, C. D. (1985). The interaction of size and experience in dominance relationships of juvenile steelhead trout (*Salmo gairdneri*). *Behaviour*, *92*(3–4), 241–253.

Barlow, G. W., & Ballin, P. J. (1976). Predicting and assessing dominance from size and coloration in the polychromatic Midas cichlid. *Animal Behaviour*, *24*, 793–813.

Chebanov, N. A. (1979). Behavior and mate selection among chum brood stock of different sizes with a predominance of males in the spawning grounds. *Soviet Journal of Ecology*, *10*(2), 141–146.

Chiszar, D., Drake, D. W., & Windell, J. T. (1975). Aggressive behavior in rainbow trout (*Salmo gairdneri* Richardson) of two ages. *Behavioral Biology*, *13*, 425–431.

Cole, K. S. (1982). Male reproductive behaviour in spawning and success in a temperate zone goby, *Coryophopterus nicholsi*. *Canadian Journal of Zoology*, *60*(10), 2309–2316.

Cole, K. S., & Noakes, D. L. G. (1980). Development of early social behaviour of rainbow trout, *Salmo gairdneri* (Pisces, Salmonidae). *Behavioural Processes*, *5*(2), 97–112.

Dill, P. A. (1977). Development of behaviour in alevins of Atlantic salmon, *Salmo salar*, and rainbow trout, *S. gairdneri*. *Animal Behaviour*, *25*(1), 116–121.

Gleick, J. (1987), *Chaos*. New York: Viking.

Hartman, G. F., & Gill, C. A. (1968). Distribution of juvenile steelhead and cutthroat trout (*Salmo gairdneri* and *S. clarki clarki*) within streams of southwestern British Columbia. *Journal of the Fisheries Research Broad of Canada*, *25*(1), 33–48.

Heland, M. (1979). The ontogenesis of territorial behaviour in the trout fry (*Salmo trutta* L.). *Bulletin de Centre Etudiants pour Recherche Scientifique (Giarritz)*, *12*(3), 564–565.

Henderson, D. L., & Chiszar, D. A. (1977). Analysis of aggressive behaviour in the bluegill sunfish *Lepomis macrochirus* Rafinesque: Effects of sex and size. *Animal Behaviour*, 25, 122–130.

Henry, M. G., & Atchison, G. J. (1979). Influence of social rank on the behaviour of bluegill, *Lepomis macrochirus* Rafinesque: Effects of sex and size. *Animal Behaviour*, 25, 122–130.

Itzkowitz, M. (1979). Territorial tactics and habitat quality. *American Naturalist*, 114(4), 585–590.

Jenkins, T. M., Jr. (1969). Social structure, position choice and microdistribution of two trout species (*Salmo trutta* and *Salmo gairdneri*) resident in mountain streams. *Animal Behaviour Monographs*, 2(2), 57–123.

Jobling, L. M., & Wandsvik, A. (1983). Effect of social interaction on growth rates and conversion efficiency of Arctic charr, *Salvelinus alpinus* L. *Journal of Fish Biology*, 22(5), 577–584.

Keen, W. A. (1982). Behavioural interactions and body size differences in competition for food among juvenile brown bullhead (*Ictalurus nebulosus*). *Canadian Journal of Fisheries and Aquatic Science*, 39(2), 316–320.

Kohda, Y., & Watanabe, M. (1982). Agonistic behaviour and color pattern in a Japanese fresh water serranid fish, *Coreoperca kawamebari*. *Zoological Magazine of the Zoological Society of Japan*, 91(1), 61–69.

Kuenzer, P. (1982). Undecided fights, behaviour induced colour change and social organization in the pencilfish *Nannostanus beckfordi* (Teleostei, Lebiasinidae). *Zeitschrift fur Tierpsychologie*, 58(2), 89–118.

Lewis, S. L. (1969). Physical factors influencing fish populations in pools of a trout stream. *Transactions of the American Fisheries Society*, 98(1), 14–19.

McIntyre, D. C., & Healy, L. M. (1978). Effects of telencephalon damage on intraspecies aggression and activity in rainbow trout (*Salmo gairdneri*) juveniles. *Behavioral and Neural Biology*, 25, 490–501.

McNicol, R. E., & Noakes, D. L. G. (1981). Territories and territorial defense in juvenile brook charr, *Salvelinus fontinalis* (Pisces: Salmonidae). *Canadian Journal of Zoology*, 59(1), 22–28.

Moyle, P. B. (1976). *Inland fishes of California*. Berkeley: University of California Press.

Newman, M. A. (1956). Social behaviour and interspecific competition in two trout species. *Physiological Zoology*, 29, 64–81.

Noakes, D. L. G., & Leatherland, J. F. (1977). Social dominance and interrenal cell activity in rainbow trout, *Salmo gairdneri* (Pisces, Salmonidae). *Environmental Biology and Fisheries*, 2(2), 131–136.

Rhijn, J. G., & Vodegel, R. (1980). Being honest about one's intentions. An evolutionary stable strategy for animal conflicts. *Journal of Theoretical Biology*, 85(4), 623–641.

Stringer, G. E., & Hoar, W. S. (1955). Aggressive behaviour in underyearling Kamloops trout. *Canadian Journal of Zoology*, 33, 148–160.

Wiley Driscoll, J., & Welanko, P. R. (1981). Dominance relationships in female *Herotilapia multispinosa* (Pisces: Cichlidae). *Animal Learning and Behavior*, 9(2), 164–168.

Yamagishi, H. (1962). Growth relations in some small experimental populations of rainbow trout fry, *Salmo gairdneri* Richardson, with special reference to social relations among individuals. *Japanese Journal of Ecology*, 12, 43–53.

Part V

SENSORY PLEASURE AND MOTIVATION

_____ chapter 10 _____

What Is Sensation?
"γνῶθι σαυτόν"

MICHEL CABANAC
Laval University, Québec

_____

SYNOPSIS AND COMMENTS
Neil V. Watson and Roderick Wong

At first sight you may find it curious that a chapter on "What is sensation?" is included in a volume that emphasizes motivated behavior. As you read beyond Cabanac's delightful philosophical and historical excursion into sensation, perception, and cognition and their relationships, you will encounter some of his original views on the affective aspects of sensation. Each organism is, in essence, the prisoner of its sensorium. Because attainment of the state of positive affect or pleasure is necessarily transduced via the sensory organs, a more precise model of the cognitive and motivational aspects of sensation is warranted. The ecological basis of motivated behaviors has been discussed in many of the earlier chapters in this volume, particularly in those on feeding, flavor neophobia, and maternal behavior. One of the implications of Cabanac's analysis is that any consideration of the ecological factors influencing motivated behaviors necessarily includes assumptions about the information content of the animal's environment, but, in fact, the sense filters this input. Consequently, information processing by cognitive adaptations of the sort urged by Cosmides and Tooby (this volume) should be concerned with the "filtered" environmental variables. The weighting given to these variables vis-à-vis pleasure achievement may constitute the proximate basis of motivated behavior. These weighting mechanisms are undoubtedly domain-specific devices subject to selection pressures themselves.

Cabanac's basic hypothesis is that any afferent fiber has the capacity to elicit a sensation. In contrast to the lists of many different sorts of sensations with different attributes categorized by traditional theories, Cabanac lumps various categories of sensations into a single class. This scheme suggests a fundamental unit of the functioning of the central nervous system. This approach relates sensation to the stimulus via physiology; from stimulus to action potential, and from action potential to sensation. If a sensation depends on the action potentials aroused by a stimulus, then the intensity of a sensation is related to the frequency of spikes arriving at neural centers. Perception consists of the summation of multiple simultaneous sensory inputs provoking a sensitivity that emerges into consciousness. It also involves a cognitive input from memory.

Cabanac proposes a model of sensation as four-dimensional space, ordered along the four continua: quality, intensity, affectivity, and duration. He regards quality as a nominal dimension in which elements appear as categories, and viewed intensity, affectivity, and duration as parametric, quantitative dimensions. Attributes can take place within each of the three dimensions of sensation. Although Cabanac did not consider this possibility, one may wonder if each four-dimensional position is representative of a unique cognitive adaptation. We raise this question because in order to understand the means by which an animal discerns pleasurable events, and thus wellbeing, it is necessary to develop an objective system for indexing the psychological dimensions of sensations.

Cabanac's four-dimensional model has the potential to integrate the role of sensory events, affect, motivation, and cognition in behavior, but in its present form, it may require further elaboration. Although quality is regarded as a nominal variate, Cabanac nevertheless orders quality along a continuous dimension in his model. It is unclear how one might discern where a particular type of sensation resides along this dimension. This model might be modified by dealing with sensations in terms of the ordinal dimensions of affective tone, amplitude, and duration. The quality of the sensation constitutes a dimension per se. Thus, within a dimension such as "sweet," each different quality of sweetness can be characterized in terms of degree, duration, and pleasantness. Although this modification of the model makes the practical aspects of the indexing of sensations quite complicated, it allows for the interaction of concurrent sensations. These interactions occupy interdimensional space. The simultaneous interaction of olfaction and gustation, which often provokes a qualitatively new sensation, provides a good example of this formulation. These interactive sensations might then be modeled as a sort of "psychological fractal" (e.g., Grilly, Earnshaw, & Jones, 1991).

According to Cabanac's formulation, a *sensitivity* is not a *sensation* unless it reaches consciousness. There are many instances in which the information never goes higher than the spinal cord, yet it can still direct behavior (e.g., the control of lordosis in the female rat by flank palpation). How does one measure consciousness in nonhumans? Do insects have any consciousness? If not, do they thereby have no sensation? There is the problem in ascertaining when consciousness begins and ends. An alternative formulation would be that a sensation occurs when the transduced environmental signal is presented to a biological information-processing adaptation, without regard to the conscious apprehension of the sensation.

Cabanac's definition rules out the use of *sensation* and *sensory* in the absence of a nervous substratum. Thus he would exclude these processes in organisms at the level of bacteria, where no such substratum has been described. In the absence of a substrate, and thus the absence of sensation, how does a paramecium manage to hunt? Pain has a nervous substrate; therefore, pain is a sensory event. One could also argue that although there may be a substrate for time sensation in the suprachiasmatic nucleus, it is cognitively impenetrable.

Cabanac believed that the intensity of sensation by the density of action potentials remains largely theoretical because there have not been sufficient advances in physiology to bridge the gap between stimuli and sensations. Recent developments on physiological signal-processing mechanisms, such as the existence of reafferent loops within the central nervous sytem and efferent innervation of the sensors, complicate the process. However, if one considers the mechanism as a preamplifier wherein afference copy acts as a gain control and efference modulation as a tone control, this problem may be resolved in principle. These variables may act as weighting factors added to the transduced signal and could be incorporated into the model, because these are the processed signals submitted to cognitive adaptations.

The part of Cabanac's essay that is of central significance for this volume is its discussion of the role of sensory pleasure on behavior. *Pleasure* is defined as the state of mind aroused by a pleasant cause, presumably from sensory stimulation. Pleasure and displeasure are part of a gradient of affectivity (Young, 1959). When the organism is in contact with incentives, the wisdom of the body leads it to seek pleasure and avoid displeasure. This results in behaviors that are beneficial to the organism's physiology (Cabanac, 1971). He links pleasure with usefulness and displeasure with harm or danger. This notion is supported by the results of his research demonstrating that the pleasure derived from a skin thermal stimulus can be predicted from knowledge of the core temperature. Other research from his laboratory shows that the same flavor can be described as pleasant when the subject is hungry, and unpleasant when the person is satiated.

In the preceding examples, the affective dimension depends directly on the usefulness of the stimulus to the subject. The seeking of pleasure and the avoidance of displeasure lead to behaviors with useful homeostatic consequences. This issue is elaborated in Schulze's chapter in this volume. Pleasure provides the motivation for eliciting behavior that optimizes physiological processes as well as serving a reward function. The emission of behavior adapted to biological goals is influenced by the affective dimension of the sensation aroused, and this occurs as soon as the relevant stimulus is discerned. Cabanac takes the unusual extra step of linking pleasure and displeasure to the well-being of the organism. Although there is a sound basis for this general principle, an exception can be noted in instances of "harmful pleasure" such as opiate addiction.

There is no doubt that Cabanac's chapter will generate much interest and discussion. Following Duncker's (1940–1941) suggestion that a search for the ultimate motives of behavior cannot disregard pleasure, the present chapter makes the case that affective processes are motivational in nature. The distinction between hedonists for whom pleasure is the fundamental motive and the "hormists" for whom pleasure is the outcome is an extremely important one. The latter notion articulates well with ideas about evolution that regard striving (to maximally reproduce) as a goal in itself (e.g., Wilson, 1975).

References

Grilly, A. J., Earnshaw, R. A., & Jones, H. (Eds.). (1991). *Fractals and chaos.* New York: Springer-Verlag.

Wilson, E. O. (1975). *Sociobiology: The new synthesis.* Cambridge, MA: Belknap Press of Harvard University Press.

INTRODUCTION

"The importance of clearly defining (and redefining) terms that describe behavioral processes as our knowledge of the underlying physiological mechanisms advances has repeatedly been emphasized" (White, 1989, p. 181). This statement applied recently to reward and reinforcement (White, 1989) and to physiological psychology (Milner & White, 1987) seems applicable to sensation.

Sensation has always been a matter of interest to philosophers. In the fourth century B.C., Plato held that sensation and opinion are the main screens masking truth, but the opposite view tended to dominate both before and after him. A century earlier, Heraclitos taught that knowledge comes to man "through the door of the senses," and Protagoras that the entire psychic life consists only of sensations. Aristotle, Plato's pupil, returned to the sophists' view that sensation is the gate of the soul. This notion can be traced through history to the present. Hobbes (1651/1904, p. 1) wrote: "There is no conception in man's mind which hath not at first, totally or in parts, been begotten upon the organs of senses." Condillac (1754), taking the theoretical example of an inert statue, showed that the progressive attribution of the senses would allow the development of a complete mind in the statue. Thus, he made it clear that the mind must use the senses to know and understand the world, and that the senses are necessary and sufficient to develop a mind. This notion was also accepted by Kant (1781), for whom, however, the senses were one of the two sources of human knowledge, the other one being understanding. "Sensationalism is the theory that all knowledge originates in sensations; that all cognitions even reflective ideas and . . . intuition can be traced back to elementary sensations" (Titchener, 1909, p. 23).

"All science, whatever the realm of application, has a common origin: the immediate experience of the observing person of the scientist himself" (Spence, 1948, p. 68). The scientific process then proceeds in the sharing of evidence by two or more persons. Both processes take the sensory channels. The study of this obligatory channel is the origin of experimental psychology (Geldard, 1972).

The concept of the senses as portals of the mind has therefore turned to a commonplace statement among modern psychologists (Marks, 1974). However, Plato's image of sensation as a screen masking truth can be recognized as arising again from two problems: the difference between sensation and perception and the complexity of attributes.

Sensation and Perception

Psychologists of the 18th century started to distinguish sensation from perception. For Reid (1785) a sensation occurs when an organ of sense is stimulated, and perception depends upon sensation but also includes a conception of the object perceived and an immediate and irresistible conviction of the object's actual existence. These definitions are still accepted today: Levine and Shefner (1981, p. 1) clearly define *sensation* as "the process of detecting a stimulus (or some aspect of it) in the environment," and *perception* as "the way in which we interpret the information gathered (and processed) by the senses. . . . In a word, we sense the presence of a stimulus, but we perceive what it is."

However, Schiffman (1982) considers as somewhat obsolete the differentiation between sensation and perception yet brings a useful light to it: Sensation is equated to physiology, and perception to psychology. This explains how two attitudes have developed until now.

For the first group, a stimulus associated with a context acquires a meaning (Titchener, 1909) and, to make perception still more complex, an adequate behavioral response to a stimulus carries a meaning and may modify perception (Tolman, 1918). The extreme of that tendency is gestalt perception, which, by definition, incorporates sensation and content into a global experience (Koffka, 1935). Without going to such extremes, many psychologists think that the distinction between sensory discrimination and perceptual discrimination is theoretical but not factual, because it is not possible to dissociate the two elements (Corso, 1967; Pradines, 1928) and because bare sensation does not exist but rather is always included in complex perception (Merleau Ponty, 1945).

An explanation of this refusal to recognize sensation as a real entity might be found in the stimuli used to arouse perception. The psychologists concerned with perception refer almost exclusively to the auditory and visual perceptions (Banks, 1991). Hearing and sight are the main channels of communication; stimuli reaching the mind via these gates are therefore the most prone to bear a context-related message. Other sensory inputs (e.g., from the skin) are less complex and more amenable to be described as sensations.

The second attitude accepts the theoretical separation of sensation from perception. Huxley (1954), in his experiment with mescaline, reported that the drug modified his perception but that his sensations remained intact. Indeed, some psychologists (Geldard, 1972; Levine & Shefner, 1981; Marks, 1974) have no problem with the concept of sensation, perhaps because the stimuli they use—light, sound, temperature, pressure, and chemical stimuli—are only slightly context related or not related at all. Yet the refusal to recognize sensation as an entity, simpler and thus different from perception, pinpoints some weakness in the definition of both sensation and perception and justifies this chapter. We shall return briefly to this point after having examined the problem of attributes. "A great deal of confusion would be avoided if psychologists at large recognized the fact that the sensation of experimental psychology is a simple, meaningless (or rather nonmeaningful) process definable only by an enumeration of its attributes" (Titchener, 1909, p. 214).

Attributes

"An attribute of sensation . . . is any aspect or moment or dimension of sensation which fulfills the two conditions of inseparability and independent variability" (Titchener, 1908, p. 8). It follows from this definition that the attributes are always given when a sensation is given, and that the nullifying of any attribute annihilates the sensation.

Wundt (1874) described sensation initially with two attributes: *quality* and *intensity*. He added *affectivity* in 1893 in the 4th edition of *Physiologische Psychologie*, but then he withdrew it and returned to two attributes in 1896 (ref. in Titchener, 1908, p. 345). Two attributes of sensation were added by Külpe (1893). To quality and intensity attributes of all five senses he added *duration* for the five senses and *extension* for vision and touch. Titchener (1908) added *clearness* to the list of attributes. Pleasure and pain were considered as plain sensations by J. Mill (1869), but affectivity was considered as an attribute of sensation by Ziehen (1924). On the other hand Külpe denied that pleasure–displeasure can be an attribute of sensation because it has attributes of its own (quality, intensity, duration) and because a sensation can exist without being pleasant nor unpleasant, which contradicts the definition of attributes. For Yokoyama (1921), the hedonic tone is phenomenally distinct from the usually accepted sensory qualities. Beebe-Center (1932) considered affectivity as an attribute but not a necessary attribute of sensation.

As is the case with pleasure, the other attributes also possess attributes of their own: Vision has light and color (color has three attributes of its own: hue, brightness, and saturation); audition has pitch and volumeness as proposed by Titchener (1908). The list of attributes therefore tends to branch on and on. This complexity, however, is not the main problem raised by the attributes of sensation. Boring (1942) listed four difficulties that contradict the theory of attributes:

1. It is not clear that vision has the attribute of intensity.
2. It is not possible to find an independent variability between visual brightness and visual intensity.
3. Some sensations are too complex to fit within the rigid limit of the attributes.
4. The question remains as to whether the attributes are not really separable.

Nowadays the psychophysicists are less concerned with the attributes of the sensations, because they have developed methods of multidimensional scaling in which they devise a single psychological unit that can serve to measure simultaneously several or all of the attributes (Ennis & Mullen, 1986). This bypasses rather than suppresses the complexity of the attribute problems. One way to obtain such a result is to ask a subject how similar are two stimuli. Thus, as underscored by Marks (1974, p. 205), "multidimensional scaling is concerned with *psychological* relations, the relations of various sensory (psychological) attributes or dimensions to each other" (emphasis in original).

In using the word *attributes* we have met a first difficulty. The list of at-

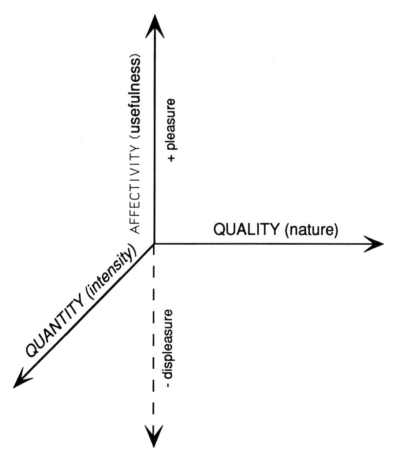

FIGURE 10.1. Theoretical model of sensation as a multidimensional experience in response to a stimulus. The fourth dimension, duration, cannot be represented graphically. Quality describes the nature of the stimulus, a nonparametric dimension. Quantity describes the intensity of the stimulus. Affectivity, positive (pleasure), negative (displeasure), or nil (indifference) describes the usefulness of the stimulus. Pleasure can be modified by the subject's internal state or past history.

tributes has grown longer and is heterogeneous. There is need for clarification and simplification.

A Simpler Descriptive Model of Sensation

Rather than describing sensation as having attributes it seems more logical to me, from both the points of view of objective criteria and of sheer introspective evidence, to describe sensation in a mathematical way. Sensation can be described as a multidimensional space. Four dimensions define this space; quality, intensity, affectivity, and duration. Quality is a nominal dimension where elements appear as categories. Intensity, affectivity, and duration are parametric, quantitative dimensions. Attributes can take place within each of the first three dimensions of sensation represented by the X, Y, and Z axes of Figure 10.1.

QUALITY OF SENSATION

It is neither obvious nor simple to explore the X axis of Figure 10.1 and to list sensations. According to Aristotle animals and humans possess five senses (Table 10.1). This concept of sensation as originating only from the five senses has endured more than two millennia without much questioning. The philosophers of the 18th century and the psychologists of the 19th have not added to the short list of the five senses, and modern textbooks on sensation study the five senses almost exclusively. Sensation is not limited to the five senses, however, and two trends have appeared in modern times.

The first trend can be considered as physiological. It consists in studying organs, the tongue, the skin, the inner ear, and so on, rather than sensations. For example, Levy-Valensi (1933) followed this trend in a treaty of physiology. Many psychologists adopt the same point of view (Geldard, 1972). Having described sensory organs, the physiologists more or less deliberately tend to incorporate them as sources of sensation. Indeed, because they are not concerned with mental experience, the physiologists have identified and studied electrically and functionally numerous afferent pathways without making a clear difference between an afferent path and sensation. Thus the list of sensations of Table 10.2, most commonly listed in modern textbooks (e.g., Wolfe, 1988), tends to increase beyond the five senses.

The other trend is the perceptual way to look at sensation with less concern for the sensory organs. This trend qualifies as psychological because it starts with an introspective step. Pain, on top of this approach, can be elicited from free nerve endings in all parts of the body without a clearly identified receptor organ. Time

TABLE 10.1. Aristotle's Five Senses

Eye	Ear	Nose	Tongue	Skin

TABLE 10.2. Beyond the Five Senses

Sensation	Sensor, organ
Vision	retina, eye
Audition	cochlea, inner ear
Gustation	gustatory buds, tongue
Olfaction	olfactory neurons, C fibers, nasal mucosa
Thermal	nerve free endings, derm
Tactile	nerve endings, hair and Paccini's Meisner's and Krause's corpuscles, derm
Spatial	labyrinth, inner ear; muscle spindles, muscles; Golgi endings, tendons
Algic	free ending C fibers, everywhere

After Wolfe (1988).

(Boring, 1942; Schiffman, 1982), orientation (Schiffman 1982), kinesthesia (Corso, 1967; Geldard, 1972; Ludel, 1978; Schiffman, 1982), perception of space (Schiffman, 1982), and organic sensation (visceral, hunger, third; Geldard, 1972) have thus been proposed as sensations in addition to the five senses. However, the common feature of these perceptions is precisely to be vague and to pertain to perception as defined earlier rather than to sensation *sensu stricto*.

It is possible to reconcile both trends by following the methods of physiology as well as introspection as advocated by Titchener (1909) and Strauss (1963). This process must take a semantic first step to differentiate sensation from sensitivity.

In the following discussion we shall call *sensitivity* the capacity of an afferent neuron to detect a physical or chemical change occurring at its endings and to transmit this information to the nervous centers. The sensor part of the neuron can sometimes be identified histologically with a specific organ, sometimes as a free nerve ending, and sometimes histologically unidentified. The afferent pathway can be constituted by only one neuron but most of the time contains a chain of neurons. *Sensation* can be defined neither in terms of chemistry or physics nor in terms of neuron function, but as a cognition. The brain possesses properties that can no more be explained by its neuronal constituents than life can be explained by the atomic or molecular properties of the constituents of the living cell (Bunge, 1989). Consciousness is one such property and sensation can be defined as the emergence of sensitivity into consciousness (Figure 10.2).

This definition rules out the use of *sensation* and *sensory* in the absence of a nervous substratum such as in bacteria (Miller, Mekalanos, & Falkow, 1989) or in the immunology system (Deschaux, 1988), and when no such substratum has been described as is the case with time. On the other hand, it conforms with the definitions found both in the Webster and the Oxford English dictionaries. Both dictionaries define sensation as the mental process due to stimulation of a sense organ. The next problem will then be reduced to identifying the sensor organs.

CONSCIOUSNES

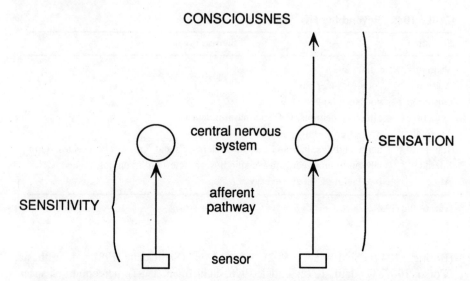

FIGURE 10.2.   Theoretical representation of the elements of sensation. Sensitivity is the set of elements composed of a specialized sensory organ, messages to the central nervous system, and afferent pathway. If the message reaches consciousness, an emerging property of the central nervous system, then sensitivity becomes sensation.

An important inference to be drawn from this definition is that sensation is not limited to the five senses. We know, from clinical evidence, that pain can be felt from any locus in the body with a small number of exceptions: skin on the center of the cheek and on the olecranon, and the nervous tissue of the brain. Pain is not the sole sensation aroused from inside the body. Mere introspection tells me that if I close my attention to the outside world and concentrate on my own body, I can feel slight visceral sensation from my limbs, trunk, chest, neck, and head. During disease, pains can be aroused in any part of the body, but in addition during health I can also feel vague and obscure messages from my viscera, heartbeat, throbbing, movements in the abdomen, and of course, hunger pangs and need to urinate or defecate. Therefore, it may be stated as a new postulate that any of the various afferent pathways discovered by the physiologists is potentially a source of sensation.

This hypothesis regarding the origin of sensations calls for four remarks:

1. The sensory window open to the outside world is limited to less than the short list of Table 10.2. Undoubtedly, it would be useful to be able to detect and sense more than these variables. For example, we could make use of a sensitivity for speed rather than acceleration (included in Wolfe's spatial sensation), to perceive ionizing radiations, to be able to analyze more completely the air and the

TABLE 10.3. List of the Nervous Sensors within the Organism

Sensor	Location	Sensed variable
Mechanoreceptors	Big arteries sino-aortic	blood pressure
	cardiac	cardiac repletion
	Pulmonary	(blood volume)
		pulmonary tension, volume
	Venous	venous volume
	Digestive tract	digestive tube repletion
	Muscular	muscle length
	Tendinous and articular	tension
Chemoreceptors	Big arteries: glomus,	blood PaO_2
	aorta, carotid art.	
	Digestive tract	content of digestive tract
	Medulla	blood $PaCO_2$, pH
	Hypothalamus	blood hormones
	Liver	portal glucose
Thermoreceptors	Hypothalamus	local temperature
	Spinal cord	local temperature
	Digestive tract	local temperature
Osmoreceptors	Hypothalamus	osmotic pressure
	Liver	osmotic pressure

water in our environment and foods, and finally to sense time, if time exists. Yet the existing spectrum of sensitivities and sensations has proven efficacious enough to ensure the survival of the species up to now, but our understanding of the universe is not facilitated by the limited information sensed.

2. In addition to information on the outside world, the brain also receives a vast amount of information about the physiological state of the milieu interieur. Table 10.3 lists the nervous sensors identified so far that sense physical and chemical variables from within the body. Most of these afferent pathways are limited to a bundle of only a few neurons, often C fibers. The contrast between this meager input and the large avenues of the classical senses may explain how the latter have dominated psychology. A whole vagus nerve collecting mechanical, chemical, thermal, and pain information from all the viscera contains no more than 40 000 afferent fibers, whereas olfactory sensation collects information from over a hundred million fibers, vision from 1.2 million fibers in the optic nerve. One cochlea alone contains 30 000 afferent myelinated fibers. In addition a qualitative step that would increase the relative importance of the five senses may exist between large, fast, and frequent spikes in A fibers and small, slow, and infrequent spikes in C fibers. It is not surprising, therefore, that the sensations in our viscera are only episodic and imprecise, as compared to the five senses, and have long been disregarded as sensations.

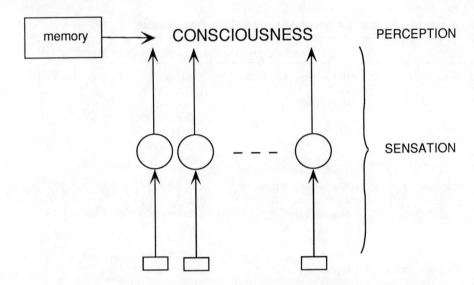

FIGURE 10.3.   Consciousness is not limited to sensation. Perception above sensation incorporates the sensory messages with information from other sensory modalities and also with information stored in memory.

3. The quality of a sensation is determined by anatomy, but the pattern of action potentials within an afferent pathway might also account for this dimension.

4. The identification of a sensation is likely to depend on the existence of a semantic support as a conceptual medium. The short list of tastes—sweet, salt, bitter, and sour—has been extended recently by adding one sensation: umami (Yamaguchi, 1987). When no word is available to describe a sensation, probably we tend to ignore this sensation.

Figure 10.2, which sketches the previous definition of sensation as a sensitivity which emerges into consciousness, can be completed now to incorporate perception by adding multiple simultaneous sensory inputs and, overall, a cognitive input from memory (Figure 10.3).

INTENSITY OF SENSATION

The second advantage of defining *sensation* as the emergence of a sensitivity into consciousness is to relate sensation to the stimulus in two steps, via physiology: from stimulus to action potential, and from action potential to sensation. If a sensation depends on the action potentials aroused by a stimulus, then the intensity of sensation is related to the frequency of spikes arriving at the centers (Adrian, 1928). In turn, the total number of spikes depends on the individual frequency in each afferent fiber and on the spatial summation in the group of activated afferent fibers.

The rate of discharge of many peripheral sensors is time dependent, or, to use the physiological terminology, they *adapt quickly*. In other words, the firing frequency of the peripheral senses is a derivative of the time:

$$\text{Firing rate} = \delta\text{stimulus}/\delta\text{time}$$

This property of the sensor is transferred to sensation. Thus, the sensory modalities, such as olfaction, that are equipped with such a quick adaptation become rate sensitive. This amplifies the sensation of directional gradients and permits anticipating regulatory responses.

The previous physiological definition of intensity solves some problems aroused in sensory modalities in which the borderline between quality and intensity is not easily defined on psychological grounds only, for example, the controversy about the intensity of white, grey, and black (Boring, 1942, p. 132). There are cases in which ambiguities have developed, probably in relation with inadequate semantics. The best-known case is that of Newton (1974), who equated brightness and intensity until Helmoltz (1860) straightened the case. Yet the explanation of the intensity of sensation by the density of action potentials remains largely theoretical, because physiology has not accumulated enough knowledge to bridge the gaps between stimuli and sensations. On the contrary, new knowledge tends to make the understanding of the magnitude of sensation more difficult. Modern physiology has confirmed the existence of reafferent loops within the central nervous system, and of efferent innervation of some sensors.

The discipline of *psychophysics*, a word coined by Fechner (1860), is devoted to the quantitative measurement of the relations between stimuli and sensations. Fechner measured the sensations of the senses (*sinnliche Empfindungen*) using sensation with the usual meanings of this word. He was mainly interested in matching sensation with the actual intensity of the physical stimuli presented to the subjects. Psychophysics is interested in measuring the threshold and the magnitude of a sensation in response to a stimulus. To treat psychophysics in one chapter would be out of place, and interested readers should satisfy their curiosity in the reading of specialized textbooks (Atkinson, Herrnstein, Lindzey, & Luce, 1988; Galanter, 1962; Manning & Rosenstock, 1968; Marks, 1974; Moskowitz, 1974; Stevens, 1975) and reviews on the senses, olfaction (Cain, 1988), taste (Bartoshuk, 1988), and audition (Green, 1988).

AFFECTIVITY OF SENSATION

Pleasure is the state of mind aroused by a pleasant cause. Titchener (1908) took great efforts to refute the hypothesis that pleasure is a peripheral sensation. This refutation entails that pleasure may reside in any kind of mental experience. As stated by Nafe (1924, p. 540): "All sensory modalities, with the possible exception of pain, involve both pleasant and unpleasant qualities." Duncker (1940–1941) listed four types of causes of pleasure: (a) sensory enjoyment (or displeasure)—enjoying a stimulus or the consequences of behavior; (b) aesthetic enjoyment—pursuing greater understanding; (c) desire (for a steak, a book, a love, etc.), not a reaction to but the fulfillment of a need; and (d) pleasure in achievement, or victory; the dynamic joy of succeeding. Nafe's statement, as well as Duncker's first category, justifies the description of sensation as being tridimensional (see Figure 10.1).

The adjective *pleasant* qualifies a cause that arouses pleasure. *Pleasantness* describes the quality of a pleasant cause. It is possible to share with others the pleasantness of a cause, but we are never sure that they share the pleasure aroused. The antonyms of *pleasure, pleasant,* and *pleasantness* are *displeasure, unpleasant,* and *unpleasantness. Pleasure* and *displeasure* merge into *indifference,* then into one another, along an affective gradient (Young, 1959) from extremely negative (distress) to extremely positive (delight). Affective and affectivity apply to the realm of pleasure and displeasure. Following Beebe-Center (1932), *hedonic* has tended to replace *affective* in the literature, but these adjectives are synonymous and, in my opinion, *affective* is better suited because the Greek root *hedone* means pleasure only. There is no place for displeasure under the word *hedonic,* yet the avoidance of displeasure is pleasurable and is therefore similar to the seeking of pleasure.

The *affective process* was defined by Wundt (1902) and he proposed three dimensions to the affective process: pleasantness–unpleasantness, excitement–inhibition, and tension–relaxation. However, Titchener (1908) showed that judgements of pleasantness and unpleasantness are direct, easy, and natural. Young (1959) defines the affective process from its three attributes: sign because the experience can provide pleasure or displeasure, intensity, and duration. Yet these attributes are not necessary when we define *sensation* itself as tridimensional (plus duration).

Sensory Pleasure and Behavior

In the commerce of a subject with incentives, it has been shown experimentally that the wisdom of the body leads the organism to seek pleasure and avoid displeasure and thus achieve behaviors that are beneficial to the subject's physiology (Cabanac, 1971). Relations exist between pleasure and usefulness, and between displeasure and harm or danger. For example, when subjects are invited to report verbally, the pleasure aroused by a skin thermal stimulus can be predicted knowing deep body temperature (Attia, 1984; Cabanac, Massonnet, & Belaiche, 1972). A hypothermic subject will report pleasure when stimulated with moderate heat, and displeasure with cold. The opposite takes place in a hyperthermic subject. Pleasure is actually observable only in transient states, when the stimulus helps the subject to return to normothermia. As soon as the subject returns to normothermia, all stimuli lose their strong pleasure component and tend to become indifferent.

Sensory pleasure and displeasure thus appear especially suited to being good guides for thermoregulatory behavior.

The case of pleasure aroused by eating shows an identical pattern. A given alimentary flavor is described as pleasant during hunger and becomes unpleasant or indifferent during satiety. Measurement of human ingestive behavior confirms the previously mentioned relationship of behavior with pleasure. It has been repeatedly demonstrated in the case of food intake (Fantino, 1984) that human subjects tend to consume foods that they report to be pleasant and to avoid those that they report to be unpleasant. Pleasure also shows a quantitative influence: The amount of pleasurable food eaten is a function of alimentary restrictions and increases after dieting. The result is that pleasure scales can be used to judge the acceptability of food.

Thus, in the cases of temperature and taste, the affective dimension of sensation depends directly on the usefulness of the stimulus to the subject. This was already noticed by Aristotle (quoted by Pfaffmann, 1982). The word *alliesthesia* (Cabanac, 1971) was coined to describe the fact that in response to a given stimulus, a sensation is not necessarily constant but can move on the Z axis of Figure 10.1. The affective dimension of sensation is contingent. Alliesthesia underlines the importance of this contingency in relation to behavior: A given stimulus will arouse either pleasure or displeasure according to the internal state of the stimulated subject. The seeking of pleasure and the avoidance of displeasure lead to behaviors with useful homeostatic consequences. The behavior of subjects instructed to seek their most pleasurable skin temperature could be described and predicted from their body temperatures and the equations describing their behavior were practically the same as those describing autonomic responses such as shivering and sweating (Attia & Engel, 1981; Bleichert, Behling, Scaiperi, & Scaiperi, 1973; Cabanac et al., 1972; Marks & Gonzalez, 1974;

It is possible from verbal reports to dissociate pleasure from behavior and to show, thus, that the seeking of sensory pleasure and the avoidance of sensory displeasure lead to behaviors with beneficial homeostatic consequences. Pleasure therefore indicates a useful stimulus and simultaneously motivates the subject to approach the stimulus. Pleasure serves both to reward behavior and to provide the motivation for eliciting behavior that optimizes physiological processes. One great advantage of this mechanism is that it does not take rationality or a high level of cognition to produce a behavior adapted to biological goals. As soon as a stimulus is discriminated, the affective dimension of the sensation aroused tells the subject, animal or human alike, that the stimulus should be sought, avoided, or ignored.

Experimental evidence in the narrow field of sensory pleasure thus confirms the Epicurean general principle, which states that pleasure and displeasure are linked to the well-being of the organism (Lehman, 1914) and according to which: "when it helps and encourages (the vital movement) it is called pleasure, satisfaction, well-being, which is nothing real but a movement in the heart" (Hobbes, 1772/1971, p. 65).

Pleasure as Seen by Philosophers and Psychologists

The relation of pleasure to behavior was regarded as obvious by the Greek philosophers Aristotle (284–322 B.C.) and Epicurus (241–170 B.C.; see Conche, 1977): "Life and pleasure, as we can see now, are not separable; for without behavior there is no pleasure, and pleasure improves behavior" (Aristotle).

After the Greeks, many philosophers and thinkers, such as St. Augustine (354–430), Montaigne (1533–1592), Gassendi (1592–1655; see Bloch, 1971), or Sulzer (1751), recognized in the affective experience a great role, if not the essential role, as a motivation. Bentham (1742–1832, see Bowring, 1838/1962) based his "greatest happiness principle" on pleasure, "the spring of action." Kant (1788/1983) and J. S. Mill (1863/1951) were more concise but equally clear on this point. For Freud (1920/1951) the "pleasure principle" determines the aim of life. An important analysis of the role of the affective process in behavior has been carried out by Duncker (1940–1941, p. 391):

> A search for the ultimate motives of human conduct cannot disregard pleasure which many eminent minds have considered to be the fundamental motive, or at least an important one. Others, to be sure, have held that pleasure is the outcome rather than the motive or goal of human striving. ... There cannot be the slightest doubt that many human strivings bear some kind of reference to pleasure, and likewise that many pleasures bear some reference to striving.

It is therefore generally assumed that a motivated behavior is oriented by the incentives received by the subjects (Killeen, 1962; Nutin, 1975; Toates, 1968). "From every point of view the affective processes must be regarded as motivational in nature" (Young, 1959, p. 117). Yet pleasure has never been popular in history for moral reasons. In addition the excesses of psychoanalysis have led to the rejection of all mentalistic explanations of behavior. As a result, pleasure is shunned by most recent textbooks of psychology and even of philosophy, a drawback of behaviorism in modern literature. According to the part they attribute to pleasure, Duncker (1940–1941) has sorted philosophers into two schools: *hedonists*, for whom pleasure is the fundamental motive, as opposed to *hormists*, for whom pleasure is the outcome. *Hormism* was coined from McDougall's (1923) *hormic force* (a force that urges us to strive). One can easily recognize in hedonism and hormism the ancient opposition of the philosophers of the Garden, the Epicurists, and those of the Portico, the Stoicists, or, with Plé (1982), the morals of pleasure, as opposed to the morals of duty. This opposition has lasted through the centuries. It is interesting to notice in this duality of looking at pleasure, an internal fracture within most societies, families of thought, and churches. Eventually, duty always wins its struggle against pleasure. One good reason for the rejection of pleasure from the realm of science was the lack of experimental evidence and the fact that the philosophers' conclusions were based on their own introspection only. Rejection of hedonism may be based on earlier approaches to these phenomena but, "as new techniques are developed, our ideas often have to be revised to encompass the new informations obtained" (Teitelbaum, 1964 p. 464). Analyzing the cause for the dominant rejection of pleasure is out of place here. Interested readers will find it together with a historical review of epicurism in Plé (1982). Additional documentation on the relation of pleasure to behavior will be found in Toates (1986) and in Lea, Tarpy, and Webley (1987).

CONCLUSIONS

Once one accepts the *cogito ergo sum*, the whole of scientific knowledge bears on two postulates: (1) a world exists around me, and (b) I can exchange evidence with others.

Both of these postulates need the channel of sensation. Therefore, our knowledge of the world, including ourselves, is filtered twice—once by the narrow chemicophysical window of the senses, and once by the biological and cultural format of our brains. The way we see sensation might have, therefore, some repercussion on the way we think.

The first hypothesis proposed here, according to which any afferent fiber is susceptible to arousing a sensation, presents several advantages. First, the theory is simple. Then all the various categories of sensations are lumped into one single class, whereas classical categorization listed many different sorts of sensations with different attributes. Thus is suggested a fundamental unity of the sensory input to the central nervous system.

The second hypothesis presented here regarding the structure of sensation can be examined from the points of view of both phylogeny and ontogeny. This chapter was devoted to human sensation, but we may step back a little in phylogeny and try to guess about the origin of sensation. Medicus (1987) has reflected on the process from a behavioral point of view. Sensation emerged from a purely reflective behavior. A Darwinian approach tells us that sensory messages became conscious when this emergence proved useful to the organisms that first acquired it. To be useful, sensations needed to describe the quality, the intensity, and above all the usefulness of environmental stimuli; therefore, it is likely that sensation was immediately multidimensional, as defined earlier. Thus, sensation gave decisional advantages to the first animals that possessed it, by freeing them from the need for an infinitely complex hardware reflex network in their nervous systems.

Finally, if, as we saw in the introduction, sensation as the gate to the soul is commonplace for psychologists and philosophers, it remains that the structure of sensation has an important consequence. If sensation is the phylogenic and ontogenic origin of the conscious experience, then any conscious event is likely to bear fundamentally the same structure. Indeed, introspection tells me that this is the case, and that any conscious feeling has quality, intensity, affectivity, and duration.

REFERENCES

Adrian, E. D. (1928). *The basis of sensation.* London: Christophers.

Atkinson R. C., Herrnstein, R. J., Lindzey, G., & Luce, R. D. (Eds.). (1988). *Stevens' handbook of experimental psychology: Vol I. Perception and motivation* (2nd ed.). New York: Wiley.

Attia, M. (1984). Thermal pleasantness and temperature regulation in man. *Neuroscience and Biobehavioral Reviews, 8,* 335–343.

Attia, M., & Engel, P. (1981). Thermal alliesthesial response in man is independent of skin location stimulated. *Physiology and Behavior, 27,* 439–444.

Banks, W. P. (1991). Perception. *Annual Reviews of Psychology, 42,* 305–331.

Bartoshuk, L. M. (1988). Taste, In R. C. Atkinson, R. J. Herrnstein, G. Lindzey, & R. D. Luce (Eds.), *Stevens' handbook of experimental psychology: Vol. I. Perception and motivation* (2nd ed.). New York: Wiley.

Beebe-Center, J. G. (1932). *The psychology of pleasantness and unpleasantness.* Princeton NJ: Van Nostrand.

Bleichert, A., Behling, K., Scarperi, M., & Scarperi, S. (1973). Thermoregulatory behavior of man during rest and exercise. *Pflügers Archiv, 338,* 303–312.

Bloch, O. R. (1971). *La philosophie de Gassendi.* La Haye: Martinus Nijhoff.

Boring, E. G. (1942). *Sensation and perception in the history of experimental psychology.* New York: Appleton Century Crofts.

Bowring, J. (1962). *The works of Jeremy Bentham published under the superintendance of his executor (1838–1843).* New York: Russell & Russell. (Original work published 1838)

Bunge, M. (1989). From neuron to mind. *NIPS, 4,* 206–209.

Cabanac, M. (1971). Physiological role of pleasure. *Science, 173,* 1103–1107.

Cabanac, M., Massonnet, B., & Belaiche, R. (1972). Preferred skin temperature as a function of internal and mean skin temperature. *Journal of Applied Physiology 33,* 699–703.

Cain, W. S. (1988). Olfaction. In R. C. Atkinson, R. J. Herrnstein, G. Lindzey, & R. D. Luce (Eds.), *Stevens' handbook of experimental psychology: Vol I. Perception and motivation* (2nd ed.). New York: Wiley.

Conche, M. (1977). *Epicure: Lettres et maximes.* Villers sur Mer: Editions de Mégare.

Condillac, E. Bonnot de. (1754). *Traité des sensations.* Paris: Arthème Fayard.

Corso, J. F. (1967). *The experimental psychology of sensory behavior.* New York: Holt, Rinehart and Winston.

Deschaux, P. (1988). Neuroimmunologie: Le système immunitaire est-il un organe sensoriel? *Archives Internationales de Physiologie et de Biochimie, 96,* A78–A89.

Duncker, K. (1940–1941). On pleasure, emotion, and striving. *Philosophical and Phenomenological Research, 1,* 391–430.

Ennis, D. M., & Mullen, K. (1986). Theoretical aspects of sensory discrimination. *Chemical Senses, 11,* 513–522.

Fantino, M. (1984). Role of sensory input in the control of food intake. *Journal of the Autonomic Nervous System, 10,* 347–326.

Fechner, G. T. (1966). *Elemente der Psychophysik* (H. E. Adler, Trans.; D. H. Howes & E. G. Boring, Eds.). New York: Holt, Rinehart and Winston. (Original work published 1860)

Foucault, M. (1901). *La psychophysique.* Paris: Félix Alcan.

Freud, S. (1951). *Beyond the pleasure principle.* In *Essais de psychanalyse* (S. Jankelevitch, Trans.). Paris: Payot. (Original work published 1920)

Galanter, E. (1962). Contemporary psychophysics. In R. Brown, E. Galanter, E. H. Hess, & G. Mandler (Eds.), *New directions in psychology* (pp. 87–156). New York: Holt, Rinehart and Winston.

Geldard, F. A. (1963). *Fundamental of psychology* (2nd printing). New York, London: Wiley.

Geldard, F. A. (1972). *The human senses* (2nd ed.). New York: Wiley.

Green, D. M. (1988). Psychophysics and perception. In R. C. Atkinson, R. J. Herrnstein, G. Lindzey, & R. D. Luce (Eds.), *Stevens' handbook of experimental psychology: Vol 1. Perception and motivation* (2nd ed., pp. 327–376). New York: Wiley.

Helmoltz, H. L. F. von. (1962). *Physiological optics* (3rd ed.). P. C. Southall (Ed. and Trans.) New York: Dover. (Original work published 1866)

Hobbes, T. (1971). *Human nature, or the fundamental elements of policy,* Baron d'Holbach (Trans.). Paris: J. Vrin. (Original work published 1772)

Hobbes, T. (1904). *Leviathan.* Cambridge, UK: Cambridge University Press. (Original work published 1651)

Huxley, A. (1954). *Les portes de la perception.* Paris: Éditions Pygmalion.

Kant, I. (1983). *Kritik der praktischen Vernunft, Part I,* F. Picavet, Trans. (1983), Paris: Presses Universitaires de France. (Original work published 1788)

Killeen, P. R. (1962). Incentive theory. In D. J. Bernstein (Ed.), *Nebraska Symposium on Motivation, 1981. Response structure and organization.* Lincoln: University of Nebraska Press.

Koffka, K. (1935). *Principles of Gestalt psychology.* New York: Harcourt, Brace & Co.

Külpe, O. (1893). *Grundriss der Psychologie.* Leipzig: W. Engelmann

Lea, S. E. G., Tarpy, R. M., & Webley, P. (1987). *The individual in the economy.* Cambridge, UK: Cambridge University Press.

Lehman, A. (1914). *Die Hauptgesetze des menschlichen.* Leipzig: Gefühlslebens, D. R. Reisland.

Levine, M. W., & Shefner, J. M. (1981). *Fundamentals of sensation and perception.* Reading, MA: Addison-Wesley.

Levy-Valensi, J. (1933). Sensibilité et motricité In *Traité de Physiologie normale et pathologique.* Paris: Masson.

Ludel, J. (1978). *Introduction to sensory processes.* San Francisco: W. H. Freeman.

Manning, S. A., & Rosenstock, E. H. (1968). *Classical psychophysics and scaling.* New York: McGraw-Hill.

Marks, L. E. (1974). *Sensory processes, the new psychophysics.* New York: Academic Press.

Marks, L. E., & Gonzalez, R. R. (1974). Skin temperature modifies the pleasantness of thermal stimuli. *Nature, 244,* 473–475.

McDougall, W. (1923). *Outline of psychology.* New York: Scribner's.

Medicus, G. (1987). Toward an etho-psychology: A phylogenetic tree of behavioral capabilities proposed as a common basis for communication between current theories in psychology and psychiatry. *Ethology and Sociobiology, 8,* 131S–150S.

Merleau-Ponty, M. (1945). *Phénoménologie de la perception.* Paris: Gallimard.

Mill, J. S. (1951) Utilarianism. In *Utilitarianism, Liberty, and Representative Government.* New York: Dutton & Co. (Original work published 1863)

Mill, J. (1967). *Analysis of the phenomena of the human mind.* Ed. with additional notes of J. S. Mill. New York: Kelley. (Original work published 1869)

Miller, J. F., Mekalanos, J. J., & Falkow, S. (1989). Coordinate regulation and sensory transduction in the control of bacterial virulence. *Science, 243,* 916–922.

Milner, P. M., & White, N. M. (1987). What is physiological psychology? *Psychobiology 15,* 2–6.

Moskowitz, H. R. (1974). *Sensation and measurement.* Dordrecht: D. Reidel

Nafe, J. P. (1924). An experimental study of the affective qualities. *American Journal of Psychology, 35,* 540.

Newton, I. (1952). *Opticks* (4th ed.). New York: Dover Publications. (Original work published 1721)

Nutin, J. (1975) La motivation. In P. Fraisse & J. Piaget (Eds.), *Traité de psychologie expérimentale* V (3rd ed.). Paris: Presses Universitaires de France.

Pfaffman, C. (1982). Taste: A model of incentive motivation. In D. W. Pfaff (Ed.), *The physiological mechanisms of motivation.* New York: Springer Verlag.

Plé, A. (1982) *Par devoir ou par plaisir.* Paris: Editions du Cerf.

Pradines, M. (1928–1934). *Philosophie de la sensation* (3 vols.). Paris: Les Belles Lettres.

Reid, T. (1969). *Essays on the intellectual powers of man.* Cambridge, MA: M.I.T. Press. (Original work published 1785)

Schiffman, H. R. (1982). *Sensation and perception an integrated approach.* New York: Wiley.

Spence, K. W. (1948). The postulates and methods of "behaviorism." *Psychological Reviews, 55,* 67–78.

Stevens, S. S. (1975). *Psychophysics* New York: Wiley.

Strauss, E. (1956). *Vom Sinn der Sinne, ein: Beitraz zur Grundeluing der Psychologie* (2nd ed.). Berlin: Springer.

Teitelbaum, P. (1964). Appetite. *Proceedings of the American Philosophical Society 108,* 464–472.

Titchener, E. B. (1908). *Lectures on the elementary psychology of feeling and attention.* New York: Macmillan.

Titchener, E. B. (1909). *Lectures on the experimental psychology of the thought-prices.* New York: Macmillan.

Toates, F. (1986). *Motivational systems.* Cambridge, UK: Cambridge University Press.

Tolman, E. C. (1918). Nerve process and cognition. *Psychological Reviews, 25,* 423–442.

White, N. M. (1989). Reward or reinforcement: What's the difference? *Neuroscience and Biobehavioral Reviews, 13,* 181–186.

Wolfe, J. M. (1988). Introduction. In J. M. Wolfe (Ed.), *Readings from the Encyclopedia of Neurosciences. Sensory systems II* (pp. xi–xiv). Boston: Birkhaüser.

Wundt, W. (1874). *Grundzüge der physiologischen Psychologie.* Leipzig: Engelmann.

Yamagauchi, S. (1987). Fundamental properties of umamai in human taste sensation. In Y. Kawamura & M. R. Kare (Eds.), *Umami: A basic taste.* New York: Marcel Dekker.

Yokoyama, M. (1921). The nature of the affective judgement in the method of paired comparison. *American Journal of Psychology, 32,* 357–369.

Young, P. T. (1959). The role of affective processes in learning and motivation. *Psychological Reviews, 66,* 104–123.

Ziehen, T. (1924). *Leitfaden der physiologischen Psychologie* (12th ed.). Jena: G. Fischer.

Epilogue

RODERICK WONG
University of British Columbia

Although this volume is modest in length and scope and offers only a selective sampling of topics, I hope that your interest in biological perspectives on motivation has been whetted as a result of the presentations contained in it. As you have noticed, there is a mix of chapters: Some provide valuable comprehensive literature reviews of selected topics (e.g., Porter & Lévy on olfactory mediation of mother–infant interactions; Raible on feeding behavior in rodents), while others combine reviews along with the presentation of current studies from their laboratories (e.g., Cheal on multiple factors affecting motivated behavior; Chew on order and chaos in fish agonistic behavior; R. Wong on flavor neophobia in rodents; and Valle's critique of the role of associative factors in the control of "normal" drinking in the rat). In addition, there are theoretical articles that deal with mechanisms of motivation (e.g., Cabanac on sensory pleasure; Schulze on homeostatic mechanisms and motivated behavior; Tooby & Cosmides on selection for proximate mechanisms).

Although the chapters deal with selected topics in the field, general issues on motivation are also discussed, along with the detailed analysis of the specific process. For example, in order to analyze the mechanisms controlling "secondary" or "normal" drinking, Valle first deals with material on "primary" or thirst-motivated drinking and discusses its relationship to "normal" drinking. Similarly, Porter and Lévy's chapter on olfactory mediation of mother–infant interactions covers a wide spectrum of issues. When analyzing the role of olfactory cues on these interactions, the authors also deal with more fundamental issues concerning the analysis of maternal behavior at both functional and proximal levels.

Some of you may notice the absence of a chapter dealing specifically with the preeminent motivational system, that of sex and mating systems. The main reason for this omission has to do with the substantial number of excellent sources that deal with reproductive behavior; these include edited volumes by Adler, Pfaff, and Goy (1985), Clutton-Brock (1985), Crews (1987), Komisaruk, Siegel, Cheng and Feder (1986), and the book by Daly and Wilson (1983). In Dewsbury's (1990) volume on *Contemporary Issues in Comparative Psychology*, a section of the book is devoted to mating behavior, and many chapters in Leger's (1988) volume also cover this area. These sources incorporate material on both function and mechanisms.

With the exception of Dewsbury's (1990) book and a recent textbook by Leger (1992), there are few sources that relate functional considerations to proximate causal mechanisms of motivated activities such as feeding, drinking, parent–offspring interactions, early experience effects, frustration, and agonistic behavior, together in one volume. I hope that you have found the discussions on these topics informative and refreshing.

A motivational system is one that is responsible for the animal's goal-oriented commerce with particular biologically important incentives (Toates, 1988). In that respect, such a system may play just as crucial a link between evolution and behavior as do information-processing systems. The common feature shared by motivational systems involves a state that causes a behavior sequence resulting in a change in the animal's relationship to the external environment from what prevailed in the absence of that motivational state. The animal is moved toward and/or away from external stimuli. The mechanisms controlling such movements are discussed in the chapter by Cabanac as well as that by Schulze. The state is a general one, and how it is manifested in behavior depends upon the fine-grained features of the situation.

A goal is associated with motivation, although behavior need not be specifically directed toward some internal representation of that goal (McFarland, 1989). The motivational state persists until the goal has been attained or until a more common goal comes into expression. The success of this motivated action results from either a change in the animal's relation to the external world, a change in its internal state, or both. This can be illustrated by the situation in which water balance of an organism is disturbed. Cellular dehydration arising from intracellular or osmotic thirst (see Valle's chapter for details) gives rise to the disposition to seek and ingest water as well as precipitating the associated release of antidiuretic hormone which facilitates the retention of body water.

It is interesting that themes of the Cosmides and Tooby chapter recur in the presentations of the other contributors even though none, except for Schulze and R. Wong, wrote with that particular source as a "target article." Yet the substance of their arguments, as well as the supporting evidence, is integral and germane to many of the issues raised in the aforementioned article. I have made some specific references to these connections in my synopsis/commentary on each chapter, although I did not initially foresee that degree of congruence.

An examination of the current literature on motivation reveals a strong representation of studies that were designed to reveal the physiological mechanisms underlying various motivational activities. This is reflected in many chapters of this volume, especially those on feeding, drinking, and parent–offspring interactions. However, McFarland (1989) doubts whether a detailed account of physiology is needed for explanations of proximal causes, any more than a detailed circuit diagram of the computer is needed by programmers. Instead, he regards hardware-independent explanations as more appropriate, although he concedes that physiological implications would arise from such models, and cannot be ignored. This control systems approach explains goal-achieving behavior by analogy and is independent of the hardware employed by the organism. Nevertheless, there is justification for a physiological approach if one adopts the perspective that the biological analogues of "software" and "circuits" are one and the same. It should be noted that none of the authors in this volume take the position that the physiological level is the only valid one for the analysis of behavior. Functional considerations are raised in every chapter in this book.

The chapter whose orientation as well as substance meshes best with McFarland's (1989) views on control systems and behavioral regulation is the one by Schulze on homeostatic mechanisms. Cosmides and Tooby also voice some reservations about explanations focusing solely on physiological mechanisms. Different mechanisms can accomplish the same adaptive function. They argue that physiological studies do not address the level that describes what a mechanism does. Instead, such an approach is restricted to questions of how the mechanism does it. We hope that the material in this book will encourage other researchers to continue asking "why" along with "how" questions at many different levels, when probing the sources of motivated behavior.

REFERENCES

Adler, N. T., Pfaff, D. A., & Goy, R. W. (Eds.), (1985). *Handbook of behavioral neuroscience: Vol. 7. Reproduction.* New York: Plenum Press.

Clutton-Brock, T. H. (Ed.). (1988). *Reproductive success: Studies of individual variation in contrasting breeding systems.* Chicago: University of Chicago Press.

Crews, D. (Ed.). (1987). *Psychobiology of reproductive behavior: An evolutionary perspective.* Englewoods Cliffs, NJ: Prentice Hall.

Daly, M., & Wilson, M. (1983). *Sex, evolution and behavior.* Boston: Willard Grant Press.

Dewsbury, D. A. (Ed.). (1990). *Contemporary issues in comparative psychology.* Sunderland, MA: Sinauer Associates.

Komisaruk, B. R., Siegel, H. I., Cheng, M. F. & Feder, H. H. (Eds.). (1986). *Reproduction: A behavioral and neuroendorine perspective* (Vol. 474). New York: Annals of the New York Academy of Sciences.

Leger, D. W. (Ed.). (1988). *Comparative perspectives in modern psychology.* Lincoln: University of Nebraska Press.

Leger, D. W. (1992). *Biological foundations of behavior: An integrative approach.* New York: Harper Collins.

McFarland, D. (1989). *Problems of animal behavior.* Essex: Longmans.

Toates, F. M. (1988). Motivation and emotion from a biological perspective. In V. Hamilton, G. H. Bower, & N. Fridja (Eds.), *Cognitive perspectives on emotion and motivation.* Dordrecht: Kluwer Academic Publishers.

Author Index

Subject Index